PERILS OF DOMINANCE

Perils of Dominance

Imbalance of Power and the Road to War in Vietnam

GARETH PORTER

UNIVERSITY OF CALIFORNIA PRESS

Berkeley   Los Angeles   London

University of California Press
Berkeley and Los Angeles, California

University of California Press, Ltd.
London, England

First paperback printing 2006
© 2005 by The Regents of the University of California

Library of Congress Cataloging-in-Publication Data

Porter, Gareth, 1942–.
    Perils of dominance : the United States, Vietnam, and the imbalance
of power / Gareth, Porter.
        p.   cm.
    Includes bibliographical references and index.
    ISBN-10 0-520-25004-4 (pbk. : alk. paper)
    ISBN-13 978-0-520-25004-8 (pbk. : alk. paper)
    1. United States—Foreign relations—Vietnam.   2. Vietnam—Foreign
relations—United States.   3. United States—Foreign relations—
1961–1963—Decision making.   4. United States—Foreign relations—
1963–1969—Decision making.   5. Balance of power—History—20th
century.   6. National security—United States—History—20th century.
7. Kennedy, John F. (John Fitzgerald), 1917–1963.   8. Johnson, Lyndon B.
(Lyndon Baines), 1908–1973.   9. Vietnamese Conflict, 1961–1975—
Diplomatic history.   10. United States—Foreign relations—1953–1961.
I. Title.

E183.8.V5P67   2005
959.704'32—dc22   2004024697

Manufactured in the United States of America

14   13   12   11   10   09   08   07   06
11   10   9   8   7   6   5   4   3   2   1

The paper used in this publication meets the minimum
requirements of ANSI/NISO Z39.48-1992 (R 1997)
(Permanence of Paper).

Contents

Preface

Nearly three decades after the end of the Vietnam War, neither historians nor international relations specialists have satisfactorily explained why the United States chose to fight a major war in that unfortunate country. The reader interested in understanding the mystery of the Vietnam War is likely to come away from the scholarly literature on the war with little more than the suggestion that Cold War ideology was to blame. Whether explicitly argued or not, the assumption underlying virtually every account of the Vietnam War has been that the primary motivating force was adherence to Cold War strategic doctrine about the threat of communism and the need to resist it by force if necessary. In a review of the literature on the war some years ago, Robert J. McMahon observed that unquestioning adherence to such Cold War doctrines had become the dominant historical explanation for U.S. Vietnam policy.[1]

The Cold War consensus explanation can no longer be reconciled, however, with the documentary record on Vietnam that is now available to scholars, which contradicts it at every turn. This study of the making of Vietnam policy is aimed at providing a clear alternative to the Cold War consensus explanation for the war. It reflects a hypothesis about the reasons for the U.S. policy decisions leading eventually to war in Vietnam that I began to formulate more than twenty-five years ago when I was assembling a documentary history of the war.[2] I did not pursue that germ of a hypothesis, however, until the past few years.

My hypothesis is that a dramatic imbalance of power between the United States and the Soviet Union had emerged by 1954, and that the new power relationship shaped the policies of both sides in the Cold War toward Vietnam for the next decade. In examining the proposition that unequal power relations had a decisive impact on Cold War foreign policy decisions,

I have drawn on the work of Melvyn P. Leffler and Marc Trachtenberg, who have challenged the assumption that there was a rough balance of power between the superpowers during the entire Cold War period. Most scholars have rejected the idea that the United States held a position of military dominance over the Soviet Union in any meaningful sense, despite its substantial numerical superiority in strategic forces, on the grounds that both sides believed that nuclear weapons were unusable in practice. The image of a Cold War bipolar balance of power based on the ability of both superpowers to cause unacceptable destruction of the other's society has therefore dominated the interpretation of that period of the Cold War, and the interpretation of U.S. policy toward Vietnam has been based on that assumption.

I began to doubt the assumption that the road to war in Vietnam was marked by a rough East-West balance of power because of the striking evidence that, from 1954 through the early 1960s, the USSR and the People's Republic of China were acting with regard to the Vietnam issue like subordinate states in a distinctly hierarchical system of international power relations. When I began to inquire into the East-West military balance from 1953 to 1965, I found abundant evidence for the persistence of a dramatically unequal power relationship between the United States and the Soviet Union, focused in particular on strategic forces. Even more important, the historical record showed that both sides in the Cold War were keenly aware of the dramatically unequal power relationship. This consciousness of the new imbalance of power, I argue, exerted a strong influence on the policies of all the major actors toward Vietnam at key decision points during the period.

My account of U.S. policy toward Vietnam shows that from the Eisenhower administration through the Johnson administration, the exaggeration of the threat of Communism out of ideological rigidity, as suggested by the Cold War consensus explanation, was not a significant factor in making the key policy decisions. In all three administrations, in fact, the understanding of the relationship between Vietnam and Southeast Asian realities was a good deal more sophisticated than is suggested by the "domino theory."

The ideological explanation for the war has also assumed a high degree of consensus between presidents and their national security advisers on the importance of South Vietnam to American security and thus the necessity for preventing its loss to anti-U.S. forces. I shared that view when I began my research. As I examined the evidence on Vietnam policy making, however, it became apparent to me that there was no such consensus between presidents and advisers and that the imbalance of power did not influence all the players in the policy-making process on Vietnam in the same way. The differences between President Eisenhower and Secretary of State John Foster Dulles in understanding the relationship between the U.S. power advantage over the Communist states and the Vietnam issue were subtle rather than dramatic. But during the administrations of John F. Kennedy and Lyndon B. Johnson, differences over the usefulness of U.S. military dominance in Vietnam emerged as a major point of contention between the presidents and their principal national security advisers. In urging the president to use force, most national security officials relied heavily on the relative weakness of the Communist states and their reluctance to resist U.S. military moves, whereas both Kennedy and Johnson were inclined to be very skeptical about relying on that factor.

A second theme that is central to the understanding of the U.S. road to war in Vietnam, is, therefore, the acute struggle between Presidents John F. Kennedy and Lyndon B. Johnson, on one hand, and their national security advisers, on the other, over Vietnam policy. For both Kennedy and Johnson, deciding against the use of force in Vietnam involved extraordinary political risks, and both presidents sought to reduce those risks by sharing responsibility for that decision with their principal national security advisers, or at least averting open opposition by those advisers to the decision. A central dynamic in the Vietnam policy-making process, therefore, was the pressure on Kennedy and Johnson by their national security advisers to commit U.S. military power in Vietnam and the resistance by both presidents to that course of action. Although previous studies have provided some evidence of such resistance to war by both presidents, I found the pattern of pressure, resistance, and compromise far more dramatic and significant than has been suggested in the literature.

Because my overall thesis about unequal power relations and the path to war in Vietnam is outside the mainstream of scholarship on the war, it is important to clarify it as much as possible at the outset by stating some major qualifications. I do not deny that factors other than the global imbalance of power influenced policy decisions on Vietnam, nor do I argue that the power imbalance was the critical factor in every decision on Vietnam, much less on every foreign policy decision in general. The public perception that the United States and the Soviet Union were engaged in a global struggle for dominance certainly facilitated the advocacy of militarily aggressive policies in Southeast Asia. I would argue, however, that this was an enabling factor but not the primary reason for U.S. military intervention in Vietnam.

American political opinion on Vietnam clearly weighed heavily in the making of Vietnam policy throughout the period. The widely shared view that France was fighting a colonialist war in Indochina, which would taint the United States if it became directly involved, was a key factor in President Eisenhower's thinking about intervention. On the other hand, the strongly interventionist cast of domestic opinion in the early 1960s made Presidents Kennedy and Johnson very cautious about putting on record any decision against the use of force in Vietnam that could be used against them by opponents.

Another major consideration for policy makers that had nothing to do with the external configuration of power was the political-military situation in Vietnam. When Communist military fortunes were at a low ebb, and even when the insurgents were in an early stage of mobilization, presidential advisers relied on the dominance of U.S. power to urge a more aggressive use of force in Vietnam. Both in the 1954 Indochina crisis and in the final decision for open-ended deployment of ground troops, however, the strength of the Communist resistance was more important than the global imbalance of power for most of the presidents' national security advisers.

By highlighting the degree to which the national security bureaucracy was able to compel presidents to become more involved militarily than they would have preferred, I do not mean to imply that the national security bureaucracy was uniform in its policy preferences regarding the use of military force in Vietnam. The Joint Chiefs of Staff were willing to accept much higher risks and costs in the use of force in Vietnam than were the civilian advisers, and the JCS therefore pushed consistently for even more aggressive military actions than most civilian advisers would support. Furthermore, not all senior civilian officials agreed on the likely consequences of major deployments of ground troops, and at least one, George Ball, expressed dissenting views on both bombing and ground forces. Nevertheless, at key policy decisions under Kennedy and Johnson, the principal national security advisers did reach a consensus on pressing the president to use U.S. combat forces to ensure victory in South Vietnam, to put military pressure on the North, and, finally, to deploy limited combat forces.

Finally, in focusing on the influence of a "structural" or impersonal influence on the policy decisions that took the United States down the road to war, I am not arguing that the outcome of the policy-making process on Vietnam was inevitable or predetermined. I will show that the individual and personal factors, including the experiences, attitudes, and values of both John F. Kennedy and Lyndon Johnson, and the personal relationships between presidents and their key advisers, were vitally important in the policy-making process, and that the policy decisions were the outcome of a struggle between two very different sets of interests and values.

Because the actual and perceived configuration of power between the two major protagonists in the Cold War during the period under study is so central to my thesis, I begin by documenting the asymmetry in the military balance between the United States and the Soviet Union from 1953 to 1965 and reconstructing the perceptions of that power relationship on the part of Eisenhower, Kennedy, Khrushchev, and Mao. In these accounts, I strip away some of the conventional assumptions about the views of the leaders of the United States, the USSR, and the PRC about the power balance during that period.

In order to develop and highlight the theme of the linkages between the imbalance of power and policies toward Vietnam with the greatest possible clarity, I have chosen to trace the development of the policies of the Soviet Union, China, North Vietnam, and the United States separately rather than integrating them all into a common narrative. In chapter 2, I show how the Soviet and Chinese governments adjusted their policy to their weakness relative to the United States by acquiescing to the U.S. assertion of its interest in keeping South Vietnam in the American sphere. Soviet and Chinese acquiescence took the form of passivity in the face of U.S. moves and pressure on the North Vietnamese not to disturb the status quo in South Vietnam.

The Communist states' appeasement policies, aimed at avoiding the risk of a clash with the United States at any cost, played a pivotal role in the calculations of the Eisenhower administration. Chapter 3 presents a reinterpretation of the Eisenhower administration's policy toward Vietnam before and after the Geneva Accords of 1954 as a response to the newly emerging imbalance of power with the USSR and to the signals sent by Soviet and Chinese policy. The chapter addresses one of the enduring issues of historical interpretation of the road to war in Vietnam: why the Geneva agreement failed to bring a peaceful settlement. It shows how the imbalance of power created the opportunity and therefore the incentive for Secretary of State John Foster Dulles to ignore and effectively undermine the Geneva framework for a settlement through free elections.

The narrative in chapter 4 traces the role of the global and regional balance of power in the evolution of North Vietnam's strategy in the South from 1954 to 1965. It views the leadership of the Vietnamese Communist Party in the North as initially divided by two conflicting pressures—one from the USSR and PRC to avoid challenging the United States in South Vietnam, the other from the Vietnamese party's own followers in South

Vietnam to approve the use of armed struggle to protect them from Diem's repression. The chapter shows how, from 1961 to 1965, North Vietnamese concern about U.S. military intervention in Vietnam compelled Hanoi to accept political-diplomatic objectives falling far short of reunification.

The account of the Kennedy administration's Vietnam policy in chapter 5 highlights the sharp conflict between Kennedy and the national security bureaucracy over U.S. policy toward Vietnam and Laos. It documents the linkage between the awareness of Kennedy's advisers of the decisive U.S. power advantage and their position on the use of force. Another theme developed in the chapter is Kennedy's determination to reverse his approval of the U.S. counterinsurgency war role in November 1963 by opening a channel for peace negotiations and by pushing behind the scenes for a phased withdrawal of U.S. troops by the end of 1985.

Chapters 6 and 7 recount the struggle between Johnson and his advisers over the bombing of North Vietnam and Johnson's abortive attempt to hold the line against pressures for an open-ended troop commitment to South Vietnam. These two chapters document a pattern of repeated efforts by Johnson's advisers, influenced by the unequal Cold War power relationship, to get Johnson to commit the United States to widening the war to North Vietnam and of Johnson's repeated refusal to do so. Chapter 7 also examines the decisions on ground troop deployments, culminating in the final decision for a major ground troop deployment in mid 1965. In the account of these decisions, I trace the influence of the global imbalance of power, as well as that of the Byzantine domestic politics of blame for any future defeat in South Vietnam.

Chapter 8 takes on more directly the familiar assertion that strategic beliefs, however mistaken, about the Communist threat to the entire Southeast Asia region anchored the chain of U.S. policy decisions that led to war in Vietnam. The chapter traces the evolution of the "domino theory" and "bandwagon" thesis from genuine beliefs to useful arguments for various political and diplomatic purposes. I conclude that presidential advisers during the Kennedy and Johnson administrations did indeed attribute strategic importance to the outcome in South Vietnam, but that this was far less compelling than the arguments that have often been presumed to have driven the United States into war.

In the concluding chapter, I recapitulate the evidence for the critical influence of unequal power relations on the four crucial Vietnam policy decisions. Then I examine the implications of this revisionist history of Vietnam policy for understanding the nature of national security policy making in a state with dominant power in the international system. The account in this study, I argue, definitively contradicts the comforting view that "the system worked" in making policy on Vietnam.[3] I discuss the emergence of a "dysfunctional" process of national security policy making accompanied by unprecedented political tensions and a pattern of dishonesty and deception within the executive branch in the struggle over Vietnam policy. Finally, I examine the lessons to be gleaned, in the present "unipolar moment" in global politics and U.S. foreign policy, from the path to war in Vietnam that was traversed by the United States in a Cold War era that was also effectively unipolar.

Acknowledgments

As an independent scholar, I have been even more dependent on the support and generosity of friends and colleagues than one who has an institutional base. I am particularly grateful to Dan Ellsberg for his support and encouragement of the project, and for hours of stimulating discussion of issues of interpretation of the evidence on the 1964–65 period, as well as for detailed comments on earlier drafts of selected chapters that pointed out weaknesses in the analysis. Marilyn Young also read a series of drafts of the same chapter, and her comments helped me realize the need for greater clarity in addressing issues that had been neglected in those drafts—especially the Gulf of Tonkin affair. Kai Bird was extraordinarily generous in allowing me to borrow his file of William Bundy documents, declassified at his request, for an extended period.

Fred Logevall also encouraged me to pursue the project during the critical first year and read earlier drafts of some chapters and provided useful comments. Robert Jervis and Chester J. Patch Jr., who read the entire manuscript, made suggestions that helped bring sharper focus to the final draft. Conversations with my editor at University of California Press, Monica McCormick, were also instrumental in trimming what was not essential to the main themes of the book and making it more accessible than it might otherwise have been.

The Lyndon Baines Johnson Foundation provided a small grant, which covered my expenses in traveling to and staying in Austin to use the archives of the LBJ Library in 2004. John Wilson, senior archivist at the Johnson Library got me started and helped me make the most of my limited time in using the collection. At the John F. Kennedy Library, reference archivist Stephen Plotkin facilitated my research and deftly handled all my questions. And at the National Defense University's man-uscripts collection, Susan Lemke made my task much easier by locating the portions of the Maxwell Taylor papers that were relevant to my research.

Selected Abbreviations

NOTE: Universally known abbreviations such as USSR and CIA are omitted from this list, as are the initials JFK and LBJ, used in note citations to refer to Presidents John F. Kennedy and Lyndon B. Johnson.

ARVN	Army of the Republic of Vietnam
CDEC	Combined Documents Exploitation Center
CINCPAC	Commander in Chief, Pacific
CPSU	Communist Party of the Soviet Union
DOD	Department of Defense
DRV	Democratic Republic of Vietnam
FBIS	Foreign Broadcast Information Service
FRUS	*Foreign Relations of the United States*
GVN	Government of Vietnam
ICC	International Control Commission
JCS	Joint Chiefs of Staff
JFKL	John Fitzgerald Kennedy Library, Boston
JPRS	Joint Publications Research Service
LBJL	Lyndon B. Johnson Library, Austin, Texas
MAAG	Military Assistance Advisory Group
MACV	Military Assistance Command Vietnam
NARA	National Archives and Records Administration
NIE	National Intelligence Estimate
NLF	National Liberation Front
NSC	National Security Council

NSF	national security files, JFKL
OSD	Office of the Secretary of Defense
OSDH	Office of the Secretary of Defense, Historical Office
PKI	Partai Komunis Indonesia [Indonesian Communist Party]
PL	Pathet Lao
PLA	People's Liberation Army
PLAF	People's Liberation Armed Forces
PRC	People's Republic of China
RG	record group
RLG	Royal Lao Government
RVN	Republic of Vietnam
SEATO	Southeast Asia Treaty Organization
SMM	Saigon Military Mission
SNIE	Special National Intelligence Estimate
VNA	Vietnam National Army
VPA	Vietnam People's Army
VWP	Vietnam Workers' Party

1 The Imbalance of Power, 1953–1965

For decades, no distinction was made between different periods in the diplomatic history of the Cold War, because no one had noted any marked change in the fundamental relationship between the two major antagonists. Since the late 1980s, however, a few scholars have established that a key turning point in U.S. Cold War policy occurred during the Korean War and that this was directly attributable to the achievement by the United States of clear-cut dominance over the Soviet Union in strategic weapons.[1]

The emergence of the United States as strategically dominant vis-à-vis the Soviet Union changed the relationship between the two superpowers so profoundly that no Cold War issue remained untouched. Once it became clear that the Soviet Union could not provide a counterweight to U.S. military power, the United States had a new freedom of action, which translated into more aggressive and interventionist policies. The U.S. path to a major land war in South Vietnam was closely related to this new global distribution of power.

Prior to the U.S. military breakthrough, the East-West balance of power was ambiguous and unstable. Both sides viewed the power balance primarily in a European context, as major powers had done before World War II.[2] Despite the U.S. atomic monopoly from 1945 to 1949, moreover, the role of nuclear weapons in the power balance was not yet clear to either Moscow or Washington. Notwithstanding the destructive power of the atomic weapons of that period, the U.S. military did not view them as capable of destroying either U.S. or Soviet society.[3] As late as 1949, the idea that the United States could use atomic weapons either to fight a war with the USSR or to influence Soviet behavior was still seriously questioned by many U.S. officials.[4] Furthermore, U.S. intelligence vastly exaggerated Moscow's ability to wage war beyond its existing security sphere in Eastern Europe.[5]

During the 1949–50 period, the Soviet Union exploded its first atomic bomb, the Chinese Communists established the People's Republic of China, and the USSR at first at least countenanced and then actively supported the North Korean invasion of South Korea. Meanwhile, the PRC gave military assistance to the Communist-led Viet Minh war of resistance to the French in Indochina. This period of Sino-Soviet initiative in the Cold War coincided with the high point of fear in Washington that the USSR might launch a "global war." Many U.S. military officials and some civilians felt that war with the Soviet Union was likely and that the United States should attack first. They also believed, however, that the United States could not take such a step until the balance of power was more favorable, particularly in regard to atomic weapons and strategic bombers.[6]

The Truman administration had decided even before the Korean War on a massive military buildup that would decisively change both the reality and the perception of that distribution of power. Secretary of State Dean Acheson later recalled that the administration's response to the Soviet atomic bomb test in 1949 was to "make a colossal effort" at rearmament, creating "real power" in order to have a "psychological impact on the Soviets."[7] According to NSC 68, the official blueprint for U.S. Cold War policy adopted by the Truman administration prior to the Korean War, the objective of the military buildup was to create a "situation to which the Kremlin would find it expedient to accommodate itself, first by relaxing tensions and pressures and then by gradual withdrawal."[8]

The idea that a dramatic imbalance of military power would compel the USSR to withdraw from Eastern Europe vastly exaggerated its potential impact. Nevertheless, the massive rearmament carried out during the Korean War brought about a far-reaching transformation of U.S. Cold War policy and the dynamics of U.S.-Soviet relations. No one particular moment after the start of the Korean War can be identified as the point at which this transformation was complete. Rather, the period of the Korean War marked a transition from one distribution of power to another. By late 1952, the leading U.S. military and civilian policy makers of the Truman administration were already confident that the United States held a commanding superiority over the USSR in strategic forces. That conclusion led, in turn, to a new willingness on the part of the administration to make a military commitment to Iran and to pursue a much more aggressively interventionist policy within Iran, including a possible coup against the nationalist regime of Premier Mohammed Mossadegh, despite the risk of Soviet intervention and military confrontation with the USSR. The new policy was based on the confidence that the USSR would be deterred by fear of war with the United States.[9]

The new imbalance of power altered the incoming Eisenhower administration's definition of its diplomatic objectives as well. Secretary of State John Foster Dulles believed in early 1953 that the United States was now in a far stronger position to get the Korean armistice terms it wanted "in view of our much greater power and the Soviet Union's weakness currently."[10] The Joint Chiefs of Staff similarly believed in late 1953 that the United States was now strong enough in relation to the USSR to fully assert its rights in Berlin, whereas they believed it had not been strong enough to do so in 1948–49.[11] "They must be scared as hell," Eisenhower said of the Soviet leadership shortly before the end of the Korean War.[12]

U.S. AND SOVIET POWER CAPABILITIES

The U.S. achievement between 1950 and 1952 of a commanding military superiority over the USSR, particularly in strategic weapons, was made possible by the much larger, more technologically advanced, and more efficient economy of the United States. The differences between the U.S. and Soviet economies were therefore a crucial factor in the changing distribution of power during this period. In 1953, the U.S. gross national product was 2.6 times larger than that of the Soviet Union, and ten years later, it was still almost 2.2 times larger, according to a recent estimate.[13] Even more important, the Soviet economy suffered from a huge "productivity gap" in relation to the U.S. economy, getting only an estimated 20 percent of the U.S. output per unit of labor and capital input using Soviet domestic prices, and 45 percent when dollars are used.[14] And the Soviet technological lag behind the United States was estimated to be twenty-five years on average across all sectors, which further increased the disparity between the economic bases of the two states.[15] Thus an index of *effective* economic power, combining GNP with productivity and technological prowess, would show the U.S. economic power base in the 1950s and 1960s to have been several times greater than that of the Soviet Union.

In theory, the stark contrast in their respective power bases need not have ruled out a balance of power between the two superpowers. Nations have a certain capability to mobilize resources for national defense or the exercise of international power, based on the degree of popular understanding and support for national objectives, but also on the relative cost of the objectives to the population. An increased mobilization of resources may be achieved, as Thomas J. Christensen has shown in the case of U.S.

Cold War policy in the late 1940s and early 1950s, by increasing popular support through political strategies.[16] But in the Soviet Union after Stalin's death in 1953, the economy was too weak, and popular demands for a better life were too strong, to permit Moscow to mobilize the resources to compete with the United States in military power, either by coercion or by ideological or nationalist appeals. The USSR was under very strong domestic pressure, therefore, to acquiesce in U.S. military superiority over a relatively long period in order to achieve rapid economic growth and to meet the demands of its population for consumer goods.[17]

Soviet military spending during the first four years of Khrushchev's leadership (1955–59) thus remained stable or may even have declined— and certainly declined precipitously as a proportion of Soviet GNP. But the continued buildup of U.S. strategic power, leading to more intense pressure from the Soviet military and political leadership for a greater military effort, ultimately forced Khrushchev to increase defense spending by more than a third between 1960 and 1963.[18] The result was a drastic reduction in the annual rate of Soviet economic growth, from an average of 6.6 percent in the 1958–61 period to just 2.2 percent in 1962.[19]

It has long been accepted that the United States enjoyed an overall quantitative superiority over the Soviet Union in military power during the 1950s and 1960s. A methodology developed in the early 1980s for comparing the two military establishments' combined indices for total firepower, manpower, and mobility of conventional forces with indices for the diversity, lethality, and precision of strategic weapons systems. Based on this systematic comparison, in 1955, the index of U.S. military power was forty times greater than the index of Soviet power, and a decade later, after both sides had multiplied their striking power several times over, the index of U.S. military power was still more than nine times greater than that of the Soviet Union.[20] This disparity in measurable military power between the two superpowers was far greater than any other disparity between the strongest power and its strongest rival, or group of rivals, since the modern state system came into existence in the seventeenth century.[21]

But even this quantitative comparison does not adequately reflect the significance of the *qualitative* differences between the U.S. and Soviet military establishments in both strategic forces and power projection from 1953 to 1965. Only the United States had strategic and power projection capabilities to credibly threaten the use of force in developing regions of the world. Those qualitative differences in military capabilities translated into a sharp contrast between the two superpowers in their ability to influence Cold War issues.

The Persistence of Strategic Asymmetry

In the logic of the nuclear age, the primary military questions for each of the superpowers were (a) the relative vulnerability of its cities to nuclear attack and (b) the strength of its secure second-strike retaliatory force—one that was capable of surviving a first-strike attack and retaliating with devastating effect. By both of these criteria, the United States held something approaching absolute strategic dominance during the period under study. The USSR did not possess a reliable minimum second-strike force until after 1965. In fact, even its ability to carry out a damaging *first strike* against U.S. society was very much in doubt as late as the early 1960s.

By 1953, the United States already had 329 B-47 Stratojets with a range of more than 3,000 miles without refueling and thus capable of hitting Soviet economic and military targets on two-way missions from European and Japanese bases. That number increased rapidly to 1,086 B-47s by 1955. In 1955, SAC also began to deploy B-52 bombers that could refuel in midair and reach targets in the Soviet Union from the continental United States, increasing the number from 18 to 538 over the next five years. The number of B-47s also continued to rise during that period. By 1960, SAC had a total of 1,735 strategic bombers that could deliver nuclear weapons on Soviet targets.[22] Moreover, U.S. B-47s based on the periphery of the Soviet Union were capable of penetrating the porous Soviet system of anti-aircraft defenses.[23]

Before 1955, Moscow did not even pretend that it had the capability to carry out a strike against the United States but relied for deterrence exclusively on the threat that its bombers posed to Western Europe.[24] The Soviet strategic bomber force consisted entirely of Tu-4 "Bulls," which were unable to reach U.S. targets on a two-way mission, even from forward bases in the Arctic, because of their short range and the lack of in-flight refueling. Even on one-way missions from Arctic bases, they would have taken thirteen hours to arrive over any U.S. targets, giving U.S. interceptors several hours to prepare for them. And this first generation of strategic bombers could have been shot down easily because of its slow speed.[25]

From 1955 through mid 1959, the USSR produced about 175 long-range jet-propelled "Bison" and turboprop "Bear" heavy bombers and several hundred two-engine "Badger" medium bombers.[26] But the Bisons were slow, lumbering aircraft, which were incapable of reaching the continental United States on two-way missions, even with refueling. Even on one-way missions, they would have been highly vulnerable to attack by U.S. air defense capabilities.[27] Nikita Khrushchev recalls in his memoirs that when the aircraft designer reported in the early 1950s that the bomber could "bomb the United States and then land in Mexico," the Soviet leaders asked, "What do you think Mexico is—our mother-in-law? You think we can go calling any time we want?"[28] The Soviet inability to mount two-way intercontinental bombing missions made the Kremlin's deterrent highly unreliable at best.[29]

Although they were much faster than the Bulls, the Badgers could only have reached a small portion of the United States on one-way suicide missions from Arctic bases. The Bears, on the other hand, could have reached North America on a two-way mission from advanced Arctic bases, but they were turboprop aircraft and so slow that they would have been very vulnerable to U.S. interceptors. With each passing year, moreover, Soviet heavy bombers became progressively less capable of penetrating the constantly improving U.S. air defense system.[30]

The Soviet bomber force was not only incapable of mounting an effective first-strike attack on the United States but also vulnerable to a U.S. disarming first strike. According to official documents on U.S. strategic planning that have become available to scholars, the U.S. Air Force was prepared throughout the 1950s to carry out a first strike that could prevent any Soviet nuclear retaliation even against Japan or Western Europe.[31] The Soviet Air Defense System continued to improve in the late 1950s but was considered incapable of coping with a large-scale U.S. attack even in the early 1960s.[32] General Curtis LeMay, chief of the Strategic Air Command during the 1950s, later recalled that SAC had the capacity to destroy all of the Soviet war-making capabilities "without losing a man to their defenses."[33] Soviet strategic bombers, including those targeted on Western Europe and Japan, were deployed at only sixty airbases at most, and they had no ground or airborne alert procedures. Nuclear warheads were not even stored at airbases.[34] Moreover, these bombers were not deployed at the advanced Arctic bases from which they would have had to take off to be able to attack the United States.[35] And if they had been deployed at those bases, a U.S. first strike would have been particularly effective against them, because the Arctic bases would have had very little warning time before being hit.[36]

Even when the USSR began producing intercontinental ballistic missiles in the early 1960s, it did not alter the strategic imbalance. By late 1962, Moscow had deployed fewer than two dozen ICBMs, compared with 284 U.S. ICBMs.[37] Equally important, even the second generation Soviet

ICBMs, the SS-7 and SS-8 missiles, were unprotected and extremely slow to prepare for launch. By September 1961, U.S. intelligence had very accurate data on the location of Soviet missile bases. And although the USSR now had about 100 bombers capable of reaching the United States by refueling on two-way missions from Arctic bases, the entire land-based Soviet strategic force was highly vulnerable to a U.S. first-strike attack.[38]

Soviet sea-based missiles added nothing to the Soviet strategic deterrent in the early 1960s. Two-thirds of these missiles were on diesel-powered submarines that were so noisy they could be easily detected by the U.S. submarine fleet. The rest were limited by the long transit time from their home bases, the short range of their missiles, and their inability to launch until after surfacing and going through a time-consuming procedure.[39] And the nuclear submarines had weapons systems that were so unreliable that, in the first years of the program, they were sent to sea armed with conventionally armed missiles. All ninety-seven of these relatively short-range ballistic missile submarines were in Soviet waters at the time of the Cuban Missile Crisis.[40]

At the time of the Cuban Missile Crisis, according to a classified 1981 Pentagon-sponsored study of the history of the strategic arms race, the Soviet ability to retaliate against a U.S. first strike was extremely precarious at best. "By standards of strategic force survivability and effectiveness that became commonplace a few years later," it concluded, "the Soviet strategic situation in 1962 might have been judged little short of desperate."[41] Between early 1963 and late 1964, the USSR took steps to make its strategic forces more survivable by hardening silos, increasing launch mobility, and dispersing the missile sites. The first forty-two hardened missile silos for the new SS-9 ICBMs were in place by late 1964. The actual deployment of the SS-9s in the hardened sites did not occur until later, however. The evidence from Soviet sources suggests that it was only in 1966 that the USSR acquired a credible minimum deterrent force in the form of ICBMs that were reasonably well protected from a U.S. first strike.[42]

Power Projection Forces: Two Global Powers or One?

During the 1953–65 period, an era of conflicts and crises in the Middle East and Southeast Asia, the ability to project military force into conflict zones was crucial to political-diplomatic influence. Qualitative comparison of the geographic reach of the two superpowers is just as starkly revealing as comparison of their strategic forces. The United States had the capability to send naval and air forces as well as ground troops into zones of conflict anywhere in the developing world, whether to intervene in an existing military conflict or to exert leverage on the conflict. The USSR, on the other hand, lacked the means to project power any significant distance beyond Soviet territory.[43]

Starting with the military buildup that began with the Korean War and continuing into the mid 1950s, the United States created a vast overseas network of 3,000 military facilities and dozens of base complexes that allowed it to project power into the Middle East and Asia. Six U.S. Army divisions within the continental United States provided a central reserve force that could be used abroad, and at least three divisions were assigned the explicit task of responding to non-Soviet contingencies in Asia or the Middle East. And with three divisions of troops and its own tactical air force, the Marine Corps was capable of carrying out amphibious landings and combat in any part of the world.[44] A fleet of fifty-nine C-124 Globe-masters provided the ability to move tens of thousands of troops quickly over long distances.[45]

The U.S. Navy had uncontested control of the seas during the 1953–65 period. The Sixth Fleet's control of the Mediterranean Sea, the availability of 1,800 marines fully capable of amphibious landings or introduction by helicopters and tactical airpower located at airbases in Greece, Turkey, Saudi Arabia, and Libya ensured U.S. military dominance in the Middle East. In East Asia, the United States had established forty-five military base complexes in Japan, Okinawa, South Korea, and Taiwan, including sixteen major airbases for both U.S. strategic bombers and tactical fighter aircraft and base complexes in Okinawa and Japan's home islands that pro-vided logistical support. By 1958, the Seventh Fleet had three naval task forces, with a total of more than 140 ships, including seven aircraft carriers, patrolling the western Pacific, ready to intervene in local conflicts.[46]

During the Eisenhower administration, three army divisions were deployed to the Pacific to support U.S. policy around the Sino-Soviet perimeter in East Asia, and two marine divisions were at the disposal of the commander in chief of U.S. forces in the Pacific (CINCPAC).[47] The Kennedy administration further strengthened its power projection capa-bilities in order to be able to fight two major wars—one in Europe and one in Asia—simultaneously while also responding to a smaller "brushfire" war in the Caribbean. These forces were to allow the administration to fight a major war in Asia and to intervene quickly with large-scale forces. Thus from 1961 to 1963, the United States expanded its "strategic reserve" from three divisions to eight (in addition to the five divisions in Europe, two divisions in Korea, and one division in Hawaii) and added the airlift capability to deploy two divisions to the Middle East or Southeast Asia within three weeks.[48] The Kennedy administration also carried out a new buildup of airpower in Southeast Asia aimed at preparing for an air war on the Asian mainland. In April 1961, it redeployed a detachment of F102 fighter planes from Japan and Okinawa to Thailand to fly reconnaissance missions in Laos and began construction on four major airbases in that country. From 1961 to 1964, the United States carried out a buildup of airpower in Thailand that would permit air offensives against targets either in Vietnam or in China.[49]

The USSR, meanwhile, was unable to project military power outside its sphere of influence in Eastern and Central Europe. Until 1959, it did not possess the capability to airlift even a small number of troops to neighboring Middle Eastern countries. The An. 12, which was introduced into service in 1959, was able to carry sixty-five paratroopers or twenty tons of cargo, but its range was limited to 750 nautical miles with maximum payload.[50] Thus it was able to airlift troops as far as Iraq or Syria, but not as far as the Suez Canal, because it lacked rights for intermediate refueling stops and overflights in neighboring countries.[51]

Because the Soviet Union had no military bases in the Middle East, Africa, or Asia, it also lacked the capability to support troops with tactical air cover in any more distant military operation. The most modern tactical aircraft in the Soviet fleet, the Su-7, the Mig-21, and the Yak-28, which were introduced in 1959, 1962, and 1964, respectively, all had combat radii of between 200 and 300 miles. This meant that none of the strategically important Middle Eastern countries—Iran, Iraq, Syria, and Egypt—were within range of Soviet tactical aircraft. Only the northwestern tip and the northeastern region of Iran and a limited area of western Afghanistan were within reach of Soviet fighter planes.[52] The marines, the only Soviet forces capable of making amphibious landings, were reduced by Khrushchev from 100,000 to approximately 15,000, then disbanded, and finally reconstituted in the early 1960s with only 6,000 men. But their role was to operate close to Soviet territory, where air cover could be assured, not to project Soviet power abroad.[53]

There was no Soviet military presence outside the Soviet Union and its Eastern European satellites until the deployment of some 40,000 troops and forty-two IL-28 light bombers (later withdrawn) to Cuba in 1962.[54] But even Soviet bases in Cuba depended on the ability to resupply them by air from bases outside the Soviet Union—something that the USSR still lacked. Because so many regimes in Africa and the Middle East were heavily influenced by the United States and its allies, it was difficult for the

USSR to obtain permission for its planes to land and refuel. When the United States imposed a naval blockade around Cuba during the 1962 missile crisis, the USSR needed to refuel aircraft in either Guinea or Senegal to be able to resupply its personnel in Cuba. Under pressure from Washington, however, both countries refused to allow this, leaving Cuba and the Soviet forces there at the mercy of the U.S. blockade.[55]

The Soviet Union lacked the capability either to challenge U.S. naval power or to initiate a naval show of force on its own.[56] The post-Stalin Soviet leadership halted Stalin's ambitious plans for a major surface fleet, ending the naval aircraft carrier program and the construction of cruisers that was already under way. Three hundred seventy-five surface ships were mothballed, and the thirteen largest ship-building facilities were shifted from construction of military vessels to building fishing and merchant ships.[57] The new ships with surface-to-surface missiles that were added to the fleet from 1957 through 1964 were intended solely for defense against an attack by U.S. aircraft carriers, not to influence the course of a conflict abroad.[58]

Without any aircraft carriers, the Soviet surface fleet could not provide the air cover and other key combat capabilities to support a larger war effort and had very limited ability to resupply at sea.[59] A U.S. intelligence estimate before the 1956 Suez crisis pointed out that the Soviet Navy was "deprived of the mobility traditionally needed by naval powers," because of the "wide separation" of its sea frontiers and the fact that the Baltic and Black Sea fleets, which represented 60 percent of Soviet naval power, could not exit into the Atlantic or the Mediterranean without the approval of the NATO powers.[60] Although the Soviet Black Sea fleet began to sail into the Mediterranean in 1964, until the late 1960s, military experts believed it could have been sunk by the Sixth Fleet within five minutes.[61] And the inability of the USSR to project power into East and Southeast Asia impelled Khrushchev to propose to Mao Zedong in 1958 a joint Sino-Soviet submarine fleet based at Chinese ports, which the latter rejected.[62] In fact, the Soviet Union did not even begin to function as a global power in terms of its naval forces until the latter half of the 1960s at the earliest.[63]

U.S. PERCEPTIONS OF THE GLOBAL POWER BALANCE

The Eisenhower Administration's Two-Level Assessment

Statements by President Dwight D. Eisenhower about possible nuclear war have sometimes been cited as evidence that he began relatively early in his presidency to view the strategic balance in terms of mutual deterrence rather than clear-cut U.S. superiority.[64] Closer examination of the statements supporting the "mutual deterrence" thesis suggests, however, that they either were acknowledging the likelihood that a situation of mutual deterrence would emerge in the future or were aimed at opposing the proposals for the aggressive use or threat of military force directly against the USSR or what Ike considered wasteful spending on more missiles. Such statements must be weighed against other indications that both Eisenhower and Dulles appreciated the situation of strategic asymmetry with the Soviet Union and its political advantages to the United States in the Cold War. In effect, they held two quite distinct levels of assessment of the strategic balance, each one serving a different policy purpose.

The very first documented statement by a leader in the Eisenhower administration suggesting mutual deterrence was clearly intended to fend off policy proposals by the JCS that Eisenhower and Dulles believed would have been dangerously provocative. The JCS asserted in June 1954 that the United States should exploit is strategic superiority over the USSR to confront the Soviet leaders with the threat that a failure to meet U.S. demands would "involve grave risks to the maintenance of their regime."[65] This proposal for an ultimatum to the USSR had been hovering in the background of U.S. foreign policy since the Project Solarium exercise convened by John Foster Dulles in mid 1953, when one of the three teams had argued that the United States should take as its foreign policy objective the "overthrow of the Communist regime in China" and the "reduction of Soviet power and militance [sic] and the elimination of the Communist conspiracy." Eisenhower and Dulles found such a policy far too risky, and their portrayal of a nuclear exchange with the Soviet Union was aimed at strengthening the case against it.[66] In mid November 1954, Dulles argued in a memorandum that "the increased destructiveness of nuclear weapons and the approach of effective atomic parity are creating a situation in which general war would threaten the destruction of Western civilization." He concluded that the United States should therefore avoid "actions that would generally be regarded as provocative."[67]

Beginning in mid 1955, Pentagon strategists began to predict the arrival of mutual deterrence within a few years. For the next five years both Dulles and Eisenhower conceded that mutual deterrence was indeed the reality the United States would face. But that acknowledgment was always related to a situation that would emerge some years in the future and was therefore an issue for planning future military budgets and posture, not about the implications of the *existing* strategic balance. In that context, Eisenhower embraced the results of the worst-case nuclear war scenario at several NSC meetings in 1956. He emphasized what he called a "transcendent consideration—namely, that nobody can win in a thermonuclear war."[68] That statement was not merely an expression of Eisenhower's horror at nuclear war. Eisenhower was engaged in a political struggle with General Maxwell Taylor and other military leaders over their demands for a buildup of conventional forces, which the president resisted in large part for budgetary and economic policy reasons. It was precisely the unacceptability of the damage that would occur to both sides in a nuclear war, Eisenhower argued, that would deter local military conflicts in peripheral areas. Taylor complained that Eisenhower's focus on the worst-case scenario of nuclear devastation was misplaced, because it was the least likely contingency the United States faced.[69] But the worst-case scenario of nuclear war was useful to Ike in holding the line against vast new spending for fighting local wars around the world.

In November 1959, Eisenhower again invoked the image of mutual deterrence, deriding the possibility of using U.S. forces to limit the damage of a nuclear exchange. "All we really have that is meaningful is a deterrent," he declared. But his statement was in the context of a budgetary struggle over proposals by the air force and navy to spend more on ICBMs and submarine-launched missiles in order to build a "second strike counterforce" capability.[70] His resort to the worst-case scenario again served his interest in fending off the arguments of those who wanted to spend more on defense than he believed was necessary.

Despite their use of worst-case nuclear war scenarios to argue against budgetary and policy proposals they opposed, Eisenhower and Dulles never believed that the United States had lost the decisive strategic advantage over the USSR that it possessed in the early to mid 1950s. Although they anticipated that the USSR would acquire a credible deterrent within a few years, Eisenhower and Dulles understood that in the meantime, Soviet strategic capabilities were still vulnerable to a U.S. first strike and that this profoundly influenced Soviet responses to conflicts in which the United States might become involved. This view was clearly supported by a National Intelligence Estimate (NIE) in late 1955 that found that the conciliatory policies being followed by the Soviet leadership were prompted by the "realization of . . . the fact that at present U.S. nuclear capabilities greatly exceed those of the USSR." The estimate concluded that "as long as this gap exists the Soviet leaders will almost certainly wish to minimize the risk of general war."[71] An NIE in mid 1956 that analyzed the power balance from the *Soviet* perspective reflected a clear awareness that Soviet leaders had reason to be fearful of U.S. strategic forces. "Their stated fear of the influence of 'aggressive-minded' leaders in the United States may be in some degree real," it said. "They probably feel therefore that there is a background of latent danger against which they must calculate, in each instance, the particular risks attending the policy decisions they make."[72]

Scholars have argued for decades that Khrushchev's claims of having achieved an ICBM capability between 1958 and 1961 deceived the Eisenhower administration and tilted the perceived power balance in Moscow's favor.[73] But analyses based on internal documents of the Eisenhower administration show that Eisenhower never abandoned his earlier view of the military balance.[74] In early 1958, Eisenhower learned that no Soviet missile tests had taken place since the previous September and told the NSC he was "inclined to think the Soviets were having some missile trouble."[75] When he learned a year later that U-2 flights had found no ICBM launch platforms at all in the Soviet Union, his suspicions that Khrushchev was simply bluffing about his missile capabilities were confirmed.[76] In mid 1959, the Joint Chiefs of Staff were telling the president that the United States still enjoyed military superiority over the USSR, and Eisenhower in turn told Lyndon Johnson, "If we were to release our nuclear stockpile on the Soviet Union, the main danger would arise not from retaliation but from fallout in the earth's atmosphere."[77]

Summarizing the latest intelligence estimates on Soviet missiles in January 1960, CIA Director Allen Dulles told Eisenhower that there was no evidence that the USSR was carrying out a crash program of missile construction, confirming what Eisenhower already believed. Continuing U-2 flights aimed at photographing potential Soviet sites over the next seven months failed to identify a single site, as reported in an August 1960 intelligence estimate.[78] As Eisenhower's second term in office drew to a close, he had no reason to believe that the imbalance of military power favoring the United States had yet been seriously eroded.

The knowledge of strategic asymmetry and of the pattern of Soviet conciliatory policies that had ensued from 1953 onward played a key role in the attitudes of Eisenhower and Dulles toward the risk of war in Cold War crises. In planning for a major landing of conventional forces in Lebanon as a show of force in the Middle East in response to the overthrow of the pro-Western Iraqi regime in July 1958, Eisenhower discounted the probability of any Soviet military reaction. He was more concerned about the "attitude of people in the area" toward the U.S. intervention, he said, than about "the Russian question." Eisenhower and Dulles agreed that the USSR was not ready to "risk general war," because it lacked long-range missiles and was "far inferior [to the United States] in long-range aircraft."[79]

In early December 1958, Dulles expressed the view that U.S. strategic superiority gave the United States a decisive political edge over the USSR in the Berlin crisis. The USSR, according to Dulles, had "an inadequate supply of missiles" and would not resist a U.S. "show of force" because of this "relative weakness." The mortally ill Dulles told his successor, Christian Herter, in March 1959 that if the United States held to its position on access to Berlin, "there is not one chance in 1000 the Soviets will push it to the point of war." Both State Department and Defense Department officials agreed with this assessment.[80] And in the 1958 Taiwan Strait crisis, putting likely Soviet behavior in the context of U.S. strategic superiority, Dulles gave a background briefing to the press in which he said that the USSR would not necessarily come to China's aid, despite its security treaty obligation, even if the United States bombed Chinese airbases.[81]

The Kennedy Administration's Two-Level Assessment

In his summit meeting with Soviet Premier Nikita Khrushchev in Vienna in June 1961, John F. Kennedy suggested that a rough parity existed between the superpowers, a political gesture that infuriated the JCS when they learned about it.[82] Kennedy's action has been interpreted as reflecting his own assessment of the power balance as roughly equal, based on his belief that the USSR held a lead in missile production.[83] Recently published evidence has revealed, however, that Kennedy knew from the beginning of his administration that there was no missile gap, contrary to his own statements. He had been briefed by Allen Dulles in August 1960, on the basis of intelligence assessments showing that not a single Soviet ICBM site been found, despite repeated U-2 flights. And in late January and early February 1961, Secretary of Defense Robert S. McNamara personally reviewed the photographic evidence from satellite reconnaissance since August 1960 and concluded that the United States was in fact still far superior to the Soviet Union in ICBMs. Kennedy got the same message from a briefing by Jerome Weisner in early February, and conceded in a telephone conversation with Charles Hitch of the RAND Corporation a few days later that there was no missile gap.[84] Kennedy and McNamara both knew, therefore, that the United States still held overwhelming strategic dominance over the USSR when all delivery vehicles on both sides were taken into account.

In July, the CIA had passed on to John F. Kennedy and the State Department a report by a CIA "mole" in the Soviet government, Lieutenant Colonel Oleg Penkovsky, based on his conversation with a high-ranking

Soviet marshal, that the USSR had built virtually no missiles and that Khrushchev's public statements implying a readiness for war were simply a "bluff."[85] Immediately after Kennedy's hard-line Berlin speech signaling U.S. readiness for war on July 25, moreover, he was told of a study by his White House strategic arms specialist Carl Kaysen that showed that a "disarming first strike" against Soviet strategic forces could be carried out with a high level of confidence that it would catch them all on the ground.[86] U.S. intelligence had pinpointed the location of the Soviet missile sites, and, as Roger Hilsman, director of the State Department's Bureau of Intelligence and Research, recalled, "[t]he whole Soviet ICBM system was suddenly obsolescent."[87] Defense Secretary McNamara and an interagency group both recognized that the submarine-based missiles that U.S. intelligence had expected the USSR to deploy in the early 1960s had not materialized and were unlikely to do so anytime soon.[88]

As for the Soviet bomber force, which had always been dismissed by U.S. analysts, the intelligence community concluded that it would have only "some prospect" of having enough bombers survive a U.S. first strike to be able to mount any retaliation. Those that did survive, moreover, would probably be located at a few bases in the Arctic and would have to be launched in "successive waves" over a number of hours, making them vulnerable to U.S. air defenses.[89] Kennedy and his advisers also knew that the USSR could not count on having any second-strike capability, and that this weakness would affect the Soviet position on a wide range of issues, particularly U.S. intervention in peripheral areas. The reality of strategic asymmetry gave the United States a marked political advantage over the Soviet Union, and McNamara and others in the administration were happy to exploit it.

On November 11, 1961, McNamara outlined the overwhelming nuclear superiority of the United States and concluded, "We have less reason to fear all-out nuclear war than do the Soviets." Assistant Secretary of Defense Paul Nitze also emphasized in a speech that U.S. nuclear superiority, "particularly when viewed from the Soviet side," was "strategically important in the equation of deterrence and strategy."[90] In testimony before the Senate Armed Services and Foreign Relations Committees in February 1962, McNamara described the strategic balance explicitly in terms of asymmetry. The entire Soviet strategic force, he said, was "vulnerable to attack, being deployed at fixed, soft bases," and U.S. bombers had sufficient knowledge of the locations and limitations of Soviet air defenses to "avoid or neutralize them." McNamara declared in September 1962 that the decisive superiority enjoyed by the United States would last "for at least the next few years." Kennedy's military adviser, General Maxwell Taylor, wrote to him in August 1962 that

Soviet leaders "must appreciate their inferiority . . . particularly in numbers of strategic weapons and delivery vehicles and in early warning." Their "growing appreciation of the effectiveness of U.S. reconnaissance capabilities," he added, "has probably been a shock."[91]

In apparent contradiction to the administration's recognition that the strategic balance dramatically favored the United States and was seen as such by Moscow, Secretary of Defense Robert S. McNamara also seemed to assert that a nuclear standoff existed between the superpowers. McNamara told colleagues that he had concluded that it would not be technically feasible to disarm more than 90 percent of Soviet strategic forces, and that massive U.S. casualties could not be avoided, even if the United States struck first. And in an NSC meeting in late 1963, McNamara declared that in a nuclear exchange the losses on each side would be from fifty to a hundred million lives.[92]

As in the case of statements by Eisenhower emphasizing the certainty of mutual destruction in a nuclear war, however, these statements should be interpreted in light of their relationship to a struggle between civilians and the military—particularly the air force—over strategic forces budget and policy issues. In 1962, air force officials were expressing confidence in the first-strike capabilities of the United States. One general declared privately at the time of the Cuban Missile Crisis that the air force was "quite sure" of being able to hit close to 100 percent of the Soviet missiles and long-range bombers in such a strike.[93] Kennedy, McNamara, and national security adviser McGeorge Bundy realized that their acceptance of the position that a successful first strike was feasible would mean that the JCS would continue to demand much larger strategic forces in order to support the first-strike option, which would in turn provoke Moscow to produce a much larger ICBM force and invite an open-ended arms race. McNamara, with Kennedy's support, resisted the JCS demands for the much larger numbers of ICBMs needed to maintain a first-strike capability.[94] The assertion that tens of millions of Americans would perish in any nuclear war was integral to McNamara's argument for a more limited force.

The position that McNamara took on the debate with the JCS on the feasibility and desirability of actually initiating nuclear war must be distinguished from the views of Kennedy, McNamara, and Bundy on how the strategic balance affected superpower relations more generally. They all recognized that asymmetry between U.S. and Soviet strategic forces was a reality and that it created serious insecurity for Khrushchev, constraining his options far more than those of the United States on a wide range of Cold War issues.

Kennedy's statement about the nuclear balance during the Cuban Missile Crisis reflects an instrumental use of mutual deterrence to fend off pressures for war. During an "Executive Committee" (ExComm) meeting, Kennedy said: "I think [Khrushchev] thinks he's got enough to cause such damage to us that one wouldn't want to accept that danger unless the provocation was extreme."[95] During those crisis deliberations, Kennedy was arguing against the aggressive military course advocated by most of his advisers—a massive air strike against Soviet missiles and forces in Cuba. Thus his statement suggesting that Khrushchev was confident about having a second-strike capability was clearly aimed at discouraging a military action against Soviet forces in Cuba that might begin a process of mutual escalation. Kennedy feared irrational behavior on both sides in such an escalating conflict more than any confidence by Khrushchev in his second-strike capabilities.[96]

A number of Kennedy's advisers did not, however, share his caution about assuming a risk of nuclear war by attacking Soviet forces in Cuba. According to an account written soon after the Cuban Missile Crisis, based on interviews with the participants in the ExComm meetings, most of Kennedy's advisers believed that it was "unlikely that the Soviets would retaliate, especially since the SAC would be on a full alert condition." Paul Nitze, Douglas Dillon, and Maxwell Taylor doubted the USSR would respond militarily to air strikes to take out the Cuban missile bases, citing the decisive U.S. strategic advantage. Taylor wrote to McNamara on October 26, "We have the strategic advantage in our general war operations. This is no time to run scared."[97]

Kennedy and McNamara, like Eisenhower and Dulles before them, had two different assessments of the strategic balance for different purposes. They assessed it as one of mutual deterrence for the purpose of fending off extreme proposals from the military and hard-liners in the administration, including the proposals from most of Kennedy's advisers in the Cuban Missile Crisis for a massive air assault against Soviet bases in Cuba. But they also recognized that the existence of strategic asymmetry conferred an overall advantage to the United States in the Cold War by constraining Soviet aggressiveness in many areas of conflict. Some of Kennedy's advisers, moreover, were so impressed by the existence of strategic asymmetry that they did not hesitate to take the risk of escalation with the USSR during the missile crisis.

Assessing the Breakup of the World Communist System

Thus far, this account of the U.S. assessment of the East-West balance of power has been confined to its military aspect. The Kennedy administration also took into account other major dimensions of the global situation, however, including the Sino-Soviet conflict, the deepening Soviet economic crisis, and the trend toward the breakup of the world system of Communist parties. By late 1962, these elements of the global power situation, taken together, represented a further shift of seismic proportions in the distribution of power.

The Sino-Soviet conflict captured the imagination of Kennedy's national security advisers from the beginning of the administration. "The surfacing of acute Sino-Soviet differences validates the existence of a major variable in our strategic calculations, which we should take fully into account," a White House national security staff aide, Robert W. Komer, noted soon after Kennedy took office.[98] Kennedy and his top foreign policy advisers discussed the Soviet worry about China, especially regarding atomic weapons, and agreed that improving relations with the Soviet Union would exacerbate the split between the Communist powers. In preparing Kennedy for his meeting with Khrushchev at the Vienna Summit in early June, therefore, the president's advisers recommended trying to get Soviet agreement to restrain Chinese aggressiveness, and encouraging joint superpower interest in a "stable viable world order."[99]

By the end of 1961, the CIA was already beginning to assess the global and regional power balance in triangular rather than bipolar terms. The Office of National Estimates issued a memorandum asserting that the Sino-Soviet conflict was really "a clash of national interests," and that a "showdown of historic proportions may be imminent."[100] Two months later, the CIA's Office of Current Intelligence went farther, arguing that the USSR and Communist China "have already broken."[101] This put Khrushchev's policy in a new perspective. As they watched the Sino-Soviet struggle unfold, administration officials actually began to debate whether the Khrushchev regime still had any revolutionary ambitions. At Secretary of State Dean Rusk's policy planning meeting on January 2, 1962, former U.S. ambassador to the Soviet Union Charles Bohlen likened the Soviet leadership under Khrushchev to the Mensheviks during the Russian Revolution, and the Chinese to the Bolsheviks. Khrushchev had already provoked opposition from orthodox figures in Moscow by "changing the ideology," Bohlen suggested.[102]

Testifying in executive session before the Foreign Relations Committee in early 1962, Rusk acknowledged the advantage that the conflict between the Communist powers gave the United States, expressing doubt that the USSR wanted China to have sophisticated weapons, least of all nuclear weapons. He also noted that both the USSR and the PRC were "putting considerable energy and effort" into competing with each other, "and that, I suppose, works to our advantage."[103] The May 1962 NIE on Soviet Foreign Policy similarly suggested that "Soviet energies now directed against the West may be diverted to combating Chinese policies in various areas." A full-fledged power rivalry with China, moreover, would cause Moscow to see interests on some issues that "parallel those of the West."[104] Senior officials then began to discuss how the United States could best take advantage of the Sino-Soviet conflict to move either or both of the Communist giants further toward explicit accommodation with U.S. interests.[105]

Another new theme that emerged in the post–missile crisis power assessment was that the Soviet Union did not have the economic capabilities to compete with the United States. Assistant Secretary of Defense William P. Bundy told attendees at a Pentagon strategy seminar in mid 1963 that the Soviet Union was "in a very drastic resource pinch," and that it was therefore unable to compete with the United States in the arms race without danger to its own economy. In early 1964, the CIA focused on the central importance of the economic factor in the power balance for the first time. It portrayed Khrushchev as having been forced by serious economic pressures and by the "dramatic demonstration of the unfavorable relations of power" in the Cuban Missile Crisis to "find ways to contain the arms race and reduce its burden on the Soviet economy," and thus to undertake a major shift in foreign policy, signaled by the Test Ban Treaty.[106]

The new clarity about the power relationship with the USSR was explicitly linked with Soviet defensiveness and respect for the status quo. In March 1963, a CIA intelligence memorandum portrayed Khrushchev as worried that the balance of power had shifted decisively against the Soviet Union and restated its pre-Kennedy assessment that the USSR had no interest in helping local Communists gain power anywhere in the world. A mid-1963 estimate declared that the Soviet leaders now understood that this was a period "when they are relatively weak and their enemy feels strong." The Cuban missile ploy was viewed as having been "in considerable part due to Soviet recognition of this trend." The estimate went so far as to declare that "the task of Soviet diplomacy is primarily to pursue defensive tactics until a more favorable correlation of forces can be brought about."[107]

The fundamental shift in world politics was so clear by the time Lyndon Johnson entered the White House in November 1963 that he referred at an NSC meeting to "the basic improvement in the balance of power which had taken place in the last three years."[108] The Kennedy and Johnson administrations thus had a decidedly more optimistic view of the East-West power relationship than the Eisenhower administration had held. National security officials now understood that the USSR neither represented a revolutionary force in world politics nor exercised real control over other Communist movements. Indeed, they had reason to believe that the USSR now shared some important political-military interests with the United States. The images of a monolithic Communist movement and implacable Soviet hostility had been replaced by an image of a much more pluralistic and inherently less threatening world.

SOVIET AND CHINESE ASSESSMENTS

Moscow and the Emergence of Strategic Asymmetry

The Soviet assessment of the balance of power in 1953–54 can be inferred from the combination of domestic and international policies that Stalin's successors put in place to deal with the reality of the massive U.S. military buildup and the growing gap between the superpowers in the strategic asymmetry that had emerged. The chairman of the Soviet Council of Ministers, Georgy Malenkov, argued that the mere existence of nuclear weapons in the hands of the two superpowers, and the fact that nuclear war would mean the end of civilization, forced both camps to seek peaceful coexistence. Based on this premise, Malenkov called for deep cuts in military spending. Although that argument seemed to suggest that Malenkov believed that a situation of mutual deterrence or "existential deterrence" existed, the Soviet leadership clearly knew that the situation was one of strategic asymmetry. Malenkov was in effect accepting that asymmetry for a relatively long period in order to restore a seriously unbalanced Soviet economy. He had no choice but to sacrifice any notion of competing with the United States in the Cold War and to seek an accommodation with the United States.

Soviet weakness, especially in relation to the United States, thus determined the Kremlin's grand strategy. This causal relationship was further underlined when Malenkov's Politburo rival Nikita Khrushchev immediately adopted Malenkov's national security strategy as soon as he began his ascent to power in late 1954. Khrushchev now accepted the reduction of tension with the United States and the Western alliance through negotiations and avoidance of confrontation as the central aim of Soviet diplomacy. He even justified his new position by adopting Malenkov's rationale that the leaders of the United States were reasonable men who were committed to peaceful coexistence with the Soviet Union.[109]

It has long been a staple of Cold War historiography that Khrushchev believed that the East-West power balance or "correlation of forces" had shifted in favor of the Soviet Union in the 1957–61 period, allowing Communism to go on the offensive against the capitalist world. That assumption has continued to inform even more recent works on this period of the Cold War.[110] A review of the evidence confirms, however, that Khrushchev's assessment of the global structure of power was utterly realistic and that it did not change between 1956 and the early 1960s.

Official Soviet statements in the late 1950s and early 1960s never actually claimed that the military balance favored the Soviet Union, or even that the USSR was equal to the United States. The most thorough study of Soviet statements on the issue observed that Moscow's assessment of the "correlation of forces" carefully avoided taking a clear position on the actual global power balance. And despite Khrushchev's own remarks to the press about having long-range missiles, Soviet commentators refrained from claiming that the Soviet Union had achieved military superiority or even parity with the United States. What they did claim was that the United States and the other capitalist states were now deterred by Soviet military might from attacking the Communist bloc—exactly the same position that had been taken by Soviet officials *before Sputnik*.[111] These statements hardly constitute evidence of Soviet confidence in a favorable "correlation of forces" in the world, much less in the military balance.

Furthermore, in his discussions with other Communist parties, Khrushchev did not to claim that the global correlation of forces had tilted toward the Soviet bloc, much to the chagrin of the Chinese. The Chinese Communist Party's *Renmin ribao* (People's Daily) complained after the 1957 Moscow conference of Communist parties—held after the Soviet *Sputnik* triumph—that the USSR had argued that the principal element in the correlation of forces between the two blocs was not military power but economic productivity, that the socialist camp was still behind the capitalist world in industrial productivity and technology, and that the Soviet Union had no lasting edge in missile technology. That account is consistent with Khrushchev's public presentation of the international strategy of the world Communist movement at the Twenty-first Congress of the CPSU in 1959. In that speech, Khrushchev asserted that the fundamental problem for the Communist bloc was to overtake the capitalist world in the competition for both overall volume of production and per capita output. Khrushchev predicted that, by 1970 or shortly thereafter, the Communist bloc's economic growth would tip the global "correlation of forces" decisively in its favor.[112]

It is not at all clear, however, that Khrushchev really believed that the Soviet Union could catch up to the United States economically in such a short period. One of Khrushchev's speechwriters, Fedor Burlatsky, has revealed that Khrushchev made the commitment to surpassing the United States against the advice of his own economic planners and that he simply fabricated statistics to support that goal.[113] This suggests that he adopted it for reasons other than confidence about the Soviet Union's ability to defeat the United States in economic competition. It reinforces other indications that Khrushchev viewed the military trends in East-West relations as extremely unfavorable and was also aware that competing with the United States in political-military power would have been both dangerous and probably futile. That appears to be his real reason for deliberately shifting the focus of East-West struggle from the military balance to the economic sphere.

Khrushchev revealed in his memoirs just how keenly aware he was of the strategic asymmetry between the superpowers, recalling that the real reason the Soviet Union could not agree to the Eisenhower administration's proposal in the mid 1950s for on-site inspection and reconnaissance was that the United States would have "discovered that we were in a relatively weak position, and that realization might have encouraged them to attack us."[114] Khrushchev knew very well that the Soviet strategic bomber force did not constitute a real retaliatory force against U.S. targets, which is why Soviet leaders never talked about their bomber force in connection with the Soviet nuclear deterrent against the United States.[115] Those same fears motivated his later claims to have ICBMs that did not yet exist. Khrushchev told his son that in order to "prevent an attack," he had exaggerated Soviet missile production to make the United States believe the USSR had more of a strategic deterrent than it actually did.[116]

In at least two Cold War crises following his missile breakthrough claim, moreover, Khrushchev referred explicitly to his fear that the United States might go to war or even attack the socialist states and shied away from any risk of confrontation with Washington. In July 1958, when the United States mounted a major show of force in Lebanon, which Moscow believed was aimed at overthrowing the new regime of General Abdul Karim Kassem in Iraq, Egypt's President Abdel Nasser demanded that the USSR issue a deterrent threat regarding any U.S.-inspired military move against Iraq. But Khrushchev flatly refused. According to an eyewitness account, Khrushchev told Nasser he thought "the Americans had gone off their heads" and said, "Frankly we are not ready for confrontation. We are not ready for World War III."[117] And after Mao had initiated the Taiwan Strait crisis a few months later, Khrushchev told the Chinese ambassador in Moscow that he considered the U.S. policy of nuclear "brinksmanship" to be "extremely dangerous," and warned that the United States might even wage an aggressive war against the socialist countries.[118]

Starting with his report to the CPSU's Twentieth Congress in 1956, Khrushchev's international line, not only for the Soviet Union, but for the entire socialist camp, was expressed in the slogan of "maintaining peace." That slogan was in turn linked with Khrushchev's insistence that Communist parties use peaceful forms of struggle in their quest for power, arguing that the peaceful coexistence between the two blocs made a "peaceful transition" to socialism increasingly possible. The Soviet draft of the final statement of the 1957 Moscow conference of Communist parties said nothing about military means, holding up the peaceful parliamentary path to power as the *only* appropriate revolutionary strategy for all Communist parties. The final text of the conference declaration was modified to read that the question of peaceful or nonpeaceful transition did not depend entirely on the revolutionary side only at the insistence of the Chinese and Vietnamese parties, in order to avoid an open breach with those parties.[119] The Soviet Party had never actually agreed to that position.

The 1958 coup against the pro-Western Iraqi regime brought the most serious test of Khrushchev's international line up to that point. The Iraqi Communist Party (ICP), which had become the single most powerful political force in the country, began a campaign in spring 1959 to demand participation in the new government. After local communists in one key city carried out an uprising against anti-Communist elements, the Iraqi premier, General Kassem, began arresting and murdering hundreds of rank-and-file members. The ICP then abruptly ended its campaign for inclusion in the government and criticized that policy as too leftist, explicitly citing the internal and international constellation of power.[120] The evidence indicates that the CPSU put pressure on a divided Iraqi Communist Party to retreat from its bid for a share of political power, a course the USSR attacked as "irresponsible."[121]

A Soviet spokesman openly criticized the Iraqi party's bid for power in 1960 as an example of "premature slogans of socialist transformation . . . where conditions for them have not yet matured." Even more revealing was his pointed suggestion that the lessons of the Iraqi experience should be heeded by "some Communist parties of the East and Latin America, if they are faced with basically the same task."[122] This was a warning to those parties that still had aspirations to attain power through means other than parliamentary elections.

Khrushchev frequently implied that the risk of U.S. intervention in response to a Communist bid for power, and of the subsequent escalation of such a war, was the overriding concern behind this international line. Khrushchev's slogan "A small imperialist war can develop into a world nuclear war" was a veiled warning to Communist regimes and parties against the use of armed force. Occasionally, Moscow was explicit about the reason for opposing armed struggle. An article in a 1960 Soviet journal stated flatly that revolutionary change had to be brought about by means that would not lead to "military clashes of the two antipodal systems."[123] In the final declaration of the 1960 Moscow conference, the only reference to "national liberation wars" suggested that it was a term reserved for armed struggles by colonial peoples fighting for independence.[124] And although the statement allowed the "possibility" that a violent transition to socialism might be necessary, it reiterated that a peaceful transition was possible in many countries. Most important from the Soviet perspective, however, the text bound all the Communist parties to pay "due regard to the international situation" in deciding on their revolutionary strategies. This codicil was scarcely disguised code wording for the Soviet insistence that Communist parties—and especially parties in divided states—should not violate the Soviet international line of maintaining peace.[125]

Khrushchev apparently had very accurate intelligence on the Kennedy administration's strategic force deployments and future plans. A retrospective Pentagon analysis nearly twenty years later concluded that Soviet projections in mid 1961 of the U.S. deployments through 1965 had come very close to the actual deployments.[126] Equally important, Khrushchev's hopes for creating the illusion in the United States that Moscow already had a credible deterrent were threatened by developments in U.S. intelligence from mid 1960 onward. When the U-2 spy plane was shot down over the Soviet Union in May 1960, Soviet intelligence learned from film recovered from the plane just how precise the U.S. photo intelligence was.[127] Just a month later, KGB chief Aleksandr Shelepin personally informed Khrushchev of an intelligence report that the United States thought it had the capability to destroy the Soviet strategic force in a first strike, although the Defense Department believed that the opportunity would soon disappear.[128]

Since the demise of the Soviet Union, a number of Kremlin insiders have recalled that in 1961–62, Soviet Party and government leaders, and Khrushchev in particular, had concluded that the United States now believed that Soviet strategic forces were vulnerable to a first strike.[129] In April 1962, Soviet intelligence passed on another report, which it believed to be credible, indicating that the United States had made plans in June 1961 for a first strike against Soviet bombers and missiles later in 1961 but had called it off after the USSR exploded a new 50-megaton weapon in the autumn of 1961.[130]

Khrushchev himself later said that he took the risk of introducing medium-range ballistic missiles into Cuba in 1962 because he lacked a strategic deterrent and perceived the United States as increasingly inclined to exploit the situation of strategic asymmetry. Khrushchev said the Americans had not "faced such a real threat of destruction" until the emplacement of missiles in Cuba.[131] This point is further underlined by a statement in Khrushchev's memoirs that was deleted from earlier volumes and published only in 1990: "To tell the truth, I have to say that if the Americans had started a war at the time we were not prepared to adequately attack the United States."[132]

The evidence indicates, therefore, that in 1956–57, Khrushchev shifted the focus of the official Soviet assessment of the "correlation of forces" in the world from military to economic prowess precisely because he knew that the USSR would not be able to achieve strategic symmetry for many years. From 1958 on, he was acutely aware of the parlous condition of the Soviet deterrent. After mid 1960, moreover, he had strong reason to believe that the United States had full knowledge of Soviet weakness, and his anxiety—and that of the Communist Party and military leadership—grew accordingly.

Mao and the Military Balance: "Paper Tiger" or Hegemonic Power?

Did Mao Zedong determine his international line in the late 1950s and early 1960s in the belief that the Soviet Union had achieved military superiority over the United States after the launching of *Sputnik*, as has sometimes been argued?[133] This enduring interpretation of the Cold War in East Asia in the late 1950s and early 1960s does not hold up in light of the wealth of evidence now available. It is now clear that Mao did not underestimate the economic or military might of the United States in relation to the USSR, and that he fully acknowledged the necessity for Chinese restraint in the face of U.S. power.

Mao had every reason, of course, to want Khrushchev to publicly exaggerate Soviet strategic power in relation to the United States, because until 1960, China was heavily dependent on the Soviet strategic deterrent as a counterweight to U.S. military power.[134] That dependence explains why, at the 1957 Moscow conference, Mao defended a strong leading role in the Communist bloc for the USSR on the grounds that it was strong enough to protect the other members of the bloc.[135] In short, Mao wanted the USSR to act as though it represented a strong military counterweight, regardless of the truth.

New documentation on Mao's thinking during this period suggests that, after the USSR demonstrated its advances in rocketry by putting *Sputnik* into space, Mao assumed it would soon have intercontinental missiles but did not believe that the military balance now favored the Communist bloc or even that Soviet military power could effectively counterbalance the United States in world politics. More important, that incipient development caused Mao to become concerned that the USSR would discount the value of its alliance with the PRC and seek détente with the United States. Thus, Mao's strategic response to the development of Soviet ICBMs was not to shift Chinese foreign policy toward more aggressiveness, but to begin to plan for the Great Leap Forward, with the aim of building up China's own economic and military power at a much more rapid pace in order to make the PRC more self-reliant.[136]

This interpretation is supported by Mao's public arguments at the time. Despite Chinese exploitation of Soviet rocket development for propaganda purposes, Mao's two speeches in Moscow during the 1957 conference did not suggest a power balance favorable to the Communist world but rather underlined his concern that the U.S. threat to China be taken seriously by the Kremlin. His November 6, 1957, speech emphasized that the possibility of war would continue "so long as imperialism exists" and strongly opposed a Yugoslav suggestion that East-West differences were now of reduced importance. A second major speech, on November 18, predicted the eventual fall of U.S. imperialism but emphasized that "strategically we should despise all enemies, and tactically take them seriously. . . . [I]f we do not attach importance to the enemy in specific questions, in every question concerning every enemy, we will commit the mistake of adventurism." Thus Mao was not arguing that the Communist states were now in a position to taken the offensive against the United States but was urging both vigilance and caution in the face of U.S. power and aggressiveness, which he implied would not be substantially diminished by any Soviet triumphs in rocket science.[137]

Mao's statement at the 1957 Moscow conference that the "East Wind Prevails over the West Wind" and his characterization of the United States as a "paper tiger," which have often been cited as evidence that he believed that the strategic military balance had actually shifted in favor of the Communist bloc, were actually expressions of Mao's long-term optimism about the greater social and political strengths of socialism. In fact, Mao had always deliberately downplayed the role of military power in his analysis of the "relationship of forces" between socialism and imperialism, precisely because he knew that the United States held such overwhelming military superiority over the Communist bloc. Mao had advanced the idea that the "forces of socialism" were already stronger than those of the imperialists and referred to the United States as a "paper tiger" as early as 1946, based on nothing more than the Soviet victory over Nazi Germany and the Chinese Communist prospect for defeating the Kuomintang.[138]

The use of the term "paper tiger" certainly did not mean that Mao believed China could openly challenge U.S. power in East Asia, even with Soviet backing. Indeed, Mao's conduct of the 1958 Quemoy crisis was aimed at raising international tensions while avoiding actions that might provoke the United States actually to go to war.[139] After the crisis, Mao rebuked those who had mistakenly thought that he had been denigrating the military power of the United States in using the term "paper tiger." These people, Mao said, "did not understand the paper tiger problem."[140]

After the Korean War, the Chinese leadership believed that the United States probably would not attack China for at least a period of years but remained concerned about the possibility of the United States using Taiwan and/or South Korea to launch such an attack.[141] The PRC first began to display overt fear of a U.S. nuclear attack after public U.S. threats to use nuclear weapons against China over the offshore islands in mid January 1955. Chinese officials directed the population to begin preparing for a possible U.S. nuclear attack on China, and the phrase "sudden atomic attack" began to appear in descriptions of Chinese military training exercises. In July 1955, Marshall Ye Jianying warned the Chinese people to be prepared for a sudden attack by the "imperialists" and admitted that, in a nuclear war, the Chinese army would be at a serious disadvantage in relation to the aggressors. In mid 1957, the PLA's chief of general staff called for broader precautions against such an attack, including dispersal of industrial bases, prevention of overconcentration of population in urban areas, and stronger civil defense.[142]

Statements by Mao that he was unconcerned about U.S. nuclear power cannot be taken at face value, because of his need to maintain Chinese morale and to convince the Americans that China could not be bullied. Mao believed that displaying fear of the enemy would not help prevent war. "If we show fear," he said in 1955, "the enemy will consider us weak and easy to bully. In other words, if we give them an inch they will take a mile and intensify their military expansionism."[143] Thus Mao's bravado about nuclear war was a deliberate tactic by the leader of a weak and vulnerable state to resist what the Chinese viewed as nuclear blackmail by a power that had publicly vowed to work for the overthrow of the PRC.[144]

From 1958 to 1962, Mao believed that a U.S-led invasion of the mainland or nuclear attack on China was unlikely, at least in the short run, provided that China did nothing to provoke such an attack. He reasoned that the United States would not risk its position of dominance in non-Communist Asia and the rest of the world, which is what he believed it really wanted, by launching an aggressive war against China. But even during that period, Mao always warned that China could not rule out the possibility of a surprise attack by the United States and had to be prepared for it. In an unpublished 1958 speech, for example, he spoke resignedly about the possibility that the United States might go so far as to launch a nuclear war against China. He urged the Chinese people to be prepared for a "great catastrophe, a scene of utter devastation and unrelieved disaster" if that should happen.[145]

The summary of a conversation between Mao and the Soviet ambassador to the PRC in October 1959, found in Soviet archives in the 1990s, shows that the Chinese leader clearly recognized the extent of U.S. military dominance in Asia and Washington's willingness to use force rather than give up any of its power positions in the region. With typical Maoist overstatement, he declared that "everything" in Asia, "beginning with Taiwan and ending with Turkey," was the "American world," and that the Americans would "try . . . to hold on to everything, not wishing to let anything escape their grasp, not even our Chinese island Quemoy." Faced with this American power and determination, Mao said, China would not "touch them, even in places where they are weak."[146] These comments underline the fact that Mao took into account not just the local power balance in each country but the overall distribution of power that favored the United States so heavily. Indeed, the evidence available indicates that Mao had always regarded the offshore islands as untouchable and had no intention during the period under study of testing the U.S. commitment to protecting them, much less the U.S. commitment to the defense of Taiwan itself.[147]

Mao's ideologically tinged optimism about the ultimate defeat of U.S. global power was based on the belief that U.S. domination would be opposed over time by an increasing number of states, as well as by popular movements around the world. During the late 1950s and early 1960s, his strategy for opposing U.S. global power represented a revised version of his earlier concept of an "intermediate zone" in world politics. It was aimed not at pushing forward Communist revolution but at obtaining as many allies as possible against U.S. military deployments and U.S. diplomatic and economic isolation of China, including advanced capitalist states such as France and Japan, bourgeois nationalists, and, at least in Asia, even reactionary, but independent, rulers.[148] This was not a strategy reflecting a sense that the world situation favored an offensive by the world Communist movement, but a defensive strategy for coping with the threat of U.S. power.

The massive failure of Mao's "Great Leap Forward" campaign of 1957–58, with its attendant food shortages and social unrest, was soon followed by the emergence of the Sino-Soviet conflict, which resulted in the withdrawal of Soviet economic assistance and also left the Soviet defense commitment to China in serious doubt. This series of blows to China's power potential and security left the Chinese leaders feeling far more vulnerable to U.S. attack in the early 1960s than they had felt in the second half of the 1950s. The balance of power undoubtedly seemed to be at its most unfavorable for the Chinese regime in 1962. At the end of 1961, mass starvation had begun to occur in many provinces. From early 1962 until midyear, the Chinese Nationalist regime stepped up its threat to invade the mainland in 1962, provoking Chinese fears of a new U.S.-Jiang plan to stimulate a domestic uprising that could be the occasion for a U.S. invasion.[149] During that period, Chinese military leaders saw two possibilities: first, that there would be no war for several years, and second, that the United States would engage in a "military adventure" against China, which might take the form of a surprise nuclear attack.[150]

The Chinese were also confronted in 1962 with a new military aggressiveness by India on the Chinese border and with Soviet and American military assistance to India for use against China.[151] In a conversation with a British diplomat in late 1962, Zhou Enlai seemed "intensely nervous" about China's national security. Zhou described the strategic situation as one of the United States "encircling China," citing U.S. troops in Taiwan, Thailand, and Vietnam, and "the new U.S. military relationship with India."[152]

During the early 1960s, therefore, Mao assessed the balance of power between the United States and the PRC—now without the assurance of Soviet diplomatic, much less military, support in the event of a military confrontation—in the context of a dramatic worsening of both the domestic and international situations. If Mao's attitude before this turn of events, as expressed to the Soviet ambassador in 1959, was one of acceptance of U.S. hegemonic power in Asia, his view of the power balance in the world and in East Asia after 1959 was certainly far more pessimistic.

THE IMBALANCE OF POWER
AND THE DYNAMICS OF THE COLD WAR

This chapter has marshaled the evidence that a situation of unambiguous U.S. military dominance emerged during the Korean War that was recognized by the leaders of the United States, the Soviet Union, and China throughout the period between that war and the major U.S. combat intervention in

Vietnam. Although Eisenhower, Dulles, and McNamara all made statements that asserted the existence of mutual deterrence, they were calculated in each case to discourage policy or budget initiatives by the military leadership, particularly the air force, that were regarded by the president as provocative. Both Presidents Eisenhower and Kennedy and their chief advisers were well aware of the weakness of the Soviet deterrent and the fact that it reduced Soviet willingness to risk confrontation with the United States.

The stark imbalance of power shaped the basic pattern of Cold War policy both in Washington and in the Communist capitals. For the USSR, the option of trying to compete with the United States for global power and military preeminence was quite unrealistic, given the fact that the U.S. power base was many times larger, and that any assertiveness by the USSR in conflict areas would risk a war with the United States. Thus Malenkov and the post-Stalinist collective leadership and, by late 1954, Khrushchev sought to reach an understanding with the United States that would avoid any possibility of military confrontation and allow the Soviet Union to become a modern industrial power, while consolidating its control over its security sphere in Eastern and Central Europe. That strategy called not only for avoiding actions that would provoke the United States but for actively seeking to curb the ambitions of Communist parties to win power by means other than parliamentary elections. Apart from Iraq's abortive bid for power in 1958–59, the primary example of such ambitions that needed to be curbed was the Vietnamese Communist drive to oust the U.S.-supported regime in South Vietnam beginning in 1960.

For the Eisenhower administration, on the other hand, the asymmetry of power provided a strong incentive to pursue a more assertive policy in relations with the USSR, as well as in areas of conflict on the periphery of the Soviet Union and China. A major problem for Eisenhower and Dulles, in fact, was the insistence by the U.S. Joint Chiefs of Staff on making demands on the Soviet Union and China that were so extreme as to risk war. Both Ike and Dulles favored exploiting U.S. supremacy for political-diplomatic advantage but opposed the policy of presenting ultimatums to Moscow and Beijing, advocated by the military.

In the early 1960s, a new set of trends—the Sino-Soviet conflict, the independence of Communist parties from Moscow, and the faltering of the Soviet economy—tilted the East-West power relationship even more sharply in favor of the United States. The impact of these developments on the thinking of U.S. national security officials can scarcely be overestimated. With world Communism seriously divided and a vastly weakened

Soviet Union shifting to a more ambiguous position between the United States and China in world politics, U.S. national security officials were bound to conclude that the United States had a free hand to assert its power in Southeast Asia.

Looking back on the evolution of U.S. views on the East-West power balance during the period between the Korean and Vietnam wars, therefore, we see two distinct formative periods in which U.S. perceptions were undergoing major changes: the first, from 1953 through mid 1955, and second, from 1961 through 1964. The first period was associated with the fundamental shift in Soviet and Chinese policies toward accommodation in conflict regions of the world. The second was linked to the shift from a bilateral struggle between the United States and the Communist bloc to a triangular political structure involving the United States, the Soviet Union, and China. It is not merely coincidental that it was during these two periods of change in the reality and perception of the configuration of power in the world that the United States made the policy decisions that took it down the path that ultimately culminated in a major war in Vietnam.

2   The Communist Powers Appease the United States

Accounts of U.S. Vietnam policy only rarely refer to the Vietnam policies of the USSR and China. Given the Cold War rationale for U.S. policy, the marginal role of the Communist powers in the story of the U.S. road to war in Vietnam would appear to be anomalous. It is easily explained, however, by the imbalance of power that had emerged by 1953. A wealth of evidence now available from Soviet, Chinese, and Vietnamese sources makes it clear that the Communist powers acted consistently from 1954 through the early 1960s to shore up the status quo of a divided Vietnam in order to avoid conflict with the United States over Southeast Asia. In other words, the Communist powers pursued a conscious policy of appeasement of the United States on Vietnam. In doing so, they invited the United States to pursue a more aggressive policy in Vietnam.

THE GENEVA NEGOTIATIONS AND THE IMBALANCE OF POWER

During the first five years of the Democratic Republic of Vietnam (DRV), from 1945 to 1950, Joseph Stalin responded to Vietnamese pleas for diplomatic support for their independence from France with icy indifference. Initially, Stalin hoped for a French government dominated by the French Communist Party and was unwilling to risk its interests in postwar relations with France by opposing that country on the issue of Indochina. But even after the French Communists left the French government in May 1947, Stalin refused to respond to Vietnamese letters asking for at least diplomatic support.[1] Meanwhile, in contrast, the Soviet Union defended the right of the non-Communist Republic of Indonesia to independence from the Dutch, supported its resistance war in the United Nations in mid 1947, and even became the first major power to extend de facto recognition to it in 1948.[2] The Soviet indifference toward the revolutionary regime in Vietnam was thus an anomaly in Soviet Southeast Asian policy.

Soviet archival documents and Vietnamese historians have revealed the reason for Stalin's lack of interest in the DRV: Stalin had deep doubts about Ho Chi Minh's loyalty to Moscow. Ho is said to have antagonized Stalin in the 1930s by giving too much emphasis to national liberation at a time when the Comintern line emphasized proletarian social revolution.[3] Ho's enemies in the Indochinese Communist Party further exacerbated Stalin's suspicions of Ho in 1948–49 by secretly denouncing him to the Central Committee of the CPSU as an ideological deviant.[4] This attack on Ho occurred in 1948, just when Stalin was expelling Yugoslavia's Communist leader, Josip Broz Tito, from the Cominform and launching a struggle against "nationalist" deviations within the world Communist movement.[5] Stalin's foreign minister, Vyacheslav M. Molotov, who had also denounced Tito in 1948, continued for the rest of his life to regard Ho and DRV Prime Minister Pham Van Dong as "stubborn men, interested only in Vietnam and not in the international movement."[6] Stalin thus suspected Ho Chi Minh of being guilty of the same "nationalist" deviation as Tito.

The leaders of the Chinese Communist movement had a very different perspective on the DRV. When they took power in October 1949, they believed that the PRC had an international obligation to assist "the Communist parties and people in all oppressed nations in Asia."[7] But the DRV was also a buffer against a hostile imperialist power. The Chinese saw military threats from the United States on three different fronts—the Taiwan Strait, Korea, and Vietnam—and Chinese troops had been deployed so that they could move in any of the three directions. As both the Chinese foreign minister, Zhou Enlai, and Liu Shaoqi told Ho in early 1950, if Vietnam were reoccupied by the imperialists, China's southern border would be exposed to a direct threat.[8]

Stalin was happy to let Mao take the responsibility for helping the Vietnamese against the French. In 1949, Stalin and Mao reached an understanding that China would have responsibility for assisting "national democratic movements" in colonial and "semi-colonial" countries, while the Soviet Union's responsibility was for the European theater.[9] When Ho Chi Minh requested Soviet military and economic assistance and diplomatic support in 1950, Stalin therefore informed him that it was up to China to aid Vietnam.[10]

Both Chinese and Soviet interest in supporting the Vietnamese struggle against French colonialist forces increased as the fortunes of the Viet Minh rose from 1950 to 1953. Chinese military assistance to the Viet Minh in 1950–54 was an important factor in the Vietnamese military success against the French, helping to counterbalance the much larger direct and indirect military and financial assistance that Washington provided to the French war effort.[11] The Chinese leaders were involved directly with Ho Chi Minh and the Vietnamese Workers' Party's Political Bureau in deciding on the military objectives of major campaigns, including the strategy adopted in 1953 to defeat the Navarre Plan and the decision to besiege the French base at Dien Bien Phu.[12]

As Vietnam became a major front in the Cold War, Stalin also began to take a personal interest in the progress of the war. By 1952, Stalin was engaged in discussions with both Ho Chi Minh and Liu Shaoqi on the military strategy for the Indochina War.[13] The Soviet engagement in the Vietnamese struggle in the last three years of Stalin's life reflected its importance to Soviet prestige at the global level. From the Soviet perspective, the growing involvement of the United States in the French war against the Viet Minh had made Vietnam an important point of struggle between the Sino-Soviet bloc and the U.S.-led capitalist bloc.

After Stalin's death in March 1953, the Soviet Union and China both began their own reevaluations of the balance of benefit and risk involved in support for the Vietnamese Communist cause. The larger context of that policy issue was the fundamental shift in the East-West military balance that had occurred during the Korean War, which had made the United States much more willing to take the risk of war and thus prepared to pursue aggressive policies on the periphery of the Sino-Soviet bloc. Beyond the strictly military element of the power balance, of course, the obvious need for both Moscow and Beijing to be released from the economic pressures of arms competition or ongoing military conflict was a major factor constraining both Communist powers.

By the time a truce agreement had been reached in July 1953 ending the Korean War, both regimes were in the process of carrying out major shifts in foreign policy that emphasized peaceful coexistence between socialist and capitalist states, reduction of East-West tensions, and negotiation of differences to eliminate potential causes of violent conflict. The Chinese Communist leadership was shifting its focus to domestic problems, and also to the aim of breaking the U.S. economic embargo and diplomatic isolation of the PRC. Immediately after the Korean truce, the USSR and the PRC both signaled that it could be the model for a similar peace agreement in Indochina, apparently without having consulted previously with the Vietnamese leadership.[14]

Although the Chinese were eager to bring the war in Vietnam to a swift end, they were aware that the outcome of the negotiations would reflect the situation on the battlefield. The Chinese supported an offensive by the Viet Minh aimed at producing a victory on the battlefield that would strengthen the Viet Minh negotiating position. The Vietnamese Political Bureau agreed with a plan proposed by Chinese military advisers to draw French main forces into the defense of Laos, which resulted in the Viet Minh siege of a vulnerable French base at Dien Bien Phu near the Laotian border.[15] Both Moscow and Beijing viewed the Vietnamese battlefield victory as providing the basis for negotiating a compromise peace settlement in the Indochina phase of the Geneva Conference. In the context of their larger foreign policy strategies, they regarded the Geneva negotiations as the first opportunity to demonstrate the two primary principles of the Communist bloc's new international line: that all international disputes could be resolved peacefully, and that "different social systems could coexist peacefully."[16]

Even before the United States appeared to threaten military intervention in Indochina, Moscow and Beijing were already preparing to make far-reaching concessions to the French in order to ensure an end to the war. The USSR had interpreted Dulles's speech in January 1954, in which the secretary of state referred to the United States as having "a great capacity to retaliate instantly, by means and at places of our choosing," in the event of a war on the Sino-Soviet periphery, as signaling the intention of the United States to use its strategic superiority for coercive purposes.[17] In early March, the Kremlin broached the notion of partitioning Vietnam at the sixteenth parallel, and its overall diplomatic line at the Geneva Conference in April was based on that idea. In conversation with Chinese Foreign Minister Zhou before the negotiations, Molotov said the Chinese should not expect too much from the Geneva Conference, because the imperialist countries had "unshakeable interests" in the outcome.[18]

The PRC, too, was weighing the threat from the United States at the same time that it was making a broader shift from the offensive revolutionary strategy for the region that it had pursued since 1949 to a defensive strategy. Beijing recognized that American intervention in Vietnam was possible in a worst-case scenario, which might lead to U.S. forces approaching the Chinese border. Meanwhile, Chinese leaders were focusing on launching a five-year plan for economic growth after years of warfare that had drained China's resources. They knew that they could not succeed if the Indochina conflict, and Chinese involvement in it, escalated because of U.S. intervention. In early March, therefore, the Chinese had agreed to the Soviet proposal for the partition of Vietnam at the sixteenth parallel.[19]

Against this background, Dulles's March 29 "United Action" speech also had a direct impact on the meetings of Molotov, Zhou, and Ho Chi Minh on April 3 and again on April 13 to plan their strategy for the Geneva negotiations. At a meeting of the three delegations on April 13, Zhou warned the Vietnamese that if the United States intervened directly in the conflict, Vietnam could not count on China to assist it openly, much less participate directly in the war. Zhou also cited Chinese fears that if the United States intervened and China had to become more directly involved, the United States would be able to establish an anti-Chinese organization in Asia "stretching from India to Indonesia."[20] Immediately after the tripartite meeting, on April 17, Mao told Chinese military leaders that because of the danger of a military confrontation with the United States, China could no longer train Vietnamese artillery regiments in China.[21]

Vietnamese Defense Minister Vo Nguyen Giap later told a delegation of Hungarian officials that the USSR, the PRC, and the Vietnamese had all assessed the threat of U.S. intervention as real.[22] In a discussion of the American attempt to prevent a settlement, *Nhan Dan,* the organ of the Vietnamese Communist Party, even suggested in late April that the United States had "displayed its hydrogen bomb threat."[23] When the Geneva Conference on Indochina began in late April 1954, therefore, the decisive U.S. military advantage over the USSR was already a potent factor in shaping Communist policy in the negotiations.

A major diplomatic issue in the Geneva negotiations was the future of the Khmer and Lao resistance forces. Relying heavily on Vietnamese troops, the Pathet Lao controlled roughly two-thirds of Laos by the time of the Geneva Conference, and the Khmer Issarak controlled one-third of Cambodia.[24] The DRV sought the delineation of formal zones of control in those countries, but the French delegation insisted that the Lao and Khmer resistance forces had to be withdrawn completely from their respective countries, because they represented "foreign aggression."[25] The Vietnamese knew that, in the absence of such zones of control, the Khmer Issarak organization would have to be disbanded, and the former resistance fighters would face the choice of leaving the country with the departing Viet Minh forces or risking arrest or worse at the hands of the government.[26] Even more vital to the Vietnamese, however, was obtaining a Pathet Lao regroupment zone that would run along the entire length of the Bolovens plateau region of northeastern and southern Laos, which forms the Laotian border with Vietnam.[27]

Such a regroupment zone, once translated into a zone of control, would have assured the Vietnamese of secure lines of communication between the northern and southern zones of Vietnam in the event of a new armed struggle.

At a meeting of the three Communist delegations on June 15, Zhou proposed that the French-sponsored governments in Laos and Cambodia be recognized and that the resistance movement in Cambodia not be given any regroupment zone. When the Vietnamese refused to go along with the Chinese on the issue, Zhou told both the British and the French that China was willing to recognize the royal governments in Cambodia and Laos anyway. Zhou assured the British that China's only concern in either country was to exclude U.S. military bases that might be used for an "assault on China" from those countries.[28]

The status of Khmer and Lao resistance movements, the date for an election, and the location of the demarcation line between the two Vietnamese administrative zones were all still unresolved when Zhou met with Ho Chi Minh and General Giap in southern China on July 3–5. Zhou pressed the Vietnamese delegation to drop its resistance to far-reaching concessions on the partitioning of the country, citing Vice President Nixon's April 16 speech as evidence that the United States would fight rather than accept a total Communist takeover. According to the Chinese records of the meeting, Zhou also argued that even if the war continued without direct U.S. military intervention, the United States would take advantage of the fighting to get control over the royal governments in Laos and Cambodia and would proceed with Britain to set up a military alliance in the region. Zhou also appealed to Ho to support the government of the Radical Socialist French premier Pierre Mendès-France, "so that we can prevent warlike elements in France from overthrowing the moderates."[29]

Ho accepted the need to avoid giving the United States an opportunity to enter the war and to differentiate between factions within French politics, but he would only agree to the sixteenth parallel as the demarcation line between the two zones, not to the seventeenth parallel, as Zhou had wanted. When the negotiations in Geneva turned to the demarcation line, the DRV premier, Pham Van Dong, proposed an S-shaped line around the thirteenth parallel, then, two days later, offered the fourteenth parallel. Finally, after another two days, he agreed to the sixteenth parallel. But French diplomatic reports show that Zhou met with Mendès-France on July 17 and told the French premier that the DRV did not, in fact, need to have the line as far south as the sixteenth parallel. Then two days later, the

Chinese delegation informed the French that Zhou "accepts and has made the Viet Minh accept" a line very close to the seventeenth parallel.[30]

More important was Zhou's unilateral concession to the French over the concept of regroupment zones in Laos. The French had been holding out against any reference to such zones, fearing that they would be the basis for more permanent Pathet Lao administration of the areas. The French wanted the text to refer only to "provisional assembly areas" in each province, from which the Pathet Lao would be transferred to the two provinces of Phong Saly and Xam Neua. In a meeting with Mendès-France and the British prime minister, Sir Anthony Eden, on July 19, Zhou agreed to the French position, provided that there were "precise guarantees" for the Pathet Lao pending general elections. The French text was adopted in the final agreement, with only an article prohibiting reprisals or discrimination against the Pathet Lao and guaranteeing their "democratic freedoms" to compensate them for the absence of any recognition in the agreement.[31]

The single most important issue of all in the negotiations for the political future of Vietnam was the date for national elections. The Vietnamese delegation had reason to fear that the United States would try to exert pressure on the French to block elections. They believed that a few months either way in the date fixed by the agreement might make a difference in whether the United States would be able to establish sufficient influence in South Vietnam to sabotage the elections. Based on this calculation, Pham Van Dong had demanded from the beginning that elections take place within six months of the agreement. That was the position that he took at the July 13 negotiation session with Mendès-France. In a meeting of the three Communist delegations, however, Zhou recalled that he had proposed three options to Ho Chi Minh: elections to be held no later than June 1955, elections to be held during 1955, or both sides to decide the date of the elections no later than June 1955. Zhou claimed that Ho had endorsed the third alternative, suggesting that Dong abandon his inflexibility on the point. What Zhou did not reveal is that he had already told Mendès-France in a meeting three weeks earlier that the elections could be after a relatively long period, without suggesting a date.

Molotov also suggested that the Vietnamese accept the more flexible formula of allowing the date to be negotiated by the two sides. In a private meeting with Mendès-France on July 15, Molotov initially took that position, then proposed as an alternative that the date be sometime before the end of 1955. On July 16, Molotov again suggested to Pham Van Dong a date to be negotiated later, but the Vietnamese premier continued to insist on a specific date for elections. The following day, Dong offered a further concession on the demarcation line and demanded a fixed date for the elections in return. In the tripartite meetings, Zhou supported Dong's position, while Molotov again suggested the compromise formula. On July 19, however, Zhou secretly instructed his deputy Wang Bingnan to inform the French delegation that the elections could be postponed until sometime in 1956, with the exact date to be determined by negotiations between North and South Vietnam.[32]

Mendès-France thus knew he would not have to agree to a date earlier than 1956, and he stuck doggedly to that position. The result was that the July 1956 date fixed in the text of the Final Declaration was actually six months later than the date the French had hoped to achieve in planning their negotiating strategy in June.[33] By systematically undermining the Vietnamese negotiating position on the election date, Zhou and Molotov gave the United States more time to intervene in South Vietnam to ensure that the elections could not take place.

The decision by the two Communist powers to push the date for elections back from the date preferred by the Vietnamese and to agree to regroupment zones in Laos that would not allow the Vietnamese access between North and South Vietnam after a partition reflected their longer-term strategic interests. The larger pattern of Chinese diplomacy at the conference indicates, in fact, that China wanted a longer-term partition of the country. Zhou signaled his government's interest on the reunification issue when he indicated at a meeting with Mendès-France that he was urging the Vietnamese to become "reconciled . . . with the Vietnam of Bao Dai." And at a dinner immediately following the end of the Geneva Conference, to which all the Indochinese delegations were invited, Zhou called for peaceful coexistence of the two Vietnamese states and invited the representative of the French-sponsored State of Viet-Nam to establish a legation in Beijing.[34]

One of Beijing's motives in pushing for a settlement that reduced the likelihood of Vietnamese reunification was undoubtedly a longer-term Chinese great power interest in avoiding having to deal with a united Vietnam, whose dominant influence in Southeast Asia, especially in neighboring Laos and Cambodia, would be in conflict with that of China.[35] But the USSR had no such geopolitical conflict with the Vietnamese, and both Beijing and Moscow also had to consider the implications of a settlement that would promote the reunification of Vietnam in the face of U.S. determination to keep South Vietnam part of the American sphere of influence in Asia. Both Communist powers recognized that the more the agreement appeared to favor reunification, either by election or by other means, the more likely it was to lead to a clash between the United States and North Vietnam. The Soviet-Chinese undermining of the Vietnamese negotiating positions on national elections and Laotian regroupment zones was only the beginning of a consistent pattern over the next several years of Soviet and Chinese opposition to any move by Hanoi to change the status quo of a divided Vietnam.

Both Communist states were signaling to the West that, despite their Marxist-Leninist ideological heritage, they had abandoned their earlier ambitions for revolutionary gains in Southeast Asia. Moscow's efforts to moderate Vietnamese aims at Geneva were such a dramatic departure from previous Soviet behavior that the British concluded that the Soviet Union was now a "satisfied power," which was anxious to maintain rather than disrupt the international status quo.[36] In the immediate aftermath of the Geneva agreement, Mao sought to convince foreign delegations that China wanted a peaceful environment and pledged that it would no longer support revolutionary armed struggles in Southeast Asia.[37] Soviet and Chinese diplomacy at Geneva was a prelude to a much longer period of appeasing the United States on Vietnam in the hope of averting direct military conflict with the dominant power.

ADVISING HANOI ON THE STRUGGLE IN SOUTH VIETNAM, 1955–1963

By late July 1955, it was already clear that the Diem regime, with U.S. backing, would not enter into consultations on the general elections for Vietnam called for in the Geneva Agreement, and that no such elections were going to take place in the absence of a new diplomatic understanding on Vietnam. From mid 1955 onward, the DRV sought to put pressure on the United States and Diem to implement the political provisions of the Geneva agreement. But both the Soviet Union and China gave little, if any, diplomatic support to the North Vietnamese demands.

As co-chair, with the United Kingdom, of the Geneva Conference, the Soviet Union was in a position to bring diplomatic pressure to bear on the United States and the Diem government in South Vietnam on the issue of the electoral provisions of the accord, as well as its military provisions forbidding reprisals against former combatants or supporters of either side. Its ultimate leverage was the threat to reconvene the Geneva Conference, where the DRV would be able to make its case before world opinion. But the USSR exhibited no interest in lending diplomatic support to that aim. It did not want to rock the boat in East-West relations or create any obstacle to a reduction of tensions. At the four-power summit in Geneva in July 1955, the instructions to the Soviet delegation limited it to making a pro forma statement that the implementation of the military clauses of the agreement had created a favorable situation for a political settlement. The delegation was expressly forbidden to criticize the U.S. policy of approving Diem's stance of rejecting electoral consultations. Eden promised at the conference that Britain, France, and the United States would recommend to Diem that he communicate his position on elections directly to the DRV. That was good enough for Molotov, who suggested that Hanoi request the co-chairs to urge the Saigon government to agree to a consultative conference with the DRV.[38]

By early 1956, after it had become very clear that the United States was not supporting the consultations, the North Vietnamese pushed Moscow to support the reconvening of the Geneva Conference. When the VWP's secretary-general, Truong Chinh, sought Soviet support for that objective during a visit to Moscow, the Soviet Foreign Ministry professed to be supportive, but questioned whether it would be feasible to convene it, because of Western obstructionism.[39] Supported by the Chinese, Hanoi requested the reconvening of the Geneva Conference anyway, and Moscow then issued a statement of support for the proposal. In consultations with the British in London in April 1956, however, Soviet Foreign Minister Andrei Gromyko tacitly agreed with the British that there was no point in reconvening the Geneva Conference and that the cease-fire should be maintained. While appearing to support its ideological ally Hanoi, Moscow was in fact colluding with the West to support the political status quo in Vietnam.[40]

Khrushchev regarded support for the status quo not just as a short-term policy but as the long-term solution to the problem of Vietnam. Moscow signaled a desire to minimize the possibility of the reunification issue arising in the future by proposing in January 1957 that both President Ngo Dinh Diem's Republic of Vietnam and the DRV be admitted to the United Nations, as "two separate states." The proposal, which was made public without prior consultation with Hanoi, brought a personal protest from Ho Chi Minh, who pointed out to the Soviet ambassador that the proposal amounted to a de facto Soviet recognition of the U.S. client regime in South Vietnam, and therefore to the "liquidation," in effect, of the Geneva Accords.[41]

At that point, Chinese and Soviet diplomatic policies toward Vietnam converged. The official Chinese media welcomed the Soviet proposal, suggesting explicitly that the Diem regime represent South Vietnam in the United Nations. The Chinese chargé d'affaires in Hanoi told the Soviet ambassador that the Vietnamese were too sensitive about proposals that could be interpreted as de facto recognition of the Diem regime by the Communist bloc. Later, the Soviet ambassador in Hanoi and his Chinese counterpart discussed the fact that Vietnam would have to remain divided over a "more or less long period of time" and urged that the two states coordinate their respective policies on the issue of Vietnamese unification.[42]

The USSR and the PRC also pursued parallel policies in their private diplomatic and party-to-party communications with the North Vietnamese from 1956 through 1958. Moscow told the Vietnamese party leadership that the correlation of forces between the Communist bloc and the U.S.-led imperialist camp was one of "contention," and that the Soviet Union was still far from equal to the United States in either strategic forces or industrial production and technology. The obvious conclusion was that the time was not ripe for the Communist bloc to take the offensive against U.S. imperialism. Moscow emphasized that, given the unfavorable balance of power at the global level, socialist states in countries divided by the Cold War (Germany, Korea, and Vietnam) not only had to avoid armed conflict that might provoke U.S. intervention but had to pursue a line of peaceful coexistence with their non-Communist counterparts. To sweeten this bitter pill, the USSR argued that successful economic development of North Vietnam would ultimately be the decisive factor in the liberation of South Vietnam, which meant in effect that consideration of reunification should be postponed for many years. In essence, Moscow informed the Vietnamese that they had to sacrifice the goal of reunification because of the danger of U.S. intervention and possible escalation of the war.[43]

The Chinese party leaders supported this Soviet line on the division of Vietnam, and they also referred directly to the unfavorable global balance of power as the decisive factor in the situation. In a letter to the Vietnamese Communist Party in 1956, the Chinese Communist Party Central Committee said the "national democratic revolution" (the Marxist-Leninist term for the overthrow of the U.S.-sponsored government in South Vietnam) "cannot yet be achieved by revolutionary means," and that the Vietnamese party should "use appropriate methods: long-term lying in ambush, accumulating our own strength, making connections with the masses, waiting for a favorable opportunity." The Chinese letter suggested that the division of Vietnam "may last a long time, and only when the situation in Asia and in the world undergoes major changes, or when Vietnam itself experiences fundamental changes, can the division be changed."[44]

In a meeting with Ho and Pham Van Dong in November 1956, Zhou echoed the Soviet rationale for long-term postponement of any initiative to carry out the liberation of South Vietnam. According to a Vietnamese Foreign Ministry specialist on China, Zhou repeated Khrushchev's line on the global "correlation of forces" to justify his position. He explained that the global correlation of forces between the imperialist and socialist camps in the world was still in a state of "contention," meaning that it did not permit the Communist bloc to go on the offensive, and that it was therefore necessary to maintain the demarcation lines already established between the two camps.[45] Zhou suggested that reunification be regarded as a "long-term struggle," and that only after North Vietnam had been "consolidated" would it be possible to talk about "how to win over the South and how to unify the country."[46] His definition of "consolidation" clearly implied a degree of economic development that was very far in the future.

In the summer of 1958, Hanoi's leaders again consulted with their Chinese counterparts on revolutionary strategy in South Vietnam, based on the proposal by some VWP Political Bureau members that it was time to resume armed struggle there. This was a period during which the Chinese international line strongly emphasized the importance of support for anti-imperialist struggles around the world, especially in the Middle East. But this radical line did not extend to Vietnam. According to Chinese sources, the Chinese message to the Vietnamese said, "The realization of revolutionary transformation in the South is impossible at the current stage." The Vietnamese were again advised to follow the strategy of "long-term lying in ambush" that had been suggested in the 1956 letter from the Chinese party leadership.[47]

A January 1959 policy memorandum outlining Soviet positions for discussions with North Vietnam and China again explicitly accepted the existence of two Vietnamese states and made it clear that Moscow no longer looked to the Geneva Accords as a basis for dealing with the problem. The memorandum argued that the North Vietnamese should wait for fundamental change in South Vietnam independent of Communist efforts or a change in the relations between the two camps. In the meantime, it suggested that Hanoi continue to work for the normalization of relations with the existing regime in South Vietnam so that the two states could enter the United Nations.[48]

When the Communist-led Pathet Lao resumed a limited armed struggle in Laos in 1959, it was the first use of arms by an orthodox Communist party since the end of the Indochina War in 1954. The Pathet Lao (PL) had been pursuing a strategy of peaceful political competition since a November 1957 coalition agreement with the neutralist Premier Souvanna Phouma, and the PL had won a third of the seats contested in the 1958 elections. But the Royal Lao Government (RLG), led by right-wing figures who had entered the government at the instigation of the United States, arrested and imprisoned leading PL figures who had been living and working in Vientiane. In a letter to the Vietnamese party leadership, the Laotian Communist leadership said that the party's Central Committee had decided to organize secretly for armed struggle. The Vietnamese initially opposed that policy, but agreed after the Chinese wrote to them supporting the concept of "defensive" armed struggle in Laos. In May 1959, two PL battalions escaped encirclement by the RLG, and some PL units, armed and equipped by the North Vietnamese, carried out attacks in the old PL regroupment area of Sam Neua province, near the border with North Vietnam, in July and August, causing general panic among government troops. The RLG charged that North Vietnamese troops had invaded Laos, but a UN investigating team found no evidence of this.[49]

Khrushchev denied these charges in a September 1959 public statement, but he added that the Soviet Union was opposed to "the existence of even the smallest source of war in Laos which could give food to the aggressive forces." In a conversation with Mao on October 2, 1959, Khrushchev argued that DRV assistance to an armed struggle by the PL could lead to a U.S. attack on North Vietnam, with grave risks of a general war. He pressed Mao to join him in opposing armed struggle by the PLA and in discouraging the Vietnamese from giving direct military assistance to the PL, meaning that its military activities should cease. Apparently, Khrushchev's determined interparty diplomacy worked. The North Vietnamese informed the USSR in early 1960 that the Vietnamese leaders had concluded, "after consulting with Soviet and Chinese comrades," that military support for the PL "would not be in the interest of the common good and could lead to dangerous international consequences."[50]

Not surprisingly, neither the Soviet Union nor China was consulted by Hanoi in advance of its decision in early 1959 to approve the limited use of armed force in South Vietnam.[51] Vietnamese leaders were evasive in response to Soviet requests for information on the 1959 Vietnamese party plenum resolution on the struggle in South Vietnam.[52] Once the signs of insurgency appeared in South Vietnam, however, the USSR warned the Vietnamese that any guerrilla war could draw in the United States, and that U.S. intervention could escalate into a nuclear war. A Soviet Foreign Ministry memorandum in July 1960 derided the Vietnamese view that the United States would "agree with the loss, in favor of the socialist camp, of such a first-class strategic position in Southeast Asia like South Vietnam."

The memorandum argued that the United States would certainly intervene militarily in Vietnam to prevent the revolutionary overthrow of the
Diem regime. The memorandum reiterated the theme that the USSR had
always emphasized after the Geneva Accords turned out to be of no value:
"the issue of the unification of Vietnam in the ways envisioned by the
Vietnamese friends is a part of the issue of correlation of forces between
the two world camps."[53] In mid 1961, the Vietnamese Political Bureau concluded that the United States probably would not send ground troops to
Vietnam.[54] But the Soviet party and government held to their much more
pessimistic assessment. In June 1961, in conversation with the Polish delegate to the International Control Commission in Laos, the Soviet chargé
d'affaires in Laos challenged the Vietnamese assumption that the United
States would not send the troops needed to save the Diem government.[55] A
Vietnamese Lao Dong Party Central Committee member later recalled
that the USSR had argued in the early 1960s that Hanoi should not support a guerrilla war in South Vietnam, because U.S. intervention would
begin a process of escalation and "a guerrilla war could lead to a world
war."[56]

Soviet opposition to armed struggle in Vietnam was part of a larger
Soviet global strategy of respecting U.S. spheres of influence in the hope
that the United States would respect the Soviet zone of influence in Central and Eastern Europe. Polish diplomat Mieczyslaw Maneli later recalled
that Soviet officials based their private discussions of Communist bloc
strategy with Polish officials on the premise of the division of the world
into spheres of influence. The USSR did not want to disturb the U.S.
sphere, according to Maneli, because they thought that "the Communist
camp will not allow any link, such as Hungary or East Germany, to be
plucked away. Neither will the Americans permit South Vietnam to be
taken over by [the Communists]."[57] In effect, the Soviet Union, as the
weaker power, was seeking to appease the stronger power by offering no
opposition to its move to obtain greater geopolitical advantage in Southeast Asia, hoping that the stronger power would leave the core interests of
the weaker state alone.

The Chinese leadership also continued to oppose any resumption of
armed struggle in South Vietnam when Hanoi gave the go-ahead for the
limited use of armed force in South Vietnam in 1959. Chinese policy
remained unchanged despite the Chinese approval of a Vietnamese proposal that the Pathet Lao be allowed to resume limited and defensive armed
struggle. An alternate member of the Chinese party's Political Bureau
agreed in a conversation with Vietnamese party secretary Le Duan in mid

1959 that the same policy should apply to South Vietnam, but he was quickly overruled by Mao and the party leadership.[58]

After popular uprisings had taken place across wide areas of South Vietnam in early 1960, the Chinese leadership abandoned its previous position of opposition in principle to any armed struggle in South Vietnam. In meetings with Vietnamese leaders in May 1960, Zhou and Deng Xiaoping agreed for the first time that armed struggle was correct on an ideological plane. They insisted, however, that the Vietnamese restrict military operations to the platoon level.[59] This Chinese response established a pattern that would continue over the next four years, in which Chinese advice was given to the Vietnamese on the apparent understanding that Beijing was an implicit partner with Hanoi in establishing policy for the revolutionary struggle in South Vietnam.

Chinese officials also bluntly advised the Vietnamese that Hanoi should not provide military assistance to the South Vietnamese revolutionaries at first, but should instead instill "self-reliance" in them. Later, in the course of a protracted struggle, Hanoi could supply a certain number of arms secretly, the Chinese said, but "in general you shouldn't help them." Finally, the Chinese warned that, "even if Diem falls, you can't unify immediately, because U.S. imperialism won't allow it."[60] Zhou's speech on the occasion of the fifteenth anniversary of the founding of the DRV on September 2, 1960, pointedly reminded the Vietnamese that the Chinese "have always been concerned for peace in Indochina and wish to see this region bordering on China become an area of peace."[61] Although the Chinese claimed to be supporting armed struggle in South Vietnam in principle, they thus remained closely aligned in practice with the Soviet policy of warning Hanoi not to challenge U.S. strategic interests there.

As the Communist-led forces began to step up their military operations in South Vietnam during 1961, the Chinese became even more insistent that military actions be limited to the platoon level. According to a Vietnamese source, Zhou told Pham Van Dong in 1961 that South Vietnamese revolutionaries should be "like termites," suggesting very low-level guerrilla activity and the avoidance of large-unit battles.[62] A Chinese account of the meeting between Ho Chi Minh and Chinese leaders on November 14, 1961, confirms that Deng and Zhou again called for limiting the scope of the war to avoid provoking U.S. intervention, but Zhou is said to have favored "medium level fighting," presumably suggesting something above the platoon level, while Deng insisted that it should be kept at the platoon level, as recommended in 1960. Deng and Zhou also appear to have called for efforts to negotiate a coalition government as a relatively long-term solution in South Vietnam.[63]

Meanwhile, the Vietnamese were not abiding by such strict limits on their operations in South Vietnam. Although platoons were still the most common military unit in the Communist armed forces in South Vietnam, some provinces had already organized company-sized units by the end of 1961.[64] More important, the Vietnamese were waging guerrilla warfare in the heavily populated areas of the Mekong Delta and the coastal plain of Central Vietnam, whereas the Chinese wanted armed struggle to be confined to less populated areas. Colonel Bui Tin, who participated in meetings with a visiting Chinese military delegation to Hanoi in December 1961, recalls in his memoirs that PLA Marshal Ye Jianying told his Vietnamese colleagues that guerrilla warfare in South Vietnam should be limited to the mountains, and that even there the revolutionaries should attack only in platoon or company strength. Chinese Defense Minister Luo Ruiqing explained to Vietnamese People's Army (VPA) officers that the Chinese wanted to keep the war at a low level because a U.S. attack on North Vietnam might force China to intervene, as had happened in the Korean War.[65]

The Chinese knew that the Vietnamese were not following their advice, and were troubled by the fact. At the National Conference on Foreign Affairs in December 1961, a Chinese official criticized the fighting that was taking place in South Vietnam, declaring that the Vietnamese Communists had already "exposed themselves too much." The official said that the Vietnamese should plan to expand their forces only over three to five years, or possibly even over ten years.[66] This unhappiness with the Vietnamese refusal to limit the guerrilla campaign geographically explains in part why the Chinese carefully avoided any public pronouncements in support of the armed struggle in South Vietnam from 1960 through 1961. In published commentaries on developments in South Vietnam, the Chinese hinted at their desire to see the struggle in South Vietnam remain an irritant but not a full-scale challenge to the Saigon regime.[67] Tellingly, after the armed struggle's political arm, the National Liberation Front, was created in late 1960, Beijing chose to give it only slight coverage in its media.[68] Apart from trying to discourage the Vietnamese Communists from having the ambition to seize a share of power in South Vietnam, the Chinese did not want to give the United States any pretext for blaming China for the guerrilla war.

Given their opposition to using armed struggle to change the status quo in South Vietnam, neither Moscow nor Beijing was sympathetic to the idea of providing arms for the South Vietnamese insurgents. The Soviet embassy in Hanoi raised the possibility of discussing with the DRV what kinds of arms and equipment might be sent to the insurgents in South Vietnam in late 1961. But Moscow rejected the idea decisively, on the grounds that it would encourage an even higher level of armed struggle, which would certainly lead to deeper U.S. involvement there, thus creating a "sharp knot of international tension." Even the argument that Moscow's neglect was causing North Vietnam to move closer to China did not sway Khrushchev and the Kremlin's foreign policy makers.[69] Khrushchev's son recalled that in the early 1960s, the Soviet leader was "afraid that the Chinese would try to force a confrontation between us and the Americans" over Vietnam, and that he was "in no hurry to provide military assistance" even to the North Vietnamese, much less to South Vietnam.[70]

Soviet archival sources and recently published Chinese accounts of the period both indicate that the USSR gave no military assistance to the North Vietnamese during the entire period from 1960 to early 1965, except for a few thousand World War II–era German weapons provided in 1962.[71] These were presumably part of the stocks of weapons the USSR had been providing to the Pathet Lao and Laotian neutralists prior to the neutralization agreement of July 1962. The earlier acquisition by VPA troops of outdated Soviet arms intended for Laotian forces in the spring and summer of 1961 caused serious friction between the USSR and North Vietnam after aides to the neutralist Souvanna Phouma complained to the USSR that the Vietnamese were keeping significant amounts of the outdated arms and ammunition themselves.[72] U.S. intelligence concluded that the Kremlin, perturbed by the increasingly pro-Chinese trend in Vietnamese policy, "virtually cut off aid" to the DRV from 1962 through 1964.[73]

The Soviet reluctance to be drawn into support of North Vietnam's effort to oust U.S. influence from South Vietnam extended even to Hanoi's negotiating strategy. When the North Vietnamese launched a concerted effort to gain international support for a negotiated settlement in South Vietnam in early 1962, the Chinese were apparently actively involved. Khrushchev refused, however, to use the USSR's position as co-chair of the Geneva Conference to help promote a negotiated settlement. The March 17 Soviet statement on Vietnam omitted any mention of consultations between the co-chair and the participants in the 1954 Geneva Conference, in contrast to a DRV diplomatic note just two days earlier. The USSR also failed to repeat DRV and PRC charges that U.S. activities in South Vietnam threatened DRV security. These omissions suggest that Moscow was determined to avoid any diplomatic position that would put it directly at odds with the United States in Southeast Asia at a time when the two superpowers were cooperating on negotiation of an agreement to neutralize Laos. The Soviet refusal to support North Vietnam's request for consultations on South Vietnam also had the effect of lending encouragement to officials in the U.S. State Department who were determined that no diplomatic talks should proceed on the conflict in South Vietnam.[74]

LAOTIAN NEUTRALIZATION
AND SOVIET-VIETNAMESE CONFLICT

The USSR became actively involved in the Laotian conflict in early December 1960 after General Phoumi Nosavan's right-wing army, which was being supplied and advised by the United States, advanced on Vientiane to oust the neutralist regime of Souvanna Phouma. Before Souvanna left the capital, he requested arms assistance from Moscow. The Soviet airlift of arms and supplies to Souvanna's government began just before the right-wing forces occupied the capital and continued after the neutralist army was forced into alliance with the Pathet Lao.[75]

This dramatic departure from the prior Soviet policy of passivity in Laos was understood at the time by the Kennedy administration primarily as an effort to avoid an East-West escalation into general war by keeping the option of a neutral Laos under Souvanna open. Later, some studies of the episode explained Soviet intervention as an effort to keep the allegiance of North Vietnam in the growing Sino-Soviet competition for leadership of the socialist camp or to placate critics of Khrushchev's conciliatory line on the Cold War within the CPSU.[76] The subsequent record of Soviet diplomacy, however, makes it clear that the initial U.S. interpretation was correct: Moscow was acting in the hope of heading off a Laotian war that could result in a U.S. attack on North Vietnam and increase the U.S. military presence on the mainland of Southeast Asia. The replacement of Souvanna's regime by a right-wing military regime signaled the beginning of an armed conflict between Phoumi's forces, backed by the United States, and the Pathet Lao, supported by the North Vietnamese and the Chinese. The external states were bound to become more deeply involved in the fighting, and Chinese involvement in the war was an obvious possibility.

In early January 1961, the USSR sent letters to neutralist leaders worldwide calling for a new conference on Laos. When the conference convened in Geneva, Gromyko insisted at a meeting with the Chinese foreign minister, Chen Yi, and the North Vietnamese and Pathet Lao Communist delegations that they must not give the West any pretext to accuse them of bad faith in observing a cease-fire. Chen Yi agreed and recommended that the PL be advised against engaging in any further military operations. The USSR then urged the Vietnamese chief military adviser to the PL to follow a similar line.[77] In a conversation with U.S. Ambassador Charles Trimble in early March, Souvanna said that both Mao and Zhou had told him that they understood that a Communist Laos would only bring insecurity to China, because the United States "would not accept it."[78]

Khrushchev was not merely using the negotiation of a coalition government as a cover for a Communist takeover. The USSR later leaned hard on the Vietnamese and Pathet Lao to be more responsive to Souvanna's interests and to make long-term commitments to cooperation with him and his neutralist faction. In September 1961, the CPSU sent the Vietnamese and Chinese parties a memorandum complaining that the PL had not yet made a clear commitment to full participation in a coalition government or to long-range support for Souvanna and the neutralist faction. The implication of the CPSU memorandum was that Moscow had no intention of supporting a bid by the PL and Vietnamese for sole power. At a November 1961 meeting with the Vietnamese and PL representatives at Khang Khay, Soviet Ambassador Alexander Abramov pressed for more concessions to Souvanna. A confidential Soviet Foreign Ministry memorandum written around that time described Soviet policy in Laos as a "struggle for the extermination of the hotbed of international tension in that region and the neutralization of the country."[79]

The negotiations on a Laotian peace agreement in 1961–62 revealed major conflicts between the Vietnamese and their major allies, just as the negotiation of the 1954 Geneva Accords had eight years earlier. The main Soviet political interests in the conflicts in Laos and South Vietnam were to avoid military confrontation with the United States, to establish cooperative relations with Washington, and to promote a neutral zone in Southeast Asia that would minimize the East-West conflict and reduce the U.S. military presence in the region.

During the Geneva negotiations, however, the USSR and Vietnamese disagreed sharply over the negotiating issues in the Laos agreement most closely linked to the struggle in South Vietnam: Vietnamese troops in Laos and the use of jungle trails down the length of eastern Laos to send men and supplies from North to South Vietnam. By late 1961, some 8,000 North Vietnamese troops had been introduced into Laos to help the Pathet Lao in the intensified fighting against both Lao and Thai troops with U.S. CIA advisers and to help develop and maintain the supply routes to South Vietnam through Laotian territory.[80] In its discussions with the Soviet Union, Hanoi was prepared to withdraw its combat forces from Laos as part of an agreement under which all foreign forces withdrew from the country, but it insisted that the agreement not interfere with its use of mountain supply routes through Laos in support of the insurgents in South Vietnam. On October 10, 1961, Nguyen Co Thach told Soviet Deputy Foreign Minister Georgi M. Pushkin that the DRV wanted to keep noncombat troops in Laos under the agreement for the purpose of maintaining those supply trails. Pushkin firmly rejected the Vietnamese request on the grounds that it would undermine the agreement. If they signed an agreement, he said, "we should unconditionally observe the neutrality of Laos. Therefore, there must be no DRV troops in Laos."[81] Pushkin clearly wanted to ensure that the North Vietnamese not be able to use those supply trails in order to escalate the war in South Vietnam.

Averell Harriman, the leader of the U.S. delegation, had already begun in September 1961 to press Pushkin for inclusion of a provision forbidding the use of Laotian territory to interfere in other countries. Pushkin balked when Harriman demanded fixed inspection teams that would stay in the southern part of Laos's eastern panhandle to deter use of it for transit between North and South Vietnam. He agreed in principle, however, that there could be well-equipped mobile teams that would stay for relatively long periods in areas of suspected military violations of the agreement.[82] And Pushkin ultimately agreed to the U.S. proposal for a provision forbidding the use of "the territory of the Kingdom of Laos for interference in the affairs of other countries." In return, Harriman agreed to compromise language by member-states of the Southeast Asia Treaty Organization (SEATO) acknowledging explicitly that Laos did not want that organization's protection.[83]

The Soviet-American bargain went much further than agreement on this wording, however. The USSR also offered to ensure full North Vietnamese compliance with the neutralization agreement on Laos. In September, Pushkin asserted, under questioning by Harriman, that the USSR "could and would control North Vietnam and continue to support Souvanna against possible Pathet Lao political or military aggression," and he added that the USSR could "guarantee" that Hanoi would live up to whatever agreement was reached on the eastern Laos corridor.[84] On the very day he rejected Thach's request that Hanoi's interests in the corridor be protected, Pushkin also rejected a written Soviet-American agreement guaranteeing the implementation of the agreement by their respective sides, but he agreed to a change giving the two co-chairs responsibility for "seeing to the observance of obligations" by the signatories. In November, Pushkin again assured Harriman that, once the agreement went into effect, "corridor traffic through Laos to South Vietnam will not be permitted."[85]

The Vietnamese were determined that, unlike with the 1954 Geneva negotiations, in which they acquiesced to Soviet and Chinese concessions, this time they would not allow the outcome of the negotiations be determined by larger Soviet and Chinese strategic interests.[86] Despite the Soviet commitment to Washington, the Vietnamese continued to use the corridor through eastern Laos to send cadres and supplies to South Vietnam. Six years later, at the U.S.-DRV Paris talks on a Vietnam peace agreement, Harriman asked Vietnamese negotiators why they had failed to comply with this provision of the 1962 Laos neutralization agreement. According to Harriman, they replied that they would not honor any agreement that was "forced down our throats by the Russians."[87] But the Vietnamese also based their rejection of the Harriman-Pushkin agreement on a legal point that neither of the superpowers had considered. Ha Van Lau, who was one of the Vietnamese negotiators at the 1962 Geneva Conference, has pointed out that the wording of the provision in question refers only to "interference in the affairs of other countries," rather than to the two zones of Vietnam. "The U.S. point of view . . . considered North and South as two separate states," Lau recalled. "We considered North and South one state. The U.S. and USSR may have reached such an agreement in their private talks, but Vietnam had no such commitment."[88]

Did Khrushchev really intend to carry out the Soviet commitment on Laos? The evidence strongly suggests that he and other Soviet officials believed that they could do so, but that they seriously miscalculated the Soviet ability to influence Vietnamese policy. They apparently believed in late 1961 that the CPSU still had some political authority over the Vietnamese leaders. After all, the Vietnam Workers' Party had remained loyal to the Soviet line despite Chinese attacks: it was still continuing to support Soviet views on negotiating agreements with the United States and pledging to "consider the interests of the safeguarding of world peace" in determining methods of revolutionary struggle.[89] Moscow assumed that, in the end, the Vietnamese would fall in line if the USSR was fully committed to a policy.

In its dealings with the Vietnamese, Moscow tried to invoke what it assumed was still a hierarchical relationship between the two Communist parties. In November 1961, when the Vietnamese resisted Soviet Ambassador Abramov's efforts to get more Pathet Lao support for Souvanna, he reminded them, according to Marek Thee, the Polish representative on the International Control Commission (ICC), which was responsible for monitoring compliance with the Geneva Accords, that he was "acting on instructions from the Soviet government and the Central Committee of the Communist Party of the Soviet Union, and in accordance with the line agreed to by the international communist and workers movements." Neither the Vietnamese nor the Laotians gave ground, however, and the USSR soon learned that the Vietnamese would no longer follow Soviet dictates on matters related to Laos. Nevertheless, in a final meeting with Thee before leaving Laos, Abramov emphasized that "the execution of the Geneva Agreements on Laos depended to a great extent on the corridor running through Laos."[90]

The bargain struck between Harriman and Pushkin closely paralleled the 1954 Geneva agreement that had traded Vietnamese strategic interests in Laos for general assurances that the United States would not integrate Laos and Cambodia into its military bloc in Southeast Asia. The Kremlin was again conceding South Vietnam to the U.S. sphere of influence in return for assurances that Laos would not be part of the pro-U.S. military bloc. But unlike the role played by the USSR at the earlier Geneva settlement, this time Moscow was actually cooperating directly with the dominant power by pledging to the Americans to ensure that the North Vietnamese would carry out the provisions of this understanding on the Laotian corridor. The eagerness with which the Kremlin accepted this task reflected both the legacy of Moscow's hierarchical relations with Communist parties in the past and the subordinate state role that the USSR had accepted in light of the global imbalance of power.

The Soviet Union viewed the Laotian agreement as a major diplomatic victory that made the neutralization of the region a possibility and apparently had hopes that the United States might agree to a neutralist settlement in South Vietnam if adequate guarantees could be worked out against a Communist takeover. In the final days of the Geneva Conference on Laos in July 1962, Pushkin suggested to Harriman that the Laotian neutralization agreement should serve as the basis for a similar settlement in South Vietnam, and referred to a "third force" emerging in South Vietnam that could play the neutralist role in the coalition.[91] Eighteen months later, a Soviet diplomat in Washington suggested that Khrushchev had nurtured hopes that the Laotian settlement would lead the United States to accept conferences on Cambodia and Vietnam, leading to the neutralization of all of mainland Southeast Asia through U.S.-Soviet diplomatic cooperation.[92]

CHINA, ARMED STRUGGLE, AND THE U.S. WAR THREAT, 1962–1964

Did China abandon the caution that had marked its Vietnam policy up to 1962 and encourage the escalation of the conflict by North Vietnam over the next two years? A new interpretation of Chinese policy portrays Beijing as having provided arms in 1962 for the Communist forces in South Vietnam and risked confrontation with the United States. That interpretation is based on the idea that Mao reasserted his leadership in foreign policy and insisted on much more militant support for the guerrilla war in South Vietnam.[93]

The evidence does not support the argument that Chinese policy lurched from advising Hanoi to be very cautious about the armed struggle to a readiness to risk war with the United States over Vietnam. Although Chinese rhetorical support for the armed struggle intensified from late 1962 onward, the Chinese fear of a direct U.S. attack on North Vietnam or even China remained the dominant factor in Chinese policy toward Vietnam. The PRC adopted a threefold strategy during the 1962–64 period for coping with the threat of a possible U.S. attack: first, to prepare militarily for the contingency of a U.S. military attack against North Vietnam or China, or both; second, to exert influence on the North Vietnamese leadership to limit the war in South Vietnam so as to minimize the risk of provoking the United States; and third, to try to deter the United States from widening the war into North Vietnam by threatening to fight on the side of the DRV in that event.

Mao did reject a policy proposal by Deputy Foreign Minister Wang Jiaxiang to Deng and Zhou in early 1962 calling for a greater effort to improve relations with the United States, the Soviet Union, and India. Motivated by China's desperate internal socioeconomic situation in 1961–62, Wang also advocated retrenchment in assistance to national liberation movements, based on the argument that China could be drawn into another Korea-type war in Vietnam.[94] Mao accused Wang of promoting a "revisionist" line, and at the next party plenum in September 1962, he called for support of the insurgencies in South Vietnam and Laos, which he called "excellent armed struggles."[95]

The current orthodox interpretation of Mao's rejection of Wang's proposed foreign policy line goes well beyond what the evidence supports. Although he was rejecting Wang's proposal for a fairly radical turn in Chinese policy toward conciliation on all three major fronts, Mao did not propose a major change in Chinese policy toward Vietnam. Mao's major concern at the Tenth Plenum was clearly not a new level of support for national liberation movements generally or the South Vietnamese armed struggle in particular, but class struggle within China and, by extension, revisionism at home and abroad. He adopted the leftist line on external armed struggle in order to discredit internal opponents of his plans for radical revolution within China.[96] Mao used support for the South Vietnamese and Laotian armed struggles as a litmus test of ideological soundness, but that does not mean that he had decided to support an escalation of the war in South Vietnam.

Central to the notion of a radical shift toward risk-taking in China's policy toward Vietnam is the claim that China provided military assistance to the insurgents in South Vietnam in the summer of 1962. That claim was first advanced by the PRC for explicitly political reasons at a time when it was defending itself against Vietnamese charges of Chinese hostility to Vietnamese reunification. The former Vietnamese ambassador Hoang Van Hoan, who had just defected to the PRC, asserted in 1979 that Ho Chi Minh and Vietnamese Political Bureau member Nguyen Chi Thanh had requested military assistance during a visit to Beijing in mid 1962, and that Beijing had agreed to provide 90,000 rifles and machine guns to the South Vietnamese insurgents. China's media gave prominence to this assertion as part of its propaganda output in regard to the Sino-Vietnamese conflict.[97]

More recent Chinese accounts, however, indicate that the Vietnamese leaders were in Beijing to inform their Chinese counterparts of the danger that the American escalation of the conflict in South Vietnam might lead to a U.S. attack on North Vietnam. The Chinese then responded, according to these Chinese sources, by agreeing to send the arms to equip 230 battalions of the VPA to defend the North—not to increase the level of the insurgency in South Vietnam.[98]

These accounts are consistent, moreover, with other evidence that Chinese leaders were extremely concerned about the new level of U.S. military involvement in Vietnam. Chinese leaders viewed the introduction of U.S. helicopters, fixed-wing aircraft, and pilots into the conflict and the formal establishment of the U.S. Military Assistance Command Vietnam (MACV) in Saigon in February 1962 as signaling an increased likelihood of an eventual U.S. attack on North Vietnam.[99] The Chinese Foreign Ministry issued a statement on February 24 to the effect that the mounting U.S. military role in South Vietnam "constitutes a direct threat to the security of North Vietnam [and] seriously affects the security of China and the peace of Asia."[100]

The visit by Ho and Thanh came in the context of a series of Chinese public statements that focused not on the importance of armed struggle in South Vietnam but on the theme that aggressive U.S. moves in Southeast Asia posed a serious threat to the security of China.[101] The Chinese reasoned that the stronger North Vietnam was militarily, the less likely the United States would be to attack the North, or, if it did attack, the less

American troops would be able to push all the way to the Chinese border, as they had in the Korean War.[102] The VPA had been reduced in the late 1950s to fewer than 100,000 troops, a number that was clearly inadequate to cope with a possible attack by the United States. By 1963, however, the strength of the VPA was increased to 173,500, reflecting in part the additional modern weaponry provided under the Chinese military assistance agreement.[103]

Equally important, the timing of the visit by Ho and Thanh does not jibe with the interpretation that it represented a Maoist radicalization of Chinese foreign policy. Although Chinese sources have never revealed the exact dates of the North Vietnamese leaders' visit, they report it as having occurred during the summer. Since such a visit had to be planned some weeks in advance, it is clear that the decision to invite the North Vietnamese leaders to discuss additional military assistance came well before Mao's attack on Wang preceding the Tenth Central Committee Plenum in late September.[104]

Even after Mao's reemergence as a force in Chinese foreign policy, Chinese preoccupation with U.S. military intentions and the problem of strengthening North Vietnam as a buffer against U.S. military power continued to grow. In March 1963, Chinese concern about a possible U.S. attack on North Vietnam prompted Beijing to send a Chinese military delegation led by People's Liberation Army Chief of Staff Luo Ruiqing to tell Vietnamese leaders for the first time that, if the United States attacked North Vietnam, China would come to its defense.[105] Nine months later, the Chinese sent the deputy chief of staff of the People's Liberation Army to work with General Giap and the VPA to prepare North Vietnam's defenses against a possible U.S. attack, including plans for construction of naval bases and other defense works.[106] The agreement on military assistance reached during the summer of 1962 thus reflected a broad consensus between Mao and more moderate Chinese leaders that something had to be done to strengthen the PRC's southern flank against a possible U.S. attack.

Furthermore, the North Vietnamese had no reason to request such major arms assistance for South Vietnam in mid 1962, because they were not planning for a rapid growth of their full-time fighting forces in South Vietnam. The Vietnam Workers' Party Political Bureau decided in February 1961 to build a revolutionary main-force army in South Vietnam of from ten to fifteen regiments, which would have been roughly 25,000 to 40,000 men.[107] They expected to arm them, however, with Western-produced weapons captured or purchased in South Vietnam, rather than with Chinese-made weapons, in order to avoid giving the United States a justification for direct intervention in the war. In late February 1962, the Political Bureau issued a new resolution on operations in South Vietnam, again emphasizing that the development of armed forces in South Vietnam should be based on "self-reliance," and repeating the explicit directive that captured enemy weapons should be the main source of supply.[108] At the time of the visit by Ho and Thanh, therefore, we know that both Hanoi and Beijing were urgently concerned about the ability of the VPA to resist a possible U.S. attack on North Vietnam, rather than about arming new battalions in the South with Chinese weapons.

Finally, the Chinese opposed a shift to main-force warfare in South Vietnam when the issue arose in the latter half of 1963. As the political crisis of the Diem regime and then its overthrow by a military coup increased the opportunities for rapid military gains, the Vietnamese party and military leaders debated whether or not to shift the emphasis of the armed struggle from guerrilla warfare to main-force warfare. Those favoring the former course argued that the Ho Chi Minh trail through eastern Laos should be kept small, so that it would be harder to bomb, limiting its capacity to a level required to support guerrilla warfare. The proponents of a main-force strategy argued that it should be widened to accommodate heavy weapons, including 75-millimeter guns. According to Vietnamese Colonel Bui Tin, the Chinese response to this Vietnamese debate was again to press Hanoi to limit forces sent to South Vietnam to platoon-sized units, because escalating the conflict in South Vietnam might provoke the United States into direct military intervention. Bui Tin, who was involved in planning for the main-force stage of the war in South Vietnam, recalls that Zhou and Mao advised the Vietnamese in late 1963 and early 1964 "not to send big units [to South Vietnam] or to widen the [Ho Chi Minh] trail, because this would incite the United States to send more troops to South Vietnam."[109]

This Chinese effort to dissuade the Vietnamese from the new policy line was reflected in the publication of a major article in late 1963 on "National Liberation War" that warned against a "quick victory" strategy and urged "protracted guerrilla war" instead. The article recalled that Mao's "main strategic principle in guiding the Chinese revolutionary war had been to exhaust every possibility of developing guerrilla warfare on a large scale and only under given circumstances, when sufficient strength had been built up, to turn guerrilla warfare into regular warfare." Guerrilla fighting during the anti-Japanese war, the article said, was "for the most part, not interior-line operations in conjunction with regular armies but independent exterior-line operations."[110] Although the author of the article avoided

any direct allusion to the situation in Vietnam, the article was clearly referring to the issue of whether the emphasis should shift from guerrilla warfare to main-force warfare, which had been under discussion between the
Chinese and Vietnamese during 1963. The publication of this article at
such a crucial moment left no doubt as to the importance that the Chinese
accorded to limiting the scale of the fighting in South Vietnam.

According to Bui Tin, the Vietnamese leadership decided after the
Vietnamese Party's Ninth Central Committee Plenum in December 1963
to send company- and battalion-sized groups of cadres—but not main-
force units—south to reinforce the PLAF in order to make large-unit
main-force warfare possible. But they knew that the Chinese would be
strongly opposed even to that increase in the flow of military personnel to
South Vietnam, because it presaged a further buildup of revolutionary
forces. Fearing the political fallout of such a decision in their relations with
the Chinese, Bui Tin recalled in an interview, "We didn't inform China of
the level of battles in the South or of the units sent to the South."[111]

Despite the new level of rhetorical support for the armed struggle in
South Vietnam, therefore, China's policy toward the insurgency remained
essentially unchanged from mid 1962 through the beginning of 1964: the
Chinese still wanted the Vietnamese to carry out a protracted guerrilla war
primarily at the platoon level, which would ensure against provoking a
direct U.S. military intervention in South Vietnam and possibly an attack
against North Vietnam or even China. Mao's ideological militancy did not
lead him to take any increased risk of military confrontation with the
United States.

Escalation of U.S. military involvement in Laos and Vietnam in 1964
prompted Chinese leaders to implement all three strategies for dealing
with the possibility of a U.S. attack on China or North Vietnam. In March,
the United States began a major buildup of U.S. airpower at bases in
Thailand, sending six F100s to Thailand, which were followed by a dozen
more over the next five months. In May, the United States began low-level
reconnaissance flights over Pathet Lao headquarters in the Plain of Jars
and added armed escorts when they were fired on by antiaircraft guns. In
early June, Thai pilots flying Lao Air Force planes strafed Pathet Lao headquarters and hit the Chinese Economic and Cultural Mission there, killing
one Chinese and wounding five others, and bombing attacks on the Plain of
Jars continued for weeks. Also in June, the United States leaked to the press
plans for an air attack against the DRV and issued both public and private
threats to Hanoi that it would be the target of a U.S. bombing campaign
unless it called off the war in South Vietnam.[112]

On June 24, 1964, PRC Foreign Minister Chen Yi issued China's first statement aimed at deterring the United States from carrying the war to North Vietnam, warning that China would "not sit idly by while the Geneva agreements are completely torn up and the flames of war spread to their side."[113] On the same day, Mao told visiting VPA Chief of Staff General Van Tien Dung that China would send volunteers to the DRV if the United States invaded.[114] The Chinese press asserted in July that U.S. threats to blockade North Vietnam or carry out a bombing campaign against it would be regarded as threats to China's security. And in late July, Zhou issued a more explicit public threat to intervene in the war if the United States invaded North Vietnam.[115]

The U.S. military moves in 1964 also prompted much more concrete Chinese military planning for the contingency of a U.S. assault on North Vietnam. At a joint planning meeting of Chinese, Vietnamese, and Pathet Lao leaders in Hanoi on July 3–5, the Chinese agreed that the United States would continue to send more forces to South Vietnam and that it might attack North Vietnam with airpower. At this meeting, the Chinese offered to support the DRV "by all possible and necessary means" if the United States attacked it.[116] That meeting was followed immediately by a visit by Zhou to Hanoi, in which Zhou expressed the Chinese view that there were two possibilities: either the United States would intensify its "special warfare" in South Vietnam or it might turn the conflict into a local war with direct deployment of U.S. troops and either bombing or an invasion of the DRV. The Chinese premier confirmed that if the United States invaded North Vietnam, China would send its own troops to resist the Americans.[117]

But Chinese documents make it clear that the Chinese also responded to the perception of increased threat by stepping up their pressure on the Vietnamese to maintain the insurgency at a low level of violence that would not precipitate a major U.S. military intervention. In a meeting with Pham Van Dong on July 3–5, 1964, to maximize the impact of Chinese policy on the Vietnamese, Zhou used language suggesting that China regarded itself as a full partner in the conduct of the insurgency in South Vietnam. "Our principle for the struggle [in South Vietnam]," he declared, "is to do everything we can to limit the war to the current scale," while at the same time preparing for a possible U.S. war against North Vietnam.[118]

The first U.S. bombing of North Vietnam following the alleged second naval incident in the Gulf of Tonkin in August 1964 created the first real war crisis in Beijing. Immediately after the U.S. air strikes, on August 6, Mao told a Chinese party official that "war is coming" and immediately canceled an inspection trip to the Yellow River scheduled for the latter half of the year to work on the Vietnam crisis.[119] The PRC immediately began to take urgent steps to prepare for war with the United States. Mao stated flatly to an August 17 meeting of the CCP's Central Secretariat that the United States was planning a new war of aggression against China, and that China had to prepare for such a war.[120] It was at this meeting that the Chinese decided to put the country on an urgent war footing. The party leadership had already established what it called the "three-front strategy" in the event of possible military attack by the United States. The provinces of coastal and central China constituted the first and second fronts, whereas the interior provinces of southwestern and northwestern China were the third front. Industrial investment in the third-front provinces was aimed at turning them into a firm base area in the event of an invasion by the United States.[121] At the August 17 meeting, Mao called for, and the leadership approved, the dramatic acceleration of the construction of industrial facilities in the interior provinces, based on his assessment that a large-scale war was an immediate possibility.[122] From then on, preparation for war with the United States was a dominant theme throughout Chinese society, all the way down to the village level.[123]

The PLA leadership recommended that troops in southern China be put on alert for a possible U.S. invasion, and that four air divisions and one antiaircraft division be dispatched to border provinces and put on high alert. Mao immediately approved the recommendations, which were implemented within a few weeks.[124] The Chinese Air Force then began construction of a number of new airbases in southern China in response to the new level of threat of U.S. military escalation in Vietnam.[125] At an October 5, 1964, meeting with Pham Van Dong, Mao discussed what the Vietnamese should do to prepare for a possible U.S. invasion of North Vietnam. He advised Dong to "construct defensive works along the coast" like those China had built during the Korean War. He also advised the Vietnamese to avoid a direct military confrontation with the invading forces, preserving their own main forces while letting the Americans penetrate deep into their territory.[126]

There can be no doubt, therefore, that the Chinese leadership took the threat of a U.S. attack on North Vietnam, and even of an attack on China, with the utmost seriousness from mid 1964 on.[127] Despite the preparations for war, however, some historians have cited a remark made by Mao at a meeting with VWP Secretary Le Duan on August 13, 1964, as evidence that he was encouraging Hanoi to escalate the war, on the premise that it need not fear that the United States would go to war over South Vietnam.[128] According to the transcript of the conversation with Le Duan,

Mao said, "It seems that the Americans do not want to fight a war, you do not want to fight a war, and we do not necessarily want to fight a war," and "because no one wants to fight a war, there will be no war."[129]

Mao certainly did not intend this statement as an encouragement of Hanoi to escalate the war in South Vietnam. In fact, when his remark is read in its full context, it becomes clear that he had the opposite intention—to convince the Vietnamese leaders that they should not carry out the major escalation of the war in South Vietnam that they were planning. Le Duan had just informed Mao that the Vietnamese party leadership had concluded that the United States intended to attack the North, and that the Vietnamese were therefore planning to dispatch an entire VPA division to South Vietnam. Mao then expressed disagreement with the North Vietnamese view that it was clear that the United States intended to attack the North or to send a large number of troops to South Vietnam.[130] Mao cited Chinese intelligence indicating that the August 4 incident and the subsequent U.S. bombing represented a "mistaken judgment" by the United States based on misinformation, rather than a more aggressive intent. A Vietnamese official then said the United States was making "outcries to attack North Vietnam," to which Mao responded that if the Americans were to do so, they should remember that the Chinese also "had legs" and could also go to North Vietnam. Mao went on to indicate that China would deploy 300,000–500,000 troops to provinces bordering on North Vietnam to be prepared for a possible U.S. ground assault.[131]

When Mao met with Pham Van Dong on October 5, his opening statement to the Vietnamese premier indicated his desire to reopen the issue: "According to Le Duan, you had [a] plan to dispatch a division [to South Vietnam]. Probably you have not dispatched that division yet. *When should you dispatch it? [T]he timing is important.* Whether or not the United States will attack the North, *it has not yet made the decision.* If it attacks the North, [it may need to] fight for one hundred years, and its legs will be trapped there. *Therefore it needs to consider carefully* [emphasis added]."[132]

Finally, Mao suggested that Americans would not "run after" the North Vietnamese as long as U.S. warships were not attacked, which again referred to the Chinese contention that the Tonkin Gulf incident was not part of a broader U.S. plan to attack North Vietnam. In the context of Hanoi's intention to carry out a major escalation of the war in South Vietnam, Mao's intention here is clear: the United States had not yet decided what it was going to do about Vietnam, and the North Vietnamese should therefore wait until U.S. intentions were absolutely clear before sending a full division of troops to South Vietnam.

Pham Van Dong not only understood that this was Mao's intention but expressed agreement with his argument. Dong said it would "not be easy for [the United States] to expand the war," and that therefore the Vietnamese "should try to restrict the war in South Vietnam to the sphere of special war" and "should not provoke" the United States. He concluded by informing Mao that this was the decision that had been reached by the Vietnamese party politburo.[133] Thus the Vietnamese premier implied strongly that the Vietnamese would hold back, at least for the time being, on the dispatch of the division of troops to South Vietnam.

Mao's suggestion that the United States might not really intend to attack North Vietnam was thus in consonance with the long-standing Chinese policy of advising the Vietnamese not to dispatch large units of the VPA to South Vietnam. Chinese policy toward Vietnam in the final three years before the United States began its bombing campaign against North Vietnam was dominated by the fear that the Americans would take advantage of the Vietnam conflict to make a thrust toward China. Chinese leaders were still trying to reduce the likelihood of such a military confrontation with the United States by simultaneously warning the United States against such a course and persuading Hanoi to restrain its own military presence in South Vietnam.

SOVIET POLICY BEFORE AND AFTER KHRUSHCHEV'S FALL

After the Laotian neutralization agreement failed to bring peace to Laos or to contribute to a stabilization of the situation in Vietnam, the brief blooming of Soviet diplomatic activism in Indochina quickly faded. Neither the increased U.S. and Thai military presence in Laos nor the escalation of U.S. military involvement in South Vietnam provoked any further Soviet effort to check U.S. intervention in the region. Instead, Khrushchev began a systematic retreat from any involvement in the Southeast Asian conflicts. The disappearance of Laotian neutralism and the escalation of violence in both Laos and Vietnam signaled an increased danger of confrontation with the United States, while underlining the reality that the USSR itself had no real influence in the area.

An early indication of the strict limitation on Soviet willingness to try to counterbalance the U.S. role in mainland Southeast Asia was Khrushchev's decision to discontinue the direct Soviet role in airlifting supplies to neutralist and Pathet Lao forces in Laos, even as CIA supply operations to forces fighting against the Pathet Lao and North Vietnamese continued.[134] The

Soviet Foreign Ministry explained to the Chinese that a Soviet failure to live up to the Geneva agreement would negatively affect the Soviet proposal to guarantee free city status for West Berlin.[135] In December 1962, the USSR delivered the first of nine transport planes that were to be distributed evenly among the three Laotian factions. From then on whatever bargaining leverage the USSR had derived from their operational role was gone. They also turned over to the North Vietnamese the Ilyushin-14 aircraft that had been ferrying supplies from Hanoi to the Plain of Jars.[136]

The end of the Soviet transport role did not have to signify an end to a Soviet diplomatic role in Southeast Asia. Within a few months, however, developments in both countries eliminated Khrushchev's ability to achieve Soviet goals in the region. The key to Soviet policy in Laos had been to support a neutralist regime under Souvanna Phouma as a check against both escalation of the conflict and U.S. political-military domination. After the Geneva agreement was signed in July, however, Souvanna was pressured by the United States into accepting the continuation of U.S. supply flights to the CIA-sponsored guerrilla fighters under Vang Pao. That action compromised his neutrality in the eyes of the Pathet Lao, as well as in those of many of the neutralist officers and troops. Fighting between anti-Souvanna and pro-Souvanna neutralist forces, the assassination of left-wing neutralist personalities, and the withdrawal of the Pathet Lao from Vientiane to the safety of the Plain of Jars destroyed the coalition government and left Souvanna a virtual prisoner of right-wing military figures in the capital.[137]

The end of Souvanna's centrist role and friendly relations with the Pathet Lao eroded what was left of any common interest between the USSR and its erstwhile Laotian and Vietnamese allies. The United States wanted to press Khrushchev to do something to curb the leftists on the Plain of Jars in mid April 1963, but State Department officials recognized that the USSR had only "slight leverage on the DRV and Pathet Lao, as they are currently giving them little aid."[138] Meanwhile, Chinese support for the DRV against a possible U.S. attack persuaded the Vietnamese leaders to associate themselves openly with Chinese positions attacking the Soviet international line. In July 1963, the Vietnamese began to criticize the Soviet Union more or less openly, without naming it, for being "afraid of the United States" and for believing that "firm opposition to U.S. imperialism would touch off a nuclear war." In August 1963, Hanoi sided with China on the nuclear test ban treaty, beginning a process of harsh criticism of the Soviet international line.[139]

By mid 1963, Khrushchev had lost all interest in Southeast Asia. When Secretary of State Dean Rusk visited him at his dacha in August 1963,

Khrushchev expressed both frustration and resignation over the Soviet inability to influence the parties in Laos to maintain the cease-fire and the tripartite neutralist government. Khrushchev admitted that the Soviet ambassador "had no contact with the Pathet Lao and no influence there." He asked rhetorically what the Soviet Union could do—"send its troops?" Khrushchev commented acidly, "It was the US that had experience in such matters. . . . But the Soviet Union could do nothing if the Laotians want to fight." He made it clear that he saw no future Soviet involvement in the Laos issue, because "he had enough of his own responsibilities and problems."[140]

The Soviet Union continued to serve as co-chair of the Geneva Conference. But in late July 1964, it threatened to abandon that responsibility entirely. Moscow had issued a renewed proposal for an international conference on Laos in June 1964, but the United States had refused to support it. On July 25, the USSR again sent messages to the fourteen nations participating in the Geneva Conference on Laos to request that the conference be reconvened in August. *Pravda* warned that if other states failed to support the proposal, the Soviet Union would have to review its role as co-chair.[141]

The subtext of Khrushchev's threat to withdraw from the Geneva co-chairship appears to have been a combination of his anger with North Vietnam and his genuine alarm at the increased likelihood of a major military confrontation between the United States and China in Southeast Asia. Khrushchev had clearly given up on North Vietnam because of its support for Chinese positions and harsh criticism of Soviet positions on issues in conflict between the Communist giants. In a meeting with UN Secretary-General U Thant in Moscow in July, Khrushchev said he wanted to "wash his hands" of Vietnam, because it was "too far away and too close [to] Peking."[142]

Under these circumstances, Khrushchev did not want to be in the position of having to choose sides in the war that appeared to him to be looming. The United States had just carried out the bombing of Pathet Lao headquarters on the Plain of Jars in early June, provoking the first major public Chinese threat. In a speech on July 8, Khrushchev reverted to the theme that "local wars" could "lead to a large conflict, and could even provoke a world conflagration."[143] The threat to withdraw from the Geneva Conference co-chairship was thus part of a larger pattern of Soviet disengagement from Southeast Asia in order to minimize the costs and risks of a wider war. In the same period, Khrushchev also wrote off the Indonesian Communist Party, which had once been aligned with the Soviet line, after he failed to persuade its leader, D. N. Aidit, to abandon key

Chinese positions in the worldwide Communist schism.[144] Khrushchev preferred to allow the Chinese to have dominant influence over East Asian Communist regimes and parties rather than to try to maintain tenuous influence in the region at the risk of coming into conflict with the United States.

Khrushchev's response to the U.S. bombing of North Vietnam in reprisal for the alleged second North Vietnamese attack on a U.S. warship in the Gulf of Tonkin further demonstrated that he was not willing to get involved in war in Southeast Asia. In a letter to President Lyndon Johnson, he pointedly refrained from associating himself with any DRV response to the bombing. He emphasized that "no one has asked the Soviet Government to address you in connection with the developments near the coast of the DRV and the CPR." He referred to the possibility of a response from "the other side," underlining the fact that the Soviet Union had nothing to do with North Vietnam's policies. Nor did Khrushchev endorse the DRV version of events in the area, suggesting that he was suspicious that Hanoi—and China—intended to provoke war with the United States. In an obvious allusion to the Chinese influence on the DRV, the letter refers to the "influence" of "those quarters and persons who do not conceal their desire to inflame the passions, to pour oil on the flame and whose militant frame of mind one should regard with great caution and restraint."[145]

Two months later, Khrushchev was removed from power. Recognizing that Khrushchev had virtually cut all political ties to Hanoi, his successors quickly moved to try to reduce the chasm separating the Soviet Union and the DRV. One of their first moves was to fill the post of ambassador to the DRV, which had been vacant for months. After the 1964 U.S. presidential election, the new Soviet ambassador in North Vietnam, Ilya S. Scherbakov, advised Moscow that the North Vietnamese were already planning to escalate the war in South Vietnam by sending VPA troops in larger numbers, and that they would certainly ask the USSR for military assistance. At two Central Committee meetings in November and December 1964, the new Soviet leaders weighed the issue of extending new military assistance to Hanoi. The initial result of these deliberations appears to have been a decision to try to deter the United States from unleashing a bombing campaign against North Vietnam by informing the Johnson administration that Moscow would extend military assistance to the DRV in the event of a U.S. attack. On November 27, *Izvestia* solemnly warned: "Those who nurture adventurist plans in the Indochinese peninsula must be aware that the Soviet Union will not remain indifferent to the fate of [a] fraternal socialist country and is prepared to extend to it the necessary assistance." Soviet officials and media reiterated this position several times during December. Significantly, however, when Foreign Minister Andrei Gromyko met with Secretary of State Dean Rusk on December 8, and they sparred over Vietnam, he made no reference to that warning, and when he met with President Johnson on the same day, he did not bring up Vietnam at all.[146]

But neither did Rusk warn Moscow against assisting Hanoi. Five years earlier, such a Soviet move would have been regarded by both sides in the Cold War as a bold challenge to U.S. power in Southeast Asia and would have been treated in Washington as something of a crisis. But now the Soviet declarations brought no response at all from Washington—no threat of serious consequences, or even a mild diplomatic warning. Something had clearly happened to cause Washington to avoid a confrontation with Moscow over Vietnam.

The new development was not a change in the military balance between the two superpowers but a shift in the structure of global politics from bipolar to triangular. The United States now regarded the USSR as closer to the United States than to the PRC in global politics, and on the Vietnam War in particular. Between 1961 and 1963, the U.S. national security bureaucracy had increasingly come to view the USSR less as an enemy than as a potential adjunct to U.S. policy on Vietnam. By failing to issue any warning to the USSR over the issue of military assistance to Hanoi, the United States had conveyed indirectly to Moscow that it would not oppose and might even welcome an increase in Soviet influence in Hanoi, in preference to exclusive North Vietnamese dependence on the Chinese. The dominant analysis in Washington was now that Soviet military and economic aid would be necessary to enable Hanoi to end the insurgency in South Vietnam and thus sacrifice the aid it received from China. In late February 1965, Ambassador Maxwell Taylor cabled a proposal from Saigon that the United States tell Moscow "that we would not oppose a continuous Soviet role in DRV, to replace dominant influence of Chicoms."[147]

Although the U.S. perception of the Soviet role in the Southeast Asia conflict was not necessarily the same as the Soviet perception, Moscow's interest was indeed to promote a peaceful settlement and less dependence on the Chinese. At least originally, therefore, Soviet willingness to provide military assistance to North Vietnam in the event of a U.S. attack on it was linked with getting Hanoi's approval of a major peace initiative. When Soviet Premier Alexei Kosygin visited Hanoi on February 6–8, 1965, he was apparently pushing for a new international conference on South Vietnam, which Kosygin wanted in order to prevent a widening of the war to North Vietnam. One week after Kosygin's return to Moscow, the Soviet Foreign

Ministry presented the North Vietnamese and Chinese ambassadors with a formal proposal for an international conference on Vietnam, based on the principle of "unconditional discussions," which the USSR hoped would make it acceptable to the United States.[148]

While Kosygin was in Hanoi, however, the United States carried out its first bombing attack against North Vietnam since August 1964, ostensibly in reprisal for a Viet Cong attack on a U.S. base in Pleiku. The Kremlin was bitter about the U.S. decision to carry out the bombing while the Soviet head of government was in the country, and the visit ended with a joint communiqué that was undoubtedly tougher than what Moscow had planned. It confirmed that the two countries had "reached an understanding on the steps that will be taken to strengthen the defense capacity of the D.R.V." and for the first time expressed full support for the South Vietnamese, who had been "forced to wage an armed struggle for their liberation."[149]

The North Vietnamese immediately rejected the wording of the Soviet proposal for an international conference and insisted that the United States accept the condition that it would not bomb North Vietnam during the conference. The USSR was then forced to modify the proposal to reflect Hanoi's demand, and it presented the amended proposal to the French government on February 23.[150] Ten days later, the United States began daily bombardment of North Vietnam, and the first U.S. combat troops began arriving on March 9. Party Secretary Le Duan and Defense Minister Vo Nguyen Giap were then invited to Moscow in April to discuss the size and scope of Soviet military assistance. Only after that meeting did the USSR begin to dispatch modern weapons, including MiG fighter planes and surface-to-air missiles, to North Vietnam.[151]

The sharp change in Soviet policy during the first six months after Khrushchev's ouster, therefore, also marked the transition in global politics from an ostensibly bipolar structure that hid actual triangular dynamics to a fully articulated triangular structure. The Vietnam War was clearly not a struggle between the Communist world and the U.S.-led coalition of anti-Communist states. The Soviet Union now played an ambiguous role that combined supplying arms to the North Vietnamese and taking a position in the larger geopolitical contest that was closer to that of the United States than to that of China.

·　·　·

In the interwar period of the Cold War, no issue in Soviet or Chinese policy was so clearly influenced by the global configuration of power as was Vietnam. The power advantage that the United States enjoyed in relation to both Communist powers was so commanding that Moscow and Beijing both adopted a policy of anticipatory concessions to U.S. interests in Vietnam. That approach not only precluded overt actions that might provoke a U.S. military response in Southeast Asia but involved actively seeking to create conditions that would minimize the risk of any conflict with the United States over the issue of South Vietnam. That meant pressing Hanoi to accept the division of Vietnam for an indefinite period, while signaling to the United States their tacit acceptance of its dominant role in South Vietnam.

The acquiescence by both Communist powers to the consolidation of power by the United States and its client regime in South Vietnam demonstrated the use of appeasement of a stronger state by weaker states in the hope of establishing a status quo that would be acceptable to the former. The USSR and the PRC both repeatedly pointed to the unfavorable correlation of forces in the world as the key factor in their choice of strategy toward Vietnam, leaving no room for doubt about the influence of the imbalance of power on the issue. The behavior of the Soviet Union and China thus conformed to what would be expected from subordinate states in an international system lacking a balance of power.

For several years, the Soviet-Chinese strategy of placating the United States achieved the desired objective of eliminating the threat of a potentially uncontrollable conflict over Vietnam. It ultimately failed, however, because it required the compliance not only of Hanoi but of the former Viet Minh and others in South Vietnam subjected to physical repression at the hands of the U.S.-supported regime. Like the United States, the Communist powers underrated the likelihood of a breach in the international hierarchy of power from the bottom up.

The Communist powers did not even attempt to use the Geneva Accords as a framework within which they might be able to broker a creative diplomatic compromise with the United States that could have avoided the use of force in South Vietnam. They understood that the United States, as the dominant power, would be impervious to any compromise on the issue. Pushing for any kind of a new settlement, therefore, would only have the effect of increasing tensions with Washington, while raising unrealistic hopes in Hanoi. The configuration of power created incentives on the part of the subordinate states to take the line of least resistance, which was to placate Washington and lean on Hanoi.

3 Eisenhower and Dulles Exploit U.S. Dominance in Vietnam

In keeping with the Cold War consensus explanation for the U.S. road to war in Vietnam, interpretations of Eisenhower administration policy during the Indochina crisis of 1954 have attributed its nonintervention in the war to its inability to meet stiff congressional conditions for a multilateral military operation with its allies and to opposition from the British.[1] This conventional view of the Eisenhower administration's policy assumes that either President Dwight D. Eisenhower or Secretary of State John Foster Dulles actually had wanted to intervene to save the faltering French military effort against the Viet Minh or even to replace the French forces with U.S. forces. This chapter argues, however, that both Eisenhower and Dulles were determined from the start to avoid actual military intervention to save the French. What they did intend was to exploit the newly decisive power advantage that the United States now enjoyed over the USSR to induce the PRC to back away from its support for the Viet Minh and, later, to influence the Geneva talks.

It was the Eisenhower administration's decision to ignore and undermine the Geneva Accords that created a ticking time bomb for future administrations, not any intention on its part to intervene militarily in 1954 or later, under the pact that established SEATO. The Geneva Accords, negotiated under what the Communists believed was the threat of U.S. intervention, offered a peaceful solution, based on free elections for a Vietnamese government. But Eisenhower and Dulles decided to ignore the political provisions of the accords in 1955 and instead tried to determine the future of South Vietnam unilaterally by destroying the Viet Minh political organization in South Vietnam. The explanation for those decisions, which led to the resumption of armed hostilities five years later, can be found in the dramatic imbalance in the East-West power relationship that Eisenhower and Dulles found when they came into office.

THE 1954 INDOCHINA CRISIS:
DECODING "UNITED ACTION"

Did the Eisenhower administration believe the threat of a Viet Minh victory in Indochina was so grave that it had little choice but to use force to prevent it? Eisenhower and Dulles certainly wanted to avoid the defeat of the French in Indochina, believing that it would be a blow to U.S. containment policy. But their policy preference was not determined primarily by their definition of the Cold War threat. Even more important was their keen awareness of the colonial character of the Franco–Viet Minh war. The general perception that the French were fighting for their colonial interests in Indochina made the idea of U.S. military intervention in Indochina politically unpopular. Virtually every senator engaged in the issue—whether Democrat or Republican, liberal, moderate, or China-first conservative— held this view of the conflict in Indochina as well. Undersecretary of State Walter Bedell Smith, testifying before the Senate Foreign Relations Committee in February 1954, alluded to the strong popular opposition to any U.S. military intervention on the side of the French, noting: "You yourselves are under great pressures in connection with this thing."[2]

Furthermore, Eisenhower and Dulles did not believe the war could be won under the existing political circumstances. Eisenhower declared at an NSC meeting in May 1953 that without clear French willingness to concede independence, "nothing could possibly save Indochina," and that U.S. assistance "would amount to pouring our money down a rathole." He reported to the NSC in early 1954 that the ambassador of the French-sponsored State of Viet-Nam had told him that only "perhaps 2 or 3 percent" of the Vietnamese people believed in French promises of independence.[3] Undersecretary Smith told the Senate Foreign Relations Committee that it was "impossible to persuade any people to fight if they think they are fighting for colonialism, and to die if they think they are dying for an overseas power which controls their political destinies." Even many military leaders were very strongly opposed to going into Indochina. General Curtis LeMay told an interviewer in March 1954 that he would not fight a war in Indochina, because it was a "political squabble that could be settled by political action," namely "offering independence to their people ultimately."[4]

The record of discussions involving Eisenhower and Dulles makes it clear that neither of them seriously considered sending U.S. forces to fight in Indochina at any time during the 1954 crisis. Their antipathy to U.S. intervention is unmistakably clear from both their words and their actions throughout the crisis. That pattern began to take shape with the National

Security Council (NSC) policy review on Indochina, NSC 177, a draft of which had been completed on December 30, 1953. On January 8, the NSC discussed a Special Annex that referred to courses of action open to the United States in two contingencies that had not been covered in NSC 177: first, a French move to negotiate a settlement in the absence of a U.S. offer to participate in the war, and, second, a French move to end the war, even if the United States was willing to join it.[5]

That discussion provided the first indication of the depth of Eisenhower's opposition to any military intervention in Indochina. He opened the discussion by declaring "with great force" that he "couldn't imagine putting ground forces anywhere in Southeast Asia except possibly in Malaysia, which we would have to defend as a bulwark to our off-shore island chain." Sending troops anywhere else, he said, was "simply beyond his contemplation." There was "no sense in even talking about United States forces replacing the French in Indochina," Eisenhower continued. "If we did so, the Vietnamese could be expected to transfer their hatred of the French to us." He concluded this remarkable statement by saying, "with vehemence," according to the minutes, "I cannot tell how bitterly opposed I am to such a course of action."

Support for intervention came from JCS Chairman Admiral Arthur Radford, who called for at least U.S. air strikes to save the French base at Dien Bien Phu, already besieged by Viet Minh forces. He suggested that putting just one squadron of U.S. planes over Dien Bien Phu for "as little as one afternoon might save the situation" and argued that the U.S. stake in the outcome made the gamble worthwhile. Eisenhower countered that the CIA might organize "a little group of fine and adventurous pilots" who could help the French covertly, but again ruled out the United States being involved "directly" in the war, which he warned would be a "dangerous thing."[6]

Having served notice that military intervention was out of the question, Eisenhower and Dulles began preparing a fall-back position to adjust to the possible defeat or negotiated surrender of the French. At the next NSC meeting, they revealed one of the tactics they had in mind to make their acceptance of Viet Minh victory more palatable to hard-liners in and outside the administration. Dulles suggested that "an opportunity would open up to us in Southeast Asia even if the French are finally defeated by the Communists." The United States could then "raise hell," and the Communists would "find it just as expensive to resist as we are finding it." Dulles was proposing the U.S. plan for supporting guerrilla resistance against the Viet Minh regime as an alternative to planning for military intervention.

Eisenhower again expressed his approval of Dulles's suggestion, saying the United States "should have done something like that" after the Communist takeover in China.[7]

On January 16, 1954, after approving NSC 5405, which authorized the dispatch of more U.S. planes to the French and mechanics to keep them flying, Eisenhower ordered five leading national security advisers—Radford, Undersecretary of State Walter Bedell Smith, Deputy Secretary of Defense Roger Kyes, CIA Director Allen Dulles, and Special Assistant to the President C. D. Jackson—to form a special committee to come up with an "area plan" for Southeast Asia. He specifically directed them to include in the plan "possible alternative lines of action to be taken in case of [a] reverse in Indochina or elsewhere in the area." One of the ideas discussed at the meeting was that Thailand could "constitute a bastion if Indochina fell," providing the "secure, sympathetic-to-the-U.S. base" for a possible Thai-Burmese-Cambodian regional defense pact.[8]

Eisenhower was clearly preparing to accept a French defeat in Indochina. At a press conference on February 10, he stated his strong objection to the idea of U.S. military intervention in Southeast Asia publicly, using almost the identical phrasing as in his remark in the NSC. "No one could be more bitterly opposed to even getting involved in a hot war in that region than I," he said. "Consequently every move that I authorize is calculated, as far as humans can do, to make certain that that does not happen." Thus he explicitly included air and naval forces in his objection to the use of force in Indochina.[9]

Meanwhile, John Foster Dulles was continuing to think about how best to exploit the obvious weakness of both the Soviet Union and China, especially in relation to the United States. After the review of U.S. containment policy in mid 1953 that was dubbed "Project Solarium," Dulles had considered the U.S. strategic invulnerability to Soviet attack as the key to getting favorable settlements in both Europe and the Far East. In a memorandum for the president in early September, he suggested that it was a "propitious time" to seek far-reaching concessions from the USSR and the PRC. The key to such a strategy, he wrote, was that the United States would be "operating from strength rather than weakness," and he cited as evidence the Korean armistice "in an atmosphere of our willingness to enlarge the war unless the armistice was accepted." On his list of issues to be addressed by exerting such diplomatic pressures on the USSR and the PRC Dulles included "Indochina–Formosa–Red China."[10]

The global policy statement adopted by the NSC in October 1953 reflected Secretary Dulles's views on exploiting the favorable power balance.

It called for "measures to impose pressures on the Soviet bloc" to "create conditions that will induce the Soviet leadership to be more receptive to acceptable negotiated settlements," as well as "selective, positive actions to eliminate Soviet-Communist control over any areas of the free world." Supporting that policy decision was an NIE in October 1953 that referred to the "unique position" of the United States in the "East-West strug-gle"—meaning the absence of a Soviet capability to retaliate against the United States with nuclear weapons—and asserted that it was already in the process of disappearing.[11] Dulles believed that pressure could be brought to bear on China to withdraw its support for the Viet Minh war effort by the use of nuanced military threats. Both he and Eisenhower believed that the warning they had conveyed to the Chinese in 1953 about extending the Korean War had helped push the PRC to agree to U.S. terms for the Korean truce, even though it had not involved an explicit threat to launch an attack on China or to use nuclear weapons, and even though the Eisenhower administration had no real evidence that the message had even gotten through to the Chinese before the truce agreement.[12]

The United States not only had the capability to bomb Chinese military targets and population centers with impunity; it had at its disposal 350,000 Chinese nationalist troops. Of these, 150,000 troops had been trained by the CIA during the Korean War to carry out harassing raids from Taiwan, and they now had the capability, with U.S. air and logistical support, to ini-tiate large-scale amphibious operations against the mainland.[13] According to an NSC decision in November 1953, these forces were to be used "for such offensive operations as may be in the U.S. interests" and "would con-tinue to represent a threat to Communist China."[14] Dulles thus had a range of options for threatening China.

Dulles later recalled that at the Berlin Conference in January and Feb-ruary, he had gotten the "feeling of some apprehension on the part of the Russians that . . . they were not particularly anxious to have the Chinese Communists get out of hand to any extent which would cause risk, at least, of a general war." By late February, he had already begun to enter-tain the hope that this Soviet "apprehension," combined with the anxi-eties of the Chinese Communists about their vulnerability to U.S. air attacks and harassment from the Nationalist Chinese forces, could be par-layed into a successful strategy of pressuring the Chinese to withdraw from the Viet Minh war. Testifying before the Senate Foreign Relations Committee on February 24, Dulles dismissed the possibility of a negoti-ated settlement of the Indochina conflict, but he then added, "I do not consider that it is entirely impossible that that [Chinese Communist] aid might be cut off." He suggested that this could lead to a situation in which most of the French forces could pull out, leaving it to Vietnam, Laos, and Cambodia to deal with the Viet Minh. He conceded that this was a "rosy prospect" but said, "I think it is certainly worth trying for."[15]

Dulles's hope for a strategy of exploiting Communist fears of a possible U.S. expansion of the war was in line with the analysis of Soviet and Chinese policy being done under his brother Allen at the CIA. A National Intelligence Estimate in mid March emphasized the extreme caution of both Communist powers toward any course that would raise the risk of war with the United States. It concluded that the USSR and the PRC would seek to attain their objectives in Asia by means that would not subject Communist China to "severe economic strains" or "invoke serious risk of attacks on the Chinese mainland." In a March 23 press conference, Secretary Dulles returned to the idea that China might opt out of the war. Responding to a question about the prospects of a peace settlement at Geneva, he suggested that they would greatly increase "if the Chinese Communists are willing to cut off military assistance."[16]

Meanwhile, despite Eisenhower's unambiguous policy of nonintervention, Radford and Smith had not given up on getting him to use U.S. forces in Indochina. In a memo to Secretary of Defense Charles Wilson on March 12, the JCS recommended that the NSC "consider now the extent to which the United States would be willing to commit its resources in support of the Associated States [Vietnam, Laos, and Cambodia] in the effort to prevent the loss of Indochina to the Communists either: (a) in concert with the French; or (b) in the event the French elect to withdraw, in concert with other allies, or if necessarily, unilaterally."[17]

This was followed by a report by the chairman of a subcommittee of the special committee, retired Marine General Graves B. Erskine, which represented a consensus of JCS and DOD participants on the subcommittee, but not of the State Department representatives, who had "reserved their positions" on the report, presumably on orders from Dulles. The paper presented three courses of action in Indochina, all of which were in support of U.S. military intervention: to take "the political steps" to ensure agreement among the United States, the United Kingdom, and France on Indochina at the Geneva Conference; to "determine the extent of U.S. willingness . . . to commit U.S. air, naval and ultimately ground forces to the direct resolution of the war in Indochina with or without French support," and to take steps to sell a possible U.S. military intervention in Indochina to domestic and international opinion, which it acknowledged was far from ready to accept such intervention.

Finally, the paper addressed the subject of "the development of a substitute base of operations"—a reference to Eisenhower's initial order to the group to come up with "possible alternative lines of action to be taken in case of reverse in Indochina or elsewhere in the area." Contrary to Eisenhower's explicit wishes, the subcommittee urged the NSC to "consider whether this course of action is acceptable as a substitute" for military intervention, arguing that it would involve major expenditure but could only bear fruit in the long run.[18] The special committee, which Eisenhower had intended to provide an alternative to military intervention, had essentially tried to bring bureaucratic pressure to bear for U.S. military action to prevent a Viet Minh victory.

Wilson transmitted both the JCS and military subcommittee papers to Dulles on March 23 with a cover note declaring that the recommendations of both papers "represent the views of the DOD." Eisenhower and Dulles were not swayed, however, by the errant behavior of at least some members of the special committee. Meeting on March 24, they agreed that the United States should not get involved in combat in Indochina in the absence of "political preconditions for a successful outcome." Eisenhower mused tentatively that he would not "wholly preclude the possibility of a single strike, if it were almost certain this would produce decisive results." But he knew very well that it couldn't, and that it might easily lead to deeper involvement. When Dulles responded that it would be "preferable to slow up the Chinese Communists in Southeast Asia by harassing tactics from Formosa and along the seacoast, which would be more readily within our natural facilities than actually fighting in Indochina," Eisenhower immediately agreed.

Dulles then revealed to Eisenhower that he was thinking of including a statement in his March 29 speech that "we could not look upon the loss to Communism of that area with indifference." Dulles hoped this traditional, unspecific diplomatic warning to the Chinese, which would leave plenty of room for further maneuver, might well frighten the PRC and help convince the USSR to bring pressure to bear on its Chinese ally to back away from the Viet Minh military campaign.[19] This was the origin of what would become the "united action" speech.

At the NSC meeting on March 25, Eisenhower approved the JCS-DOD recommendation that the Planning Board study the question of intervention. This action has been viewed by some as evidence that Eisenhower remained open to unilateral intervention in Indochina. The larger pattern of Eisenhower's policy toward Indochina clearly indicates, however, that this was merely a bureaucratic maneuver to keep the pro-interventionist

officials on board without actually accepting their policy recommendation. More significant was Eisenhower's move at that meeting to play
his political trump card in the struggle with Radford and DOD officials
over Vietnam policy: congressional opposition to military intervention in
Indochina. Noting that Congress would have to approve any military
action, Eisenhower instructed Dulles to explore with Congress what support could be expected. Eisenhower certainly knew that there was virtually
no possibility of congressional approval of unilateral intervention, and that
stringent conditions would undoubtedly be attached to any military action
that was authorized.[20]

Dulles was opposed to Eisenhower's maneuver, because he viewed a
congressional resolution as an important element in his strategy of diplomatic coercion of China. He suggested that the NSC needed to do more
work before approaching Congress and said there was plenty of time to
"work out some kind of suitable United Nations action." But Eisenhower
was unmoved. He managed in the same NSC meeting both to put himself
on record as keeping the intervention option open and to effectively block
any such intervention by invoking the requirement for congressional
approval.

At a cabinet meeting the following day, Dulles dismissed the ongoing
battle between the French and the Viet Minh at Dien Bien Phu as of "only
the slightest importance." Then he suggested that the United States might
have to take "fairly strong action" on Indochina, carrying definite risks,
and that "these risks will be less if we take them now rather than waiting
several years."[21] He believed the risk was low and controllable, because of
the strategic asymmetry with the USSR, which he hoped would lead
Moscow to put pressure on the PRC to halt its aid to the Viet Minh. Dulles
knew that the risks of the same action would be greater in a few years,
because the existing U.S. strategic invulnerability was expected to give way
to a state of mutual deterrence.[22] The "fairly strong action," as would
become clear in the days to come, was not actual military intervention but
a carefully formulated threat to China.

At the Overseas Press Club on March 29, Dulles initiated his public
strategy of coercive threat. In the operative sentences of the address, he
declared, "Under the conditions of today, the imposition on Southeast Asia
of the political system of Communist Russia and its Chinese Communist
ally, by whatever means, would be a grave threat to the whole free community. The United States feels that that possibility should not be pas-
sively accepted, but should be met by united action."[23] Dulles apparently
impressed on Republican Senator H. Alexander Smith of the Senate Foreign

Relations Committee shortly before giving the speech that it was aimed not at paving the way for military intervention but at exerting strong diplomatic pressure on the USSR and the PRC from a position of commanding strength. After Dulles had shown him the text of the speech, Smith wrote in his diary, "If we are firm, Russia will have to yield."[24]

Although Eisenhower was broadly supportive of Dulles's strategy of diplomatic pressure, he was not willing to feign readiness for U.S. military intervention publicly. Asked at a press conference two days after the Dulles speech whether "united action" meant that U.S. forces might be used in Indochina, Ike said each case would have to be judged on its own merits, but he was unable to restrain himself from expressing his own strongly felt objection to fighting in Indochina. "I can conceive of no greater disadvantage to America," he said, "than to be employing its own ground forces, and any other kind of forces, in great numbers around the world, meeting each little situation as it arises."[25]

Dulles's aim of pressuring the Chinese to back away without war was then integrated into the text of the draft congressional resolution prepared, on Dulles's orders, in support of the "united action" strategy. The draft alluded clearly to the intention to use the threat of force as a means of coercion. It read, in part: "Whereas peace and order may be restored and this aggression ended if it is known that the United States is prepared, in pursuance of a decision or recommendation of the United Nations, or by united action with other free nations or in the exercise of the inherent right of individual or collective self-defense recognized by Article 51 of the UN Charter, to restrain and retaliate against such armed attack." The draft authorized the president to "employ the naval and air forces of the United States to assist the forces which are resisting aggression in Southeast Asia."[26]

Meeting with the ambassadors of India and the United Kingdom on April 2, Dulles revealed the outlines of his strategy of diplomatic coercion. He conveyed a distinct but very low-key threat to the Chinese through the Indian ambassador, telling him that he "did not wish to specify" what he had in mind in his speech, but that "military action was always the last resort." Dulles said he "hoped military activity would not spread" from the Indochina battlefield but added that it was not excluded.[27] Despite the fact that Dulles knew he would be meeting the following day with congressional leaders who would want to know what the British were willing to contribute to a military intervention in Indochina, when he met with the British ambassador, Sir Roger Makins, on April 2, Dulles made no effort to probe the British willingness to join in such an intervention. He did not even bring up "united action" and fended off a question about exactly what it meant, saying he could not discuss it in detail. Instead, Dulles proposed what he called a "deterrent action" directed at compelling Communist China to end its aid to the Viet Minh, in the form of a joint U.S.-British warning to the PRC of air action against the Chinese coast if the aid were not stopped. Dulles linked this proposal to the asymmetry between the United States and the USSR in vulnerability to strategic attack, which he pointed out might "decline over the next four years," and to U.S. military superiority in East Asia. In addition, Dulles wanted the United States and Britain to consider "security arrangements" to "keep Southeast Asia out of the hands of the Communists irrespective of what position the French might finally adopt."[28]

Most accounts of the meeting with the congressional leadership on April 3 have assumed that Radford and Dulles were working closely with each other on a U.S. strategy rather than being in conflict. When Dulles and Radford had met with Eisenhower and Defense Secretary Wilson the day before, however, Dulles had called attention to the "differences in approach" between Radford and himself on getting congressional support. Dulles said his view was that congressional authority was "designed to be a deterrent" and to help get support for an international coalition, whereas Radford saw it as a means of carrying out a "strike," irrespective of allied unity on the issue. Radford confirmed the difference, noting that future military developments "might call for more active U.S. participation" in Indochina.[29]

At the April 3 meeting, Radford talked of the possibility of using U.S. planes for a single strike to save Dien Bien Phu, but Dulles did not refer to military action at all. Instead he emphasized again that the mere passage of a congressional resolution might make it unnecessary to actually use military force. The congressional leaders did not respond to Dulles's suggestion, but unanimously insisted that there could be no congressional action until Dulles actually had commitments "of a political and material nature from our allies" regarding an international military operation. Once that was done, they said, a congressional resolution could be passed authorizing the use of force in the area.[30]

Dulles's conversations with other allied diplomats indicate that he was increasingly thinking of using a joint warning to influence the Geneva negotiations. Meeting with French Ambassador Henri Bonnet on April 3, Dulles said it was important to form an international coalition before the Geneva conference began to "permit us to go to Geneva with the required strength." And he drew a direct parallel with Korea, recalling that he and

Eisenhower had "obtained an armistice in Korea primarily because the Chinese feared that we would knock out their industrial area North of the Yalu." The formation of an international coalition, he said, would "give us an alternative in Geneva without which we are lost."[31]

Dulles and Eisenhower were both involved in drafting a letter from the president to British Prime Minister Winston Churchill on April 4 seeking his support for "united action" in Indochina. Past accounts have emphasized the seemingly martial tone of the final paragraph invoking the pre–World War II failure to "halt Hirohito, Mussolini and Hitler," but the letter actually suggested the probability of affecting Chinese policy without going to war. "If we grasp this one together," wrote Eisenhower, "I believe that we will enormously increase our chances of bringing the Chinese to believe that their interests lie in the direction of a discreet disengagement."[32]

Meeting with a Filipino diplomat on April 5, Dulles said nothing about an international military action in Indochina but did refer to the desirability of forming a "loose coalition" of Western and Asian states. He said he did not have in mind a "permanent Pacific type of alliance," but only a temporary coalition for the purpose of influencing the outcome of the Geneva Conference "through such a device as a joint declaration of purpose."[33] At an NSC meeting the following day, Dulles again said that it was not primarily about military intervention in Indochina, but "an effort at building up strength in the Southeast Asia area to such a point that military intervention might prove to be unnecessary." If he could organize a regional grouping before the Geneva Conference, he said, they could go to Geneva "with a good hope that we would come out of the conference with the Communists backing down." Eisenhower also indicated clearly at that meeting that he had no intention of planning for intervention in Indochina, suggesting that the regional organization he and Dulles envisioned "would have for its purpose the defense of Southeast Asia *even if Indochina should be lost* [emphasis added.]"[34]

If the U.S. effort to build an international coalition for "united action" were to fail, Dulles said, it would be necessary to "contemplate armed intervention," and he reiterated his view that "there were certain risks which we could take today which we might not be able to take later." Earlier in the same meeting, however, Dulles had informed the NSC that it would be impossible to get congressional authorization for unilateral intervention in Indochina. Again, Dulles was actually referring not to the risk of entering into combat in Indochina but to the risk of threatening China.

Dulles was not counting on the success of an international coalition for "united action" to accomplish his political-diplomatic objectives but hoped that his speech and the press and diplomatic reports speculating on U.S. intervention would by themselves moderate Communist demands and stiffen the French position in Geneva. On April 7, he told Alexander Wiley, the chairman of the Senate Foreign Relations Committee, that his aim was to "hold the Communists at Geneva."[35] Dulles's hope was encouraged by French Ambassador Bonnet and the U.S. ambassador in Moscow, Charles E. "Chip" Bohlen. Bonnet told Dulles that Dulles's "united action" speech had created "a strong impression" in Paris, and probably elsewhere, that the United States would intervene in Indochina by itself, if necessary, to prevent Indochina from falling to the Communists. In a message to Dulles on April 12, Bohlen further bolstered Dulles's hopes of persuading the Communists that he was bent on intervention, if necessary. "Recent indications of firmness in American policy in regard to Indochina," reported the ambassador, "appear to have produced characteristic uncertainty on the part of the Soviet government when faced with real determination." Bohlen suggested that "a solution on our terms is not totally out of the realm of possibility."[36]

Dulles left Washington for London and Paris on April 10 to seek the support of both allies for his plan for a joint coalition warning aimed at influencing the Chinese. As Dulles expected, however, British Foreign Secretary Anthony Eden declined to be drawn into any coalition warning to China over the Indochina war. Eden concluded in a paper he prepared for the meeting with Dulles that no U.S. threat would be "sufficiently potent to make China swallow so humiliating a rebuff as abandonment of the Viet Minh." Eden also knew, however, that the USSR had no bombers that could reach the United States, and he believed that the generalized threat of U.S. intervention in the conflict and the attendant risk of escalation exerted pressure on the USSR to make concessions at the Geneva negotiations to avoid any resumption of hostilities. He offered to explore the idea of a defense organization for Southeast Asia as a whole, but he wanted to see how the negotiations would play out first, thinking that such a military pact might not be necessary. The French government, under Prime Minister Joseph Laniel, also insisted that the Western powers wait and see what would happen at Geneva before making any commitments to a military coalition.[37]

Even after the European trip failed to generate any immediate support for the idea of a joint warning to China, Eisenhower and Dulles went on trying to persuade the Communists and the French that the United States was contemplating joint military action. When asked at a press conference in London what he would regard as a "satisfactory settlement" in Indochina,

Dulles suggested that he had not considered any compromise with the Communists at Geneva. Back in Washington, Dulles told Eisenhower's press secretary, James Hagarty, that the Communists "do not know whether we will attack if they move . . . and we want to leave it that way." In an April 19 conversation with Vice President Richard Nixon, Dulles said he had told Eisenhower that the administration had to follow a course that would avoid war, but that "one cannot explain everything to our own people, as it also explains things to the enemy." The next day at a State Department briefing on Indochina, Dulles said that there was a "fair chance that the ambitions entertained by the Communists would be written off." Recalling Stalin's cutoff of assistance to the Greek Communists, Dulles said that the Communists were "without scruples when it came to cutting off an adventure that was not paying off."[38]

Conferring with Republican congressional leaders on April 26, Eisenhower provided another clear indication that the administration was engaging in strategic deception in its "united action" strategy. He informed the Republicans that Dien Bien Phu could fall any day and then warned against putting even a single combat soldier into Indochina and committing U.S. prestige to the contest. What was important, he said, was that the administration should "not let the Russians think that we might not resist in the event that the Communists attempted to step up their present tactics in Indochina and elsewhere." He hinted broadly that the policy was a bluff, saying, "[I]t was not well to tell the Russians everything as to what we would or would not do."[39]

While Dulles was attending the Geneva Conference on April 29, proponents of military intervention took the offensive within the NSC. The most outspoken war hawk, Harold Stassen, argued that the American people and Congress would support U.S. intervention. That provoked Eisenhower to raise the issue of colonialism, which he said would exist even if the United States replaced the French in Indochina. Then Eisenhower brought out his main argument against any proposal for intervention, expressing his "conviction" that unilateral intervention would "mean a general war with China and perhaps with the USSR." Conveniently for Ike, Dulles had just reported from Geneva that Soviet Foreign Minister Molotov's attitude and a statement by Zhou the previous day had led him to "rate more highly than heretofore the probability that any open US intervention would be answered by open Chinese intervention with consequences of general war in Asia." Ike denounced unilateral military intervention as "an attempt to police the entire world" and said the United States would be "everywhere accused of imperialistic ambitions."[40]

Upon his return from Geneva, Dulles's primary concern shifted to justifying Ike's nonintervention policy. He told the NSC on May 6 that he doubted the wisdom of U.S. "belligerency" in Indochina unless the French agreed to grant the Associated States genuine independence; to give the United States a much more active role in training indigenous armed forces; to share responsibility for military planning; and to stay in the fight in Indochina. Both Eisenhower and Dulles then added that they would insist on having Asian states included in the coalition, rather than limiting it to France, Britain, Australia, and New Zealand. They were setting the bar for U.S. intervention considerably higher, therefore, than the congressional leadership had done. Dulles then returned to his assertion that China and Russia were now feeling "much greater confidence in the strength of their position than we had earlier estimated" and argued that if the U.S. intervened in Indochina without the British, there was a "much greater chance of Chinese overt intervention than . . . if the British were in with us."[41]

In a briefing for congressional leaders that same day, however, Dulles pronounced the issue of intervention, whether unilateral or multilateral, to be closed. The issue of participation by other allies in such an intervention was now "academic," he said, because France had "not fulfilled the prerequisite." Dulles revealed that he had now turned his attention to the development of what he called a "Southeast Asia community," which was not for the purpose of supporting future military intervention in Vietnam but offered a "fair chance" to "insulate the rest of Southeast Asia" from the possible loss of Vietnam.[42]

Even after declaring the issue closed, Dulles and Eisenhower continued to build a case against intervention, relying primarily on the danger of Chinese counterintervention. Dulles had a paper prepared for a meeting with Eisenhower on May 11 that marshaled the arguments against any U.S. military intervention in Indochina or expansion of the war to China. "All estimates agree," it asserted, "on at least a 50 percent chance of Chinese Communist reaction to U.S. intervention." If the United States expanded the war to China and the USSR became involved, according to the paper, it would endanger British and NATO bases. The paper warned, furthermore, that there could be no intervention in Indochina without U.S. ground forces, which might be "larger under some contingencies." Dulles sent a telegram to the U.S. embassy in Paris suggesting that intervention "might involve consequences of utmost gravity," because the reactions of the Communist bloc "could not be predicted."[43]

The allegedly high risk of a Soviet or Chinese military response to U.S. intervention that became the centerpiece of the justification for nonintervention had all the marks of an instrumental argument created by Dulles out of whole cloth. Dulles's sudden pessimism about Soviet and Chinese willingness to go to war with the United States came just in time to serve the immediate policy need to counter the pressure from administration hawks for the use of force in Indochina. The speech by Zhou cited by Dulles as evidence that the risk of war with China had increased contained no threat of counterintervention by the PRC: Zhou merely complained about unidentified threats to the "peaceful development and security" of the PRC.[44] No other intelligence supporting such a fundamental shift ever came to light. Nor would the absence of British support for a U.S. intervention have had any logical bearing on whether the Chinese would send troops into Vietnam to counter U.S. air and naval power.

Furthermore, the paper's claim that intelligence estimates supported this new assessment does not appear to be accurate. The Special National Intelligence Estimate on the question issued by the CIA in mid June actually came to the opposite conclusion. Although the NIE was based on the dubious premise that the Chinese would regard any intervention by U.S. air and naval forces as presaging the destruction of the Viet Minh, it nevertheless judged that the Chinese probably would not respond by sending troops into Vietnam.[45]

Dulles continued to act in the hope that Soviet and Chinese fear of war might still be great enough to influence the Communist diplomatic position in Geneva, even in the absence of any clear international coalition, which was at odds with the alleged Chinese readiness to face war with the United States. In his May 11 press conference, Dulles suggested that the regional security pact would include Vietnam, and that once the pact was signed, "it would then be appropriate to use force to put down attacks such as are going on there."[46] Testifying the following day in executive session before the Senate Foreign Relations Committee, however, Dulles again related the pursuit of regional collective security primarily to possible influence on the Geneva negotiations. "We felt the chances of salvaging something out of the Geneva Conference would be very much greater," he said, "if there was open evidence of activity in terms of the collective security of the area." On May 20, Dulles told the NSC that the "only ray of hope would be Communist fear of U.S. intervention in Indochina or of general war," which he said "might conceivably induce the Communists to moderate their demands on the French in Geneva."[47]

It is now clear that Dulles's hard line against any diplomatic compromise in Geneva and his determination to remain aloof from the Geneva negotiations were aimed primarily at reinforcing Soviet and Chinese fears that the United States might continue the war if the Geneva settlement was not acceptable to Washington.[48] In response to entreaties by Eden and French Prime Minister Mendès-France in Paris on July 13 to return to the Geneva Conference to support the allied negotiating position, Dulles argued that staying away from the negotiations could help persuade the Communists to end the war on more favorable terms by implying a more warlike posture by the United States. "Perhaps the French negotiating position would be strengthened," Dulles said, if it could portray the United States as the "wicked partner" lurking in the background. When Eden reacted strongly against that idea, Dulles suggested that any allusion to threatening U.S. intentions "might be implicit rather than explicit."[49]

Interpretations of Dulles's organization of the Southeast Asian collective security pact have long suggested that he was ensuring that he would have a legal cover for a possible military intervention in Vietnam.[50] But the record of the crucial discussions of U.S. policy toward SEATO belies any such intention. Both Dulles and Radford agreed that, after the Geneva agreement was signed, the most likely form of "aggression" would be subversion. Dulles told Eisenhower that the risk of subversion could be "largely countered by some buildup of local forces, as in Thailand, by some token participation of the coalition and by economic and social measures," which he pointed out would be "infinitely" cheaper than building a "major military defense in the area." In discussions with Thai Foreign Minister Prince Wan Waithayakorn and Ambassador Pote Sarasin, Dulles portrayed the new pact as drawing a new defense line in the region that would include Thailand, Burma, Laos, and Cambodia, and "perhaps part of Vietnam." He explained that the parties to the pact would agree to "guarantee against foreign aggression" but that they would agree only to "assist" countries covered by the treaty in the event of subversion.[51]

The earliest draft of the Southeast Asian security pact, approved by Dulles on July 9, made a fundamental distinction between the obligations of the parties to the treaty to respond to "overt Communist aggression" and to subversion. In case of the former, the obligation was to "take in accordance with its constitutional processes such action as it deems necessary including the use of armed force." But in the case of subversion, it was only to "consult together in order to agree on the measures which should be taken."[52] That fundamental distinction remained in the final version of Article IV of the "Southeast Asia Collective Defense Treaty," signed in Manila on September 8, 1954.[53] Ike and Dulles thus deliberately wrote the treaty so as to exclude any U.S. military commitment to use force in the circumstances they knew were most likely to arise in Vietnam.

After the Geneva agreement partitioned the country, the focus of U.S. policy toward SEATO on subversion became clearer. The South Vietnamese regime was extremely vulnerable to subversion and guerrilla warfare, whereas the danger of a North Vietnamese invasion of the South seemed remote. In the debate in the NSC on U.S. policy, therefore, the central issue was how the United States would respond to an armed insurgency arising *within* a country covered by the pact. The NSC staff drafted two alternative paragraphs on the issue for the draft statement of policy under discussion. The first presented the JCS preference for an ultimatum to Communist China that subversive war would "not be tolerated," and that its continuance "would in all probability lead to the application of military power not necessarily restricted to conventional weapons against the source of the aggression (i.e., Communist China)." The other said that the United States should be "prepared, either unilaterally or under the terms of the Southeast Asia Treaty, if requested by a legitimate local government, to assist by military force, if necessary and feasible, to defeat local Communist subversion or rebellion which does not constitute external armed attack."[54]

Dulles and Eisenhower, however, rejected both of the proposals from the national security bureaucracy. Dulles suggested that they would "add commitments which U.S. armed forces could not carry out at their present levels." Eisenhower added that he was "frankly puzzled by the problem of helping defeat local subversion without turning the United States into an armed camp." The problem, he said, was one of "defining conditions under which the President would go to Congress and ask for a declaration of war." At the following NSC meeting, Dulles introduced revised language that he said was aimed at avoiding "a fixed or automatic commitment to seek authority to intervene in Southeast Asia." The revised language said that the president "should at once *consider* requesting Congressional authority to take appropriate action [emphasis added]."[55] The Eisenhower-Dulles language did not commit the president to do anything in the event of a subversive war in South Vietnam.

Eisenhower made it clear that he would distinguish clearly between local subversion and Chinese Communist–inspired subversion. "If subversion in Southeast Asia was strictly local in inspiration," he said, "the United States would not be able to intervene, but if such subversion were the result of Chinese Communist motivation, the President would be quite right in seeking Congressional authorization for the United States to intervene." Dulles repeated in testimony on the Southeast Asia treaty that if there were a revolutionary movement in Vietnam or in Thailand, the United States would consult with other SEATO members but had "no undertaking to put it down." Dulles reassured the Senate Foreign Relations Committee that the administration would not use a "subterfuge" to permit military involvement in such a war. That testimony accurately reflected the position of both Eisenhower and Dulles.[56]

When the record is reviewed in its entirety, therefore, it does not support the view that Ike and Dulles organized a regional security pact in Southeast Asia in order to make the option of military intervention in Vietnam possible. Robert Bowie, who worked closely with Dulles on Indochina policy during that period as head of the State Department's Policy Planning staff, has called the "united action" policy a "grand charade of deterrence."[57] The record of statements and actions by both men confirms his characterization of the policy. When pressures for such intervention did come from the national security bureaucracy and others in the government, Eisenhower and Dulles mounted an energetic bureaucratic counterattack featuring a major emphasis on the threat of Chinese and Soviet military intervention and of general war. And neither of them tried to establish a justification for future military intervention against a Vietnamese Communist insurgency in negotiating the Southeast Asian pact.

REPRESSING THE COMMUNISTS IN THE SOUTH

The U.S. "Basic National Security Policy" adopted in early 1955 called for "destroying the effectiveness of the Communist apparatus in the free world," but specified that "direct action against the Communist apparatus must rest largely with the local governments concerned, although the United States should be able to help significantly, chiefly through covert means."[58] The adoption of that policy only codified, however, what the United States was already doing in both Iran and Vietnam.

The Tudeh Party in Iran had become one of the most effective Communist movements in the world and had mobilized large numbers of followers in previous years. Furthermore, it operated on the border of the Soviet Union, in a country where anti-Communist forces had been weakened. Until the latter half of 1952, U.S. policy had been to eschew any military commitment to Iran and avoid provoking a possible Soviet military response by refraining from intervention in the country's turbulent and highly nationalist domestic politics. But once the new U.S.-Soviet power balance became clear in the latter half of 1952, the NSC assumed that the USSR would be constrained by fear of war with the United States from responding to U.S. moves to establish a position of power in Iran. That assumption was the basis for the NSC decision in November 1952 to carry out "special political operations" aimed at restoring stability in Iran and using covert operations, if necessary, to reverse any coup carried out by the Tudeh Party. That broad policy led to the decision to organize the coup to overthrow Mossadegh and restore power to the shah in March 1953.[59] Beginning in September 1953, the CIA worked with the government of the shah to ferret out the membership of the Communist-controlled Tudeh Party.[60]

The decision to eliminate the Tudeh Party as a political force followed logically, especially after the USSR made no threatening response to the coup. On the contrary, the USSR refused to support the Tudeh Party's efforts to organize a popular front against the new pro-U.S. regime, and instead tried to establish normal relations with that regime.[61] The Iranian experience thus indicated that the United States could carry out covert operations that not only put a pro-Western government in power but effectively eliminated the Communist Party organization from a state right on the Soviet periphery without risk of any riposte from the Communist bloc.

The decision to seek to severely damage the Communist organization in South Vietnam, however, responded to a separate set of signals on the impact of the imbalance of power on Soviet and Chinese policies in Southeast Asia, beginning with the stunning diplomatic concessions made by the Communist delegations in the final days of the Geneva Conference in July 1954. At that time, the CIA's assessment of the outcome had concluded, "Communist willingness to reach agreement for an armistice in Indochina was probably derived in substantial part from the Communist estimate that: (a) an effort to win a total military victory in Indochina might precipitate US military intervention, and (b) the objective of gaining political control over all Indochina could be achieved as a result of the armistice agreement." The Communist bloc, it said, probably considered that the resumption of large-scale war from North Vietnam would "negate the political and psychological advantages the Communists could have gained by negotiating a settlement and could involve grave risk of expanded war."[62]

Two days after this CIA estimate, in early August 1954, Dulles affirmed at an NSC meeting that the Communists "had settled for less than they could have obtained at Geneva, one reason for this being the possibility of U.S. intervention in Indochina." It was "unlikely that the Communists would make a major military move anywhere in the world," he said. "The Communists would probably not violate the armistice in Indochina, but would use subversive means to gain control."[63] Dulles thus interpreted

Communist behavior at the Geneva Conference as reflecting a decisive U.S. power advantage over the Communist bloc and predicted that the defensive posture of the Communists in the region would continue indefinitely.

Dulles's view of Soviet and Chinese policy in Southeast Asia was further strengthened by indications in late 1954 and early 1955 that the new Soviet leadership was interested in consolidating the existing superpower spheres of influence, with South Vietnam allocated to the U.S. sphere. A CIA estimate in November portrayed the Sino-Soviet desire to reduce tensions in Asia as motivated by the need to "lessen the dangers of full-scale US military action against mainland China." It suggested that the Communist bloc's overall strategy would probably sacrifice "the ambitions of local Communist parties," if necessary, to serve Sino-Soviet interests. Meanwhile, the dependence of the North Vietnamese regime on the Communist bloc for technical, military, and economic assistance would give the USSR and the PRC considerable leverage over its policies, so Vietnamese Communist policy toward the South was expected to "reflect a consensus of Sino-Soviet views."[64] That estimate dovetailed with new evidence presented by CIA Director Allen Dulles in a paper in mid November 1954 that the USSR wanted to "make a deal" to secure Western acquiescence to Soviet domination in Eastern Europe in return for an undertaking by the USSR not to "expand the Communist orbit by force."[65]

These assessments indicate that, when Secretary Dulles and his brother Allen authorized an effort to repress the Communist organization in South Vietnam in November or December 1954, they had a high level of confidence that they could do so without any serious risk of a North Vietnamese or Chinese military response. The operation began when Lieutenant General John W. O'Daniel, head of the U.S. Military Assistance Advisory Group (MAAG) in Vietnam, began to staff what was then called the Advisory Training and Organization Mission. Air Force Colonel Edward G. Lansdale, a CIA specialist on political and psychological warfare, who already headed a CIA group in the U.S. embassy in Saigon, called the Saigon Military Mission (SMM), was named as head of the "national security" division of the training mission. One of the first things O'Daniel did was to begin developing a plan for the "pacification" of former Viet Minh areas by the South Vietnamese army. The plan, which was drafted by Lansdale, was issued by Prime Minister Ngo Dinh Diem as the "National Security Action (Pacification) Directive." Lansdale was then given the authority to coordinate all U.S. civil and military efforts related to this pacification work.[66]

At that stage of implementation of the pacification plan, the United States regarded the Vietnam National Army (VNA) as the primary instrument for tracking down and capturing suspected Communists. As General O'Daniel explained in early 1955, "The Army will be, above all, according to American ideas on the subject, a police force capable of spotting Communist guerrillas and Communist efforts at infiltration."[67] The VNA carried out the first major reoccupation of a Viet Minh base area in early 1955, when it swept through the Viet Minh zone in the Ca Mau peninsula. This was followed later in 1955 by operations in Quang Ngai and Binh Dinh provinces in Central Vietnam, two of the strongest political bases of the Viet Minh during the war. Two more major pacification campaigns, called Operation Thoai Ngoc Hau and Operation Truong Tan Buu, were carried out in provinces west of Saigon in 1956. The Vietnamese commander of these operations, General Mai Huu Xuan, stated explicitly that one of the purposes of these sweeps was to destroy the political organization left behind by the Viet Minh.[68] General Tran Van Don, who was then chief of staff of the Vietnam National Army, later described in his serialized memoirs in a Saigon newspaper how U.S. officials working under Lansdale collaborated closely with him and other VNA staff officers in planning these pacification operations and were directly involved in their execution as advisers.[69]

U.S. involvement in operations against civilian activists was not limited to military sweeps, however. Beginning in mid 1955, "Civic Action" teams began to arrive in the wake of the occupying troops. The Civic Action Program was one of the main activities developed and supported by Lansdale's SMM team. Conceived of originally by a former Viet Minh officer, Kieu Cong Cung, and using university-trained anti-Communist refugees from North Vietnam dressed in black pajamas, the program was further modified by Lansdale based on his experience in the Philippines. Rufus Phillips of Lansdale's national security team helped write a training and operations program, and Lansdale got seed money from the CIA to support its start-up. The Civic Action Program was established in January 1955, and by May 1955, 1,400 cadres organized in mobile teams were already working in ten provinces that had been occupied by the army. Eventually there were 1,800 cadres in over 100 teams in the field.[70]

In mid 1955, Diem launched an "Anti-Communist Denunciation Campaign," which the Civic Action teams implemented in former Viet Minh villages newly occupied by government troops. As Lansdale described it, "Diem ordered the teams to start working directly with Army commands in pacification campaigns, as civil government 'troops' in what were essentially combat zones."[71] In explaining the Civil Action Program to the State Department, Lansdale acknowledged the role of these teams in what he called the "race between our counter-subversives and the communist-subversives" and referred in guarded terms to a "civilian watch group . . . being developed to help report on the communist groups." A Saigon newspaper's account of the military's pacification operation in the delta in 1956 confirmed that the troops were accompanied by black-clad Civic Action teams who were involved in countering "dissident activities" in the former Viet Minh villages.[72]

Two sources sympathetic to the pacification program in South Vietnam later recounted that the Civic Action teams staged what they called "people's courts," in which residents were pressured to denounce those in the village who had been identified as pro-Communist. The victims of these "people's courts" were sometimes subjected to what the official characterized as a "brutal and physically painful ordeal."[73] These mock trials organized by the Civic Action teams targeted anyone who had been associated with Viet Minh during the resistance war, including those who had sons who had fought with the Viet Minh and had regrouped to the North, or who even had relatives known to be associated with the Viet Minh.[74] Most of those accused of connections with the Viet Minh in the Anti-Communist Denunciation Campaign sessions were sent without formal charges for various periods to "reeducation camps," but those suspected of being actual party members were generally either sentenced to long prison terms or summarily executed.[75] The Anti-Communist Denunciation Campaign was curtailed only in late 1956 by Diem's powerful brother Ngo Dinh Nhu, who did not want a politically sensitive program being run by an independent figure with U.S. backing. By 1957, the Civic Action Program's functions, including the Anti-Communist Denunciation Campaign, had been reassigned to Nhu's National Revolutionary Movement.[76]

Meanwhile, U.S. intelligence analysts and policy makers saw no evidence that Hanoi or its erstwhile major power allies were doing anything to disrupt the Diem regime's consolidation of power, and felt increasingly confident that no such efforts would be forthcoming before the July 1956 deadline for elections. In an August 1955 message to U.S. Pacific headquarters, General O'Daniel asserted that, at least until mid 1956, the Viet Minh would "probably confine their paramilitary activities to resisting efforts by the natl [national] army to destroy them." When that deadline passed without further evidence of a Communist response to the repression, the CIA noted the clear disinclination of the Soviet Union and China to support resumption of armed conflict and confidently predicted that the VNA would be able to "pacify and extend government authority into many areas of Communist influence."[77]

Meanwhile, in early 1956, the NSC had approved the even more sweeping objective of "destroying or neutralizing the international Communist apparatus in the free world."[78] That revised objective regarding the targeting of local Communists reflected the success of the covert operations to repress Communist organizations in both Iran and South Vietnam and the absence of any Communist response. The destruction of the Tudeh Party had been virtually completed by then and had still brought no noticeable change in the new soft Soviet line toward Iran.[79] The more ambitious aim of complete destruction or neutralization was yet another response to the shifting incentives brought about by the stark imbalance of power.

The repression of the Communist organization did indeed come close to eliminating the Communists as a political force in South Vietnam. Based on internal party documents and the testimony of prisoners and defectors, the situation of the party organization after nearly four years of Diemist repression can be described as desperate. In the Central Interzone, where there had been 12,000 party members and cadres at the time of the Geneva Accords, only 2,000 remained by the end of 1959. In the Mekong Delta, only 5,000 party members remained of 60,000 at the time of the Geneva settlement, and many lowland districts had no party organization left. According to detailed statistics gathered by Vietnamese military historians, during the 1955–59 period, in Zone 5 of the Mekong Delta, twelve districts had no party bases at all, and in some districts only two or three party members continued to operate. A cadre who had escaped the repression later recalled that "only one or two cadres were left in every three to five villages." In one village in the western Mekong Delta, which appears to have been typical of the region as a whole, the party organization was broken up three times during the 1954–59 period; three party members were killed and more than one hundred taken into custody. By 1959, only one party member was left, and he was isolated from the people. Most party members remaining in the Delta had to hide in the jungle or in underground tunnels.[80]

The human cost of the choice of physical repression of suspected Communists rather than the implementation of the Geneva Accords can only be estimated. The DRV liaison with the International Control Commission charged in 1959 that nearly 5,000 "former resistance fighters" were known to have been executed or had disappeared and were believed to have been killed. That figure is consistent with the estimate by the party's headquarters in the South in an internal document that "thousands" of party members had been killed by late 1959.[81] The VPA sent dozens of complaints to the ICC on specific incidents of the killing and disappearance of hundreds of former Viet Minh and supporters. The Diem government generally refused to allow the ICC to investigate allegations of summary executions of former Viet Minh. Sherwood Lett, the head of the Canadian delegation to the ICC, noted in late 1954 that investigations by mobile teams "provide an ugly picture of beatings, torture and murders of former members of the resistance." Canada did little or nothing to press for investigations, however, on the grounds that the physical repression of Communists was related to their refusal to submit to government authority in rural areas.[82] In December 1955, however, the South Vietnamese military liaison officer with the ICC admitted to a U.S. embassy official that local security forces in Quang Nam Province had indeed rounded up and massacred forty villagers for being pro–Viet Minh, as the VPA had alleged, and that the bodies had been thrown in the river.[83]

LETTING THE GENEVA ACCORDS "DIE A NATURAL DEATH"

The Geneva Accords consisted of two documents: a cease-fire agreement, signed by France and the Viet Minh on July 20, 1954, and a "Final Declaration of the Geneva Conference," dated July 21, 1954, which was not signed but was approved by oral statements at the final plenary session of the Geneva Conference.[84] For decades, the failure of the accords to settle the Vietnam conflict peacefully has been explained by an allegedly fatal legal defect in the Final Declaration. Because he had signed the agreements, according to this explanation, the State of Viet-Nam's Premier Ngo Dinh Diem refused to be bound by the electoral provisions of the Final Declaration, and his position was then supported by the Eisenhower administration.[85]

The full record of U.S. policy making in this period, however, provides a different explanation for the refusal of the Diem government to participate in North-South consultations on all-Vietnam elections. These documents point to the lopsided East-West imbalance of power, not the legal defects of the agreement or the personal stubbornness of Diem, as the main factor that doomed the Geneva Accords. They show that the sudden emergence of the United States as the arbiter of the political future of South Vietnam, combined with Dulles's reading of a lopsided power imbalance, gave Washington both the opportunity and the incentive to frustrate the intention of the Geneva Accords.

The cease-fire agreement provided for the creation of two temporary administrative zones on either side of the demarcation line at the seventeenth parallel and the regroupment of all forces in the northern and southern zones. In the same agreement, each party pledged to "refrain from any reprisals or discrimination against persons or organizations on account of their activities during the hostilities and to guarantee their democratic liberties." Finally, the cease-fire agreement explicitly recognized that the demarcation line between the two zones was only "provisional," and the Final Declaration added that this line "should not in any way be interpreted as constituting a political or territorial boundary." The Final Declaration provided for "free general elections by secret ballot" throughout the country to be held by July 20, 1956. The Final Declaration was accepted by all participants in the conference except for the United States and the still French-dependent State of Viet-Nam.

The U.S. policy of ignoring the electoral provisions of the Geneva Accords has often been defended on the grounds that they were not binding on South Vietnam.[86] But that argument was so fundamentally flawed that the State Department's own legal experts rejected it as dangerous. In late 1961, the State Department's Office of the Legal Adviser wrote in a memorandum that it had "never accepted the argument that South Vietnam is not bound by the Geneva Accords of 1954 because it did not sign them." It noted that the agreement had been signed by the French on behalf of the French Union Forces, and "since the State of Viet-Nam was part of the French Union, it would seem to be bound by the French signature." The memorandum pointed out that the argument that South Vietnam was not bound by the agreement led to "very undesirable consequences, for if the South Vietnamese are not parties to the Accords and not bound by them, they would seem to have no legal basis for demanding compliance by the Viet Minh with obligations under the Accords such as respect for the demarcation line and the cease-fire."[87]

The Diem government implicitly acknowledged in 1956 that it was inheriting the French obligations under the agreement when it agreed to replace the French liaison mission to the International Control Commission. And when the United States was contemplating a large combat commitment to South Vietnam in April 1965, the State Department again acknowledged privately that the argument that the GVN was not bound by the electoral provisions of the Geneva Accords because it was not a party to them was "plainly dangerous in that both GVN and we base our central case on other key elements in same Accords."[88]

The central reason for the failure of the Geneva Accords was not their legal defects but the extreme imbalance of power that facilitated the U.S. replacement of France as the dominant power in South Vietnam. The political pemises on which the accords were based—that France and the Viet

Minh would end the war and allow an internationally supervised election to determine the future of Vietnam—were undermined by the U.S. assumption, within a few months of the Geneva agreement, of dominant power over the State of Viet-Nam.

The dependent character of the State of Viet-Nam made it relatively easy for the United States to accomplish the transference of real power in the southern zone of Vietnam from Paris to Washington. Since its creation by the French in 1949, the State of Viet-Nam had not been given control over essential services, such as immigration, communications, industry, and customs, much less military and foreign policy. More important, it lacked the financial means to sustain its state machinery and was completely dependent on French military forces to protect it from the Viet Minh resistance. At the time of the Geneva agreement in July 1954, the State of Viet-Nam was still far from having genuine independence. France was not even scheduled to turn over essential services that it had promised to turn over to the State of Viet-Nam until the end of 1954.[89] The Vietnamese National Army (VNA) created by the French in 1948 was still under French command, and the French paid all of its costs, including the salaries of the officers and troops. After the Geneva agreement, therefore, the higher-ranking Vietnamese officers, from major to general, continued to operate on the assumption that the French army would play the same leading role in South Vietnam that it had played during the war.[90]

Operating in a sociopolitical system that had been mobilized by the Viet Minh during the war, the State of Viet-Nam could not exist without the patronage of a major power. Had its policy depended primarily on France, Diem would certainly have been obliged to participate in consultations on countrywide general elections between the State of Viet-Nam and the Democratic Republic of Vietnam by July 1955. French governments were strongly inclined toward using the Geneva framework to establish a new relationship with Ho Chi Minh's government, in the hope of reducing its dependence on the Soviet Union and China and permitting Ho Chi Minh to practice a form of Asian "Titoism." French Premier Pierre Mendès-France declared in March 1955 that France "must appeal to [Ho's] national, even to his nationalistic inclinations and not push him toward a dependency that many Vietnamese, even the Communists wish to avoid."[91] Even after Mendès-France was replaced as premier by the more conservative Edgar Faure, France continued to press the United States to support electoral consultations between North and South Vietnam. In Washington, the first secretary of the French embassy told the State Department on May 4, 1955, that the French, "because of their commitments to Geneva, were obliged to support elections in July 1956 between the North and South Vietnam on the subject beginning July 1955." He pressed for early tripartite U.S.-French-British agreement on the specifics of all-Vietnam elections and left a paper that outlined key questions about the elections to be resolved.[92] Both the French and the British governments tried to persuade Washington to adopt a common tripartite policy on the electoral provisions of the Geneva Accords in a tripartite meeting with the United States in April 1955.[93]

What France failed to anticipate was that the United States would move within only a few months after the Geneva Accords to replace France as the real arbiter of power in the southern zone. By 1954, France was dependent on the United States for nearly 80 percent of the costs of the war against the Viet Minh, and it counted heavily on American willingness to provide France with the funds to pay the salaries of the administrative personnel of the State of Viet-Nam and, in particular, the salaries of the VNA, in order to maintain continued French political-administrative domination in South Vietnam.[94] In a meeting with the French in Washington in late 1954, the United States insisted on providing its assistance directly to all three Associated States in Indochina, thus taking over the French political role in Saigon.[95] In January 1955, the United States began paying the salaries of the South Vietnamese military directly through the State of Viet-Nam. Symbolizing the abruptness of the transfer of hegemony over the South, in January 1955, the Americans took a check for $28 million into the presidential palace and handed it to an official of Diem's finance ministry, but the check left the building in the pocket of the French financial adviser. The National Bank of the State of Viet-Nam was still tied to the French franc.[96]

Whoever paid the expenses of the South Vietnamese military would determine the Diem government's policy toward the all-Vietnam elections, and after Geneva, the United States was paying 90 percent of those costs.[97] Diem understood that reality as soon as he became premier in July 1954, and he was prepared to bow to U.S. wishes on the Geneva agreement. A few days before the final Geneva settlement, Diem asked U.S. Ambassador Donald Heath how the United States would react if he rejected that agreement. Heath suggested that this would be a "grave decision."[98] After that, Diem was prepared to go ahead with the consultations, however reluctantly, in the belief that that was what the United States wanted. He continued to take that stance until Washington suddenly shifted its policy and told him that he could refuse to participate in the process.

What has confused historians about the reason for the U.S. rejection of the Geneva elections is that John Foster Dulles did not decide on that policy until the very last minute. For nearly eleven months after the Geneva Accords, Dulles believed that the all-Vietnam elections could be finessed with relative ease, because the government in North Vietnam would never agree to the conditions that the United States and South Vietnam would demand for such elections. In October 1954, Dulles told a group of State Department officials that there was "no possibility of free elections in the North and that, when the time comes, we would have ample grounds for postponing or declining to hold them in the South. The problem is not one of getting ready for an election but [of] combating subversion and infiltration in the immediate future."[99] When an NSC planning board recommendation on "careful preparations to meet the eventuality of the all-Vietnam elections" came up at a January 1955 meeting of the NSC, Dulles asserted that there were "techniques, many of which were very familiar to the Soviets, for preventing the holding of those elections."[100] Dulles said Diem could simply demand such stringent conditions for free elections that Hanoi would reject them, thus providing "ample grounds for postponing or declining to hold [elections] in the South."[101] He could not believe that Ho Chi Minh's government had built such a strong base of popular support that it could accept whatever conditions of genuine free choice might be demanded by Saigon.

With Dulles's full support, the United States was on a course in May 1955 to reaffirm its existing policy of support for free elections under stringent conditions and international supervision to reunite divided countries. That course had been accepted despite the argument by Kenneth Young, the head of the State Department's Office of Philippines and South Asia Affairs and a former Asian specialist for the Defense Department, that the policy would certainly result in the loss of South Vietnam. Young realized that Ho Chi Minh's government would win any election in Vietnam no matter how rigorously the conditions for free choice were defined. Young's position was based on an analysis in February 1955 by the State Department's Division of Research, which had concluded: "Almost any type of election that could conceivably be held in Vietnam in 1956 would, on the basis of present trends, give the Communist[s] a very significant if not decisive advantage." The analysis observed that the establishment of "conditions of electoral freedom . . . might operate to favor the Communists more than their opponents," and that maximizing the degree of electoral freedom and international supervision "might well . . . allow considerable Communist strength in the South to manifest itself at the polls."[102]

Young had echoed this conclusion in his draft policy statement on all-Vietnam elections in early April 1955, which said, "It is probable that any type of election which could be held in Viet-Nam in 1956 would produce a victory for the Communists." The Communists held "significant and probably decisive advantages" over the Diem regime, Young observed, including "(a) a greater popular appeal derived from their long identification with the struggle for independence and the subordination of communist practices to nationalist ideals; (b) the greater organizational capacity of the Communists to influence elections through propaganda, control and coercion; (c) continuing difficulties of the South Viet-Nam government in consolidating its political control."[103]

Although Young was determined to persuade the administration to find a way to avoid going ahead with consultations on all-Vietnam elections, he faced an uphill battle, because support for free elections in divided countries had played such a key role in Eisenhower's foreign policy. Young had to concede that the "overall U.S. position in the world would be harmed by U.S. identification with a policy which appeared to be directed toward avoidance of elections." He also admitted that "world opinion, and for that matter domestic opinion," would have difficulty in understanding why the United States would "oppose in Viet-Nam the democratic procedures which the United States advocated for Korea, Austria and Germany." He even conceded that U.S. refusal to support free elections would encourage the Viet Minh to "undertake early political and military activity in South Vietnam," and that they would "be in a position to justify such activity on the grounds of [South] Vietnamese violation of [the] Geneva Accords." Such a policy would also forfeit the support of the British and French for a SEATO military response to a resumption of hostilities by the Viet Minh. "Neither the British nor the French would interpret such Viet Minh renewal of hostilities as calling for action under the Manila Pact obligations," he wrote.

The only way out of this dilemma that Young could suggest was for the United States and Diem to demand conditions for elections that would be tantamount to turning control of the country over to an international organization, which would be unacceptable to any sovereign Vietnamese government. He proposed that the United States demand that an international commission supervising the elections have the power to "supervise, direct and control all civil officials," including the judiciary, the military, and the police of the two zones, in order to stall long enough for Diem to consolidate his power in the South. When Diem's powers were consolidated sufficiently, Young suggested, Diem might agree to a negotiating formula under which the two governments maintained control over the electoral process in their zones of control.

This extreme position did not prevail in the State Department, however. It was not Young but State Department Counselor Douglas MacArthur II who drafted the memorandum on the issue of all-Vietnam elections for the Far Eastern Bureau in early May. MacArthur's memo put the Geneva Accords elections in global perspective, declaring: "The United States believes that the conditions for free election should be those which Sir Anthony Eden put forward and the three Western powers supported at Berlin in connection with German reunification." The paper provided a long list of guarantees of freedoms that would be demanded by the United States, and presumably by Diem, along with a demand that the elections be for the purpose of establishing a "joint constitutional assembly" to draft a constitution for the entire country, and that pending the adoption of the constitution, full government power remain in the hands of the two existing regimes.[104]

Dulles still believed that this position could be used as the basis for refusing to actually agree to the elections themselves. In a telegram to the State Department from Paris on May 13, he wrote that both the United States and the South Vietnamese government "should envisage the holding of free elections in 1956 under genuine conditions of freedom, without intimidation before or reprisals after." Dulles recalled that he had "expressed himself in this sense in Saigon in March and this continues to be U.S. policy."[105] U.S. views on free elections in Vietnam, based on the MacArthur draft, were shared with British and French foreign ministry officials separately in Paris, and representatives of both governments indicated that the U.S. position was in line with their own thinking.[106]

A draft policy statement on all-Vietnam elections was prepared on May 17 for consideration by the National Security Council, calling for the United States to assist Diem in adopting terms for the election that would avoid a Communist takeover of the South and, at the same time, "to the extent feasible . . . maintain a position generally consistent with that adopted by the Free World in other areas such as Korea and Germany." Still assuming that the North Vietnamese would reject the terms for elections that the United States and Diem would demand, the statement acknowledged that the policy might result in a resumption of war, and it fell back on the superior military power that the United States could bring to bear under those circumstances, combined with the assumption that the USSR and the PRC would stay out of the conflict. If the policy resulted in a renewal of warfare by the Communists, the policy statement said, the United States "should be prepared to oppose any Communist attack with U.S. armed forces, if necessary and feasible consulting with Congress in advance if the emergency permits—preferably in concert with the Manila Pact allies of the U.S., but if necessary alone."[107] On May 27, Dulles instructed the U.S. embassy in Saigon to outline the American position on elections orally to Diem, based on the May 17 position paper.[108]

Diem, meanwhile, was still prepared to comply with U.S. policy if it was decided to go ahead with consultations on elections under the Geneva Accords. Although Ngo Dinh Nhu, Diem's brother and political adviser, had told Tilman Durdin of the *New York Times* that the regime did not regard the State of Viet-Nam as bound by the Geneva Accords, he also acknowledged, by implication, that it could not take a position on the question of elections without regard to the views of the United States, Britain, and France. Nhu suggested that these three powers and the Diem government discuss "what should be [the] attitude [of] Free Viet Nam toward [the] Geneva requirement of 1956 elections." The minister attached to the presidency also told U.S. Ambassador Randolph Kidder that Diem wanted to hold National Assembly elections before any consultations on elections and did not plan to announce any plans for conversations with the Viet Minh. However, he thought that Diem "would make such a declaration if we thought it desirable, but in any case would not do [so] without consulting us."[109]

The policy paper on elections was to be considered by the NSC at its June 9 meeting. Eisenhower's special assistant for national security, Dillon Anderson, wrote a "briefing note" repeating the official assumption of the draft NSC decision that the vagueness on election procedures allowed the United States to insist on conditions for free elections that were consistent with the U.S. stand on Germany and Korea but that would be impossible for the North Vietnamese to accept.[110]

The day before the scheduled meeting, however, Young wrote his own "briefing paper" on the NSC policy paper over Deputy Assistant Secretary of State William J. Sebald's signature aimed at heading off its approval and also asked for a meeting with Dulles to discuss it. The paper repeated Young's warning that the "Viet Minh," as he called the Democratic Republic of Vietnam, would put forward "seemingly plausible and moderate proposals" for free elections, and that the French, British, and Indians would therefore put pressure on Diem and the United States to "accept a compromise with the Viet Minh." The problem, therefore, was that "it may become increasingly difficult to demonstrate . . . that the failure to secure free elections is the fault of the Communists."[111]

In a meeting in Dulles's office the same day as Young wrote his memo, Dulles accepted Young's argument that the existing U.S. position could lead to the loss of South Vietnam. Privately, he was less concerned about preserving the U.S. position on free elections to reunify Germany than he had been when the State Department policy paper on Vietnamese elections was adopted, because he had learned that the USSR did not oppose free elections in Germany per se, provided Germany was neutralized with security guarantees.[112] The real issue for Dulles, however, was whether, if Diem did not conform to the provisions of the Geneva Accords, and the Viet Minh invaded "Free Viet-Nam," the United States would "consider the Viet Minh action a breach of the accords and . . . come to Diem's aid . . . by invoking the Manila Pact." Dulles was obviously unsure about whether Eisenhower would be willing to commit U.S. forces to saving a South Vietnamese regime that had so openly flouted the Geneva agreement. That question remained unanswered at the end of the meeting.[113]

Dulles's uncertainty over that issue provided Young with a new idea for derailing the existing policy paper on all-Vietnam elections. On the morning of June 9, the day the NSC was to discuss the policy paper, Young drafted a memorandum, again over Sebald's signature, urging Dulles to postpone consideration of the NSC paper on Vietnam, "at least until certain aspects of it can be clarified, *and with no definite date set for reconsideration* [emphasis added]."[114] Young hoped to persuade Dulles that the United States could threaten a firm military response to a resumption of war by the "Viet Minh," regardless of Diem's policy toward the Geneva Accords, without any serious risk of a Viet Minh attack. Dulles could then argue that U.S. policy on the defense of South Vietnam need not be influenced by whether or not Diem had violated the Geneva Accords. Furthermore, he argued, Diem might not go along with consultations with the Viet Minh, and Washington should have a "clearer and more precise view of the Vietnamese position than at present." Young concluded that it would be "better to proceed with our exchange of view[s] in Saigon with Diem, as well as with the British, French and Canadians before fixing a draft statement of policy."

After reading Young's memo, Dulles seized on Young's idea of taking the decision off the NSC agenda. By the time the NSC met on June 9, Dulles had already spoken with Eisenhower about postponing consideration of the policy paper on all-Vietnam elections. When Anderson began briefing the NSC on the policy paper on the issue, Eisenhower asked Dulles if this was not the report that Dulles wanted to postpone. Dulles explained that he had suggested postponement because the situation was "not sufficiently clear to warrant Council action at this time." Deliberately misrepresenting the diplomatic situation, he reported that the British, the French, and Diem "had not yet made their positions clear with respect to the election problem."

Special Assistant Anderson then hinted at a private agreement with Dulles that the election problem should not be considered by the NSC at all. He told the NSC that "he, too, had entertained doubts as to whether the technique and details of the election problem in Vietnam were properly in the realm of NSC policy."[115] The issue before the NSC was not "the technique and details" of elections in Vietnam, of course, but whether the United States was to support free elections or prevent them from taking place—a decision with the most far-reaching implications for the future of Vietnam. Defining the issue in such narrow terms was therefore merely a tactic to help Dulles justify keeping it off the NSC agenda.

Having gotten a green light from Dulles, Young then drafted yet another position paper, this time aimed at providing the rationale for a wholly different policy toward the elections. Young argued that the United States could discount the likelihood of any military response by the Vietnamese Communists to Diem's renunciation of electoral consultations, citing two main points:

> (a) There probably will be pressures upon the Viet Minh by Moscow and Peiping to avoid actions which might precipitate world conflict;
>
> (b) Viet Minh capabilities in [the] South—while great—are probably insufficient at this time to overthrow the Free Viet-Nam regime without direct Viet Minh military support from across the 17th Parallel.[116]

Young was suggesting that the Communists would have to resort to an attack across the border in order to overthrow Diem, and that the USSR and the PRC would probably not stand for such an overt military response by the North Vietnamese. In short, Hanoi was not in a position to challenge Diem if he simply refused to participate in electoral consultations.

Young's argument that a North Vietnamese attack was extremely unlikely was in line with Dulles's own thinking. On May 15, 1955, Dulles had taken the opportunity of a meeting with Molotov on restraining the PRC with respect to Taiwan to test this new assessment. Dulles suggested to Molotov that the two superpowers needed "a situation where, as in Germany, Korea and Vietnam, it was agreed that unification would not be sought by force." Dulles had thus sought confirmation that the USSR was indeed prepared to commit informally to restraining its Communist allies in divided countries. Molotov had not taken exception to Dulles's statement, responding that the USSR "wanted peace."[117] Meanwhile, Allen

Dulles was accumulating evidence that the Soviet leaders had adopted a soft foreign policy because they were "particularly concerned over their relative disadvantage during the next few years until they have acquired nuclear weapons and delivery capabilities sufficient to counterbalance those of the U.S."[118]

Young also argued that Diem would oppose consultations until he had secured an agreement with France on the retreat of French forces and a National Assembly had been elected. On the same day that Young was making this assertion, however, Diem, who still believed the United States was supporting the electoral consultations, was telling a group of correspondents that his government was willing to discuss the question of national elections with North Vietnam, explaining that "it all depends on the conditions under which the elections are held." A source close to Diem was further quoted as saying that Diem would demand extensive third-party supervision and detailed procedures for ensuring a secret ballot, including the stationing of military forces in concentration areas away from voting stations to ensure that no pressure was brought to bear on civilians in the vote. The source also said that the results of any decision on organizing elections would be submitted to the National Assembly to decide whether the South would participate in unification elections.[119]

Dulles approved Young's proposal on June 14, setting in motion a train of events that removed any possibility that the electoral provisions of the Geneva Accords could be implemented. Dulles immediately informed the U.S. embassies in Paris and London that the United States had given Diem a "summary of our general thinking" on the electoral consultations issue, based on an "informal paper," referring to a version of the paper that Young had written. The substance of the new policy was also conveyed immediately to the British and French. The U.S. embassy in London immediately reported that the British Foreign Office had expressed "great disappointment" at the State Department's message and had warned prophetically that "such peace as Indo-China now enjoys stems from Geneva and breach of agreements must inevitably lead to breach of peace."[120]

Dulles was clearly taken aback when he read the report of Diem's apparent readiness to participate in electoral consultations, which contradicted one of the premises of Young's paper. On June 16, the day after the *New York Times* had reported Diem's remark about willingness to discuss conditions for national elections with the North, Dulles sent a summary of the *Times* story to the U.S. embassy in Saigon and asked whether this represented a change in Diem's attitude toward elections and consultations, and why Diem had chosen to make a public statement at that time.[121] But his decision was already made, and Diem's position on consultations was a secondary issue. The decision was clearly based primarily on his assessment of the broader international context. If the North Vietnamese were effectively constrained by Soviet and Chinese fears of war with the United States, Dulles evidently felt there was no serious downside to scrapping the elections called for by the Geneva Accords.

The image of the Dulles-Eisenhower relationship that has prevailed in recent decades is one of a secretary of state who "did not keep information from Eisenhower's attention, nor . . . make important decisions solo."[122] But this portrait of Dulles's role does not tell the whole story. Eisenhower's aide Emmett John Hughes observed that Dulles believed it was necessary for him occasionally to protect Eisenhower from what Dulles regarded as his "naivete."[123] Dulles did make the fateful decision to reverse U.S. policy on the elections called for by the Geneva Accords without ever having submitted it for NSC or presidential approval.

Up to that point, Dulles and Eisenhower had been in fundamental agreement on Vietnam policy. Both had been prepared to let South Vietnam go if Diem could not handle a domestic insurgency, rather than intervene to save the regime from such an armed uprising, and both had assumed that an overt invasion by North Vietnam would be met with a swift U.S. military response under SEATO. Dulles was obviously doubtful, however, that Eisenhower would be willing to defy the British and French to save South Vietnam if Diem were to defy the electoral provisions of the Geneva Accords. He also worried that Ike would not be willing to violate his administration's own principles on free elections in states divided by Cold War conflict, which was central to the rationale of the existing draft policy. Dulles had strong reason to believe that Soviet concerns about the overwhelming military dominance of the United States made a renewal of major warfare in Vietnam extremely unlikely, but he could not be sure that Eisenhower would approve ignoring the Geneva electoral provisions based on that calculation.

Having gotten a clear signal at last of U.S. intentions on the Geneva elections provisions, Diem reversed his position on the electoral consultations issue. On July 16, Diem announced publicly for the first time that the State of Viet-Nam did not regard itself as bound by the Geneva agreement. "[I]t is out of the question for us to consider any proposal from the Vietminh, if proof is not given us that they put the superior interests of the national community above those of communism," he said.[124] On July 19, Ho Chi Minh and Pham Van Dong sent a joint message to Diem in which they invited him to nominate a representative to North-South consultations on elections. That prompted the British and French foreign ministers to bring new pressures on Dulles in Geneva on July 22 to agree that the three Western embassies in Saigon would advise Diem to "contact [the] Viet Minh and assure him [sic] our support on genuinely free elections."[125] Dulles then instructed the U.S. embassy in Saigon to tell Diem that "some Vietnamese response to the authorities of Hanoi is necessary," but that the United States would help Saigon decide what kind of reply would be sent.[126]

The result was a declaration by the Diem government on August 19 that referred to the note from the "Vietminh authorities" but announced Diem's refusal to consult on the Geneva elections provisions, because "nothing constructive . . . can be achieved as long as the Communist regime in North Vietnam does not allow each Vietnamese citizen to enjoy the democratic freedoms and the fundamental rights of man."[127] Dulles then publicly supported Diem's position that the State of Viet-Nam was under no obligation to abide by the Geneva Accords' electoral provisions, because it had not signed the agreement.[128]

Meanwhile it was becoming increasingly clear to the Eisenhower administration that the Communist bloc was acquiescing in the United States's consolidation of its power position in South Vietnam. A CIA estimate issued at the time of the first anniversary of the Geneva Accords emphasized that the USSR and the PRC would "prevent the DRV from openly invading the South during the period of this estimate." Although it assessed the chances of a resumption of guerrilla warfare as greater if Diem refused to consult on elections, the estimate found such guerrilla warfare unlikely in any case prior to the 1956 election deadline.[129]

The USSR communicated its intentions clearly to the United States by failing to raise the issue of consultations on all-Vietnam elections at the heads of state summit conference in Geneva in July. Young, who was a member of the U.S. delegation to the conference, reported to the U.S. embassy in Saigon, "The Russians never pressed the issue and Bulganin treated it quite perfunctorily in his opening and closing statements."[130] Three weeks after this signal of Moscow's passivity, Dulles declared publicly for the first time that the Diem regime had no responsibility to consult on all-Vietnam elections.

Dulles continued to suggest privately that Diem take "minimum steps to give [the] appearance of consultations on [a] technical level in order to lessen international pressures now building up."[131] State Department officials were confident, however, that the United States was now in the clear in scrapping the Geneva agreement. In a letter to U.S. Ambassador Frederick

Reinhardt in Saigon in October, Young enumerated all the reasons for having the utmost confidence in the new policy: "Judging by such indications as the passing of July 20 without major incident, the rather leisurely pace which all communist leaders have so far followed regarding the consultations issue, and the hints from the Viet Minh on zonal 'autonomy,' one can now speculate that Communist diplomacy will not put unbearable pressure regarding the issue."[132]

In late October, an aide to Dulles summarized for him a new national estimate, NIE 63.1–3–55, which predicted that the Viet Minh would not even undertake guerrilla warfare against Diem unless such a policy were "consistent with overall Bloc policies" and unless Hanoi "estimated it would not provoke SEATO counter-action."[133] In early November, with Vietnam obviously in mind, the CIA explicitly related the Communist bloc policy to the overall East-West imbalance of power, concluding that, "at least so long as the USSR suffers a marked inferiority in nuclear capabilities, neither Peiping nor Moscow is likely to undertake or sponsor any local aggression which in their judgment would involve appreciable risk of general war."[134] At the four-power foreign ministers' conference in Geneva in November, as Paul Kattenburg, then the Vietnam desk officer at the State Department, later recalled, the USSR actually asked that Indochina be taken off the agenda. USSR treatment of the issue in Geneva, according to Kattenburg, "provided confirmation for those in the U.S. government who believed that the USSR . . . intended the Vietnam partition to continue into the indefinite future."[135]

By the beginning of December, Dulles was ready to dispense with the Geneva framework entirely, including the International Control Commission, which he derided for its "intermeddling" in the "consultations problem." The situation in Vietnam, he wrote to the U.S. embassies in London, Paris, and Saigon, had been "fundamentally altered since Geneva," and the "present deterrent on [the] Communists lies less in [the] thin mechanism [the] Commission maintains on [the] ground" in Vietnam than in "policies [of the] governments principally concerned on [the] Free World side." In other words, the United States could guarantee unilaterally through its dominant power that the status quo would not be disturbed. Although the United States would "take no positive steps [to] speed up [the] present process [of] decay [of the] Geneva Accords," Dulles wrote, neither would it "make [the] slightest effort to infuse further life into them." From Paris, Ambassador Douglas Dillon agreed that the Geneva Accords "should be allowed to die [a] natural death."[136] In early February, Dulles reported to Eisenhower that U.S. policy was aimed at "preservation of peace and security under some new arrangement which would permit gradual termination of the old Geneva Accords."[137]

U.S. intelligence estimates of the Communist states' Vietnam policies continued to support Dulles's cavalier attitude toward the Geneva Accords. The CIA issued a new NIE just days before the second anniversary of the Geneva Accords, concluding that the DRV would not attempt either an open invasion of the south or a "large scale guerrilla warfare effort" in the near future, "because of the danger of US or possibly SEATO counteraction and because such action would prejudice Bloc emphasis on peaceful coexistence elsewhere." The estimate posited that a key factor governing Soviet and Chinese thinking was that U.S. intervention in any future conflict "would make it difficult to limit the conflict to Vietnam." It observed that both Soviet and Chinese diplomacy during the first half of 1956 had made it clear that neither of the Communist powers would press for "strict implementation of the Geneva Agreements," which in turn strengthened "international acceptance of the status quo in Vietnam and . . . confidence in the future of South Vietnam."

Despite its presumed disappointment with Soviet and Chinese policies, the DRV was said to be "firmly committed to the policies of the Sino-Soviet Bloc, even to the extent of subordinating or postponing the pursuit of its local or regional objectives in the interest of over-all Bloc tactics and strategy." This loyalty to the Soviet bloc's international line, it explained, was a consequence of the "fact that DRV objectives can only be realized with Sino-Soviet Bloc support." The chances of a DRV military action against South Vietnam "in the absence of assured Bloc support" were thus assessed as "extremely small."[138]

The confidence of administration policy makers in the effectiveness of U.S. military dominance over the Communist bloc was at its zenith as the date set in the Geneva Accords for Vietnamese elections approached. After Admiral Radford briefed the NSC in early June 1956 on U.S. plans for responding to any Viet Minh attack across the partition line, Eisenhower noted that although Zhou Enlai had repeatedly said that China would retake Taiwan by military means, if necessary, "nothing quite comparable to this has been said by the Viet Minh in reference to South Vietnam."[139]

The clarity of the imbalance of power and its impact on the Communist powers discouraged any serious debate within the administration over scrapping the Geneva elections provisions. A few working-level officials at the State Department and the CIA regretted the fact that the United States had chosen to turn its back on free elections in Vietnam. But as Paul Kattenburg later recalled, it was politically impossible to argue that the

United States should uphold the electoral provisions of the Geneva Accords.[140] No serious cost or risk could be cited for a policy of simply ignoring those provisions, because of the obvious Soviet acceptance of the fait accompli in South Vietnam. The lopsided U.S. power advantage over the Communist states thus skewed the discourse on Vietnam, encouraging the advocates of a more assertive U.S. policy in South Vietnam, while effectively silencing those who had doubts.

Tragic ironies surround the fateful decision to scrap the Geneva Accords. Both Eisenhower and Dulles were prepared to let South Vietnam go Communist rather than intervene militarily if Communist resistance in the South threatened the Saigon regime. And Dulles doubted whether either he or Eisenhower would be willing to respond with force even to a North Vietnamese invasion in the context of a refusal by Diem to carry out the electoral consultations called for in the Geneva Accords. It was only because Dulles also believed that such an invasion was so improbable, regardless of Diem's policy, that he had the confidence to decide—without consulting Eisenhower—to ignore the electoral provisions of the accords. Even more ironic, the administration's policy toward the elections, right up to the eve of the NSC meeting in June 1955 that was to have approved the policy, advanced a series of demands that the administration considered extreme. We now know, however, that the North Vietnamese regime was prepared to accept all the demands.

4 North Vietnamese Policy under the American Threat

REUNIFICATION, LEADERSHIP POLITICS, AND THE NEW POWER BALANCE

When he explained the new line of the Vietnam Workers' Party (VWP) at the Sixth Central Committee Plenum in mid July 1954, just before the final phase of the Geneva negotiations, Ho Chi Minh was confronting the first dramatic shift in global power relationships since the triumph of the Chinese Communists in late 1949. In his report to the Sixth Plenum, Ho explained why it was necessary to accept an agreement at Geneva that represented a major retreat from the aims of the resistance and why the party's primary task had to shift from military victory over the French to "secur[ing] and consolidat[ing] peace." Ho told the Central Committee that it was the new U.S. threat to intervene that compelled the Vietnamese to agree to a temporary partition of the country and the ceding of large areas of the South that had been under Viet Minh control to the enemy in return for a pledge from the French for a specific date for elections.[1]

At that moment of bitter disappointment, Ho did not mention the role played by the policies of Moscow and Beijing in the decision of the leadership of the VWP to make such a far-reaching concession. Eleven years later, however, Party Secretary Le Duan explained to a cadre conference that the sudden shift in party line on reunification in mid 1954 had been forced on the leadership by three factors: the threat of U.S. intervention, the refusal of Vietnam's socialist allies to support reunification by armed force, and popular war weariness after nine years of insurgency, which made it necessary to "consolidate the rear."[2] The first two of these three factors added up to a starkly unfavorable external balance of power, to which Ho and his colleagues had been compelled to adjust.

In light of the new situation in the world, the Vietnamese Communist leadership could hardly have been confident about the prospects for reunification of the country in the short run. The evidence indicates, however, that during the first year after the signing of the Geneva Accords, Hanoi hoped that the French government would carry out their electoral provisions.[3] As discussed in chapter 2, Pham Van Dong had bargained hard in the Geneva negotiations to move the date of elections as close to the Geneva Accords as possible, calculating that it would give the United States less time to elbow the French aside in South Vietnam. Ho had agreed with Zhou in early July 1954, however, that the Communists should cooperate as much as possible with Mendès-France in the hope of keeping a moderate government in power in Paris. The implication was that Mendès-France would maintain an Indochina policy independent of the United States. In June 1955, however, the leadership of the VWP admitted publicly that it had been in error in seeing only the "contradictions" among the French, the United States, and Diem, and not their fundamental agreement.[4]

As the first anniversary of the Geneva Accords approached, the DRV leadership knew that the United States had replaced the French and was consolidating Diem's power. Hanoi was certainly growing more pessimistic about the chances of nationwide elections in 1956. Nevertheless, they were still hoping to persuade the French government to use its influence with the United States and Diem in regard to elections. In early July, Premier Pham Van Dong told a top aide to Jean Sainteny, the French representative in Hanoi, that his government was willing to "go very far" toward guaranteeing truly free choice for Vietnamese voters, because it was confident that it would win 80 percent of the vote in the North and 55 percent of the vote in the South if elections were free.[5] In a letter to Canadian Secretary of State for External Affairs Lester Pearson in November, Pham Van Dong listed the freedoms the DRV was prepared to guarantee in preparation for the elections, including "the freedom to make propaganda throughout the nation by meetings, tracts, newspapers, etc."[6]

By late 1955, Hanoi knew there was no chance of reunification through elections, because of Soviet unwillingness to support that aim and U.S. ascendance in the South. So the Vietnamese leaders were compelled to make a far-reaching concession to the anti-Communists in the South, which they hoped would be seen by the Soviet government—and the United States—as more realistic. In a conversation with a Soviet diplomat, Vietnamese Party Secretary Truong Chinh revealed that the North Vietnamese were prepared to agree that the national elections would lead to what he called a "partial" or "pro forma" unification of the country. He explained that the elections would be for a national assembly that would choose a national government and draw up a constitution for the entire country, but that the constitution would have to be accepted by both zones and would permit the "Southern authorities" to maintain a separate regime in which they "would see that they still retained their positions and advantages."[7] This was precisely what the U.S. State Department had intended to demand before Dulles decided not to implement the electoral provisions of the Geneva Accords. The global power balance was so inhospitable to the revolutionary side that Hanoi was willing to accept the very demands that Dulles had been sure it would reject.

The same unfavorable global power balance, combined with the desperate poverty of North Vietnamese society, continued to exert a dominating influence on Hanoi's policy toward South Vietnam for the next five years. That influence operated through the internal politics of the Central Committee of the VWP and its Political Bureau. North Vietnamese policy emerged from a process of compromise and adjustment not only between the DRV and the Communist powers but between different views among Vietnamese leaders, some of whom were far more willing than others to acquiesce to the position of the Soviet Union and China on South Vietnam.

A major issue in the North Vietnamese debate on reunification policy was the emergence of the new Soviet global strategy of peaceful coexistence. At its Seventh Enlarged Central Committee Plenum in August 1955, the Vietnamese party leadership explicitly endorsed the Soviet strategy of "maintaining peace," agreeing that "countries having different political and social systems can coexist in peace" and that "all conflicts in the world can be resolved by negotiations."[8] But when Khrushchev in 1956 introduced a new doctrine that it was possible to carry out a "peaceful transition" to socialism, eschewing armed struggle entirely, it provoked an intense debate among Vietnamese Communist leaders. When the Vietnamese Central Committee held its next plenum in April 1956, Ho insisted on adding a major codicil to the doctrine: "While recognizing that in certain countries the road to socialism may be a peaceful one, we should be aware of this fact: in countries where the machinery of state, the armed forces and the police of the bourgeois class are still strong, the proletarian class still has to prepare for armed struggle."[9]

Despite its stand on defending the ideological principle at stake, however, the VWP leadership was seriously divided over its policy toward South Vietnam. According to a party analysis written many years later, the Central Committee concluded that the line on South Vietnam urged on Hanoi by both the USSR and the PRC represented "liquidationism,"

meaning that it would result in the liquidation of the revolutionary struggle in the South.[10] Le Duan revealed to cadres during the war against the
United States, however, that a minority of the leadership had been prepared to accept something very close to just such a policy a decade earlier.[11]

In sharp contrast to the Chinese Communist Party, which tended to
polarize between leftist and moderate political lines during the 1950s and
1960s, the leaders of the VWP had adopted a decision-making style in which
Political Bureau members were expected to compromise rather than to split
into ideologically warring factions. That tendency, which reflected Ho Chi
Minh's influence on the party leadership's style of operation, gave a few
Political Bureau members the ability to wield a veto over a party policy. That
appears to have happened in the case of DRV policy toward the South.[12]

The central issue in the debate on policy toward the South was whether
to allow any use of arms for self-defense in support of political struggle. Le
Duan revealed later in his talk to party cadres that those party leaders most
closely associated with the Soviet-Chinese line had argued against the use
of armed units, even to protect the political struggle, on the ground that
the strength of the United States and Diem arrayed against the party in the
South was too great, and that any armed resistance would simply increase
the level of repression by the Diem regime. Le Duan made it clear that
he had strongly disagreed and had argued that such armed propaganda
units, with support from a company of combat troops in each region, would
help relieve the pressure on the party structure.[13] In the end, those who
were opposed to any use of armed force, even for self-defense, had to make
some concessions to Le Duan's point of view. The resulting compromise,
however, was still weighted heavily on the side of a policy that was almost
completely ineffective in protecting party cadres from Diem's repression.

That compromise was reflected in a directive to the party in the South
in late 1956. Although the document was written by Le Duan, it clearly
reflected a policy that had been negotiated between groups within the
party leadership with very different views on the issue. The document
asserted that a peaceful transition in the South was possible and cited the
Khrushchev rationale for this: "If the world situation can maintain peace
due to a change in the relationship of forces in the world in favor of the camp
of peace and democracy, the [world] revolutionary movement can develop
following a peaceful line, and the revolutionary movement in the South
can also develop following a peaceful line." The directive conceded that
some in the party believed that the repression of the party in the South
could destroy it to the point where a political struggle could not develop—
an argument that certainly came from those still in the South, as well as

from party leaders in the North reflecting their interests. This view was "incorrect," however, according to the directive, because "the U.S.-Diem regime has no political strength in the country worth mentioning. . . . Its cruelty definitely cannot shake the revolutionary movement, and it cannot survive for long." The U.S.-Diem regime "cannot destroy the masses," the directive asserted. "Therefore, they cannot annihilate the cadres leading the mass movement."[14]

As confirmed by a regional committee meeting in the South in December 1956, armed self-defense was to be waged not by guerrilla units but by "armed propaganda units," organized only in squads and platoons. These units were supposed to "intimidate low-level administrative personnel and spies so that they shrink from their duties without the knowledge of the higher level." That meant in part carrying out the selective killing of "tyrants" (those responsible for the repression of revolutionaries and their families). We know from a later critique by the regional committee for the South, however, that the actual guidelines for the armed propaganda units in the lowland areas called for them to "avoid intensifying the situation," and that they were given no clear "action plan" for achieving their objective, thus severely restricting their impact. The policy adopted also included the formation of three companies, one in each of the central, western, and eastern zones, which were supposed to support the armed propaganda units. These units were located in mountainous areas and remained in hiding most of the time, according to the critique, in order to "preserve the forces." As a result, when the armed units did operate in populated areas, they often simply made matters worse, because people were afraid of retaliation by government forces.[15]

The slogan promoted by the party in the South in carrying out this policy ("not exposing our forces for a long period, accumulating our own strength, long-term lying in ambush, accumulating our own strength, making connections with the masses, waiting for a favorable opportunity for a general uprising to liberate the South") is even more revealing, because it is word for word the formula proposed in a Chinese Communist Party Central Committee letter in 1956.[16] A few years later, the VWP's southern regional committee strongly criticized the peaceful struggle line adopted in the 1956 directive as a "major mistake" with a "rightist" orientation. It charged that the directive had applied the peaceful transition thesis to South Vietnam despite the fact that the CPSU had specified that it could be achieved only in "some capitalist countries which already had democratic institutions." The regional committee concluded that the party leadership should have allowed it to organize real armed struggle—not just halfhearted armed propaganda—once it became clear that the Geneva Accords would not be honored.[17]

Even though the southern wing of the Vietnamese party opposed a policy based on an analysis of the power balance on both practical and ideological grounds, that analysis was clearly the primary influence on Hanoi's policy toward South Vietnam. Because the Vietnamese party based its policy on Marxist-Leninist ideology, the natural tendency to pay attention to power relationships was strongly reinforced by the practice of formal analysis of the "relationship of forces" worldwide, as well as in Vietnam, in considering its broad lines of strategy, both foreign and domestic. In line with Ho Chi Minh's own style of realistic analysis of power relationships, the U.S. capability for intervening militarily in Indochina and the appeasement of the United States by the USSR and the PRC were inevitably defining factors in this Vietnamese analysis. In a 1982 interview, then Foreign Minister Nguyen Co Thach confirmed that the party leadership had felt it had little choice but to go along with Soviet and Chinese views in making its own analysis of the global "relationship of forces" during the 1954–60 period. "In China and the Soviet Union," he recalled, "there was an evaluation of the strength of the United States—the myth of its invincibility—that led to the desire for peace at any price." That Soviet-Chinese evaluation of U.S. power, he said, "was very bad for us."[18]

When the VWP's Central Committee Plenum convened in April 1959, the party organization in the South was in grave danger of being completely destroyed, and the party leadership was under heavy pressure from its leadership organ in the South to approve a change in party line to permit the use of force. But the Central Committee had no intention of launching a new guerrilla war to overthrow the Diem regime; it would resort to armed force only to end the wholesale destruction of the party in the South. As the Political Bureau was working out the details of the new line for the South, Prime Minister Pham Van Dong explained privately to a visiting Hungarian delegation that it would be "folly" to begin an armed struggle in the South "before North Vietnam was strong enough to back it up and before the situation is ripe in the South."[19]

The secret party plenum resolution on the South actually reaffirmed the commitment of the party leadership to take advantage of any possibility of nonviolent change in the South. "[W]e must see that the revolution in the South still has the possibility of peaceful development," it said, "that is, the possibility of gradually changing the political situation in the South to the advantage of the revolution. That possibility is small at present, but the Party does not reject that possibility, but must make every effort to achieve it."[20] The "main task" of armed force was still to "serve the political struggle," just as it had been under the previous line, but some of the previous restraints on its use were to be relaxed. Force could be used not only to kill those who hunted down former Viet Minh but for "clearing out and destroying concentration centers of the enemy" and even to resist armed attacks by Diem's forces. But these military functions would be allowed only "to a certain degree and in a certain number of localities." The regional party committee in the South made it clear to party members, however, that, although the new line was referred to as "armed struggle," it was still "not guerrilla warfare, nor is it long-term warfare, fighting to liberate zones and to establish a government as at the time of the resistance."[21] Protracted guerrilla warfare, according to a party training document in the South, would mean "to taking the armed forces . . . as the main element in overthrowing the enemy, as during the 1945–54 resistance war or the long war of China to overthrow the United States and Chiang."[22]

Nor did the new line mean that the political objective of the struggle was necessarily to overthrow the Diem government. The party had to be alert to any "peaceful possibility," however small, to force the "U.S.-Diem" regime to "carry out a number of conditions in our government's diplomatic note, acquiescing in economic, cultural and postal exchanges and travel, etc."[23] Hanoi was still strongly committed to peaceful coexistence with Diem if he would agree to negotiate such arrangements.

The new line was used by local party organs in the South to carry out local uprisings to seize power in the villages, however. From early 1960 to the end of the year, such uprisings took place in over 800 out of the nearly 1,300 villages in the Mekong Delta. Of those 800 villages, according to the party's figures, only 100 were able to get rid of the local government presence entirely, but another 560 formed local guerrilla squads or platoons.[24] In most of the villages in the Delta, therefore, an intense struggle continued between local armed groups and government forces.[25]

The regional party committee, evaluating the first few weeks of implementation of the new line in March 1960, complained that local party organs in these contested villages were "getting into rash adventures," which were "destroying the legal status of the population." The report mentioned such actions as "dissolving local administrative machinery, guiding people to tear up their ID cards, pushing them to commit provocative actions such as taking over posts, setting fire to village offices, cutting down trees, digging up roads, setting up obstacles."[26] These "provocative" actions, which drew the attention of the Saigon military and thus escalated the conflict, were condemned as going beyond the new party line.

The success of the revolutionary upsurge and the apparent weakness of the Diem regime in the rural areas nevertheless touched off a new debate among party leaders about the role of military struggle in the South. Some began to argue for a Maoist strategy of using the countryside to encircle the urban centers. Others, including the head of the southern regional party committee, Nguyen Van Linh, were interested primarily in the possibility of a political crisis in Saigon that might be parlayed into a "general uprising" in the capital. They downplayed the need for building up military forces and base areas on the grounds that seizing opportunities for a general insurrection did not depend on the party's military strength.[27]

Meanwhile, the Army of the Republic of Vietnam (ARVN) introduced a new factor into the equation. It carried out several "mopping up operations" each month, and at least twenty large-scale operations of regimental or division strength against areas that had been under revolutionary control as a result of the 1959–60 uprising. In one province, 20,000 ARVN troops were sent to encircle three villages that had been taken over by the Communists.[28] This military escalation by the Diem regime made it much clearer to Hanoi leaders that defeating the Diem regime through political struggle would not be possible without developing real military forces. In 1960, the party had only about 1,000 men under arms, compared with 136,000 regular troops at the disposal of the Diem government, not including 95,000 armed members of the Civil Guards and the Self-Defense Corps. The revolutionary organization was therefore extremely vulnerable to attack by Saigon's forces.[29] Le Duan argued that, for political struggle to succeed, the revolutionaries had to be able to control the strategic areas of the South militarily.[30]

The Political Bureau agreed with Le Duan's assessment, and in January 1961, it directed the party in the South to put military struggle on an equal footing with political struggle in the plains and to make it the dominant form of struggle in the mountains.[31] In concrete terms, the new party line called for creating a total of eighteen battalions in South Vietnam during 1961. As a result, the full-time strength of the new People's Liberation Armed Forces (PLAF) increased to about 17,000 men by the end of 1961.[32] The longer-term strategy of the armed struggle in the South, however, was constrained by concerns about U.S. intervention. The Political Bureau resolution on military tasks in the South warned, "We must act cleverly to avoid a big armed intervention by imperialism, restraining and defeating the United States in the South."[33] Early in 1961, Le Duan explained in a letter to party leaders in the South the difference between the Maoist three-stage people's war strategy, which had guided the development of the anti-French resistance war, and the strategy chosen by the party for the struggle in the South. The armed struggle had to be conducted "in the Vietnamese way," he said, "by partial insurrection, building revolutionary bases, launching guerrilla warfare and then a general insurrection, chiefly by the use of political forces combined with armed forces to seize power for the people."[34]

Meanwhile, some Vietnamese leaders were watching international developments for any evidence of political and other constraints on U.S. use of military force that they could use to refute the Soviet thesis that a Communist guerrilla war posed serious risk of a nuclear confrontation. Events in nearby Laos, where the Laotian neutralist paratrooper Captain Kong Le had ousted the U.S.-backed rightist government in August 1960 without any U.S. military response, were cited by those who wanted to challenge what they considered the excessively conciliatory Soviet strategy.[35] By mid 1961, a majority of the Politburo was arguing that the United States was unlikely to do more than send additional advisers to South Vietnam. The evidence was the U.S. failure to defeat the Cuban government at the Bay of Pigs and its decision to respond to the 1960–61 surge in revolutionary activity in South Vietnam by sending only advisers and more aid rather than troops.[36]

Thus the Political Bureau developed its own distinct assessment of the global power balance that deemphasized the importance of the military balance between the two camps and played up the role of the worldwide "national liberation movement." The theory was that the United States was not as capable of intervening in Vietnam as previously feared, because it could not afford to get too bogged down in one place in a world rocked by anti-imperialist revolution. The world revolution was now viewed for the first time as being in a "strategic offensive posture," whereas U.S. imperialism was seen as being in a "strategic defensive posture."[37]

Even as it distinguished its own analysis from that of the Soviet Union, however, the party leadership remained acutely aware of the threat of U.S. military intervention. The October 1961 resolution of the conference of the party's Central Committee directorate for the South on the new situation in the struggle against the Diem regime noted that the U.S. ability to intervene militarily in the South had "many limitations," citing opposition that would come from the socialist camp, the national liberation movement, and neutralist states, as well as from Gaullist France. But it also reflected the basic Soviet-Chinese view of the correlation of forces, warning that the threat of a big war against U.S. forces imposed major limits on how far the revolution could push by force of arms. The resolution maintained that it would take "a long time before we can advance toward the General Uprising," and that revolutionaries in the South would have to "wait until a change takes place in the world or in the country to intensify the revolutionary movement and quickly overthrow the Diem Government."[38]

Only a few weeks after that conference, a major development in the war underlined the need for caution. The announcement of the introduction by the United States of helicopters and pilots into the war in late 1961 confronted the North Vietnamese with a new military challenge and, more important, with new evidence of the U.S. determination to hold on to South Vietnam. In February 1962 a resolution issued by the Political Bureau warned the party that, despite favorable changes in the relationship of forces between the two sides, increasing U.S. intervention would "create many difficulties for the Southern revolution." The resolution called for the leadership in the south to "cleverly protect and hide our forces and oppose adventurism and impatience." It suggested that the war could end in a number of ways, including a change in the existing—and implicitly unfavorable—global power balance, but that all of them would involve a negotiated settlement:

> Either the enemy will be defeated by our army and people . . . and will have to end the war and recognize the sovereignty and independence of our people (similar to the circumstances after the Dien Bien Phu battle) or the enemy will fall into passive position from which he cannot escape but which becomes more unfavorable the longer it is protracted, and will be forced to negotiate peace with us on the basis of our independence and sovereignty (as in the case of the Algerian war at present); or this could happen because of the rapid strengthening of the socialist camp, and of peace, democracy and national independence in the world and because our forces within the country are constantly growing stronger.[39]

It warned that, regardless of the circumstances in which the war ended, a negotiated settlement would yield far less than a decisive victory. A diplomatic agreement with the United States would represent only the first in a series of stages on the way to final reunification:

> We must know how to defeat the enemy but we must know how to do so step by step, and to make each stage another step on the path leading to complete victory. Now we fight while demanding a true coalition government, real elections, peace, and neutrality. That will only make later steps easier, further isolating the warmongers and winning over those within the enemy camp inclined to negotiate peace.[40]

The Hanoi leadership had become so much more concerned about the rapid increase in U.S. military personnel and technology in the war—even before their impact had been felt—that it had already planned for a political settlement that would fall short of the goal of eliminating the U.S.-sponsored regime. That anticipatory response underlines the extreme sensitivity of the North Vietnamese to any evidence affecting the intentions of the United States toward Vietnam. The actual impact of the U.S. military presence strengthened the desire of the North Vietnamese leadership to find a negotiated solution to the war. When ARVN began using helicopter assault tactics to go on the offensive in the Mekong Delta, and increased the number of sweep operations against areas where the revolutionaries had taken power, the "liberated areas" began to shrink, and party members and cadres in affected areas were forced to hide in rice paddies during daytime. In the Mekong Delta and southern Central Vietnam, main-force units had to be broken up into smaller subunits to avoid being caught in sweep operations.[41]

The new U.S. military presence in South Vietnam further sharpened the Hanoi leadership's fear that the United States might move to what it called "limited war," defined as the deployment of 250,000 or more U.S. troops. Le Duan wrote another letter to the party leaders in the South in early July 1962 that made it clear the Politburo had reversed its 1961 view and now agreed that the United States would not accept the loss of South Vietnam to the Communists. He acknowledged that the U.S. decision against sending troops to Laos in 1960–61 was not an indicator of its likely behavior in South Vietnam, as the majority had argued in 1961. Le Duan observed that Laos shared a border with China, which had made the United States reluctant to send troops there, whereas South Vietnam had no common border with China, so the United States "doesn't regard confrontation with North Vietnam as dangerous in the same way that it does a confrontation with China." Because the United States was "determined to protect South Vietnam to the end," he warned, the struggle was bound to become "increasingly fierce and complex."[42]

The Vietnamese leadership now put greater emphasis on both limiting the war in the South and limiting the Communist side's negotiating demands once that phase of the conflict began. This concern pointed to the strategy that had been followed in Laos as a model for conducting revolutionary struggle under the threat of direct U.S. intervention. Le Duan recalled how the Vietnamese party had advised the Lao People's Revolutionary Party to "restrict the war in Laos and not let it develop into a big war between the two sides." The Pathet Lao had halted their military momentum after the victory at Nam Tha and had gone on to achieve an "important victory" in the international neutralization of Laos. If the Pathet Lao had "pushed the revolutionary struggle, especially the military struggle, too far," he wrote, it would "not have conformed to what the relationship of forces permitted." In other words, the United States would not have accepted it. The lesson of Laos for the South Vietnamese revolution, according to the Vietnamese party chief, was that "if . . . we don't assess the relationship of forces between the enemy and us correctly and push the struggle beyond the necessary level during this period, it will produce bad results."[43]

The main problem, Le Duan explained, was that the revolution "must limit the ever-increasing intervention of U.S. imperialism, and not let the enemy turn 'special war' into 'local war' and broaden the war to the entire nation." The southern revolutionaries had to emulate the Pathet Lao, who had "only defeated the US puppet army to a certain degree and not completely" and had "won a political victory." The southern revolutionary army, he wrote, could only partially defeat the Saigon army. The key to Hanoi's strategy, therefore, was the hope that it could use world opinion to "isolate and force the enemy to negotiate with us." Le Duan reflected the Politburo's understanding that the overall power balance favored the United States, reducing its incentive to make major concessions to Hanoi. The DRV negotiating demands, he wrote, would have to "cause the enemy to consider it an acceptable loss, a loss that would not push it into a dangerous situation."[44]

POWER ASSESSMENT AND NEGOTIATING POLICY, 1962–1963

As shown by these internal communications from Le Duan to party leaders in the South, the Vietnamese party leadership had concluded by mid 1962 that the United States would fight for South Vietnam rather than allow it to be lost to the Communist bloc, and that the Communist side would have to avoid terms for a settlement that would be regarded by Washington as too onerous. This fundamental assessment of the vastly unequal power relationship set the context for North Vietnamese efforts from 1962 through 1964 to promote a negotiated solution to the conflict.

Hanoi began its campaign for negotiations on the neutralization of South Vietnam in early 1962 at the same time that it recognized that the United States was becoming much more deeply involved in the war and that the danger of a much larger U.S. intervention had increased. The neutralization initiative sought to take advantage of the progress that had been made on negotiating the neutralization of Laos by applying a similar formula to South Vietnam. Hanoi orchestrated support for the initiative from China and, the neutralist leaders of Laos and Cambodia, Souvanna Phouma and Prince Norodom Sihanouk. The leaders of the VWP appear to have decided, however, that the public advocacy of the neutralization proposal should come mainly from the South Vietnamese National Liberation Front, which held its first congress in early 1962. The decision to give the NLF the primary role in calling for neutralization was evidently aimed at giving it greater credibility as an entity independent of Hanoi.

According to both U.S. intelligence and former National Liberation Front sources, Hanoi and the NLF officials approached Sihanouk about supporting a neutralization agreement for South Vietnam.[45] In its January 17, 1962, program, the NLF called for the formation of a "peace and neutrality zone comprising Cambodia, Laos and South Vietnam" and welcomed Sihanouk's initiative. DRV Foreign Minister Ung Van Khiem then sent a formal note to Britain and the Soviet Union, co-chairs of the 1954 Geneva Conference, on March 15, 1962, requesting that they "proceed to consultations with the interested countries so as to find effective steps designed to preserve the 1954 Geneva Agreements and safeguarding peace in Vietnam and in Southeast Asia." But Hanoi wanted to avoid the identification of the neutralist solution as a North Vietnamese proposal. Ho Chi Minh declared in an interview with a Chinese newspaper that the DRV had always favored negotiations between the two zones for national elections to achieve reunification, but that it was "up to the people in South Vietnam to decide whether South Vietnam is to have a neutral regime or any other regime."[46]

Sihanouk repeated his own call for an international conference to negotiate a peace agreement on South Vietnam based on the Laos model in late March and early April, explaining that the Chinese had encouraged him to do so. On April 13 and 14, Hanoi and Beijing both released the manifesto of the first NLF congress, held several weeks earlier, which called for the neutralization of South Vietnam. On April 19, a DRV Foreign Ministry spokesman called for "consultations" on Vietnam, leaving the door open to various approaches to negotiations on a settlement of the war. The following day, the head of the DRV National Reunification Commission and Vice Minister of Defense Nguyen Van Vinh called for a reconvening of the Geneva Conference "to discuss the Vietnamese question." British diplomats reported that Hanoi was prepared to negotiate directly with Diem to bring about a peace settlement.[47]

Meanwhile, Souvanna Phouma, who was soon to become prime minister of the tripartite neutralist Laotian regime, understood that, given North Vietnam's insistence on the use of the corridor through eastern Laos, the Laotian settlement would not end the fighting in Laos without an end to the conflict in Vietnam. In June 1962, Souvanna began to tell foreign diplomats in Vientiane about the need for the neutralization of South Vietnam. He then traveled to Hanoi on June 16, where he discussed his ideas about a tripartite neutralist solution in South Vietnam and the establishment of a neutral zone on the Indochinese peninsula with Pham Van Dong. Even the Soviet Union, which had been reluctant to press for negotiations on South Vietnam in March, then supported Hanoi's neutralization initiative. In the final days of the negotiations on the Laotian agreement, Soviet Deputy Foreign Minister Pushkin met with Averell Harriman and suggested that the Laotian formula could also be applied to South Vietnam, arguing that a South Vietnamese neutralist movement had now materialized.[48]

Despite this concerted diplomatic campaign for the neutralization of South Vietnam, Hanoi stopped campaigning publicly either for convening a Geneva Conference on South Vietnam or for the neutralization of Vietnam. Various explanations have been advanced for Hanoi's failure to continue to press diplomatically for such negotiations: that it was satisfied with the way the war in the South was progressing; that it was only interested in negotiations on terms that would guarantee a Communist takeover in the South, or that it was beginning to fall under Chinese ideological influence.[49] The evidence suggests a much simpler explanation, however, for Hanoi's suspending its campaign for the neutralization of South Vietnam. After British diplomatic efforts to dissuade Sihanouk from advocating an international conference on Vietnam in May, the North Vietnamese knew that the British would block the convening of any such conference.[50] And as Colonel Ha Van Lau, a veteran of the Vietnamese delegations to both the 1954 Geneva Conference and the 1962 Geneva Conference on Laos, explained to Marek Thee, Hanoi believed that the Kennedy administration was still thinking in terms of military victory in South Vietnam. A meeting between DRV Foreign Minister Ung Van Khiem and the head of the U.S. delegation to the Geneva Conference, Averell Harriman, on July 22, 1962, just after the signing of the Laos neutralization agreement, reinforced the North Vietnamese conviction that the United States was not interested in negotiations. In that meeting, Harriman demanded an end to armed resistance before any discussions on the political future of South Vietnam could begin.[51]

After Geneva, the North Vietnamese shifted the focus of their diplomatic strategy from the United States to France. The immediate object of Hanoi's diplomacy was South Vietnamese exiles in France whose close ties with the former colonial power could be helpful in persuading the government of President Charles de Gaulle to play an active role in bringing about the neutralization of South Vietnam. French support for a neutral South Vietnam would in turn help gain political support from the South Vietnamese elite for that aim. Premier Pham Van Dong explained the neutralization strategy to a French journalist in late 1961. "The [South Vietnamese] intellectuals and the bourgeoisie," he said, "remain very attached to France. Thus the solution largely depends on an understanding between you and us that would permit joining the masses to the intelligentsia and to the middle class in order to establish a democratic rule. Oh, if only Paris would play its role and contribute to peace."[52]

Hanoi's strategy was to encourage Vietnamese neutralists in exile in France who were completely independent of the Communists to become active on the international political-diplomatic stage. In this regard, the North Vietnamese were willing to accept even the most anti-Communist Vietnamese as representatives of a neutralist tendency, provided that they were independent of the United States.[53] In August 1962, DRV Foreign Minister Ung Van Khiem (himself a former professor in Saigon and a leader of the southern resistance) met in Geneva with Tran Van Huu, a former prime minister of the French-sponsored State of Viet-Nam from 1950 to 1952 and a naturalized French citizen. Some in the party found Huu objectionable as an interlocutor because they still remembered his government's repression of an anti-war demonstration in Saigon in 1950. Nevertheless, Khiem suggested to Huu that he could be the "Souvanna Phouma of South Vietnam." A few days after meeting with Khiem, Huu traveled to London, where he unveiled a neutralization plan for South Vietnam.[54]

Hanoi's courting of pro-French exiles did not lead to any political breakthrough either in Paris or in Saigon. But in 1963, a new opportunity to make an end run around the United States arose when Ngo Dinh Diem's brother Ngo Dinh Nhu took the initiative in contacting the North about a rapprochement. A reconstruction of the origins and development of this episode in North-South Vietnamese diplomacy reveals both the fluidity of the political forces in South Vietnam and the lengths to which Hanoi was willing to go to reach an accommodation with the South.

Although many accounts have attributed Nhu's contacts with the Communists to his desire to gain leverage over the Americans, the evidence indicates that, at least initially, Nhu hoped to gain greater leverage over

Hanoi by negotiating limited steps toward normalization between North and South Vietnam. At the end of March 1963, he told a South Vietnamese diplomat, Tran Van Dinh, then deputy ambassador in Washington, that Dinh would have the opportunity to negotiate with North Vietnam on the issue of normalization of relations. Ambassador Dinh, who was trusted by Diem and Nhu as a fellow native of the former imperial city of Hue, was the only South Vietnamese diplomat to have dealt directly with the DRV. In 1957–58, he had served as Diem's ambassador to Burma where both North and South Vietnam had full diplomatic representation. During his service there, the DRV ambassador in Rangoon had proposed to Dinh the formation of a joint committee to explore eventual reunification, with no prior conditions imposed on the talks. Dinh had recommended to Diem that the RVN agree to such a joint committee, but Diem had rejected the proposal. In the March 1963 conversation, however, Nhu said that Dinh would soon be able to accomplish what he had talked about earlier, although he gave no further details.[55]

In mid September, Nhu told Dinh that the Communists were interested in a modus vivendi with the Diem regime, because North Vietnam was under intense pressure from China in the Sino-Soviet conflict and needed a "period of real non-alignment."[56] In addition, Nhu thought that the North's need for rice from the South gave him real bargaining leverage with Hanoi. In March 1963, some U.S. officials in Saigon had informally discussed a possible initiative on normalization of such matters as postal communication and travel between North and South with Diem and Nhu. The assumption underlying these discussions was that the Communist insurgents were on the defensive and that the steps toward normalization of relations might be a bargaining counter in an eventual cease-fire agreement.[57]

Nhu's willingness to take steps toward normalization of relations also reflected his confidence that the Diem regime could defeat the Communist guerrillas without U.S. military advisers. The transcript of a meeting of the Inter-Ministerial Committee for Strategic Hamlets in late August 1962 provides a fascinating glimpse of his thinking. A counterguerrilla policy, Nhu said, was only a stage on the way to organizing his own "basic guerrilla establishment." The developed nations "can have no concept of guerrilla warfare," Nhu observed, so their military aid "belongs entirely to the counter-guerrilla concept, not at all to the guerrilla concept." Therefore, he concluded, "We must depend on ourselves alone."[58]

Nhu made no secret of his self-reliant strategy. At the height of the Buddhist crisis in late August 1963, he defended his readiness to fight the war without depending on U.S. assistance to the top generals in the South

Vietnamese army. He argued that the RVN could survive without U.S. assistance because of the success of the Strategic Hamlet program. And in any case, he said, the United States, having just signed the test ban treaty, was moving toward its own accommodation with the Communist bloc and might reduce its assistance to South Vietnam.[59]

Nhu took advantage of a visit by Polish ICC delegation chief Mieczyslaw Maneli to Hanoi in May 1963 to convey his proposal for steps toward normalization to Hanoi. The proposal went much farther than what Nhu had discussed with American officials, offering to establish normal North-South trade relations—South Vietnamese rice for North Vietnamese coal.[60] Nhu correctly assumed that North Vietnam's desperate food situation gave him a major bargaining chip in negotiations with Hanoi. The 1960–64 DRV five-year plan, following the formation of low-level collectivization of agriculture, had brought a sharp decline in rice production. After reaching a peak of 335 kilograms of rice per capita in 1959, production had averaged only 254 kilograms per capita over the period of the plan—a decline that had been only partially offset by increases in production of other crops—and the decline may have been much worse than these official figures indicate.[61] Meanwhile, Hanoi had increased the size of the VPA from just 120,000 in 1962 to 174,000 troops in 1963, with the capability to mobilize an additional 90,000 troops within fifteen days if necessary and even more in the event of full-scale war with the United States.[62] That substantial increase in the DRV's requirements for state-controlled grain came just as North Vietnam's food crisis had worsened in the early months of 1963, when adverse weather had caused a reduction in per capita production of the fifth-month crop to less than 240 kilograms for the first time since 1954.[63]

Pham Van Dong responded to Maneli's presentation of Nhu's message by telling Maneli that Diem could "prove his good faith" by agreeing to a renewal of economic and cultural relations between North and South Vietnam.[64] Because Diem had flatly refused to discuss economic relations between the two zones when Hanoi had proposed them from 1956 to 1958, the Hanoi leaders recognized Nhu's proposal as a sign of genuine change in Diem's attitude and of serious differences between Diem and the United States.

The North Vietnamese leaders also knew that the PLAF was still very far from achieving military equality with the ARVN. The buildup of main-force units that had been planned for 1962 had not met expectations, and the combat tactics adopted by the PLAF had not kept up with the rapidly changing realities of the southern battlefield in 1963, according to a party military history. A Political Bureau resolution in December 1962 had set as its military objective building "concentrated forces" to become one-fifth as large as the main forces of the ARVN and guerrilla forces as large as Diem's armed Republic Youth organization within two or three years.[65] Hanoi was thus faced with the prospect of a long and difficult war in the South and a potentially disastrous economic situation if it had to escalate its involvement in the war in the South, on top of the threat of U.S. military intervention and widespread destruction of the North.

Immediately after receiving the offer of steps toward normalization from Nhu, therefore, the Political Bureau of the VWP met to decide on the outlines of a new initiative for negotiations with the Diem regime. The new peace proposal was conveyed through an interview with Ho Chi Minh by the Australian leftist journalist Wilfred Burchett that was published in Moscow's *New Times* at the end of May. Ho told Burchett that a cease-fire "could presumably be arranged between the Diemist forces and those of the patriotic National Liberation Front of South Vietnam." He then addressed the political element of a settlement: "Conditions must be created in which the people of South Viet-Nam can freely elect a government of their own choice." North Vietnam would then negotiate with the new government to normalize trade, communications, and cultural relations. The United States would have to withdraw its military forces from the South, and the new government in the South would renounce military bases and membership in military blocs.[66]

Ho's interview with Burchett was the most important interview on foreign policy granted by Ho in the decade since he had signaled the DRV's readiness to begin peace negotiations with France in a December 1953 interview with the Swedish newspaper *Expressen*.[67] The new peace proposal went considerably beyond the previous formula of a tripartite neutralist regime in making political concessions to Diem. By omitting the standard demand for the overthrow of Diem and by offering a cease-fire without conditions, Hanoi's new negotiating position left open the possibility that Diem could remain in power during the organization of an election in the South. Maneli recounts that Pham Van Dong and Ho Chi Minh at first had refused to concede before any negotiations began that Diem could actually remain as president of the Republic of Vietnam, but did agree to that point under his prodding that summer.[68]

Sometime before mid September, Maneli carried a message to Diem to the effect that Hanoi was willing to negotiate a peace agreement on generous terms. In an interview with Joseph Alsop in mid September, Nhu referred to a message from Pham Van Dong that proposed negotiations on the basis of "Ho Chi Minh's ceasefire proposal," meaning the proposal for a cease-fire and negotiated settlement in Ho's interview with Burchett. Nhu said "many details were spelled out," making it "almost an attractive offer." Nhu claimed, of course, that he had rejected the offer, saying, "I could not open negotiations behind the backs of the Americans. . . . That was out of the question."[69] For his part, Maneli tried to keep his role secret. He denied that he had carried a message "from Pham Van Dong to the South." Nevertheless, Tran Van Dinh, Nhu's diplomatic confidant in 1963, confirmed that Nhu had received a letter from North Vietnam through Maneli, although he did not know who had signed it.[70] A Vietnamese Central Committee member confirmed in an interview in 1974 that some weeks before Diem's overthrow and assassination, Ho Chi Minh himself had sent a personal letter to Diem about a possible peace agreement.[71]

According to the Vietnamese party official, Diem had not answered the letter when he was killed on November 1, 1963. Evidence from several sources indicates, however, that Nhu had also been in direct contact with top-ranking NLF representatives in the South during 1963. Ambassador Frederick Nolting recalls that, in the spring of 1963, Nhu told him that he had just finished meeting with a prominent Viet Cong leader, and that other Viet Cong leaders had also come to his office under a "gentleman's agreement" that they would not be arrested.[72] After the overthrow and assassination of Diem and Nhu, a series of investigative articles in a South Vietnamese newspaper reported that Nhu had met with General Tran Van Tra, then commander of the southern B2 Region of South Vietnam. The same investigation revealed that Nhu had also met with representatives of the Communists on at least three other occasions, once at Gia Long Palace, once in Phan Rang, and once in War Zone D.[73] But Nhu's most important contact with the Communist side, which he revealed to Tran Van Dinh in September, was with the chairman of the NLF Foreign Affairs Commission, Tran Buu Kiem, who had tentatively approved the outlines of the peace plan described above.[74]

Finally, Diem himself informed Dinh in late September that he had agreed with the North on the outlines of a peace settlement that would include a cease-fire, the departure of all U.S. forces, the acceptance of NLF representatives into his government, and an election in which the Communists could participate. Diem confirmed that Dinh would go to New Delhi in November to begin the negotiations. Once agreement was reached, Dinh was to inform Indian Prime Minister Jawaharlal Nehru himself, who would immediately call a news conference to announce it.[75] Nhu and Diem told Dinh that he was to conclude the negotiations as quickly as possible and even arranged for a code that would signify the completion of the negotiations, in the belief that U.S. intelligence would be monitoring the government's cable traffic. If Dinh cabled that the prospects for concluding an economic treaty were excellent, it would mean that the negotiations had been successful, because South Vietnam had no economic relations with India.[76]

MILITARY WEAKNESS, ESCALATION, AND NEGOTIATIONS, 1964–1965

The overthrow of the Diem regime by a military coup on November 1 prompted the VWP's Ninth Central Committee Plenum in early December to reassess its strategy in the South. The new military regime and the complex political-military situation in the South, along with the assassination of President Kennedy and his replacement by Lyndon Johnson, presented the most important changes in the situation since the United States's new military role in late 1961 and early 1962. This situation elicited a new level of debate over the party's strategy in the South and, for the first time, over the participation of North Vietnamese regular forces in the war.

The testimony of knowledgeable Hanoi officials and the text of the plenum resolution both indicate that the Central Committee responded to the overthrow of Diem and a likely weakening of the Saigon government's war effort by adopting a strategy aimed at building up the revolutionary forces in the South while postponing a decision on whether to begin sending large-scale combat units to the South. VPA staff officer Colonel Bui Tin recalled in a later interview that the assassinations of Diem and of Kennedy had considerable impact on Hanoi's thinking about the likelihood of the United States sending its own forces. North Vietnamese leaders viewed Lyndon Johnson as more likely to change the character of the war from "special war" to "limited war," he recalled, and Hanoi perceived in late 1963 and early 1964 that the United States was actively debating whether to send its own troops. "We felt we had to have a policy to deal with that possibility," Tin said.[77] Another knowledgeable military source also recalled that party leaders were becoming increasingly concerned that the United States would send its own troops and that "there would be a big war in the South."[78]

While suggesting that the United States would be constrained from full-fledged intervention in the South by the fear of being "bogged down" in a war there, the Ninth Plenum resolution nevertheless predicted that the United States might "bring in from fifty to a hundred thousand additional troops to South Vietnam."[79] Weighing the likelihood that the United States was already planning to send combat troops to fight in Vietnam, the leaders of the VWP judged the revolutionary forces in the South still too weak to wage regular army battles against the ARVN, let alone deal with a U.S. military intervention. The resolution asserted that, although the PLAF had "absolute political superiority" over the Saigon regime, the revolutionary forces were "inferior to the enemy in weapons, ammunition, equipment and war facilities." Furthermore, the Americans were expected to increase the strength of the Saigon army and try to retake the offensive.[80]

A major conclusion of the Ninth Plenum resolution was, therefore, that a U.S. transformation of the war into a "limited war" would "become more probable if the revolutionary movement in the South is not strong enough."[81] Clearly, the Central Committee intended to strengthen the revolutionary forces, but how and with what aim? The Central Committee debated at the Ninth Plenum how far and how fast to build forces that could wage regular warfare, and whether and when to commit regular VPA units to the war. One specific issue under debate was whether to widen the Ho Chi Minh trail network, the logistical system running through eastern Laos that had been used to send men and supplies to the South. The trail was then only wide enough for bicycle traffic. The more cautious view in the debate was that the trail should remain small, so that it would be harder to bomb, but opponents of that position argued that it would mean limiting its capacity to the level required to support guerrilla warfare. The other position was that the trail should be widened to accommodate trucks and heavy weapons, as well as whole VPA regiments.[82]

Contrary to the interpretation of the Ninth Plenum resolution as authorizing a strategy of striving for a quick victory, the text of the resolution shows that Hanoi's leaders had not in fact decided on such a strategy.[83] The Central Committee plenum agreed only to a "gradual advance" by the PLAF to "mobile warfare" and to changing the military balance so as to gain "victories" in "not too long a period of time." It called for the forces in the South to "strive to attain victory step by step and gradually push back the enemy before reaching the General Offensive and Uprising to win complete victory." The plenum strongly reaffirmed the line of protracted war, explaining that the southern armed struggle had to be protracted, "because we are a small people having to fight [the] imperialist ringleader which is the U.S.A."[84]

In identifying the goal of mobile warfare in the South, the Central Committee left open the question of whether Hanoi would widen the trail network and send regimental-sized units to the South. That decision was postponed until the completion of a study mission in the South that had already been set in motion in October 1963, two months before the Ninth Plenum. Colonel Bui Tin left for the South in late December to study the feasibility of widening the trail network, as well as whether it was necessary to help the PLAF create a change in the military balance. He would then remain in the South to help "prepare the battlefield" for the possible entry of large-scale American forces into the war.[85]

In mid March, after an eighty-day trip down the trail on foot, Tin arrived at the southern party headquarters in Quang Ngai province. Some weeks later, he sent a letter, which was carried on foot back to Hanoi, reporting his conclusion that the trail could be widened to accommodate regular army regiments. Tin's report also confirmed the fears expressed at the plenum that the PLAF would not be able to win major battles against the Saigon army without substantial help from the VPA. He found that the PLAF had just formed its first regiments, and that they were neither big enough nor strong enough to fight against American forces. The differences he found in training between northern and southern combat units, moreover, were dramatic. He concluded that it would be impossible to liberate the South without deploying northern units in the South.[86]

The Central Committee decision to widen the trail and send VPA regiments or divisions to the South followed signals by the Johnson administration that it was planning an attack on North Vietnam. In late March 1964, Secretary of Defense McNamara, who had just returned from a trip to South Vietnam with General Maxwell Taylor, told an NBC interviewer that the he and Taylor had reported to President Johnson that one option was "the initiation of military action . . . against North Vietnam." That warning coincided with an acceleration of commando raids against the North, which had been going on since 1961.[87] These threats to carry the war to the North prompted Hanoi to accelerate its own contingency plans for a U.S. escalation of the conflict. The VPA High Command shifted a portion of the Air Force to wartime status, formed antiaircraft cells, and began building bomb shelters to protect state agencies. The Political Bureau issued instructions on June 1 to prepare for "acts of provocation and aggression against North Vietnam" by "enemy air forces."[88]

In June, the United States made a series of more explicit public and private threats to attack North Vietnam. On June 18, the State Department released testimony by Assistant Secretary of State William Bundy before a House Appropriations Subcommittee on May 4, in which he said, "We are going to drive the Communists out of South Vietnam," even if it meant "attacking countries to the North."[89] Meanwhile, a Canadian diplomat,

J. Blair Seaborn, passed on a U.S. message to Pham Van Dong that U.S. patience was growing "extremely thin." Finally, in late June, in retaliation for the shooting down of an escort plane earlier that month, U.S. fighters accompanying low-level reconnaissance missions over the Pathet Lao zone in Laos attacked two PL military installations at PL headquarters and Khang Khay and in the process hit the Chinese mission at Khang Khay.[90]

Against this backdrop of U.S. threats and a growing direct military role in Southeast Asia, the U.S. bombing of North Vietnam for the first time on August 5 convinced the Vietnamese party leadership that Washington believed that the ARVN was going to be defeated without U.S. intervention and had decided not to accept such a loss. Party leaders now believed the United States would probably not only attack North Vietnam but intervene with large numbers of troops in the South. According to three knowledgeable Vietnamese sources, the party Central Committee convened an extraordinary plenum a few days after the U.S. bombing raids to reassess the likelihood of a shift to "limited war" and to decide how to respond to the new situation.[91]

General Nguyen Chi Thanh, then the most influential figure in the leadership on the war in the South, estimated that the United States might send 100,000 troops in the relatively short-term future. Nguyen Co Thach recalled, however, that the Central Committee plenum had discussed the need to be prepared for a worst-case contingency of as many as one million American troops in South Vietnam.[92] The Political Bureau assumed that, if the United States entered the war in the South, it would also carry out systematic attacks on the North. The first thing that the DRV government ordered in the aftermath of the Tonkin Gulf bombings, therefore, was the evacuation of children from Hanoi, which occurred very quickly. The only question was how far the United States would go. The secret plenum discussed the possibility that the United States would invade and try to occupy part of North Vietnam, especially the southernmost provinces.[93]

The prospect of a war against the world's most powerful army provoked expressions of doubt by some Central Committee members, who wondered how the revolutionary forces could defeat the United States.[94] The only time a Communist army had fought significant U.S. forces had been in the Korean War, when the Chinese had done the heaviest fighting. In this war, the North Vietnamese understood that there would be no Chinese troops involved in combat.[95] One party leader proposed that the party send a mission to North Korea to learn from their experiences in fighting the Americans. Ho Chi Minh vehemently disagreed, however, telling the conference, "If you are determined to win, you will have all the wisdom to win. If you are determined to run away, you will have all the wisdom to run away." Ho told the plenum that he could not say how they would win, but that he was sure they would win.

In the end, the Central Committee supported Ho's standpoint with little or no dissent. The main theme of the Central Committee's still unpublished decision, according to Thach, was the party's determination to "win the war within an appropriate period of time," which represented no sharp departure from the existing protracted war line.[96] The Political Bureau apparently got approval from the Central Committee for a tentative decision to dispatch a division of VPA troops to the South in anticipation of a U.S. decision to intervene. On August 13, presumably immediately after the secret Central Committee meeting, Le Duan flew to Beijing for a meeting with Chinese leaders on the new situation. The Vietnamese party secretary told Mao that the Vietnamese were now certain that the United States intended to send combat forces to South Vietnam and to widen the war to the North, and that they had decided to send a VPA division to the South.[97]

In the weeks that followed Le Duan's visit to Beijing, however, Vietnamese leaders had second thoughts about their interpretation of U.S. policy, as well as about sending troops to the South in advance of the dispatch of a major U.S. combat force. In the second half of August, moreover, the USSR conveyed a proposal from UN Secretary-General U Thant to Hanoi for a secret meeting with U.S. officials, presumably along with his belief that he had been encouraged to arrange such talks at a meeting with Johnson and Rusk on August 6. Ho Chi Minh reportedly personally accepted the proposal in a letter to U Thant in early September.[98]

When the Political Bureau met on September 26–29, 1964, it had moderated its hasty and alarmist conclusion following the Gulf of Tonkin bombing raids. It now believed that the United States had not intended to provoke the North with its combination of naval patrolling and commando raids. Party leaders concluded that the United States was "studying and striving to prepare for" the dispatch of expeditionary forces to South Vietnam and for a war of destruction against the North, but that major U.S. military intervention was "a possibility that our army and people must do our best to prevent and take precautions against." While acknowledging that Vietnam had "an important position in the overall strategy of the United States," the Political Bureau now suggested that international and internal constraints on the United States would inhibit the Johnson administration from being able to "mobilize the maximum level of military power" for the war in Vietnam.[99] That meant that it doubted the United States would actually take over the war, turning it into what the VWP called a "limited war."

The Political Bureau was also unclear about whether the Johnson administration intended to negotiate. A summary of its conclusions transmitted to the regional party committee in the South suggested that U.S. officials were discussing the possibility of negotiations but did not intend to negotiate the withdrawal of U.S. troops. As for the Vietnamese leadership's own policy on negotiations, the same document indicated that "the problem of negotiation is very complicated," because it meant "solving the problem of the balance of power and attaining victories." In other words, the revolutionary forces had not yet achieved a military balance that would make possible a settlement that would represent a step forward. The summary observed that they had not yet obtained victories such as those won by the Viet Minh prior to the Geneva settlement of 1954.[100] The Political Bureau resolution was quite forceful on that point. "The main-force units in the South," it said, "are still weak and are not well prepared to carry out concentrated operations to destroy the puppet main forces." The Political Bureau resolution indicated that the "best method to win a victory for the South Vietnamese revolution" was to rapidly build up military forces in the South and partly destroy the ARVN in an effort to "completely defeat the puppet army before the United States jumps into the war." But the document later explained that winning a "decisive victory" in the South could only be accomplished "within a few years."

The resolution made it clear that the South Vietnamese revolutionary forces would not be capable of achieving this by themselves. The Political Bureau therefore decided to send the equivalent of a division of regular VPA troops to the South.[101] It also apparently authorized the widening of the Ho Chi Minh trail network to accommodate mechanized traffic, for which the VPA had been clamoring since spring.[102] However, Hanoi had to reconcile the need to move large regular army units to South Vietnam with its desire to avoid provoking an American takeover of the war. When Pham Van Dong met with Mao in early October to report on the Political Bureau meeting the previous week, Dong agreed with the Chinese leader on the need to avoid any action that would give the United States a pretext for a larger intervention. "We should try our best not to let the U.S. imperialists turn the war in South Vietnam into a limited war," said the Vietnamese prime minister, "and try our best not to let the war be expanded to North Vietnam. We must adopt a very skillful strategy, and should not provoke [the United States]."[103]

We now know that the "skillful strategy" to which Dong referred was to deploy and utilize the regiments of the 325th VPA division and the

545th Viet Bac Battalion in such a way as to minimize their detection by U.S. and ARVN intelligence. According to a July 1965 U.S. Defense Department study, the deployment of the first large North Vietnamese regular army units in the South involved two major changes from the normal deployment of such units that considerably reduced their offensive capacity. The first was to deploy the division's infantry regiments without the artillery regiment that would normally have accompanied them. The second was to break up the division into battalions and to disperse them among existing PLAF units, rather than reconstituting it as a division in the South.[104] The 320th Regiment began the journey from its North Vietnamese base at Dong Hoi in October, arriving in the South sometime in late November or December. The other three regiments (the 18th, 95th, and 101st) did not leave North Vietnam for another two months, arriving in the South in February.[105] These regiments were also broken up into battalions, which were dispersed among larger local Viet Cong units. Elements of a battalion of the 18th Regiment, for example, were integrated into a Viet Cong sapper squad that carried out an attack on Danang Airbase on July 1, 1965.[106]

Once they had finally verified that North Vietnamese troops were indeed in the South in mid 1965, Pentagon analysts puzzled over the lack of a division structure and the dispersal of the 101st Regiment's battalions among existing Viet Cong units. They were also surprised by the absence of combat on the part of North Vietnamese forces. Although the 101st and 320th Regiments overran or forced withdrawal from a series of small border outposts in Pleiku and Kontum provinces in early 1965, they avoided further contact with the ARVN for the next few months. The only breach in the secrecy surrounding the northern troops in the South was a single soldier who surrendered to South Vietnamese authorities on March 23 and identified himself as a member of a battalion of the 101st Regiment. His story was only accepted by U.S. intelligence after he passed two polygraph tests. Even in mid 1965, the 320th Regiment still had not been identified by U.S. intelligence, which confirmed only the 101st Regiment as definitely present in South Vietnam, with two others (the 18th and 95th) considered "unconfirmed but probable." Military analysts concluded in mid July that Hanoi had chosen to make a considerable sacrifice in the offensive capacity of the Communist forces against the ARVN in order to hide the presence of regular VPA forces in the South.[107] Had Hanoi been less concerned about the U.S. military response to the North Vietnamese presence in the South, it would certainly have sent a full division with its normal strength and structure to take on the ARVN directly.

The Political Bureau's recognition that the military balance in the South was not favorable enough to support a negotiated settlement did not mean that it was pulling back from diplomacy. The Political Bureau meeting in September 1964 also led to a significant new diplomatic initiative. While it waited for Washington to respond to the U Thant proposal for bilateral secret talks, the DRV began clarifying its terms for a settlement, evidently hoping to encourage a positive U.S. response. In conversations with Wilfred Burchett in Phnom Penh toward the middle of the month, a North Vietnamese diplomat repeated that the National Liberation Front was willing to negotiate directly with the Saigon government, rather than demanding its replacement, and that it was ready to agree to a prolonged period of a separate regime for South Vietnam. Then he added an entirely new element to DRV-NLF negotiating terms. Although Hanoi had insisted on U.S. military withdrawal as part of a settlement, it had never indicated when that withdrawal had to take place. Now the North Vietnamese official specified that the United States could keep its military presence in South Vietnam until *after* a neutralist coalition government was formed, suggesting that it could guarantee the implementation of an agreement, at least for some period of time.[108]

After Pham Van Dong met Polish party chief Władysław Gomułka in Moscow on November 9, the Polish Foreign Ministry conveyed a similar clarification of Hanoi's negotiating terms to the British ambassador in Warsaw. The British were assured that the North Vietnamese would accept a non-Communist regime in the South, and that the U.S. withdrawal could be carried out in stages, again suggesting that the U.S. military presence could be allowed to remain for some period after a coalition government was established. Later in the month, Cambodian Foreign Minister Huot Sambath visited Hanoi and reported that Ho had told him that the North Vietnamese were willing to postpone reunification with a neutralist regime in the South for ten to fifteen years.[109]

In late December, the DRV ambassador in Paris, Mai Van Bo, met with French Foreign Office officials, who posed three questions to the North Vietnamese diplomat: would Hanoi accept and join in guarantees for a neutral and completely independent South Vietnam? Would it agree to end political and military subversion in South Vietnam? And would it accept international control with wider powers than the existing International Control Commission? Bo unequivocally answered yes to the first and third questions, while remaining evasive on the second, which would have required a public admission of having interfered in South Vietnam. In January, Bo again met with French officials to listen to their views on a negotiated settlement.[110] In February both Ho Chi Minh and Pham Van Dong asked the

French delegate-general in Hanoi to relay to Paris their request for French assistance in convening a Geneva-type conference on South Vietnam.[111]

North Vietnamese policy was still based on the hope that the United States might choose to limit its military intervention in South Vietnam. Le Duan confirmed in a February 1965 letter to party headquarters in the South that the Political Bureau still saw a possibility that the United States would not take over the war, and that Hanoi would do its best to maximize that possibility. "If we restrain ourselves in the 'special war,'" he wrote, "when the U.S. has to end the war, it can withdraw with little loss of honor compared with being bogged down in a limited war."[112]

Le Duan's plan for ending the war was based not on the expectation of defeating the Saigon regime militarily but on doing enough damage to the ARVN to discourage Washington from believing in a military solution, while organizing a political uprising in Saigon and other cities. That combination, he wrote, might lead to the creation of a left-leaning neutralist regime in Saigon, but not one that would be under the control of the Communists.[113] His focus on a neutralist solution was in part a response to the constant political turmoil and rising neutralist sentiment in Saigon and to the predilection of even some top Saigon officials—including the chief of the military junta, General Nguyen Khanh, himself—for a neutralist solution.[114] But it also reflected Le Duan's analysis of the configuration of power surrounding the struggle as of early 1965.

Le Duan observed that, unlike the situation in which the 1945 August Revolution had brought the DRV to power, the situation in the South did not yet allow a general uprising to install a Communist-led regime. At the time of the August Revolution, he recalled, the Japanese fascists had just surrendered and could not oppose the revolution, but now the Saigon regime could rely on the United States and a "rather large army," with at least the capacity to "maintain security." He noted that the Binh Gia battle in January had been called a "little Dien Bien Phu," because it had shown that the southern revolutionary forces had "the capability to destroy the main forces of the puppet army."[115] This did not mean, however, that the PLAF was on its way to rapidly destroying the ARVN. The briefing to a January 1965 cadre conference in the PLAF headquarters by the chief of staff of the PLAF command, General Le Duc Anh, indicated that the party's military line was still to fight a protracted war. The protracted war line, he explained, was based on the "balance of forces between the enemy and us." The PLAF had made great strides but was still "not strong enough to destroy the enemy completely within a short period of time."[116]

Le Duan's strategy was to build up the regular forces in the South by as much as 30,000 troops in order to improve the ratio between the PLAF and the ARVN. He promised that the dispatch of forces from the North would be "more urgent and stronger," indicating that more regular-army units would be sent to the South in the future. The objective, according to Le Duan, would be not to defeat the ARVN completely but to instigate a general uprising, combined with mutinies in some ARVN units to turn them into a "neutralist army" that might bring a neutralist regime to power. The regime that the strategy was aimed at achieving would not necessarily follow the tripartite Laotian model, but it would include some NLF representatives, some still-secret sympathizers, pro-French figures from Paris, and pro-U.S. figures—including those in the current Saigon regime—supporting a peaceful solution. That regime would call for an end to the war and for a neutralist policy, including the reconvening of the Geneva Conference to discuss guarantees of neutralism for South Vietnam. With this strategy, Le Duan wrote, "we can create circumstances that will allow the United States to accept its withdrawal" and "reduce the chances of the United States sending its expeditionary forces to carry out 'limited war' to the lowest level possible."

In late February, the United States openly admitted that U.S. planes were now carrying out bombing throughout the South Vietnamese battlefield. Continuous bombing of North Vietnam by U.S. planes began on March 3, and the first two battalions of U.S. Marines splashed ashore at Danang on March 8 and 9. A little more than two weeks later, the Central Committee met to assess these new developments. The plenum resolution noted that the United States had caused its "special war" in the South to "develop to a high degree, with some elements of 'limited war,'" but it concluded that the character of war "still has not changed fundamentally." This was consistent with the Vietnamese party leadership's definition of a "limited war" as one that involved 250,000 U.S. troops.[117] The March 1965 Central Committee resolution asserted that the "lines and directions for winning victory in the South put forward in previous resolutions have not fundamentally changed." It said the "fundamental task" of the party in the South was still to "actively limit and defeat the enemy in the high level 'special war' in the South," to take advantage of the favorable opportunity to win a victory in the South in a "relatively brief period," and to "be prepared to cope with and win a limited war . . . if the enemy creates it."

The day after the systematic bombing of the North began on March 3, Mai Van Bo had told the French Foreign Ministry that the bombing had "changed the situation," and that negotiations were "no longer a matter for consideration at this time."[118] Just two weeks after the plenum, however, Pham Van Dong made the first public North Vietnamese negotiating proposal on ending the war since Ho's interview with Burchett in 1963.

Hanoi's four-point statement presented its position on a peace settlement at a level of broad principles, rather than calling for the neutralization of South Vietnam. It called for withdrawal of U.S. troops and bases, strict respect for the military provisions of the 1954 Geneva agreements, settlement of South Vietnam's internal affairs by the South Vietnamese people themselves without foreign interference, and peaceful reunification by the Vietnamese without foreign interference. Furthermore, it called these four points the basis for the "soundest political settlement," a formula that seemed to leave open the possibility of other proposals. Finally, the statement suggested that an international conference similar to the 1954 Geneva Conference could be convened if "this basis is recognized."[119] Pham Van Dong's Four Points were probably aimed at winning over public opinion in the West and in neutral countries rather than at beginning the actual negotiating stage. Contrary to American convictions that the North Vietnamese were too confident of victory to make major concessions at the negotiation table, Hanoi's leaders were actually afraid that their bargaining position was still too weak to compel the United States to consider even a neutralist regime that the Communists themselves would not necessarily control. They believed that the PLAF would have to become much stronger before they could hope to achieve such an outcome.

For many years, the debate over the 1964–65 period revolved around whether North Vietnamese regular troops entered the South before or after the United States began its bombing of the North. This debate missed the most significant points about the party leadership's decisions in late 1964 and early 1965: first, its political-diplomatic objective was limited to neutralization of the South because of its assessment of the unfavorable balance of power; second, it was driven to send regular-army units to the South for fear that it would not even be able to achieve that limited objective without doing so; and, third, it did so in a way that reflected its strong desire to avoid provoking a major U.S. intervention in the South and an air war against the North, even if it meant reducing the damage that was likely to be inflicted on the ARVN. Hanoi was very clear about the need to make far-reaching concessions to U.S. interests and believed that it had to do much more militarily just to get a neutralization settlement that would fall far short of the ultimate goal of reunification.

POWER RELATIONS AND THE FEASIBILITY
OF NEUTRALIZATION

As Fredrik Logevall has noted, the literature on the Vietnam conflict has had little of substance to say about the possibility of a political-diplomatic compromise aimed at creating a neutral South Vietnam.[120] The lack of such discussion is not surprising, given the obvious difficulties of describing in any depth the evolution of a counterfactual agreement. Nevertheless, an examination of the problem from the perspective of the profound imbalance of power surrounding the conflict provides important clues to the question of whether such an agreement would have been durable or simply a cover for a quick takeover of the South by Hanoi.

The history of Hanoi's policy toward the South after the Geneva Accords, as this chapter has shown, was one of continuous adjustment to an unfavorable global balance of power by making a series of accommodations with its own erstwhile Communist allies, with the United States, and with the South Vietnamese regime. Because North Vietnam was a small, vulnerable, and desperately poor region of a developing country, the Vietnamese Communist leaders had to balance their responsiveness to demands from southerners for support for armed struggle against the need to avoid provoking U.S. military intervention in Vietnam. Once the insurgency arose in South Vietnam, moreover, that consideration first constrained Hanoi's willingness to escalate the war, then its readiness to send northern troops to the South, and finally the manner in which they did so.

The shadow of U.S. power over North Vietnam also compelled Hanoi to accept terms for a settlement that pushed any prospect for reunification far into the future. The North Vietnamese knew from the beginning that attempting to defeat the Saigon government in a way that would assure early reunification meant the likelihood of a U.S. bombing campaign that would destroy the fragile economic gains it had made in the post-Geneva period and consequently lead to a severe economic crisis in the North. They also knew that the result was likely to be a long, bloody war for the South that would be far more dire in its consequences for Vietnam than the war against the French.

Any temptation on the part of the North Vietnamese to use a neutralization agreement to engineer a takeover in the South would have been checked by the threat of U.S. military reprisals and reentry into South Vietnam; by Hanoi's powerful need for economic cooperation with the South; and by pressure from the USSR and the PRC, on whom the North Vietnamese would still have been dependent, not to provoke renewed U.S. military intervention.

To this list of constraints on Hanoi's policy must be added a fourth: had such a settlement been reached anytime between 1962 and spring 1965, it would have rested on a military balance that Hanoi strongly believed still favored the Saigon side. In sharp contrast to the view in Washington, Hanoi's internal assessment throughout that period was that Communist forces in the South were far from being able to achieve a favorable military balance in the foreseeable future. The VPA study mission to the South in early 1964 was pessimistic enough about the PLAF being able to actually destroy regular ARVN units that it assumed that North Vietnamese units would have to be sent to the South to have any chance of defeating Saigon—something the North Vietnamese leadership was not yet prepared to do. That pessimistic assessment of PLAF strength was reaffirmed by the Political Bureau in September 1964. In early 1965, Le Duan assumed that it would take a major buildup of regular Communist troops in the South, as well as many thousands of troops from the North, just to destroy enough of the ARVN to bring about even the establishment of a neutralist government that would not be under the control of the Communist Party.

A curious feature of the diplomatic situation, therefore, is that the North Vietnamese leadership appears to have had substantially greater respect for the ability of the Saigon regime to survive a peace settlement than did U.S. policy makers. This may be attributable in part to the extremely cautious approach adopted by most North Vietnamese leaders. Because the potential costs and risks of a full-scale war with the United States were so high, Le Duan and his allies in the Political Bureau undoubtedly tended to err on the side of extreme conservatism in assessing the likelihood of achieving a complete victory. But it also reflected the pessimism of the VPA's own officers about the capabilities of the PLAF.

The evolution of political forces and dynamics in South Vietnam under a neutralization regime could hardly have been predicted. The political collapse of the ARVN and of non-Communist civilian resistance to a Communist takeover, to which U.S. officials referred in opposing neutralization, would have been one possible outcome of such arrangements. It is far more likely, however, that an international agreement on neutralization of South Vietnam, which would have given new legitimacy to the anti-Communist segment of a neutralist government by removing the taint of dependence on the U.S. military presence, would have strengthened the position of both the military and civilian leaders of the anti-Communist faction in South Vietnam rather than weakening it.

What is far more certain is that, had the United States agreed to neutralization arrangements such as those proposed by Hanoi in actual negotiations, Hanoi would have had strong incentives for carrying it out faithfully, rather than risking everything in an effort at an early takeover of South Vietnam. Hanoi's offers to accept a long period of non-Communist rule in the South were not mere propaganda positions but accurately reflected the North Vietnamese leadership's assessment of the power balance both within the South and at the global level. Even assuming that the neutralization would have weakened rather than strengthened the legitimacy and cohesion of anti-Communist forces in South Vietnam, therefore, the international elements in Hanoi's power calculus would have remained in place as long as U.S. interest in the agreement did not wane.

5 Kennedy's Struggle with the National Security Bureaucracy

No issue in the interpretation of U.S. policy on the road to war in Vietnam has stirred as much controversy as the role of John F. Kennedy. For decades, historians portrayed Kennedy as a militant anti-Communist who believed that defeating communism in Vietnam was vital to U.S. national security.[1] In the past few years, that picture of Kennedy as Cold War zealot has begun to change, as new accounts of his policies in the Cuban Missile Crisis and toward Vietnam have shown that, whatever his faults as a leader, he was willing and able to step outside the Cold War consensus.[2]

What has been missing from the story of the Kennedy administration's Vietnam policy is the intense pressure brought to bear on Kennedy by the national security bureaucracy to use military force in Laos and Vietnam. That pressure, from both military and civilian advisers, clashed with Kennedy's own political instincts and created an unprecedented political struggle between the president and his advisers over a major issue of war and peace. Kennedy blocked the policy emanating from the bureaucracy of committing the U.S. forces necessary to win in South Vietnam, but he was thwarted by the bureaucracy in pursuing the policy he preferred.

Contrary to his contemporary image as an ideologically committed anti-Communist and swashbuckling interventionist, Kennedy's approach to Vietnam was informed primarily by his unusual independence of mind and his skepticism about most conventional Cold War thinking. As a senator he had been open-minded in his view of America's Cold War adversaries, and he had quietly adopted operational principles in foreign policy that were aimed at avoiding unnecessary conflict. During Kennedy's presidential campaign, his foreign policy line had oscillated between a sophisticated critique of Eisenhower's Cold War policy as unnecessarily provocative and attempts to portray himself as tougher on Communism than the

Eisenhower administration had been. Privately, however, he had expressed the desire to "break out of the confines of the Cold War."[3]

When it came to Vietnam, moreover, Kennedy relied more on his own personal experience than on the advice of his national security team, and not on Cold War doctrine at all. His visit to Indochina as a young congressman in 1951, which impressed on him the explosive power of Vietnamese nationalism and the enormous gulf between the official French view of the war and the political reality at the village level, was most important in this regard. His travel diary reveals that he believed that Ho Chi Minh had popular support, and that the French would certainly lose.[4] In a Senate speech on April 6, 1954, Kennedy warned that "no amount of American military assistance in Indochina can conquer an enemy which is everywhere and at the same time nowhere, 'an enemy of the people' which has the sympathy and covert support of the people."[5]

Another side of Kennedy's political style that was central to his role on Vietnam, however, was his habit of taking a harder line on Cold War issues in public than he did in private. As a young politician, he had learned that hard-line anti-Communist stances were more popular than evenhandedness. He had even refused to condemn Senator Joe McCarthy (R-Wisc.) after the rest of the Senate was censuring him, despite the fact that he knew McCarthy was wrong, because he believed that McCarthy remained popular in Massachusetts. Even more important, he concluded from his campaign for the presidency that presenting a carefully reasoned approach to Cold War issues simply invited charges of weakness and appeasement by his opponents and important sections of the media.[6] Just after entering the White House, he told his national security team, "The American people are very bellicose in their attitudes and objectives in respect to Russia and Cuba, but at the same time, they very strongly do not want to go to war."[7] This perception of the politics of foreign policy led him to downplay or even hide his true beliefs in favor of Cold War rhetoric for political protection. For example, he warned Chester Bowles, who was preparing for his confirmation hearings on his appointment as undersecretary of state, to "play down the differences between my ideas about China and the generally accepted wisdom generated by the partisans of Chiang Kai-shek."[8]

When Kennedy encountered a national security bureaucracy that seemed bent on military intervention in Southeast Asia, therefore, his political instinct was to avoid any move that might be used by enemies inside or outside the administration to accuse him of being soft on communism. He never made a formal decision against military intervention in either Laos or Vietnam. Nor did he ever go on record at any of those meetings to the effect that he would abandon the anti-Communist U.S. client regime in Laos. Instead, he spoke on the record only of conditions for agreeing to military intervention that were in fact so stringent as to make it impossible.[9] And in the end, Kennedy concealed his real policy toward Vietnam not only from the public but from most of his own national security bureaucracy.

RESISTANCE AND ACCOMMODATION, 1961

Kennedy's struggle with his national security advisers began with fundamental differences over Laos. By March 1961, Kennedy had already made up his mind that military intervention was a disastrous idea, and although he ruled out "visible humiliation" in Laos, he was determined to try to negotiate the neutralization of the country, which meant putting Prince Souvanna Phouma back in power.[10] After four years of determined efforts by the State Department and the CIA to oust him from power, Souvanna had been driven from Vientiane in December 1960 by the forces of General Phoumi Nosavan, supported by the CIA. This prompted an airlift of supplies by the USSR to Souvanna's army, which then allied itself with the Pathet Lao against Phoumi.[11]

At the first indication of Kennedy's willingness to support the neutralization of Laos, both Secretary of State Dean Rusk and National Security Adviser McGeorge Bundy expressed strong opposition to Souvanna's return to power, warning that the neutralization of Laos could prove disastrous for South Vietnam.[12] On April 29, Kennedy's national security advisers, alarmed about Pathet Lao military gains, were in nearly complete agreement among themselves that the United States should intervene with combat troops in Laos if no cease-fire between the Pathet Lao and the forces of General Phoumi was quickly forthcoming. In the NSC meeting that followed, White House adviser Walt W. Rostow and Deputy Undersecretary of State U. Alexis Johnson advocated the occupation of the Mekong Valley of Laos by U.S. troops. On May 2, Secretary of Defense Robert S. McNamara and his deputy, Roswell Gilpatric, similarly recommended the deployment of U.S. forces to Laos if the Pathet Lao did not agree to a cease-fire after a time limit had elapsed. The same position was taken in a paper drafted jointly by the State and Defense Departments at Kennedy's request.[13]

The possibility of a military response by the PRC to the deployment of U.S. troops in Laos had been noted by the CIA in February. However, that possibility was not taken very seriously by Kennedy's advisers.[14] As McGeorge Bundy's assistant Robert W. Komer observed in April 1961, "During the last decade the ChiComs . . . essentially lacked the resources (without Soviet support) to do more than make nasty gestures toward us."[15] By 1960, moreover, Mao's disastrous "Great Leap Forward" had caused a precipitous fall in national income that was almost unprecedented in history. In the first days of the administration, Komer, Rostow, and Bundy discussing organizing a briefing for Kennedy on how China's serious economic difficulties had reduced its military strength. Komer noted that such problems would make "Chicom intervention in Southeast Asia" much less likely "unless we push them very far." He concluded that the weakness of the PRC and the "problematic nature of Soviet support" both argued for "a cautious Communist approach in Southeast Asia."[16]

Eisenhower's outgoing secretaries of state and defense had assured the new administration, moreover, that the Communists were not prepared to risk a major war in Southeast Asia, even though they would "continue to make trouble right up to that point." McNamara and Gilpatric wrote that the Soviet Union would probably act to bring about a cease-fire in Laos, because it "would not wish to see an uncontrollable situation develop." Komer called Bundy's attention to a paper by a Soviet specialist in the administration concluding that Moscow was "highly reluctant to get involved in even local direct military confrontations."[17]

Most of Kennedy's advisers did not believe the Chinese could fight effectively in Laos in any case. The Laos Task Force, which included Deputy National Security Adviser Walt W. Rostow, Undersecretary of State U. Alexis Johnson, and Assistant Secretary of Defense for International Security Affairs Paul Nitze, concluded that the formidable logistical problems faced by the Chinese and North Vietnamese would severely limit the number of troops they would be capable of supporting in Laos. Johnson later recalled his conviction, which he believed was shared by Rusk, that if the United States moved to deploy forces in Laos, it would probably not be necessary to use them in combat, because the Communists would back down rather than fight.[18]

Top Pentagon officials also believed that the Chinese and North Vietnamese were unlikely to intervene in Laos, given U.S. military dominance. The memorandum co-signed by McNamara and Gilpatric said, "[T]he U.S. has overall military superiority now against which all courses of action must ultimately be weighed. Our strengths impose greater risks on the Communist Bloc than theirs do on us." Even if Chinese or North Vietnamese troops intervened, they believed, the United States would prevail at any level of escalation. "If North Viet-Nam attacks, we must strike North Viet-Nam," the memorandum said. "If Chinese volunteers intervene, we will have to go after South China."[19]

The configuration of power was thus a powerful inducement for the national security bureaucracy to recommend sending combat troops into Laos. Kennedy, on the other hand, questioned the fundamental wisdom of introducing troops into a country bordering on China. Like Eisenhower and Dulles in 1954, he justified his position by emphasizing the likelihood of a land war with China if U.S. troops were sent to Laos. On April 6, Kennedy gave a background briefing on Laos in which he mentioned the danger of an "intervention by the Viet Minh and possibly by Red China." Meeting with congressional leaders on April 27, Kennedy again evoked the specter of overwhelming numbers of Communist troops to indicate his doubts about the wisdom of intervening. And in a conversation with Richard Nixon a few days later, Kennedy spoke of fighting "millions of Chinese troops in the jungle."[20] Although he clearly implied that he was not prepared to send troops, however, Kennedy avoided making an explicit decision on the issue when he met with his advisers on May 2.[21]

Less than two weeks after the Geneva co-chairs, Britain and the Soviet Union, agreed on April 24 for the reconvening of the Geneva Conference to negotiate a settlement in Laos, the Pentagon began to press for putting U.S. troops into South Vietnam as well. At a meeting of the newly created Vietnam Task Force, Gilpatric expressed the fear that such a conference "could result in a freeze of forces into and out of the area" and indicated that the DOD wanted to get troops into South Vietnam before the May 12 start of the conference.[22] The May 6 draft of the Vietnam Task Force report announced a study of various options for U.S. troop deployment to South Vietnam as "preparation for possible commitment of U.S. forces to Vietnam, which might result from an NSC decision following discussions between Vice-President Johnson and President Diem." The task force report also called for a bilateral U.S.–South Vietnamese military alliance, "which might include stationing of U.S. forces on Vietnamese soil."[23]

These pressures for an early deployment of U.S. troops to South Vietnam came only days after Kennedy had refused to commit airpower to an invasion of Cuba and then had refused to send troops to Laos against the virtually unanimous recommendation of his military advisers. The JCS already held Kennedy personally responsible for the failure of the Bay of Pigs operation, creating what Maxwell Taylor, investigating the Bay of Pigs fiasco for Kennedy in late April, called a "crisis" in relations between the Kennedy and the JCS.[24] Kennedy carefully avoided a direct confrontation with his national security team over the issue of troop deployments to South Vietnam at an NSC meeting on May 11. He approved a study of troop deployment "in the case of a possible commitment of U.S. forces to

Vietnam," but added that it should examine the "diplomatic setting within which this action might be taken." As would later become clear, this obscure formula was Kennedy's way of making a troop commitment conditional on the support of Britain and France. Kennedy authorized negotiation of a "new bilateral arrangement" with Diem in principle, but he also insisted that no commitment could be made without his prior approval.[25]

The JCS tried to use Diem to corner Kennedy on the troop deployment issue. On May 10, the JCS responded to a request from Gilpatric for their views on the troop deployment issue by recommending that Diem be "encouraged" to request "immediate deployment of appropriate U.S. forces to South Vietnam," citing the new threat in Laos. During a meeting between Vice President Johnson and Diem, the chief of the U.S. Military Assistance Advisory Group, General Lionel McGarr, asked Diem if he would accept U.S. combat troops "for direct training purposes," to which Diem assented.[26] When the official record of the presidential decision appeared on May 20, however, Kennedy had changed the troop deployment study into a study of "the diplomatic setting within which a possible commitment of U.S. forces to Viet-Nam might be undertaken"—the same phrase he had used ten days earlier to pose the condition that the British and French had to be on board. Three days later, the DOD study of combat deployment reappeared in a message from the State Department to the U.S. embassy in Saigon, reflecting renewed pressure from the Pentagon. [27]

Having artfully resisted the efforts of his advisers to intervene militarily in both Laos and South Vietnam, Kennedy initiated a year-long effort to negotiate a tripartite neutralist regime in Laos. In an extraordinary demonstration of presidential diplomacy, he named Averell Harriman his personal envoy to the talks and proceeded to carry out what was essentially an end run around the State Department's Far Eastern Bureau. That office was still run by hard-line holdovers from the Eisenhower administration who remained adamantly opposed to his neutralization policy. Kennedy intervened repeatedly in the negotiations by calling Harriman in Geneva to make sure that they stayed on track. After his meeting with Khrushchev, in which both leaders agreed that Laos should be neutralized, Kennedy told Harriman in a phone conversation, "Did you understand? I want a negotiated settlement in Laos. I don't want to put troops in."[28]

The State Department and the JCS did their best to obstruct the negotiation of a neutralist regime in Laos. Rusk went along with the hard-liners in the Far Eastern Bureau, instructing Harriman to pressure Souvanna to form a government only with anti-Communist figures approved by the United States, and if that failed, to push for a tripartite territorial division of the country. In late June, Rusk pressed Kennedy to reject Souvanna as the head of the Laotian government, insisting that a neutralist regime would be "difficult, if not impossible to establish." The hard-liners called for preparations to implement a JCS contingency plan called "SEATO Plan 5," under which U.S. forces would occupy lowland Laos, if necessary, to support the more ambitious negotiating aims they were advocating.

When Phoumi visited Washington at the end of June, Kennedy strongly hinted at his intention to negotiate a neutralist regime built around Souvanna. "We cannot get everything we want in Laos," he told Phoumi. "[W]e must therefore seek the best arrangement we can obtain." But Rusk encouraged Phoumi to continue to reject a neutralist coalition under Souvanna, and the JCS promised to increase the size of his army, encouraging him to resume the offensive once the rainy season ended in September. When Phoumi returned to Laos, he made it clear he would prolong the three-way talks and would start fighting with a stronger army in September. At an interagency meeting in late July, the national security bureaucracy was in agreement that Phoumi should be urged to continue to take an uncompromising position in negotiations with Souvanna.[29]

After it became clear to them that Kennedy and Harriman were indeed supporting Souvanna, State Department hard-liners viewed the policy as selling out an anti-Communist ally to appease the USSR. Johnson recalled later that he had led a group of officials in the State Department who were "expressing great concern" over Harriman's negotiating stance and calling for a "somewhat stronger stand" on Souvanna and his followers. In fact, Johnson knew very well that the policy emanated from the White House, and he took the group's complaint directly to Kennedy. To Johnson's dismay, however, Kennedy invited him to participate in a three-way conversation with Harriman, in which Kennedy approved Harriman's recommendations for accepting Souvanna's position in the negotiations. Johnson concluded that Kennedy's policy was the result of a secret deal on Laos that he had reached with Khrushchev in Vienna.[30]

Explaining the bitterness in the Far Eastern Bureau over Kennedy's policy in Laos, Deputy Assistant Secretary of State John Steeves recalled that Phoumi "was a bastard, but he was our bastard, and that was the trouble." He and others on Harriman's staff in Geneva referred caustically to that policy as "Cave with Ave," and Steeves remarked at one point that the next cable from Harriman's mission "would probably be signed by Pushkin"—a reference to the head of the Soviet delegation in Geneva, Georgi Pushkin. Both State Department officials and the JCS were furious at Kennedy for essentially ignoring the views of the permanent bureaucracy. As one of the military chiefs later complained, Kennedy had "operated out of his shirt pocket" on Laos, revealing his policy only to certain people. Steeves bitterly resented what he regarded as Kennedy's reaching "a kind of private agreement" with Harriman on Laotian neutralization "without sanctifying it in a proper state paper."[31]

Meanwhile, General Maxwell Taylor, who became Kennedy's personal military representative in June, joined with Johnson and Rostow in trying to turn Kennedy away from negotiations toward the use of force in Southeast Asia. Their working assumption, according to Rostow, was that "a break in the cease-fire would present us with a nice clean-cut case for intervention." On July 18, the three discussed both "aggressive limited military action against North Viet-Nam" and attacking and occupying the Laotian panhandle, although they recognized that neither would be possible as long as the Laotian negotiations were under way.[32] Working with Steeves, who had been appointed to head the newly formed Southeast Asian Task Force, they developed a strategy aimed at forcing Kennedy's hand.

At a meeting at the White House on July 28, Johnson presented a new plan to the president on behalf of Rusk, Assistant Secretary for East Asia Walter McConaughy, Steeves, Taylor, and Rostow. It proposed acquiescence to Phoumi's demand for the defense and interior positions, which they knew was unacceptable to Souvanna, and an inflexible demand for an intrusive International Control Commission, which they thought would be unacceptable to the USSR. If U.S. demands were not met, and the negotiations broke down, Johnson said, "we should then go, not for a re-establishment of the status quo, but for a strong new position . . . in Southern Laos." The plan called for a Vietnamese-Thai-Laotian "mop-up" operation in Southern Laos, with U.S. Special Forces in the lead, if the fighting resumed.[33]

Kennedy parried the Rostow–Taylor–State Department proposal by questioning the feasibility of the plans for military intervention and by insisting that the United States not "get ourselves badly separated from the British" in the negotiations—which the proposal would clearly have done. When Johnson asked him to indicate at least a willingness to "decide to intervene if the situation seemed to him to require it," Kennedy refused to give a direct answer.[34] As he had from the beginning, Kennedy carefully sidestepped any direct confrontation over intervention. Instead, he maintained a stance of deliberate ambiguity about whether he might intervene under some circumstances. Meanwhile, however, he was countering the pressures from the bureaucracy for using U.S. troops by bringing General Douglas MacArthur to Washington to meet with congressional leaders.

Kennedy knew that the highly respected war hero would argue strongly against sending American troops to Southeast Asia on the grounds that they would be overwhelmed by larger numbers of Chinese troops.[35]

Nevertheless, the Taylor-Rostow-Johnson group persisted. On September 23, Taylor sent a memo to Kennedy arguing that U.S. troops could intervene effectively in southern Laos. He insisted that North Vietnam would be unable to reinforce its troops in southern Laos with major units because of logistical problems and noted that Hanoi was "highly vulnerable" to air attacks. As for the PRC, Taylor said that its reinforcement capabilities in the area were so limited that "the possibility of a Chinese Communist intervention on the ground tends to lose significance." The threat of Chinese air attacks on targets in Southeast Asia could be kept to "manageable proportions" by U.S. air capabilities in East Asia, reinforced by U.S. carrier-based aircraft. "We are not talking about a war which might approach in size the Korean operation," Taylor assured the president.[36]

The same group also agitated for the use of U.S. combat forces in South Vietnam as well. At an NSC meeting in October, Kennedy was presented with two new troop deployment plans. A JCS plan estimated that 40,000 U.S. troops would be needed to defeat the Viet Cong and another 128,000 to deal with a possible North Vietnamese and Chinese intervention. A second intervention plan for South Vietnam presented to Kennedy was an effort to get him to accept a change in the rule of unanimity among member-nations required to approve a SEATO military action. Kennedy would only agree, however, to sending an air force squadron to South Vietnam on a training mission.[37]

As always, while rejecting the recommendations of his advisers for military intervention in Southeast Asia, Kennedy handled them with kid gloves to avoid overt disaffection with his policy. He agreed to send Taylor and Rostow to South Vietnam to make recommendations but made it clear in his instructions to Taylor that he did not want any recommendations for use of U.S. combat forces. Kennedy said Taylor should "bear in mind that the initial responsibility for the effective maintenance of the independence of South Vietnam rests with the people and government of that country," and that his evaluation recommendations should be formulated "with this fact in mind."[38]

Despite Kennedy's admonition, the Taylor-Rostow mission's recommendations, cabled to Kennedy on November 1, included the introduction of a U.S. military task force of about 8,000 men into South Vietnam. The task force would not take on the insurgents directly but would have the mission of "raising national morale and showing to Southeast Asia the seriousness of the U.S. intent to resist a Communist takeover," as well as providing an "emergency reserve." Taylor admitted that it might lead to further deployments but minimized the risk of "backing into a major Asian war by way of SVN." North Vietnam's vulnerability to conventional bombing could be used to put pressure on Hanoi to "lay off SVN," he argued, and the North Vietnamese and Chinese faced "severe logistical difficulties which we share but by no means to the same degree." Because of Hanoi's fear of U.S. retaliatory attacks, the insurgents could not "safely engage their forces against the GVN regulars," nor could North Vietnam "engage its division strength." Taylor cited starvation in China as evidence that its leaders would be discouraged from using military force beyond its borders for many years to come. For these reasons, Taylor wrote, he had concluded that introducing the task force "offers definitely more advantage than it creates risks and difficulties."[39]

The overwhelming U.S. power advantage over the Communist states was thus central to the rationale for the troop deployment recommendation. Taylor's analysis was further buttressed, moreover, by the intelligence estimates of that period. A special CIA estimate in September had for the first time raised the possibility of an economic collapse on the Chinese mainland. Another CIA estimate had concluded that neither the Chinese nor the North Vietnamese would respond to such a deployment by sending regular units to fight SEATO forces, and that both would want to avoid U.S. forces. All three Communist states, it noted, "would almost certainly be concerned over the increased risks for each of them of broadened hostilities involving US forces." The CIA had also concluded that Hanoi wanted to retain a strong Soviet presence to avoid being completely dominated by the PRC. And the CIA, relying on years of experience on the issue, believed that the USSR still exercised "considerable restraint" on any decision by Hanoi that would risk "the broadening of hostilities and raise the issue of USSR or US participation."[40]

The knowledge that the Taylor-Rostow recommendations would be considered at a meeting with the president on Vietnam policy galvanized agreement among Kennedy's national security advisers on the need for a military commitment to defeat the Communist insurgency and for threatening to attack North Vietnam. The JCS, under Chairman General Lyman Lemnitzer, now became more active in advocating the use of force in Vietnam. In a meeting with McNamara, who had not been personally involved in Vietnam policy up to then, the JCS argued that the 8,000 troops recommended by Taylor and Rostow probably wouldn't be enough to save South Vietnam. Furthermore, they called for a warning to Hanoi that the

United States would hit North Vietnam unless it halted its support for the Viet Cong.[41]

McNamara quickly adopted the JCS position, demonstrating a tendency to placate the country's military leadership on Vietnam. Two days after that meeting, he sent a memorandum to Kennedy on behalf of himself, Gilpatric, and the JCS arguing that the chances were "probably sharply against" preventing the fall of South Vietnam without "the introduction of U.S. forces on a substantial scale." The memorandum insisted that the United States could convince "the other side" that "we mean business" only if an initial force deployment were combined with a "clear commitment" to preventing the fall of South Vietnam and a warning to Hanoi that continued support of the Viet Cong would "lead to punitive retaliation against North Vietnam." It also echoed Taylor's key argument that, even in the worst case, Communist logistical difficulties would reduce the maximum number of U.S. troops required to six divisions, or about 205,000 men.[42]

Just before the November 11 NSC meeting on the issue, Rusk and McNamara sent a joint memo that reflected their awareness that Kennedy was not ready to send troops. They again recommended a commitment to prevailing in South Vietnam with U.S. forces if necessary and urged Kennedy to warn Moscow that the United States was determined to "prevent the fall of South Viet-Nam to Communism by whatever means is necessary." But instead of the Taylor recommendation of an 8,000-man task force, they called for the preparation by DOD of plans for deployment of U.S. forces for various purposes.[43] At the November 11 meeting, both McNamara and Lemnitzer repeated that "further action" beyond the Taylor-Rostow recommendation would be required.[44]

Taylor told his colleagues that Kennedy had revealed to him that he was "instinctively against introduction of U.S. forces." At the NSC meeting on November 11, however, Kennedy was less candid. He called the deployment of U.S. troops "a last resort" and insisted that they be SEATO forces.[45] This invocation of SEATO must be understood in light of the fact that the SEATO Council had adopted at its first meeting in 1955 the rule that SEATO itself could act in response to armed aggression only by unanimous vote. Kennedy's advisers had chafed at the SEATO unanimity rule, which prevented the United States from using SEATO cover, given British and French opposition to combat intervention by the organization. The Interagency Task Force on Laos, Rostow, McNamara, William Bundy, and the JCS had all recommended during 1961 that the United States organize its own intervention force in Laos independent of a SEATO decision and that it nevertheless be billed as a SEATO force. But Kennedy had never responded to such proposals. An earlier draft of the memorandum that McNamara and Rusk sent to the president on November 9 had urged once again that the U.S. commitment of troops to South Vietnam not be "contingent upon SEATO agreement thereto."[46] In line with his broad strategy for dealing with the national security bureaucracy, Kennedy's invocation of the requirement for a SEATO imprimatur on U.S. intervention was clearly another ploy to fend off pressures for armed intervention.

At the November 15 NSC meeting, Kennedy went much farther in expressing fundamental misgivings about the nature of the conflict itself than at any other time in his presidency. Whereas Korea had been a clear-cut case of aggression, Kennedy said, the South Vietnamese case was "more obscure and less flagrant." He also compared the "obscurity" of the issue in the Vietnamese conflict with the "clarity" of the issue in Berlin. Kennedy also challenged his advisers' reliance on the overwhelming U.S. superiority in power. "[F]irmness in Vietnam in the manner and form of that in Berlin," Rusk argued, "might achieve desired results in Vietnam without resort to combat." McNamara similarly contended that U.S. power could be successfully "applied against sources of Viet Cong power including those in North Vietnam." But Kennedy insisted that Vietnam could not be approached in terms of conventional power relations. In a rhetorical echo of his April 1954 Senate speech, he referred to actions by "guerrillas, sometimes in a phantom-like fashion" and again described it as "more a political issue," which was of a "different magnitude" and "less defined" than Korea.[47] Kennedy was rejecting the idea that the strategic importance of South Vietnam could be likened to that of Cold War issues on which the United States had been willing to go to war, as well as the assumption that U.S. military dominance over the Communist bloc would assure success in Vietnam.

Kennedy approved all the other recommendations in the McNamara-Rusk memo regarding a large increase in the number of military advisers, as well as helicopters and fixed-wing aircraft to be flown by U.S. pilots in a training role. Those recommendations also included the establishment of a new military command in Saigon, the Military Assistance Command Vietnam (MACV), aimed at giving U.S. military personnel increased influence over how the war would be fought. It was a very serious step toward war. But Kennedy was not committing himself to doing whatever was necessary to save South Vietnam. He told John McCloy the week before the NSC meeting that he could approve the new U.S. role in the counterinsurgency war "without making an irretrievable commitment."[48]

Kennedy's approval of a very large U.S. counterinsurgency role in South Vietnam reflected at least in part his need to maintain a minimum of political unity in his own administration. He believed that open criticism of his Vietnam policy by elements of the national security bureaucracy—if he rejected its recommendation—was a real possibility. Apart from the bad blood that already existed between Kennedy and the JCS as a result of the Bay of Pigs fiasco, he knew that most national security officials were opposed to his effort to negotiate a neutralization agreement in Laos. Kennedy revealed to his close friend Paul Fay in early 1962 that he was afraid that some military leaders had begun criticizing him privately after the Bay of Pigs, and that, if a second "Bay of Pigs" occurred, they would regard him as unfit to be president.[49] Kennedy had reason to believe that the JCS would regard a rejection of the counterinsurgency war in South Vietnam as another "Bay of Pigs."

After the second NSC meeting, McGeorge Bundy reminded Kennedy that the recommendation for a military commitment to South Vietnam that he had rejected represented the unanimous advice of his top advisers and the heads of the special mission he had sent to Vietnam. Relying heavily on the obvious U.S. power advantage, Bundy wrote that the odds were "almost even that the commitment would not have to be carried out" if he made that decision, and certainly would not lead to escalation, "since the Communists do not want this kind of test." Bundy suggested that Kennedy was merely postponing an unpleasant decision that he would ultimately have to make. "I am troubled by your most natural desire to act on other items now without taking the troop decision," he wrote. Bundy then suggested that Kennedy change the cable going out to Ambassador Frederick E. Nolting Jr. in Saigon to say that U.S. combat troops would be sent to South Vietnam "when and if the U.S. military recommend it on persuasive military grounds."[50] Bundy was clearly speaking for Kennedy's whole national security team in expressing consternation over this rejection of their unanimous advice on the use of force in Vietnam.

THE HIDDEN STRUGGLE OVER PEACE DIPLOMACY

The one thing on which past accounts of Kennedy's Vietnam policy have agreed is that Kennedy rejected the idea of any negotiated settlement on Vietnam.[51] The evidence now shows, however, that Kennedy maneuvered to ensure that he would have someone in the lead position in the bureaucracy on Vietnam policy who could be expected to pursue a diplomatic option on Vietnam, and that he tried to open secret diplomatic channels with North Vietnam or China. And when those efforts were blocked, he switched policy makers yet again to maintain the option of negotiating the neutralization of South Vietnam.

Kennedy showed his displeasure with the way the bureaucracy had relentlessly pushed the option of military intervention leading up to the November decision by making significant personnel changes. On November 15, a memo from Bundy to the president indicated that Kennedy had already made up his mind that he wanted to get rid of Assistant Secretary of State for East Asia Walter McConaughy, who had been an ally of the hawks, and replace him with Averell Harriman.[52] Within days, Harriman had become the primary policy maker on Vietnam, and Rostow and Johnson, the two most active second-level advocates of military intervention, were shunted off to jobs where they would no longer be involved in the formulation of policy on Vietnam. Johnson was replaced as undersecretary for political affairs by George McGhee, who was known to oppose sending combat troops.[53]

Kennedy thought he had reason to trust Averell Harriman to pursue such diplomatic contacts. Harriman not only had carried out his orders to negotiate a neutralization of Laos but had written a draft proposal for negotiations on Vietnam just before the November NSC meeting that would have built on the Laotian agreement. The Harriman proposal would have sought Pushkin's support for a meeting of a subset of the members of 1954 Geneva Conference in order to "see how compliance can be secured and how they can be strengthened to meet today's needs."[54] Hanoi would have been required to accept "for the time being . . . the division of Viet-Nam with non-interference of any kind by one side in the other's affairs," the mutual renunciation of force by both regimes, and a "strengthened and modernized" international control commission or some other mechanism for enforcement of these provisions. In return, Hanoi would have been allowed to trade with the South. But Harriman also added, "We should not preclude a restudy of the possibility of elections as a matter of strategy." The United States, he suggested, "might be prepared to adhere to the Accords as revised." And as peace stabilized, Harriman wrote, the United States would reduce U.S. military aid and advice.[55] Kennedy's memo to Rusk and McNamara asked them to "consider" the Harriman plan and even raised the possibility that Harriman might initiate discussions with Pushkin as soon as he returned to Geneva.[56]

Instead of helping Kennedy draw Moscow into a diplomatic track on Vietnam, however, Harriman lost no time in communicating to Pushkin in Geneva that the administration was not interested in negotiations. In a series of private one-on-one meetings with Pushkin between November and January, he raised the subject of South Vietnam. But in sharp contrast to what he had proposed to Kennedy, he took a line that was so unyielding as to preclude any bargaining with Hanoi. In a conversation on November 20, Pushkin suggested that the "only real solution lay in elections to achieve national unity," to which Harriman retorted that it would be "impossible to conduct valid elections in North Vietnam," so the 1954 accords "could not be implemented."[57]

Harriman thus reversed his earlier position that the United States should remain open to a return to the original and complete Geneva Accords. Harriman must have known that Kennedy would not approve his diplomatic line with Pushkin, because he did not inform Kennedy or the State Department about the conversation with Pushkin. He reported a two-hour conversation with Pushkin on November 20 in a message to the State Department and in his "weekly evaluation" of the talks, but omitted any mention of a discussion on South Vietnam.[58]

In further meetings with Pushkin in December and January, Harriman repeatedly ruled out any possibility of implementation of the political provisions of the 1954 agreement or any other political compromise in the South. Pushkin asked whether Washington would consider other solutions, such as "democratization (not communization) of the Diem regime, . . . neutralization of the South, or reunification via elections." But Harriman would only discuss the issue of all-Vietnam elections, which he rejected out of hand, on the grounds that the Geneva Accords posed "certain conditions for free elections which did not now exist in view of Northern behavior." He insisted that elections were "a matter for the distant future."[59]

Harriman's instant transformation from advocate to determined foe of negotiations on Vietnam is not difficult to explain. He had supported such negotiations in November only as a temporary tactic to save the Laotian neutralization talks, in which his own prestige had become invested. In a meeting of Kennedy's principal advisers on November 9, Harriman had urged a negotiating conference of Geneva Conference member states, to be organized with Soviet concurrence, *before* U.S. troops were introduced into South Vietnam. He argued at that meeting that putting U.S. forces into Vietnam before negotiations would "blow open" the Laotian negotiations.[60] That argument and Harriman's November 11 proposal for Vietnam negotiations were both explicitly based on the assumption that Kennedy would approve the early dispatch of some combat troops to South Vietnam, as was being urged by his entire national security team, and that it would happen quickly unless negotiations could be initiated first.[61] After Kennedy rejected the troop deployment to Vietnam, and there was no threat to completing the neutralization agreement in Laos, Harriman immediately reverted to the view of the issue commonly held by the national security bureaucracy.

Meanwhile, the resistance of the national security bureaucracy to Kennedy's policy of negotiating a compromise political settlement in Laos continued. The State Department, the JCS, and the CIA all encouraged General Phoumi to take the offensive against the Pathet Lao in October and November, in violation of the cease-fire, insisting that it was unacceptable to abandon their Laotian military client. In early January, the JCS began pushing openly for the United States to "exploit the improving military balance" in Laos by backing an offensive by Phoumi's forces. CIA Director John McCone had told Kennedy, moreover, that the CIA considered a government dominated by Souvanna's men as "an open road for North Vietnam to South Vietnam."[62] Despite this JCS-CIA resistance to his policy, Kennedy strongly implied at a meeting on January 6, 1962, that he wanted Harriman to go ahead with the negotiation on Souvanna's terms. But he was careful not to put any statement on the record that might be used by the military or other opponents of his policy in the bureaucracy to accuse him of having "sold out" an anti-Communist ally.[63]

Nevertheless, Kennedy quietly tried to open a diplomatic alternative to war on Vietnam, as he had done on Laos. In the first half of 1962, he approved probes of Chinese or North Vietnamese willingness to negotiate on four separate occasions. The first was an initiative proposed by Chester Bowles in February 1962 to discuss the feasibility of a regional neutralization agreement with Premier U Nu of neutral Burma, who enjoyed good relations with the Chinese leaders. Bowles would explore with the Burmese leader whether the PRC would be willing to give formal guarantees of support for peaceful change in Southeast Asia in exchange for long-term credits for the import of grain to cover its food deficit. According to Bowles, Kennedy agreed to his exploring such a deal as "ideas he had discussed in general terms" with the president, although not as a formally approved policy. The initiative had to be canceled, but only because the U Nu government was overthrown unexpectedly on the eve of Bowles's departure from Delhi for Rangoon.[64]

In March 1962, North Vietnam indicated for the first time that it was interested in peace negotiations on South Vietnam. The British sent a note to Washington suggesting that the interest of the North Vietnamese in reconvening the Geneva Conference on South Vietnam might reflect increased concern about the risk of "full-scale intervention by the United States if they enlarge their own activities" and doubt that they could get "all they want by means of armed subversion."[65] Responding to the same diplomatic signals, John Kenneth Galbraith, the U.S. ambassador to India, a longtime friend of Kennedy's, proposed in a letter to him on April 4, 1962, that the United States put out specific peace feelers to the North Vietnamese through both Moscow and New Delhi. Galbraith suggested offering a "phased American withdrawal" in return for Hanoi's willingness to "call off the Viet Cong activity." Galbraith also suggested that the United States offer some North-South trade and "general and non-specific agreement to talk about reunification after some period of tranquility" as an inducement for Hanoi to come to terms. Galbraith proposed that the United States use the occasion of a forthcoming International Control Commission (ICC) report on violations of the Geneva Accords by both Vietnams to demand "steps to re-establish compliance with the Geneva accords," which could "eventually" include a reconvening of the Geneva Conference. As a starting point, the United States would agree to a standstill on introduction of men and matériel in return for a suspension of Viet Cong activity.[66]

Kennedy was especially interested in the Indian element of Galbraith's proposal. The day after he received the proposal, Kennedy discussed it with Harriman. Harriman expressed opposition to the idea of an international conference and to any "neutral solution" to the Vietnam conflict. He suggested that an approach to Hanoi through India "might be worthwhile," but only if the ICC report was strong enough, and he wanted to wait until the ICC report before deciding on an initiative. Kennedy agreed that the initiative should await the report, but he insisted that Harriman should send instructions to Galbraith on an Indian approach to Hanoi "with a view to exploring the possibility of getting them to withdraw from Viet-Nam in conjunction with us." Furthermore, he wanted to see the instructions personally before they went out. Kennedy concluded the meeting by declaring that he wanted to "be prepared to seize upon any favorable moment to reduce our involvement, recognizing that the moment might be some time away."[67]

Michael Forrestal, the NSC staff specialist on Southeast Asia, who also happened to be a protégé of Harriman's, wrote a memo to Kennedy on April 17 suggesting that Harriman brief him on "our reaction to the pressures from various sources (principally Sihanouk) for an international conference on Vietnam" and explaining that Harriman was opposed to such a conference "at this time."[68] Kennedy responded, however, by ordering Harriman to act on the instructions to Galbraith on the Indian initiative without further delay. Someone in the White House communicated

Kennedy's order to Harriman that same day. The message said, "The President wants to have instructions sent to Ambassador Galbraith to talk to [Indian Foreign Secretary M. J.] Desai telling him that if Hanoi takes steps to reduce guerrilla activity, we would correspond [sic] accordingly." If Hanoi were to "stop the activity entirely," it continued, "we would withdraw to a normal basis." The message ended by reminding Harriman, "The President will want to see the message before it is despatched [sic]."[69]

By offering a proposal for mutual de-escalation, Kennedy was adding a further diplomatic nuance, which suggested greater flexibility, to the original Galbraith proposal. Harriman's displeasure at Kennedy's new instructions is clear from the fact that he struck the language on de-escalation from the message with a heavy pencil line.[70] Harriman immediately dictated instructions for Deputy Assistant Secretary for Southeast Asia Edward Rice about drafting a telegram to Galbraith. But those instructions were very different from what Kennedy had ordered. Harriman wrote, "The President wants [Galbraith] to explore with Desai whether he thinks it would be a good idea to take up with Hanoi the question of stopping the guerrilla activity and indicating the President's position as he has spoken of it." Harriman then indicated the line he wanted Rice to take in the draft: "[I]f they behave themselves we won't escalate, but if they do not it will be dangerous, etc."[71]

Harriman thus changed the purpose of the instructions from authorizing the use of Desai as an intermediary to explore mutual de-escalation with Hanoi to exploring with the Indians *whether* to take up the issue with Hanoi. Even more subversive of Kennedy's purpose, he also changed the mutual de-escalation approach into a threat of U.S. escalation of the war if the North Vietnamese refused to accept U.S. terms. Harriman was evidently concerned that the offer of mutual de-escalation would lead to talks on a broader framework for a settlement, including the inducements of trade relations and eventual discussions of all-Vietnam elections that Galbraith (and Harriman himself) had suggested. His instructions to Rice represented an outright sabotage of Kennedy's effort to establish a diplomatic track on Vietnam.

Rice apparently understood that Harriman had not accurately reflected Kennedy's instructions, perhaps because he spoke directly with Forrestal. He drafted instructions to Galbraith that ignored Harriman's orders. The draft began, "The President wants you to explore with Desai the feasibility and desirability of serving as channel for discreetly communicating to responsible leadership North Vietnamese regime President's position as he indicated it to you." It went on to suggest that the United States would reciprocate de-escalation by the North Vietnamese with a "phasing back to normal" of U.S "support activities."[72]

Harriman was determined to prevent any such approach from going forward. After crossing out Rice's sentence, Harriman simply killed the telegram altogether. No instructions to Galbraith were ever sent in response to Kennedy's reminder.[73] The following week, Harriman sent cables to Galbraith and the U.S. ambassadors in Saigon, Paris, and Phnom Penh declaring: "[T]he U.S. is not rpt not in favor of an international conference on Viet Nam at this time. Believe therefore we should seek to reduce all incipient pressures behind conference."[74]

Kennedy's interest in the diplomatic option remained undiminished. In response to a query from Kennedy about how a speech by Undersecretary of State George Ball asserting the strategic importance of South Vietnam to U.S. interests had been approved, McGeorge Bundy wrote on May 1 that the "tone and content" of Ball's speech "would not have been cleared, simply from the point of view of maintaining a chance of political settlement."[75] Harriman, meanwhile, enlisted Gilpatric to help dissuade Kennedy from trying to make diplomatic contact with the North Vietnamese. At a meeting on May 1, Gilpatric, who had obviously been prompted by Harriman, characterized the Galbraith initiative disingenuously as "a recommendation that we negotiate a coalition-type neutralized South Viet-Nam," despite the fact that Galbraith's plan did nothing of the sort. Harriman and Hilsman argued that Kennedy should reject the Galbraith plan, and Hilsman's draft memorandum of the meeting, which indicated that Kennedy had agreed with them, has been cited as proof that Kennedy flatly rejected negotiations on Vietnam.[76] But Kennedy had not changed his mind. The following day, he agreed only that "we should await the report of the ICC in Vietnam before considering indirect approaches to Hanoi on the Vietnam conflict."[77]

Galbraith, meanwhile, continued to pursue the Indian channel on his own. On May 5, he reported a conversation with G. Parthasarathi, the Indian ICC delegate and chairman, a frequent visitor to Hanoi. Parthasarathi had suggested another variant on a mutual de-escalation deal with the North that would ultimately result in a phased U.S. withdrawal after six months of peace. And a few days later, Galbraith wrote a private letter to Harriman revealing that he had just told Parthasarathi that "if he ever felt Hanoi had anything to say to you or the President they should feel free do so and could do it through me."[78]

Harriman must have been alarmed that the Indian diplomat would soon be shuttling between Galbraith and Hanoi. This time, Harriman did write to Galbraith himself, but deliberately misled him about Kennedy's policy. Harriman said the president was authorizing him to "continue informal conversations" with the Indians on the "manner in which they suggest Co-Chairmen could institute informal talks on stabilization, compliance and peace." Harriman sent the draft to Forrestal with a note explaining that the telegram was "designed to calm Ken down" and to "cover [the] point the President had in mind regarding possible usefulness of Desai-Hanoi approach." This was quite disingenuous, because he knew that Kennedy's desire for approaches to Hanoi through intermediaries, and especially the Indians, had not changed. Nevertheless, Forrestal agreed, and the telegram was dispatched to Galbraith.[79] Harriman had substituted the Geneva co-chair formula for the Indian intermediary role in the knowledge that the British would veto any Soviet move toward negotiations on South Vietnam.[80]

Harriman then went even further in substituting his own hard-line diplomatic stance on Vietnam publicly for Kennedy's approach. In a magazine article published in late May, he wrote that the United States would withdraw its "augmented forces" from South Vietnam only after the insurgents had withdrawn "behind the seventeenth parallel."[81] Appearing just one week before the expected issuance of the International Control Commission's report, which Kennedy had indicated on May 1 he would await before pursuing a diplomatic initiative with Hanoi, this obviously extreme position amounted to a preemptive strike against any subsequent diplomatic probe of Hanoi's intentions.[82]

Harriman pursued the same preemptive approach in a meeting with the North Vietnamese foreign minister, Ung Van Khiem, in Geneva on July 22, 1962, which had been initiated by Undersecretary for Foreign Affairs James Barrington. Harriman agreed immediately to meet Khiem without first informing the president or the State Department.[83] Harriman's deputy William Sullivan claims in his memoirs that Harriman probed the North Vietnamese willingness to settle the conflict peacefully but was "incessantly rebuffed" by Khiem.[84] His memorandum of conversation on the meeting, however, reveals that Harriman only talked about North Vietnamese non-compliance with the Laotian agreement and never asked Khiem about Hanoi's views on a negotiated settlement. It was Khiem, not Harriman, who turned the discussion to South Vietnam by condemning the U.S. military intervention there. Harriman then declared: "The way that peace could be brought to Vietnam would be for the North Vietnamese to cease their aggression against South Vietnam, and to stop guerrilla activity. Then the status envisaged by the 1954 Agreements could be reestablished and the possibilities of dealing with other difficulties could be explored."[85]

Harriman's formulation of demanding an end to all "guerrilla activity" before any talks could even begin was not aimed at opening a diplomatic dialogue with Hanoi, as some accounts have suggested, since it could only discourage Hanoi from any further efforts to explore a peace settlement with the United States.[86] After the meeting, Harriman directed Sullivan to draft an assessment of the meeting "in bleak, unpromising terms," to be passed on to the president.[87] After seeing Sullivan's memorandum of conversation, Harriman wanted it sent to the CIA, Galbraith, and McGeorge Bundy in particular.[88]

In September, Galbraith reported new evidence of North Vietnamese interest in negotiations to Harriman, based on talks with India's consul-general in Hanoi. "Some in Hanoi's government," he wrote, "would welcome a standstill in hostilities with prospective American withdrawals from the South." While acknowledging Hanoi's "passionate, almost religious hope for unification," Galbraith observed that the development of North-South trade would be "of great importance" to the North Vietnamese leaders, suggesting a further opening for diplomacy. Harriman responded coolly: "I am afraid we are going to have to discourage the Communists a bit more before they will be willing to give up their aggression."[89]

Chester Bowles, meanwhile, had been working on a much more sweeping diplomatic initiative aimed at the neutralization of all of mainland Southeast Asia, including both North and South Vietnam. In a memo to Kennedy in early April, Bowles proposed that China provide guarantees against internal subversion in the region in return for grain shipments to help with its food deficit.[90] According to Bowles, Kennedy responded enthusiastically to his preliminary concept of neutralization of the region, and Harriman also told Bowles that he favored the idea.[91] Kennedy, who had expressed keen interest in Bowles's argument in early 1962 that the PRC's dependence on foreign grain sources offered the United States the opportunity to increase its leverage on PRC policy, asked Bowles to update his analysis of China's food situation in June.[92]

Bowles was not alone in believing that China's economic weakness and dependence on the West for foodstuffs might provide a degree of leverage over PRC policies. The Chinese had quietly indicated their interest in buying grain from a private U.S. company in March 1962, prompting Rostow's Policy Planning office at the State Department to observe that "several circumstances suggest at least a possibility that Peiping may consider it useful to establish, within narrowly confined limits, a new relationship with the West, including the United States." A State Department policy paper drafted jointly by several offices had suggested that the United

States use the possibility of trade liberalization as leverage to demand unidentified changes in Beijing's behavior.[93]

Harriman believed that there were undoubtedly leaders in Beijing who were interested in more conciliatory policies, and that a political initiative would tend to strengthen their hand. But Harriman and Rusk were then fending off suggestions by the CIA station chief in Taipei, Ray Cline, to support dropping several teams of 200–300 Nationalist Chinese commandos on the mainland. They could hardly give serious consideration to a proposal to negotiate with China on regional peace and security at a time when the administration still feared being blamed by the Right for failing to support Jiang's ambitions.[94] The imbalance of power in relation to China, which encouraged continued U.S. efforts to destabilize the Chinese Communist regime, precluded diplomatic accommodation of any kind with Beijing.

Bowles nevertheless pressed the case for at least canvassing Southeast Asian leaders on the concept. On July 12, Bowles outlined to Rusk his plans for "the mission to Southeast Asia which you suggested I undertake," which would include meetings with Indonesia's Sukarno, Cambodian Chief of State Norodom Sihanouk, Philippine President Diosdado Macapagal, and Malaysian Prime Minister Tunku Abdul Rahman.[95] But Harriman stepped in to stop it. In a meeting with Rusk on July 30 and in a follow-up memorandum later the same day, he argued that the Bowles proposal was "based on the assumption that a Laos-type of international agreement is possible and enforceable for the whole of Southeast Asia" and that it would "require another Geneva meeting." The following day, Harriman told Rice to inform Bowles's staff that the political situation in the region was in such "turmoil" that the visit then being planned by Bowles would be "counterproductive."[96] Harriman then interceded directly with Kennedy to call off the trip. Kennedy informed Bowles that, in light of Harriman's strong opposition to the trip, it would have to be "abandoned or postponed."[97]

Harriman's sabotage of Kennedy's diplomatic probe of Hanoi and his sidetracking of the Bowles initiative were both related to the strongly held belief among national security officials that the United States should not be thinking about diplomatic compromise on South Vietnam. The initial draft of the November 1961 memorandum for the president intended for signature by Rusk, McNamara, and the JCS had made the explicit linkage between the U.S. power advantage and the danger of negotiations on South Vietnam. The Communists "would insist upon some sort of settlement comparable to that in Laos," it said, adding, "We do not believe this is desirable or necessary, given the scale of Viet Cong action and the stronger position of the GVN *and the greater accessibility of Viet-Nam to the United States and SEATO* [emphasis added]."[98]

Harriman shared the consensus view that in South Vietnam, unlike Laos, the United States could bring its power advantage to bear. In a letter to Arthur Schlesinger Jr. in October 1961, he had disparaged the idea of sending U.S. troops to Laos, but had then added, "Of course, South Vietnam is quite different as the logistics are in our favor, and that country is of enormous political, strategic and economic importance."[99] In mid 1962, Harriman publicly cited, as a major consideration in U.S. policy, the ease with which the United States could intervene in South Vietnam, if necessary, because of a "lengthy seacoast which favors the accessibility and utility of American air and sea power."[100]

In a broader sense, South Vietnam was "accessible" to U.S. forces because the global and regional imbalance of power gave the United States such complete freedom of action to intervene militarily. The U.S. assessment of the rapid widening of the chasm between the Soviet Union and China in late 1961 and early 1962, and its implications for Soviet policy, increased that freedom still further. The CIA concluded in December 1961 that "a showdown of historic proportions" between the two Communist giants "may be imminent" and that it could "lead to a breakdown of Bloc cooperation" in Southeast Asia. Less than two weeks later, State Department officials recognized for the first time that the Sino-Soviet conflict conferred significant advantages on the United States. On April 2, 1962, Rostow sent Rusk a paper from Policy Planning suggesting that the United States could draw the Soviet leaders further in that direction and proposing exploring Khrushchev's willingness to "take joint positions with us" on both nuclear weapons and Southeast Asia. In May, a CIA estimate predicted that the USSR would "urge a gradualist strategy" on the North Vietnamese.[101]

The national security bureaucracy was even more confident in 1962 than it had been in 1961 that China would not risk a confrontation over South Vietnam. In mid January 1962, Rusk told the Senate Foreign Relations Committee that "some extremely good intelligence" indicated that Beijing knew that China would not get any additional Soviet assistance if there were to be a confrontation with the United States.[102] McNamara, testifying before the same committee in early February, referred to new evidence that the Chinese military was being "adversely affected" by the economic chaos in the country, which had deprived it of supplies, food, and petroleum it needed to maintain combat effectiveness.[103] The CIA concluded in February that Chinese determination to minimize the risks of U.S. military intervention not only made it unlikely that Beijing would use military force in Southeast Asia but also constrained its support for the insurgents in South Vietnam.[104] When the U.S. delegation to the Geneva Conference on Laos discussed China's future on the day the agreement was signed in July, moreover, everyone agreed, in Harriman's words, "that the Chinese would be in a weakened economic condition for a number of years which would reduce their aggressive attitude."[105]

It might be argued that Kennedy lost interest in negotiating on Vietnam, as indicated by his failure to press Harriman on the Indian channel after the ICC report in June, and by his acquiescence in Harriman's insistence on canceling the Bowles mission. Kennedy was undoubtedly aware by mid-summer that Harriman was opposed to such negotiations and did not believe he could pursue a diplomatic track on Vietnam without the support of the administration's key policy maker on East Asia. By then, however, he had shifted his attention from negotiations to a plan for phasing out the U.S. military presence in South Vietnam as his main policy line.

In any case, Kennedy had not lost interest in a possible negotiated outcome in South Vietnam. When Galbraith reported a January 1963 conversation with the Polish foreign minister, Adam Rapacki, in which the latter had suggested that Ho Chi Minh would be willing to call off the insurrection in the South if a "liberal government" were to come to power in South Vietnam, Kennedy directed him to pursue the subject further with Rapacki. It was too late: Rapacki had already left Delhi, and Galbraith had no way to pursue the issue from India.[106]

In March 1963, Kennedy replaced Harriman as assistant secretary of state with Roger Hilsman, whom he could expect to be far more responsive to his wishes on Vietnam policy. According to Hilsman, Kennedy indicated to him that if the South Vietnamese failed, he would "go to Geneva and do what we did with Laos."[107] Hilsman's recollection is supported, moreover, by Robert F. Kennedy's statement to Daniel Ellsberg in 1967 that his brother would have arranged "a Laotian type solution, some form of coalition government with people who would ask us to leave," rather than send troops to Vietnam.[108]

Kennedy's determination to leave the door open to the neutralization of South Vietnam can also be inferred from Kennedy's response to the suggestions of his advisers on how to respond publicly to Charles de Gaulle's August 29, 1963, statement on the neutralization of Vietnam. Before Kennedy's interview with Walter Cronkite of CBS News, McGeorge Bundy drafted and Hilsman and Forrestal cleared four alternative possible comments that Kennedy might use, three of which made it clear that the United States disagreed with de Gaulle, while the remaining one simply called attention to the lack of French support for the counterinsurgency war. But instead Kennedy refused to express any irritation with de Gaulle's views. "I think anything De Gaulle says should be listened to," Kennedy said to Cronkite, "and we listened."[109]

KENNEDY'S TROOP WITHDRAWAL PLAN

Historians have generally remained skeptical of the idea that Kennedy pursued a firm policy of phasing out U.S. troops from South Vietnam.[110] That rejection has rested on four grounds: the absence of any internal documentation of such a policy, at least until October 2, 1963; a record of public statements that seems to contradict it; Kennedy's alleged rejection of the idea of peace negotiations on South Vietnam; and the denial by Robert F. Kennedy in an oral history interview that the president had seriously considered withdrawal.[111]

The fact, documented above, that Kennedy secretly tried to initiate diplomatic contacts with the North Vietnamese to begin peace talks addresses one of these objections. And Robert F. Kennedy's denial should not be regarded as disposing of the matter, because the oral history interview in question was given in April 1964, after the situation in South Vietnam had gone into a serious downward spiral, the Kennedy withdrawal policy had been repudiated by Johnson, and the mood in the country still leaned toward preventing the loss of South Vietnam. Furthermore, Robert Kennedy was weighing whether to make a bid to become Lyndon Johnson's vice presidential running mate or to run for a Senate seat in New York. He was determined to protect his brother's reputation for anti-Communism—and his own—which he feared would be tarnished by an admission that John F. Kennedy had promoted a policy of withdrawal from Vietnam, regardless of the outcome.

Kennedy's Secretary of State, Dean Rusk, observed in a later interview that Kennedy had never mentioned a phase-out of U.S. troops from South Vietnam in any of their "hundreds" of conversations on Vietnam. Similarly, McGeorge Bundy could not recall any involvement by Kennedy in the withdrawal issue before October 1963.[112] Furthermore, Kennedy repeatedly emphasized in public statements in 1963 the necessity to stay the course in South Vietnam. The absence of reference by the president in the records of meetings with advisers to his intention to pursue a particular policy and a series of public statements that appear to contradict it would normally be sufficient to rule out the thesis that a president was pursuing such a policy.

In the case of Kennedy's policy toward withdrawal from South Vietnam, however, both of these indicators must be examined more closely. Kennedy was extremely cautious about revealing positions that he knew were at odds with the national security bureaucracy, and he had come to believe that revealing his intentions on withdrawal from Vietnam to the public or even to his own National Security Council was too risky. Kennedy had reason to believe that neither Rusk nor Bundy would have been sympathetic to a complete military withdrawal by 1965.[113] Furthermore, Kennedy's decision to handle the withdrawal plan outside the normal policy channels was in line with his exclusion of Rusk and Bundy from the policy of negotiating Laotian neutrality, which both Bundy and Rusk had opposed and which Kennedy had handled directly with Harriman. As in the case of Laos, Kennedy hoped to minimize the possibility that the withdrawal policy would be undermined by opposition from high-ranking officials.

Furthermore, Kennedy feared that being associated by the media and the public with the withdrawal plan would risk a serious political campaign against him if the war in South Vietnam were then to go sour. That fear must have been strongly reinforced, moreover, by the fierce political attack on Kennedy in September and October 1962, primarily but not exclusively by Republicans, for his failure to take forceful action against the Soviet military presence in Cuba.[114] Kennedy was determined, therefore, to shift the public responsibility for the withdrawal policy to McNamara and the JCS.

Kennedy's decision to generate a plan for withdrawal of U.S. troops was apparently prompted by new pressure from the military to deploy combat forces to South Vietnam if necessary to avoid defeat. On January 3, in a meeting with the JCS, Taylor, U.S. MACV Commander Paul Harkins, McNamara, and Gilpatric, Kennedy reiterated that "the U.S. military role there was for advice, training and support of the Vietnamese Armed Forces and not for combat."[115] Ten days later, however, the JCS sent McNamara a memorandum that forcefully reopened the issue of a commitment to save the South Vietnamese regime by sending combat troops, if necessary. It asserted that, if the Viet Cong could not be brought under control, the JCS saw "no alternative to the introduction of US military combat forces" into South Vietnam.[116]

The memo was a political challenge to Kennedy's policy of opposing the deployment of combat troops in Vietnam. Although he was determined to keep the United States from sliding into a major war in South Vietnam, Kennedy anticipated a political attack by the military leadership if he moved openly to reverse the direction of Vietnam policy, especially if the Communists appeared to be on their way to gaining power as a result. In response to this dilemma, Kennedy came up with a clever strategy, which was to get the JCS themselves to take responsibility for a withdrawal plan. The first indication of that strategy comes from the fragmentary record of a March 1, 1962, meeting involving Kennedy, McNamara, and the JCS. Kennedy announced that he wanted a "contingency plan for South Vietnam in the event our present efforts fail." This request is remarkable as a reflection of his lack of confidence in the proposed escalation of U.S. military involvement before it had even started to take hold. McNamara then volunteered, "We need a plan for the introduction of U.S. forces before the loss of the total interior of South Vietnam, if such a catastrophe were about to overtake us." The partial notes of the meeting, however, record Kennedy's rejoinder to McNamara as follows: "An important item in this planning . . . is the timing of a decision for US action *and the factors that go into such a decision* [emphasis added]."[117]

The meaning of Kennedy's elliptical wording "the factors that go into such a decision" becomes clear if it is recalled that in May 1961, he had insisted that the Pentagon's study of possible U.S. troop deployments had to include the "diplomatic setting within which this action might be taken." That mysterious phrase had been a coded signal that he would not approve military intervention without British and French concurrence through SEATO—a possibility that was already understood in the administration to be virtually nonexistent. Against the background of his consistent opposition to deployment of combat forces, this phrase indicates that Kennedy was requesting not a contingency plan for combat troop deployment but rather a contingency plan for the actions that would have to be taken if Britain and France refused to support intervention. Those actions would obviously have included a timetable for the orderly withdrawal of U.S. advisers, hence the importance of the word "timing." In effect, Kennedy was seeking to impose on the JCS the responsibility for coming up with a schedule for withdrawal of U.S. advisers if it became clear that such a withdrawal was necessary.

Within a few weeks of that March 1 meeting, as the U.S. military was exulting over the early results of the deployments of troops and aircraft, an even better route to the same objective appeared to open up. McNamara began to push openly for the formulation of a plan for the orderly withdrawal of U.S. advisers on a fixed time schedule. At the fifth Honolulu conference on the war on May 8, McNamara asked Harkins for a phased plan to complete the training of the South Vietnamese and the withdrawal of

U.S. forces on a schedule, and suggested that 1965 would be an appropriate target date for the end of the phase-out.[118] On July 26, at another Honolulu conference, the decision became official, and directives were issued for a "comprehensive plan" for the replacement of U.S. advisers with trained South Vietnamese personnel "during the next three year period."[119]

McNamara has never admitted publicly that Kennedy was behind these proposals.[120] Asked by the author in early 2004 if Kennedy did indeed direct him to initiate the withdrawal plan, McNamara replied, "I don't remember."[121] McNamara's refusal to acknowledge Kennedy's role in the origins and evolution of the withdrawal plan is certainly related to his desire to take full credit for the withdrawal policy. After all, McNamara bore the responsibility for it during 1962 and 1963, while Kennedy chose to remain in the shadows. It is hardly plausible, however, that Kennedy, who had just ordered McNamara a few weeks earlier to negotiate a "contingency plan" with the JCS and who was at that very moment trying to open a diplomatic channel to Hanoi, was a passive spectator to the policy.[122]

McNamara's precipitous transition from the hard-line position of the JCS in November 1961 to Kennedy's withdrawal policy in 1962 was certainly facilitated by the shallowness of McNamara's views on Vietnam and his tendency to take foreign policy positions for reasons of political convenience. But it was also deeply rooted in McNamara's sense of loyalty to President Kennedy, as well as to the Kennedy family. McNamara felt strongly that he owed a personal debt to Kennedy because he had failed to warn the president against the ill-fated Bay of Pigs invasion plan, and because Kennedy had then taken all the blame for it publicly. McNamara not only admired Kennedy for that but privately vowed that he would not "let him down again."[123]

McNamara's relationship with Kennedy was unusually close for a president and a cabinet member; a biographer refers to his "reverence" for Kennedy and his tearful response to the memory of it. Also cementing his loyalty to the president, however, were his close friendships with Robert and Jackie Kennedy, which had made him a member of the extended Kennedy family. McNamara's friendship with Robert F. Kennedy had already begun to develop during 1961 but would be further cemented by their comradeship during the Cuban Missile Crisis.[124] McNamara's extraordinary personal loyalty explains why Kennedy told both his brother and *Washington Post* publisher Philip Graham in late 1962 and 1963 that he was seriously considering replacing Rusk with McNamara as secretary of state after the 1964 election. "McNamara would have been a good Secretary of State," Robert F. Kennedy explained, "because President Kennedy knew so much about it that he could make the major decisions."[125]

Some historians have minimized the significance of the phase-out plan on the grounds that it was contingent on success in bringing the insurgency under control.[126] As McNamara asserts quite forcefully in his memoirs, however, the phased withdrawal he proposed in 1962 was considered "justified" whether U.S. training of the ARVN was successful or not.[127] Nearly a decade earlier, in an oral history for the Office of the Secretary of Defense, he had been even more explicit, recalling: "I believed that to the extent we could train those forces, we should do so, and having done it, we should get out. To the extent those trained forces could not handle the problem—the subversion by North Vietnam—I believed we should not introduce our military forces in support of the South Vietnamese, even if they were going to be 'defeated.'"[128]

The military questioned McNamara's timetable for withdrawal from the beginning. The plan proposed by MACV and submitted by the JCS to McNamara in March 1963 was heavily back-loaded to minimize the risk of a major setback. It would have resulted in a few thousand troops being brought home during calendar 1964, but would have kept U.S. strength at a peak of 12,200 as late as mid 1965. That number would have been reduced by half over the next year, to nearly 6,000 advisers remaining in South Vietnam by mid 1966, and would have left 1,600 advisers even in 1967.[129] McNamara rejected that plan, insisting that the withdrawal should be completed by the end of FY 1965, that the end result be that U.S. personnel should be used strictly in an advisory role, and that total U.S. strength in country should be 500–700 people.[130]

At the May 6, 1963, Honolulu conference, McNamara again insisted that the JCS withdrawal plan was "too slow" and that "we should try to get U.S. numbers down to a minimum level earlier than FY 66." He directed CINCPAC to develop a revised plan that would accelerate the training of helicopter pilots so that "we may give the Vietnamese our copters and thus be able to move our forces out." The guidelines included training the minimum number of South Vietnamese forces "necessary to cope with reinsurgency and [to] permit timely introduction of U.S. forces *in the event of overt aggression* [emphasis added]." On May 9, the JCS directed CINCPAC to redraft the withdrawal plan to conform to McNamara's guidelines. That prompted CINCPAC Admiral Harry Felt to complain that it was "overly optimistic to assume that insurgency can be controlled as early as FY65."[131]

Meanwhile, Kennedy had decided to begin the withdrawal earlier than he had originally planned, presumably so that the policy would be established well before the 1964 presidential primary season began. In early 1963, Kennedy told Senate Majority leader Mike Mansfield, who had just returned from Vietnam with a highly critical report, that he would "begin pulling troops out on the first of the next year."[132] In early April, anticipating that, he told Harriman and Forrestal that the administration should be "prepared to seize upon any favorable moment to reduce our commitment, recognizing that the moment might yet be some time away."[133] Later that month, Kennedy told the journalist Charles Bartlett, "We don't have a prayer of staying in Vietnam."[134]

Kennedy was pessimistic about the outcome, but determined to take advantage of the optimism of the U.S. command in Saigon to begin the withdrawal. On April 29, 1963, McNamara told the JCS he wanted to explore "the feasibility of bringing back 1,000 troops at the end of this year." McNamara directed the JCS to develop a plan on the "general assumption that such a course of action would be feasible." At the Honolulu conference a few days later, he went much further, declaring such a plan to be "a matter of urgency" and repeated that it should be "based upon the assumption that the progress of the counterinsurgency campaign would warrant such a move." McNamara specifically proposed to select two or three Vietnamese units for intensive training, so that they could replace U.S. units. General Harkins, who had been wildly optimistic in his reporting about progress in the war, objected that a further speedup in the training schedule was not feasible and that "it would have a bad effect on the Vietnamese, to be pulling out just when it appears they are winning." Nevertheless McNamara insisted that a plan should be "laid down quickly, within the next couple of weeks, for training the RVNAF" in order to make the 1,000-man withdrawal possible.[135]

On August 20, the JCS forwarded to McNamara a plan from Admiral Felt for withdrawing 1,000 troops in three or four increments before the end of 1963. But instead of endorsing McNamara's position that the withdrawal should be based on the assumption that "progress would warrant such a move," Felt wrote that it should take place "only if progress in the counterinsurgency campaign warrants such action." Felt noted that the political tensions in South Vietnam and the "highly volatile situation in Laos" made it "prudent to delay [the] decision as long as possible." Under Felt's plan, half of the 1,000 men to be withdrawn would be accounted for not by military units but by individual soldiers. The JCS also agreed to the withdrawal timetable, but only for planning purposes, with the final decision to be contingent on a reevaluation of the situation by the JCS themselves by October 31. They also agreed on a detailed plan, in which the "emphasis would be on withdrawal of units rather than individuals."[136]

This insistence by the JCS on retaining the right to veto the 1,000-man withdrawal if the counterinsurgency campaign was not making sufficient progress threatened Kennedy's whole withdrawal strategy. Immediately after the JCS memorandum was received, moreover, the Diem regime's raids on Buddhist pagodas initiated a new period of intense political crisis in South Vietnam, which further dimmed the prospect of JCS approval of the withdrawal. McNamara held off on his own response to the JCS memorandum for two weeks, and it appears that Kennedy tried to get the JCS to soften their position. Between August 28 and 30, Taylor held three "special meetings" and one "executive session" of the JCS on the subject of Vietnam. After one more meeting with McNamara on Vietnam on September 2, Taylor met again on September 3 with Kennedy and McNamara.[137]

Later that same day, McNamara officially accepted the August 20 JCS plan, and implicitly its demand for a late-October review of the issue, but requested a document from the JCS that would specify the precise numbers and dates for withdrawal and the strength levels that would result between the end of October and the end of December. Eight days later, Taylor delivered a memo confirming that the level of U.S. forces in Vietnam would fall by exactly 1,000 from 16,732 troops on October 30 to 15,732 on December 30. In the meantime, however, the JCS had written to CINCPAC on September 6 reaffirming that the withdrawal plan had been accepted "for planning purposes pending final decision on or about 31 Oct."[138] Kennedy thus had no assurance that the JCS would approve even the first stage of the withdrawal, much less the complete withdrawal by the end of 1965, which still languished in CINCPAC.

The pattern of Kennedy's decisions on Vietnam in late August and September makes sense only in light of his concern about promoting both the plan for a phased withdrawal by the end of 1965 and the proposed withdrawal of the first 1,000 men by the end of 1963. The intensified political crisis of the Diem regime beginning in late August made it more difficult to get JCS and CINCPAC support for both plans, but it also opened up new possibilities for advancing a withdrawal strategy. After the Diem regime's raid on Buddhist pagodas in Saigon on August 21, Kennedy was acutely aware of the relationship between the Diem regime's negative image in the United States and his room for maneuver on Vietnam. When George Ball called Kennedy on August 21 about the draft State Department public response to the pagoda raid, which distanced the United States from Diem, Kennedy objected only to a sentence pledging to "continue to assist Vietnam to resist Communist aggression and maintain its independence." Kennedy wanted it stricken from the statement, saying it was "sort of almost a non-sequitur."[139]

Implicit in that reaction was the assumption that the U.S. commitment could be invalidated by the policies of the regime.

On August 24, Kennedy allowed the Harriman-Hilsman cable, which was aimed at encouraging the South Vietnamese generals to move against Diem, to be sent to Saigon if senior officials at State and Defense cleared it. By the following Monday, however, Kennedy had begun to move in the opposite direction, opposing any U.S. encouragement of the South Vietnamese generals to overthrow Diem. At a meeting with his advisers, he asserted that the United States should not move against Diem simply because of "media pressure"—a reference to *New York Times* correspondent David Halberstam's account of the raids on the pagodas—and rejected Hilsman's appeal for immediate action to reaffirm the August 24 cable. The following day, he said it was not too late to pull back from the August 24 cable and ordered that a cable be sent to newly arrived Ambassador Henry Cabot Lodge asking his advice on whether to do so. On August 29, Kennedy insisted in a cable to Lodge that he reserved the right to "reverse previous instructions."[140]

From the end of August until mid September, Hilsman and Lodge used diplomatic and intelligence reports of contacts between Ngo Dinh Nhu and the North Vietnamese to strengthen their argument for encouraging Diem's overthrow.[141] Kennedy was well aware of the reports and speculation on a possible deal between Nhu and the North Vietnamese, but he did not share the concern of the pro-coup group in the administration about such a possibility, according to McGeorge Bundy.[142]

On September 3, Kennedy took a decisive step toward accommodation with Diem, declaring that he wanted no further contacts with the coup group, and ordered a shift to "a diplomatic route" in regard to Diem. Two weeks later, he rejected the draft cable by Hilsman that would have directed Lodge to take a confrontational approach to Diem and ordered that the more conciliatory alternative be sent. In his September 17 cable to Lodge, Kennedy wrote that there was "no good opportunity to remove the present government in the immediate future," and that the United States would have to settle for "whatever modest improvements on the scene may be possible."[143] On the same day that he chose the conciliatory line with Diem, Kennedy announced that he was sending McNamara and Taylor to South Vietnam to study the situation and make recommendations. In his final meeting with McNamara and Taylor before their departure on September 23, Kennedy repeated that he opposed a cutoff of aid to Diem and that only "small changes" in the South Vietnamese regime were likely to be achievable.[144]

Why was Kennedy so insistent that the United States work with Diem, despite the entreaties of the State Department and Lodge to pull back and encourage the military to move against him? It was not because he was optimistic about the regime's success in bringing the Communist insurgency under control, for he repeatedly said, both publicly and privately, that the Diem regime's loss of political support would probably seriously affect the course of the war if it continued.[145] Nor is there any reason to believe that he was more optimistic than his advisers about the likelihood that Diem would agree to Nhu's removal. The evidence suggests that Kennedy strongly preferred that Diem remain in power because he believed that political failings of the Diem regime provided another rationale for U.S. military withdrawal if the regime stumbled in the war. It was the "favorable moment" to reduce the U.S. commitment to which he had referred five months earlier.

The Kennedy decision to send McNamara and Taylor to Saigon at the end of September has been interpreted as a means by which Kennedy intended to encourage the generals to take action against Diem, or, alternatively, as a way of bridging the gap between the pro-coup faction in his administration (Harriman and Hilsman) and those who opposed a coup (McNamara, Taylor, and McCone).[146] Kennedy's overriding purpose in sending the McNamara-Taylor mission, however, appears to have been to obtain a recommendation from his most senior national security advisers for complete withdrawal by the end of 1965 and the withdrawal of the first 1,000 men by end of the 1963. After it had become clear in early September that the JCS was insisting on a veto over the plan for a first-stage withdrawal, Kennedy had to find another way of committing his national security team to an entire withdrawal plan.

In McNamara and Taylor, Kennedy had two top national security advisers whom he trusted to come back with the policy recommendations he needed, because of their personal ties to him and the Kennedy family. He had chosen Taylor to replace General Lyman Lemnitzer as JCS Chairman in October 1962 not only because he thought Taylor could be effective in controlling the JCS but because Taylor had unusually close friendships with both Robert F. Kennedy and McNamara. Taylor later recalled that the four service chiefs had known when he became chairman that "I was very close to McNamara" and "would never bring a [JCS] paper that the Secretary wouldn't support."[147]

While quietly pulling the strings on the withdrawal plan, Kennedy was deliberately conveying the opposite impression to the public through his statements on Vietnam. On March 6, responding to a question on the

Mansfield report's recommendation for a reduction in the U.S. role in Vietnam, Kennedy told a press conference, "I don't see any real prospect of the burden being lightened for the U.S. in Southeast Asia in the next year if we are going to do the job and meet what I think are very clear national needs." When Kennedy was asked on May 22 about Ngo Dinh Nhu's criticism of the size of the U.S. military advisory corps, however, he replied, "We are hopeful that the situation in South Viet-Nam would permit some withdrawal in any case by end of the year, but we can't possibly make that judgment at the present time." His answer indicates that he knew and approved McNamara's seeking approval for a 1,000-man withdrawal by the end of 1963. But Kennedy wanted to be associated in the public mind with toughness in Vietnam, not with withdrawal. On July 17, he began to define "withdrawal" as *immediate* withdrawal, and expressed his opposition to it. "For us to withdraw from that effort," he said, "would mean a collapse not only of South Viet-Nam, but Southeast Asia. So we are going to stay there."[148] These public statements have been cited as further evidence that Kennedy had not decided to support the phased withdrawal of U.S. troops. Read in light of everything we know now about the broader pattern of Kennedy's Vietnam policy, however, they simply show that he was conveying to the public a different course of policy from the one he was pursuing behind the scenes.

Kennedy was quite explicit about the new rationale for withdrawal when he met with McNamara and Taylor on September 19, with no one else present, and no notes taken. The result of that meeting, which had been preceded by two meetings between McNamara and Taylor on September 18 and 19, was an understanding about how the troop withdrawal plan would be handled during and after the trip. Many years later, Taylor revealed to an interviewer that he and McNamara had been "charged" by Kennedy with telling Diem, "Unless you do certain things we have described, we are going to pull out in a relatively short time." He explained that the withdrawal recommendation "was part of our pressures on Diem to get him to do certain things, which, if done, we believed would make possible a termination of the [U.S. troop presence] situation in about two years."[149] That was what McNamara conveyed to Diem in essence during a meeting on September 28.[150]

Taylor's memoirs make it clear, moreover, that Kennedy did not intend merely to make an idle threat in order to pressure Diem. Explaining the rationale for the recommendation for a withdrawal plan on which he and McNamara had an understanding with Kennedy, Taylor wrote: "If further deterioration of the political situation should occur to invalidate the target date, we would have to review our attitude toward Diem's government *and our national interests in Southeast Asia* [emphasis added]."[151] In other words, the withdrawal would be *accelerated* if it could be argued that Diem's political failures had caused the planned turnover of the war to Saigon to fail. Bobby Kennedy, who was presumably well aware of his brother's thinking, had alluded to this new rationale for a more rapid withdrawal from South Vietnam at a meeting of Kennedy's advisers on September 6 from which the president himself was absent. In response to Rusk's statement that the United States would have to respond with "a massive military effort" if the situation in South Vietnam continued to deteriorate, he said Diem would have to "do things we demand or we will have to cut down our effort as forced by the U.S. public." If the war was not winnable, he added, "it would be better to get out now rather than waiting."[152]

The Taylor-McNamara report concluded that the war could be won if the necessary political reforms were made, but suggested that "further repressive actions could change the present favorable military trend." It suggested that a "return to more moderate methods of control and administration," which would help mitigate the political crisis, was "unlikely." This was exactly the position that Kennedy had outlined before they departed, and it was consistent with their private understanding with Kennedy that the withdrawal plan would apply whether the war went well or not.[153]

Forrestal, William Sullivan of the State Department, and William Bundy of DOD all strongly dissented from the withdrawal dates during the trip, and Sullivan threatened to write a dissenting view on the issue. Taylor and McNamara agreed to remove the end of 1963 date for the initial phase of the withdrawal from the draft report, but the end of 1965 date for completing the withdrawal remained.[154] There was never any question, however, about dropping either deadline from the report. On the morning of their arrival in Washington in October, Taylor and McNamara met privately at 9:40 A.M., fifteen minutes before a meeting of the entire mission, to discuss a "change in draft trip report for the President."[155] The result of their brief meeting was that both deadlines were in the draft report when the meeting with the other members of the mission began.

That meeting quickly erupted into heated debate over the withdrawal deadlines, particularly the end of 1965 deadline for complete withdrawal.[156] McNamara thought he had achieved a consensus among members of the mission on the withdrawal deadlines, but some officials who were not on the trip—presumably Harriman and McGeorge Bundy—objected, and some members of the mission joined them.[157] However, in the White

House briefing of Kennedy by McNamara and Taylor that followed, attended by Harriman, McCone, McGeorge Bundy, and Ball, no one challenged the withdrawal openly. Kennedy left it to Taylor and McNamara to defend the end of 1965 target date, appearing to be noncommittal. "If it doesn't work out," Kennedy said, "we'll get a new date." Taylor expressed confidence that the insurgency could be brought under control by the end of 1965, but McNamara said he "wasn't entirely sure" that it could be accomplished by then. Nevertheless, he argued that the administration could withdraw "the bulk of our U.S. forces according to the schedule we've laid out," because "we can train the Vietnamese to do the job." Kennedy then agreed that the policy statement to be issued should say that there "may continue to be a requirement for special training forces," and that "we believe that the major United States part of the task can be completed by the end of '65."[158]

Kennedy's apparent skepticism about the withdrawal was political theater to complete the fiction that he was only responding to urging of his top national security advisers. When McGeorge Bundy and Chester Cooper of the CIA complained to William Bundy, who had been the drafter of the report, about including the withdrawal deadline in the statement to be issued to the press, William Bundy said he agreed but was "under instructions" by McNamara on the issue. McGeorge Bundy then called McNamara to try to persuade him to take the deadline out of the public statement but was told that the president wanted it to stay.[159]

The purpose of the announcement of the withdrawal deadline was to prevent Bundy and other opponents from seeking to reverse the policy. Apparently referring to McGeorge Bundy's effort to delete the reference to the 1965 deadline from the statement to be issued to the press, McNamara later recalled, "The people who were opposed to the decision didn't want to announce it, because they thought that they would live to fight another day and win the battle." The opponents of the withdrawal, he said, "believed, as I did, that if it were announced, it would be in concrete."[160]

The text of the statement to be issued publicly was already decided, therefore, before the NSC meeting that evening, which lasted only half an hour and was clearly intended to formalize the decisions already reached in the morning.[161] At that meeting, Kennedy was still pretending to be undecided. Nevertheless, he referred to the same rationale for an even more rapid withdrawal that he had conveyed to McNamara and Taylor before the trip. "To cut off completely would not be wise," he said, "*unless the situation really begins to deteriorate more.*" McNamara repeated the line he had taken in the morning meeting with Kennedy: "We need a way out of

Vietnam. This is a way of doing it." Kennedy again expressed the reservation that "if the war doesn't continue to go well, it will look like we were overly optimistic." He added, "I'm not sure what benefit we get at this time by announcing a thousand." Offering a public rationale for such announcement, McNamara suggested that, if the war didn't go well, "we can say that these thousand would not have influenced the course of action."[162]

Kennedy insisted that the policy statement derived from the Taylor-McNamara report should be attributed not to him but to his advisers. "This ought to be their statement," he said, which he would then support in a press conference. He also suggested that the entire NSC go on record as supporting the policy, and that his own role would be that of accepting the unanimous recommendation. Kennedy proposed that the policy statement given to the press say that the president had accepted the McNamara-Taylor recommendations "on the advice of the NSC."[163] That is exactly what happened that evening. When Press Secretary Pierre Salinger released the policy statement on Vietnam, he attributed Kennedy's formula on completing "the major part of the military task by the end of 1965" to McNamara and Taylor. Salinger told the press that their conclusions had been "endorsed by all members of the [National] Security Council this afternoon" and that the policy statement had been "approved by the President on the basis of recommendations received from them and from Ambassador Lodge."[164]

Kennedy's maneuvering on October 2 involved yet another level of deception. Although the withdrawal endorsed by the NSC and announced to the public referred only to the "major part" of the U.S. military presence being withdrawn by the 1965 deadline, Kennedy, McNamara, and Taylor had already agreed that the withdrawal plan that would actually be carried out would reduce the number of advisers to a bare minimum. McNamara recalls that, when he referred to the end of 1965 withdrawal date in the October 2 meeting, it was based on the plan to which JCS had agreed in May 1963.[165] That was precisely what Taylor referred to when he sent a memo to the JCS two days after the NSC decision calling for all planning to be "directed towards preparing Republic of Vietnam forces for the withdrawal of all United States special assistance units and personnel by the end of calendar year 1965." It called for the "Comprehensive Plan" to be revised to "bring it into consonance with these objectives, and to reduce planned residual (post-1965) MAAG strength to approximately preinsurgency levels."[166]

Kennedy thus used multiple levels of deception to make the two-year phase-out of U.S. troops official administration policy while making it appear to have been the initiative of his two top national security advisers and the NSC. That triumph of Machiavellian maneuvering was Kennedy's response to a powerful momentum toward military intervention that he had seen coming from national security bureaucracy. It succeeded, at least in the short run, because he was able to draw McNamara and Taylor into his scheme by playing on their personal ties to the Kennedy family.

Kennedy's withdrawal strategy was based, however, on the premise that the Diem regime would not be overthrown by a military coup, and that its repressive character and political weakness probably would provide a convenient rationale for early withdrawal. Immediately after Kennedy had achieved the objective of legitimizing the withdrawal plan, the CIA reported on October 5 that Saigon generals were now moving ahead with a coup plan. Kennedy was reluctant to oppose a coup plan that had already been set in motion. Instead, he tried to tread a fine line between not "thwarting" a coup and encouraging such a coup. Once the United States decided to establish liaison with the coup plotters, however, this line was meaningless. Even though Kennedy tried to insist shortly before the coup that Lodge discourage the generals unless it was certain to succeed, the administration was irrevocably compromised by such contacts.[167]

Immediately after the overthrow and assassination of Diem and Nhu, Kennedy realized that the new regime might not be any more successful in prosecuting the war than the Diem regime had been, as indicated by the private reflections he taped on November 4.[168] He also realized that it would be far more difficult to explain a rapid pullout if the new regime stumbled militarily than it would have been had Diem and Nhu remained in power. Significantly, within the space of eleven days, Kennedy twice indicated that he was rethinking his strategy of relying on working only behind the scenes and only on the basis of the existing phase-out plan. Instead, he suggested that he was moving toward making a broader public case for withdrawal. On November 12, he told Wayne Morse (D-Ore.), the most aggressive Senate foe of the Vietnam War, that he agreed with him and was in the midst of a review of Vietnam policy that would support Morse's position, and wanted to discuss it with him when he was finished. Then Kennedy told Forrestal on November 21, less than twenty-four hours before he was cut down by an assassin's bullet, that he wanted to start a "complete and very profound review of how we got into this country; what we thought we were doing; and what we now think we can do." Kennedy concluded, "I even want to think about whether or not we should be there."[169]

In light of the increased risk of rapid decline of the Saigon government and Kennedy's abiding interest in the diplomatic option, these conversations appear to indicate that he was now thinking seriously about negotiating a political settlement in South Vietnam before the situation had deteriorated too far. The counterfactual debate over whether Kennedy would have proceeded with a unilateral withdrawal of U.S. troops once his administration encountered the reverses in South Vietnam that did come in 1964–65 may therefore have focused on the wrong question. Kennedy probably would not have attempted to carry out the withdrawal plan for which he had obtained NSC approval in late 1963, but he almost certainly would have resumed the effort to establish a diplomatic channel for peace negotiations on Vietnam that he had begun in 1962. He would have faced opposition from within his own administration to the neutralization of South Vietnam, and the path to a negotiated settlement would not have been straight. But Kennedy's use of the McNamara-Taylor mission to legitimize the withdrawal scheme shows that, when he was sure of what he wanted, he was capable of Machiavellian political manipulation in order to achieve it.

6 Johnson, McNamara, and the Tonkin Gulf Episode

Were Lyndon Johnson's Cold War beliefs and insecurity the primary reasons the United States went to war over Vietnam in 1965? That is the overwhelmingly dominant interpretation in the literature on U.S. Vietnam policy.[1] The focus on Johnson is not surprising. He lacked Kennedy's analytical bent and had little patience with diplomacy. Furthermore, he exhorted his aides during 1964 to do more to defeat the Communist insurgency *within* South Vietnam—something Kennedy had never done.[2] Finally, once he regarded himself as irrevocably committed to war in Vietnam in mid 1965, Johnson fiercely defended that course. The frustrations of the war took a heavy toll on him both physically and mentally, and as he became increasingly reliant on alcohol to quell his anxieties, Johnson became surly even with his closest confidants and expressed paranoia about Communists among his critics.[3]

Robert S. McNamara states quite categorically in his memoirs that Lyndon Johnson was "determined" to prevent the loss of South Vietnam and "felt more certain than President Kennedy that the loss of South Vietnam had a higher cost than would the direct application of U.S. military force." He has also said that Johnson came to the presidency with a "hawkishness" on Vietnam that had not changed since his time as vice president.[4] But this portrayal of Johnson does not withstand careful scrutiny. Consciously or unconsciously, McNamara has remembered what he needed to shift the responsibility for going to war over Vietnam from his own shoulders to those of Lyndon Johnson.

For all his personal insecurities, bluster, and crudeness, Lyndon Johnson was never held in thrall by any Cold War doctrine that required the United States to do whatever was necessary to save South Vietnam. Johnson's opposition to U.S. military intervention in Vietnam, like Kennedy's, went all the way back to the early 1950s. As Senate majority leader, he had played politics with the issue in 1954 by criticizing the Eisenhower administration's failure to save Indochina, while carefully avoiding an explicit public position on military intervention.[5] In the crucial meeting of congressional leaders with Eisenhower and Dulles on April 3, 1954, however, Johnson had joined Senator Richard B. Russell Jr. (D-Ga.) in demanding substantial commitments in advance from Britain and France as conditions for congressional approval of the use of force in Indochina—a position that he knew was likely to rule out U.S. military intervention. He had told four Democratic senators immediately after the meeting that he had "pounded the table" in the Oval Office to emphasize his opposition to sending U.S. troops to Indochina.[6]

Johnson still felt passionately that U.S. forces should not be committed to Vietnam when he became vice president in 1961. He expressed that view with extraordinary forcefulness in a report to Kennedy after his visit to South Vietnam in May 1961:

> We should make clear, in private, that barring an unmistakable and massive invasion of South Viet Nam from without we have no intention of employing combat U.S. forces in Viet Nam or using even naval or air support which is but the first step in that direction. If the Vietnamese government, backed by a three-year liberal aid program cannot do this job, then we had better remember the experience of the French who wound up with several hundred thousand men in Vietnam and were still unable to do it. . . . Before we take any such plunge we had better be sure we are prepared to become bogged down chasing irregulars and guerrillas over the rice fields and jungles of Southeast Asia while our principal enemies China and the Soviet Union stand outside the fray and husband their strength.[7]

Johnson's personal beliefs were strongly at odds, therefore, with the idea that the United States had to use force to resist a Communist takeover in South Vietnam. Like Kennedy, however, Johnson had a strong political need to get his national security advisers to share the responsibility for a policy of nonintervention that could result in defeat in South Vietnam. And the same national security advisers who insisted in 1961 that Kennedy send U.S. troops to South Vietnam also pushed Johnson to carry out an air war against North Vietnam and then to put a limited ground combat force into South Vietnam. Lyndon Johnson's decisions for war were the result of a continuing struggle between Johnson and his principal advisers—and particularly with Robert S. McNamara—over escalation of the war. The full story of that struggle shows that the national security bureaucracy's pressures on Johnson for war were much stronger and more persistent—and Johnson's resistance more remarkable—than has ever been recorded.

MCNAMARA PUSHES FOR THE BOMBING OPTION

McNamara had loyally carried out John F. Kennedy's policy of phased withdrawal from Vietnam, but after Kennedy's murder, he felt no personal loyalty to Lyndon Johnson. Johnson had no clear policy of his own, moreover, when he succeeded to the presidency, and was far more dependent on his advisers, and particularly on McNamara, than Kennedy had been. McNamara had a deep-seated need to impose his own policy preference on major issues, which he had kept under control, at least on Vietnam, during the Kennedy administration.[8] But with a new president who lacked Kennedy's self-confidence in foreign affairs, the opportunity presented itself for McNamara to increase his influence on Vietnam policy.

McNamara's new aggressiveness on Vietnam was abetted by the fact that JCS Chairman General Maxwell Taylor, who had also been drawn into JFK's policy because of his close relationship with Robert F. Kennedy, was also free of any loyalty to Lyndon Johnson and was in basic agreement with McNamara on the need to escalate the war. Their instinctive desire to be associated with a winning cause, combined with the incentives inherent in the unequal Cold War power balance, led them both to urge the use of U.S. military power to put pressure on North Vietnam.

McNamara had already wanted to see increased military pressures on North Vietnam even before Kennedy was assassinated. At the Honolulu Conference on November 20, 1963, just two days before Kennedy traveled to Dallas, McNamara argued strongly that a "full-fledged effort" at covert operations carried out by the Pentagon, rather than the CIA, could do "serious damage" to North Vietnamese military efforts. Despite opposition to the idea by William Colby of the CIA, he ordered MACV and the CIA to prepare a twelve-month plan for operations against North Vietnam of graduated intensity, to include actions by U.S. forces.[9] McGeorge Bundy knew, however, that Kennedy would not approve of planning for any covert operations that included U.S. air attacks on North Vietnam, because Kennedy had expressed his opposition to such a policy on at least two occasions earlier in 1963.[10] Bundy returned from the Honolulu meeting with a draft of NSAM 273 that said, in paragraph 7, "with respect to action against North Vietnam, there should be a detailed plan for the development of additional Government of Vietnam resources, especially for seagoing activity," which would "indicate the time and investment necessary to achieve a wholly new level of effectiveness in this field of action."[11]

This cautious language limited the scope of any operations against North Vietnam to South Vietnamese forces. Sometime between November 21 and 24, however, Bundy made a major change in the draft NSAM. In a draft dated November 24, paragraph 7 no longer clearly limited covert operations against the North to the South Vietnamese forces. The new draft stated:[12]

> Planning should include different levels of possible increased activity, and in each instance there should be estimates of such factors as:
>
> A. Resulting damage to North Vietnam;
>
> B. The plausibility of denial;
>
> C. Possible North Vietnamese retaliation;
>
> D. Other international reaction.

This new language, which was clearly intended to be broad enough to cover planning for actions by U.S. as well as South Vietnamese forces, was then included in the text of NSAM 273 adopted on November 26.[13] Bundy later claimed that this change in policy was prompted by Johnson's directives on November 24.[14] But the evidence belies Bundy's claim. Johnson did direct Lodge to tell the South Vietnamese generals that he "would not be the first president to lose a war" and that he would "stand by our word." But he was seeking to reassure Saigon, not signaling that he was prepared to take responsibility for the war. At a meeting with Lodge and his principal advisers that same day, Johnson said nothing to indicate that he would change Kennedy's policy, and he offered no opposition when most—though not all—of these advisers said the United States could withdraw most of the troops by the end of 1965. Johnson told Bill Moyers after the meeting that he had agreed to the request for "a hundred or so million" and "more if they need it." He made it clear, however, that he was demanding that the South Vietnamese "get off their butts and get out in those jungles and whip hell out of some Communists." And he left no doubt that he was determined to avoid a U.S. takeover of the war: "I want 'em to leave me alone," he told Moyers, "because I've got some bigger things to do right here at home." Two days later, Johnson approved NSAM 273, which explicitly endorsed the aim of withdrawing the bulk of U.S. military personnel from Vietnam by the end of 1965.[15]

Johnson had no interest in opening the door to direct U.S. military actions against North Vietnam. As McNamara concedes in his memoirs, Johnson was "[g]rasping for a way to hurt North Vietnam *without direct U.S. military action* [emphasis added]."[16]

It was McNamara who was pushing for a policy of much stronger pressures against North Vietnam, including direct U.S. military pressures. In messages to U.S. MACV Commander Paul Harkins and Ambassador Henry Cabot Lodge on December 10 and 12, respectively, McNamara demanded that plans for covert operations make it clear that "the United States will not accept a Communist victory in South Vietnam and that we will escalate the conflict to whatever level is required to ensure their defeat."[17] The plans drawn up by the military and the CIA at McNamara's behest did indeed include air strikes against the North in phases II and III. A CIA message later described the three phases of attacks in the plans as being of "increasing intensity," with "prospects of immense destruction."[18] General Victor Krulak wrote that they included "destruction of major resources by raid or bombing." The premise of the plans was that North Vietnam would first be warned that it would be "punished"; the United States would then "proceed with selected elements of an escalation program."[19]

One of the main purposes of the trip by McNamara and JCS Chairman General Maxwell Taylor to Saigon on December 19 and 20 was to discuss this plan with the U.S. commander in Vietnam, the CIA station chief, and the embassy. As a result of the discussion, McNamara decided that this program would be studied by an "interdepartmental group" and that the specific operations it selected would be submitted to the "Special Group," or "303 Committee," which had authority to make decisions on most covert operations.[20] After meeting with Johnson on December 21, however, McNamara submitted a memorandum to the president that struck a notably less aggressive note. "I believe we should aim to select those [operations] that provide maximum pressure with minimum risk," he wrote. His memo also indicated that Johnson had specifically directed that the interagency group present its program directly to the president for approval—not to the 303 Committee. The same day, Johnson wrote a formal directive that an interagency committee should select from the twelve-month plan only "those operations which are most feasible, and which provide greatest return for the least risk."[21] He was moving swiftly to contain any move to commit the United States to a wider war in Vietnam.

The three-phase program of operations prepared by the interdepartmental committee reflected McNamara's desire to escalate the war, including air strikes against military targets in North Vietnam. But on January 16, Johnson authorized only the first phase of the plan, thus excluding air attacks, whether carried out by U.S. or South Vietnamese pilots.[22] Although Johnson did not explicitly reject the second and third phases of the plan, it was clear to McNamara and Taylor that the president was not prepared to support the military escalation McNamara had tried to maneuver Johnson into adopting.

Less than a week after Johnson's decision, Taylor sent a memorandum to McNamara on behalf of the JCS declaring that the covert operations that had been approved by Johnson would not have a "decisive effect" on Hanoi. "[W]e must be prepared fully to undertake a much higher level of activity, not only for its beneficial tactical effect, but to make plain our resolution, both to our friends and to our enemies," Taylor said. In a move clearly coordinated in advance with McNamara, Taylor called for readiness to bomb North Vietnamese targets using "U.S. resources under Vietnamese cover" and for commitment of U.S. forces "as necessary in direct actions against North Vietnam."[23]

It was only after Ambassador Lodge called for retaliatory attacks on the North for any further terrorist attacks on Americans in South Vietnam on February 20 that Johnson made any move to authorize direct planning for possible U.S. military pressures on North Vietnam. Johnson, who viewed Lodge as a potential Republican critic of his policy with presidential ambitions, told Bundy he was determined to "build a record" of having been responsive to Lodge's recommendations. Otherwise, as he later told McNamara, "we are caught with our britches down." At a meeting with his advisers at which a response to Lodge was on the agenda, Johnson agreed that contingency planning for "pressures on North Vietnam" should be "speeded up," with particular attention to "shaping such pressures so as to produce the maximum credible deterrent effect on Hanoi."[24]

That same day, however, Johnson made it clear that he did not intend to escalate the war. In a conversation with McNamara on how he wanted Vietnam to be handled in a speech scheduled for a week later, he said, "It's their war and it's their men." Johnson then talked about U.S. Vietnam policy as though it were McNamara's policy rather than his own: "McNamara's not fighting a war. But he's training men to fight a war, and when he gets them through high school, they will have graduated from high school, and will have twelve grades behind them next year, and he hasn't taken on any agreement to keep them for the rest of their life. He's just made a commitment to train them to fight. And if he trains them to fight and they won't fight, he can't do anything about it. Then he's got to choose whether he fights or lets them have it."

McNamara responded: "That is the problem exactly, and what I fear is that we're right at that point."[25] McNamara wanted a decision from Johnson that he was ready to fight for South Vietnam, if necessary. But Johnson was far from ready to concede that the United States should save the Saigon government by taking over the war.

McNamara had already decided to recommend a plan for bombing North Vietnam well before he had left on another trip to South Vietnam in early March. On March 1, Assistant Secretary of Defense William P. Bundy wrote the first draft of a memorandum to serve as a "framework" for McNamara's report to the president upon his return from Vietnam.[26] Bundy's draft recommended a bombing campaign against targets in North Vietnam, including "key rail lines to Communist China" and "key industrial complexes." The primary objectives of the attacks would be to get Hanoi to "stop, or at least sharply cut down, its supply of key items to the Viet Cong" and to "stiffen the Khanh government, completely assure it of our determination, and discourage moves toward neutralism in South Vietnam."

Bundy's central argument for the use of force against North Vietnam, however, was the low risk that it would involve. If the United States clearly stated its aims in attacking North Vietnam to be "limited and punitive," the draft argued, the Chinese, fearful of U.S. reprisals, would not respond with large-scale ground or air involvement. Similarly, it expressed confidence that North Vietnam's dual fear of potential devastation by the United States and of a major Chinese military force on its territory inhibited any escalation by Hanoi of the war in the South. "They make bold noises," wrote Bundy, "but there are plenty of indications that they fear US action against them, are not confident they could deal with it by themselves, and at the same time do not want to have to call on Communist China."[27]

Bundy's and McNamara's assumption that Soviet and Chinese passivity and North Vietnamese fears made attacking North Vietnam an extremely low risk reflected a broad consensus in the national security bureaucracy about the implications of the East-West power balance. If the United States carried out air attacks on North Vietnam, the JCS advised McNamara, the USSR "would probably be highly concerned over possible expansion of the conflict" and would "initiate no action which, in the Soviet judgment, would increase the likelihood of nuclear war."[28] The CIA agreed, predicting that the USSR would "refrain from military action in the area and would not provoke a major crisis with the U.S. elsewhere."[29] The interagency study of military pressures on North Vietnam calculated that Moscow would "avoid any commitment that would embolden Hanoi" and would probably do nothing to defend North Vietnam, "at least up to the point where [the] USSR considered the existence of a Communist regime in North Vietnam directly threatened."[30]

Indeed, most of the national security bureaucracy now viewed the USSR as aligned more with the United States than with China. The CIA believed that the Kremlin leaders saw their own interests as "paralleling those of the West rather than those of their communist ally."[31] As early as mid 1963, Bill Bundy had told a group of Pentagon officials, "Although we continue to use [the Soviet leaders], to try to get them to do whatever is possible to restrain [the North Vietnamese], they do not control the situation." Deputy Assistant Secretary of State for Southeast Asia Marshall Green explained to a German official that the United States and the Soviet Union were pursuing "somewhat similar policies" toward Communist China: "Moscow contains Peiping on the North and West, while we contain it on the other side."[32]

Given Chinese economic and military weakness and the absence of a Soviet deterrence threat, Johnson's advisers saw only a slight possibility of a major Chinese military response to a U.S. bombing offensive against the DRV. The JCS believed that the most China would do in response to a U.S. air assault on North Vietnam was to offer the DRV fighter aircraft, antiaircraft units, and volunteers, and perhaps commit aircraft to its defense. DOD had concluded, moreover, that the withdrawal of Soviet military assistance had severely reduced the Chinese Air Force's flying proficiency and supply of air-to-air missiles. The CIA agreed. "Communist China almost certainly would not want to become involved in hostilities with U.S. forces," it concluded, and would therefore "proceed with caution." Rusk, too, believed that the Chinese could no longer count on Soviet support, and that it was therefore "highly questionable whether they would want to face our power."[33]

The knowledge that China would soon test a nuclear device only reinforced the national security bureaucracy's belief that China would have to exercise caution in the face of systematic U.S. attacks on North Vietnam. Although the CIA expected China to explode a nuclear device sometime in 1964, it predicted that the PRC would probably not have sufficient nuclear striking capability to deter U.S. military action against China for "decades." Khrushchev's shrewd observation to Harriman in mid 1963 that the Chinese would be even more careful to avoid provoking the United States once they had nuclear weapons had been widely accepted in the administration.[34] The State Department's Policy Planning staff pointed out that the Chinese had been "very sensitive to the possibility of an attack on the mainland," and that the acquisition of nuclear weapons would probably make the Chinese even more cautious in that respect.[35]

The national security bureaucracy also believed that the broader imbalance of power sharply constrained Hanoi's options in the South. The CIA had reckoned in mid 1963 that Hanoi's fear of a "major military confrontation" with the United States put "an upper limit on the scale and tempo of Hanoi's militancy in South Vietnam and Laos." A paper for the interagency study group in early 1964, reflecting a CIA view that would be repeated throughout the year, noted that Hanoi could not be sure whether the United States would occupy areas in the North, or even whether its leadership might be "decimated in an attack on Hanoi." It concluded that there was at least a 50–50 chance that the North Vietnamese would temporarily reduce the effort in the South if Hanoi were convinced that the United States would go ahead with serious air attacks on the North.[36]

The belief that a decisive U.S. power advantage reduced the risks of bombing the North to a very low level created a powerful incentive for McNamara and other national security advisers to advocate that option. Since it was seen as an opportunity to demonstrate the willingness and ability of the United States to use its military power to punish its Communist foes, the bombing appeared to most national security officials to be a good bet, even if the chances that it would force Hanoi to change its policy toward the South were poor, as some analysts believed.

The evidence is now clear, however, that Johnson forced McNamara to drop his plan for recommending a bombing program even before he left for South Vietnam. Johnson met with Rusk and McNamara on March 3 specifically to discuss the McNamara mission to South Vietnam. Before the meeting, McGeorge Bundy urged Johnson to "explore with McNamara his own increasing concern that we simply cannot count on our current policies to carry us through the year without stronger steps of some sort." Johnson's position in that meeting, for which no notes are available, can be deduced from the fact that, two days after that meeting, William Bundy rewrote the draft memorandum so that it now marshaled the arguments *against* the "overt extension of operations in the North" in the immediate future: the Communists might respond by escalating the war, pressures for negotiations would increase, and the attacks would be "mounted from an extremely weak base which might at any moment collapse and leave the posture of political confrontation worsened rather than improved."[37]

Johnson also called McNamara on March 5 at 8:10 P.M. for a last conversation before the secretary's departure. That same evening McNamara had dinner with the British ambassador, Lord Harlech, who reported to London that the secretary seemed "despondent" about the war. In contrast to previous conversations, in which McNamara had talked confidently about "hurting the North Vietnamese," this time McNamara confided to him that no recommendation for air attacks against the North was likely to be forthcoming from his trip.[38]

After their visit to South Vietnam on March 8–12, McNamara and Taylor met with the NSC on the revised McNamara report, with its arguments against attacking the North. In a scene that obviously reflected a prior understanding between them, Johnson asked McNamara whether his recommendation would be sufficient to "turn the tide" in South Vietnam, to which McNamara gave the positive answer he knew Johnson expected. Johnson then accepted McNamara's report without changing a single word, as NSAM 288.[39] Johnson had again used his presidential power to outmaneuver McNamara.

Nevertheless, Johnson was beginning to feel real pressure from the military. In a meeting with the JCS on March 4, at which the military leadership called for a naval blockade and the destruction of military and economic targets in North Vietnam, Johnson begged off. As he described the meeting to McGeorge Bundy, he pleaded, "[W]e haven't got any Congress that will go with us, and we haven't got any mothers that will go with us in a war" and added, "I've got to win an election." Two weeks later, White House aide Michael Forrestal advised McGeorge Bundy that the JCS believed that Johnson was avoiding the "correct decisions" on Vietnam in order to assure his election.[40] Later that month, Johnson's military aide Brigadier General Chester Clifton warned the president that the JCS regarded a refusal to put stronger military pressure on the North as an "Asian Bay of Pigs" and were already registering their dissent, so that they could not be blamed later if the policy ended in defeat.[41] "They're trying to get me in a war over there," Johnson complained to Richard Goodwin in early April.[42]

Soon after McNamara's return from Vietnam, Johnson fed political speculation by telling columnist James Reston that he would consider McNamara as his vice presidential running mate. In an interview with a *New York Times* reporter around the same time, Johnson praised McNamara as "the best utility man" in his administration and said he was ready to make him secretary of state or secretary of transportation "tomorrow."[43] Such unstinting praise and hints of higher office have been interpreted as expressions of Johnson's admiration for McNamara. Johnson's motives were far more complex, however. Johnson knew that McNamara was a very close friend of Robert F. Kennedy's, a powerful political rival whose allies were already trying to pressure Johnson into putting Kennedy on the ticket as vice presidential candidate. One aim of these leaks, as well as of the later offer of the vice presidential nomination and yet another offer to name McNamara "number one executive vice-president in charge of the cabinet," was certainly to cement McNamara's loyalty.[44] But Johnson also must have thought seriously about finding a way to move McNamara out of the Pentagon, so that he would no longer be pushing for escalation of the war. In any case, McNamara turned him down, leaving no easy way to solve the problem.

In mid May, for the first time in Johnson's presidency, Johnson's principal advisers—McNamara, Rusk, McGeorge Bundy, CIA Director

John McCone, and Taylor—constituted themselves as the Executive Committee of the NSC, or "ExComm."[45] The political significance of that decision can hardly be overestimated. The ExComm had been convened in the Kennedy administration only at Kennedy's direction during the Cuban Missile Crisis and then in late August 1963 over the political crisis in Saigon, and in both cases, the president had attended almost all the meetings of the group. Johnson's five principal advisers, however, used it as a mechanism to develop a strategy for getting him to escalate the war. Those meetings produced the first intense pressures from the national security bureaucracy on Johnson to make a commitment to the use of direct U.S. military force against North Vietnam.

The first result of these meetings was that McNamara, McCone, and Assistant Secretary of State William Bundy joined in warning Johnson on May 18 that the chances were now "at least 50–50" that, unless he took action against North Vietnam, the situation in both South Vietnam and Laos would "deteriorate by the latter part of this year to a point where they would be very difficult to save." Johnson then agreed to look at two different plans—one for "interlarding" U.S. personnel with South Vietnamese, the other for "graduated action against North Vietnam."[46]

At a series of three meetings of the new ExComm on May 24–25, including one with the president, Johnson's advisers discussed a thirty-day scenario that would begin with a warning to North Vietnam through a Canadian intermediary and would include passage of a congressional resolution authorizing the use of force in Vietnam, followed, just two weeks later, by air strikes by U.S. aircraft against military and industrial targets in North Vietnam and—should China enter the conflict—the possible use of nuclear weapons.[47] The ExComm did not present Johnson with a choice between widening the war and inserting U.S. officers in the South Vietnamese army; instead, the latter option was incorporated into the scenario leading to an air campaign in the North. At the ExComm meeting on May 24, without Johnson, McNamara complained that the president appeared to regard more and better actions in South Vietnam "as an alternative or a substitute for the use of force." McNamara insisted that such proposed actions within South Vietnam were "not a substitute for the use of force." They could "ride through for a few additional weeks, even with further weakening," he said, but they might have to use military force eventually.[48]

Meeting with Johnson on May 24, McNamara and Rusk agreed that striking the North was "necessary," and McNamara argued for putting U.S. ground troops into Southeast Asia to deter the Chinese Communists and the DRV from moving their own troops into Laos or elsewhere in response. Johnson temporized, saying he wanted to be "ready, if other efforts fail, to go on to air attacks against North Vietnam." He insisted, however, that the United States "attempt to get a UN peacekeeping operation first."[49] It was only the first of several arguments Johnson would use to avoid authorizing the use of force.

Johnson's advisers knew that Johnson was not going to agree to start the bombing while he was campaigning for the presidency. What they wanted from him was precisely what they had sought from Kennedy. On May 25, McGeorge Bundy wrote to Johnson on behalf of McNamara and Rusk seeking a commitment to "selected and carefully graduated military force against North Vietnam." McNamara and Rusk called for a formal decision that the United States "cannot tolerate the loss of Southeast Asia to Communism" and commitment of the necessary military deployments to the region to back it up. The rationale for such a policy was again that it carried such low risk, given the dominance of U.S. power. Bundy argued, as he had to Kennedy, that such a commitment offered "the best present chance of avoiding the actual use of such force." Bundy said the "hope and best estimate of most of your advisers" was that limited air strikes on North Vietnam would not draw "a major military reply from Red China or the Soviets." Two days later, Bundy even suggested that Johnson could "do what I think Kennedy did at least once, which is to make the threat without having made your own internal decision that you would actually carry it through."[50]

Johnson carefully avoided putting an outright rejection of the option of force on the record. Instead, he told his advisers on May 26 to discuss the matter further with Lodge and the military leadership at a conference in Honolulu.[51] Johnson was far from being convinced by their argument for the use of force. The following day, in a phone conversation with Bundy, he railed against his advisers' confidence that the Chinese would not intervene. "I believe the Chinese Communists are coming into it," he asserted. "I don't think that we can fight them 10,000 miles away from home and ever get anywhere in that area." And he derided the idea that the United States should fight for Vietnam. "What the hell is Vietnam worth to me?" he demanded. "What is it worth to this country?" The United States had a treaty, he admitted, "but hell, everybody else's got a treaty out there and they're not doing anything about it." Johnson concluded, plaintively, "I don't think it's worth fighting for and I don't think we can get out."[52]

In an unscheduled meeting with McNamara, Rusk, Bundy, and White House aide Jack Valenti on June 5, Johnson told a story that clearly signaled his refusal to make a commitment to the use of force to save South Vietnam. He recalled how he had led a group of schoolboy friends in a physical confrontation with a teacher whom they all disliked and thought would be easy to intimidate. When the teacher turned out to be more prepared to fight than they had expected, Johnson recalled, he turned to find that all of his friends had fled, and he, too, beat a hasty retreat. "What I am saying," he explained, "is if I have to turn back I want to make sure I am not in too deep to do so."[53]

The ExComm meetings also led to the development of a congressional resolution authorizing the use of force in Southeast Asia. Contrary to the popular notion that the main purpose of the resolution was to get Congress to support a war policy that was already settled, the real target of the resolution was Lyndon Johnson himself. William Bundy, who led the drive for such a resolution, rejected an early draft of a resolution written by the State Department's former legal adviser that had included the phrase "if the President determines the necessity thereof" in the operative paragraph on possible use of arms. The operative provision of a draft resolution prepared during the second week in June was not a statement of congressional support at all. Instead, it formalized a military commitment to Southeast Asia that the president had strongly resisted in May. One alternative for the operative paragraph of the resolution stated that the United States "is determined to prevent by whatever means may be necessary, including the use of arms, the Communist regime in North Viet-Nam, with the aid and support of the Communist regime in China, from extending, by force or threat of force, its aggressive or subversive activities against any non-Communist nations in Southeast Asia." As Bundy later recalled, the argument against the resolution was that it would have committed the president to a much more ambitious policy than he was ready to embrace.[54]

The leading opponent of the resolution was the president himself. Before the meeting on June 15 to discuss the resolution, McGeorge Bundy, obviously acting on Johnson's behalf, circulated a paper that listed a series of actions to be taken on the presumption that there would be no decision to carry out the escalation against the North and no congressional resolution. The participants in the meeting understood clearly that Johnson was again moving indirectly to reaffirm his opposition to widening the war.[55]

TONKIN GULF: THE USURPATION
OF PRESIDENTIAL POWER

For decades, the Tonkin Gulf has been a symbol of deceit in the service of aggressive war. As documented in increasing detail over the years, the alleged North Vietnamese attack on U.S. warships on August 4, 1964, which was used by the administration to justify the bombing and a congressional authorization for the use of force, never occurred at all.[56] Robert S. McNamara, who had insisted strongly for decades that the evidence supported his conclusion that the attack had taken place, finally conceded, after meeting DRV General Vo Nguyen Giap in 1998, that no such attack had in fact occurred.[57]

The literature on the Tonkin Gulf episode has always assumed that Lyndon Johnson was in command on August 4 and decided to bomb North Vietnam, despite the knowledge that top military authorities had doubts about the authenticity of the attack.[58] The evidence now available, however, suggests that Johnson was never informed on August 4 that both the task force commander of the U.S. warships and the commander in chief, Pacific (CINCPAC) had called for further review of the incident before deciding on any action. Thus, Johnson was deliberately prevented from making an informed decision on whether to go ahead with bombing attacks decided on earlier in the day.

Despite an attack by North Vietnamese patrol boats on the USS *Maddox* on August 2, Johnson ruled out retaliation, because he did not believe the incident was the result of a deliberate policy by Hanoi. He told McNamara that he wanted fifteen to twenty members of the Senate Armed Services Committee and Foreign Relations Committee briefed, because Senate minority leader Everett M. Dirksen (R-Ill.) and others were calling for tougher U.S. action against North Vietnam. McNamara suggested that the OPLAN 34 covert operations be revealed to congressional leaders and mentioned that the North Vietnamese "undoubtedly" had interpreted the U.S. naval patrol as connected with the covert attack on two North Vietnamese islands by the U.S.-sponsored South Vietnamese boats just twenty-four hours earlier. "Well, say that to Dirksen," Johnson replied.[59]

The most serious pressure for military action in the Gulf came not from the Republicans but from Johnson's own national security team. Maxwell Taylor, Johnson's new ambassador in Saigon, sent a telegram on August 3 complaining that the administration's response would suggest to the world that the United States "flinches from confrontation with the North Vietnamese" and proposing retaliatory air attacks. Although McNamara thought Taylor was overreacting, both Undersecretary of State George Ball and McGeorge Bundy felt that his reaction "reflects a mood out there."[60]

On August 4, McNamara was clearly determined that the administration should take full advantage of any second naval incident in the Tonkin Gulf to bomb the North. Well before the first report of an attack on U.S.

vessels on August 4, McNamara called Johnson to alert him to the intercept of a North Vietnamese message indicating that some kind of naval action was imminent. Then, thirty minutes later, he called again to discuss changes in the military rules of engagement in the Gulf and to recommend retaliation against North Vietnamese targets in response to a second attack. McNamara began discussions with the Joint Staff, in which he pushed for the option of mining the North Vietnamese coastline, and ordered that mines by brought from Subic Bay in the Philippines to Danang Airbase in Vietnam. All this happened before the first report of firing of torpedoes at the U.S. destroyer *Maddox* arrived at the Pentagon at 11:18 A.M.[61]

At a lunch meeting following a briefing by McNamara on the alleged torpedo attack, Johnson accepted McNamara's recommendation that strikes be carried out against the PT boat base and the fuel depot at Vinh, and that they be launched at 7:00 P.M., pending agreement with the Joint Chiefs. Even before that meeting broke up, however, the earlier accounts from the U.S. task force commander in the Gulf, Captain John J. Herrick, of the *Maddox* dodging torpedoes from unidentified vessels was beginning to unravel. Herrick sent a message to CINCPAC Admiral Grant Sharp reporting that "freak weather effects" on the ship's radar made the earlier torpedo reports questionable and that no North Vietnamese boats had actually been sighted. Herrick suggested the need for a "complete evaluation" before any action was taken in response. McNamara read the Herrick message during the hour after he arrived back at the Pentagon at 3:06 P.M., according to his 1968 congressional testimony.[62]

At 3:44 P.M., Johnson called McNamara from the mansion, which meant that the conversation was not recorded. McNamara called back to the mansion just seven minutes later.[63] McNamara's behavior over the hour following those calls provides compelling evidence that he did not inform Johnson about Herrick's call for further investigation before taking action. When McNamara called Admiral Sharp twenty-five minutes later, at 4:08 P.M., it was not to launch such an investigation but to see if he could get a statement from him that the attack had definitely taken place.

McNamara had every reason to expect that Sharp would dismiss Herrick's doubts about the attack. Sharp had already told director of the Joint Staff Lieutenant General David Burchinal earlier in the afternoon that he was certain that it had occurred, even after he had read the Herrick reappraisal.[64] McNamara also knew that Sharp was eager for the opportunity to strike at North Vietnam. That morning, Sharp had urged that U.S. forces be authorized in advance to destroy any bases used by vessels attacking U.S. ships.

Despite his knowledge of the Herrick report, McNamara did not bring it up with Sharp. Nevertheless, Sharp informed him of yet another report from Herrick, which was based on further checking with the crew of the *Maddox*. Sharp said Herrick's "summation SITREP" indicated "a little doubt on just exactly what went on." Instead of asking further about the details of the new report, however, McNamara asked him an obviously leading question: "There isn't any possibility there was no attack, is there?" Sharp conceded that a "slight possibility" existed that there had been no attack. He added that he was "trying to get it nailed down," because "the Task Group Commander . . . says we need a daylight recce [reconnaissance] of the whole situation, and the situation's in doubt, he says."

McNamara said, "We obviously don't want to do it until we are damn sure what happened." But he did not direct Sharp to undertake a thorough investigation of what had happened. Instead, he invited Sharp to suggest how they should proceed. Sharp then recommended that McNamara "hold this execute"—the strike execute order from McNamara to CINC-PAC and the Seventh Fleet—"until we have a definite indication that this happened," adding that he thought he could have such a "definite indication" within an hour.

McNamara rejected Sharp's proposal. "If you get your definite information in two hours," said McNamara, "we can still proceed with the execute and it seems to me we ought to go ahead on that basis: get the pilots briefed, get the planes armed, get everything lined up to go. *Continue the execute order in effect, but between now and 6 o'clock get a definite fix and you call me directly* [emphasis added]."[65] McNamara did not want to delay the execute order, because he would then have to explain the delay to Johnson, which might well have led to the cancellation of the strike pending a full investigation. Instead, McNamara insisted on proceeding with the strike execute order even before the earlier reports of torpedo attacks on U.S. vessels had been verified.

It was the responsibility of the president—not that of the secretary of defense—to decide to go ahead with an order for the bombing of a foreign country when new information made it unclear whether U.S. ships had been attacked or not. Yet the president's log of phone conversations for August 4 shows that McNamara did not call Johnson following that crucial conversation with Sharp.[66] Instead, he proceeded with his own plan to issue the execute order. At 4:49 P.M., according to the Pentagon's subsequent chronology, the strike execute message was transmitted from the Pentagon to CINCPAC headquarters in Hawaii for retransmission to the Seventh Fleet.[67] One minute after that message had been sent, the president's phone log indicates that he called McNamara from the mansion.[68] Again, that call was not recorded, but the subsequent phone conversation between McNamara and Johnson shows that McNamara still did not alert Johnson to the latest developments.

At 4:45 P.M., both AP and UPI put on the ticker the news that congressional leaders had been informed of a meeting at the White House at 6:45 P.M. and that it was presumed to be a briefing on a second attack on U.S. warships in the Tonkin Gulf.[69] McNamara quickly learned about the story, and he called Johnson at 5:09 P.M. to tell him that "the story has broken" and to urge him to authorize a statement by the Pentagon about an attack on U.S. warships. McNamara had already drafted the statement, and he recited it: "[D]uring the night . . . two destroyers were attacked by the patrol boats. The attack was driven off. No casualties or damage to the destroyers. We believe several of the patrol boats were sunk. Details won't be available till daylight."[70]

Johnson immediately approved his proposed statement, and asked, "Anything further?" McNamara told him that former Treasury Secretary Douglas Dillon was supportive of retaliatory strikes—indicating that he had talked with Dillon, based on the premise that the torpedo attack was not in question, since previously talking with Johnson at 3:51—and that he had been unable to contact Robert F. Kennedy. The conversation ended without any reference to the problem of uncertainty about the alleged attack on U.S. vessels. At 6:00 P.M., Assistant Secretary of Defense Arthur Sylvester issued a statement to the press that was very similar to the one outlined by McNamara.[71]

The record of that McNamara-Johnson conversation indicates that McNamara had withheld from Johnson in the earlier, unrecorded conversations the information he would have needed to make an informed decision on whether to continue with the retaliatory strikes. Had McNamara informed Johnson in the earlier conversation about the uncertainties of Herrick and Sharp, and about Sharp's promise to get back to him with confirming evidence, Johnson presumably would at least have asked whether it was necessary to make a public announcement before hearing further from Sharp.

McNamara denied to the author in February 2004 that he had kept Johnson uninformed of the doubts of Herrick and Sharp on August 4, but he did not claim that he had informed Johnson by phone. He noted that telephone calls were not the only way he had to communicate with Johnson, and said he "could have" told Johnson about the military's unresolved doubts at the NSC meeting at 6:15 that night.[72] According to the notes of that meeting,

McNamara again asserted unequivocally that the attack had taken place. "The North Vietnamese PT boats have continued their attacks on two U.S. destroyers in international waters in the Gulf of Tonkin," he said. "No enemy aircraft was involved. Our efforts to learn the exact situation and protect the Patrol have been complicated by a very low ceiling. One of the destroyers was fired on by automatic weapons and lit up by searchlights."

USIA Director Carl Rowan then put McNamara on the spot: "Do we know for a fact that the North Vietnamese provocation took place?" he asked. "Can we nail down exactly what happened? We must be prepared to be accused of fabricating the incident." McNamara's response hinted at the truth while carefully skirting it. "We will know definitely in the morning," he said. "Only highly classified information nails down the incident. This information we cannot use and must rely on other reports we will be receiving."[73] This was as close as McNamara came to revealing that there had been any question about the evidence for an attack. McNamara insisted to the author that the official notes of the meeting, which were written by Bromley Smith of the NSC staff and marked "Top Secret Sensitive; For the President Only," were "not complete."[74] But it is hardly plausible that Smith would have omitted any statement admitting that the task force commander and CINCPAC had expressed doubts about the torpedo attacks from notes for the president's use. Furthermore, McNamara cites those same notes as documentation for his own recollection that he "outlined the evidence supporting our conclusion and presented our proposed response."[75]

McNamara had seized on an intercepted North Vietnamese message referring to the loss of two of its vessels as the sole basis for his assurance that an attack on U.S. vessels had indeed occurred without making any effort to analyze the document. Based on the time-date group of the intercepted message alone, intelligence analysts quickly determined that it could not have been referring to the August 4 incident.[76]

In an interview with CNN in 1996, McNamara asserted that Johnson had decided to go ahead with the strike despite uncertainty about what had happened in the Gulf. On August 4, he said, "we thought it highly probable but not entirely certain" that an attack on U.S. vessels had taken place. "And because it was highly probable—and because even if it hadn't occurred, there was strong feeling we should have responded to the first attack, which we were positive had occurred—President Johnson decided to respond to the second."[77]

This account, which McNamara did not relate in his own memoirs, is at odds with the documentary record of McNamara's behavior that afternoon.

Furthermore, if Johnson had ordered McNamara not to attempt to confirm the attack, Johnson should have acted in the aftermath of the bombing to suppress any information on what had actually happened in the Tonkin Gulf. In fact, however, Johnson almost immediately did the opposite. Even before the Gulf of Tonkin Resolution was passed overwhelmingly by Congress, Johnson ordered McGeorge Bundy—not McNamara—to launch a major inquiry into the alleged attack on U.S. ships and the way in which decisions had been made. On August 7, Bromley Smith of McGeorge Bundy's staff began collecting what he called "proof of attack" messages that had come from Herrick.[78] On the same day, Bundy himself requested "all intercepts which preceded or related to the second attack" from the intelligence community, indicating that Johnson wanted an independent analysis of whether they really showed what McNamara had claimed.[79]

Johnson also wanted a full accounting of communications between CINCPAC and DOD on August 4–5—suggesting a suspicion that he had not been fully informed about what McNamara knew. A preliminary chronology of McNamara's actions during the episode was written in McNamara's office as early as August 6, with a handwritten note at the top: "Answer to inquiry only!"[80] A few days later, McNamara's office received a set of questions that referred to the chronology on which someone had written by hand "How to transmit to WH [White House]."[81] The chronology was to be based in part on the original tapes of all such communications, which were tracked down and transcribed.[82] McNamara clearly exercised personal control over its content, making revisions in the third draft by hand.[83] It was submitted to Johnson on September 4 and was never used by the White House for propaganda purposes.[84] Johnson's intense interest in getting the full facts on what had happened and what McNamara had known suggests that Johnson felt he had been kept in the dark.

Furthermore, the Pentagon chronology was written specifically to hide certain key facts from Johnson. The conversation between McNamara and Sharp was central to an understanding of McNamara's actions on the afternoon of August 4, and the chronology was deliberately misleading in its description of that conversation. Instead of quoting McNamara's leading question to Sharp from the actual transcript of the conversation ("There isn't any possibility there was no attack, is there?"), the chronology had McNamara wanting to know "if there is a possibility that no attack occurred." The account of that conversation also failed to mention Sharp's revelation that Herrick considered the "whole situation" to be "in doubt" and was now calling for a "daylight recce." Most important, however, the chronology portrayed McNamara as agreeing with Sharp that the execute order should be withheld until confirming evidence was found. Without using quotation marks, it showed McNamara suggesting to Sharp that, "if definite confirmation of an attack is not forthcoming for another 2 hours, an hour would still remain and the execute order could then be issued." What McNamara had actually said was that they could "still proceed with the execute." Although it quoted McNamara's statement about making preparations for a strike, the Pentagon account carefully omitted the crucial words that followed: "*Continue the execute order in effect.*" [85]

McNamara used the chronology to make the case that he had weighed the evidence with the Joint Chiefs before concluding that the *Maddox* and the *C. Turner Joy* had been subjected to a second North Vietnamese PT boat attack. The chronology shows McNamara beginning a meeting with Deputy Secretary Cyrus Vance and the Joint Chiefs of Staff at 4:47 P.M. to "marshal the evidence to overcome the lack of a clear and convincing showing that an attack on the destroyers had taken place." It claims that McNamara and the JCS based their conclusion about the attack on five kinds of evidence, the most important of which were an intercepted North Vietnamese message, which supposedly indicated that two North Vietnamese PT boats had been sunk, and Sharp's satisfaction an attack had taken place.[86]

But unfortunately for McNamara's case, the chronology also showed that the strike execute order to CINCPAC had gone out at 4:49 P.M.—just two minutes after the meeting had supposedly begun. It also showed that McNamara did not learn about the supposedly crucial intercept of the North Vietnamese message until after a phone call from Sharp to Burchinal that began at 5:23 P.M., more than thirty minutes after his decision to send out the execute order and fourteen minutes after his request to Johnson for a public statement that an attack had occurred.[87]

The transcript of Sharp's conversation with Burchinal confirms that McNamara had already made up his mind before Sharp's call to justify the strike without any additional evidence. Burchinal was the officer on whom McNamara relied all that day to keep track of communications from CINCPAC and the task force commander as well as intelligence intercepts. He told Sharp he had not yet seen the specific intercept to which Sharp was referring but added that it didn't matter, because McNamara was already "satisfied with the evidence."[88] But that key piece of information, too, was omitted from the chronology.[89]

Sharp's determination that an attack had taken place also came after McNamara had made up his mind. When Sharp called Burchinal at 4:40 P.M., *before* McNamara's alleged meeting with the JCS, he repeated his previously expressed view that "it may be just as well to wait an hour or so, if we have to, to be certain"—a statement that was also omitted from the chronology.[90] Sharp's statement that he was "satisfied with the evidence" came only in the call to Burchinal at 5:23 P.M., in which Burchinal told him that McNamara was already satisfied with the evidence.

Contrary to the image of the Tonkin Gulf episode as moving U.S. policy firmly onto a track for military intervention, it actually widened the differences between Johnson and his national security advisers over Vietnam policy. Within days of the episode, Johnson had learned enough to be convinced that the alleged August 4 North Vietnamese attack probably had not occurred, and he responded by halting both the OPLAN 34A raids and the DESOTO patrols. In meetings with McNamara after August 4, Johnson referred, in a "sort of kidding way," according to George Ball, to his own doubts that the attack had actually taken place.[91]

Johnson's advisers, on the other hand, were encouraged by the bombing of North Vietnam to begin a new round of planning for a broader campaign of retaliatory strikes and ultimately systematic military pressure—none of which had Johnson's authorization. Within hours of the August 5 air strike, McNamara, Rusk, and Bundy had approved a telegram to Taylor that said, "We will be reviewing the whole gamut of operations against North Vietnam with particular view to those most justifiable in terms of activity against South Vietnam." Within days, Bundy began drafting a proposal for a sequence of actions that would lead to more retaliatory attacks on the North.[92]

Johnson's national security team wanted to use the combination of 34A sabotage operations and naval patrols to provoke further incidents with North Vietnamese naval forces. In an August 27 memorandum, the JCS urged intensification of OPLAN 34A operations and the naval patrols in the Gulf of Tonkin. A memorandum drafted by William Bundy for a meeting of the principals on August 31 proposed carrying out further commando attacks against targets on North Vietnam's coast while running the DESOTO patrols close to or within North Vietnam's territorial waters in a "defensible but challenging mode" in the hope that the North Vietnamese might be provoked into military action once again. A few days later, Assistant Secretary of Defense John McNaughton proposed the same provocative strategy in a memorandum to McNamara.[93]

Before visiting Washington for discussions in light of further political upheavals in Saigon in early September, Taylor provided a key argument for such a strategy: the United States could not realistically hope for a much stronger, more stable government in Saigon and couldn't wait until the beginning of 1965 to attack the North. Taylor called for exploiting "any opportunities presented by the Communists (such as Gulf of Tonkin attacks)" to help "hold South Vietnam together" as well as to produce "mounting pressures on the will of Hanoi." William Bundy then formulated an explicit provocation strategy for a meeting at which a presidential decision was expected. His draft suggested that naval patrols could be run outside the twelve-mile limit at first, but that if they had not "aroused a reaction" within a couple of weeks, they might be run "increasingly close to the North Vietnamese coast" or be "associated with 34A operations."[94]

The plan to maneuver Johnson into accepting a deliberately provocative policy came to an abrupt halt after Taylor met privately with Johnson on September 8. When Johnson's principal advisers met with Taylor later that day, they decided to rule out "deliberately provocative elements" as long as the Saigon government was still "struggling to its feet." They agreed that such actions could be reconsidered in October, "depending on GVN progress"—a position quite different from what Taylor had argued before his arrival. At a meeting with the president and his advisers on September 9, Taylor explicitly reversed his own earlier position and said that the GVN was too weak to contemplate retaliatory attacks in the immediate future. Johnson now became more assertive on the issue. "The proper answer to those advocating immediate and extensive action against the North," he declared, was that "we should not do this until our side could defend itself in the streets of Saigon." McNamara, Rusk, and McCone then went on record as endorsing Johnson's policy of postponing such attacks indefinitely.[95]

In mid September, Johnson agreed to a resumption of the DESOTO patrol in the Tonkin Gulf, but this time without any 34A operations, and only on a track that remained at least twenty miles from the North Vietnamese mainland.[96] Nevertheless, on September 18, McNamara and Rusk claimed yet another naval attack in the Gulf and urged U.S. retaliatory strikes. That morning, McNamara told Johnson that there was "considerable"—although not "conclusive"—evidence that North Vietnamese PT boats had carried out "an intentional attack" on a U.S. destroyer in the Gulf. He urged a retaliatory response and outlined the option favored by the JCS: two distinct waves of bombing over thirty-six hours. McNamara further urged that they make a decision and put out a statement within three or four hours, because news of the incident would soon leak out.

Johnson's reaction was to express both skepticism and frustration about such alleged incidents, recalling numerous instances of dubious claims of such attacks by the military over his thirty years of experience. "It would make us vulnerable if we conclude these people attacked us and it developed that it wasn't true at all," he said, insisting that he wanted "more caution from the admirals" on such claims of an attack. Then he needled McNamara about his claim of an attack on August 4. "You just came in a few weeks ago and said they're launching an attack on us—they're firing at us," he recalled, "and we got through with the firing and concluded maybe they hadn't fired at all." Confronted with Johnson's resistance, McNamara retreated, suggesting that the strike order be canceled pending an investigation.[97]

The next day, however, McNamara returned to the offensive, presenting new evidence of an attack, which again relied primarily on a communications intercept that appeared to suggest that DRV ships—not U.S. ships—were under attack. Rusk put the probability of an attack at 99 percent and stressed "the importance of not seeming to doubt our naval officers on the spot." But Johnson refused to reinstate the strike order, insisting again on finding out "exactly what happened." Despite McNamara's requests to resume the DESOTO patrols, Johnson suspended them indefinitely.[98]

After McNamara had misled him and then tried to maneuver him into another round of bombing against North Vietnam, Johnson began to challenge McNamara sharply on the bombing issue in White House meetings in September and October. According to accounts given by Assistant Secretary of Defense John McNaughton to his assistant Daniel Ellsberg, Johnson referred to the proposal for systematic air attacks against North Vietnam as "your bombing bullshit," and McNamara defended the bombing option primarily on the grounds that it was a "bargaining chip" to use in eventual negotiations with Hanoi.[99] Johnson also invited George Ball to "shoot holes" in McNamara's bombing plan, which resulted in a long memorandum by Ball on October 5 that criticized the escalation option and called for a political settlement. By early October, the degree of Johnson's disaffection with the bombing option had become a matter of concern to the White House national security staff. Noting Johnson's reluctance to use force on Vietnam, Robert Komer urged McGeorge Bundy to "bring home to him why he's got to fight."[100]

**Bureaucratic Pressures
and Decisions for War**

CONFRONTATION AND COMPROMISE
ON THE BOMBING

When they set about formulating a recommendation on Vietnam on November 3, 1964, Lyndon Johnson's principal advisers already knew what policy they wanted the president to approve, and now that Johnson had won the presidential election, they believed he would approve the policy they would recommend. Just five days into the exercise, Secretary of State Dean Rusk sent a cable to General Maxwell Taylor, who had succeeded Henry Cabot Lodge as U.S. ambassador in Saigon, describing the "present high-level tendency, not yet discussed at highest levels," to support adoption of a program of four to six weeks of "reprisals against any repetition of spectacular VC action in the south." If that immediate policy change did not produce signs of a change in Hanoi's stance, Rusk said, "we would initiate in January a program of slowly graduated military moves against the North in conjunction with negotiating moves in which we would seek throughout to keep alive a clear threat of additional action if the Communist side does not modify its position." Rusk wrote that they hoped to get a "government decision firmly laying the immediate program and deciding on our long-range course of action" soon after November 19.[1]

In the policy options paper drafted by William Bundy, who headed the working group on the Vietnam policy recommendation, this option of "slowly graduated military moves" against North Vietnam became "Option C"—also called "progressive squeeze-and-talk"—in a menu of three broad options. The other two options were a continuation of existing policies ("Option A"), defined as including reprisal bombings in response to "any recurrence of VC 'spectaculars' in South Vietnam," and a program of more rapid escalation of bombing of targets aimed at achieving the goal of "getting Hanoi completely out of South Viet-Nam" ("Option B"), also labeled the "fast/full squeeze."[2]

The incentive for systematic bombing of the North was underlined by a new intelligence estimate in October that reemphasized the importance of U.S. military dominance over North Vietnam and China. "We are almost certain," said the estimate, "that both Hanoi and Peiping are anxious not to become involved in the kind of war in which the great weight of U.S. weaponry could be brought against them." If U.S. attacks continued for some time, the estimate asserted, "Hanoi's leaders would have to ask themselves whether it was not better to suspend their support of Viet Cong military action rather than suffer the destruction of their major military facilities and the industrial sector of their economy." The estimate concluded that the implicit U.S. nuclear threat would play an important role in the thinking of North Vietnamese and Chinese policy. "Even if Hanoi and Peiping estimated that the US would not use nuclear weapons against them," the estimate suggested, "they could not be sure of this." The assumption that global military dominance would tend to intimidate Hanoi and Beijing was then integrated into the intelligence panel's analysis on likely Communist reactions to Options B and C for the Bundy working group. The draft added that the USSR would not risk "trying the American temper" by provoking a crisis elsewhere in the world.[3]

Writing on the same day as the intelligence panel, McNaughton also doubted that either the DRV or China would invade South Vietnam or Laos or conduct air strikes. Two days later, William Bundy wrote an analysis of Option C focusing on Hanoi's possible responses. He suggested that the North Vietnamese were unlikely to "yield visibly" but that a "major degree of military retaliation" by Hanoi was less likely than Hanoi simply "holding firm" or just "avoiding major new attacks in South Vietnam." Bundy concluded that the advantage of Option C was that, even if South Vietnam were lost, "our having taken stronger measures would still leave us a good deal better off than under Option A" in regard to Thailand's "willingness to stand firm."[4] Bundy later recalled that the participants in the November 1964 discussions had held some hope that the Communist leaders would seek a respite and reduce support, and perhaps even order the Viet Cong to go underground, as they had in 1954.[5]

At a meeting on November 24, McCone, McNamara, Rusk, and McGeorge Bundy agreed that the situation in South Vietnam "would deteriorate further under Option A even with reprisals, but stands a significant chance of improving under Option B or Option C." All four principals also agreed that "major targets," especially airfields, should be hit "at once" rather than waiting until they were used for attacks on U.S. or South Vietnamese forces. And they all agreed with the premise that "the purely military aspects of the VC could be contained."[6] This confidence reflected the intelligence community's belief that North Vietnam would be deterred from sending its regular units to the South, and that the Viet Cong would be reluctant to engage in main-force battles, fearing that its units might be "chewed up" more easily by the ARVN if it did so.[7]

Thus the unanimous recommendation by the principals for a program of escalating strikes against military targets was based on their confidence that they need not fear a major escalation of the war in the South in response to the bombing. They had not given up the hope that Hanoi might actually withdraw from the battlefield in the face of superior power. But in the end it was not the expectation of success in South Vietnam that made it appear such an attractive option to Johnson's advisers. As William Bundy later recalled, "The costs of carrying on seemed moderate," in large part because they did not "include the possibility that large U.S. ground forces would be needed."[8]

Four days later, the principals met again and decided to scrap the existing options paper and replace it with a draft national security action paper focusing on actions to be taken under Option C during the initial thirty-day period and beyond. The action paper prepared by William Bundy on November 29 called for "retaliation against any major or spectacular Viet Cong action in the south for a period of 30 days," after which "first phase actions may be continued without change, or additional military measures may be taken, including the withdrawal of dependents and the possible initiation of strikes a short distance across the border against infiltration routes from the DRV." The paper described this as a "transitional phase" to a possible second phase of bombing:

> Thereafter, if the GVN improves its effectiveness to an acceptable degree and Hanoi does not yield on acceptable terms, or if the GVN can only be kept going by stronger action, the US is prepared—at a time to be determined—to enter into a second phase program . . . of graduated military pressures against the DRV. Such a program would consist principally of progressively more serious air strikes, of a weight and tempo adjusted to the situation as it develops (possibly running from two to six months).

The paper suggested that this bombing program was aimed at eliciting a "sign of yielding by Hanoi." Accompanying the paper was a list of actions to be taken immediately upon approval of the new policy, which included a

White House statement, publication of evidence of North Vietnamese infiltration, and a major presidential speech or statement of policy.[9] Thus Bundy's draft asserted the view of Johnson's advisers that systematic bombing would be justified if it appeared to be the only way to avoid demoralization and the emergence of a neutralist policy in Saigon.

On November 30, the Bundy draft was discussed by the principals in preparation for a meeting with the president on December 1. Before submitting the paper, they made a fundamental change in William Bundy's draft. The clause "or if the GVN can only be kept going by stronger action," which had been inserted to justify beginning the second phase of military actions against North Vietnam, was eliminated. That meant that the phase of bombing to put political pressure on Hanoi would not go ahead except in the unlikely event that political stability was established in South Vietnam—just what Johnson had been insisting on for two months. William Bundy himself later observed that this and other changes were "almost certainly" the result of Johnson's "guidance."[10] The paper Johnson approved on December 2 did not commit him to anything beyond retaliation for specific Viet Cong terrorist incidents, at his discretion—the existing policy that Johnson's advisers were insistent on changing.[11]

At the December 1 meeting, Johnson affirmed that the "policy decision" was that "there will be reprisals" but that he would "decide exactly what at the time." As for more systematic bombing, he established tough conditions even more firmly than before. According to William Bundy, he "laid it down flatly that he would never consider stronger action against the North unless he was sure that the United States had done everything it could to help in the South." He insisted, moreover, that there was no point in hitting the North if the South was "not together" and used the metaphor of South Vietnam as a patient to explain why he wasn't ready to bomb North Vietnam. "I am hesitant to sock my neighbor," he said, "if my fever is 104 degrees." Finally, Johnson wanted all U.S. dependents moved out of Saigon before any sustained attacks on the North, sharply differing from his principal advisers, who felt that it would have a demoralizing effect on Saigon.[12] Johnson's instructions to Taylor on December 3 restated his position that "certain minimum criteria of performance" would have to be met by the Saigon government before "new measures against North Vietnam would be either justified or practicable."[13]

Many in the national security bureaucracy had concluded that Johnson's failure to retaliate for the Viet Cong attack on the U.S. air base at Bien Hoa on November 1 signaled his refusal to fight for South Vietnam. In December, the prowar columnist Joseph Alsop wrote that there were "plenty of discouraged Americans in Saigon who think the President is consciously prepared to accept defeat here." Since Johnson refused to do what was needed to avert defeat, "they suspect that he is simply planning to wait until the end comes and then to disclaim responsibility," Alsop wrote.[14] The Viet Cong bombing of a U.S. officers' billet at the Brinks Hotel in Saigon on December 24 further heightened the tension between Johnson and his advisers. Both Bundys, among others, felt that that bombing was so serious that Johnson should launch retaliatory strikes.[15] But Johnson rejected a reprisal attack as unjustified because of the "general confusion in South Vietnam" and even complained about receiving repeated recommendations for "large-scale bombing," which he said he had never felt would win the war.[16] Alsop then reported that Taylor had asked for a U.S. air attack against the DRV in reprisal for the Bien Hoa attack in November, but that Johnson had rejected the request. Johnson feared that that Taylor himself was the source of leaks to Alsop, and he asked McGeorge Bundy to investigate.[17]

On January 6, Taylor proposed to Johnson that the minimum political criteria for establishment of a government that would justify Phase II air strikes against the DRV should be "the ability of the government to speak for and to its people, to maintain law and order in its principal cities, to make plans for the conduct of operations and assure their effective execution by military and police forces completely responsive to its authority." Johnson refused to comment directly on these minimal political criteria for Phase II, but he indicated that his readiness to begin such bombing would depend not only on "political stability" but on "experience in reprisal actions" and "joint efforts to achieve victories within South Vietnam." Taylor then complained, in diplomatic terms, that Johnson was adding even more conditions for starting Phase II and warned that the Saigon regime was so weak that the United States would "have to be satisfied with little more than continued existence of a government in whose name we can act."[18]

William Bundy had concluded that Johnson was deliberately holding back on retaliatory bombing. He wrote to Rusk on January 6 that the "very shaky" morale in the Saigon government was directly related to "a widespread feeling that the US is not ready for stronger action and indeed is *possibly looking for a way out* [emphasis added]." Bundy complained that the United States appeared to the Vietnamese, as well as many elsewhere in Asia and in Europe, "to be insisting on a more perfect government than can reasonably be expected, before we consider any additional action—and that we might even pull out our support unless such a government emerges."[19] Bundy was clearly implying that he shared that suspicion himself.

Johnson's advisers were particularly suspicious of the president's insistence throughout January 1965 that U.S. dependents be removed from Saigon before he could consider bombing the North, on the grounds that American women and children should not be exposed to the risk of war. Taylor agreed in January, provided that the withdrawal of dependents was followed immediately by the start of Phase II bombing, but, according to William Bundy, "the answer came back that the President had made no decision and was not committing himself to any." Bundy and others considered Johnson's position on U.S. dependents as "a stalling tactic" to give him more time while he waited for a "dramatic new event"—such as the emergence of a neutralist government in Saigon.[20] McGeorge Bundy, too, concluded that the president was in effect "coming to a decision, a decision to lose."[21]

The tension over Johnson's inaction arose against a background of fears that the Saigon government would negotiate its own peace with the Communists—or be replaced by one that would do so—unless the United States initiated attacks on North Vietnam. Taylor had raised the threat of a neutralist peace in his very first report from Saigon in August, and it had been highlighted in national intelligence estimates on September 8 and again on October 1 and in a November 6 draft by McNaughton.[22] The national security bureaucracy was firmly opposed to allowing the emergence of a neutralist regime to frustrate U.S. objectives in Vietnam. The State Department's Vietnam Working Group had produced a contingency plan calling for the use of U.S. forces, if necessary, to reverse any seizure of power by a "neutralist coup group."[23] Taylor had explicitly urged bombing the North at the end of December to reduce the likelihood of such a negotiated solution.[24]

Johnson's advisers could only conclude that Johnson was holding off on the bombing in the hope that a neutralist regime would emerge in Saigon to negotiate a peace settlement with Hanoi. That was also the perception of Vice President Hubert Humphrey, who told an NSC aide, James Thomson, in mid January that he was convinced that, before any bombing was carried out, a neutralist government would come to power in Saigon that would request U.S. withdrawal.[25]

The suspicions that Johnson was deliberately biding his time were not without foundation. Johnson regarded a request from the South Vietnamese government for U.S. withdrawal as the one way out of the war that would be politically acceptable. In response to McGeorge Bundy's concern in March 1964 about a coup in Saigon resulting in the United States being "invited out," Johnson had said, "I don't know what we can do if there is. . . . What alternatives do we have then? We're not going to send our troops in there, are we?" Johnson had told Russell in May 1964, "I don't know how in hell you're going to get out *unless they tell you to get out* [emphasis added]." Three weeks later, he repeated the same point in a conversation with McNamara. He had also made it clear at the end of November that U.S. policy should not foreclose the possibility of peace negotiations by a South Vietnamese government. The November 29 draft of Bundy's policy paper had included a sentence that the United States should "seek to control any negotiations and would oppose any independent South Vietnamese efforts to negotiate." That sentence was removed, however, before it went to the president, evidently reflecting Johnson's wishes.[26]

Another reason for Johnson to resist going to war over Vietnam was that he was focused on what would be the greatest political accomplishment of his career: getting an unprecedented, sweeping program of domestic reform passed by Congress. Johnson believed that he had perhaps six months of "honeymoon" with Congress in which to get it passed, and he knew that a war in Vietnam would probably destroy the historically unique political momentum that he had behind his legislative program. Johnson was both preoccupied with his legislative program and protective of it.[27]

In late January, a strong upsurge of the Buddhist movement in South Vietnam, with its anti-American and neutralist overtones, produced an accord between the Buddhists and the military strongman Nguyen Khanh. The emergence of a Saigon regime that pursued a neutralist policy now appeared to be a much shorter-term prospect than ever before. On January 26, the U.S. embassy reported that Khanh was about to overthrow the weak government of Tran Van Huong.[28]

The following day, McGeorge Bundy and McNamara brought the simmering tension between Johnson and his advisers to a head. They sent Johnson an extraordinarily blunt criticism of his inaction on Vietnam. "Our best friends have been somewhat discouraged by our own inactivity in the face of major attacks on our installations," they wrote. The Vietnamese "see the enormous power of the United States withheld, and they get little sense of firm and active U.S. policy. They feel that we are unwilling to take serious risks." They made it clear that they found it unacceptable to wait for a neutralist regime to request U.S. withdrawal, which Johnson's advisers had concluded was Johnson's strategy. The "worst course of action," they wrote, would be to "continue in this essentially passive role which can only lead to eventual defeat and an invitation to get out in humiliating circumstances." Johnson either had to "use our military power in the Far East . . . to force a change of Communist policy" or negotiate to "salvage what little can be preserved."[29]

For Johnson, the McNamara-Bundy memo raised the possibility that his refusal to make war on North Vietnam would lead to serious division in his administration. Johnson had regarded both McNamara and Bundy from the beginning as Kennedy men who had no loyalty to him, and the distrust of Bundy persisted, although he apparently believed he had succeeded in cementing McNamara's loyalty in 1964.[30] Now both men had put on paper an indictment of his policy that strongly implied that responsibility for U.S. "humiliation" in South Vietnam would rest squarely on the president's shoulders if he continued to pursue his policy of "passivity."

Lyndon Johnson had good reason to fear a campaign of political retribution from the Republican Right and their allies in the media if he failed to use force to prevent the loss of South Vietnam. When he met with a group of ten Republican senators in late May 1964, every one of them agreed that the United States would have to intervene in South Vietnam with combat forces if necessary to prevent its loss.[31] And in a *Reader's Digest* article in August 1964, Richard Nixon had signaled that he was ready to lead the charge against the Johnson administration if its policy failed to exhibit the "will to win" in Vietnam. Nixon had made it clear he regarded the use of airpower against North Vietnam as the key to victory.[32]

The specter of a Republican attack on him over the loss of South Vietnam would have been serious enough even if Johnson's national security advisers had been united in support of the policy. But Johnson knew that the JCS would seek to put the blame for the loss of South Vietnam directly on his shoulders. Political aide Jack Valenti had advised him in late November to cover his flank on Vietnam by getting the JCS to "sign on" to his policy, "so there can be no recriminations" by the military leadership if things should "go wrong later."[33] Even that threat might have been manageable had McNamara been prepared to defend his policy. But McNamara, Taylor, and Bundy all appeared to be ready to turn on him if he failed to launch a bombing campaign against North Vietnam and the war in South Vietnam were lost.

The Bundy-McNamara memorandum had an immediate and dramatic effect on Johnson's attitude toward the bombing. Meeting with McNamara, Bundy, Rusk, and Ball the same morning that he received it, he responded directly to the memorandum and expressed a willingness to give up his precondition on bombing North Vietnam. "[S]table government or no stable government," he vowed, "we'll do what we ought to do." He also agreed to send McGeorge Bundy to Saigon to investigate what could be done. Bundy wrote to Johnson later that day to express satisfaction on behalf of both McNamara and himself with "your comments this morning in response to our memo."[34]

Just as Johnson was close to capitulating to his advisers, however, a series of messages from Taylor on February 2 and 3 gave him new courage to insist on political stability in Saigon as a precondition for Phase II bombing. General Khanh had just taken full power, after having reportedly signed an agreement with the Buddhists, and Taylor did not regard him as sufficiently reliable in his determination to prosecute the war to represent the armed forces. The ambassador warned Johnson of a "likely trend toward neutralism and anti-Americanism" under Khanh's rule and declared that his government did not represent "even that minimum stability which would allow us to continue the struggle against the Viet Cong and Hanoi at present levels of success."[35] Johnson seized on Taylor's views on the new government, which suggested that it might even turn toward neutralism, as a sufficient basis for holding off on the bombing. That same day, Johnson ordered McCone to send a message to Bundy in Saigon saying, "President continues to feel that a stable Saigon government is an essential prerequisite to other activities."[36]

Bundy told White House staff aide Chester Cooper, who accompanied him on the Saigon trip, that it would not be possible to begin the systematic bombing of North Vietnam without a Communist attack that was "so atrocious" that it would justify the new policy.[37] Anticipating that such an opportunity would arise, Bundy worked with McNaughton and others on his mission to craft a policy that cleverly collapsed the distinction between reprisal attacks and systematic pressure on the North, calling it a policy of "sustained reprisals."

Before Bundy left South Vietnam, Viet Cong sappers attacked the U.S. base at Pleiku, killing eight and wounding one hundred U.S. troops. Bundy immediately talked by phone with Johnson and his advisers assembled in the cabinet room, arguing that Hanoi had "thrown down the gauntlet" by colluding with the USSR to test the U.S. reaction by attacking a U.S. base while Bundy was in South Vietnam and the Soviet premier, Alexei Kosygin, was visiting Hanoi. Such collusion would have been technically impossible, of course, since planning for the operation would have begun long before Bundy's presence in Vietnam could have been known. Bundy had not gotten that idea from anyone in the U.S. mission, and certainly not from the intelligence analysts.[38] He had simply contrived the argument to make it more difficult for Johnson to reject his "sustained reprisals" policy.

Nevertheless, Bundy's tactic of turning the Pleiku attack into a personal test worked with Johnson, who had already been admonished that he could not expect support from his national security team if he rejected the bombing policy. After approving retaliatory strikes on North Vietnam later that night, Johnson summoned James Reston to the White House. Still emotionally distraught, Johnson recounted his conversation with Bundy and vowed to Reston that he would "lean on" the North Vietnamese "hard." The *Times*'s diplomatic correspondent, Max Frankel, then reported that Johnson had acted on the assumption that North Vietnamese troops had participated in the planning of the attack, and that he was being "tested" by the North Vietnamese. The following day, Johnson told a group of congressional leaders that the administration would not limit future actions to "retaliating against Viet Cong attacks."[39]

Johnson now embraced the key argument of the bombing proponents he had rejected so emphatically for months. In his message to Taylor later that same day, Johnson said he was "impressed by argument the building of a minimum government will benefit by some private assurances from us to the highest levels that we do now intend to take continuing actions." He authorized Taylor to use that intention as an inducement for South Vietnamese political figures to establish a more effective government.[40]

Johnson was reluctant, however, to yield his last room for maneuver on the bombing. On February 16, he told a meeting of his principal advisers that he was authorizing the start of reprisal bombings in three days, "hoping out of hope" that it would "draw people in Saigon closer together." But he rejected the idea of bombing the North to force it to capitulate, asserting that "bombers won't bring the [North Vietnamese] to their knees unless we do something we wouldn't do. We'll be called warmongers." Then he summed up his policy: "They hit our barracks, our hotel, and we hit theirs."

A deeply frustrated Bundy sent a memorandum to Johnson that same day pointing out that the policy Johnson's advisers had advocated "amounts to a decision to mount continuing pressure against Hanoi by use of our air and naval superiority." It was "not the same as a policy of episodic retaliation for particular attacks against large numbers of Americans," he wrote. "It is very different indeed, and the difference is just what we are counting on as the one possible means of turning around a desperate situation which has been heading toward a disastrous U.S. defeat."[41] Bundy tried once more to commit Johnson to the beginning of Phase II bombing by drafting a cable to Taylor saying, "We have recommended, and the President has concurred in, continuing air and naval action against North Vietnam whenever and wherever necessary." But Johnson changed the draft, in his own handwriting, to read, "We have recommended, and we think the President will concur in," that policy.[42]

While the President stubbornly refused to commit himself irrevocably to a campaign of military pressure on North Vietnam, the start of the bombing campaign, called Rolling Thunder by the Pentagon, was repeatedly delayed over the next two weeks. The initial reason for delay was the political struggle unfolding between Khanh and his opponents among the South Vietnamese generals. Taylor had been secretly plotting, with General William Westmoreland's support, to oust Khanh since the beginning of the month, but by February 19–20, the U.S.-supported coup plan had failed, after threatening a serious split in the military.[43]

But another reason for delay in scheduling the air strikes was Johnson's consideration of peace negotiations. On February 17, British Ambassador Lord Harlech discussed with Rusk a Soviet government proposal for a joint initiative by the Geneva Conference co-chairs (Britain and the USSR) for a Vietnam settlement. Rusk responded negatively, asserting that Washington was not interested in negotiations unless it could be assured that they would achieve the U.S. goal of ending the threat from the Communists. The following day, after discussions with the Bundy brothers, Ball, and Llewellyn Thompson, Johnson decided to encourage the British to propose to Moscow that the co-chairs ask the relevant parties for their views on peace—a process that would be well short of negotiation—and also decided that air strikes would be postponed until the Soviet Union had responded to the British.[44]

Johnson was also informed by UN Ambassador Adlai Stevenson on February 17 of a proposal from UN Secretary-General U Thant for a conference of the five great powers (the United States, the USSR, Britain, France, and China) and the two Vietnams.[45] On the same day, Johnson and his advisers met with Eisenhower, and the president referred to the fact that some in his administration were prepared to go to "an early conference." He asked Ike's advice on the matter, and the former president warned against "negotiation from weakness."[46]

The main stumbling block to peace negotiations, however, was Rusk. Sensing that Johnson would be tempted to negotiate a settlement, Rusk had never informed him that Hanoi had agreed privately to U Thant's suggestion for unconditional secret talks with the United States the previous September and that the secretary-general had conveyed to Stevenson Hanoi's willingness to enter into secret talks in Rangoon as late as January 1965.[47] Even though he had been led to believe that Hanoi had expressed no interest in negotiations, Johnson had asked Rusk in early February to come up with a peace proposal. But Rusk was determined to discourage any move toward negotiations. On February 18, Rusk made a special point of expressing his "misgivings with respect to an approach to the UN at this time." Unless there was "some prospect that negotiations would be meaningful," he said, it would be "a dangerous situation." He insisted that no "significant signals" of a Communist readiness to engage in "meaningful negotiation" had been received. Johnson responded that he would "rather talk than fight" but agreed it was "terribly important that the GVN not get the wrong impression that the U.S. is seeking negotiations prematurely."[48] At a meeting with French Foreign Minister Couve de Murville the following day, Johnson expressed doubt that Hanoi wanted to negotiate, citing an intelligence report on a hard-line statement by a North Vietnamese official.[49] Johnson was prepared to negotiate, therefore, but did not believe that the North Vietnamese had any interest in a compromise solution.

Rusk and McCone ensured that Johnson would receive only information that would reinforce that belief. When Johnson told Rusk on February 23 that he might call a meeting that afternoon, Rusk immediately called McCone to ask for a "wrap up" of the evidence regarding Hanoi's and Beijing's interest in negotiating a peaceful settlement of the conflict.[50] McCone advised Rusk that there was "no reliable evidence" that Hanoi and Beijing were prepared for a settlement that would achieve the "abandonment of aggression." Rusk then incorporated the CIA assessment into a broader paper for the meeting, declaring that a "formal and public negotiation" would "simply register the impossibility of a peaceful settlement."[51] Reflecting the decisions reached at that meeting, Rusk gave a press conference two days later in which he publicly dismissed for the first time the whole idea of a peace conference, calling it merely "procedural" and of no interest to the administration.[52]

Meanwhile, on February 20 and 21, the U.S. military command in South Vietnam twice intervened in the military leadership struggle to arrange for rump sessions of members of the Armed Forces Council against Khanh. There is no evidence that these extraordinary interventions to get rid of Khanh were cleared by the White House or even reported to the State Department.[53] With General Khanh's departure from Vietnam on February 25 and the issue of entering into peace negotiations settled, the last possible reasons for delay in bombing were removed. After several more delays because of weather, Rolling Thunder began on March 2.

Within three days, Taylor was expressing his dissatisfaction with the targets hit, complaining that, in Hanoi's eyes, the bombing campaign had probably been "merely a few isolated thunder claps." He and Westmoreland called for a bombing program that would begin to "move northward up the target system" in order to break Hanoi's will. Only after this challenge from both Taylor and Westmoreland did Johnson concede on March 15 that the strikes would no longer be related specifically to "VC atrocities" and that field commanders would have flexibility in the exact timing of particular strikes.[54]

But Johnson continued to limit the target list to interdiction targets south of the twentieth parallel, and he insisted on personally approving every target at a weekly meeting with Rusk and McNamara. He closely questioned his advisers about any target that appeared to be near a populated area, asking about the risk of civilian casualties and whether it was justified, according to McNamara's deputy, Cyrus Vance.[55] Johnson's rejection of even the threat of massive devastation to try to put pressure on the North Vietnamese made the bombing policy very different from what had been envisioned by the national security bureaucracy.

THE RISE AND COLLAPSE OF THE LIMITED COMMITMENT OPTION

Johnson's cable to Taylor on December 30 suggested that more U.S. "rangers and Special Forces and Marines, or other appropriate military strength on the ground and on the scene" would be more effective than bombing the North. This statement has been cited as evidence that Johnson had no problem with sending combat troops to South Vietnam.[56] But Johnson had very clear limits in mind, and he was unwilling to go as far as McGeorge Bundy wanted. Bundy's original draft of Johnson's cable offered to double the number of U.S. troops in South Vietnam, which would have brought the number to about 46,000, but Johnson changed that to a "substantial increase." After Taylor reported a week later on Westmoreland's estimate that a total of 75,000 U.S. troops would be required, Johnson dropped the whole subject of ground troops.[57] When he met with congressional leaders on January 22, Johnson was certainly not contemplating a major U.S. ground combat role in the war. "The war must be fought by the South Vietnamese," he said. "We have to count on *them* fighting *their* war." No more U.S. troops would be needed, he said, "short of a decision to go to full-scale war."[58]

Johnson knew when he approved the systematic bombing of the North that he would be pressed to protect airbases in South Vietnam from guerrilla attacks with U.S. ground troops. On February 22, Westmoreland requested that two battalions of marines be sent to South Vietnam to protect the airbases from which the strikes were being launched. Although the Pentagon's account reported that Johnson had approved the request four days later, the evidence now indicates that he was still agonizing over the decision two weeks later. On March 5, he told McGeorge Bundy he hadn't made the decision about the marines and was "still worried about it." He told his advisers to "clear it with the Congressmen" later that same day, explaining to Dick Russell he was afraid "everybody is going to give me hell for not securing them" if U.S. airbases were attacked. But he also feared the marines were "going to get in a fight, just sure as hell. . . . Then you're tied down."[59]

Meeting with Army Chief of Staff Harold Johnson before his visit to South Vietnam on March 2, Johnson tried to head off military demands for more large-scale troop deployments. He said he would approve more U.S. troops than the initial Westmoreland request, but insisted that he would not be able to support a large-scale troop deployment, given his domestic political concerns.[60] McGeorge Bundy and McNamara, meanwhile, gravitated rapidly toward the ground force option as their hopes for the bombing faded. After a meeting of the three principals on March 5, Bundy reported that he and McNamara thought the chances of "turn-around" in the war were less than even, despite the bombing. Nevertheless, they joined Rusk in suggesting that a "substantial allied ground force" placed in central and northern South Vietnam could "have a substantial breaking effect on any possible Communist escalation" and urged that it be given "serious further exploration."[61] Less than two weeks later, even Rusk seemed to CIA Director McCone to be "depressed" about the outlook for the war in light of the unexpected strength shown by the Viet Cong."[62]

McNamara and McGeorge Bundy saw ground force deployments as offering a chance for avoiding defeat and positioning the United States for an eventual settlement. On March 16, Bundy wrote a memo for a discussion of a regular meeting of the Tuesday Group at the White House, arguing that an increased U.S. ground combat presence would improve the "eventual bargaining position" of the United States, because it would probably "reinforce both pacification efforts and Southern morale, while discouraging the VC from their current expectation of early victory."[63] And two weeks later, he advised Johnson that the combination of U.S. troops preventing the Viet Cong from making "real headway" in the South and the bombing of the North would eventually move Hanoi to the "political track."[64]

McGeorge Bundy's readiness to try a limited troop commitment was based on the hope and belief that the North Vietnamese would not respond by intervening with significant regular forces in the South. That view from the conventional power relations perspective still dominated in the national security bureaucracy, including the CIA, which had issued a special estimate on February 18 predicting that the North Vietnamese "would recognize that to launch . . . an invasion [of the South] would be to invite further major destruction upon the DRV."[65]

In the same memo, Bundy assured Johnson that a major North Vietnamese invasion of the South in response to the bombing was unlikely "for the moment," but he then raised the question of going to full-scale ground war against the Communists. "We do not feel confident," said Bundy, "that we know just what our actual decisions should be and would be if there were North Vietnamese ground movements over the demarcation line or large movements of Chinese forces into North Vietnam, or both." Instead, Bundy sought Johnson's guidance on "whether and when you would authorize landings of a number of U.S. divisions in South Vietnam."[66] Bundy was strongly implying that he and the other two advisers were not ready to recommend such landings. That revelation underlines how crucial the belief in the U.S. ability to deter North Vietnamese intervention in the South was to their recommendation that a substantial, but limited, number of ground troops be deployed.

By then, however, another factor was driving Johnson's principal advisers toward the ground force option. On March 16, McGeorge Bundy wrote to Johnson that a major ground force deployment "may soon be necessary for both military and political reasons." And in notes on the U.S. stake in South Vietnam on March 21, Bundy wrote, "If we visibly do enough in the South (whatever that may be), any failure will be, in that sense, beyond our control." He then asked, "In terms of U.S. politics, which is better: to 'lose' now or to 'lose' after committing 100,000 men? Tentative answer: the latter."[67] Bundy thus viewed the deployment of combat troops primarily as a means of protecting himself politically when the eventual collapse of the Saigon regime occurred.

In the consultations with Taylor on possible troop deployments at the end of March, the main concern was that the presence of U.S. divisions would provoke anti-American sentiment in South Vietnam. Johnson's advisers recommended conducting an experiment with U.S. troops in combat on a much smaller scale in an "enclave strategy" that would limit the range of combat to the area surrounding their bases on the coast. Initially, the experiment with U.S. troops would be located in the Bien Hoa–Vung Tau area, but two or three additional coastal enclaves would be added later. U.S. forces would be confined to a defensive role in a strategic sense and could be withdrawn easily, because they would have their backs to the sea.[68]

At an enlarged meeting at the White House on April 1, Johnson deferred a decision on a JCS request for two full divisions, while agreeing to the two-battalion request from Westmoreland and CINCPAC Admiral

Grant Sharp and allowing U.S. combat forces already in South Vietnam for base security to participate in counterinsurgency operations. Nevertheless, the military leadership continued to insist on enough troops to achieve the military initiative against the Communists. On April 13, the JCS went back to the president to ask for the same three-division deployment, as well as for a more immediate deployment of two additional brigades (about 8,000 troops). Johnson approved the two additional brigades but again rejected the request for three divisions, this time citing both congressional and enemy reaction. He affirmed the April 1 decision that "something else on a smaller scale would have to be tried." And in a reference to the possibility that his national security advisers would blame him for the eventual loss of South Vietnam, he warned them that he would "share" the blame for the continued deterioration of the situation "with those who had been giving him advice."[69]

Nevertheless, Westmoreland, General Earle C. Wheeler, and Sharp pressed again for the three-division deployment at a conference in Honolulu on April 20. McNamara, with Taylor's support, again said no, agreeing to deployment of three more battalions, while leaving open the possibility of division strength deployments later. That would increase U.S. troop strength from 33,000 to 82,000 men. McNamara claimed a consensus for a strategy to "break the will of the DRV/VC by denying them victory." Sharp later denied, however, that there had been such a consensus.[70] The military wanted enough troops to take the offensive. But Johnson finally approved only 69,000 troops to be deployed permanently, thus reaffirming the enclave strategy.

Given their reluctance to deploy troops on a large scale and the apparent dramatic shift in the military balance in favor of the Communists, Johnson and his principal advisers knew that they would eventually have to negotiate some kind of settlement with Hanoi. Yet the administration made no move to adopt any realistic negotiating strategy. The only negotiating proposals produced in the administration in March and April demanded either the disarming of the Viet Cong units in the South or their withdrawal to North Vietnam. Taylor even wrote, without a trace of irony, "The VC units could depart honorably with their arms and colors flying."[71]

This lack of interest in crafting more realistic terms for a diplomatic settlement can be understood at two distinct levels. At one level, Johnson's advisers were consciously or unconsciously avoiding realistic proposals in order to avoid a collapse of morale within the national security bureaucracy. They associated negotiations with compromise and compromise with defeat. Dean Rusk explicitly refused to do any planning for negotiations because it would "make defeat more likely." Even though the possibility of what Bundy called a "sharp deterioration" would require negotiations, they decided to think about it only among the three of them and their deputies, with nothing to be committed to paper.[72]

At a deeper level, however, both Johnson and his advisers were able to postpone serious consideration of negotiations only because they assumed that the U.S. bargaining position would improve substantially once the United States had applied its power in the air and on the ground. Bundy advised Johnson on March 6, "My own opinion . . . is that we can always get to the conference table when we need to, and there is no great hurry about it right now." Johnson told his advisers on March 10 that he was interested in "any honorable basis" for negotiations but doubted that the North Vietnamese were ready to negotiate seriously, because "we've not done anything yet." On March 16, Bundy wrote that it was "quite likely" that the "eventual bargaining position" would be strengthened by additional ground force deployments.[73]

Once again, the expectation of a better bargaining position depended in large part on the assumption that Hanoi's fear of U.S. destructive capabilities would deter North Vietnam from sending its own troops to the South, even if it did not force Hanoi to reduce the military effort. The CIA reaffirmed this thesis in its estimates of Hanoi's likely response to U.S. troop deployments. After the decision to increase U.S. troops to 82,000 in April, the CIA concluded that Hanoi and Beijing would "probably recognize that that the chances of overrunning South Vietnam in overt military operations had receded" and would calculate that the United States "probably would not accept defeat without expanding the war to the DRV and China, perhaps using nuclear weapons." It predicted that Hanoi was more likely to "resort to political measures" than to "launch a major ground invasion."[74]

When McCone presented the estimate at a White House meeting on April 22, McNamara declared his agreement with that conclusion, even though McCone personally dissented from the idea that Hanoi would be deterred from deeper military involvement in the South.[75] McNamara believed in the efficacy of using the threat of overwhelmingly superior U.S. military power to prevail through coercion. Based on both the Berlin and Cuban crises, he had concluded that preparatory moves signaling U.S. determination to prevail might well persuade Hanoi to reduce its demands. It was an idea that he had broached in congressional testimony in 1964 and again in conversation with McCone in March 1965.[76] As early as April 1963, he had considered moving a carrier task force into the Gulf of Tonkin off Hanoi as a direct threat to North Vietnam.[77]

McNamara's interest in signaling to Hanoi about possible use of nuclear weapons was galvanized by a meeting with Eisenhower on February 17 at which the former president recounted how he and Dulles had used an indirect nuclear threat to end the Korean War. Ike told Johnson and his advisers how he had passed on three messages to North Korea and China warning that, failing a satisfactory armistice, "we would remove the limits we were observing as to the area of combat and the weapons employed." If the United States let it be known that it would not be bound by restrictions against the use of nuclear weapons in Vietnam, Eisenhower suggested, the North Vietnamese "will not come in great strength." McNamara picked up on the idea of exploiting the potential for threatening such devastation. "We should try to induce them to get out of the war," he said, "without having their country destroyed and to realize that if they do not get out, their country will be destroyed."[78]

Two months later, McNamara did exactly what Eisenhower had suggested. In a background briefing for the press on April 22, he cited current "inhibitions" on the use of nuclear weapons in Vietnam and suggested that they might eventually be lifted. His speculation about possible future use of nuclear weapons in Vietnam was reported in a front-page story in the *New York Times* a few days later, citing an unnamed U.S. official as the source.[79] McNamara's confidence that the United States could deploy ground forces to South Vietnam without being caught up in a much larger war reflected his faith that dominant military power would provide a bargaining edge with Hanoi.

There was another major threat to the strategy of committing a limited ground force aside from the possibility of a much bigger North Vietnamese military involvement in the South: the pressures by the U.S. military leadership for an open-ended troop commitment. That threat materialized on June 7, when General William Westmoreland requested ten more U.S. battalions as soon as possible, and a delay in the scheduled withdrawal of the 173d Airborne Brigade until the additional battalions arrived in late August. Four days later, the JCS called for deployment of all ten battalions requested by Westmoreland, along with logistics, combat support, and tactical fighter squadrons that would increase total U.S. strength from 70,000 to 117,000 troops.[80]

Johnson and his advisers clearly understood that this request was a fork in the road between capping the U.S. commitment to South Vietnam and sliding into constantly escalating war.[81] Their reaction was to gravitate toward a strategy of limiting the U.S. ground troop deployment. At the meeting between Johnson and his advisers, including Taylor, on June 8, McNamara advocated what he called a "limited cost and limited risk" option, which would involve substantially fewer troops than Westmoreland had requested. George Ball asked at what point the additional troops requested would make Vietnam a "white man's war" and suggested that more than 100,000 troops would have that effect. Taylor agreed, and Johnson referred to political problems with Congress and U.S. allies that such an increase would cause.[82]

The underlying assumption of the discussion on troop deployments over the next few days was that the administration's military commitment to Vietnam would remain limited. In a phone conversation with Johnson on June 10, McNamara said, "I have a very definite limitation on commitment [of U.S. ground troops] in mind," he said. "I don't think the Chiefs do. In fact, I *know* they don't." McNamara recommended that, "unless we're really willing to go to a full potential land war, we've got to slow down here and try to halt, at some point, the ground troop commitment." Johnson's language also suggested that he was thinking in terms of a limited commitment. When McNamara suggested that Taylor might explain to Congress "that there's been this continued Vietcong buildup and we have to respond to it," Johnson responded, "Well, I wouldn't say we have to respond. I'd say there been this constant buildup, and *we must protect ourselves as best we can* [emphasis in original]."[83]

On June 10, McNamara called for approving only half of Westmoreland's short-term request (i.e., five battalions, which he asserted would bring the total to 93,000) and none of his longer-term requests. Rusk and Taylor concurred with that recommendation. Johnson asked his advisers, "How do we extricate ourselves?" to which one of the proponents of the limited increase in troop deployment answered that there was "still room to pull back, or even out, if ARVN could not carry on."[84] The following day, Johnson seemed to be positioning himself to hold the line on troop deployments. "We have a treaty obligation and we intend to keep our commitment," he said. "Some say we should get out of Vietnam while others say we should do more. We should seek ways of holding the situation so that we can carry out what we are committed to do." Defining the issue in terms of the legal issue of the U.S. treaty commitment rather than in terms of preventing a Communist victory was a way of limiting the U.S. commitment. In his summation of the meeting, Johnson explicitly defined the U.S. commitment as falling short of taking responsibility for the outcome of the conflict: "We must delay and deter the North Vietnamese and Viet Cong *as much as we can and as simply as we can,*" he declared, "*without going all out.* When we grant General Westmoreland's request, it means that we get in deeper and *it is harder to get out* [emphasis added]."[85]

At that moment, Johnson, McGeorge Bundy, and McNamara were all aware of the real possibility of an early Communist victory over the Saigon government. On June 14, Johnson said the United States was in a "very precarious position" in Vietnam.[86]McNamara recalled in a later oral history that during the summer of 1965, he was convinced that the United States was "on a certain course of defeat," and that "it wasn't clear to me that we could avoid defeat by any action in our power."[87] McGeorge Bundy similarly believed that the limited U.S. troop deployment being discussed in June would not avert an ultimate Communist victory. When he forwarded Ball's memo advocating gradual disengagement from the Saigon government on June 23, Bundy appended a note suggesting that the United States should take advantage of any neutralist regime in Saigon to withdraw—the same course that he had denounced so unequivocally in his January memo to Johnson. And he asked McNamara a few days later, "[Do] we want to invest 200 thousand men to cover an eventual retreat? Can we not do that just as well where we are?" William Bundy also recalls that the assumption among Johnson's advisers in late June was that the chance of an "early failure" was "substantial" regardless of the additional deployments.[88] Among the inner circle of Johnson's advisers, only Rusk appears to have believed that a limited U.S. combat deployment could prevent a U.S. defeat. Rusk was convinced that American troops could discourage the Communists by achieving a military "stalemate."[89]

On June 17, McNamara proposed a revised plan that actually increased the total number of battalions to be deployed from ten to twelve by canceling a decision to withdraw the two battalions of the 173d Airborne Brigade. His proposal made it appear to reduce the number of additional battalions by subtracting the three battalions of the brigade of the 101st Airborne Division that were already scheduled to return to the United States and had not even been counted in the total of thirteen approved battalions used in the original JCS plan. McNamara also added another 4,000 troops in combat support and logistics and in additional personnel for the four tactical air squadrons to be sent under the JCS plan. McNamara's plan actually increased total strength by 4,000 above the JCS request. The JCS agreed the following day to that revised plan, but imposed an additional condition—that the decision to withdraw the brigade of the 101st Airborne Division "will be reviewed in light of the situation existing at that time."[90]

The following day, Johnson met with McNamara, Bundy, and Rusk to discuss the troop deployment issue and made a crucial decision. The extremely fragmentary notes by McGeorge Bundy, which are the only documentation of that meeting, show that the decision was to deploy the eight battalions of the Airmobile Division, but with the "intention" to withdraw six battalions by September 1, subject to review in light of the circumstances at the time.[91] Assuming that all six battalions were to be withdrawn, that decision would have meant that only six of the ten additional U.S. battalions requested by Westmoreland would have been approved—a dramatic change from the McNamara proposal. Johnson also indicated that Westmoreland's short-term request (for about 120,000) was to be the "upper threshold" of the U.S. troop commitment, from which the six-battalion reduction would be carried out. McNamara, however, was dissatisfied with that decision. He was "concerned with the size of U.S. forces" and questioned whether "we can assure security," according to Bundy's notes. This apparent difference in view suggests that Johnson was still clinging to the idea of limiting the commitment, whereas McNamara had already begun to retreat from that option.[92]

During the few days before and after that decision, Johnson was also thinking once more about the possibility of a negotiated settlement. Anticipating a scheduled meeting between Rusk and Soviet Ambassador Anatoly Dobrynin, Johnson told Ball on June 14 to get the views of Senate Foreign Relations Committee Chairman J. W. Fulbright on a peace settlement so that he could pass on the information to Rusk. Johnson expressed his willingness to support a plan Ball had proposed in May, which would have sanctioned a standstill cease-fire, allowing the Communists to maintain their administrative control over villages and to participate in elections as individuals.[93]

He referred to Fulbright's suggestion that the United States ask the Russians, "What can you live with?" and Fulbright's belief that the answer would be "Tito," meaning a Communist-leaning regime independent of the Communist bloc. Johnson asked Ball to send Fulbright what he called the "Tito" memorandum, written by McGeorge Bundy a few weeks earlier, adding that he didn't know "how we could sell something like this in this country." Finally, he told Ball to offer to help the Senate Foreign Relations Committee write its own Vietnam policy, with the assurance that Johnson would try to carry it out.

On June 18, the same day he made his decision on troop deployments, Johnson received a memorandum from Ball on how to prevent control over Vietnam policy from falling into the hands of the military. Ball urged the president to authorize an increase in U.S. forces to no more than 100,000 and to instruct McNamara, Rusk, and possibly Wheeler that he was not committing U.S. forces "on an open-ended basis to an all-out land war in South Vietnam," but was instead "making a controlled commitment for a trial period of three months." Ball drew parallels between the confidence of the U.S. military in its ability to fight the Vietnamese successfully and French confidence in Indochina more than a decade earlier. If U.S. troops could not fight successfully on the Vietnamese battlefield with acceptable losses, he argued, Johnson still had the option to limit the defense perimeter of U.S. forces to cities and major towns and to "subtly . . . withdraw moral and political support from the Government in Saigon."[94]

Ball has often been portrayed as being Johnson's designated in-house skeptic or "devil's advocate," primarily to convey to the media and critics of the war the impression that he listened to different points of view.[95] In June 1965, however, Ball's memorandum was clearly taken very seriously by Johnson, McNamara, and the JCS. On June 21, Johnson's Special Assistant Bill Moyers told Ball that the president "agrees in substance with most of the memo—one or two slight changes possibly." Moyers quoted Johnson as having told him earlier that day, "I don't think I should go over 100,000, but think I should go to that number and explain it. I want George [Ball] to work for the next 90 days—to work up what is going to happen after the monsoon season."[96] Either the same day he read Ball's paper or the following day, Johnson ordered his political aide Jack Valenti to request a new intelligence memorandum from the CIA on the evolution of the North Vietnamese and Chinese positions on peace negotiations.[97]

Ball sent the memorandum only to Johnson and Rusk. However, McNamara quickly got a copy of it, presumably from Rusk, and he was perturbed that Johnson had not chosen to send it to him or to discuss it with his principal advisers.[98] McNamara's concern must have been heightened by his telephone conversation with Johnson on June 21, in which the president said that he was worried about whether it would be possible to "prosecute effectively" a war so far away with the "divisions that we have here and particularly the potential divisions." Johnson went on to say that he had been "very depressed," because he saw "no program from either Defense or State that gives much hope of doing anything except praying and grasping to hold on during [the] monsoon season and hope they'll quit. And I don't believe they're ever goin' to quit." Johnson even raised the possibility of implementing the policy advocated by Senator Russell to "use one of these changes [of government] to get out of there," but concluded that he didn't think "we can get out of there with our treaty like it is," because the United States would "just lose face in the world."[99] McNamara perceived Johnson as "tortured" and desperate for a way out of the war.[100] Knowing the contents of the Ball memorandum, which Johnson had *not* mentioned to him on June 21, McNamara evidently believed Johnson was seriously weighing Ball's plan to use the troop deployment cap to keep open the option of withdrawing political support from the Saigon government.

Just two hours after that conversation with Johnson, McNamara met with the JCS.[101] Although no records of McNamara's meetings with the JCS have been found, McNamara clearly informed the military chiefs of Johnson's rejection of their proposals and his decision to withdraw two brigades, as well as the content of the Ball memo and McNamara's disturbing conversation with LBJ earlier that day. Undoubtedly the most disturbing information passed on by McNamara, however, was that Johnson regarded the total troop strength that would be reached under the deployment plan before the withdrawal of the three to six battalions as the "upper threshold" of the U.S. ground commitment.

The official reaction of the JCS to McNamara's revelations was to send a message to Westmoreland inviting him to repudiate the troop deployment agreement and to argue once again for the full request for ten additional battalions. The message from Wheeler alluded indirectly to the June 18 decision and linked it directly with Ball's argument about the parallel with the French war: "Thought here in some areas is to the effect that introduction of U.S. troop units over 10,000 [100,000] (some 20,000 fewer than already requested) will convert the war into a second Vietnamese/French war in which we would play the role of the French." Wheeler urgently requested Westmoreland's "personal views for upcoming discussions" and his "assessment of need for additional U.S. forces, their locations and missions, and an assessment of what they could accomplish in South Vietnam." Wheeler further requested his views on new actions against the DRV.[102]

McNamara not only encouraged the JCS to break with Johnson on the troop deployment decision of June 18 but immediately renounced it himself. At the next meeting of the principals with Johnson on June 23, Ball argued, along the lines of his memo, for stopping at 100,000 troops and for "plans for cutting our losses and shifting our focus of action in Southeast Asia to Thailand." But McNamara signaled that he had fundamentally changed his position on troop deployments. Abandoning the idea of a limited commitment of troops, he called for "a lot more force in the South and possibly selectively in the North as well," while supporting more intensive efforts at negotiations.[103]

Westmoreland's response to Wheeler's request on February 24 insisted on the retention of both brigades that were subject to withdrawal under the June 18 decision and "possibly at least another U.S. infantry or airborne division to provide an offensive punch." Westmoreland also called for the use of B-52s against "isolated military targets remote from civilian populations" in North Vietnam, the destruction of the rail lines to China, and the mining of Haiphong Harbor.[104] Wheeler requested another meeting with McNamara on the morning of June 24, after Westmoreland's telegram had arrived in Washington. Later that day, McNaughton wrote a draft memorandum to the president for McNamara's signature that supported not only the request for the two brigades to stay in Vietnam but the additional division that Westmoreland had requested, thus accepting all of Westmoreland's original 34-battalion request. The memo justified this position by referring to the urgent need for more "immediate reinforcements" reported by Westmoreland and the JCS.[105] It was the first draft of what would become McNamara's July 1 memorandum to the president.[106]

The final version of that memo called for the deployment of 175,000 troops and clearly anticipated much larger requests for troops in 1966. But the memo reflected a remarkable lack of conviction about the likely results of such a deployment. In contrast to McNamara's position in April, it warned that, even if the United States were able to halt the Communist offensive in the South, the North Vietnamese might "seek to counter it by sending larger numbers of men into South Vietnam." It raised questions about whether cadres and supplies from the North could actually be cut off, whether cutting them off would "render the Viet Cong impotent," and whether the increasing number of U.S. troops would actually contribute to a nationalist backlash against both the U.S. presence and the Saigon government. Far from suggesting that increasing the troop presence would be likely to allow the United States to negotiate a favorable settlement, he portrayed the war to come as a "war of attrition" that would be a "test of endurance" not only in Vietnam but in the United States.[107] McNamara's arguments were more appropriate, in fact, to a recommendation for Ball's position than to his own recommendation.

McNamara has explained his support for the full Westmoreland request as a response to what he calls the "disquieting cable from Westy" of June 24.[108] But Westmoreland's message did not convey any new information on the military situation, nor did it provide any new rationale for increased deployments. And McNamara signaled his abandonment of the limited commitment option before that message arrived in Washington. The timing of McNamara's shift and the contradiction between his support for the full Westmoreland request for troop deployments and his pessimism about its prospects indicate that his decision was prompted, not by new information or analysis of the war itself, but by internal administration and domestic politics.

McNamara's pique at Ball and Johnson for doing an end run around the rest of the national security bureaucracy may have played a role in that decision. By mid 1965, McNamara's stake in the war had become highly personal. For three years, he had been the administration's preeminent policy maker on Vietnam, and Johnson now appeared to be preparing to opt out of the war on the advice of someone who had been a secondary figure in the policy-making process. But McNamara's sharp turn toward the JCS also was based on a political calculation that Ball's course would be politically disastrous for the administration and particularly for himself. He had seen Kennedy subjected to a political campaign accusing him of irresolution and appeasement and demanding aggressive military action against the Soviet presence in Cuba in September 1962—*before* the discovery of the IRBMs on the island. Given the political frenzy that the Republicans had generated, McNamara had concluded at that time that any public trade-off of U.S. missiles in Turkey for Soviet missiles in Cuba would have been "politically infeasible," even though he had agreed privately that it should be considered.[109]

Now McNamara evidently felt that the same was true of a policy that would inevitably be portrayed by some as a deliberate decision to surrender South Vietnam. As McNamara told the British ambassador on June 29, none of Johnson's advisers "talk about winning a victory" in Vietnam, but it was impossible to tell the American people that the war could not be won.[110] He knew that it would take no more than a statement by the JCS to Congress accusing the administration of a "no-win" policy in South Vietnam to touch off a frenzy of recrimination of the kind that had prevailed in 1962. McNamara had thus chosen to align himself with the JCS in his recommendations both to head off and to separate himself clearly from any decision on Vietnam that could have made him politically vulnerable.

McNamara's memo had not yet been transmitted to Johnson when the latter spoke with McNamara by phone on June 30. Nevertheless, Johnson already knew from McNamara's position at the June 23 meeting and from Bundy, who had read an earlier draft, that McNamara had renounced the limited commitment option. "I don't see anything to do," Johnson said "except give them what they need, Bob, do you?" McNamara confirmed that he was calling for the full Westmoreland request.[111] Without McNamara's support to provide political cover, trying to hold the line against pressures from the military for an open-ended commitment appeared impossible. Johnson was a political realist who knew when the risk was too great, and he had already dropped the discussion of such an option.

Johnson went through an elaborate formal process of discussion of the alternative courses on the war. Beginning with a July 1 meeting and culminating in a marathon NSC session on July 21–22, George Ball presented the case for cutting U.S. losses, and McNamara and Rusk repeated the worst-case scenario arguments against any retreat from Vietnam.[112] But it wasn't a genuine decision-making process. William Bundy later called the July 21–22 conference a "set piece," which "you felt had been staged to a degree."[113] Many years later, it was revealed that Johnson had already informed McNamara four days before that meeting through Deputy Secretary of Defense Cyrus Vance that he had decided to go ahead with the full request from Westmoreland for thirty-four battalions.[114]

Thus Lyndon Johnson's final effort to avert an open-ended general war in Vietnam ended with political theater. Johnson had demonstrated in that episode of decision making an openness to searching for a new way out of the war that had been absent in the February and April episodes. And he had shown a new firmness of purpose in indicating that he wanted to make the high-water mark of troop deployment levels resulting from the June 18 decision the upper limit on the U.S. commitment. It has often been observed that Johnson tried to maintain a middle path on Vietnam between the extremes of escalation and withdrawal. But he seemed willing to take political risks in that final episode in order to avoid war, provided he had the support of his national security advisers, and particularly of McNamara. It was not the middle ground that he sought, but the least warlike ground he could occupy without having to face criticism from his own secretary of defense.

McNamara abandoned the limited commitment option just as Johnson was trying to make it official policy, because of his unwillingness to put himself at odds with the JCS on the issue of troop deployments. He realized that the administration was in a politically precarious situation in which the public expected a victory in Vietnam. His proposal to the JCS for a deployment plan, which departed so sharply from his initial proposal to Johnson, signaled that he was already moving away from the limited commitment option he had helped to fashion. That defection by McNamara was the final act in the five-year drama of pressure, resistance, and accommodation on Vietnam policy that had been played out between two presidents and their national security advisers. It opened the last gate on the road leading to seven and a half years of major U.S. combat.

8 Dominoes, Bandwagons, and the Road to War

The account of U.S. policy making with respect to Vietnam in this study sharply contradicts the conventional interpretation that successive administrations blindly followed Cold War doctrines about containing Communism down the road to war. It shows that the national security bureaucracy was attuned to the signals of U.S. military dominance over its adversaries rather than to the threat of Communism in Southeast Asia. Most readers will nevertheless wonder whether it ignores evidence that presidents and national security advisers alike were led astray by the belief that the loss of South Vietnam would lead to dire consequences in Southeast Asia. After all, wasn't the "domino theory" generally believed by top policy makers on the long road to war in Vietnam?

The domino theory held that most or all of Southeast Asia would be at risk of following South Vietnam into the Communist camp. It suggested both highly unstable and weak regimes and tight linkages between the outcome in Vietnam and the potential vulnerability of neighboring countries to demoralization, destabilization, subversion, and guerrilla warfare. The less familiar "bandwagon effect" thesis suggested that in the event of a U.S. defeat in or withdrawal from Vietnam, non-Communist Southeast Asia would view the PRC as the rising power in the region and hence would align with Beijing.

These arguments are not merely relics of past history. It has been argued that U.S. officials had sound reason to believe in the logic of bandwagoning in the case of Vietnam and Southeast Asia, because bandwagoning is a fundamental tendency of international politics in an anarchic world.[1] Others have challenged the applicability of this thesis to the Cold War generally, however, citing evidence that "balancing" behavior—alignment with opponents of the state that appears to be strongest or most threatening—was far more prevalent than bandwagoning behavior in the Middle East during that period of the Cold War.[2] Whether weaker states tend to balance or band-wagon under different international circumstances has been a significant theoretical issue in the international relations literature.[3]

Another approach to understanding domino and bandwagon thinking in U.S. policy, advanced by Robert Jervis and other theorists, is to treat it as a manifestation of "motivated bias." These analysts have suggested that a definition of threat that responds to a policy maker's personal and political needs rather than to the objective situation is a cognitive bias motivated by the need for rationalization of a policy option preferred for other reasons that are less legitimate or more painful to acknowledge. This approach to interpreting domino and bandwagon thinking treats it is a subconscious or semiconscious device rather than a conscious political tactic.[4]

This chapter examines a third hypothesis about domino and band-wagon arguments: that neither of them ever actually motivated policy makers in the Eisenhower, Kennedy, and Johnson administrations to make decisions affecting Vietnam, but that they were deliberately manipulated for a variety of political and diplomatic objectives. These strategic doc-trines undoubtedly reflected the genuine beliefs of the national security bureaucracy in 1949–50, but the objective realities in Southeast Asia and in the global distribution of power changed so markedly over the next three years that, by early 1954, it was recognized that they no longer reflected those realities. The shift in the global power balance and the diminution of the threat from China and local Communists was so clear after 1953 that few in the national security bureaucracy were unable to grasp the new realities. The story of domino and bandwagon arguments in the politics of Vietnam is therefore one not of credulousness or ideologi-cal zeal, as has long been assumed, but of strategic behavior by policy makers.

THE ORIGINS AND EVOLUTION OF THE DOMINO THEORY

The idea of a chain reaction in the rest of Southeast Asia resulting from the loss of Indochina first appeared in late 1949 and early 1950, when U.S. per-ceptions of the worldwide threat from the Soviet Union were at their height. The emergence of that definition of threat in relation to the Franco–Viet Minh war can be explained by the convergence of three fac-tors: the ambiguity of the global power balance, the high tide of Commu-nist armed struggle in Southeast Asia, and the Truman administration's ignorance about Chinese military capabilities and intentions.

With the triumph of the Chinese Communists on the mainland in October 1949, the international Communist movement, assumed by the administration to be unified under Soviet control, now appeared to have the Chinese Communist army at its disposal in seeking to extend control over Southeast Asia. A key premise of the extreme definition of threat to Southeast Asia was a vastly exaggerated estimate of Communist China's military capabilities and an assumed Chinese proclivity to use them outside the Chinese mainland. U.S. officials assumed that Chinese forces were ready and able to intervene in Vietnam and elsewhere in Southeast Asia. Central to the sense of power imbalance in favor of China and the Soviet bloc was the fact that the United States was not yet in a position to commit any U.S. military forces to the defense of the region.

In February 1950, NSC 64 articulated the official perception that there were "Communist plans to seize all of Southeast Asia" and that mainland Southeast Asia had no defense against such a plan except for the French army in Indochina. Indochina, it said, was the "only area adjacent to Communist China . . . which contains a large European army."[5] That was before the Korean War and the Chinese entry into the war, which lent more credibility to Chinese military moves in the region. In September 1950, the CIA asserted that China had the forces necessary to move simultaneously against Indochina, Korea, Taiwan, Tibet, Hong Kong, and Macao.[6]

Non-Communist Southeast Asia was seen as a power vacuum waiting to be filled by the Communists, with support from China. An NSC staff study in 1951 warned that Chinese military success would "lend greater effectiveness to the ordinary communist techniques of penetration and subversion and cause many Asians to remain on the side lines during the present phase of the struggle." The vulnerability of non-Communist Southeast Asian states was considered to be very high because of political instability, weak leadership, and the twin problems of "prejudice against colonialism and Western 'interference' and the insensitivity to the danger of communist imperialism."[7]

Furthermore, by 1950–51, Communist insurgencies in Burma, Malaya, and the Philippines were at their height, with a total of roughly 50,000 guerrillas in armed resistance in the three countries combined. The insurgents in Burma numbered 25,000, there were between 12,000 and 13,000 in Malaya, and the Communist insurgency in the Philippines numbered roughly 13,000.[8] It was in large part because of the apparent seriousness of Communist insurgencies in non-Communist Southeast Asia that the CIA predicted in an estimate in December 1950 that Viet Minh control of Indochina "would eventually entail control of all mainland Southeast Asia in the absence of effective Western resistance [in] other countries of the area." It portrayed Burma as besieged by internal Communist pressures backed by Chinese and Indochinese military forces, and Malaya as vulnerable to increased military assistance to the Communist insurgents there, which would also "strengthen indigenous Communist movements" in the Philippines and Indonesia.[9]

In the early 1950s, therefore, U.S. policy makers undoubtedly held a genuine strategic belief that a chain reaction in Southeast Asia was likely to result from a Viet Minh victory over the French in Indochina. This strategic belief was expressed consistently over time in a series of studies, estimates, and analyses by the national security bureaucracy.[10]

As congressional impatience with the lengthening war in Indochina mounted, however, the Eisenhower administration began to use the idea of a chain reaction in the region following the loss of Indochina as its key argument for continuing to support the French. In March 1953, Secretary of State John Foster Dulles referred to Indochina as being "in some ways more important than Korea because the consequences of loss there could not be localized, but would spread throughout Asia and Europe." Two months later, he referred in congressional testimony to a "chain reaction throughout the Far East and Southeast Asia." And in late December 1953, Vice President Richard Nixon repeated the chain reaction argument upon his return from a trip to East Asia.[11]

While the administration continued to invoke the strategic perceptions of Indochina and Southeast Asia that it had inherited from its predecessor to prevent erosion of congressional and public support for the policy of assistance to the French war effort, the strategic context of the Indochina conflict—and the administration's appreciation of it—had began to shift significantly during 1953. Administration officials realized that the United States was now in a far stronger position, and that China was not able to threaten the region militarily. Furthermore, non-Communist Southeast Asia no longer appeared so weak as to automatically change sides or simply roll over before internal or external Communist threats. Reflecting these shifts, the CIA issued an estimate in mid November 1953 that took a far more nuanced view of the consequences of a Viet Minh victory than it had three years earlier. The estimate said the loss of South Vietnam would be a "major blow to U.S. power and prestige in Asia," but that the impact on non-Communist Southeast Asia would depend on "a number of contingent developments such as subsequent policies and action of the United States, Communist China and the new Indochina." It noted that local Communist movements in the region outside Indochina were "not now capable of overthrowing existing governments" and would be less likely to affect non-Communist governments' policies toward Communism than the degree of pressure from outside and the "assessment of the power balance in Asia."[12] The CIA thus suggested for the first time that the notion of an inevitable "chain reaction" might no longer apply.

By early 1954, confronted with the greatly increased likelihood that the French might withdraw from Indochina, and unwilling to intervene militarily in the war, Eisenhower and Dulles began to think about strengthening Thailand militarily and making regional defense commitments to other Southeast Asian states.[13] They believed that the region could be stabilized even if Indochina were lost. As Eisenhower began preparing for the anticipated fall of Indochina, he and Dulles therefore began to distance the administration from the "chain reaction" argument.

In executive session testimony before the Senate Foreign Relations Committee on January 7, 1954, the day before the NSC was to discuss the subject of possible French withdrawal from the war, Dulles presented Southeast Asia as a region that could hold out against future Communist efforts with U.S. help. Far from being a domino that would be toppled by a Viet Minh victory, he said, Thailand was "in a good mood" to combat any new efforts at subversion that might arise in the future, and "in the main, the situation in Thailand is fairly satisfactory." Referring to the administration's past use of the chain reaction image, Dulles said the Thais were insisting that "we should stop talking that way, because they don't intend to go if Indochina goes, and it is very demoralizing . . . to have it said that 'We have no independent capacity to stand up.'"[14]

Undersecretary of State Walter Bedell Smith, who had previously testified before the Senate Foreign Relations Committee that the loss of Indochina would cause the collapse of Southeast Asia "like one of those houses of cards that children build," returned to the committee in mid February 1954 to retract his earlier statement. "I do not believe that now," he said. "I think that, even at the worst, part of Indochina might be lost without losing the rest of Southeast Asia." Smith cited the willingness of the Thais to increase the number of men under arms and referred to the possibility of a defense pact with Thailand, Burma, and "possibly" Cambodia. What would be really disastrous, Smith told the committee, would be "if Indochina were to fall without any such effort having been made in the rest of the region."[15] The chain reaction argument was being officially retired.

By 1954, the senators who were most deeply involved in U.S. Indochina policy were not persuaded by the familiar chain reaction argument either.

For most of them, the taint of colonialism attached to the Franco–Viet Minh war had rendered the contention that supporting the French was vital to American security highly suspect. Senator Barry Goldwater (R-Ariz.), for example, simply refused to "imagine Vietnam as vital to American interests."[16] When the Eisenhower administration began to signal its rejection of intervention in Indochina in early 1954, it dealt a final blow to the credibility of the chain reaction argument in the eyes of key members of Congress. When Dulles testified in February 1954, both Republican and Democratic senators pointed out the contradiction between the claim that holding Indochina was "more important than Korea" and the administration's obvious reluctance to intervene with U.S. forces to save the French. "If it is that important," asked Senator Homer Capehart (R-Ind.), "and it is important for us to go to war in Korea, then what are we waiting for now? Who is kidding whom and why?" Senator Hubert Humphrey (D-Minn.) said he had the same question.[17]

Beginning in late March, however, administration policy entered a new phase, in which Dulles's primary concern was to convey to the USSR and the PRC that the United States was prepared to intervene militarily as part of a "united action" with its allies and to put pressure on the British, in particular, to cooperate with Dulles's strategy.[18] Those objectives required that the administration once again maximize the strategic stakes for the United States in Indochina for public consumption. At the same time, however, Eisenhower and Dulles also wanted to discourage any buildup of political pressures for unilateral armed intervention and gain support for actions aimed at strengthening the rest of Southeast Asia, both of which required a more realistic definition of the stakes. The president thus had to face both ways at once on the chain reaction argument.

Pursuing these two contradictory political purposes, Eisenhower *both* voiced a new formulation of that argument *and* refuted it in the course of the same NSC meeting on April 6. When Treasury Secretary George Humphrey expressed concern that the United States was "trying to prevent the emergence of Communist governments everywhere in the world," Eisenhower defended the plan for a regional grouping in Southeast Asia by invoking a new image of Indochina as "the first row of dominoes." If that row fell, he said, "its neighbors would shortly thereafter fall with it, and where did the process lead?"

In response to arguments by Admiral Arthur Radford, chairman of the JCS, and Allen Dulles for unilateral U.S. military intervention in Indochina, however, Eisenhower "expressed his hostility to the notion that because we might lose Indochina we would necessarily have to lose all the rest of

Southeast Asia." In an obvious swipe at Walter Bedell Smith and Radford, who had used a special committee he had created to make the argument for unilateral intervention in Indochina, if necessary, Eisenhower
recalled that the NSC had set up the special committee "to recommend
measures for saving the rest of Southeast Asia in the event Indochina
were lost."[19]

At his press conference the following day, in the context of explaining
his administration's policy of pursuing "united action," Eisenhower dram-
atized Indochina's strategic importance by putting forward the memorable
image of falling dominoes. "You have a row of dominoes set up," he said,
"you knock over the first, and what will happen to the last one is the
certainty that it will go over very quickly. So you have a beginning of dis-
integration that would have the most profound influences." Eisenhower
suggested that the strategic consequences could include the loss of the
defensive island chain of Japan, Taiwan, and the Philippines.[20]

Eisenhower's recasting of the chain reaction argument would stick in
the minds of journalists for many years to come as the official rationale for
military intervention in Southeast Asia. What the media did not understand was that the use of the falling dominoes image was part of a larger
strategy to convince the USSR and the PRC that the administration was
contemplating intervention and trying to get the British to back Dulles's
"united action" initiative on Indochina. It was so effective that it convinced
not only the press and public but successive generations of historians that
the administration was planning to intervene militarily in concert with its
allies. Only when the archival documents of that period were finally published could Ike's real strategy be understood.

After the fall of Dien Bien Phu, however, as proponents of going to war
in Indochina went on the offensive within the NSC, Ike and Dulles apparently decided that the greater danger was the increased pressure for military intervention.[21] Dulles then reverted publicly to the more moderate
view that Southeast Asia could be salvaged despite the loss of Indochina. At
a press conference on May 11, Dulles rejected what he called "the so-called
domino theory." In its place, he advanced a countertheory that the security
pact he was planning for Southeast Asia would attract the countries of the
region: "As the nations come together, then the 'domino theory,' so called,
ceases to apply."[22] Testifying in executive session to the Senate Foreign
Relations Committee the next day, Dulles again referred to Thai resent-
ment at their country being regarded as a falling domino. He added that
neither the Burmese nor the Indonesians felt that they would "be lost" in
the event that Indochina was lost. "I am determined," said Dulles, "not to

make Indochina a symbol for all of Southeast Asia, so if Indochina is lost, we assume that the whole game is up."[23]

The irony of the domino theory's status as an unchallenged strategic belief of the Eisenhower administration as well as its successors, therefore, is that Ike's original formulation was not a reflection of Eisenhower's and Dulles's strategic beliefs but an instrumental argument for short-term diplomatic purposes. Before, during, and after the planning for "united action," in fact, both Dulles and Eisenhower believed that non-Communist Southeast Asia would survive the shock of a Communist victory.

No further allusion to anything like the domino effect in Southeast Asia appears in the public or private record of the Eisenhower administration. But the administration did have available assessments of the strategic consequences of the unification of Vietnam under Ho Chi Minh's government. In September 1955, the CIA was asked to analyze the consequences of a failure by the United States to respond to an open invasion of South Vietnam by North Vietnamese troops, even after having made strong public threats to respond militarily—the most serious scenario possible for impacts on Southeast Asia. Even with this worst-case premise as the basis for its estimate, however, the CIA rejected not only the domino thesis but the bandwagon logic as well. Instead, it argued that the likely consequence of a North Vietnamese military conquest of the South would be a set of negotiated accommodations by non-Communist Southeast Asia with Communist China, going beyond carefully balanced neutralism but still short of alignment with China. The Chinese Communists would "demand an accommodation to the Bloc going beyond the benevolent neutralism that is the current goal of Communist strategy," and mainland Southeast Asian countries would "become increasingly inclined to attempt to maintain their independence through negotiated understandings with Peiping."

In Thailand, internal political changes would bring to power a government "amenable to an accommodation with Communist China." Burma would seek closer alignment with non-aligned India but would not become a vassal state of China. The British would want a U.S. defense commitment to Malaya, and the Philippines, South Korea, and Nationalist China would remain allied with the United States, as would Japan, despite "grave doubts" about the future and increased neutralist sentiment in Japan. European allies would be, on balance, relieved that the United States had not gone to war over Vietnam, although the broadening of the shaky anti-Communist defense arrangements in the Middle East might be more difficult, because pro-Western governments would have less confidence in U.S. commitments.[24]

Political-military developments in Southeast Asia had continued to undermine the credibility of the domino argument. Communist armed insurgencies in Burma, Malaya, and the Philippines had declined with stunning swiftness in the early 1950s, and by the mid 1950s, it was clear that the high tide of Communist insurgency in Southeast Asia had receded. By 1954, mass surrenders had reduced the estimated 25,000 armed Burmese Communist insurgents to only about 1,000, including part-time guerrillas. In the Philippines, the Communist insurgency had already essentially unraveled by 1955–56, with only "widely scattered handfuls of desperate rebels" remaining. In Malaya, the insurgency had been reduced from as many as 12,000 at its height in 1951 to only 3,000 guerrillas by mid 1955.[25]

Soon after the end of the Indochina War, it was also clear that China's policy toward the region had also undergone a dramatic change. Instead of instigating or supporting subversive warfare in Southeast Asia, China shifted in 1954–55 to a new foreign policy line of *opposing* armed struggle by Communist movements in the region. During the second half of the 1950s, Chinese foreign policy strongly emphasized state-to-state relations with the anti-Communist governments of the region. In 1955, the Chinese Communist Party pressured the Malayan Communist Party (MCP) to lay down its arms, despite the fact that the British had refused the party's offer to surrender in return for legal recognition. When the Burmese Communist Party (BCP) ended a policy of peace with the Burmese government and launched a campaign of violence in 1954, the Chinese applied pressure on the party to return to a line of negotiating with the government on a peace agreement under which it would give up its armed struggle entirely, and the BCP did return to negotiating peace in 1955.[26]

U.S. intelligence analysis accurately portrayed the significance of these developments in a late 1958 intelligence memorandum attached to the NSC policy statement on Southeast Asia. It observed that both "the bloc" and local Communist parties "generally would prefer legality to continued illegal and guerrilla activity." In Thailand, South Vietnam, Malaya, and Singapore, the report said, the Communist parties were "for the most part fragmented," and their "immediate aim" was to "achieve legality and eventually to turn their governments' policies into neutralist channels."[27]

The last policy statement on mainland Southeast Asia issued by the Eisenhower administration's National Security Council in mid 1960 codified in official language the strategic assessment of the region that had emerged more clearly over the previous five years: "The loss to Communist control of any single free country would encourage tendencies toward accommodation by the rest."[28] Rather than a toppling of dominoes or band-wagoning, it was the likelihood that Southeast Asian states would refuse to be part of the U.S. network of anti-Communist political-military relation-ships that worried the national security bureaucracy as the Eisenhower administration wound down.

By the time the Kennedy administration took office, scarcely any secu-rity problem outside of Laos and South Vietnam remained to arouse anxi-ety about the stability of Southeast Asia. The precipitous reduction of China's power because of the near collapse of its agricultural economy, combined with the loss of Soviet economic and military assistance, had made the overall power balance in East Asia even less favorable to the Communist world than in the previous five years.[29] Given the nonthreat-ening character of Communist movements in Southeast Asia outside of Laos and South Vietnam, the worst that could be projected in the event that the Diem regime collapsed was that Thailand and Malaysia would be tempted to adopt a neutralist posture. The CIA issued an estimate in the first few weeks of the Kennedy administration that underlined the relative stability and security that would remain in non-Communist Southeast Asia even in the event of losses in Laos and South Vietnam. A victory by the Pathet Lao in Laos or the division of the country into Pathet Lao and anti-Communist zones would "almost certainly incline the Thais toward accommodation to Communist power in Southeast" and would cause other states in the region to feel a "strong temptation to take a neutral position between the two power blocs." The CIA estimated that the impact on non-Communist Southeast Asia if South Vietnam fell or became neutral would be "similar in kind" but "more severe."[30]

Notably absent from the CIA estimate was serious concern about the threat from domestic Communist movements in the region. By the begin-ning of the 1960s, the problem of Communist insurgency had essentially disappeared. In Burma, there were fewer than 1,000 full-time armed rebels in 1961, as had been the case for more than six years. In the Philippines, only 75 diehards were still in the jungle, only barely able to stay alive and out of jail. In Malaya, the "emergency" had officially ended in July 1960, after all but 500 of the insurgents in the field had actually surrendered. Only 100 of those remaining, moreover, were actually inside Malaya, the rest having moved into Thailand to escape apprehension.[31] Neither the Philippines nor Malaya was even mentioned in a February 1962 intelligence estimate of Communist bloc objectives and capabilities in Southeast Asia.[32]

Burma's main problem in the early 1960s was not the few Communists who were still in the jungle but burgeoning armed insurgencies by ethnic minorities—Shans, Karens, Kachins, and Chins. The only external state suspected of providing material support to those insurgents, moreover, was Thailand.[33] In Cambodia, the CIA believed that the Communist Party of Kampuchea (CPK), which was then engaged in a modestly successful parliamentary struggle, had an estimated 1,000 members and possibly 30,000 sympathizers, but noted that its activities were being "stringently curtailed" by Chief of State Norodom Sihanouk.[34]

The Indonesian Communist Party (PKI in its Indonesian acronym) was by far the largest political party in Indonesia, claiming more than two million members. But the PKI had firmly committed itself in 1952 to a strategy of a peaceful path to socialism, explicitly rejecting Mao's strategy of armed agrarian revolt and endorsing Khrushchev's peaceful transition thesis. Unlike any other Communist party in the world, moreover, the PKI maintained a policy of staunch support for a non-Communist neutralist regime in which the anti-Communist military held a powerful position. Far from representing a threat to overthrow the political system of Indonesia, the PKI had a very substantial stake in maintaining it. It was well known that the main reason for this stance was that the party was so vulnerable to physical repression by the Indonesian military.[35] The Kennedy administration's basic policy document on Indonesia in 1961 acknowledged that once Sukarno passed from the scene, the army would have the capability for "at least temporary curtailment of PKI activities."[36]

Thailand was the main concern of U.S. policy makers about non-Communist Southeast Asia, and both the CIA and the U.S. embassy in Bangkok were optimistic about its social and political stability. The Communist Party of Thailand (CPT) had never been an important political force in the country, in large part because no nationalist political mobilization had taken place during World War II. Despite numerous incidents of political protest in the poverty-stricken and culturally distinct northeastern region of the country, the CIA found in early 1962 that "no widespread indigenous Communist movement exists in Thailand," and that the "small, illegal Thai and Chinese Communist parties are relatively ineffective."[37] In early 1962, the administration's Special Group on counterinsurgency began drawing up plans to "break up" what they called "rebellious elements" in the northeast, but they regarded these as essentially nationalist rather than Communist in orientation and knew that they had no arms.[38]

When Maxwell Taylor and Walt Rostow stopped in Bangkok after their visit to South Vietnam in October 1961, therefore, the U.S. embassy gave them a briefing that emphasized the "fundamental stability of Thailand, the lack of serious economic or social cleavages, the general political docility of the Thai public, assimilationist tendencies among the Chinese, and the firm control of [military strongman] Sarit [Thanarat]." The Taylor-Rostow mission learned that the Communist movement was "small and did not have much handle to use for its work."[39]

This analysis of Thailand did not serve the needs of the Taylor-Rostow mission in building a case for U.S. military intervention in South Vietnam. In writing their report, therefore, the members of the mission simply ignored it. They submitted a paper suggesting that Thailand, along with the rest of Southeast Asia, faced a serious threat from Communist subversion and guerrilla warfare in the event of the loss of South Vietnam: "The Communists undoubtedly believe," it asserted, "and with good reason—that if the strategy succeeds in Laos and South Vietnam, the enterprise will rapidly gather momentum throughout Southeast Asia." Contradicting this depiction of Southeast Asia as under threat, however, it noted that the "interim" objective of the Communists was not to overthrow non-Communist governments but to "induce a neutralist solution, blocking the U.S. military presence, as with the proposal to deprive Laos of SEATO protection." Taylor referred to the "interim Communist goal" and did not predict an early collapse or loss of independence of non-Communist Southeast Asia. Instead, he merely observed that, depending on U.S. policy in South Vietnam, Southeast Asian states would "adjust their behavior accordingly," which was compatible with the CIA's less alarmist analysis of the region.[40]

The Taylor-Rostow group thus flirted with the image of a red tide flowing into Thailand but found that it was simply too difficult to make a credible case for either a domino or a bandwagon effect. Taylor had no scruples, however, about presenting a straightforward bandwagon argument to members of the Foreign Relations Committee, whom he apparently viewed as less sophisticated than Kennedy about Southeast Asia. Testifying on his return from a trip to South Vietnam with McNamara in September 1963, Taylor declared that a U.S. retreat from Vietnam would cause "anybody who has any faith in us in that part of the world" to "immediately try to get on the Communist bandwagon, which would result in the loss of the states in Southeast Asia."[41]

When Rusk, McNamara, and McGeorge Bundy were deciding how best to persuade Kennedy to make a military commitment to South Vietnam in November 1961 they therefore had nothing on which to hang either the domino or the bandwagon argument. Instead, McNamara and Rusk managed to invoke both falling dominoes and a bandwagon in a single sentence: "The fall of South Vietnam to Communism would lead to the fairly rapid extension of Communist control, or complete accommodation to Communism, in the rest of mainland Southeast Asia and in Indonesia," warned a November 8 memorandum to the president from McNamara, who reported this as the joint conclusion of Deputy Secretary of Defense Roswell Gilpatric, the JCS, and himself.[42] A Rusk-McNamara joint memorandum to Kennedy three days later used a slightly modified formulation: "We would have to face the near certainty," it said, "that the remainder of Southeast Asia and Indonesia would move to a complete accommodation with Communism, if not formal incorporation within the Communist bloc."[43]

The use of the phrase "complete accommodation" involved some creativity in turning the likelihood of accommodation into something much more threatening than either diplomatic reporting or intelligence analysis supported. But even that indistinct notion was apparently thought to be inadequate in justifying the dispatch of U.S. combat troops to South Vietnam, as indicated by the suggestion in the November 8 memorandum that actual Communist control of Southeast Asia, brought about by some unidentified linkage between Vietnam and Communists in each of those countries, was an equally plausible result.

It might be argued that the hold of the domino and bandwagon theories on Kennedy's principal advisers was so strong that it was immune even to intelligence analysis that directly contradicted it. That is a plausible explanation in the abstract, but the evidence suggests otherwise. Asked about the domino thesis in a 1986 oral history interview, Dean Rusk replied tersely, "I never used the domino theory." McGeorge Bundy's response to the same question sought to distinguish his own more sophisticated thinking from the crudeness of the domino thesis: "[W]hat happens in one country affects what happens in another, yes, but that you could push one down and knock the rest over, its extreme form . . . I never believed that."[44]

Historians have generally thought that Kennedy himself believed in the domino thesis, based on his statement in a September 9, 1963, television interview. When he was asked by David Brinkley of NBC News whether he doubted the "so-called 'domino theory,' that if South Viet-Nam falls, the rest of Southeast Asia will go behind it," Kennedy answered: "No, I believe it. I believe it. I think that the struggle is close enough. China is so large, looms so high just beyond the frontiers, that if South Viet-Nam went, it would give them an improved geographic position for a guerrilla assault on Malaya but would also give the impression that the wave of the future in Southeast Asia was China and the Communists. So I believe it."[45]

This was not exactly a description of a full-blown domino effect. Kennedy's statement did not indicate a chain reaction, a general collapse of the will to remain independent of China in non-Communist Southeast Asia, or a move by Southeast Asian countries to align themselves with international Communism. It provided a rationale for continued involvement in South Vietnam, but not necessarily for going to war over the issue. In any case, Kennedy's apparent endorsement of the domino theory must now be reinterpreted in light of his political strategy in 1963 of establishing his firmness on Vietnam in the public mind while he pulled the strings of the troop withdrawal negotiations from behind the scenes. Indeed, at that moment, Kennedy was thinking about how to obtain the approval of the entire NSC for a phased complete withdrawal of U.S. troops from South Vietnam by the end of 1965. Kennedy could not ignore the fact that embracing the domino theory, which was associated closely— however mistakenly—with Eisenhower, had become a symbol of anti-Communist policy in Southeast Asia. He could reasonably anticipate that any response other than a straightforward endorsement would certainly invite Republican criticism.

Despite his public obeisance to the domino theory, Kennedy had expressed skepticism about the argument in private. In a conversation with the *New York Times* columnist Arthur Krock, a longtime family friend and confidant, on October 11, 1961, Kennedy doubted that the domino theory "has much point any more because . . . the Chinese Communists are bound to get nuclear weapons in time, and from that moment on they will dominate South East Asia."[46] Coming just at a time when Kennedy was under intense pressure within his administration to take major steps toward military intervention in South Vietnam, Kennedy's response to Krock reflected his instinctive understanding that the domino theory was being used by those who wanted armed intervention in Vietnam. He was almost certainly creating his own strategic argument against the domino theory aimed at defending his policy preference for keeping U.S. troops out of Vietnam.

The role of the domino argument in U.S. policy toward Vietnam from 1954 through 1963 is therefore quite different from the one that has been so often attributed to it. The origins of the explicit domino image in the Eisenhower administration reveal that it was not a strategic belief that enthralled policy makers but a tactic for selling the French and the Communists on the determination of the United States to take action in Indochina.

By the time Kennedy became president, Eisenhower's falling-dominoes argument had taken on the odd status among civilian national security officials of a relic of the distant past that was considered crude and unsophisticated. The CIA Office of National Estimates had definitively rejected both the domino and bandwagon arguments. Kennedy's advisers toyed with using it with him, but they finally decided not to rely on an argument that clearly lacked credibility. The president cast doubt on it off the record, and Rusk and Bundy disdained it, even though Rusk consented to a statement that implied it as a possibility.

THE REVIVAL, DEATH, AND RESURRECTION OF THE DOMINO THEORY

During the Johnson administration, the domino argument became the subject of an intrabureaucratic battle between those who wished to use it to convince the president to use force in Vietnam and those who tried to discredit it as a distortion of reality. The CIA's Office of National Estimates was in the forefront of the fight against the domino theory, and it was joined by the administration's leading policy maker on Asia, William Bundy. McNamara, Rusk, and McGeorge Bundy were determined, however, to keep it as a central element in the effort to sway the president's decisions.

William Bundy was a pivotal figure in the fight over the domino theory. He was assistant secretary of defense for international security affairs at the beginning of the Johnson administration, but became assistant secretary of state for East Asian affairs in March 1964. Beginning in May 1964, he was one of the small circle of advisers continuously involved in Vietnam policy, along with McNamara, Rusk, Ball, Taylor, and his brother McGeorge Bundy. Following his changing formulations of the U.S. strategic stake in South Vietnam through 1964 provides insights into the political role of the domino and bandwagon arguments in the making of the Johnson administration's Vietnam policy.

Bundy wrote his first memorandum depicting the effect of a loss in South Vietnam on Southeast Asia after Johnson requested in early January that Rusk and McNamara provide him with "memorandums of refutation" of a proposal by Senator Mike Mansfield (D-Mont.) for a negotiated settlement of the Vietnam War.[47] Bundy immediately drafted a memorandum to the president for McNamara, arguing that the consequences of losing Vietnam, by whatever means, would cause the rest of Southeast Asia either to become "shaky" or to reach accommodations with China, or both.

> In Southeast Asia, Laos would almost certainly come under North Vietnamese domination, Cambodia might preserve a façade of neutrality but would in fact accept Communist Chinese domination, Thailand would become very shaky, and Malaysia, already beset by Indonesia, the same; even Burma would see the developments as a clear sign that the

whole of the area now had to accommodate completely to communism (with serious consequences for the security of India as well).

Basically a truly "neutral" Southeast Asia is very unlikely to emerge from such a sequence of events, even if the US itself tried to hold a firm position in Thailand and Malaysia too tried to stand firm.

In the eyes of the rest of Asia and of key areas threatened by Communism in other areas as well, South Vietnam is both a test of U.S. firmness and specifically a test of U.S capacity to deal with "wars of national liberation." Within Asia, there is evidence—for example, from Japan— that U.S. disengagement and the acceptance of Communist domination would have a serious effect on confidence. More broadly, there can be little doubt that any country threatened in the future by Communist subversion would have reason to doubt whether we would really see the thing through.[48]

McNamara submitted Bundy's memorandum to Johnson on the same day he received it without changing a word.[49] Even though Bundy's memorandum had the conscious political aim of refuting Mansfield's policy proposal, it was closer to the assessment that had consistently been offered by the intelligence community than to the November 1961 memorandums by Kennedy's advisers. Significantly, Bundy did not even argue that Thailand would choose to end its alliance with the United States. He was not predicting either falling dominoes or a realignment of the region with China.

Instead, Bundy focused on the idea that South Vietnam was a test of U.S capacity to deal with "wars of national liberation." That was a very different conception of the strategic importance of the war in South Vietnam and had less to do with Southeast Asia than with the U.S. ambition to discourage armed struggle in unstable countries around the world. The "test case" thesis was indeed a strategic belief that key officials in the Kennedy administration, including McNamara and JCS Chairman Maxwell Taylor, had embraced. It was much less concrete and much less far reaching in its claims, however, than either the domino or the bandwagon argument. As Taylor put it in a memorandum to McNamara in January 1964, "this being the first real test of our determination to defeat the communist wars of national liberation formula, it is not unreasonable to conclude that there would be [a] correspondingly unfavorable effect upon our image in Africa and in Latin America."[50]

The "test case" argument, moreover, was not simply a definition of threat. It was also a reflection of the optimism that the national security bureaucracy felt about the political advantages the United States would derive from success in defeating the Vietnamese Communist insurgency. McGeorge Bundy had suggested to Kennedy as early as November 1961 that success in South Vietnam would "produce great effects all over the world."At a State Department meeting in 1962, Rostow argued, "If we can thoroughly disabuse those who see indirect aggression as a plausible way, we will have scored heavily."[51] In short, it was seen at least as much as an opportunity for the United States as it was as a definition of threat.

In February 1964, as the national security bureaucracy was buzzing about attacking North Vietnam, the CIA came out with its first Special National Intelligence Estimate (SNIE) dealing with the strategic consequences of defeat in South Vietnam since 1961. The SNIE reaffirmed previous CIA estimates that the effect of the loss of South Vietnam would be an increased tendency toward neutralism in the region. It concluded that the outcome in South Vietnam would "have a serious effect on the future willingness of governments in Southeast Asia to adopt anti-Communist, rather than neutralist stances." It suggested that the South Vietnamese conflict was "a test, crucial for much of Southeast Asia," of "the feasibility of going along with the US response to Communist pressures rather than opting for some other course such as an attempt to negotiate livable settlements with the Communists." If the United States moved toward negotiations in South Vietnam, it concluded, "the idea of accommodation with Communist forces in the area would spread."[52]

The CIA estimate was careful to distinguish the probable "accommodation" at issue from any bandwagon effect that proponents of the use of force over Vietnam might wish to argue for. The primary effect of the loss of South Vietnam, it observed, would be a series of "livable settlements with the Communists" in much of Southeast Asia, thus explicitly denying the notion that these governments would join an anti-U.S. alignment sponsored by China. For the CIA, the only issue was whether the United States would be able to continue successfully to pursue its policy of diplomatic isolation and pressure on the Chinese Communist regime.

Despite this clear reaffirmation by the CIA that the domino theory did not apply to Southeast Asia, however, in late February, McNamara directed Bundy to draft a memorandum to the president calling for "direct U.S. action against North Vietnam." Bundy understood that he was to portray the strategic consequences of defeat in much darker tones than he had in January. To do so, Bundy had to ignore the CIA estimate that had been written only two weeks earlier, because it would have undercut the rationale for such a policy. Bundy made no reference to that estimate but instead constructed a strategic argument out of whole cloth. His paragraph on the subject is worth quoting in full:

> Unless we can achieve [our] objective in South Vietnam, almost all of Southeast Asia will probably fall rapidly under Communist dominance

(all of Vietnam, Laos and Cambodia), accommodate to Communism so as to remove effective US and anti-Communist influence (Burma), or fall under the domination of forces not now explicitly Communist but likely then to become so (Indonesia taking over Malaysia). Thailand might hold for a period with our help, but would be under grave pressure. Even the Philippines would become shaky and the threat to India on the West, Australia and New Zealand to the south, and Taiwan, Korea, and Japan to the north and east would be greatly increased.[53]

A comparison of Bundy's March 1 formulation with the January 7 version reveals no fewer than five significant changes that made the consequences of defeat appear far more serious in the later version. Cambodia was now consigned to "communist dominance"; the Philippines, not even mentioned in the previous version, were now put in the "shaky" category; Malaysia was considered to be not merely "shaky" but bound to fall under the control of Indonesia. Even more important, Bundy now presented Indonesia, which had not been mentioned in January, as a domino that would inevitably fall to Communism. Finally, Bundy added to this alarmist picture an increased—albeit undefined—threat to all of East Asia and the Pacific.

Bundy was applying domino logic to Cambodia, Thailand, Malaysia, and Indonesia, thus leaving the Philippines and Burma as the only Southeast Asian dominoes not doomed to fall. No external events in January and February 1964 can account for this dramatic transformation of Bundy's view of the consequences of an undesirable outcome in Vietnam. He was simply crafting an argument to suit the policy needs of his boss.

Can Bundy's memorandum be seen as evidence that McNamara was a true believer in the domino thesis? McNamara is the only one of Kennedy's principal advisers who claimed after the war that the domino theory caused policy makers to charge into war in Vietnam. In a 1996 interview for a television documentary, McNamara called the domino theory "the primary factor motivating the actions of both the Kennedy and the Johnson administrations, without any qualification."[54] When McNamara was asked point-blank a decade earlier whether he had subscribed to the domino theory in 1961–62, however, he did not answer the question directly. Instead, he recalled his view that the United States should train the South Vietnamese but should not intervene in support of them, "even if they were going to be 'defeated.'"[55]

At least one important piece of documentary evidence supports the view that McNamara, along with Taylor and McCone, understood that Thailand was not likely to be "gravely threatened" in the event of a Communist victory in South Vietnam, as Bundy's draft had suggested. In October 1962, McNamara and other participants in a conference on Vietnam in

Honolulu discussed the situation in Thailand and registered a consensus that it would not be "an easy target" for Communist subversion, given the stability of the government of Sarit Thanarat.[56]

McNamara's renewed embrace of the domino thesis in late February and early March 1964 was certainly opportunistic. It came just in time to justify a new proposal for the use of force to a new and untried president. McNamara may have been encouraged to invoke it by Johnson's own use of the domino theory in a conversation with the defense secretary only days earlier. Johnson had employed it, however, not as an argument for going to war in Vietnam but to frame his justification for the existing policy of assisting South Vietnam. On February 20, while suggesting to McNamara how Vietnam policy might be described in an upcoming speech, Johnson presented existing policy as the moderate alternative between two possible extremes: "We could pull out of there. The dominoes would fall and that part of the world would go to the Communists. We could send our marines in there, and we could get tied down in a Third World War or another Korea action. The other alternative is to advise them and hope that they stand and fight."[57]

A major element in William Bundy's argument was that Indonesia would go Communist and would then take over Malaysia, and that either or both of those developments would be attributable to the outcome in South Vietnam. Indonesia was the largest and arguably most important country in Southeast Asia, and connecting its potential loss with the Vietnam conflict was one way of raising the U.S. stake in the outcome of the conflict. Bundy almost certainly did not actually believe that the collapse of the Saigon government would increase the likelihood of Indonesia falling under Communist control.

The situation in Indonesia and its relationship to Southeast Asia had been under intense discussion at high levels of the administration since January. In that discussion, not a single official had suggested a linkage between the deterioration of the situation in South Vietnam and the political fate of Indonesia. On the contrary, Rusk had clearly implied the opposite in arguing at an NSC meeting that continued U.S. assistance to Indonesia was necessary. "More is involved in Indonesia, with its 100 million people," Rusk said, "than is at stake in Viet-Nam."[58]

Regardless of what happened in Vietnam, national security officials did not believe that Indonesia was in serious danger of falling under PKI control in the foreseeable future.[59] The intelligence community had been reporting for some time that the Indonesian military was a strong bulwark against an unarmed PKI. A CIA estimate in late 1963 had reaffirmed that the potential for PKI subversion or guerrilla warfare was "limited because of close military scrutiny."[60] That conclusion was confirmed by further intelligence analysis a week before the NSC meeting that considered the report incorporating Bundy's analysis of the threat in Southeast Asia.[61]

Bundy's suggestion that Indonesia was likely to take over Malaysia was sharply contradicted by the bureaucracy's own internal assessment. Bundy was well aware that Indonesia did not have the capability to do more than harass Malaysia by stirring up guerrilla actions in Sabah and Sarawak. The State Department had estimated in February 1964 that there were only 150–200 Indonesian guerrillas in eastern Malaysia, and that most of these were "inactive." It had expressed confidence that the British and Malaysian governments could "substantially eliminate them by attrition" through "quiet pressure."[62] U.S. officials also knew from intelligence analysis and diplomatic reporting that the British had the military capability to quickly destroy Indonesia's offensive capabilities if Indonesia tried to escalate the conflict.[63] Bundy was vastly exaggerating the likelihood of Malaysia being taken over by Indonesia to construct a sufficiently disturbing picture of Southeast Asia after a defeat in South Vietnam.

At the NSC meeting on March 17 that adopted McNamara's trip report, with Bundy's language on the threat to Southeast Asia, as NSAM 288, Johnson agreed that McNamara would make a major speech on Vietnam to generate more public support for the president's policy. In fact, Bundy had already drafted such a speech, and he circulated the draft on the same day to key State Department and White House officials for comment. The draft included an explicit invocation of the domino argument: "The 'falling dominoes' analogy often applied to Vietnam and its several neighbors is not an idle phrase. The ease and rapidity with which Japan's conquest of Southeast Asia was completed in 1942, when the first 'domino' fell, speaks for itself."[64] It was hardly a persuasive argument, however, since it had so little to do with the situation in the region more than two decades later.

One of the officials to receive that draft was William Sullivan, who headed the interdepartmental committee on Vietnam. Sullivan was very optimistic about non-Communist Southeast Asia; later in 1964, he would characterize Thailand and Malaysia as "remarkably sound centers of stability, economic progress and (particularly in Malaysia) political maturity."[65] He strenuously objected to the draft's "reiteration of the 'falling dominoes,'" which, he complained, portrayed non-Communist Southeast Asian states as "a row of feeble dominoes sustainable only by a constant bleeding of American human and material resources for their support." Sullivan suggested replacing it with the argument that Vietnam was a "test case" of Communist guerrilla wars.[66] The reference to the falling dominoes argument was deleted from McNamara's speech when it was presented on March 26, and was replaced, as Sullivan had suggested, by the "test case" argument.[67]

Regardless of the resistance from the bureaucracy to the use of the domino argument, Johnson's advisers continued to rely on it in pressing him on the issue of military action against North Vietnam. In late May, Johnson told his old friend and Senate colleague Richard Russell (D-Ga.) that Rusk, McNamara, McGeorge Bundy, and Harriman had all been trying to convince him that Vietnam would be "a domino that will kick off a whole list of others," and that therefore "we've just got to prepare for the worst."[68]

In a television interview on March 15, 1964, in which Kennedy's statement the previous year was invoked by the questioner, Johnson had followed in Kennedy's footsteps. "I share President Kennedy's view," he affirmed, that, if South Vietnam was lost, the "whole of Southeast Asia would be involved."[69] But was Johnson really convinced that a domino effect was likely? After getting a large dose of domino argument from his advisers, Johnson asked the CIA for a second opinion on the issue. He requested that CIA analysts answer the question, "Would the rest of Southeast Asia necessarily fall if Laos and South Vietnam came under North Vietnamese control?"[70] The wording of Johnson's question strongly hinted at a desire for a refutation of the domino thesis that would give him more room for maneuver on Vietnam.

The CIA's answer did exactly that. Sherman Kent, the director of the Office of National Estimates responded a few days after Johnson's request with a memorandum that reaffirmed the CIA's earlier conclusion that Southeast Asia would not follow Laos and South Vietnam into the Communist camp, but went even further than that in refuting domino thinking.[71] "With the possible exception of Cambodia," the memorandum said, "it is likely that no nation in the area would quickly succumb to Communism as a result of the fall of Laos and Vietnam." Nor, it added, would the further spread of Communism in the area be "inexorable." On the contrary, it observed, "any spread which did occur would take time—time in which the total situation might change in any number of ways unfavorable to the Communist cause." The CIA was sticking by the analysis it had provided in 1961 and again in early 1964.

This time, however, the CIA memorandum also took aim at the bandwagon argument as well, even though it had not been asked to address it. It admitted that the loss of control of South Vietnam and Laos would be "damaging to U.S. prestige and would seriously debase the credibility of

US will and capability to contain the spread of Communism elsewhere in the area." However, it added, "the extent to which individual countries would move away from the U.S. towards the Communists would be significantly affected by the substance and manner of U.S. policy in the period following the loss of Laos and South Vietnam."[72] Specifically in the case of Thailand, the memorandum anticipated an "almost certain shift toward a neutralist position, hoping thus to forestall any vigorous Communist move against the regime for as long as possible." Thai cooperation with the United States would be "reduced." Burma, however, would be "less affected," because it had few political-military ties with the United States. Indonesia was not mentioned as being affected by the outcome in Vietnam.

More important, the CIA analysis pointed out that U.S. military power in East Asia was based not on the mainland of Asia but on the chain of allied island states from the Philippines to Japan. "As long as the US can effectively operate from these bases," the memorandum concluded, it would "probably still be able to deter Peiping and Hanoi from overt military aggression." And the analysis predicted that all these allied states would maintain their policy of military cooperation with Washington, despite some increased political pressures on the alliance policy within the Philippines and Japan.

Thus, the CIA argued, in effect, that the U.S. losses and Communist gains from the defeat of the Saigon government would necessarily be limited by the fundamental imbalance of power in East Asia. The clarity with which it refuted the logic of the domino argument left no room for misunderstanding. This was no obscure intelligence document but a response to a specific presidential request; the CIA memorandum quickly became known in the intelligence community as the "Death of the Domino Theory Memo."[73]

This time the CIA memorandum had an impact on the discourse among Johnson's advisers. Less than a week after the CIA refutation, William Bundy retreated from his portrayal of Southeast Asia as a set of falling dominoes or countries ready to bandwagon to the Communist bloc. In a paper for a June 15 meeting on his proposal for a congressional resolution on the use of force in Southeast Asia, he redefined the security threat emanating from South Vietnam as the spread of neutralism in the region. "Pressures toward rapid accommodation with Peiping and Hanoi would intensify in every country in the region," he wrote, but then added, "This is not to say that nations would go Communist at once or that immediate changes would be apparent in the foreign policy of Southeast Asian nations." He now conceded that Thailand "might remain an ally and defensible," although internal pressures for neutralism would increase. He also conceded that Cambodia and Burma would not go Communist, as he had suggested they would a few months earlier, but would take "further steps to preserve their independence through intimate relations with Peiping and a minimization of Western ties." Malaysia, previously portrayed as likely to be engulfed by a Communist Indonesia, would "soon face a rising tide of pro-Peiping activity" from its Chinese population. But he now conceded that the Philippines would not be seriously affected and dropped the suggestion that Indonesia was likely to go Communist.[74]

Bundy was now arguing that U.S. defeat in South Vietnam would likely eventuate in the abandonment of anti-Chinese policies, but not acceptance of Chinese suzerainty, by non-Communist Southeast Asian states. Why did he follow the CIA line in June but not in March? The obvious explanation is that Bundy had changed jobs. In March, he had been writing a memorandum for the specific purpose of justifying McNamara's recommendation to the president. As assistant secretary of state for East Asian affairs, Bundy was now, in theory, at least, the administration's leading policy maker on East Asia. Bundy was able to express his own views, because, unlike McNamara, Rusk did not demand that analyses prepared for a meeting with the president conform to his personal policy views.

Despite the rejection of the domino and bandwagon arguments by the CIA and William Bundy, Johnson's advisers did not renounce them as discredited theories but continued to advocate using them to make congressional and the public opinion more amenable to the anticipated eventual use of force against North Vietnam. McGeorge Bundy again advised Johnson on July 1 that he should use the domino theory on Senator Mansfield.[75] At the end of July, even William Bundy himself advocated warning of dire consequences as a result of the loss of South Vietnam as the main argument to build public support for possible later military action. He joined with Michael Forrestal in proposing that Democratic candidates and their supporters assert during the electoral campaign that "preventing Communist domination of South Vietnam is of the highest importance to U.S. national security." The concerted campaign would argue that, if South Vietnam were lost, "Burma and India to the west and the Philippines to the east" would also go Communist, which Bundy's June 15 paper had shown he did not believe at all.[76]

When Johnson met with his advisers, including Taylor, in early September, moreover, neither the CIA's rejection of domino and bandwagon thinking nor Bundy's own retreat from it in June restrained Johnson's advisers from pressing such arguments with the president. JCS Chairman General Earle Wheeler reported the unanimous view of the service chiefs that "if we should lose South Vietnam, we would lose Southeast Asia," and then he added: "Country after country would give way and look toward Communist China as the rising power of the area." McCone and Rusk then indicated their agreement with Wheeler.[77] They did not explicitly say that Southeast Asian states would be taken over by Communist movements, or that they would ally themselves with China against the United States, but they clearly implied that one or both would occur. The argument was therefore artfully ambiguous, obscuring the difference between bandwagoning to the Chinese Communist side and neutralist accommodation with the PRC by establishing normal diplomatic and trade relations and eschewing policies that could be associated with the U.S. strategy of isolation of and pressure on China.

William Bundy was disturbed by this renewed reliance on an implied bandwagon effect in selling Johnson on going to war over South Vietnam. In October he wrote a 42-page analysis of the U.S. strategic stake in South Vietnam, dissecting the kind of argument Johnson's principal advisers had made in September, and circulated it to the four men who were Johnson's closest civilian foreign policy advisers: Rusk, McNamara, McGeorge Bundy, and Ball.[78] It was an unprecedented repudiation of the domino and bandwagon arguments by a member of the inner circle on Vietnam and the administration's top policy maker on Southeast Asia. Bundy again underlined the difference between Southeast Asian accommodations with China that would follow a victory for Hanoi in South Vietnam, or even Laos, and the assumption of the modern equivalent of "vassal states"—traditionally, smaller states that paid tribute to China, recognizing its political and cultural superiority in return for being allowed to maintain their independence.

Bundy concluded that the worst that could happen was that Thailand would abandon its alliance with the United States and reach some kind of accommodation with China and Vietnam, but he indicated that even that degree of shift in foreign policy might well be prevented in spite of defeat in Vietnam. Bundy observed that the Thai government had strengthened its security and extended its national presence throughout its territory," suggesting that it was much less vulnerable to Communist insurgency than it had been five or ten years earlier. Conceding that persuading the Thai leaders to maintain their military cooperation with the United States would be an "uphill" struggle "for a long time to come," he suggested that the United States might even have to station one or more divisions in Thailand to reassure the Thais.

As for Malaysia, Bundy suggested that defeat in Vietnam would "embolden Sukarno to increase his pressure on Malaysia," but that the

United States could reinforce Malaysia's defenses as well. This time he did not even bother to mention Indonesia in relation to a Vietnamese Communist victory. Both the CIA and the State Department were expecting a power struggle between the Indonesian army and the PKI upon Sukarno's death or removal from office, which they were certain the army would win. The CIA was so confident of the army's ability to crush the Communists that it was considering a covert action program under which its agents would provoke violence that would give the Indonesian military the pretext for taking action against the PKI.[79]

After this extraordinary challenge to the use of the domino and bandwagon arguments in the internal discourse over Vietnam, on top of the CIA's explicit repudiation of them, all of the inner circle of national security advisers knew that these rationales for war were seriously discredited. Because of William Bundy's central role in coordinating Southeast Asia policy as assistant secretary of state for East Asia, moreover, he was also in a position to ensure that his critique would be incorporated into official policy papers. That is exactly what he did as coordinator of the drafting of the papers by a "Working Group on Courses of Action in Southeast Asia" in November 1964.

Bundy personally drafted the paper on the U.S. objectives and strategic stake in the conflict.[80] This time, he went even further in dismissing the domino effect in regard to South Vietnam, writing that it would apply only if the United States did go to war in South Vietnam and this prompted the Chinese to enter Southeast Asia "in a big way," leading to South Vietnam being lost "not by collapse of the Saigon government but something akin to military defeat." Bundy also dealt with the effects of retreat from South Vietnam on U.S. military allies in East Asia—Japan, Taiwan, and South Korea. They would have to be reassured, he conceded, but the problem in Japan would not be a turn away from the military alliance with the United States. The problem with Tokyo, he argued, would be that "the growing feeling that Communist China must somehow be lived with might well be accentuated."

The gist of William Bundy's section on the U.S. strategic stake was thus that the loss of South Vietnam would threaten the ability of the United States to continue pursuing the same hard-line policy of isolation of and pressure on China, but not the survival of non-Communist Southeast Asia. He supported the bombing of North Vietnam, but he wanted to leave the door open to an eventual withdrawal if South Vietnam could not survive. The implicit message of his paper was that the bombing should not be advocated on the basis of an argument that would foreclose later flexibility.

McNamara, McGeorge Bundy, and Rusk could not allow the domino and bandwagon arguments to be dismissed in their submission to Johnson. Given Johnson's growing resistance to that option in September and October, they knew that they faced a hard sell on starting phase II of the bombing. They needed a political trump card in presenting the case for the bombing policy, which could only be the threat of the loss of all of Southeast Asia. Their response to William Bundy's analysis, therefore, was not to have a full discussion of the issue with him, as might have been expected had they held strong convictions on the matter. Instead, they simply used hardball tactics to eliminate this view on the issue from the documentation on Vietnam policy that would go to the president.

On November 24, when Rusk, McNamara, McCone, JCS Chairman Wheeler, Ball, and the Bundy brothers met to discuss the "Courses of Action" paper William Bundy had written, they reached a "consensus" that "the loss of South Vietnam would be somewhat more serious than stated in Section II of the draft paper, and it would be at least in the direction of the Joint Staff view as stated in the footnote to page 7 of the draft."[81] That referred to the JCS's argument that "early loss of Southeast Asia and the progressive unraveling of the wider defense structures would be the almost inevitable result of the loss of South Vietnam in any circumstances."[82] The issue was decided by the bureaucratic maneuver of using the official position of the JCS, whose views both McGeorge Bundy and McNamara had generally regarded as extreme, against that of William Bundy.

The suppression of William Bundy's critique of the domino thesis by McGeorge Bundy, Rusk, and McNamara in November 1964 provides further evidence that the Johnson's inner circle of advisers was not urging the use of force based on a naïve belief in Cold War doctrines of threat. The picture of those advisers that emerges from this reconstruction of the discourse on Vietnam in relation to Southeast Asia is one of coldly calculating political realists who could not afford to sacrifice an argument that they hoped would make the president hesitate to reject their recommendation for war.

THE REAL THREAT: THE FAILURE OF A STRATEGY

If Johnson's principal advisers were not driven by a belief in the domino or bandwagon effects of the loss of South Vietnam, they did have fears about the political-diplomatic consequences of a loss in South Vietnam—particularly if the United States had failed to use force to try to prevent it. To understand the real fears of the leaders of national security bureaucracy, one must put the Vietnam issue in the broader context of U.S. Cold War policy and programs in East Asia. The unifying theme of the policy and programs throughout the period of U.S. dominance had long been pressure on and isolation of China on the premise that the Communist regime would eventually fall. That fundamental strategy had been institutionalized during the 1950s and early 1960s through military alliances and cooperation with anti-Communist states in East and Southeast Asia, culminating in the establishment of a military foothold on the mainland of Southeast Asia in Thailand and the effort to suppress the Communist insurgency in South Vietnam. Despite the recognition that the Chinese Communist regime probably would not be overthrown in the foreseeable future, that essential strategy was reaffirmed officially in a November 1962 policy paper on China that called for the avoidance of any action that would "reduce pressures operating on the regime," including "pressures resulting from our military presence in the Taiwan Strait, Korea and Southeast Asia."[83]

By 1961, the U.S. national security bureaucracy had come to regard the maintenance of the political-military status quo as a vital interest. The idea that a military ally or other anti-Communist state would make an "accommodation" with China and shift to a neutralist position was regarded by U.S. national security officials as threatening to the U.S. power position on the periphery of China. The fear of neutralism was not limited to Southeast Asia but was part of the global perspective inherited by the national security bureaucracy from the Eisenhower administration. The CIA reflected that perspective in its "Estimate of the World Situation" a few days before Kennedy took office, warning that, unless reversed, the trend toward neutralism already under way in the developing world "will become so strong that it will draw away from the West some of those nations now associated with it."[84] That was a trend that national security officials strongly resisted wherever possible.

Holdovers from the previous administration argued that the Kennedy administration had to keep up the pressure on China in order to head off such accommodations. As Robert W. Komer of the White House national security staff wrote in a draft paper in April 1961, any easing of pressure on China by the United States "would greatly accelerate the already dangerous trend toward accommodation on the part of peripheral Far Eastern countries."[85] It was a perfectly circular argument, which allowed the bureaucracy to avoid having to reevaluate the reasons for the growing disparity between the belligerent U.S. policy toward China and the views of several of its Asian allies.

The fear of accommodation in the early 1960s was focused primarily on Thailand, which had become the bastion of U.S. anti-Communist policy on the Southeast Asian mainland. The United States spent $100 million from 1954 to 1962 on the building of four major airbases in Thailand from which the United States could bomb China and North Vietnam.[86] Despite Thailand's close military cooperation with the United States, however, U.S. officials viewed the Thai military regime as opportunistic and prone to accommodation with China.

Such an accommodation had already occurred, in fact, even while the Thai military regime was ostensibly committed to the anti-PRC policies of the United States in Southeast Asia. Thai military leaders had begun in 1955 to pursue a quasi-neutralist policy by secretly opening political contacts with China. They had actually reached agreement with the Chinese on eventual normalization of relations, and in 1956–57, they had partially lifted the trade embargo against China, allowed groups of businessmen and political figures to travel to China, and even encouraged the Thai press to criticize U.S. policy toward China. Even after the Thai regime had renounced this opening to China under pressure from the United States in 1957, U.S. concern about neutralism in Thailand had persisted.[87]

Even though they recognized that Thailand's internal security situation was stable in the early 1960s, senior U.S. national security officials continued to worry about the adoption by Thailand of a neutralist stance if the United States failed to hold on to South Vietnam or Laos. A Special National Intelligence Estimate in 1962 denied that Communism had any attraction for the Thais, but noted that "neutralism has certain historical roots in Thailand and considerable immediate appeal to the Thai people." On his return from a visit to Bangkok in June 1962, McCone shared with McNamara his worry that Bangkok had a "historical propensity to adjust to prevailing trends in the area" and would "move toward neutralism and seek accommodation with the Communist bloc should the U.S. position in Southeast Asia show additional signs of weakness." In September, Taylor recorded his own "hunch" that Sarit would "not leave our side unless we should lose in South Viet-Nam."[88]

As documented in this chapter, in refuting the domino theory, both William Bundy and the CIA judged that the consequences were likely to be that Thailand and other pro-Western states in the region would reach political-diplomatic accommodations with China. A move to neutralism by Thailand would in turn probably result in the loss of the only U.S. military bases in mainland Southeast Asia, the irrelevance and possible breakup of SEATO, a reduction in U.S. influence on non-Communist states in the region, and a new period of political-diplomatic fluidity. Not only the Thais, but the Malaysians, the Japanese, and perhaps the Filipinos as well would be thinking about normalizing relations with China and ending any remnants of the old Cold War hostility in their foreign policies.

In short, the larger U.S. Cold War strategy in East Asia might not survive if the United States left South Vietnam without succeeding or at least having put up a fight for it. As McNamara put it in his memoirs, "the West's containment policy"—meaning the U.S. policy of confronting and isolating China— "lay at serious risk in Vietnam."[89] Holding on to that anti-China strategy had ceased to be merely a means to the ultimate objective of U.S. foreign policy in Asia and had become an end in itself.

Both in late 1964 and in mid 1965 the threat of neutralism to U.S. containment policy was discussed explicitly by leading national security officials as the primary reason for going to war rather than cutting U.S. losses in Vietnam. When Bundy was called in by McNamara and Rusk on November 23, 1964, he had written a memorandum calling for a negotiated withdrawal from South Vietnam and had argued that the problem maintaining military cooperation with Thailand against China was not insuperable, even if the United States disengaged from Vietnam. The two secretaries argued strenuously, however, that "the problems of carrying on" after the loss of South Vietnam would be "nearly insuperable" if his advice were followed.[90] The context of that remark makes it clear that McNamara and Rusk were referring the problem of avoiding a move by Thailand toward neutralism.

In late June, as the decision on approving Westmoreland's full troop deployment request loomed, William Bundy argued with his colleagues that, even if the chances of an "early failure" of the ground troop commitment were substantial, as they all assumed, "you had to make the try." If the United States didn't "make the try," Bundy warned, the Thais would "cash in their chips," either by accommodating with China or by establishing a "leftist neutralist" government.[91] In the crucial period of decision making on Vietnam, therefore, Rusk, McNamara, and William Bundy all argued that the specter of a military ally opting out of the U.S. Cold War system was a legitimate reason for sending tens of thousands of U.S. troops into combat in South Vietnam.

The desire to avert a failure of the U.S. Cold War strategy in regard to China was not the same as the fear that the overall power balance in East Asia would shift toward Communist China, much less the Soviet Union. As shown in Chapters 5 and 6, the national security bureaucracy believed that China could not become even a great power for many years, much less challenge the overall U.S. power position in the region. Indeed, with the shift by the Soviet Union to a position in East Asian geopolitics that was somewhat closer to the United States, Lyndon Johnson's principal advisers knew that the longer-term trend of the balance of power was even less favorable to the PRC than it had been before the Sino-Soviet conflict.

Even though Johnson's advisers regarded the threat of neutralism and accommodation with China as a sufficient rationale for going to war in Vietnam, they also knew that neither the president nor the public would find it very persuasive. They had good reason to fear that Johnson would not have been willing to ask Americans to fight a war simply to prevent the failure of the policy of isolation and pressure on China. They were forced to invoke the far more dramatic images of threat embodied in the domino and bandwagon arguments for tactical political purposes.

9 Conclusion: The Perils of Dominance

I have argued in this study that it was not Cold War ideology or exaggerated notions of the threat from communism in Southeast Asia that paved the U.S. road to war in Vietnam but the decisive military dominance of the United States over the Soviet Union. The extremely high level of confidence on the part of national security officials that the United States could assert its power in Vietnam without the risk of either a major war or a military confrontation with another major power conditioned the series of decisions that finally led to war. To put it another way, the imbalance of power so constrained the policies of Moscow and Beijing toward Vietnam (and toward the peripheral countries more generally) that it created incentives for ambitious U.S. objectives in that country.

The second theme of the study has been that the imbalance of power did not have the same influence on all the actors involved in U.S. policy making on Vietnam. The values, attitudes, and interests of the national security bureaucracy were focused overwhelmingly on U.S. power and influence abroad, so it is not surprising that the signals of highly unequal power relations had a very direct influence on their policy preferences. The same cannot be said, however, of the presidents who were in office during the period under study. Eisenhower, Kennedy, and Johnson saw no reason to commit U.S. forces against an internal insurgency in South Vietnam. For those three presidents, other political values, including the avoidance of war, outweighed the desire to score a Cold War victory over the Communists. Although all three presidents were well aware of the stark imbalance of power, therefore, it did not incline them to go to war in Vietnam. During the 1961–65 period, U.S. dominance led to a consistent pattern of struggle between the president and the national security bureaucracy over Vietnam.

This study has delineated the linkage between unequal power relations and each of five U.S. policy decisions on Vietnam. During 1954–55, the imbalance of power directly shaped John Foster Dulles's response to the crisis in Indochina, but it did not lead to a decision to intervene, because both Eisenhower and Dulles thought such intervention would be a disastrous course. However, the imbalance of power did lead Dulles to exploit the *threat* of military intervention to exert pressure on the USSR and the PRC in regard to Indochina. Even more important, after the Geneva Accords, the unequal configuration of power encouraged him to carry out a "covert operation" to support the repression of the Viet Minh political organization in South Vietnam and to cast aside the Geneva Accords provisions for national elections to reunify Vietnam. The latter decision, made without consulting Eisenhower, discarded a policy on Vietnamese elections based on consistency with broader U.S. ideology and Cold War policy. We now know that North Vietnam was prepared to agree to virtually everything the United States demanded, not only on guarantees of a free election, but on continuation of a separate regime in South Vietnam for an indefinite period. The tragedy of Dulles's decision is compounded by the fact that Eisenhower had already ruled out U.S. military intervention to save South Vietnam from just the kind of internal Communist insurgency that arose in 1960 in response to the U.S.-instigated repression.

By the time Kennedy entered the White House, the initial U.S. assessment of Soviet and Chinese acquiescence in the U.S. assertion of power in South Vietnam had hardened into a fundamental assumption of U.S. policy. When the new Communist insurgency suddenly became a potentially serious threat to the Diem regime, therefore, national security officials believed that the United States had a free hand to employ U.S. military power in South Vietnam to suppress it before it could become too powerful. The Soviet Union was considered irrelevant to the Vietnam issue, China was mired in starvation and disorder, and both the Chinese and North Vietnamese were seen as intimidated by the destructive power of the United States. The absence of any external constraint led Kennedy's principal advisers to advocate the use of U.S. forces in South Vietnam with little or no debate.

Kennedy, on the other hand, explicitly rejected the overall U.S. power advantage as the framework for approaching the issue. He was inclined by his personal knowledge of the historical background to the conflict to avoid a U.S. military commitment in South Vietnam. But he was also afraid to reject his advisers' recommendation completely. The result was a compromise on the third major decision in late 1961 that allowed a major U.S. role in the counterinsurgency war by U.S. pilots but ruled out open combat by U.S. troops. Meanwhile, the earlier effect of the imbalance of power—the rejection of the Geneva Accords and of any political-diplomatic compromise with the North Vietnamese—continued to operate. Kennedy's efforts to initiate diplomatic contacts with Hanoi were resisted by the national security bureaucracy in the firm belief that South Vietnam was a place where the United States could and should effectively exert its power.

When Lyndon Johnson ascended to the White House, a fourteen-month struggle began over the third major decision—whether or not to carry out an air war against North Vietnam. As the Communist bloc disintegrated, the power relationship had continued to develop even more favorably for the United States, and U.S. officials had come to view Moscow as a potentially helpful interlocutor in getting Hanoi to retreat. The tenuous character of a series of South Vietnamese governments made bombing the North even more attractive. Because air attacks on the North were a low-risk option, provided the bombing did not threaten the regime or the Chinese border, the case for attacking North Vietnam did not even depend on the prospects for forcing Hanoi to withdraw from the war. It could also be useful as a bargaining chip, and even in the worst case, it would demonstrate that the United States was willing to use its power to punish its adversaries for challenging U.S. interests in East Asia. U.S. military dominance was thus central to the rationale for the bombing of North Vietnam.

Lyndon Johnson had strong reservations about bombing the North from the beginning, but the pattern of pressures, resistance, and compromise that had defined the major policy decision on Vietnam in the Kennedy administration repeated itself under Johnson. Johnson's advisers repeatedly pressed him to commit himself to a strategy of military pressure on North Vietnam; he refused but tried to keep his advisers "on board" his policy by suggesting that he had not rejected their recommendation completely. After Johnson's landslide election victory, the pressure on him intensified, until a compromise was finally reached between the president and his advisers in February 1965 limiting the scope of the bombing much more narrowly than the advisers had wanted by ruling out even the threat of bombing civilian targets.

The causal linkage between the imbalance of power and the fourth major policy decision on the limited deployment of ground troops in South Vietnam is more complex than in earlier decisions. When Rolling Thunder began, McNamara and McGeorge Bundy understood that the South Vietnamese government might suffer serious reverses and go rapidly downhill at any time, and they had grave doubts about whether U.S. forces could actually defeat the Vietnamese insurgency. Nevertheless, they could still imagine a peace agreement or tacit understanding that would not involve any explicit political compromise with Hanoi. They proposed to increase U.S. ground strength in South Vietnam significantly, which, they hoped, in combination with the northward movement of the bombing of North Vietnam, would signal to Hanoi the seriousness of the U.S. commitment to stay in South Vietnam. This was extremely wishful thinking on their part, which they could have entertained only because of the extraordinary U.S. power advantage. They believed U.S. ability to destroy much of North Vietnam at will would deter Hanoi from committing regular troops to the South, and a stalemate in the war was therefore possible.

The notion that the ability of the United States to threaten North Vietnam with vast destruction could be used to control Hanoi's role in the war in the South still had a strong hold on the thinking of Johnson's advisers in March–April 1965. It was based on a historical reality: the North Vietnamese had constrained their role in the South for years out of fear of U.S. retaliation. Those advisers failed to consider two new realities, however: first, the major escalation of the war in the South—and of American military involvement in it—meant that Hanoi's leaders had reached a threshold where they regarded the failure to send North Vietnamese troops to the South as having potentially irreversible consequences. Thus they were willing to accept some increased risk of U.S. bombing by late 1964 and early 1965 in order to achieve an improved military balance in the South.

Second, the U.S. threat to North Vietnam had already been considerably diluted by the beginning of the actual bombing campaign—which was very far from the kind of devastation Hanoi had feared all along—and by Lyndon Johnson's refusal to threaten devastation to cow the North Vietnamese. Even after the purpose of the bombing was officially designated as interdiction rather than pressure on Hanoi's political will on April 1, 1965, Bundy, McNamara, and Rusk seem to have relied on the residual threat to remove the existing restrictions on the bombing of the DRV to deter a large-scale North Vietnamese troop presence in the South—hence, McNamara's dabbling in nuclear threat in April.

On a path to war strewn with cruel ironies, perhaps the greatest irony is that the fifth and final decision, namely, to give the military leaders all the troops they wanted in mid 1965, was the least affected by the unequal power relationship. For McNamara and Bundy, at least, exaggerated expectations of the efficacy of dominant power in constraining Hanoi's options, while enhancing those of the United States, were still alive and well in April, but those expectations had come crashing down by early June. The prospect of either relatively short-term defeat or a long, bloody war if the United States did not choose to settle was no longer deniable. Facing that truth, Johnson, Bundy, and McNamara were all gravitating in early and mid June toward a limited commitment option that they all knew meant the acceptance of a possible defeat. Like Kennedy before him and Johnson himself during the previous year and a half, Johnson never referred directly to the acceptance of defeat either in meetings or in phone conversations with McNamara. He spoke of the need to meet the U.S. treaty obligation in Vietnam, but not of preventing the fall of the Saigon government regardless of the cost.

Johnson still hoped to avoid escalation to an open-ended ground war by establishing an upper limit on troop deployments, while hoping for an evolution of congressional sentiment that would make possible a negotiated exit from the war. But his hope of avoiding a big war depended on having the active support at least of his principal advisers, and especially of McNamara, in order to face the inevitable accusations of having lost South Vietnam. McNamara initially supported the limited commitment option, but he abandoned it within a few days when he realized that Johnson was considering an option that would make everyone associated with it even more vulnerable to the charge that he was following a "no-win" policy. Ultimately, it was the presidential need for collective responsibility for a politically unpalatable decision and his primary national security advisers' fear of taking such responsibility that put the administration on the path to an open-ended war in Vietnam.

DYSFUNCTIONAL POLICY MAKING ON VIETNAM

The Cold War consensus explanation for the Vietnam War implies that the national security institutions and the processes of policy making on Vietnam worked the way they should in a democratic system. The theme of the first major assessment of Vietnam policy making after the war was that "the system worked," because the policy consistently reflected the presumed consensus on the goal of containing Communism.[1] The present study suggests, however, that the process of making policy toward Vietnam resulted in policy decisions that did *not* reflect the best judgment of the president about Vietnam. Instead, the policy was skewed by the aggressive role of the national security bureaucracy in pushing its own policy preferences.

Students of U.S. foreign policy have long observed that the president's actual power over foreign policy does not match his formal authority.

More than four decades ago, Richard Neustadt portrayed the president as able to get his way with his subordinates only by persuading them to follow his lead, suggesting that a degree of independence was inherent in their positions as heads of bureaucracies with their own interests.[2] The bureaucratic politics model of foreign policy making views foreign policy decisions as the result of "conflict and consensus-building," in which the different goals and values of the president and leading policy makers are reconciled.[3]

Such anodyne descriptions of the process of making foreign policy fail, however, to convey the seriousness of the struggles between the presidents and their national security advisers from 1961 to 1965 over the issue of going to war in Vietnam. The idealized image of White House meetings at which the president seeks to bring his subordinates around to his viewpoint bears no relationship to the reality of the policy-making process revealed in this study. In fact, the process in respect to Vietnam was just the reverse of this image: the Defense Department, the State Department, the JCS, and even the White House national security staff played the role that students of foreign policy making have always attributed to the president, and Presidents Kennedy and Johnson were hard put to maintain control over Vietnam policy.

The tendency of national security advisers to lobby aggressively for military action did not begin with the Kennedy administration. It was already evident, albeit at a lower level of intensity, even in the Eisenhower administration in 1954. Chairman of the JCS Admiral Arthur Radford and former CIA Director Walter Bedell Smith used their positions on a task force created by Eisenhower to put pressure on him to intervene in Indochina, despite the president's explicit directive to them to provide alternative options to such intervention. Eisenhower was not really vulnerable to such pressures, because they did not represent a consensus among national security officials, and because he knew that public opinion would not support intervention in Indochina on behalf of the French. He was able to manage the pressures from the national security bureaucracy for war without the need for any substantive compromise with the hawks. Even so, he felt obliged to make the argument that intervention would risk a war with the Soviet Union and China, which appears to have been created out of whole cloth.

Not all the decisions on the road to war in Vietnam directly involved the question of using military force. U.S. policy on the Geneva settlement was one issue that involved force only indirectly, insofar as it was realized that the decision might provoke a military response by the Vietnamese

Communists. For that reason, Eisenhower did not follow the issue as closely as he would have had it more obviously been a question of war and peace. As a result, Dulles was able to take the decision on scrapping the existing policy on national elections under the Geneva Accords out of Eisenhower's hands by ensuring that it was never raised within the NSC.

By the time Kennedy entered the White House, high officials in the Defense and State Departments and the White House Office of National Security Affairs, as well as the JCS, were asserting their primacy in making Vietnam policy. Well before Kennedy had begun to focus on the problem, they had already formulated their own policy, which was to prepare for the introduction of U.S. combat forces into the war, and had begun to seek presidential authorization to carry it out. That pattern only became more pronounced over the course of 1961.

High-ranking bureaucrats and national security advisers expected the president to accede to the policy on Laos and Vietnam that they found necessary to maintain existing U.S. positions of strength in Southeast Asia. When Kennedy began to carry out his own policy of neutralization of Laos in the face of opposition from his advisers, key officials in the State Department, the CIA, and the military were outraged that Kennedy was making an end run around them. Many of them considered that he was selling out a U.S. ally to the Soviet bloc. Determined to hold on to the U.S. positions in both Laos and South Vietnam, Walt Rostow, U. Alexis Johnson, and Maxwell Taylor began meeting in the summer of 1961 to make plans to get Kennedy to drop the negotiation of a compromise on Laos and use military force in both Laos and South Vietnam.

Kennedy responded to the aggressive advocacy role of the national security bureaucracy by carefully avoiding a clear-cut rejection of the use of force in any formal meeting, encouraging his advisers to believe that he was still considering their recommendations. In November 1961, Kennedy compromised with the hawks in his administration by approving the opening wedge of U.S. combat intervention in South Vietnam, but he made it clear that he would approve the use of combat troops only under diplomatic circumstances that everyone knew were prohibitive. That decision shocked his national security advisers. Reflecting the feelings of the inner circle of national security officials, McGeorge Bundy's memorandum to Kennedy about the decision captures the feeling on the part of his advisers that a president should not reject the course of action recommended unanimously by his national security team.

Two months after Kennedy's decision, the JCS openly challenged his policy against the use of combat forces in South Vietnam in an unsolicited letter to McNamara. That action in itself reflected a dramatic change in the norms governing the role of the JCS in relation to the making of foreign policy decisions from those of the early Eisenhower years. When Radford had called a meeting of the JCS on March 31, 1954, to canvass their views on sending Eisenhower a memorandum calling for military intervention in Indochina, Army Chief of Staff Matthew Ridgeway had insisted that, unless requested by "proper authority," such a recommendation would be "clearly outside the proper scope of authority of the JCS" and would "involve the JCS inevitably in politics."[4] By 1962, however, the JCS were no longer constrained from trying to influence the president's policy toward Vietnam.

Kennedy soon realized that compromise with his advisers threatened a loss of control over the policy, making him vulnerable to pressures from military and civilian advisers alike for open-ended escalation of the U.S. military role in South Vietnam. He sought to regain control over Vietnam policy by adopting an indirect strategy of withdrawal that would not expose him to political charges of having lost South Vietnam. He exploited McNamara's personal ties with the Kennedys, using his secretary of defense to initiate planning by the military for a strict timetable for withdrawal of U.S. troops. Later, Kennedy exploited his brother's close friendship with Maxwell Taylor, whose cooperation in the plan as chairman of the JCS was vital to its success, to the same end. While the negotiations went forward, Kennedy maintained a public rhetorical stance of staunch opposition to withdrawal from South Vietnam. By drawing McNamara and Taylor into his withdrawal strategy, Kennedy succeeded in regaining a tenuous control over Vietnam policy in October 1963.

Kennedy's fear of opposition and criticism by his own national security bureaucracy and his adoption of a strategy of manipulating policy from behind the scenes limited his ability to lead, even within his own administration. After his efforts to open a diplomatic channel to Hanoi in 1962 encountered stiff resistance from Harriman, Kennedy postponed any such diplomatic probe, waiting to see how the withdrawal plan would develop and whether a diplomatic settlement would be necessary. In the final weeks of his life Kennedy apparently realized that he would have to resort to negotiations in order to avoid being sucked ever deeper into the war.

The assassination of John F. Kennedy and the entrance of a new president into the White House dramatically increased the distorting effects of the aggressive role of national security advisers on Vietnam policy. Kennedy had been able to weaken the national security bureaucracy's power over policy by using both his defense secretary and the chairman of the JCS as stalking horses. When Lyndon Johnson became president, however, neither McNamara nor Taylor was any longer constrained by personal loyalty to the president. Johnson's two top advisers were once again free to push for the use of force on Vietnam, with serious consequences for policy making.

Throughout 1964 and the early part of 1965, McNamara, Taylor, and other principal advisers used a wide range of bureaucratic devices to maneuver Johnson into agreeing to initiate military action against North Vietnam: joint warnings by the CIA, State, and Defense that Johnson had to act soon to avoid irreversible deterioration; insistence that the loss of South Vietnam would result in a falling-dominoes effect in Southeast Asia; a unanimous recommendation of bombing from his principal advisers, after they had convened as the "Executive Committee" without Johnson's authorization; and the drafting of a congressional resolution that would have formally committed the president to prevent the loss of South Vietnam by force, if necessary. Even more serious was McNamara's deliberate deceit in failing to inform Johnson about the uncertainty surrounding the alleged second attack on U.S. navy vessels on August 4. McNamara and Rusk tried again in September to mousetrap Johnson into retaliatory strikes over a nonexistent naval attack but this time were rebuffed.

There is surely no parallel in modern history to the twelve separate attempts by the national security bureaucracy over a fourteen-month period to get Johnson to authorize the use of military force against the same state. It is indicative of the acute contradiction between Johnson and his advisers, however, that Johnson rebuffed every one of them, except when he was deprived by McNamara of vital information in the Tonkin Gulf decision. Those attempts can be summarized as follows:

1. November 1963–January 1964: change of wording of NSAM; preparation of plans for covert actions that included U.S. air attacks on North Vietnam

2. February 1964: McGeorge Bundy proposes creation of an interagency group to plan military pressures on North Vietnam to Johnson; creation by Rusk of such a group without presidential authorization

3. March 1964: draft recommendation by McNamara for bombing North Vietnam to be presented to Johnson upon return from South Vietnam

4. May 1964: joint recommendation by McNamara and Rusk for commitment to use force

5. June 1964: proposal for congressional joint resolution on use of force

6. August 1964: withholding of information by McNamara on doubts about the alleged attack on U.S. ships in the Tonkin Gulf

7. September 1964: plans for a strategy of provocation

8. September 1964: effort to convince Johnson that another attack on U.S. ships had taken place

9. November 1964: recommendations for retaliation for attack on the Bien Hoa airbase

10. December 1964: unanimous recommendation for two-phase bombing policy

11. December 1964: recommendations by Taylor, McGeorge Bundy, and others for retaliation for the bombing of Brinks Hotel in Saigon

12. January 1965: McNamara-Bundy letter to Johnson insisting that present policy was unacceptable

Johnson became concerned very early in his presidency about the political implications of the aggressiveness with which the JCS and McNamara were pressing him to go to war. Like Kennedy, he was careful never to put anything on paper that could be cited as evidence of his rejection of the use of force. Once he had discovered arguments he could use to justify rejecting the bombing of North Vietnam (the threat of intervention by China, ineffectiveness in bringing North Vietnam to heel, the fragility of the South Vietnamese government, and the threat of physical harm to U.S. women and children in Saigon), Johnson was willing to defy his advisers on that issue. Johnson also had an additional motive for resisting pressures for war in the opportunity to pass a historic domestic reform program. His preoccupation with his "Great Society" agenda, moreover, came after his election in November 1964, just when his advisers were counting on their unanimous recommendation of a bombing program to finally prevail on him to implement that policy.

Despite Johnson's resistance to actually committing himself to the use of force over Vietnam, his advisers extracted one concession after another from him: first studies of covert pressures on the North, then contingency plans for bombing, then the retaliatory strike over the alleged Tonkin Gulf attacks, then a commitment to retaliate against future incidents. Johnson's advisers drew the noose progressively tighter in anticipation of a decision by the president after the election to approve the bombing program. It was after the election that the tensions between the national security bureaucracy and Johnson over Vietnam became palpable. While the president refused to budge on starting the bombing of North Vietnam week after week in December and January of 1964–65, his advisers became increasingly convinced that he was ready to let South Vietnam go and was hoping that one of the revolving-door governments in Saigon would ask the United States to leave. The reaction of top national security officials to his policy once again revealed the bureaucracy's view of its role in making policy on the defense of U.S. national security interests in Southeast Asia. They considered Johnson's refusal to pursue the policy on which they had agreed, after a long, formal interagency process, to be unacceptable. McGeorge Bundy and McNamara finally used the ultimate leverage of the national security bureaucracy on the president: the implicit threat to disassociate themselves from his policy if it resulted, as they expected, in the loss of South Vietnam.

In the month that followed the McNamara-Bundy letter, Johnson made a series of compromises with his advisers that in large part accepted their policy of systematic bombing of the North and resulted in the Rolling Thunder campaign. That compromise had far-reaching political consequences at home. Despite Johnson's insistence on avoiding any change in declaratory policy, it created the general expectation that the United States would now act to prevent the loss of South Vietnam. It also ushered in a period in which Johnson was suddenly under pressure to approve a substantial ground combat deployment as well, on the basis of quite unrealistic policy assumptions.

The April decision on troop deployment appears to have represented the apogee of influence of Johnson's inner circle of advisers. In June, with the military pressing for an open-ended commitment of troops to the war, Johnson tried to reassert presidential leadership over policy to avoid that outcome. But in the end, he felt that he could not make the decision to reject the full request for troops without the active support of McNamara. The use of force had become, in effect, a collective responsibility shared by the president and his principal advisers.

Thus the dynamics of policy making on Vietnam, in which the national security bureaucracy had powerful leverage on the president to make concessions to their preference for war, undermined a principle that should govern decisions on the use of military force in a democratic society: that such decisions are not only made formally by the president and approved by Congress but actually reflect the considered judgment of the highest elected official. Neither Kennedy nor Johnson had full control over Vietnam policy, because the national security bureaucracy acted as an independent power center within the U.S. government with the right to pressure the president on matters of war and peace.

Underlying the ability of the national security bureaucracy to wrest concessions from the president on Vietnam policy and ultimately, in the case of Lyndon Johnson, to break his resistance to going to war, was the fear on the part of both Kennedy and Johnson of political retribution over a policy decision that might lead to the defeat of the U.S. client regime in South Vietnam. The model for the kind of political attack that both presidents feared, moreover, was not the "Who lost China" campaign, with its search for subversives in the State Department who had allegedly prevented the United States from giving military aid to an anti-Communist ally, but the attack on Kennedy in September–October 1962 over his failure to use military force against the Soviet military presence in Cuba. It was not unreasonable to fear that such a campaign would appeal to public opinion because of the general assumption that the United States should be able to prevail against a third-rate Communist foe.

The perception of anti-Communist critics of U.S. policy toward Vietnam as too "soft" was most dramatically expressed by Senator Thomas J. Dodd (D.-Conn.), who declared in a 1961 Senate speech, "If the United States, with its unrivaled might, with its unparalleled wealth, with its dominion over sea and air. . . . can be laid in the dust by a few thousand primitive guerrillas, then we are far down the road from which there is no return."[5] The Republican view, still best represented by Eisenhower and Nixon, assumed that U.S. military dominance over the Communist powers and the ability to devastate North Vietnam should have been sufficient to defeat the Communist challenge in Vietnam.

A central conclusion of this study, therefore, is that the aggressiveness of the national security bureaucracy in asserting the necessity for a military approach to Vietnam in both the Kennedy and Johnson administrations was not a function of the specific personalities involved. It was a consequence of the emergence of a dramatic imbalance of power at the global level. The dominant power of the United States created a political atmosphere that encouraged the expression of certain policy approaches and discouraged the expression of others. In that atmosphere, the national security bureaucracy became increasingly self-confident, powerful, and convinced of its own right to define U.S. policy toward Vietnam. The constitutional role of the president in making foreign policy and deciding on the use of force was replaced, in practice, by a system of shared power and responsibility over the decision to use force between presidents and unelected national security managers.

LESSONS OF VIETNAM FOR THE UNIPOLAR ERA

Since the end of the Cold War, it has been universally agreed that the international system is "unipolar," meaning that no other state or possible combination of states can counterbalance the power of the United States. Beginning in the 1990s and continuing into the new century, students of international relations and international security have carried on a heated debate over whether the new situation of clear-cut U.S. dominance is likely to endure and whether it is desirable in terms of international peace and stability. Defenders of policies aimed at exploiting the "unipolar moment" have argued that the present structure is likely to be enduring, and that it is more likely than a balance of power to preserve peace, because it minimizes uncertainty. They assert that U.S. dominance ensures that weaker states will not be tempted to challenge even an expansive definition of U.S. security interests around the globe.[6]

Opponents of policies based on unipolarity, on the other hand, argue that a policy aimed at preserving and exploiting U.S. dominance is both futile, because of the fundamental tendency of states to balance against a dominant power, and dangerous, because the exploitation of dominance is likely to be seen as provocative by other states.[7] Paralleling these academic arguments over the unipolar system, of course, are sharp differences of view over the practice of unilateralism in the use of military power by the United States against a weaker "rogue" state in the absence of a consensus of the international community. The Bush administration justified the U.S. invasion and occupation of Iraq in 2003 by alleging a threat of "weapons of mass destruction." Underlying that highly inflammatory—and ultimately deceptive—claim, however, was a more fundamental issue. Defenders of using U.S. dominance to maintain a world order of Washington's own choosing saw the occupation of Iraq as minimizing the likelihood of serious threats to U.S. and international security. Opponents saw the unilateral use of force in Iraq as more likely to increase regional instability and the dangers to U.S. and global security.

These debates on the advantages and disadvantages of unipolarity and of policies that exploit it have assumed that there has never before been anything in the modern state system even remotely similar to the present global structure of power. This assumption reflects the conventional view that there was a rough bipolar balance of power between the United States and the Soviet Union throughout the Cold War. The reinterpretation of the period between the Korean and Vietnam wars offered in this study suggests, however, that the dominance of U.S. power over that period was roughly equivalent to the unipolarity of the post–Cold War period. In the earlier period, U.S. power could not be balanced by that of the Soviet Union and China. By 1964, U.S. officials had begun to view the Soviet Union less as a Cold War rival for power than as a potentially useful adjunct to U.S. efforts to impose a settlement in Vietnam at some future date. Several major states today arguably occupy analogous political roles in relation to the issue of unilateral U.S. use of military force.

The insights that can be gleaned from reassessing the dynamics of the political system and of U.S. policy making toward Vietnam during that period are highly relevant, therefore, to the present "unipolar moment." In particular, the U.S. experience on the road to war in Vietnam offers useful lessons about the ways in which the United States is mostly likely to become involved in wars in a unipolar system. The question is whether wars are more likely to arise from states that seek to make a significant change in the international balance of power, or even to disturb a regional status quo, or from the tendency of the United States to extend its power and influence too far and to provoke greater resistance and hostility to U.S. power.

In retrospect, it is clear that U.S. dominance during the interwar period of the Cold War reduced to virtually nil the possibility of wars involving the Soviet Union or China—the only second- or even third-level states in the power hierarchy who at least in theory were hostile to U.S. power interests. Neither Communist great power was willing to take even minimal risks of a military clash with the United States. The extreme imbalance of power ruled out even the encouragement by the USSR or the PRC of a direct challenge by local Communists to U.S. power interests. It is no accident that the Soviet Union and China, whose internal organization and ideology inclined them toward support for such challenges to the existing international order, both gave up their previous policy of backing revolutionary struggles just as the new power configuration emerged at the end of the Korean War. Those effects of the unipolarity of that interwar period can be counted as positive for preventing war.

The lesson of this study of the impact of unbalanced power on the Vietnam issue, however, is that the absence of challenge from second-rank or third-rank states in terms of power does not prevent the occurrence of war on the periphery. The initiative in challenging the U.S. power position in South Vietnam in 1959–60 did not come from either of the major Communist powers, after all, but from the Vietnamese Communists themselves. It was not the North Vietnamese regime, moreover, that initially pushed for an armed uprising aimed at upending the Saigon regime. The party leadership in Hanoi, under pressure from their Communist patrons and cautious in the face of the ever-present threat of U.S. military force, had been prepared to continue to support the Soviet-Chinese strategy of waging only political struggle in South Vietnam. The initiative came from the South Vietnamese victims of the Diemist repression, for many of whom the issue of armed struggle was literally one of life or death. Their motivation in taking up arms had nothing to do with Cold War power politics between the two blocs. These southern communists and former Viet Minh forced the hand of the North Vietnamese regime by threatening Hanoi with a loss of control over its followers in the South.

In the earlier unipolar power era, then, it was those with the *least* power who were willing to take the initiative to challenge U.S. power, rather than those who were closest to the United States in power capabilities. Although seemingly paradoxical, this historical fact reflected an elementary reality: these local resistance forces had the least to lose and the most to gain from challenging the status quo established by U.S. power. Furthermore, they were the least knowledgeable about U.S. power capabilities. This fact suggests that the debate over the present unipolar power structure has been too narrow in its focus on whether other major powers or potential major powers are likely to challenge U.S. dominance. The previous experience with unipolarity indicates that the United States can probably intimidate second- and third-level states, because the risks of even slight overt resistance to U.S. assertion of power beyond their borders are simply too great. One lesson of the path to war in Vietnam, however, is that war is much more likely to arise, not from a decision by those with the most to lose but from conflicts involving the vigorous assertion by the United States of its power interests abroad, even in the absence of an overt challenge by another state.

A second lesson from the path to war in Vietnam has to do with the roles of force and diplomacy in the ability of the dominant power to exert influence on potential foes. The dominance of the United States in the international politics of the interwar period was based primarily on its ability to manipulate the implicit or explicit threat to use U.S. air and naval power—including the ultimate sanction of the use of nuclear weapons—without having to actually use that power. We now know just how strongly the existence of strategic asymmetry impressed on the Soviet Union and China, as well as North Vietnam, the risks and costs of war with the United

States. During the entire period between the Geneva Accords and the major U.S. combat intervention in Vietnam in 1965, the North Vietnamese leaders were ready to make far-reaching compromises on the length of time that an independent non-Communist regime could remain in the South, provided that it was buffered from U.S. political-military power. That position was a direct consequence of the ability of the United States to threaten wholesale destruction of North Vietnamese society. For the same reason, the North Vietnamese also limited participation in the armed struggle to native southerners for the first four years of the war.

Despite the genuine fear of U.S. attack, however, the DRV became increasingly committed to the struggle in the South from 1961 on. Its gradual assumption of increasingly greater risk reflects two factors working in tandem. The first was the fact that the outcome of the struggle in the South bore on the primordial interest of the regime in national independence. The more direct reason for the escalation of North Vietnamese involvement, however, was that the United States completely shut the door on any compromise that could have allowed North Vietnam to end the war honorably.

By rejecting diplomatic negotiation, the United States threw away most of its actual ability to shape the political outcome in South Vietnam through a combination of threat, restraint, and knowing what concessions it could extract from Hanoi, short of giving up the ultimate possibility of reunification. Paradoxically, by attempting to press its advantage too far—and especially by engaging in systematic bombing of North Vietnam while blocking the possibility of diplomatic compromise—the United States sacrificed its considerable influence over Hanoi's choices.

I have argued above that the outcome of U.S. policy can be traced to the reading of power relationships by the national security bureaucracy. In opting to put in a large ground contingent and postponing any diplomatic probe of Hanoi in 1965, Johnson's national security advisers were basing their recommendations on the incentives that they presumed to be inherent in the overwhelming U.S. dominance in the power relationship with Hanoi. In doing so, they completely ignored the much more complex set of actual incentives facing Hanoi.

This episode illustrates the broader problem of the reliance by the national security bureaucracy on the absence of any external countervailing power in using force. It suggests that national security officials in the dominant state are incapable of going beyond crude signals of hierarchical power in thinking about going to war against a weaker state or sociopolitical movement in conflict with U.S. policy. The record of policy deliberations on Vietnam suggests that the advisers were simply unable to recognize that they were pressing their power advantage too far in South Vietnam in that crucial March–May 1965 period. The fateful decisions to deploy more troops and to forgo genuine negotiations were only possible because of the engrained habit of relying so heavily on the U.S. power advantage in Vietnam over a period of years. This is obviously not a tendency that is exclusive to U.S. Vietnam policy in the first half of the 1960s, moreover. It is likely that it is endemic to policy making over a prolonged period of unbalanced power and conflicts with much weaker adversaries.

In documenting the effect of the imbalance of power on U.S. policy toward Vietnam, this study illustrates the most fundamental insight of realist international relations theory: that a rough balance of power is necessary to curb the tendency of the strongest state to exploit its power advantage to the maximum at the expense of weaker states. "Unbalanced power is a danger to weak states," Kenneth Waltz once observed, adding, "It may also be a danger to strong ones."[8] Realist theory generally asserts that the tendency of the strongest state to extend its power and influence continues until it is checked by external forces or by sociopolitical forces at home that weaken its ability to do so.[9]

Until the end of the Cold War, realists generally did not apply this general principle to the United States, but in the present "unipolar moment," the issue of how to restrain the excessive use of U.S. power is unavoidable. It has now become part of the debate over the advantages and disadvantages to the United States and to the world of U.S. dominance of the international system. Waltz, for one, has suggested that peace will require not only external constraints on U.S. power but internal restraints as well.[10] Students of unipolar politics and foreign policy looking at the question of domestic restraint on the deployment of U.S. power abroad would do well to take account of the political dynamics of policy making on the road to war in Vietnam.

A recurrent theme of this study has been that the impetus for the assertive use of U.S. military power in Vietnam came overwhelmingly from the national security bureaucracy itself, rather than from the presidency. The previous section discusses the ways in which the policy-making process on Vietnam became dysfunctional because of the refusal of national security advisers to accept a presidential policy that rejected the use of military force in defense of national security interests. That earlier unipolar experience suggests that the problem of inadequate domestic restraints may be exacerbated by the tendency of the national security bureaucracy to assert itself in policy making.

Alongside these parallels between the present unipolar moment and the one that existed for at least twelve years in the 1950s and 1960s, there are obvious differences as well. Perhaps the main one is a far greater pluralism of sociopolitical and intellectual views of national security in the current phase of unipolar power than existed in the earlier period. As long as the unipolar moment persists, however, the political power of the national security bureaucracy, both within the executive branch and in the larger society, will certainly remain a challenge to domestic efforts to restrain the use of military power by the United States.

Notes

PREFACE

1. Robert J. McMahon, "U.S.-Vietnam Relations: A Historical Survey," in Warren I. Cohen, ed., *Pacific Passage: The Study of American–East Asian Relations on the Eve of the Twenty-first Century* (New York: Columbia University Press, 1996), 317.

2. Gareth Porter, ed., *Vietnam: The Definitive Documentation of Human Decisions* (Stanfordville, N.Y.: E.M. Coleman Enterprises, 1979).

3. This was the message of one of the earliest postwar interpretations of Vietnam policy making. See Leslie H. Gelb and Richard K. Betts, *The Irony of Vietnam: The System Worked* (Washington, D.C.: Brookings Institution, 1979).

1. THE IMBALANCE OF POWER, 1953–1965

1. See Marc Trachtenberg, "A 'Wasting Asset': American Strategy and the Shifting Nuclear Balance," *International Security* 13 (Winter 1988–89): 5–49; Melvyn P. Leffler, *A Preponderance of Power: National Security, the Truman Administration and the Cold War* (Stanford, Calif.: Stanford University Press, 1992); Francis J. Gavin, "Power, Politics and U.S. Policy in Iran, 1950–1953," *Journal of Cold War Studies* 1, no. 1 (1999): 56–89.

2. On the traditional Eurocentric definition of the distribution of power, see Jack S. Levy, "The Polarity of the System and International Stability: An Empirical Analysis," in Alan Ned Sabrosky, ed., *Polarity and War: The Changing Structure of International Conflict* (Boulder, Colo.: Westview Press, 1985), 48.

3. See Trachtenberg, "Wasting Asset," 21–22.

4. Greg Herken, *The Winning Weapon: The Atomic Bomb in the Cold War, 1945–1950* (New York: Knopf, 1980), 221–41, 287–97.

5. Georgi M. Kornienko, an American expert in the Soviet Foreign Ministry for forty-one years, reported in the early 1990s that when he showed the 1950

estimate of Soviet military capabilities in NSC-68 to the General Staff of the Soviet armed forces, they "could not believe that such an estimate was seriously adhered to by their counterparts from the Joint Chiefs of Staff." See "Kornienko's Commentary," in Ernest R. May, ed., *American Cold War Strategy: Interpreting NSC 68* (Boston: Bedford Books/St. Martin's Press, 1992), 135.

6. Trachtenberg, "Wasting Asset," 15–26.

7. Frank A. Ninkovich, *Modernity and Power: A History of the Domino Theory in the Twentieth Century* (Chicago: University of Chicago Press, 1994), 184.

8. Text of NSC-68, in May, ed., *America's Cold War Strategy*, 111.

9. Leffler, *Preponderance of Power*, 487–88; Gavin, "Power, Politics and U.S. Policy."

10. Trachtenberg, "Wasting Asset," 30–31.

11. David G. Coleman, "Eisenhower and the Berlin Problem, 1953–1954," *Journal of Cold War Studies* 2, no. 1 (Winter 2000): 24.

12. Memo of discussion, 148th NSC meeting, June 4, 1953, *FRUS, 1952–1954*, 2: 369.

13. Gur Ofer, *Soviet Economic Growth, 1928–1985* (Santa Monica, Calif.: RAND Corp. and UCLA Center for the Study of Soviet International Behavior, 1988), 20; Philip Hanson, *From Stagnation to Catastroika: Commentaries on the Soviet Economy, 1983–1991* (New York: Praeger, 1992), 8, table 1.1.

14. Gertrude Schroeder, "Soviet Technology: System vs. Progress," *Problems of Communism* 19 (September–October 1970): 20–21.

15. Michael Boretsky, "Comparative Progress in Technology, Productivity and Economic Efficiency: USSR vs. USA," in U.S. Congress, Joint Economic Committee, *New Directions in the Soviet Economy*, 89th Cong., 2d sess., 1966 (Washington, D.C.: Government Printing Office, 1966), pt. II-A, 149.

16. Thomas J. Christensen, *Useful Adversaries: Grand Strategy, Domestic Mobilization and Sino-American Conflict, 1947–1958* (Princeton, N.J.: Princeton University Press, 1996).

17. On the interaction of economics, politics, and military policy in the initial post-Stalin period, see C. G. Jacobsen, *Soviet Strategy–Soviet Foreign Policy: Military Considerations Affecting Soviet Policy-Making* (Glasgow: Robert Maclehose, 1972), 34–39, 56–57; Richard Cohen and Peter Wilson, *Superpowers in Economic Decline: U.S. Strategy for the Transcentury Era* (New York: Crane Russak, 1990), 34–37; Carl A. Linden, *Khrushchev and Soviet Leadership, 1957–1964* (Baltimore: Johns Hopkins University Press, 1966), 114–15; Thomas N. Nichols, *The Sacred Cause: Civil-Military Conflict over Soviet National Security, 1917–1992* (Ithaca, N.Y.: Cornell University Press, 1993), 62–81; James G. Richter, *Khrushchev's Double Bind: International Pressures and Domestic Coalition Politics* (Baltimore: Johns Hopkins University Press, 1994).

18. See Abraham S. Becker, "Sitting on Bayonets: The Soviet Defense Burden and the Slowdown of Soviet Defense Spending," in Roman Kolkowitz and Ellen Propper Mickiewicz, eds., *The Soviet Calculus of Nuclear War* (Lexington, Mass.: Lexington Books, 1986), 175, table 1.1; William T. Lee, *The Estimation of*

Soviet Defense Expenditures, 1955–75: An Unconventional Approach (New York: Praeger, 1978), 114, table 7.1; Karen Dawisha, *Soviet Foreign Policy toward Egypt* (New York: St. Martin's Press, 1979), 109, table 6.6; Bruce Russett, *The Prisoners of Insecurity: Nuclear Deterrence, the Arms Race and Arms Control* (New York: W. H. Freeman, 1983), fig. 1.2, 10.

19. Judith Thornton, "Factors in the Recent Decline in Soviet Growth," *Slavic Review* 25 (March 1966): 114, table 1.

20. M. D. Ward, "Differential Paths to Parity: A Study of the Contemporary Arms Race," *American Political Science Review* 78 (1984): 312, table 3.

21. On configurations of power among leading states since the sixteenth century, see Paul Kennedy, *The Rise and Fall of the Great Powers* (New York: Random House, 1987); George Modelski and William R. Thompson, *Seapower in Global Politics, 1494–1993* (Seattle: University of Washington Press, 1987); Karen A. Rasler and William R. Thompson, *The Great Powers and Global Struggle, 1490–1990* (Lexington: University of Kentucky Press, 1994).

22. Natural Resources Defense Council, Archive of Nuclear Data, "Table of US Strategic Bomber Forces," www.nrdc.org/nuclear/nudb/datab7.asp#sixty (accessed June 17, 2004).

23. John M. Collins, *U.S.-Soviet Military Balance, 1960–1980* (New York: McGraw-Hill, 1980), 32–36. Gen. Curtis LeMay, then commander of the U.S. Strategic Air Command (SAC), later recalled how SAC flew all of its reconnaissance jets over Vladivostok at midday in the 1950s without the slightest resistance from the Soviet Air Force. Richard Kohn and Joseph Harahan, eds., "Strategic Air Power, 1948–1962, Excerpts from an Interview with Generals Curtis E. LeMay, Leon W. Johnson, David Burchinal and Jack J. Catton," *International Security* 12, no. 4 (Spring 1988): 86.

24. Thomas W. Wolfe, *Soviet Power and Europe, 1945–1970* (Baltimore: Johns Hopkins University Press, 1970), 40.

25. NIE 11–56, "Soviet Gross Capabilities for Attack on United States and Key Overseas Installations and Forces through Mid-1959," March 6, 1956, in Donald P. Steury, ed., *Intentions and Capabilities: Estimates on Soviet Strategic Forces, 1950–1983* (Washington, D.C.: Center for the Study of Intelligence, Central Intelligence Agency, 1996), 27; Philip Klass, *Secret Sentries in Space* (New York: Random House, 1971), 5; Norman Polmar, *Strategic Weapons: An Introduction* (New York: Crane Russak, 1982), 28.

26. CIA Director Allen Dulles, briefing at NSC meeting, June 4, 1959, *FRUS, 1958–1960*, 3: 215; Collins, *U.S.-Soviet Military Balance*, 32.

27. See SNIE 11-7-58, "Strength and Composition of the Soviet Long Range Bomber Force," in Steury, ed., *Intentions and Capabilities*, 49; Raymond L. Garthoff, *Reflections on the Cuban Missile Crisis*, rev. ed. (Baltimore: Johns Hopkins University Press, 1989), 208, table 1.

28. Nikita S. Khrushchev, *Khrushchev Remembers: The Last Testament*, ed. and trans. Strobe Talbott (Boston: Little, Brown, 1974), 39.

29. In an influential study on the effect of the strategic military balance on U.S.-Soviet relations, Richard K. Betts suggested that the Soviet inability to

carry out two-way bombing missions was not of crucial importance, because in the 1950s, "it was widely assumed that many U.S. bombers would not be able to return in event of war." See Betts, *Nuclear Blackmail and Nuclear Balance* (Washington, D.C.: Brookings Institution, 1987), 148. There is an enormous difference, of course, between knowing that some planes will not return from a bombing mission and knowing that none of them will return. It is not surprising that Moscow regarded the inability to mount two-way bombing missions against North America as a crucial weakness of Soviet strategic forces.

30. CIA Director Allen Dulles, briefing to NSC, June 4, 1959, *FRUS, 1958–1969*, 3: 215; NIE 11–56, "Soviet Gross Capabilities," 27; SNIE 11-7-58, "Strength and Composition of the Soviet Long Range Bomber Force" (n.d.), in Steury, ed., *Intentions and Capabilities*, 48–49.

31. See David Alan Rosenberg, "The Origins of Overkill: Nuclear Weapons and American Strategy, 1945–1960," *International Security* 7 (Spring 1983): 66; David Holloway and Condoleezza Rice, "The Evolution of Soviet Forces: Stability and Control," in Kurt Gottfried and Bruce G. Blair, eds., *Crisis Stability and Nuclear War* (New York: Oxford University Press, 1988), 151.

32. NIE 11–3-61, "Sino-Soviet Air Defense Capabilities," July 11, 1961, *FRUS, 1961–1963*, 8: 118.

33. Thomas M. Coffey, *Iron Eagle: The Turbulent Life of General Curtis LeMay* (New York: Crown, 1986), 331.

34. Ernest R. May, John Steinbrunner, and Thomas Wolfe, "History of the Strategic Arms Competition, 1945–1972" (unpublished study, Office of the Secretary of Defense, Historical Office, March 1981), 1: 33, 474. See also Jacobsen, *Soviet Strategy*, 44–45.

35. NIE 11–56, "Soviet Gross Capabilities," 2.

36. Betts, *Nuclear Blackmail*, 166.

37. Garthoff, *Reflections on the Cuban Missile Crisis*, 208

38. NIE 11–8-64, "Soviet Capabilities for Strategic Attack," in Steury, ed., *Intentions and Capabilities*, 197; Fred Kaplan, *The Wizards of Armageddon* (New York: Simon & Schuster, 1983), 294–301; Herken, *Counsels of War*, 159–60; Lawrence Freedman, *U.S. Intelligence and Russian Military Strength* (New York: Dial Press, 1986), 99; Jacobsen, *Soviet Strategy*, 44–45; Walter Slocombe, *Political Implications of Strategic Parity*, Adelphi Paper No. 77 (London: Institute for Strategic Studies, 1971), 18–19.

39. Secretary of Defense Robert S. McNamara, testimony in U.S. Congress, Senate, *Executive Sessions of the Senate Foreign Relations Committee, together with Joint Sessions with the Armed Services Committee*, 97th Cong., 2d sess., 1962, Historical Series (Washington, D.C.: Government Printing Office, 1986), 14: 145.

40. Kaplan, *Wizards*, 295; Steven J. Zaloga, *Target America: The Soviet Union and the Strategic Arms Race, 1945–1964* (Novato, Calif.: Presidio Press, 1993), 199; Garthoff, *Reflections on the Cuban Missile Crisis*, 207–8.

41. May, Steinbrunner, and Wolfe, "History of the Strategic Arms Competition," 1: 475. See also Jacobsen, *Soviet Strategy*, 45–60; Robert G. Weinland,

"The Evolution of Soviet Requirements for Naval Forces: Solving the Problems of the Early 1960s," *Survival*, January–February 1964, 16–25.

42. Cristoph Bluth, "Defence and Security," in Martin McCarthy, ed., *Khrushchev and Khrushchevism* (Bloomington: Indiana University Press, 1987), 206; Jacobsen, *Soviet Strategy*, 74.

43. For overviews of Soviet power projection capabilities, see John Vigor, "The Soviet 'Forward Reach,'" in John Erickson and E. J. Feuchwanger, eds., *Soviet Military Power and Performance* (Hamden, Conn.: Archon Books, 1979), 106; Dennis M. Gormley, "The Direction and Pace of Soviet Force Projection Capabilities," in Jonathan Alford, ed., *The Soviet Union: Security Policies and Constraints* (New York: St. Martin's Press, 1985), 148.

44. Martin Binkin and Jeffrey Record, *Where Does the Marine Corps Go from Here?* (Washington, D.C.: Brookings Institution, 1976), 15.

45. Collins, *U.S.-Soviet Military Balance*, 26, 30.

46. Robert E. Harkavy, *Great Power Competition for Overseas Bases: The Geopolitics of Access Diplomacy* (New York: Pergamon Press, 1982), 130–41, 184; Marc S. Gallicchio, "The Best Defense Is a Good Offense: The Evolution of American Strategy in East Asia, 1953–1960," in Warren I. Cohen and Akira Iriye, eds., *The Great Powers in East Asia 1953–1960* (New York: Columbia University Press, 1990), 71.

47. Gallicchio, "Best Defense," 26.

48. Robert P. Haffa Jr., *The Half War: Planning U.S. Rapid Deployment Forces to Meet a Limited Contingency, 1960–1983* (Boulder, Colo.: Westview Press, 1984), 26–33.

49. Jeffrey D. Glasser, *The Secret Vietnam War: The United States Air Force in Thailand, 1961–1975* (Jefferson, N.C.: McFarland, 1995), 17–19; Roland Paul, *American Military Commitments Abroad* (New Brunswick, N.J.: Rutgers University Press, 1973), 105–27; U.S. Senate, *United States Security Agreements and Commitments Abroad, Part 3: Kingdom of Thailand: Hearings before the Senate Foreign Relations Committee, November 10–17, 1969*, 91st Cong., 1st sess., 1969 (Washington, D.C.: Government Printing Office, 1987), 615.

50. U.S. Department of Defense, *Soviet Military Power* (Washington, D.C.: Government Printing Office, 1987), 35–37.

51. Karen Dawisha, *Soviet Foreign Policy toward Egypt* (New York: Macmillan, 1979), 91.

52. From bases in Kirovabad, the tactical aircraft available to the Soviet Air Force before 1970 could have penetrated only about fifty miles into northern Iraq and would barely have reached the Syrian border. Keith A. Dunn, "Soviet Strategy, Opportunities and Constraints in Southwestern Asia," *Soviet Union/ Union Sovietique* 11, pt. 2 (1984), 201–2, table 1. For an official Johnson administration appraisal reaching the same conclusion, see Robert S. McNamara, memo to LBJ, December 19, 1963, *FRUS, 1961–1963*, 8: 577.

53. Gormley, "Direction and Pace of Soviet Force Projection Capabilities," 148; Lawrence L. Whetten, "Recent Developments in the Soviet Navy," in id., ed., *The Future of Soviet Military Power* (New York: Crane Russak, 1976), 98;

Ephraim Karsh, *The Cautious Bear: Soviet Military Engagement in the Middle East War in the Post-1967 Era* (Jerusalem: Jaffee Center for Strategic Studies; Boulder, Colo.: Westview Press, 1985), 20; Bruce W. Watson, *The Changing Face of the World's Navies: 1945 to the Present* (Washington, D.C.: Brassey's, 1991), 119; Collins, *American and Soviet Military Trends since the Cuban Missile Crisis* (Washington, D.C.: Center for Strategic and International Studies, Georgetown University, 1978), 181.

    54. Harkavy, *Great Power Competition*, 173.

    55. Robert F. Kennedy, *Thirteen Days* (New York: Norton, 1969), 122–23.

    56. See Kenneth R. McGruther, *The Evolving Soviet Navy* (Newport, R.I.: Naval War College Press, 1978), 73–74.

    57. Michael MccGwire, "The Rationale for the Development of Soviet Seapower," in Gerald Segal and John Baylis, eds., *Soviet Strategy* (London: Croom Helm, 1981), 213–14; Brian Moynahan, *Claws of the Bear: The History of the Red Army from the Revolution to the Present* (Boston: Houghton Mifflin, 1989), 363; Zaloga, *Target America*, 186.

    58. McGruther, *Evolving Soviet Navy*, 72. MccGwire, "Rationale for the Development of Soviet Seapower," 214; Watson, *Changing Face of the World's Navies*, 117–19.

    59. Karsh, *Cautious Bear*, 16; Harkavy, *Great Power Competition*, 242; Moynahan, *Claws of the Bear*, 363.

    60. NIE 11–4–56, "Soviet Capabilities and Probable Courses of Action through 1961," August 2, 1956, RG 263, NARA, 40.

    61. Ferenc A. Vali, *The Turkish Straits and NATO* (Stanford, Calif.: Hoover Institution, 1972), 121.

    62. Constantine Pleshakov, "Nikita Khrushchev and Sino-Soviet Relations," in Odd Arne Westad, ed., *Brothers in Arms: The Rise and Fall of the Sino-Soviet Alliance, 1945–1963* (Washington, D.C.: Woodrow Wilson Center Press, 1998), 235.

    63. James M. McConnell, "The 'Rules of the Game': A Theory in the Practice of Superpower Naval Diplomacy," in Bradford Dismukes and James McConnell, eds., *Soviet Naval Diplomacy* (New York: Pergamon Press, 1979), 240.

    64. Rosenberg, "The Origins of Overkill: Nuclear Weapons and American Strategy," *International Security* 7, no. 4 (Spring 1983): 40, 62; Andrew Erdmann, "'War No Longer Has Any Logic Whatever': Dwight D. Eisenhower and the Thermonuclear Revolution," in John Lewis Gaddis, Philip H. Gordon, Ernest R. May, and Jonathan Rosenberg, eds., *Cold War Statesmen Confront the Bomb: Nuclear Diplomacy since 1945* (New York: Oxford University Press, 1999), 87–119; Betts, *Nuclear Blackmail*, 149–58.

    65. Memo from the JCS to Secretary of Defense Charles Wilson, June 23, 1954, *FRUS, 1952–1954*, 2: 680. See also memo of discussion at 204th meeting of the NSC, June 24, 1954, ibid., 694–95.

    66. Trachtenberg, "Wasting Asset," 35–37, 41–43.

    67. John Foster Dulles, memo, November 15, 1954, *FRUS, 1952–1954*, 2: 772–76.

68. Betts, *Nuclear Blackmail*, 149–58.

69. On Eisenhower's stubborn refusal to give up his policy of reliance on the threat of retaliation for any Soviet act of war against U.S. forces, see Campbell Craig, *Destroying the Village: Eisenhower and Thermonuclear War* (New York: Columbia University Press, 1996), 53–70; Rosenberg, "Origins of Overkill," 42.

70. Rosenberg, "Origins of Overkill," 63.

71. NIE 100–7-55, "World Situation and Trends," November 11, 1955, *FRUS, 1955–1957*, 19: 132.

72. NIE 11–4-56, "Soviet Capabilities and Probable Courses of Action through 1961," 47.

73. For examples, see Arnold Horelick and Myron Rush, *Strategic Power and Soviet Foreign Policy* (Chicago: University of Chicago Press, 1966), 63–64; Stephen S. Kaplan, *Diplomacy of Power: Soviet Armed Forces as a Political Instrument* (Washington, D.C.: Brookings Institution, 1981), 5; Raymond L. Garthoff, *Deterrence and the Revolution in Soviet Military Doctrine* (Washington, D.C.: Brookings Institution, 1990), 19.

74. May, Steinbrunner, and Wolfe, "History of the Strategic Arms Competition," 1: 415; Raymond Garthoff, *Assessing the Adversary: Estimates by the Eisenhower Administration of Soviet Intentions and Capabilities* (Washington, D.C.: Brookings Institution, 1991), 47; Rosenberg, "Origins of Overkill"; Peter Roman, *Eisenhower and the Missile Gap* (Ithaca, N.Y.: Cornell University Press, 1995), 36.

75. Memo of discussion, NSC meeting, January 16, 1958, *FRUS, 1958–1960*, 3: 25.

76. John Lewis Gaddis, *Now We Know: Rethinking Cold War History* (New York: Oxford University Press, 1998), 246; see also McGeorge Bundy, *Danger and Survival: Choices about the Bomb in the First Fifty Years* (New York: Random House, 1988), 339–40.

77. Dwight D. Eisenhower, *Waging Peace, 1957–1961* (Garden City, N.Y.: Doubleday, 1963), 347–48.

78. Christopher A. Preble, "'Who Ever Believed in the "Missile Gap"?': John F. Kennedy and the Politics of National Security," *Presidential Studies Quarterly* 33, no. 4 (2003): 809, 814.

79. Memo of a conference with the president, July 14, 1958, *FRUS, 1958–1960*, 11: 212–13, 219; Eisenhower, *Waging Peace*, 282; Douglas Little, "Ike, Lebanon, and the 1958 Middle East Crisis," *Diplomatic History* 20, no. 1 (Winter 1996): 27–54; Saki Dockrill, *Eisenhower's New Look National Security Policy, 1953–61* (New York: St. Martin's Press, 1996), 239.

80. Dockrill, *Eisenhower's New Look*, 250; William Burr, "Avoiding the Slippery Slope: The Eisenhower Administration and the Berlin Crisis, November 1958–January 1959," *Diplomatic History* 18, no. 2 (Spring 1994): 190, 194; Frédéric Bozo, *Two Strategies for Europe: De Gaulle, the United States, and the Atlantic Alliance*, trans. Susan Emanuel (London: Rowman & Littlefield, 2001), 31; Coleman, "Eisenhower and the Berlin Problem," 25.

81. Gordon Chang, *Friends and Enemies: The United States, China and the Soviet Union, 1948–1972* (Stanford, Calif.: Stanford University Press, 1990), 199–200; Rosemary Foot, "New Light on the Sino-Soviet Alliance: Chinese and American Perspectives," *Journal of Northeast Asian Studies* 10 (Fall 1991): 22–23; Betts, *Nuclear Blackmail*, 71.

82. Michael R. Beschloss, *The Crisis Years: Kennedy and Khrushchev, 1960–1963* (New York: Edward Burlingame Books, 1991), 202.

83. See Gaddis, *Now We Know*, 251–52.

84. Preble, "'Who Ever Believed in the "Missile Gap"?'" 815–16; Robert S. McNamara, with Brian VandeMark, *In Retrospect: The Tragedy and Lessons of Vietnam* (New York: Vintage Books, 1996), 20; McNamara comment in James G. Blight and David A. Welch, *On the Brink: Americans and Soviets Reexamine the Cuban Missile Crisis* (New York: Hill & Wang, 1989), 135.

85. Garthoff, *Journey through the Cold War*, 111–13; Christopher Andrew, *For the President's Eyes Only: Secret Intelligence and the American Presidency from Washington to Bush* (New York: HarperCollins, 1995), 268.

86. Carl Kaysen, interview by Marc Trachtenberg and David Rosenberg, August 1988, cited in Francis J. Gavin, "The Myth of Flexible Response: American Strategy in Europe during the 1960s," *International History Review* 23, no. 4 (December 2001): 39–40, n. 36; www.utexas.edu/lbj/faculty/gavin/articles/mofr.pdf.

87. Roger Hilsman, *To Move a Nation: The Politics of Foreign Policy in the Administration of John F. Kennedy* (Garden City, N.Y.: Doubleday, 1967), 193–264.

88. "Report of the Special Interdepartmental Committee on the Implications of NIE 11-8-62 and Related Intelligence," August 23, 1962, *FRUS, 1961–1963*, 8: 367. See also McNamara's testimony in *Executive Sessions* (cited n. 39 above), 14: 145.

89. NIE 11-8-62, "Soviet Capabilities for Long Range Attack," July 6, 1962, *FRUS, 1961–1963*, 8: 182; NIE 11-8-63, "Soviet Capabilities for Strategic Attack," October 18, 1963, *FRUS, 1961–1963*, 8: 518–20; NIE 11-9-64, "Soviet Capabilities for Strategic Attack," in Steury, ed., *Intentions and Capabilities*, 197.

90. Andreas Wenger, *Living with Peril: Eisenhower, Kennedy and Nuclear Weapons* (Lanham, Md.: Rowman & Littlefield, 1997), 244–45.

91. *Executive Sessions* (cited n. 39 above), 1st sess., 14, pt. 1, 146; Maxwell Taylor, memo to JFK, August 23, 1962, *FRUS, 1961–1963*, 8: 379.

92. Paul Nitze, *From Hiroshima to Glasnost: At the Center of Decision* (New York: Grove Weidenfeld, 1987), 247; summary record of NSC meeting, December 5, 1963, *FRUS, 1961–1963*, 8: 543–44. In a conference on the Cuban Missile Crisis in 1992, McNamara said that prior to the Cuban Missile Crisis, neither he nor Kennedy had believed that a U.S. first strike could have prevented "unacceptable" damage to the United States. Comment in James G. Blight, Bruce J. Allyn, and David A. Welch, *Cuba on the Brink* (New York: Pantheon Books, 1993), 137.

93. Raymond Garthoff, comment in Blight and Welch, *On the Brink*, 29, 31.

94. McGeorge Bundy, memo to special counsel Theodore Sorensen, March 13, 1961, *FRUS, 1961–1963*, 8: 68; Theodore Sorensen, *Kennedy* (New York: Harper & Row, 1965), 609–10; memo from McNamara to JFK, September 23, 1961, *FRUS, 1961–1963*, 8: 142; Marc Trachtenberg, *History and Strategy* (Princeton, N.J.: Princeton University Press, 1991), 220; Wenger, *Living with Peril*, 187.

95. *John F. Kennedy: The Great Crises* (New York: Norton, 2001), Presidential Recordings, vol. 2, *September–October 21, 1962*, ed. Timothy Naftali and Philip Zelikow, 202.

96. Ernest R. May and Philip D. Zelikow, eds., *The Kennedy Tapes: Inside the White House during the Cuban Missile Crisis* (Cambridge, Mass.: Belknap Press of Harvard University Press, 1997), 19. Kennedy's view of the crisis anticipated the critique of deterrence theory that irrational responses might prevail in a crisis situation. See Richard Ned LeBow and Janice Gross Stein, *We All Lost the Cold War* (Princeton, N.J.: Princeton University Press, 1994), 358–59.

97. Blight and Welch, eds., *On the Brink*, 52, 147; Blight, Allyn, and Welch, *Cuba on the Brink*, 49, 88, 100; Nitze, *From Hiroshima to Glasnost*, 237; Gen. Maxwell Taylor, oral history interview with Elspeth Rostow, June 21, 1964, JFKL, 5; Nash, "Bear Any Burden?" in Gaddis et al., eds., *Cold War Statesmen Confront the Bomb*, 133; May and Zelikow, eds., *Kennedy Tapes*, 197.

98. Robert W. Komer, "Strategic Framework for Rethinking China Policy" (draft paper), April 7, 1961, NSF, Country Files, box 22, JFKL.

99. Gordon H. Chang, *Friends and Enemies: The United States, China and the Soviet Union, 1948–1972* (Stanford, Calif.: Stanford University Press, 1990), 229–32.

100. CIA Office of National Estimates, "An Appraisal of Soviet Intentions," December 21, 1961, in Gerald K. Haines and Robert E. Leggett, eds., *CIA's Analysis of the Soviet Union, 1947–1991* (Washington, D.C.: Center for the Study of Intelligence, 2001), 72, 74–75, 82–83.

101. CIA Office of Current Intelligence, "Prospects for the Sino-Soviet Relationship" (transmitted as an attachment to a memo from Walt Rostow to Dean Rusk), February 12, 1962, OCI #0360/62, 2–3; P/S files, lot files 69D121, box 208, RG 59, National Archives.

102. James C. Thomson, memo to Averell Harriman, January 12, 1962, *FRUS, 1961–1963*, 2: 177. For another summary of the discussion at that meeting, see "Highlights of Discussion at the Secretary's Policy Planning Meeting," January 2, 1962, S/P Files, lot files 69D121, box 212, RG 59, National Archives.

103. *Executive Sessions* (cited n. 39 above), 68.

104. NIE 11-9-62, "Trends in Soviet Foreign Policy," May 2, 1962, *FRUS, 1961–1963*, 5: 420, 427–29.

105. Noam Kochavi, "Washington's View of the Sino-Soviet Split, 1961–63: From Puzzled Prudence to Bold Experimentation," *Intelligence and National Security* 15, no. 1 (Spring 2000): 50–71.

106. William Bundy, "Exploring the Vulnerabilities of the Communist World," strategy seminar, July 18, 1963, 16, lot 85D240, subject files of the

assistant secretary of state for Far Eastern affairs, box 6, RG 59, NARA; NIE 11–9-64, "Soviet Foreign Policy," February 9, 1964, *FRUS, 1964–1968*, 14: 20–30.

107. "Soviet Policies: The Next Phase," March 18, 1963, OCI No. 1096/63, *FRUS, 1961–1963*, 5: 645; NIE 11–63, "Main Trends in Soviet Foreign Policy," May 22, 1963, ibid., 687, 689.

108. Ninkovich, *Modernity and Power*, 278.

109. Herbert Dinerstein, *War and the Soviet Union: Nuclear Weapons and the Revolution in Soviet Military and Political Thinking* (New York: Praeger, 1962), 66–69; Deborah Welch Larson, *Origins of Containment: A Psychological Explanation* (Princeton, N.J.: Princeton University Press, 1985), 60; Cohen and Wilson, *Superpowers in Economic Decline*, 34–35; Carl A. Linden, *Khrushchev and the Soviet Leadership: With an Epilogue on Gorbachev* (Baltimore: Johns Hopkins University Press, 1990), 30; Christoph Bluth, *Soviet Strategic Arms Policy before SALT* (Cambridge: Cambridge University Press, 1992), 60–62.

110. For statements of this thesis in more recent works, see Beschloss, *Crisis Years*, 238–39; William Curti Wohlforth, *The Elusive Balance: Power and Perceptions during the Cold War* (Ithaca, N.Y.: Cornell University Press, 1993), 148, 164–65, 179; Vladislav M. Zubok and Konstantin Pleshakov, *Inside the Kremlin's Cold War: From Stalin to Khrushchev* (Cambridge, Mass.: Harvard University Press, 1996), 193–94, 255; Vladislav M. Zubok and Hope M. Harrison, "The Nuclear Evolution of Nikita Khrushchev," in Gaddis et al., eds., *Cold War Statesmen Confront the Bomb*, 149–50.

111. William Zimmerman, *Soviet Perspectives on International Relations, 1956–1967* (Princeton, N.J.: Princeton University Press, 1969), 165–79. William Wohlforth cites statements by Khrushchev himself claiming Soviet strategic superiority and argues that official commentaries claimed that the West had "lost its superiority in power." See Wohlforth, *Elusive Balance*, 145–47. However, Wohlforth cites in support of that assertion the work of Zimmerman, whose account of official Soviet commentaries is rather different.

112. See Donald S. Zagoria, *The Sino-Soviet Conflict, 1956–1961* (Princeton, N.J.: Princeton University Press, 1962), 163–64, 236–37.

113. Fedor Burlatsky, *Khrushchev and the First Russian Spring*, trans. Daphne Skillen (London: Weidenfeld & Nicolson, 1991), 130.

114. Khrushchev, *Khrushchev Remembers*, ed. and trans. Talbott, 536.

115. Blight, Allyn, and Welch, *Cuba on the Brink*, 130. For an analysis that Khrushchev's missile deception was intended to deter U.S. exploitation of strategic asymmetry or even a possible U.S. first strike, see Arnold L. Horelick and Myron Rush, *Strategic Power and Soviet Foreign Policy* (Chicago: University of Chicago Press, 1966), 67, 69.

116. See Horelick and Rusk, *Strategic Power*, 28–29.

117. Mohamed Heikal, *The Cairo Documents* (Garden City, N.Y.: Doubleday, 1973), 133–35.

118. John Garver, *Foreign Relations of the People's Republic of China* (Englewood Cliffs, N.J.: Prentice-Hall, 1993), 58.

119. Editorial departments of *Renmin Ribao* and *Hongqi;* "Origins and Development of the Differences between Leadership of the CPSU and Ourselves— Comment on the Open Letter of the Central Committee of the CPSU (1) September 6, 1963," in William E. Griffith, ed., *The Sino-Soviet Rift* (Cambridge, Mass.: MIT Press, 1964), 396–97. For the original text of the 1957 Moscow statement, see G. F. Hudson, Richard Lowenthal, and Roderick MacFarquhar, *The Sino-Soviet Dispute* (New York: Praeger, 1961), 54–55.

120. Joe Stork, "The Soviet Union, the Great Powers and Iraq," in Robert E. Fernea and William Roger Louis, eds., *The Iraqi Revolution of 1958: The Old Social Classes Revisited* (London: I. B. Taurus, 1991), 97; Uriel Dann, *Iraq under Qassem: A Political History, 1958–1963* (New York: Praeger; London: Pall Mall, 1969), 223–28; Marion Farouk-Sluggett and Peter Sluggett, *Iraq since 1958: From Revolution to Dictatorship* (London: KPI, 1987), 69; Samira Haj, *The Making of Iraq, 1900–1963: Capital, Power, and Ideology* (Albany: State University of New York Press, 1997), 125–26; Oles M. Smolansky, *The Soviet Union and the Arab East under Khrushchev* (Lewisburg, Pa.: Bucknell University Press, 1974), 157–60; Aryeh Yodfat, *Arab Politics in the Soviet Mirror* (Jerusalem: Israel Universities Press; New York: Halsted Press, 1973), 155.

121. CIA, Office of Current Intelligence, "Soviet Policy toward the Underdeveloped Countries," April 28, 1961, OCI No. 1803/61, 84, CIA Historical Review Program, Reports on the Soviet Union, 1951–1991, RG 263, NARA; NIE 30–59, "Main Currents in the Arab World," August 25, 1959, *FRUS, 1958–1960*, 12: 230–32. For scholarly analyses reaching the same conclusion, see Hanna Batatu, *The Old Social Classes and the Revolutionary Movement in Iraq* (Princeton, N.J.: Princeton University Press, 1978), 903; Fawaz A. Gerges, *The Superpowers and the Middle East: Regional and International Politics, 1955–1967* (Boulder, Colo.: Westview Press, 1994), 148; Galia Golan, *Soviet Policies in the Middle East: From World War Two to Gorbachev* (New York: Cambridge University Press, 1990), 55; Geoffrey Wheeler, "Soviet Interests in Iran, Iraq and Turkey," *World Today,* May 1968, 199.

122. Donald Zagoria, *The Sino-Soviet Conflict, 1956–61* (Princeton, N.J.: Princeton University Press, 1962), 259–60.

123. Mark Katz, *The Third World in Soviet Military Thought* (Baltimore: Johns Hopkins University Press, 1982), 18–20; Zagoria, *Sino-Soviet Conflict,* 231, 256.

124. The final declaration of the 1960 Moscow conference asserted: "Hundreds of millions of people in Asia, Africa and others parts of the world have won their independence in hard-fought battles with imperialism. Communists have always recognized the progressive, revolutionary significance of national liberation wars; they are the most active champions of national independence." David Floyd, *Mao against Khrushchev: A Short History of the Sino-Soviet Conflict* (New York: Praeger, 1964), 302.

125. Hudson et al., *Sino-Soviet Dispute,* 177; Foy D. Kohler, Mose L. Harvey, Leon Goure, and Richard Soll, *Soviet Strategy for the Seventies: From Cold War to Peaceful Coexistence,* Monographs on International Affairs (Coral

Gables, Fla.: Center for Advanced International Studies, University of Miami, 1973), 39.

126. May, Steinbrunner, and Wolfe, "History of the Strategic Arms Competition," 1: 473.

127. Alexander Orlov, "The U-2 Program: A Russian Officer Remembers," *Studies in Intelligence,* Winter 1998–99, www.cia.gov/csi/studies/winter98–99/art02.html (accessed July 16, 2004).

128. Aleksandr Fursenko and Timothy Naftali, *"One Hell of a Gamble":* *Khrushchev, Castro and Kennedy, 1958–1964* (New York: Norton, 1997), 50–51.

129. For testimony of former Soviet officials on this point, see Marc Trachtenberg, "The Influence of Nuclear Weapons in the Cuban Missile Crisis," *International Security* 10 (Summer 1985): 139, 158–60, 229, and 258; Robert E. Quirk, *Fidel Castro* (New York: Norton, 1993), 414–15; Yuri Pavlov, *Soviet-Cuban Alliance, 1959–1991* (New Brunswick, N.J.: Transaction, 1994), 8, 31–32; Fursenko and Naftali, *"One Hell of a Gamble,"* 154–56; Blight and Welch, eds., *On the Brink,* 130, 229, 242, and 258; Bruce J. Allyn, James G. Blight, and David A. Welch, eds., *Back to the Brink: Proceedings of the Moscow Conference on the Cuban Missile Crisis, January 27–28, 1989,* CSIA Occasional Paper no. 9 (Cambridge, Mass.: Center for Science and International Affairs, Harvard University; Lanham, Md.: University Press of America, 1992), 27–29; Dale C. Copeland, "Neo-Realism and the Myth of Bipolar Stability: Towards a New Dynamic Realist Theory of Major War," in Benjamin Frankel, ed., *Realism: Restatements and Renewal* (London: F. Cass, 1996), 73–75; Anatoly F. Dobrynin, *In Confidence: Moscow's Ambassador to America's Six Cold War Presidents (1962–1986)* (New York: Times Books, 1995), 73; Oleg Troyanofsky, "The Making of Soviet Foreign Policy," in William Taubman, Sergei Khrushchev, and Abbott Gleason, eds., *Nikita Khrushchev* (New Haven, Conn.: Yale University Press, 2000), 234; Anatoli I. Gribkov and William Y. Smith, *Operation ANADYR: U.S. and Soviet Generals Recount the Cuban Missile Crisis,* ed. Alfred Friendly Jr. (Chicago: Edition q, 1994), 11.

130. Fursenko and Naftali, *"One Hell of a Gamble,"* 155. This 1962 intelligence report, while inaccurately characterizing Kennedy administration policy toward a first strike, was evidently based on the fact that a plan for a U.S. first strike was developed by civilian Pentagon officials and outside consultants in June 1961 and submitted to McNamara and, ultimately, to President Kennedy, in mid September. That document had indeed concluded that a first strike was "very feasible" and could be carried out "with high confidence." See Kaplan, *Wizards,* 249.

131. Quoted in May, Steinbrunner, and Wolfe, "History of the Strategic Arms Competition," 1: 484.

132. Nikita S. Khrushchev, *Khrushchev Remembers: The Glasnost Tapes,* trans. and ed. Jerrold L. Schecter and Vyacheslav Luchkov (Boston: Little, Brown, 1990), 182.

133. For the argument that Mao pursued a more aggressive policy based on that belief, see Gaddis, *Now We Know,* 253.

134. Alice Langley Hsieh, *Communist China's Strategy in the Nuclear Era* (Englewood Cliffs, N.J.: Prentice-Hall, 1962), 121.

135. The East German Politburo member Friedrich Ebert recounted this in a report on the meeting. See CIA, "An Assessment of International Communism's Current Objectives and Tactics" (n.d. [ca. January 1958]), 6, RG 263, National Archives. On the importance of the Soviet security guarantee to Chinese security, see Garver, *Foreign Relations of the People's Republic of China*, 68, n. 43.

136. Christensen, *Useful Adversaries*, 206–17.

137. Hsieh, *Communist China's Strategy*, 86–87.

138. David Mozingo, *Chinese Policy toward Indonesia, 1949–1967* (Ithaca, N.Y.: Cornell University Press, 1976), 133–35; John Gittings, *The World and China, 1922–1972* (New York: Harper & Row, 1974), 217–18.

139. For a careful reconstruction of Mao's policy in that crisis based on new Chinese documentation, see Christensen, *Useful Adversaries*, 227–28.

140. Allen S. Whiting, "Quemoy 1958: Mao's Miscalculations," *China Quarterly* 62 (June 1975): 266–67; Hsieh, *Communist China's Strategy*, 139.

141. Jia Qingguo, "Searching for Peaceful Coexistence and Territorial Integrity," in Harry Harding and Yuan Ming, eds., *Sino-American Relations, 1945–1955: A Joint Reassessment of a Critical Decade* (Wilmington, Del.: Scholarly Resources, 1989), 269.

142. Hsieh, *Communist China's Strategy*, 67, 69; New China News Agency, July 27, 1955, cited in Leo Yueh-Yun Liu, *China as a Nuclear Power in World Politics* (London: Macmillan, 1972), 54; Gordon H. Chang, "To the Nuclear Brink: Eisenhower, Dulles and the Quemoy-Matsu Crisis," *International Security* 12, no. 4 (1998): 108.

143. He Di, "The Most Respected Enemy," in David Hunt and Niu Jun, eds., *Toward a History of Chinese Communist Foreign Relations* (Washington, D.C.: Woodrow Wilson Center for Scholars, 1993), 44; Gordon Chang and He Di, "The Absence of War in the U.S.-China Confrontation on Quemoy and Matsu in 1954–1955: Contingency, Luck, Deterrence?" *American Historical Review* 98 (December 1993): 1516.

144. See He Di, "Most Respected Enemy," 42; Allen S. Whiting, "Mao, China and the Cold War," in Akira Iriye and Yonosuke Nagai, eds., *The Origins of the Cold War in Asia* (New York: Columbia University Press, 1977), 257–58; Michael Yahuda, *China's Role in World Affairs* (New York: St. Martin's Press, 1978), 97.

145. Christensen, *Useful Adversaries*, 216–17; Whiting, "Mao, China and the Cold War," 258–65; Gittings, *World and China*, 232; John Gittings, "New Light on Mao: 1. His View of the World," *China Quarterly* 60 (October–December 1974): 754–55. The quotation from the 1958 speech is from Mark A. Ryan, *Chinese Attitudes toward Nuclear Weapons: China and the United States during the Korean War* (Armonk, N.Y.: M. E. Sharpe, 1990), 181.

146. Soviet Ambassador S. F. Antonov, summary of a conversation with Mao Zedong, October 21, 1959, in "Soviet Policy during the Cold War: A

Documentary Sample," Cold War International History Project. On the web at www.gov.edu/~nsarchiv/CWIHP/Bulletins/b3a1.htm (accessed July 16, 2004).

147. See Whiting, "Quemoy 1958," 266–67; Thomas E. Stolper, *China, Taiwan and the Offshore Islands* (Armonk, N.Y.: M.E. Sharpe, 1985), 84–85.

148. Qiang Zhai, "Beijing and the Vietnam Conflict, 1964–1965," *Cold War International History Project Bulletin* 6–7 (Winter 1995–96): 239.

149. Qiang Zhai, *China and the Vietnam Wars, 1950–1975* (Chapel Hill: University of North Carolina Press, 2000), 113; Chen Xiaolu, "Chen Yi and China's Diplomacy," in Hunt and Niu, eds., *Toward a History of Chinese Communist Foreign Relations,* 103.

150. Alice Langley Hsieh, "China's Secret Military Papers: Military Doctrine and Strategy," *China Quarterly* 18 (April–June 1964): 81–82.

151. For the best account of these developments, by the head of the CIA's Tibetan Task Force, see John Kenneth Knaus, *Orphans of the Cold War: America and the Tibetan Struggle for Survival* (New York: Public Affairs, 1999), 255–69.

152. U.S. consul-general, Singapore, telegram to Department of State, November 13, 1962, *FRUS, 1961–1963,* 22: 323.

2. THE COMMUNIST POWERS APPEASE THE UNITED STATES

1. Christopher Goscha, "Le Contexte asiatique de la guerre franco-vietnamienne: Relations, réseaux et économie (1945–1954)" (doctoral thesis, École pratique des hautes études, Paris, November 2000), 6–14.

2. Charles B. McLane, *Soviet Strategies in Southeast Asia: An Exploration of Eastern Policy under Lenin and Stalin* (Princeton, N.J.: Princeton University Press, 1966), 287–91, 401–3; Ann Swift, *The Road to Madiun: The Indonesian Communist Uprising in 1948,* Monograph Series, no. 69 (Ithaca, N.Y.: Cornell Modern Indonesia Project, Southeast Asia Program, 1989), 33.

3. Mark Philip Bradley, *Imagining Vietnam and America: The Making of Post-Colonial Vietnam, 1919–1950* (Chapel Hill: University of North Carolina Press, 2000), 243 n. 5. See also William Duiker, *The Communist Road to Power in Vietnam,* 2d ed. (Boulder, Colo.: Westview Press, 1996), 22–23, 39–40.

4. Goscha, "Context asiatique," 22–23.

5. For evidence that Stalin's suspicions of Ho were related to this charge by Ho's internal party rivals as well as to his failure to seek Soviet consent before the declaration of independence and to wartime collaboration with British and U.S. intelligence services against the Japanese, see Janos Radvanyi, *Delusion and Reality: Gambits, Hoaxes and Diplomatic One-Upmanship in Vietnam* (South Bend, Ind.: Gateway Editions, 1978), 4–5.

6. Radvanyi, *Delusion and Reality,* 20.

7. Qiang Zhai, *China and the Vietnam Wars, 1950–1975* (Chapel Hill: University of North Carolina Press, 2000), 21.

8. Chen Jian, "China and the First Indochina War, 1950–54," *China Quarterly* 133 (March 1993): 90; Shu Guang Zhang, *Deterrence and Strategic*

Culture: Chinese-American Confrontations, 1949–1958 (Ithaca, N.Y.: Cornell University Press, 1992), 175.

9. Qiang Zhai, *China and the Vietnam Wars*, 22–23.

10. Shu Guang Zhang, *Deterrence and Strategic Culture*, 172; Qiang Zhai, "China and the Geneva Conference of 1954," *China Quarterly* 129 (March 1992): 246; Chen Jian, "China and the First Indochina War," 88.

11. For details of U.S. military and financial assistance to the French war effort, see George McT. Kahin, *Intervention: How the United States Became Involved in Vietnam* (New York: Knopf, 1986), 35–37, 43–44.

12. Qiang Zhai, *China and the Vietnam Wars*, 36–38, 43–46; Chen Jian, *Mao's China and the Cold War* (Chapel Hill: University of North Carolina Press, 2001), 124–38.

13. Qiang Zhai, *China and the Vietnam Wars*, 37.

14. Philippe Devillers and Jean Lacouture, *End of a War: Indochina, 1954*, trans. Alexander Lieven and Adam Roberts (New York: Praeger, 1969), 40.

15. Chen Jian, *Mao's China*, 134–38; Shu Guang Zhang, *Deterrence and Strategic Culture*, 181, 183–84. On the Vietnamese surprise and unhappiness regarding this turn in Soviet and Chinese policy, see Gareth Porter, "Vietnam and the Socialist Camp: Center or Periphery?" in William S. Turley, ed., *Vietnamese Communism in Comparative Perspective* (Boulder, Colo.: Westview Press, 1980), 232–33.

16. He Di, "The Most Respected Enemy," in Michael H. Hunt and Niu Jun, eds., *Toward a History of Chinese Communist Foreign Relations* (Washington, D.C.: Woodrow Wilson Center for Scholars, 1993), 38; Chen Jian, *Mao's China*, 133–34, 139–40.

17. James G. Richter, *Khrushchev's Double Bind: International Pressures and Domestic Coalition Politics* (Baltimore: Johns Hopkins University Press, 1994), 48.

18. Ilya V. Gaiduk, *Confronting Vietnam: Soviet Policy toward the Indochina Conflict, 1954–1963* (Stanford, Calif.: Stanford University Press, 2003), 18, 39; Qiang Zhai, "China and the Geneva Conference," 115.

19. Qiang Zhai, *China and the Vietnam Wars*, 54; Chen Jian, *Mao's China*, 139; Gaiduk, *Confronting Vietnam*, 18.

20. François Joyaux, *La Chine et le règlement du premier conflit d'Indochine: Genève 1954* (Paris: Publications de la Sorbonne, 1979), 70; Gaiduk, *Confronting Vietnam*, 23.

21. Yang Kuisong, "Changes in Mao Zedong's Attitude toward the Indochina War, 1949–1973," trans. Qiang Zhai, Working Paper no. 34, February 2002, Cold War International History Project, Washington, D.C., 7.

22. Radvanyi, *Delusion and Reality*, 10.

23. *Nhan Dan*, April 23–30, 1954.

24. Bernard Fall, "The Pathet Lao: A 'Liberation' Party," in Robert A. Scalapino, ed., *The Communist Revolution in Asia*, 2d ed. (Englewood Cliffs, N.J.: Prentice-Hall, 1969), 193. The Pathet Lao forces numbered at least 1,500 at the time of the Geneva conference, having grown from only two or three

hundred in 1953. See Joseph J. Zasloff, *The Pathet Lao: Leadership and Organization* (Lexington, Mass.: Lexington Books, 1973), 69. In Cambodia, the Khmer Issarak actually represented the bulk of the anti-French forces fighting in Cambodia at the close of the war, when they were estimated at about 5,000, compared with fewer than 3,000 to 4,000 Viet Minh troops in Cambodia. Ben Kiernan, *How Pol Pot Came to Power: A History of Communism in Kampuchea, 1930–1975* (London: Verso, 1985), 133.

25. Devillers and Lacouture, *End of a War*, 167, 202, 235.

26. About 1,000 Khmer Issarak, fearing reprisals by the government, left Cambodia with the departing Viet Minh forces. Sihanouk then proceeded to repress Khmer Communists in strengthening his hold on political power, and many Khmer Communists continued to hold the Vietnamese responsible for betraying them at Geneva. Kiernan, *How Pol Pot Came to Power*, 152–54.

27. Pham Binh, interview by the author, Hanoi, June 24, 1984; Robert F. Randle, *Geneva 1954: The Settlement of the Indochinese War* (Princeton, N.J.: Princeton University Press, 1969), 311.

28. Walter Bedell Smith, undersecretary of state, telegram to John Foster Dulles, June 17, 1954, *FRUS, 1952–1954*, 16: 1157–61, 1171.

29. John P. Burke and Freed I. Greenstein, *How Presidents Test Reality* (New York: Russell Sage Foundation, 1989), 99; Yang Kuisong, "Changes in Mao Zedong's Attitude," 9; Qiang Zhai, *China and the Vietnam Wars*, 58–60; Chen Jian, "China and the First Indochina War," 110; Shu Guang Zhang, *Deterrence and Strategic Culture*, 185; Chen Jian, *Mao's China*, 142.

30. Coordinator of the U.S. delegation (Johnson), memo of conversation, July 13, 1954, *FRUS, 1952–1954*, 13: 1819–20; Devillers and Lacouture, *End of a War*, 275–81; Joyaux, *Chine*, 283–86.

31. Joyaux, *Chine*, 285; "Agreement on the Cessation of Hostilities in Laos," Randle, *Geneva 1954*, app., doc. 3, 585–86.

32. Devillers and Lacouture, *End of a War*, 309; Joyaux, *Chine*, 281; Gaiduk, *Confronting Vietnam*, 46–47.

33. Devillers and Lacouture, *End of a War*, 309.

34. Ambassador C. Douglas Dillon, Paris, telegram to Department of State, June 24, 1954, *FRUS, 1952–1954*, 16: 1240–41; U.S. DOD, *United States–Vietnam Relations, 1945–1967* (Washington: Government Printing Office, 1971), bk. 1, pt. 3, ch. 2, D-5; Joyaux, *Chine*, 240–41, 296–97.

35. Qiang Zhai, *China and the Vietnam Wars*, 61.

36. Qiang Zhai, "China and the Geneva Conference," 115.

37. Yang Kuisong, "Changes in Mao Zedong's Attitude," 12.

38. Gaiduk, *Confronting Vietnam*, 72–73.

39. Mari Olsen, *Solidarity and National Revolution: The Soviet Union and the Vietnamese Communists, 1954–1960* (Oslo: Norwegian Institute for Defence Studies, 1997), 67–68.

40. Gaiduk, *Confronting Vietnam*, 82–83.

41. Kahin, *Intervention*, 92, 462 n. 58; Carlyle A. Thayer, *War by Other Means: National Liberation and Revolution in Viet-nam, 1954–60* (Sydney:

Allen & Unwin, 1989), 159–60; Gaiduk, *Confronting Vietnam,* 85; Olsen, *Solidarity,* 92–94.

42. Kahin, *Intervention,* 92, 462 n. 58; Olsen, *Solidarity,* 94; Gaiduk, *Confronting Vietnam,* 86.

43. This Soviet argument is reported in a Vietnamese party document marked "for internal circulation." See *Tai lieu huong dan hoc tap nghi quyet Dai Hoi IV cua Dang* [Guidance Document for Studying the Resolution of the Fourth Party Congress] (Hanoi: Nha Xuat Ban Sach Giao Khoa Mac-Le Nin, 1977), 86. Lt. Gen. Tran Cong Man also referred to the Soviet argument about the need to maintain the status quo in divided states in an interview with the author, Hanoi, June 23, 1984.

44. Committee to Summarize the War Experience, *Cuoc Khang chien Chong My, Cuu nuoc, 1954–1975: Nhung su kien quan su* [The Anti-U.S. National Salvation Resistance War, 1954–1975: Military Events] (Hanoi: Nha Xuan Ban Quan Doi, 1980), 34, translated in Joint Publications Research Service, JPRS 80968, June 3, 1982, 20; Hoang Van Hoan, "Distortion of Facts about Militant Friendship between Viet Nam and China Is Impermissible," *Beijing Review,* December 7, 1979, 15; Chen Jian, *Mao's China,* 206.

45. Nguyen Tien, China specialist with the Vietnamese Foreign Ministry, interview by the author, Hanoi, November 17, 1978.

46. Chen Jian, "China's Involvement in the Vietnam War 1964–69," *China Quarterly* 142 (1995): 357.

47. Ibid., 358; Qiang Zhai, *China and the Vietnam Wars,* 80.

48. Olsen, *Solidarity,* 112–13.

49. Gaiduk, *Confronting Vietnam,* 131–32; MacAlister Brown and Joseph J. Zasloff, *Apprentice Revolutionaries: The Communist Movement in Laos, 1930–1985* (Stanford, Calif.: Hoover Institution Press, 1986), 67–72; Charles Stevenson, *The End of Nowhere: American Policy toward Laos since 1954* (Boston: Beacon Press, 1972), 58–66; A. M. Halpern and H. B. Fredman, *Communist Strategy in Laos,* RM-2561 (Santa Monica, Calif.: RAND Corp., 1960), 21–51, 118–19; Bernard B. Fall, *Anatomy of a Crisis: The Laotian Crisis of 1960–1961,* ed. Roger M. Smith (Garden City, N.Y.: Doubleday, 1969), 75–81.

50. Zagoria, *Sino-Soviet Conflict,* 283; Olsen, *Solidarity,* 118; Gaiduk, *Confronting Vietnam,* 133–34.

51. "Comrade B on the Plot of the Reactionary Chinese Clique against Vietnam" (a 1979 document from the People's Army Library in Hanoi, translated by Christopher E. Goscha), available on the website of the Cold War International History Project (http://cwihp.si.edu), 14; Sergei N. Khrushchev, *Nikita Khrushchev and the Creation of a Superpower* (University Park, Pa.: Pennsylvania State University Press, 2000), 695.

52. Olsen, *Solidarity,* 114.

53. Ilya V. Gaiduk, "Containing the Warriors: Soviet Policy toward the Indochina Conflict," in Lloyd C. Gardner and Ted Gittinger, eds., *International Perspectives on Vietnam* (College Station: Texas A&M University Press, 2000), 63. In June 1961, in conversation with the Polish delegate to the International

Control Commission in Laos, the Soviet chargé in Laos, repeating the mid-1960 Foreign Ministry analysis, challenged the Vietnamese assumption that the United States would not send the troops needed to save the Diem government. See Marek Thee, *Notes of a Witness: Laos and the Second Indochinese War* (New York: Vintage Books, 1973), 146.

54. John Wilson Lewis, "China and Vietnam," in *China Briefing* (Chicago: University of Chicago Center for Public Policy, 1968), 53.

55. Foreign Minister Nguyen Co Thach and LDP Central Committee member Hoang Tung, interviews by the author, Hanoi, August 2, 1982.

56. Hoang Tung, alternate VWP Central Committee member, interview by the author, Hanoi, December 25, 1974.

57. Mieczyslaw Maneli, *War of the Vanquished*, trans. Maria de Görgey (New York: Harper & Row, 1971), 177.

58. "Comrade B on the Plot of the Reactionary Chinese Clique against Vietnam," 14.

59. Ibid., 14–15. Zhou and Deng's approval of the decision, but not their insistence that the Vietnamese refrain from military operations above the platoon level, is discussed on the basis of Chinese sources in Qiang Zhai, *China and the Vietnam Wars*, 83.

60. DRV, Ministry of Defense, Institute of Vietnamese Military History, *Victory in Vietnam: The Official History of the People's Army of Vietnam*, trans. Merle L. Pribbenow (Lawrence: University of Kansas Press, 2002), 72–73.

61. Speech by Zhou Enlai, September 2, 1960, in Gareth Porter, ed., *Vietnam: The Definitive Documentation of Human Decisions* (Stanfordville, N.Y.: E.M. Coleman Enterprises, 1979), 2: 72.

62. Pham Binh, director of the Institute of International Relations, interview by the author, Hanoi, June 21, 1984.

63. See Yang Kuisong, "Changes in Mao Zedong's Attitude," 21. This source implies that Mao advocated a more aggressive military strategy by the Vietnamese, but the opinions attributed to Mao ("there was nothing to fear" and "even if a coalition government was established, . . . war would break out sooner or later") are far from clear in this regard.

64. "Report on the SVN Situation from the End of 1961 to the Beginning of 1964" (translation of captured party document, ca. May 1964), CDEC Doc. Log No. 01–0519–70, 23.

65. Bui Tin, *Following Ho Chi Minh: The Memoirs of a North Vietnamese Colonel* (Honolulu: University of Hawaii Press, 1995), 45. The Chinese insistence on platoon- or company-strength attacks is also discussed in DRV, Ministry of National Defense, *History*, 72–73. Col. Tin's memoirs are given added credibility by the fact that he no longer reflected Hanoi's official line, having left Vietnam for Paris to become a leading critic of the regime, and therefore had no need to support the Vietnamese theme of betrayal by their erstwhile Chinese allies.

66. Qiang Zhai, *China and the Vietnam Wars*, 113.

67. George McT. Kahin and John W. Lewis, *The United States in Vietnam* (New York: Dell, 1969), 282.

68. Thee, *Notes of a Witness*, 146.

69. Gaiduk, "Containing the Warriors," in Gardner and Gittinger, eds., *International Perspectives on Vietnam*, 73.

70. Sergei N. Khrushchev, *Nikita Khrushchev*, 716. See Gaiduk, "Containing the Warriors," in Gardner and Gittinger, eds., *International Perspectives on Vietnam*, 74, for a report, based on a conversation between the Soviet ambassador in Cambodia and the pro-Communist journalist Wilfred Burchett in 1964, that the USSR had agreed in 1962 to provide 130 recoilless guns and mortars, 1,400 machine guns, 54,500 rifles, and ammunition for South Vietnamese "patriots." Given the firm and consistent Soviet opposition to any armed struggle in South Vietnam, the accuracy of the ambassador's report seems questionable.

71. See Ilya V. Gaiduk, "The Vietnam War and Soviet-American Relations, 1964–1973: The New Russian Evidence," *Cold War International History Project Bulletin 6–7* (Winter 1995–96): 250; Xiaoming Zhang, "The Vietnam War, 1964–1969: A Chinese Perspective," *Journal of Military History* 60 (October 1986): 735.

72. Gaiduk, *Confronting Vietnam*, 169–70.

73. *The Pentagon Papers: The Defense Department History of United States Decisionmaking on Vietnam. The Senator Gravel Edition* (Boston: Beacon Press, 1972), 3: 116.

74. U.S. embassy, Moscow, telegram to secretary of state, March 29, 1962, NSF, box 196, "Vietnam General 3/29/62–3/31/62" files, JFKL; U.S. embassy, Saigon, telegram to secretary of state, March 22, 1962, NSF, box 196, "Vietnam 3/13/62–3/22/62" file, JFKL; Chalmers B. Wood, memo to Averell Harriman, "Chronology of Exchanges of Notes between British and Russians," April 17, 1962, NSF, box 128, "Vietnam Security 1962" file, JFKL.

75. Stevenson, *End of Nowhere*, 92–114; Arthur Dommen, *Conflict in Laos: The Politics of Neutralization*, rev. ed. (New York: Praeger, 1971), 172–79.

76. For the Kennedy administration interpretation, see comments of Charles Bohlen, memo of conversation, January 17, 1961, *FRUS, 1961–1963*, 24: 15; Hilsman, *To Move a Nation*, 132; Arthur Schlesinger Jr., *A Thousand Days* (Boston: Houghton Mifflin, 1965), 331; David K. Hall, "The Laos Crisis, 1960–61," in Alexander L. George, David K. Hall, and William R. Simons, eds., *The Limits of Coercive Diplomacy* (Boston: Little, Brown, 1971), 43–44. For the Sino-Soviet competition and Soviet hard-line interpretations of Soviet policy in Laos, see Dommen, *Conflict in Laos*, 179–81; Hall, "Laos Crisis, 1960–61," 44; Chae-Jin Lee, *Communist China's Policy toward Laos: A Case Study, 1954–67*, International Studies, East Asian Series, Research Publication No. 6 (Lawrence: Center for East Asian Studies, University of Kansas, 1970), 74. For an interpretation suggesting that Khrushchev was aiming at both objectives, see Adam B. Ulam, *Expansion and Coexistence: Soviet Foreign Policy, 1917–73*, 2d ed. (New York: Holt, Rinehart & Winston, 1974), 699.

77. Gaiduk, "Containing the Warriors," in Gardner and Gittinger, eds., *International Perspectives on Vietnam*, 66–67; Gaiduk, *Confronting Vietnam*, 162–63.

78. U.S. embassy, Phnom Penh, message to secretary of state, March 7, 1961, in Historical Division, Joint Secretariat, Joint Chiefs of Staff, *Chronological Summary of Significant Events Concerning the Laotian Crisis, Second Installment: 1 February to 31 March 1961*, Virtual Vietnam Archive, Texas Tech University, www.vietnam.ttu.edu/star/images/250/2500118001C.pdf (last visited August 23, 2004), 47.

79. Thee, *Notes of a Witness*, 17, 166–67, 192; Gaiduk, "Containing the Warriors," in Gardner and Gittinger, eds., *International Perspectives on Vietnam*, 68–69.

80. Gaiduk, "Containing the Warriors," in Gardner and Gittinger, eds., *International Perspectives on Vietnam*, 70.

81. Gaiduk, *Confronting Vietnam*, 174; Gaiduk, "Containing the Warriors," in Gardner and Gittinger, eds., *International Perspectives on Vietnam*, 70.

82. Averell Harriman, telegrams to Department of State, September 13 and October 10, 1961, *FRUS, 1961–1963*, 24: 411, 461–62.

83. Averell Harriman, telegrams to Department of State, November 2 and 12, 1961, ibid., 497, 510. For the text of the Geneva Conference Declaration on the Neutrality of Laos, see Dommen, *Conflict in Laos*, 415–18.

84. U.S. embassy, Rome, telegram to Department of State, September 13, 1961, *FRUS, 1961–1963*, 24: 411.

85. Averell Harriman, telegram to Department of State, November 2, 1961, ibid., 497.

86. Thee, *Notes of a Witness*, 130–31.

87. Hilsman reported this Vietnamese comment, presumably based on his own conversation with Harriman, in Michael Charlton and Anthony Moncrieff, eds., *Many Reasons Why: The American Involvement in Vietnam* (New York: Hill & Wang, 1978), 63–64.

88. Ha Van Lau, interview by the author, Hanoi, June 26, 1984. The North Vietnamese position was consonant with the language of paragraph 6 of the Final Declaration of the 1954 Geneva agreement, which says, "the military demarcation line is provisional and should not in any way be interpreted as constituting a political or territorial boundary." See the text in George McT. Kahin and John W. Lewis, *The United States in Vietnam*, rev. ed. (New York: Dell, 1969), app. 2, 442.

89. Hoang Tung, "The Struggle to Safeguard Peace Is a First Responsibility," *Nhan Dan*, January 22, 1961, in Joint Publications Research Service, *Translations on North Vietnam*, no. 8423 (June 9, 1961): 50-58.

90. Thee, *Notes of a Witness*, 167, 327.

91. Ibid., 335.

92. Michael Forrestal, "Conversation with Mr. Alexander Zinchuk," memo for the record, December 16, 1963, Hilsman Papers, box 1, "Cambodia 1963–64" file, JFKL. Zinchuk was counselor of the Soviet embassy in Washington.

93. See Qiang Zhai, *China and the Vietnam Wars*, 114–16; Yang Kuisong, "Changes in Mao Zedong's Attitude," 21–22; Chen Jian, "China's Involvement in the Vietnam War, 1964–69,"*China Quarterly* 142 (1995): 362.

94. Roderick MacFarquhar, *The Origins of the Cultural Revolution*, vol. 3: *The Coming of the Cataclysm, 1961–1966* (New York: Oxford University Press and Columbia University Press, 1997), 269.

95. Qiang Zhai, *China and the Vietnam Wars*, 115; Yang Kuisong, "Changes in Mao Zedong's Attitude," 22.

96. MacFarquhar, *Origins of the Cultural Revolution*, 3: 283; Philip L. Bridgham, "The International Impact of Maoist Ideology," in Chalmers Johnson, *Ideology and Politics in Contemporary China* (Seattle: University of Washington Press, 1973), 327.

97. Hoang Van Hoan, "Distortions," 15; "More on Hanoi's White Book," *Beijing Review*, November 30, 1979, 13.

98. See MacFarquhar, *Origins of the Cultural Revolution*, 3: 368; Chen Jian, *Mao's China*, 207; Chen Jian, "China's Involvement," 359. See also Qiang Zhai, "An Uneasy Relationship: China and the DRV during the Vietnam War," in Gardner and Gittinger, eds., *International Perspectives on Vietnam*, 109, 252 n. 3, which cites the research of Chinese military historians and does not claim that the 1962 military assistance was intended for the insurgents in the South. The same author suggests in a more recent work that these same weapons would be used to support guerrilla warfare in the South, even though he points out that the arms were promised at a time when the PRC leadership was preoccupied with external threats "from several directions." See Qiang Zhai, *China and the Vietnam Wars*, 116.

99. Chen Xiaolu, "Chen Yi and China's Diplomacy," in Michael H. Hunt and Niu Jun, eds., *Toward a History of Chinese Communist Foreign Relations* (Washington, D.C.: Woodrow Wilson Center for Scholars, 1993), 103.

100. New China News Agency, February 24, 1962.

101. John Garver, "The Chinese Threat in the Vietnam War," *Parameters* 22 (Spring 1992): 77; Melvin Gurtov and Byong-Moo Hwang, *China under Threat: The Politics of Strategy and Diplomacy* (Baltimore: Johns Hopkins University Press, 1980), 160.

102. Chinese worries about North Vietnamese ability to hold off the United States remained, despite Chinese military assistance and increases in the troop strength of the VPA. In 1966, Mao and PRC Minister of Defense Lin Biao were afraid that North Vietnamese troops would be no match for the United States if it should decide to conquer North Vietnam. See Odd Arne Westad, "History, Memory, and the Languages of Alliance-Making," in Westad et al., eds., *77 Conversations between Chinese and Foreign Leaders on the Wars in Indochina, 1964–1977* (Washington, D.C.: Cold War International History Project, Woodrow Wilson Center for Scholars, 1998), 10. Westad cites "sources in Beijing with access to Mao's papers."

103. DRV, Ministry of Defense, Institute of Vietnamese Military History, *Victory in Vietnam*, 94.

104. The Tenth Plenum was held September 24–27, 1962, and the preparatory meetings took place from August 26 to September 23. See MacFarquhar, *Coming of the Cataclysm*, 283.

105. Chen Jian, "China's Involvement," 360; Qiang Zhai, *China and the Vietnam Wars*, 117.

106. Qiang Zhai, *China and the Vietnam Wars*, 120; Xiaoming Zhang, "Communist Powers Divided," 83.

107. DRV, Institute for Research on Marxism-Leninism and Ho Chi Minh Thought, *Lich Su Dang Cong San Viet Nam*, vol. 2: *1954–1975* [History of the Vietnamese Communist Party, vol. 2: 1954–1975] (Hanoi: Chinh Tri Quoc Gia, 1995), 175; Merle L. Pribbenow, "North Vietnam's Master Plan," *Vietnam* 12, no. 2 (August 1999).

108. "Nghi quyet cua Bo Chinh tri Ban Chap hanh Trung uong ve cong tac cach mang Mien Nam" [Political Bureau Resolution on Southern Revolutionary Work], February 26–27, 1962, in Vietnamese Communist Party, *Mot so van kien cua dang ve Chong My Cuu nuoc* [Some Documents of the Party on the Anti-U.S. Resistance War for National Salvation], vol. 1: *1954–1975* (Hanoi: Su that, 1985), 151; DRV, Institute for Research on Marxism-Leninism and Ho Chi Minh Thought, *History*, 174.

109. Bui Tin, *Following Ho Chi Minh*, 48–53; VPA Colonel Bui Tin, interview by the author, Hanoi, June 23, 1984. The director of Hanoi's Institute for International Relations recalled the same advice from the Chinese at that stage. Pham Binh, interview by the author, Hanoi, June 21, 1984.

110. Kao Ko, "The Victorious Road of National-Liberation War," *Beijing Review*, November, 1963, 10–13.

111. Col. Bui Tin, interview by the author, Hanoi, June 23, 1984.

112. Sandra C. Taylor, "Laos: The Escalation of a Secret War," in Jane Errington and B. J. C. McKercher, eds., *The Vietnam War as History* (New York: Praeger, 1990), 73–90; *New York Times*, June 18 and 19, 1964. On Chinese press reports on press leaks about U.S. plans for taking the war to North Vietnam, see Allen S. Whiting, *The Chinese Calculus of Deterrence* (Ann Arbor: University of Michigan Press, 1975), 172.

113. Whiting, *Chinese Calculus*, 173.

114. Qiang Zhai, *China and the Vietnam Wars*, 131.

115. Gurtov and Hwang, *China under Threat*, 160.

116. Chen Jian, "China's Involvement," 360.

117. Qiang Zhai, "Uneasy Relationship," 110.

118. Ibid.

119. Qiang Zhai, *China and the Vietnam Wars*, 141.

120. Xiaoming Zhang, "Vietnam War," 742.

121. Xiaoming Zhang, "Communist Powers Divided," 84; Barry Naughton, "The Third Front: Defense Industrialization in the Chinese Interior," *China Quarterly* 115 (September 1988): 351–88.

122. Naughton, "Third Front," 353; Qiang Zhai, *China and the Vietnam Wars*, 141–42.

123. Xiaoming Zhang, "Communist Powers Divided," 84.

124. Xiaoming Zhang, "Vietnam War," 739–40; Qiang Zhai, "Uneasy Relationship," 110–11.

125. Frank E. Rogers, "Sino-American Relations and the Vietnam War, 1964–66," *China Quarterly* 66 (June 1976): 297.

126. Transcript of Mao Zedong meeting with Pham Van Dong and Hoang Van Hoan, Beijing, October 5, 1964, in Westad et al., eds., *77 Conversations*, 74–76.

127. Naughton, "Third Front," 371.

128. William J. Duiker, *Ho Chi Minh* (New York: Hyperion, 2000), 541: David Kaiser, *Vietnam Tragedy: Kennedy, Johnson and the Origins of the Vietnam War* (Cambridge, Mass.: Belknap Press of Harvard University Press, 2000), 339. Fredrik Logevall, however, interprets them as reflecting Mao's desire to "avoid a direct military confrontation with the United States." See Logevall, *Choosing War: The Lost Chance for Peace and the Escalation of War in Vietnam* (Berkeley: University of California Press, 1999), 208.

129. Westad et al., eds., *77 Conversations*, 74 n. 117.

130. Chen Jian, one of the editors of the set of seventy-seven documents cited in n. 102 above, personal communication to author, July 11, 2000. Unfortunately, the footnote to the document quoting from Mao's meeting with Le Duan fails to inform the reader of the exchange that preceded Mao's quoted remarks. Chen Jian explained that the editors did not have permission to publish the full text of the August 13 talk between Mao and Le Duan, but that he had read the document and was able to add this crucial detail to the brief footnote on the meeting.

131. Chen Jian, *Mao's China and the Cold War*, 213; Qiang Zhai, *China and the Vietnam Wars*, 132.

132. Mao Zedong, meeting with Pham Van Dong and Hoang Van Hoan, in Westad et al., eds., *77 Conversations*, 74. Two modifications have been made to the punctuation in the text as published to clarify Mao's statement.

133. Ibid., 75.

134. On the U.S. supply operations, see documents 79–86 in Porter, ed., *Vietnam*, 2: 161–69.

135. Thee, *Notes of a Witness*, 325, 328–29.

136. Dommen, *Conflict in Laos*, 246–47.

137. See Brown and Zasloff, *Apprentice Revolutionaries*, 89–81; Gareth Porter, "After Geneva: Subverting Laotian Neutrality," in Nina S. Adams and Alfred W. McCoy, eds., *Laos: War and Revolution* (New York: Harper & Row, 1970); Dommen, *Conflict in Laos*, 232–35.

138. William Colby, memo to CIA Director John McCone, May 19, 1963, *FRUS, 1961–1963*, 24: 972, editorial footnote.

139. Excerpt from article by Political Bureau member Nguyen Chi Thanh, in Porter, ed., *Vietnam*, 2: 186: King Chen, "North Vietnam in the Sino-Soviet Dispute, 1962–1964," *Asian Survey*, September 1964, 1023–36.

140. Memo of conversation, August 9, 1963, *FRUS, 1961–1963*, 21: 1044–45.

141. Ilya Gaiduk, *The Soviet Union and the Vietnam War* (Chicago: Ivan R. Dee, 1996), 13.

142. U Thant cited this comment by Khrushchev in a meeting with U.S. Ambassador Stevenson on February 27, 1965. See Adlai E. Stevenson, memo of conversation with U Thant, February 27, 1965, LBJL. See also David Kraslow and Stuart H. Loory, *The Secret Search for Peace in Vietnam* (New York: Vintage Books, 1968), 98.

143. Daniel Papp, *Vietnam: The View from Moscow, Peking, Washington* (Jefferson, N.C.: McFarland, 1981), 35–36.

144. Nikita S. Khrushchev, *Khrushchev Remembers: The Last Testament,* ed. and trans. Strobe Talbott (Boston: Little, Brown, 1974), 328.

145. Soviet Premier Nikita Khrushchev, letter to LBJ, August 5, 1964, in Porter, ed., *Vietnam,* 2: 384–86.

146. Xiaoming Zhang, "Communist Powers Divided: China, the Soviet Union, and the Vietnam War," in Gardner and Gittinger, eds., *International Perspectives on Vietnam,* 86; Papp, *Vietnam,* 44–45; memo of conversation between Gromyko and Johnson, December 9, 1964, *FRUS, 1964–1968,* 1: 193; memo of conversation, Soviet embassy, Washington, D.C., December 9, 1964, ibid., 990–93.

147. William C. Gibbons, *The U.S. Government and the Vietnam War: Executive and Legislative Roles and Relationships,* pt. 3: *January–July 1965* (Washington, D.C.: Government Printing Office, 1988), 114. William Sullivan, U.S. ambassador to Laos, reflected the widespread understanding in the national security bureaucracy that it would be better for North Vietnam to be dependent on the USSR in a memo on June 14, 1965, opposing massive bombing of civilian targets, because "it would run counter to the proposition that we are willing to see North Vietnam remain intact but under Soviet tutelage" (ibid., 337).

148. According to the Chinese account, Kosygin discussed his proposal with Chinese officials following his trip to Hanoi. "Refutation of the New Leaders of the C.P.S.U. on 'United Action,'" *Peking Review,* November 12, 1965, 17.

149. Extract from joint statement of Kosygin and Pham Van Dong, February 10, 1965, in Gareth Porter, ed., *Vietnam: A History in Documents* (New York: New American Library, 1981), 300.

150. Logevall, *Choosing War,* 364.

151. Gaiduk, *Soviet Union and the Vietnam War,* 38.

3. EISENHOWER AND DULLES EXPLOIT U.S. DOMINANCE
IN VIETNAM

1. Leslie Gelb and Richard Betts, *The Irony of Vietnam: The System Worked* (Washington, D.C.: Brookings Institution, 1979), 50–60; John Prados, *The Sky Would Fall* (New York: Dial Press, 1983), 78–81, 104; William C. Gibbons, *The U.S. Government and the Vietnam War: Executive and Legislative Roles and Relationships,* pt. 1: *1945–1961* (Washington, D.C.: Government Printing Office,

1984), 176; George C. Herring, *America's Longest War: The United States and Vietnam, 1950-1975* (New York: Knopf, 1986), 29–40; Richard H. Immerman, "Between the Unattainable and the Unacceptable: Eisenhower and Dienbienphu," in Richard A. Melanson and David Mayers, eds., *Reevaluating Eisenhower: American Foreign Policy in the 1950s* (Urbana: University of Illinois Press, 1987), 123; George C. Herring and Richard H. Immerman, "Eisenhower, Dulles and Dien Bien Phu: 'The Day We Didn't Go to War' Revisited," in Lawrence Kaplan, Denise Artaud, and Mark Rubin, eds., *Dien Bien Phu and the Crisis of Franco-American Relations, 1954–1955* (Wilmington, Del.: SR Books, 1990), 83, 86 n. 20, 100; Melanie Billings-Yun, *Decision against War: Eisenhower and Dien Bien Phu, 1954* (New York: Columbia University Press, 1988), 38–40, 93–95, and 108; George C. Herring, "A Good Stout Effort: John Foster Dulles and the Indochina Crisis, 1954–1955," in Richard Immerman, ed., *John Foster Dulles and the Diplomacy of the Cold War* (Princeton, N.J.: Princeton University Press, 1992); Fredrick Marks III, "The Real Hawk at Dienbienphu: Dulles or Eisenhower?" *Pacific Historical Review*, 59 (August 1990): 297–322; David L. Anderson, *Trapped by Success: The Eisenhower Administration and Vietnam, 1953–1961* (New York: Columbia University Press, 1991), 17–64; James R. Arnold, *The First Domino: Eisenhower, the Military and American's Intervention in Vietnam* (New York: William Morrow, 1991), 160.

2. Gibbons, *U.S. Government and the Vietnam War*, 129–35, 203–9; U.S. Congress, Senate, *Executive Sessions of the Senate Foreign Relations Committee*, 83d Cong., 2d sess., 1954, Historical Series (Washington, D.C.: Government Printing Office, 1977), 6: 110.

3. Memo of discussion at the 143d meeting of the NSC, May 6, 1953, *FRUS, 1952–1954*, 13, pt. 1: 547–48; memo of discussion at the 183d meeting of the NSC, February 4, 1954, ibid., 1014.

4. *Executive Sessions* (cited n. 2 above), 110; David Alan Rosenberg, "'A Smoking Radiating Ruin at the End of Two Hours': Documents on American Plans for Nuclear War with the Soviet Union, 1954–55," *International Security* 6, no. 3 (Winter 1981–82): 27.

5. Prados, *Sky Would Fall*, 46; Assistant Secretary of State for Far Eastern Affairs Walter Robertson, memo to Secretary of State John Foster Dulles, January 8, 1954, *FRUS, 1952–1954*, 13: 944–45.

6. Memo of discussion at the 179th meeting of the NSC, January 8, 1954, *FRUS, 1952–1954*, 13: 949–53. Some accounts have cited Eisenhower's statement later in the same meeting that the United States should not forget its "vital interests in Indochina" as nullifying his statement opposing the deployment of U.S. combat forces in Indochina, suggesting that it implied a willingness to intervene. See Herring, *America's Longest War*, 29; Immerman, "Between the Unattainable and the Unacceptable," 123. But the latter statement suggested only that Eisenhower was motivated to assist the French, not that he was ambivalent on the issue of military intervention.

7. Memo of discussion at the 189th meeting of the NSC, January 14, 1954, *FRUS, 1952–1954*, 13: 962–63.

8. C. D. Jackson, memo to the president, January 18, 1954, *FRUS, 1952–1954,* 13: 981–82. For analysis of this move by Eisenhower, see Gibbons, *U.S. Government and the Vietnam War,* 156.

9. Dwight D. Eisenhower, *Public Papers of the Presidents of the United States: Dwight D. Eisenhower,* vol. 2: *1954* (Washington, D.C.: Government Printing Office, 1960), 250.

10. CIA Director Allen Dulles, memo, September 6, 1953, *FRUS, 1952–1954,* 2: 459–60.

11. Memo of discussion at the 165th meeting of the NSC, October 7, 1953, ibid., 530; "Review of Basic National Security Policy" (NSC draft statement of policy), September 30, 1953, ibid., 513; NIE 99, "Estimate of the World Situation through 1955," October 23, 1953, ibid., 552.

12. See Rosemary Foot, "Nuclear Coercion and the Ending of the Korean Conflict," *International Security* 13, no. 3 (Winter 1988–89): 92–93; Lawrence Freedman, *The Evolution of Nuclear Strategy* (New York: St. Martin's Press 1989), 84–85; Roger Dingman, "Atomic Diplomacy during the Korean War," *International Security* 13, no. 3 (Winter 1988–89): 82–87.

13. By September 1951, CIA agents had already trained 100,000 Chinese Nationalist troops to carry out coastal raids and in supplying and reinforcing opposition forces on the mainland. In 1951–52, the CIA sponsored a second front of attack on China by 30,000 Nationalist troops from Burma, after flying them from Taiwan and supplying them with large quantities of modern weapons. The Nationalist troops launched three unsuccessful invasions of China's Yunnan province in 1951 and 1952. See Su-Ya Chang, "Pragmatism and Opportunism: Truman Policy toward Taiwan, 1949–52" (PhD diss., Pennsylvania State University, 1988), 203; Rosemary Foot, *The Wrong War: American Policy and the Dimensions of the Korean Conflict, 1950–53* (Ithaca, N.Y.: Cornell University Press, 1995), 263; Robert H. Taylor, *Foreign and Domestic Consequences of the KMT Intervention in Burma,* Cornell University Southeast Asia Program Data Paper No. 93 (Ithaca, N.Y.: Southeast Asia Program, Department of Asian Studies, Cornell University, 1973), 10–14; Nancy Bernkopf Tucker, "John Foster Dulles and the Taiwan Roots of the 'Two China' Policy," in Immerman, ed., *John Foster Dulles and the Diplomacy of the Cold War,* 244–45.

14. NSC 146/2, "United States Objectives and Courses of Action with Respect to Formosa and the Chinese Nationalist Government," November 6, 1953, *FRUS, 1952–1954,* 14: 307–8.

15. *Executive Sessions* (cited n. 2 above), 166, 171.

16. NIE 19-2-54, "Communist Courses of Action in Asia through Mid-1955," March 15, 1954, *FRUS, 1952–1954,* 2, pt. 1: 394–95; *Department of State Bulletin,* April 5, 1954, 513.

17. JCS, memo to Secretary of Defense Charles Wilson, March 12, 1954, *FRUS, 1952–1954,* 16: 472–75.

18. "Military Implications of the U.S. Position on Indo-China in Geneva," March 17, 1954, ibid., 475–79.

19. John Foster Dulles, memo of conversation with the president, March 24, 1954, ibid., 13: 1150.

20. Memo of discussion at the 190th meeting of the NSC, March 25, 1954, ibid., 1163–68; see Billings-Yun, *Decision against War*, 93–95.

21. Prados, *Sky Would Fall*, 81; Billings-Yun, *Decision against War*, 58–59.

22. The estimate that the strategic dominance of the United States would be replaced by "mutual deterrence" sometime between 1955 and 1959 was included in a Pentagon study in June 1954. See DOD, "Estimates of the Military Posture throughout the Free World FY 1956 through FY 1959," *FRUS, 1952–1954*, 2, pt. 1: 675.

23. John Foster Dulles, extracts from speech to the Overseas Press Club of America, March 29, 1954, in Allan W. Cameron, ed., *Viet-Nam Crisis: A Documentary History*, vol. 1: *1940–1956* (Ithaca, N.Y.: Cornell University Press, 1971), 235.

24. Gibbons, *U.S. Government and the Vietnam War*, 181.

25. Eisenhower, *Public Papers of the Presidents of the United States: Dwight D. Eisenhower*, vol. 2: *1954*, 366.

26. Department of State draft, April 2, 1954, *FRUS, 1952–1954*, 13: 1212.

27. John Foster Dulles, telegram to U.S. embassy, New Delhi, April 2, 1954, *FRUS, 1952–1954*, 13, pt. 2: 1217–18.

28. Memo of conversation between Dulles and Makins, April 2, 1954, *FRUS, 1952–1954*, 13: 1214–17; Anthony Eden, *Full Circle: Memoirs of Anthony Eden* (Boston: Cassell, 1960), 102–3.

29. John Foster Dulles, memo of conversation, April 2, 1954, *FRUS, 1952–1954*, 13: 1211.

30. Chalmers M. Roberts, "The Day We Didn't Go to War," in Marcus G. Raskin and Bernard B. Fall, eds., *The Viet-Nam Reader* (New York: Vintage Books, 1965), 58; Prados, *Sky Would Fall*, 95; John Foster Dulles, memo for the file, April 5, 1954, *FRUS, 1952–1954*, 13: 1224–25.

31. Deputy assistant secretary of state (Bonbright), memo of conversation, April 3, 1954, *FRUS, 1952–1954*, 13: 1227, 1229.

32. *FRUS, 1952–1954*, 13: 1240.

33. Memo of conversation between Dulles and Emilio Abello, Philippine chargé, April 5, 1954, The Secretary's and Undersecretary's Memoranda of Conversations, 1953–1954, box 2, "January–December, 1954," RG 59, NARA.

34. Memo of discussion at the 192d meeting of the NSC, April 6, 1954, *FRUS, 1952–1954*, 13: 1254.

35. Ibid., 1255.

36. Deputy Assistant Secretary of State James G. H. Bonbright, memo of conversation, April 3, 1954, ibid., 1229; Charles E. Bohlen, *Witness to History: 1929–1969* (New York: Norton, 1973), 521.

37. Eden, *Full Circle*, 124; *FRUS, 1952–1954*, 13: 1307–8.

38. Leonard Mosley, *Dulles: A Biography of Eleanor, Allen and John Foster Dulles and Their Family Network* (New York: Dial Press / James Wade, 1978), 355; Prados, *Sky Would Fall*, 143–44; Elizabeth Brown of the Office of UN Political and Security Affairs, memo of conversation, April 20, 1954, *FRUS, 1952–1954*, 16: 536, 538.

39. James Hagarty, diary entry, April 26, 1954, *FRUS, 1952–1954*, 13, pt. 2: 1410; Assistant Staff Secretary to the President L. Arthur Minnich Jr., memo (n.d.), ibid., 1413; Richard M. Nixon, *The Memoirs of Richard M. Nixon* (New York: Grosset & Dunlap, 1978), 153.

40. Memo of discussion at the 194th meeting of the NSC, April 29, 1954, *FRUS, 1952–1954*, 13, pt. 2: 1439–45; John Foster Dulles, telegram to State Department, April 29, 1954, in *United States–Vietnam Relations, 1945–1967* (Washington: Government Printing Office, 1971), bk. 9, 398.

41. Memo of discussion at the 195th meeting of the NSC, May 6, 1954, *FRUS, 1952–1954*, 13, pt. 2: 1485–87.

42. Department of State, telegram to U.S. delegation, May 6, 1954, *FRUS, 1952–1954*, 16: 707.

43. Robert Cutler, special assistant for national security affairs, memo of conversation, May 7, 1954, *FRUS, 1952–1954*, 13, pt. 2: 1497–98; memo of discussion at 196th meeting of the NSC, May 8, 1954, ibid., 1505; Robert R. Bowie, memo, May 11, 1954, ibid., 1533–34; John Foster Dulles, telegram to U.S. embassy, Paris, May 11, 1954, ibid., 1534.

44. Robert Randle, *Geneva 1954: The Settlement of the Indochinese War* (Princeton, N.J.: Princeton University Press, 1969), 144.

45. SNIE, 10-4-54, "Communist Reactions to Certain US Courses of Action with Respect to Indochina," June 15, 1954, in Scott A. Koch, ed., *Selected Estimates on the Soviet Union, 1950–1959* (Washington, D.C.: History Staff, Center for the Study of Intelligence, CIA, 1993), 103–7.

46. *New York Times*, May 11, 1954, 6.

47. *Executive Sessions* (cited n. 2 above), 267; memo of discussion at the 198th meeting of the NSC, May 20, 1954, *FRUS, 1952–1954*, 13, pt. 2: 1588–90.

48. On Dulles's public opposition to any agreement short of complete victory over the Viet Minh, see *United States–Vietnam Relations, 1945–1967*, bk. 1, III.A.1, A-9.

49. Coordinator of the U.S. delegation (U. Alexis Johnson), memo of conversation, July 13, 1954, *FRUS, 1952–1954*, 16: 1353.

50. See Gelb and Betts, *Irony of Vietnam*, 68; George McT. Kahin, *Intervention: How the United States Became Involved in Vietnam* (New York: Knopf, 1986), 73–74; Herring, *America's Longest War*, 45.

51. Cutler, memo of conversation, May 28, 1954, *FRUS, 1952–1954*, 12: 523; John Foster Dulles, memo to the president, May 28, 1954, ibid., 528; memo of conversation between John Foster Dulles and Thai Foreign Minister Prince Wan Waithayakorn, July 2, 1954, ibid., 613.

52. U.S. draft, July 9, 1954, ibid., 693.

53. For the text, see Cameron, ed., *Viet-Nam Crisis*, 1: 343.

54. "Draft Statement of Policy Proposed by the HSC on Review of US Policy in the Far East," August 4, 1954, *FRUS, 1952–1954*, 12: 700–701.

55. Memo of discussion at the 211th meeting of the NSC, August 18, 1954, ibid., 7: 527–28.

56. Ibid., 538; Kahin, *Intervention*, 74.

57. Herring and Immerman, "Eisenhower, Dulles and Dienbienphu," 86.

58. NSC 5501, "Basic National Security Policy," January 7, 1955, *FRUS, 1955–1957,* 14: 33–34.

59. Francis J. Gavin, "Power, Politics and U.S. Policy in Iran, 1950–1953," *Journal of Cold War Studies* 1, no. 1 (1999): 67–69, 75–80, 84–86.

60. Mark Gasiorowski, "Security Relations between the United States and Iran, 1953–1978," in Nikki R. Keddie and Mark J. Gasiorowski, eds., *Neither East nor West: Iran, the Soviet Union and the United States* (New Haven, Conn.: Yale University Press, 1990), 150–53.

61. Richard Cottam, *Nationalism in Iran* (Pittsburgh: University of Pittsburgh Press, 1979), 115–16.

62. NIE 63–5-54, "Post-Geneva Outlook in Indochina," August 3, 1954, in *United States–Vietnam Relations,* bk. 10, 694.

63. *FRUS, 1952–1954,* 14: 518, editorial note.

64. NIE 10–7-54, "Communist Courses of Action in Asia through 1957," November 23, 1954, ibid., 931–32, 934, 936–37.

65. CIA Director Allen Dulles, paper, November 18, 1954, *FRUS, 1952–1954,* 2, pt. 1: 778. This conclusion was based on reports from a U.S. agent in the Soviet government. See Christopher Andrew, *For the President's Eyes Only: Secret Intelligence and the American Presidency from Washington to Bush* (New York: HarperCollins, 1995), 213–14.

66. See "Landsdale Team's Report on Covert Saigon Mission in '54 and '55," in *The Pentagon Papers as Published by the New York Times* (New York: Bantam Books, 1971), 62–63; Ronald H. Spector, *Advice and Support: The Early Years of the United States Army in Vietnam, 1941–1960* (New York: Free Press, 1985), 240–42. Unfortunately, this key document on U.S. post-Geneva policy in South Vietnam was not available to the authors of the Pentagon study and has never been declassified.

67. *New York Times,* February 13, 1955.

68. DRV, Ministry of Defense, Institute of Vietnamese Military History, *Lich su Khang chien Chong My, Cuu nuoc (1954–1975)* [History of the Anti-U.S. Resistance for National Salvation (1954–1975)] (Hanoi: Su that, 1990), 1: 29; id., *Victory in Vietnam: The Official History of the People's Army of Vietnam, 1954–1975,* trans. Merle L. Pribbenow (Lawrence: University of Kansas Press, 2002), 47; Carlyle Thayer, *War by Other Means: National Liberation and Revolution in Viet-Nam, 1954–60* (Winchester, Mass.: Unwin Hyman, 1989), 113.

69. Tran Van Don's recollections of the U.S. role in these operations are in his serialized memoirs in *Tieng noi dan toc* [Voice of the People] (Saigon), May 20, 24, and 25, 1971. On the presence of U.S. advisers in the Quang Ngai and Binh Dinh sweeps, see *United States–Vietnam Relations,* bk. 2, pt. 4, A. 5, table 2, p. 22.

70. Memo of discussion at a meeting of the Operations Coordinating Board's Special Working Group on Vietnam, November 7, 1955, *FRUS, 1955–1957,* 1: 575; Rufe Phillips, "Before We Lost in South Vietnam," in Harvey Neese and

John O'Donnell, eds., *Prelude to Tragedy: Vietnam, 1960–1965* (Annapolis, Md.: Naval Institute Press, 2001), 21–23; William Nighswonger, *Rural Pacification in Vietnam* (New York: Praeger, 1968), 35–36.

71. *United States–Vietnam Relations*, bk. 2, pt. 4, A. 5, table 2, pp. 24, 27; William Colby, with James McCargar, *Lost Victory: A Firsthand Account of America's Sixteen-Year Involvement in Vietnam* (Chicago: Contemporary Books, 1989), 62; Nighswonger, *Rural Pacification in Vietnam*, 35–36; John C. Donnell, "Politics in South Vietnam: Doctrines of Authority in Conflict" (PhD diss., University of California, Berkeley, 1964), 290. Rufus Philips, who was the CIA adviser to the Civic Action Program, denied that the teams were involved in the Anti-Communist Denunciation Campaign, insisting that the Anti-Communist Denunciation Campaign did not begin until after the CIA's involvement with the teams had ended. Rufus Philips, interview by author, June 28, 2000, McLean, Virginia.

72. Memo of discussion at a meeting of the Operations Coordinating Board's Special Working Group on Vietnam, *FRUS, 1955–1957*, 1: 575; Thayer, *War by Other Means*, 113.

73. Donnell, "Politics in South Vietnam," 290; Nighswonger, *Rural Pacification in Vietnam*, 36. Nighswonger quotes a "confidential source" who had been involved in U.S. pacification efforts during the period. Nighswonger worked in the U.S. pacification program in Central Vietnam as a provincial representative of the U.S. Agency for International Development during 1962–64.

74. According to a VPA history of the war, the government categorized each family in a village in the South according to its past or present relations with the Viet Minh. Families with relatives who had regrouped to the North were subject to arrest and torture and forced to report on who were Communists in the village; those who were believed to have sympathy for or contact with the revolutionaries were treated somewhat less harshly. See DRV, Ministry of Defense, Institute of Vietnamese Military History, *History of the Anti-U.S. National Salvation War*, 21, 25. For confirmation of the repression of "Viet Minh families," based on later interviews with prisoners, see J. J. Zasloff, *Origins of the Insurgency in South Vietnam, 1954–1960: The Role of the Southern Vietminh Cadres*, RAND Corp. memo RM-5193/2-ISA/ARPA, May 1968, 9.

75. Nicholas G. M. Luykx, "Some Comparative Aspects of Rural Public Institutions in Thailand, the Philippines and Vietnam" (PhD diss., Cornell University, 1962), 725.

76. John D. Montgomery, *The Politics of Foreign Aid* (New York: Praeger, 1962), 70–71; Colby, *Lost Victory*, 62.

77. NIE 63–56, "Probable Developments in North and South Vietnam through Mid-1957," July 17, 1956, in *United States–Vietnam Relations*, bk. 10, pp. 1079–80.

78. NSC 5602/1, March 15, 1956, *FRUS, 1955–1957*, 19: 245.

79. Cottam, *Nationalism in Iran*, 115–16.

80. DRV, Ministry of Defense, Institute of Vietnamese Military History, *History of the Anti-U.S. National Salvation War*, 29; id., *Victory in Vietnam*, 44;

"Experiences in Turning XB Village in Kien Phong Province into a Combatant Village," in Michael Charles Conley, *The Communist Insurgent Infrastructure in South Vietnam: A Study of Organization and Strategy* (Washington, D.C.: Department of the Army, 1966), doc. E-6, 348; DOD, *United States–Vietnam Relations*, bk. 2, pt. 4, A.5, table 2, pp. 50–55; "Situation in South Vietnam from the Restoration of Peace to Date" (n.d., CDEC Log. No. 01-05333-70; a translation of an internal VWP document believed to have been prepared for a conference of the VWP headquarters in South Vietnam in 1961), 34, 49.

81. See Thayer, *War by Other Means*, 117; "Situation in South Vietnam," 34.

82. See Douglas A. Ross, *In the Interests of Peace: Canada and Vietnam, 1954–1973* (Toronto: University of Toronto Press, 1984), 121.

83. U.S. embassy, Saigon, telegram to secretary of state, December 16, 1955, State Department Central Files, 751G.00/12–1655, RG 59, NARA, 1984, 121.

84. For the full texts of the two agreements, along with the verbatim record of the final plenary session of the conference, see Cameron, ed., *Viet-Nam Crisis*, 1: 288–308.

85. The earliest version of this explanation for the failure of the Geneva Accords is *The Pentagon Papers: The Defense Department History of United States Decisionmaking on Vietnam. The Senator Gravel Edition* (Boston: Beacon Press, 1972), 1: 243–45. For subsequent accounts following the same explanation, see Gelb and Betts, *Irony of Vietnam*, 61; George C. Herring, *America's Longest War: The United States and Vietnam, 1950–1975* (New York: John Wiley & Sons, 1979), 55; Stanley Karnow, *Vietnam: A History* (New York: Viking, 1983), 213–14; Kahin, *Intervention*, 89–90; Gibbons, *U.S. Government and the Vietnam War*, 299–300; R.B. Smith, *An International History of the Vietnam War*, vol. 1 (New York: St. Martin's Press, 1984), 21–24; Marilyn B. Young, *The Vietnam Wars, 1945–1990* (New York: HarperCollins, 1991), 52–53; Anderson, *Trapped by Success*, 122–25; James R. Arnold, *The First Domino: Eisenhower, the Military and American Intervention in Vietnam* (New York: William Morrow, 1991), 286–87; William J. Duiker, *Ho Chi Minh* (New York: Hyperion, 2000), 470.

86. For a polemical argument based on the premise that the Geneva Accords were not binding on Diem, see Guenter Lewy, *America in Vietnam* (New York: Oxford University Press, 1978), 9–10.

87. State Department, Office of the Legal Adviser, memo, November 16, 1961, *FRUS, 1961–1963*, 1: 632.

88. DOD, *United States–Vietnam Relations*, bk. 1, pt. 4, A.3, p. 40; Department of State, telegram to U.S. embassy, Saigon, April 15, 1965 (declassified document in the Kai Bird Collection). The author is indebted to Kai Bird for making available his extensive collection of documents declassified under the Freedom of Information Act.

89. DOD, *United States–Vietnam Relations*, bk. 1, pt. 4, A.3, p. 14.

90. Gen. Lam Van Phat, Saigon, August 11, 1971, and Nguyen Huu Co, Saigon, November 22, 1971, interviews by the author. Cited in Gareth Porter,

"Imperialism and Social Structure in Twentieth Century Vietnam" (PhD diss., Cornell University, 1976), 246.

91. Pierre Melandri, "The Repercussions of the Geneva Conference: South Vietnam under a New Protector," in Lawrence Kaplan, Denise Artaud, and Mark Rubin, eds., *Dien Bien Phu and the Crisis of Franco-American Relations, 1954–1955* (Wilmington, Del.: SR Books, 1990), 203.

92. Memo of conversation between Mr. Purnell, Department of State and Mr. Pelletier, First Secretary of French Embassy, May 4, 1955, State Department Central Files, RG 59, 751G.00/5–0455, NARA.

93. See *FRUS, 1955–1957*, 1: 13, 41, 110; DOD, *United States–Vietnam Relations*, bk. 1, pt. 4, A.3, pp. 15, 34, 38.

94. On the degree of French dependence on U.S. assistance, see Kahin, *Intervention*, 42.

95. DOD, *United States–Vietnam Relations*, bk. 1, pt. 4, A.3, pp. 14–15; Melandri, "Repercussions," 198–202.

96. Leland Barrows, chief of the U.S. Operations Mission in Saigon in 1955, interview by the author, Washington, D.C., April 17, 1972. Quoted in Porter, "Imperialism and Social Structure," 247.

97. See Leland Barrows, "American Economic Aid to Viet Nam," *Viet My* [Saigon] 1, no. 2 (December 1956): 36.

98. U.S. Ambassador Donald Heath to Department of State, July 16, 1954, *FRUS, 1952–1954*, 13, pt. 2: 1842–43.

99. "Summary Minutes of Meeting in the Office of Secretary of State," October 8, 1954, ibid., 2123. Dulles foreshadowed this position in testimony before the Senate Foreign Relations Committee on July 16, a few days before the signing of the agreement. See *Executive Sessions* (cited n. 2 above), 633–58.

100. Memo of discussion, NSC meeting, January 27, 1955, *FRUS, 1955–1957*, 1: 68.

101. "Summary Minutes of Meeting in Office of Secretary of State," October 8, 1954, *FRUS, 1952–1954*, 13: 2123.

102. Department of State, Division of Research for Far East, "Considerations Bearing on the Problem of the 1956 Elections in Vietnam," February 6, 1955, Intelligence Report no. 6818. Cited in Kahin, *Intervention*, 89.

103. "US Policy on All-Viet-Nam Elections" (draft), April 4, 1955, 1, State Department Central Files 751G.00/4–455, NARA.

104. "U.S. Views on All-Vietnam Elections," May 5, 1955 (paper attached to memo from Douglas MacArthur II to Deputy Assistant Secretary of State William Sebald et al., May 6, 1955), State Department Central Files, 751G.00/5–0655, RG 59, NARA.

105. John Foster Dulles, telegram from Paris to State Department, May 13, 1955, State Department Central Files, 751G.00/5–1355, RG 59, NARA.

106. Memo of conversation between Kenneth T. Young Jr. and Denis Allen, assistant undersecretary of state, United Kingdom, May 13, 1955; memo of conversation between Kenneth T. Young Jr. and Jacques Roux, minister in charge of

Asian affairs, France, memo of conversation, May 13, 1955. State Department Central Files, 751G.oo/5–1355, RG 59, NARA.

107. "Draft Statement of U.S. Policy on All-Vietnam Elections," NSC 5529, *FRUS, 1955–1957*, 1: 411–12.

108. Telegram from Dulles to Saigon, May 27, 1955, ibid., 422–23.

109. U.S. embassy, Saigon, telegram to secretary of state, May 23, 1955, State Department Central Files, 751G.oo/5–2355, RG 59, NARA.

110. Anderson, *Trapped by Success*, 123.

111. Deputy Assistant Secretary of State William Sebald, memo to John Foster Dulles, June 8, 1955, *FRUS, 1955–57*, 1: 436–38.

112. Marc Trachtenberg, *A Constructed Peace* (Princeton, N.J.: Princeton University Press, 1999), 134–35.

113. Department of State, memo of conversation, June 8, 1955, *FRUS, 1955–1957*, 1: 439.

114. Deputy Assistant Secretary of State William Sebald, memo to John Foster Dulles, June 9, 1955, *FRUS, 1955–1957*, 1: 441–42.

115. Ibid., 443.

116. Deputy Assistant Secretary of State William Sebald, memo to John Foster Dulles, June 14, 1955, ibid., 453.

117. John Foster Dulles, telegram to Department of State, May 15, 1955, ibid., 5: 181.

118. CIA Director Allen Dulles, memo to executive secretary of the NSC (James S. Lay), "Intelligence Comments on NSC 5524," July 1, 1955, ibid., 247–49.

119. *New York Times*, June 14, 1955, cited in Franklin Weinstein, *Vietnam's Unheld Elections: The Failure to Carry Out the 1956 Reunification Elections and the Effect on Hanoi's Present Outlook* (Ithaca, N.Y.: Cornell University Southeast Asia Program, 1966), 30–32.

120. John Foster Dulles, telegram to U.S. embassies, Paris, Saigon, and London, June 15, 1955, State Department Central Files, 751G.oo/6–1555, RG 59, NARA; U.S. embassy, London, telegram to Dulles, June 16, 1955, State Department Central Files, 751G.oo/6–1655, RG 59, NARA.

121. John Foster Dulles, telegram to U.S. embassy, Saigon, June 16, 1955, State Department Central Files, 751G.oo/6–1655, RG 59, NARA. Unfortunately, the reply to this query from the Saigon embassy on June 17 was withdrawn from the files in 1987 for reasons of "national security."

122. Fred I. Greenstein, "Presidential Activism Eisenhower Style: A Reassessment Based on Archival Evidence" (paper delivered to the 179th Meeting of the Midwest Political Science Association, January 1979), quoted in Alexander L. George, *Presidential Decisionmaking in Foreign Policy: The Effective Use of Information and Advice* (Boulder, Colo.: Westview Press, 1980), 153.

123. Emmett John Hughes, *The Ordeal of Power: A Political Memoir of the Eisenhower Years* (New York: Atheneum, 1963), 206–7.

124. President Ngo Dinh Diem's broadcast declaration on the Geneva agreement and free elections, July 16, 1955, in *The Problem of Reunification* (Saigon: RVN Ministry of Information, 1958), 30–31.

125. John Foster Dulles, telegram from Geneva to Department of State, July 22, 1955, *FRUS, 1955–1957,* 1: 494.

126. John Foster Dulles, telegram to U.S. embassy, Saigon, July 22, 1955, ibid., 495.

127. "Declaration of the Government of Vietnam on the Reunification of Vietnam," in *Problem of Reunification,* 32–33.

128. Weinstein, *Vietnam's Unheld Elections,* 32–33.

129. NIE 63.1–55, "Probable Developments in North Vietnam to July 1956," July 19, 1955, in *United States–Vietnam Relations,* bk. 10, p. 995. The estimate was summarized for Dulles in a memo by his "Special Assistant for Intelligence" on July 27, 1955. See *FRUS, 1955–1957,* 1: 498–99.

130. Kenneth Young, letter to U.S. Ambassador Frederick Reinhardt, Saigon, July 28, 1955, *FRUS, 1955–1957,* 1: 500.

131. John Foster Dulles, telegram to U.S. embassy, Saigon, September 23, 1955, State Department Central Files, 751G.00/9–2355, RG 59, NARA.

132. Kenneth Young, letter to U.S. Ambassador Frederick Reinhardt, Saigon, October 5, 1955, *FRUS, 1955–1957,* 1: 552.

133. Fisher Howe, acting special assistant to the secretary, memo to the acting secretary, October 26, 1955, State Department Central Files, 751G.00/ 10–2655, RG 59, National Archives.

134. NIE 100–7-55, "World Situation and Trends," *FRUS, 1955–1957,* 19: 138.

135. Paul Kattenburg, *The Vietnam Trauma in American Foreign Policy, 1945–1975* (New Brunswick, N.J.: Transaction Books, 1980), 63.

136. John Foster Dulles to U.S. embassy, Saigon, December 2, 1955, *FRUS, 1955–1957,* 1: 595; U.S. embassy, Paris, telegram to Dulles, December 5, 1955, State Department Central Files, 751G.00/12–0555, RG 59, NARA.

137. John Foster Dulles, memo to the president, February 10, 1956, *FRUS, 1955–1957,* 1: 642.

138. NIE 63–56, "Probable Developments in North and South Vietnam through Mid-1957," July 17, 1956, in *United States–Vietnam Relations,* bk. 10, pp. 1067, 1071, 1077–80. For an estimate in 1957 reaffirming the substance of this estimate, see NIE 63.2–57, "The Prospects for North Vietnam," May 14, 1957, ibid., 1102.

139. Memo of discussion at the 287th meeting of the NSC, June 7, 1956, *FRUS, 1955–1957,* 1: 702.

140. Kattenburg, *Vietnam Trauma,* 63. On the regrets of some CIA analysts on U.S. policy toward the elections, see Kai Bird, *The Color of Truth: McGeorge Bundy and William Bundy: Brothers in Arms* (New York: Touchstone, 1998), 178.

4. NORTH VIETNAMESE POLICY UNDER
THE AMERICAN THREAT

1. See Ho Chi Minh, "Report to the 6th Plenum of the Viet Nam Workers' Party Central Committee (July 15, 1954)," in id., *Selected Writings* (Hanoi: Foreign Languages Publishing House, 1977), 175, 177, 179.

2. Le Duan, *Ta nhat dinh thang, dich nhat dinh thua* [We Shall Certainly Win; the Enemy Will Certainly Lose] (South Vietnam: Tien Phong, 1966).

3. P. J. Honey, a longtime foe of the Ho Chi Minh government, claimed that Dong told a Vietnamese friend of Honey's right after the Geneva Conference, "You know as well as I do that there won't be elections." See P. J. Honey, *Communism in North Vietnam* (Cambridge, Mass.: MIT Press, 1963), 6. This story lacks credibility because Honey would not have been close to anyone with whom Pham Van Dong would have discussed the party's internal view of the chances for elections. Unfortunately, William J. Duiker has given this undocumented and dubious story new life by quoting it, without citing the original source, in two different books. See Duiker, *Ho Chi Minh* (New York: Hyperion, 2000), 467, and id., *The Communist Road to Power*, 2d ed. (Boulder, Colo.: Westview Press, 1996), 183.

4. This error in analyzing the international situation was revealed in a rare published admission at a cadre conference following the party's Seventh Central Committee Plenum in June 1955. See *Nhan Dan*, June 7, 1955.

5. John Gunther Dean, "Crystal Balling of the Political Future of Viet Nam" (n.d. [ca. July 1955]), State Department lot files, Records of the Vietnam Desk Officer, 1954–55, lot 58D257, box 3, microfilm C0014, roll 39, NARA.

6. *Nhan Dan*, November 17, 1955, trans. in U.S. consul, Hanoi, to secretary of state, November 17, 1955, State Department Central Files, 751G.00/17–1155, RG 59, NARA.

7. Ilya Gaiduk, *Confronting Vietnam: Soviet Policy toward the Indochina Conflict, 1954–1963* (Stanford, Calif.: Stanford University Press, 2003), 74–75.

8. Truong Chinh, *Tinh hinh hien tai va nhiem vu truoc mat* [The Present Situation and Immediate Tasks] (report read to the Seventh Enlarged Conference of the Central Committee, 1955; for internal circulation only).

9. "Speech Closing the Ninth (Enlarged) Plenum of the Central Committee of the Viet-Nam Workers Party," April 24, 1956, in Bernard B. Fall, ed., *Ho Chi Minh on Revolution: Selected Writings* (New York: Praeger, 1967), 298–99.

10. *Tai lieu huong dan hoc tap nghi quyet Dai Hoi IV cua Dang* [Guidance Document for Studying the Resolution of the Fourth Party Congress] (Hanoi: Nha xuat ban sach giao Khoa Mac-Le-Nin, 1977), 86. The only reference in Vietnamese documents to pressures on Hanoi from *both* socialist allies to pursue only peaceful struggle in the South that I have been able to find is in this 1976 study document for the party congress that year intended for internal distribution among party cadres only. I am indebted to Motoo Furuta, University of Tokyo, for providing a copy of this document.

11. Le Duan, *Ta nhat dinh thang*, 7.

12. For analyses of this characteristic of DRV leadership politics, see Gareth Porter, *Vietnam: The Politics of Bureaucratic Socialism* (Ithaca, N.Y.: Cornell University Press, 1993), 115–18; David W. P. Elliott, "North Vietnam since Ho," *Problems of Communism* 4 (July–August 1975): 41–44.

13. Le Duan, *Ta nhat dinh thang*, 7.

14. "Duong loi cach mang mien nam" [The Path of Revolution in the South] (document no. 1002 in the Jeffrey Race Collection, available on microfilm from Center for Research Libraries, Chicago), 2. William J. Duiker describes Le Duan's thesis as leaving "open the possibility that the struggle to complete the unification of the two zones might require the resumption of revolutionary war." See Duiker, *Communist Road to Power*, 190. However, the document never mentions the possibility of a return to warfare of any kind in the future, and it repeatedly refers to the "peaceful struggle line," which it defines as taking "the political forces of the people as the base rather than using people's armed forces to struggle with the existing government to achieve their revolutionary objectives."

15. DRV, Ministry of Defense, Institute of Vietnamese Military History, *Victory in Vietnam: The Official History of the People's Army of Vietnam*, trans. Merle L. Pribbenow (Lawrence: University of Kansas Press, 2002), 43; id., *Cuoc Khang chien Chong My, Cuu nuoc 1954–1975: Nhung su kien quan su* [The Anti-U.S. Resistance for National Salvation, 1954–1975: Military Events] (Hanoi: Nha Xuat Ban Quan Doi, 1980), 22 (trans. JPRS 80968, June 3, 1982); Le Duan, letter to Muoi Cuc (Nguyen Van Linh) and others, February 7, 1961, in *Thu vao Nam* [Letters to the South] (Hanoi: Foreign Languages Publishing House, 1986), 9–11; "Situation in South Vietnam from the Restoration of Peace to Date" (n.d., CDEC Log. No. 01-05333-70; a translation of an internal VWP document believed to have been prepared for a conference of the VWP headquarters in South Vietnam in 1961), Avery Collection, 27, 40, 44, 51, 52. In his letter to the southern regional committee, Le Duan responded to criticism of his "Path of Revolution in the South" directive and of the regional party committee's position when he was its chairman.

16. For the Vietnamese party slogan, which I have translated from the Vietnamese, see Carlyle Thayer, *War by Other Means: National Liberation and Revolution in Viet-Nam, 1954–60* (Winchester, Mass.: Unwin Hyman, 1989), 84. The Chinese formula is from Chen Jian, *Mao's China and the Cold War* (Chapel Hill, N.C.: University of North Carolina Press, 2001), 206.

17. "Situation in South Vietnam," 49, 51–52.

18. Nguyen Co Thach, interview by the author, Hanoi, August 2, 1982.

19. Janos Radvanyi, *Delusion and Reality: Gambits, Hoaxes and Diplomatic One-Upmanship in Vietnam* (South Bend, Ind.: Gateway Editions, 1978), 23.

20. "Resolution of the Fifteenth Plenum (Enlarged) of the Party Central Committee (2d Term): Strengthen Unity, Determinedly Struggle to Maintain Peace, Achieve National Unification," in Vietnamese Communist Party, *Mot so van kien cua dang ve Chong My, Cuu nuoc* [Some Party Documents on the Anti-U.S. National Salvation Resistance] (Hanoi: Su that, 1985), 1 (1954–65): 117.

21. "Muc tieu va phuong huong cua toan dang, toan dan ta" [The Objective and Line of the Struggle of Our Whole Party and People], *Hoc Tap* [Binh Duong Province], May 25, 1960 (Jeffrey Race Collection, Cornell University

Library, document no. 1938), translated in Gareth Porter, ed., *Vietnam: The Definitive Documentation of Human Decisions* (Stanfordville, N.Y.: E. M. Coleman Enterprises, 1979), 2: 56.

22. "22 cau hoi ve duong loi cach mang Viet Nam o mien nam," [Twenty-two Questions about the Path of the Vietnamese Revolution in the South] (captured party document no. 206 in the Douglas Pike Collection at the Library of Congress), translated in Porter, ed., *Vietnam*, 2: 52.

23. "Objective and Line of the Struggle," in Porter, ed., *Vietnam*, 2: 55.

24. DRV, Ministry of Defense, Institute of Vietnamese Military History, *Victory in Vietnam*, 65.

25. "Situation and Tasks in 1961" (English translation of document no. 241 in the Douglas Pike Collection).

26. VWP committee for South Vietnam, letter to party chapters, March 28, 1960, in Porter, ed., *Vietnam*, 2: 59–68.

27. Le Duan, letter to Nguyen Van Linh and others, February 7, 1961, in *Letters to the South*, 12, 14, 15.

28. See Vietnam Press (the Diem government's official press agency), June 9, 15, and 28, 1960, and July 22 and 26, 1960; DRV, Ministry of Defense, Institute of Vietnamese Military History, *Victory in Vietnam*, 63.

29. Le Duan, letter to Nguyen Van Linh, in *Letters to the South*, 10, 11, 27. On Diem's forces, see "Prospects for North and South Vietnam," NIE 63-59, 26 May 1959, in *United States–Vietnam Relations*, bk. 10, p. 1193.

30. Le Duan, *Letters to the South*, 14–15.

31. VWP Committee on Party History, *50 Nam hoat dong cua Dang Cong San Viet Nam* [Fifty Years of Activities of the Vietnamese Communist Party] (Hanoi: Su that, 1979), 171.

32. DRV, Institute for Research on Marxism-Leninism and Ho Chi Minh Thought, *Lich su Dang Cong San Viet Nam, Tap II (1954–1975)* [History of the Vietnamese Communist Party, vol. 2 (1954–1975)] (Hanoi: Chinh Tri Quoc Gia, 1995), 174.

33. DRV, Institute for Research on Marxism-Leninism and Ho Chi Minh Thought, *History of the Vietnamese Communist Party*, 2: 175.

34. Le Duan, letter to Nguyen Van Linh, in *Letters to the South*, 9–10.

35. Hoang Tung, interview by the author, Hanoi, August 2, 1982.

36. Foreign Minister Nguyen Co Thach, interview by the author, Hanoi, August 2, 1982.

37. *Tai lieu huong dan hoc tap nghi quyet Dai Hoi IV cua Dang*, 79–80; editorial, *Nhan Dan*, July 26, 1961, FBIS, Far East, July 26, 1961, JJJ1–2.

38. Excerpts from "Resolution of an Enlarged Conference of the Central Office for South Vietnam (COSVN), October 1961," in Porter, ed., *Vietnam*, 2: 119–20, 122. A full translation of the draft form of the same resolution is also available in the series of translations done by the Combined Documents Exploitation Center (CDEC). See "A Draft of the Resolution Adopted by R (COSVN) in Its Open *[sic]* Conference in [October] 61," CDEC Report no. 6 028 0207 70, Avery Collection, 11–12.

39. "Resolution of the Political Bureau on Revolutionary Work in the South," February 26–27, 1962, in *Mot so van kien cua dang ve Chong My, Cuu nuo,* 1: 140, 147, 156–57.

40. Ibid., 157.

41. DRV, Ministry of Defense, Institute of Vietnamese Military History, *Victory in Vietnam,* 109–10, 113.

42. Le Duan, letter to Nguyen Van Linh and COSVN, July 7, 1962, in *Thu vao Nam* [Letters to the South] (Hanoi: Su that, 1985), 51–52, 54. This letter is not included in the English-language version of the book cited in n. 27 above.

43. Ibid., 52–53. Pham Van Dong made the same point in a conversation with the Polish ambassador, Mieczyslaw Maneli, in June 1963. The Laotian agreement, he said, did not reflect the "real distribution of power" within Laos, but Hanoi had agreed to the compromise because it wanted to "show good will" and to demonstrate that "the Western powers can and must talk to us." Mieczyslaw Maneli, *War of the Vanquished* (New York: Harper & Row, 1971), 187.

44. Le Duan, letter to Nguyen Van Linh, in *Thu vao Nam,* 54–55, 62–64.

45. Thomas L. Hughes, "Communist Attitudes toward Neutralization for South Vietnam" (Department of State Bureau of Intelligence and Research, research memo, January 20, 1964, LBJL), 2; Robert Brigham, *Guerrilla Diplomacy: The NLF's Foreign Relations and the Vietnam War* (Ithaca, N.Y.: Cornell University Press, 1998), 29.

46. George McT. Kahin, *Intervention: How America Became Involved in Vietnam* (New York: Knopf, 1986), 117; U.S. embassy, Saigon, telegram to secretary of state, April 7, 1962, NSF, box 196, "Vietnam General, 3/29/62–3/31/62" file, JFKL.

47. U.S. embassy, Phnom Penh, airgram to Department of State, April 5, 1962, NSF, box 196, "Vietnam General, 4/1/62–4/10/62" file, JFKL; Cheng Guan Ang, *Vietnamese Communists' Relations with China and the Second Indochina Conflict, 1956–1962* (Jefferson, N.C.: McFarland, 1997), 222–23, 225; U.S. embassy, Saigon, Foreign Service dispatch to Department of State, May 17, 1962, State Department Central Files 751K.5/5–1762, RG 59, NARA; Fredrik Logevall, *Choosing War: The Lost Chance for Peace and the Escalation of War in Vietnam* (Berkeley: University of California Press, 1999), 8.

48. Marek Thee, *Notes of a Witness: Laos and the Second Indochinese War* (New York: Vintage Books, 1973), 283–85, 335. British diplomats attributed Souvanna's convictions that the Laos settlement could not be effective without a settlement in South Vietnam to Hanoi's "blackmail." See Logevall, *Choosing War,* 425 n. 22. On Moscow's failure to support reconvening the Geneva Conference on the subject of South Vietnam, see 40–41 above.

49. See Duiker, *Communist Road to Power,* 224 nn. 11 and 12, and 403; Logevall, *Choosing War,* 10–11.

50. The United Kingdom sent its top diplomat in Southeast Asia to Phnom Penh from May 11 to 15, 1962, to express strong opposition to Sihanouk's proposal. See Ang, *Vietnamese Communist Relations,* 225.

51. Thee, *Notes of a Witness,* 286–87; memo of conversation, Geneva, July 22, 1962, *FRUS, 1961–1963,* 24: 869.

52. Jean Lacouture, *Vietnam: Between Two Truces,* trans. Konrad Kellen and Joel Carmichal (New York: Vintage Books, 1966), 40–41.

53. William J. Duiker suggests that the Hanoi strategy was to cultivate an "under the blanket" (i.e., covert) group of Vietnamese exiles in France who would be "neutralist in name but pro-Hanoi in actuality." See Duiker, *Communist Road to Power,* 223. Although it is not cited, this is apparently based on Le Duan's letter to COSVN of July 7, 1962, which suggests allying with "progressive and prestigious personalities having sympathy for the revolution, but not yet known to the enemy, in order to use them in the struggle to establish a multifaction government later." Le Duan, in *Thu vao Nam,* 65. But this related only to personalities *within* South Vietnam. In regard to the exile community in France, the Vietnamese sought out only personalities who were neutralist but far from being pro-Communist.

54. Georges Chaffard, *Les Deux Guerres du Vietnam: De Valluy à Westmoreland* (Paris: La Table Ronde, 1969), 266–71.

55. Tran Van Dinh, interview with the author, Washington, D.C., July 27, 1967.

56. Tran Van Dinh, interviews with the author, Washington, D.C., July 27, 1967, and October 22, 1967; Ellen J. Hammer, *A Death in November: America in Vietnam, 1963* (New York: Dutton, 1987, 269–70.

57. Michael Forrestal, JFK's NSC specialist on Vietnam, interview with the author, New York, November 27, 1967. Forrestal recalled that when rumors of Nhu's negotiations with the North reached Washington, some CIA officials did not share the alarm of other U.S. officials but said, "So what? If they can negotiate without losing their shirts, what's wrong with that?"

58. Report no. 19 of the meeting of the Inter-ministerial Committee for Strategic Hamlets at Gia Long Palace, August 31, 1962 (mimeo). According to Tran Van Dinh, who was chosen by Nhu to negotiate with the North Vietnamese, Nhu had actually begun planning to set up a guerrilla base in Long An province. The guerrilla movement he had in mind would be independent of the Communists but not necessarily antagonistic to them. Tran Van Dinh, interview with the author, Washington, D.C., October 27, 1967.

59. David Kaiser, *American Tragedy: Kennedy, Johnson and the Origins of the Vietnam War* (New York: Belknap Press of Harvard University Press, 2000), 239.

60. Malgorzata Gnoiska, "Maneli and Nhu: Rumors Revisited: The United States, Poland and Vietnam, 1963" (paper presented to the Annual Meeting of the Society for Historians of American Foreign Relations, Austin, Texas, June 24–26, 2004).

61. Andrew Vickerman, *The Fate of the Peasantry: Premature "Transition to Socialism" in the Democratic Republic of Vietnam,* Yale University Southeast Asian Studies Monograph Series, no. 28 (1986), table 4, 279; Nguyen Tien Hung, *Economic Development of Socialist Vietnam, 1955–1980* (New York: Praeger, 1977), 127–28.

62. DRV, Ministry of Defense, Institute of Vietnamese Military History, *Victory in Vietnam*, 94.

63. Vickerman, *Fate of the Peasantry*, 190.

64. Geoffrey Warner, "The United States and the Fall of Diem, Part I: The Coup That Never Was," *Australian Outlook* 28 (December 1974): 248–49.

65. DRV, Institute for Research on Marxism-Leninism and Ho Chi Minh Thought, *History of the Vietnamese Communist Party*, 239–42.

66. *New Times* (Moscow), May 29, 1963: 14. Text in Porter, ed., *Vietnam*, 2: 183.

67. For the text and significance of the 1953 interview, see Porter, ed., *Vietnam*, 1: 491–92.

68. Mieczyslaw Maneli, "Vietnam, '63 and Now," *New York Times,* January 27, 1975. Maneli had held back his most important revelations about his role in helping achieve North-South peace negotiations in *War of the Vanquished*, waiting until the war was nearly over.

69. Joseph Alsop, "Very Ugly Stuff," *Washington Post*, September 18, 1963.

70. Maneli's denial is reported in *Christian Science Monitor*, October 10, 1963. Dinh's confirmation of the letter from Hanoi is from an interview with the author in Washington, D.C., October 27, 1967. Maneli went to great lengths to try to hide his role as an intermediary between the two Vietnamese regimes, claiming that he had never even seen Nhu except at a party. Maneli went so far as to beg both *New York Times* reporter David Halberstam and UPI reporter Neil Sheehan to publish his denial. They both refused to do so, because they had reason to believe that he was hiding the truth. Neil Sheehan, interview with the author, Washington, D.C., July 12, 1967.

71. Hoang Tung, editor of *Nhan Dan*, interview with the author, Hanoi, December 29, 1974.

72. Frederick Nolting, *From Trust to Tragedy: The Political Memoirs of Frederick Nolting, Kennedy's Ambassador to Diem's Vietnam* (New York: Praeger, 1988), 117–18. Nhu told the same story to two British diplomats in August. See Logevall, *Choosing War*, 6.

73. *Dong Nai* [Saigon], February 2 and 4, 1969. This very long investigative series of articles, of which these were nos. 75 and 76, was based on interviews with a large number of former officials who had worked for Nhu and Diem.

74. Tran Van Dinh, interview with the author, Washington, D.C., July 27, 1967. The contacts between the NLF and Nhu were undoubtedly very closely held by Kiem and other party members in the NLF leadership. Truong Nhu Tang, a non-Communist member of the NLF's Central Committee, recalls in his memoirs that Nhu's overtures to the NLF had been regarded as "not serious" and merely intended to "blackmail the Americans." See Truong Nhu Tang, *A Viet Cong Memoir* (New York: Vintage Books, 1985), 51. However, Tang was not privy to the thinking of the inner core of the NLF's leadership, who were party members. Indeed, Tang was not even aware at that point that Tran Buu Kiem had secretly become a party member twelve years earlier. See ibid., 69.

75. Tran Van Dinh, interviews with the author. Asked about the account given by Dinh, the Indian ICC delegate Ram Goburdhun denied any knowledge of such an understanding and said he doubted that Nhu and Diem would have negotiated such an agreement. But he admitted that Nehru might well have thrown his support behind the kind of agreement that Dinh had outlined to me. Ram Goburdhun, interview with the author, New Delhi, November 15, 1970.

76. Tran Van Dinh, interview with the author, October 21, 1967.

77. Col. Bui Tin, deputy editor, *Quan Doi Nhan Dan,* interview with the author, Hanoi, June 23, 1984.

78. Lt. Gen. Tran Cong Man, editor of *Quan Doi Nhan Dan,* interview with the author, June 23, 1984.

79. Two different translations of the Ninth Plenum resolution, based on the same captured document, are available, one of which was published by the U.S. Mission in Vietnam. The published version is "Resolution: Ninth Conference of Central 12/63," *Viet-Nam Documents and Research Notes* [Saigon], document no. 96, 8–9, 21. A different translation of the same captured document is CDEC Log No. 01–0516–70, Avery Collection. It should be noted that the translation in the published version is occasionally significantly different from the unpublished translation. The published version, which appears to be more accurate, is used for these quotations, however.

80. "Resolution: Ninth Conference of Central 12/63," *Viet-Nam Documents and Research Notes,* 12, 15, 21.

81. "Resolution: Ninth Conference of Central 12/63," 9.

82. Col. Bui Tin, interview with the author; Bui Tin, *Following Ho Chi Minh: The Memoirs of a North Vietnamese Colonel* (Honolulu: University of Hawaii Press, 1995), 49.

83. For the interpretation of the plenum decision as ordering a strategy of quick victory, see Duiker, *Ho Chi Minh,* 535; Robert S. McNamara, James Blight, and Robert Brigham, with Thomas Biersteker and Herbert Schandler, *Argument without End: In Search of Answers to the Vietnam Tragedy* (New York: Public Affairs, 1999), 183. The latter work seriously misrepresents the text of the resolution. It also quotes VPA Colonel Bui Tin's comment "We were completely lightheaded in the firm belief that victory was ours" as referring to the Ninth Plenum, whereas he was speaking, not, in fact, about the strategic assessment of the Vietnamese party leadership at the time of the Ninth Plenum, but about the attitudes of North Vietnamese military officers at the outset of the war against the United States. See Bui Tin, *Following Ho Chi Minh,* 52.

84. "Resolution: Ninth Conference of Central 12/63," 13, 15, 22, 24.

85. Bui Tin, interview with the author.

86. Ibid. For a similar account from Bui Tin, see Stanley Karnow, *Vietnam: A History* (New York: Viking, 1983), 331–32.

87. Wallace J. Thies, *When Governments Collide: Coercion and Diplomacy in the Vietnam Conflict, 1964–1968* (Berkeley: University of California Press,

1980), 22–24, quotation at 24; Robert S. McNamara, with Brian VanDemark, *In Retrospect: The Tragedy and Lessons of Vietnam* (New York: Vintage Books, 1995), 117.

88. DRV, Ministry of Defense, Institute of Vietnamese Military History, *Victory in Vietnam*, 128–30.

89. *New York Times*, June 19, 1964, 5.

90. Thies, *When Governments Collide*, 40–42; Logevall, *Choosing War*, 161.

91. Nguyen Co Thach, interview by the author, Hanoi, June 28, 1984; Col. Bui Tin and Lt. Gen. Tran Cong Man, interviews by the author, Hanoi, June 23, 1984. Thach did not attend the Central Committee plenum but had heard details of it from participants. None of the three could recall the exact date of the plenum, but Thach said that it was "perhaps one week after the bombing." It seems almost certain that the date was less than a week after the bombing. Le Duan's trip to Beijing on August 13 must have been after the plenum because it is very unlikely that Hanoi would have informed the Chinese of such a decision unless it had been already approved by the Central Committee. The existence of this plenum has never been revealed in documents published by the Vietnamese party.

92. The Nguyen Chi Thanh estimate of 100,000 troops is from the Bui Tin interview. The qualification that the estimate applied only in the relatively short run is from the Nguyen Co Thach interview. Tran Cong Man confirmed the "hundreds of thousands" estimate.

93. Bui Tin interview with the author.

94. Ibid.

95. Tran Cong Man interview with the author.

96. Nguyen Co Thach interview with the author.

97. See 60 above.

98. Kahin, *Intervention*, 243; William P. Bundy, untitled MS, OSDH, 22–18.

99. The September Political Bureau resolution has not been published in full, presumably because the VCP is still sensitive about direct discussion of the timing of the decision to dispatch regular North Vietnamese troops to the South before the arrival of the U.S. combat forces. This paragraph is based on DRV, Ministry of Defense, Institute of Vietnamese Military History, *Lich su Quan Doi Nhan Dan Viet Nam*, vol. 2, bk. 1, 243–44; id., *Victory in Vietnam*, 138; DRV, Institute for Research on Marxism-Leninism and Ho Chi Minh Thought, *Lich Su Dang Cong San Viet Nam*, 2: 267. None of these sources use quotation marks, but the excerpts that I have quoted appear to be direct quotations from the document. The party's change of mind about U.S. intentions in the Tonkin Gulf is from "Summary of an Assessment by Bac Huong Disseminated by Comrade Sau" (translation of a captured top secret party document, n.d., but presumably October 1964), CDEC Doc. Log No. 05–2400–70, October 2, 1970, 30, Avery Collection. The document reports the assessment reached by the Political Bureau at its late September meeting.

100. "Summary of an Assessment by Bac Huong," 28–30.

101. DRV, Institute of Vietnamese Military History, *History of the Vietnam*

People's Army, 245; DRV, Institute of Military History, *Victory in Vietnam,* 138. Neither source mentions the Political Bureau decision.

102. An exhibit on the Ho Chi Minh Trail that the author saw in the Museum of the Revolution in Hanoi in 1984 put the widening of the trail for mechanized traffic "at the end of 1964." The decision to widen it may have been made in principle at the Central Committee meeting in August and confirmed by the September Political Bureau meeting after further thought.

103. "Mao Zedong and Pham van Dong, Hoang Van Hoan, Beijing, 5 October 1964," in Odd Arne Westad et al., eds., *77 Conversations between Chinese and Foreign Leaders on the Wars in Indochina, 1964–1977* (Washington, D.C.: Cold War International History Project, 1998), 75.

104. The identification of VPA units is from DRV, Ministry of Defense, Institute of Vietnamese Military History, *Victory in Vietnam,* 136, 142. The analysis is from "Intensification of the Military Operations in Vietnam: Concept and Appraisal, Report of Ad Hoc Study Group, July 14, 1965," annex to Section F, Harriman Papers, National Security Archive.

105. U.S. Department of State, "Working Paper on the North Vietnamese Role in the War in South Vietnam," *Vietnam Documents and Research Notes,* no. 37 (May 1968): 12, 19.

106. "The Attack on Danang Air Base," U.S. Marine Corps Medium Helicopter Squadron 365, www.angelfire.com/de/HMM365Vietnam/hist65july.html (accessed June 18, 2004).

107. "Intensification of the Military Operations," annex to Section F.

108. Thomas L. Hughes, director of intelligence and research, Department of State, to Dean Rusk, "North Vietnam and Negotiations," research memo, RFE-29, July 28, 1965, Thomson Papers, box 27, "Southeast Asia, 1961–65": Vietnam file, JFKL

109. Thomas L. Hughes, note to Dean Rusk, "Communists Hint Interest in South Vietnam Settlement," November 20, 1964, lot files 66D93, Bureau of Far Eastern Affairs, subject files of the assistant secretary, box 1, RG 59, NARA; Allen S. Whiting, memo to William P. Bundy, December 23, 1964, lot file 66D93, Bureau of Far Eastern Affairs, subject files of the assistant secretary, box 1, RG 59, NARA.

110. U.S. embassy, Paris, telegram to Department of State, January 29, 1965, *FRUS, 1964–1968,* 2: 105–6; Hughes, research memo to Rusk, July 28, 1965.

111. Logevall, *Choosing War,* 366.

112. Le Duan, *Thu vao Nam,* 72–73.

113. The following account of Le Duan's strategy is based on *Thu vao Nam,* 73–75, 84–88.

114. On secret negotiations between the NLF and Khanh from December 1964 and January 1965, see Kahin, *Intervention,* 295–96; Brigham, *Guerrilla Diplomacy,* 36–37. On the rising demands in South Vietnam for peace and neutralism during this period, see Kahin, *Intervention,* 272, 288; Logevall, *Choosing War,* 320–21.

115. Le Duan, *Thu vao Nam,* 71.

116. "Comrade Sau's Briefing at the Cadre Congress of the Liberation Army Headquarters, held on 15 January 65" (translation of captured document), CDEC Doc. Log No. 01–0526–70, Avery Collection, 3. The document repeatedly makes the distinction between being able to win specific military victories and defeating the enemy, emphasizing that the PLAF was too weak to accomplish the latter. Ibid., 15, 17–18.

117. "Nghi quyet Hoi nghi lan thu 11 (dac biet) cua Ban Chap hanh Trung uong Dang (Khoa III)" [Resolution of the Eleventh Plenum (Special) of the Party Central Committee (3d Session)], March 25–27, 1965, in *Mot so van kien cua dang ve Chong My, Cuu nuoc* [Some Party Documents on the Anti-U.S. National Salvation Resistance], 218; Le Duan, letter to Nguyen Chi Thanh, May 1965, in *Letters to the South*, 27.

118. Ambassador Charles Bohlen, Paris, telegram to Department of State, March 4, 1965, in DOD, *United States–Vietnam Relations, 1945–1967*, Settlement of the Conflict, unpublished volumes, VI.C.1, Negotiations, 1965–1966, 26.

119. Excerpt from report of Pham Van Dong, April 8, 1965, in George McT. Kahin and John W. Lewis, *The United States in Vietnam*, rev. ed. (New York: Delta, 1969), app. 14, 506–7.

120. Logevall, *Choosing War*, xxiii. For a somewhat discursive discussion about whether neutralization of South Vietnam was possible, involving former U.S. and North Vietnamese officials, see McNamara et al., *Argument without End*, 129–50.

5. KENNEDY'S STRUGGLE WITH THE NATIONAL
SECURITY BUREAUCRACY

1. The earliest works to take this position were Louise FitzSimons, *The Kennedy Doctrine* (New York: Random House, 1972); Richard J. Walton, *Cold War and Counter-Revolution: The Foreign Policy of John F. Kennedy* (Baltimore: Johns Hopkins University Press, 1972); Leslie H. Gelb and Richard K. Betts, *The Irony of Vietnam: The System Worked* (Washington, D.C.: Brookings Institution, 1979), 69–95. Studies drawing on archival documents that view JFK's Vietnam policy as a reflection of his Cold War beliefs include Steven Pelz, "John F. Kennedy's 1961 Vietnam War Decisions," *Journal of Strategic Studies* 4 (1981): 356–85; George McT. Kahin, *Intervention: How America Became Involved in Vietnam* (New York: Knopf, 1986), 128–81; Lawrence J. Bassett and Stephen E. Pelz, "The Failed Search for Victory: Vietnam and the Politics of War," in Thomas G. Paterson, ed., *Kennedy's Quest for Victory: American Foreign Policy, 1961–1963* (New York: Oxford University Press, 1989), 251; James N. Giglio, *The Presidency of John F. Kennedy* (Lawrence: University of Kansas Press, 1991), 239–54; Gary R. Hess, "Commitment in the Age of Counterinsurgency: Kennedy's Vietnam Options and Decisions, 1961–1963," in David L. Anderson, ed., *Shadow on the White House: Presidents and the Vietnam War, 1945–1975* (Lawrence: University of Kansas Press, 1993), 63–83; George C. Herring, *America's Longest War: The United States and Vietnam, 1950–1975*,

2d ed. (New York: McGraw-Hill, 1986), 73–107; Robert Buzzanco, *Masters of War: Military Dissent and Politics in the Vietnam Era* (Cambridge: Cambridge University Press, 1996), 81–151; Fredrik Logevall, *Choosing War: The Lost Chance for Peace and the Escalation of the War in Vietnam* (Berkeley: University of California Press, 1999), 30–74; Robert D. Shulzinger, *A Time for War: The United States and Vietnam, 1941–1975* (New York: Oxford University Press, 1999), 97–123.

2. See Robert Weisbrot, *Maximum Danger: Kennedy, the Missiles and the Crisis of American Confidence* (Chicago: Ivan R. Dee, 2001); David Kaiser, *American Tragedy: Kennedy, Johnson and the Origins of the Vietnam War* (Cambridge, Mass.: Belknap Press of Harvard University Press, 2000); Robert Dallek, *An Unfinished Life: John F. Kennedy, 1917–1963* (Boston: Little, Brown, 2003); Sheldon M. Stern, *Averting the Final Failure: John F. Kennedy and the Secret Cuban Missile Crisis Meetings* (Stanford, Calif.: Stanford University Press, 2003); Howard Jones, *Death of a Generation: How the Assassinations of Diem and JFK Prolonged the Vietnam War* (New York: Oxford University Press, 2003).

3. On early signs of Kennedy's skeptical mind and capacity for critical thinking, see Dallek, *Unfinished Life*, 42, 59, 62. On his open-mindedness and his skepticism about conventional Cold War thinking—and particularly military thinking—before becoming president, see Arthur Schlesinger Jr., *Robert Kennedy and His Times* (Boston: Houghton Mifflin, 1978), 419; Harris Wofford, *Of Kennedys and Kings: Making Sense of the Sixties* (New York: Farrar, Straus & Giroux, 1980), 236–37; Weisbrot, *Maximum Danger*, 18–19, 31, 34–35, 41–43; Michael Beschloss, *The Crisis Years: Kennedy and Khrushchev, 1960–1963* (New York: HarperCollins, 1991), 70; Stern, *Averting the Final Failure*, 32–34.

4. Geoffrey Perret, *Jack: A Life Like No Other* (New York: Random House, 2001), 170; Laurence Leamer, *The Kennedy Men, 1901–1963* (New York: HarperCollins, 2001), 288–329; Denise Bostdorff and Steven Goldzwig, "Idealism and Pragmatism in American Foreign Policy Rhetoric: The Case of John F. Kennedy and Vietnam," *Presidential Studies Quarterly* 24, no. 3 (Summer 1994): 515. On the lasting influence of that trip on Kennedy's thinking about Vietnam, see memo of conversation between Kennedy and President Charles de Gaulle, May 31, 1961, *FRUS, 1960–1963*, 24: 220; Daniel Ellsberg, *Secrets: A Memoir of Vietnam and the Pentagon Papers* (New York: Viking, 2002), 196–97; Roger Hilsman, oral history interview, June 1998, National Security Archives.

5. William C. Gibbons, *The U.S. Government and the Vietnam War: Executive and Legislative Roles and Relationships*, pt. 1, *1945–1961* (Washington, D.C.: Government Printing Office, 1984), 204. On Kennedy's opposition to both French policy and U.S. military involvement against the Viet Minh, see Dallek, *Unfinished Life*, 185–87.

6. On Kennedy's political cynicism, see Leamer, *Kennedy Men*, 135; Peter Collier and David Horowitz, *The Kennedys: An American Drama* (New York:

Warner Books, 1984), 254; Arthur M. Schlesinger Jr., *A Thousand Days: John F. Kennedy in the White House* (Boston: Houghton Mifflin, 1965), 95; Dallek, *Unfinished Life,* 64. On his early anti-Communism, including his reluctance to renounce Sen. Joseph McCarthy for pragmatic political reasons, see Leamer, *Kennedy Men,* 303; Dallek, *Unfinished Life,* 159–64, 187–92; Thomas C. Reeves, *A Question of Character: John F. Kennedy in Image and Reality* (New York: Free Press, 1990), 120–22. On the conclusions drawn by Kennedy from his presidential campaign, see Weisbrot, *Maximum Danger,* 18–19.

7. Memo of conference with President Kennedy, January 25, 1961, *FRUS, 1961–1963,* 8: 13.

8. Chester Bowles, *Promises to Keep: My Years in Public Life, 1941–1969* (New York: Harper & Row, 1971), 398.

9. This pattern was noted by administration insiders. See, e.g., Theodore C. Sorensen, *Kennedy* (New York: Harper & Row, 1965), 654; U. Alexis Johnson, oral history interview with William Brubeck (n.d.), 11, JFKL.

10. Edmund F. Wehrle, "'A Good, Bad Deal': John F. Kennedy, Averell Harriman and the Neutralization of Laos, 1961–1962," *Pacific Historical Review* 67, no. 3 (1998): 349–55; Schlesinger, *Thousand Days,* 332; Kaiser, *American Tragedy,* 39–46.

11. At least one high-ranking bureaucrat who had been in the Eisenhower administration understood clearly that the United States had provoked the crisis. In a speech to military men in May 1961, William Bundy noted that the United States's "ideal objective" had been "a Laos that really was aligned with the West," but he added, with unusual candor: "Sometimes if you pursue the ideal you overplay a hand," and the result could be the "loss of your minimum acceptable objective." Deputy Assistant Secretary of Defense William P. Bundy, National War College speech, May 10, 1961, 16–17; subject files of the assistant secretary of state for Far Eastern affairs, 1961–74, box 6, lot file 85D240, RG 59, NARA.

12. McGeorge Bundy, memo to JFK, April 1, 1961, *FRUS, 1961–1963,* 24: 112–16; memo of conversation between Secretary of State Dean Rusk and the British foreign minister, Lord Hume, April 6, 1961, ibid., 119.

13. Memo of conversation, April 29, 1961, in DOD, *United States–Vietnam Relations, 1945–1967* (Washington: Government Printing Office, 1971), bk. 11, 62–66; Schlesinger, *Thousand Days,* 337; Charles A. Stevenson, *The End of Nowhere: American Policy toward Laos since 1954* (Boston: Beacon Press, 1972), 151; Robert S. McNamara and Roswell Gilpatric, memo to JFK, May 2, 1961, *FRUS, 1961–1963,* 24: 167–68; Kaiser, *American Tragedy,* 52.

14. "SNIE 58–62: Probable Communist Reactions to Certain U.S. Courses of Action with Respect to Laos," February 23, 1961, *FRUS, 1961–1963,* 24: 61.

15. Robert W. Komer, "Strategic Framework for Rethinking China Policy" (draft paper), April 7, 1961, NSF, box 22, China folder, JFKL.

16. Shigeru Ishikawa, "China's Economic Growth since 1949—An Assessment," *China Quarterly* 94 (June 1983): 247; Komer, "Strategic Framework"; Robert W. Komer, memo to McGeorge Bundy, January 27, 1961, NSF, box 321,

"Staff Memoranda Robert W. Komer 1/1/61–3/14/61" file, JFKL. See also William Bundy, oral history interview with Alfred Goldberg and Lawrence Kaplan, January 22, 1990, 18, OSDH.

17. Dallek, *Unfinished Life,* 304–5; Beschloss, *Crisis Years,* 60–61; McNamara and Gilpatric, memo to JFK, May 2, 1961, *FRUS, 1961–1963,* 24: 167–68; Komer, memo to McGeorge Bundy, January 27, 1961.

18. U. Alexis Johnson, *The Right Hand of Power* (Englewood Cliffs, N.J.: Prentice-Hall, 1984), 324; Johnson, oral history interview with William Brubeck, 4, JFKL.

19. McNamara and Gilpatric memo to JFK, May 2, 1961.

20. Schlesinger, *Thousand Days,* 337.

21. Kaiser, *American Tragedy,* 52.

22. Draft memo of conversation of the second meeting of the Presidential Task Force on Vietnam, May 4, 1961, *FRUS, 1961–1963,* 1: 118–19.

23. "A Program of Action to Prevent Communist Domination of South Vietnam" (draft), May 6, 1961, in DOD, *United States–Vietnam Relations,* bk. 11, pp. 75–76.

24. Sorensen, *Kennedy,* 607; H. R. McMaster, *Dereliction of Duty: Lyndon Johnson, Robert McNamara, the Joint Chiefs of Staff, and the Lies That Led to Vietnam* (New York: HarperCollins, 1997), 16.

25. National Security Action Memorandum no. 52, May 11, 1961, in DOD, *United States–Vietnam Relations,* bk. 11, pp. 136–37.

26. Diem apparently did not understand that McGarr was talking about a training mission as a cover for getting combat troops into the country, however. Later, U.S. Ambassador Frederick E. Nolting Jr. enquired of Diem's secretary on three separate occasions about Diem's interest in such an arrangement but got no reply. John M. Newman, *JFK and Vietnam: Deception, Intrigue and the Struggle of Power* (New York: Warner Books, 1992), 58, 73; Nolting, telegram to Department of State, May 24, 1961, Department of State Central Files, 751K.5-MSP/5-2461, RG 59, NARA.

27. Newman, *JFK and Vietnam,* 58, 73, 86; Nolting, telegram to Department of State, May 24, 1961; Department of State, telegram to U.S. embassy, Saigon, May 20, 1961, *FRUS, 1961–1963,* 1: 140–42 and editorial footnote 2, p. 142.

28. Wehrle, "'Good, Bad Deal,'" 358–62; Stevenson, *End of Nowhere,* 154.

29. Dean Rusk, telegram to Averell Harriman, June 2, 1961, *FRUS, 1961–1963,* 24: 222–23; Kaiser, *American Tragedy,* 78–80; memo of conversation between Kennedy and Gen. Phoumi, June 30, 1961, *FRUS, 1961–1963,* 24: 285; Assistant Secretary of State Paul Nitze, memo to McNamara, June 29, 1961, ibid., 273–74; Robert H. Johnson, memo to Walt Rostow, July 25, 1961, ibid., 312–13.

30. U. Alexis Johnson, oral history interview with William Brubeck, 19.

31. John Steeves, oral history interview with Dennis J. O'Brien, September 5, 1969, 28–29, JFKL; Schlesinger, *Thousand Days,* 515; U. Alexis Johnson, oral history with William Brubeck, 18; Stevenson, *End of Nowhere,* 161.

32. Walt Rostow, memo to Robert Johnson, September 29, 1961, *FRUS, 1961–1963*, 1: 314; memo of conversation by Rostow, July 18, 1961, ibid., 232–33. A note by *FRUS* researchers indicates that Rostow sent the memo to Kennedy.

33. Memo of a discussion, July 28, 1961, ibid., 252–54; chairman, Southeast Asia Task Force (John Steeves), memo to JFK, July 28, 1961, ibid., 253. The group suggested that, if the "Viet Minh" intervened in response to such an operation, U.S. forces could seize and hold Hanoi and Haiphong, driving the North Vietnamese regime from its capital.

34. Memo of a discussion, July 28, 1961, ibid., 254. In a follow-up memo, Rostow again pushed all the options presented in the previous meeting, including seizing Hanoi and Haiphong, and suggested that "we must peer all the way down the road to the nuclear threshold." Rostow, memo to JFK, August 4, 1961, ibid., 341–44.

35. Johnson, *Right Hand of Power*, 324.

36. Gen. Maxwell Taylor, memo to JFK, "Southeast Asia Planning," September 23, 1961, Taylor Papers, box 43, Archives, National Defense University.

37. *The Pentagon Papers: The Defense Department History of United States Decisionmaking on Vietnam. The Senator Gravel Edition* (Boston: Beacon Press, 1972), 2: 13, 744; Kaiser, *American Tragedy*, 100–101; "Revised Concept for the Use of SEATO Forces in South Vietnam" (marked October 11, 1961, by hand), RG 218, Wheeler Papers, box 138, NSC Files, Vietnam, NARA.

38. JFK, letter to Gen. Maxwell Taylor, October 13, 1961, in *United States–Vietnam Relations*, bk. 11, p. 327.

39. Gen. Maxwell Taylor, cablegram to JFK, November 1, 1961, in *United States–Vietnam Relations*, bk. 11, pp. 337, 341; Taylor, letter to JFK, November 3, 1961, *FRUS, 1961–1963*, 1: 478; "Evaluation and Conclusions" (paper prepared by members of the Taylor mission, attachment 2 to the Taylor letter), ibid., 485.

40. SNIE 13–2-61, "Communist China in 1971," September 28, 1961, *FRUS, 1961–1963*, 22: 139; SNIE 10–3-61, "Probable Communist Reactions to Certain SEATO Undertakings in South Vietnam," October 10, 1961, in *United States–Vietnam Relations*, bk. 11, pp. 314–15; NIE 10–61, "Authority and Control in the Communist Movement," August 8, 1961, RG 263, NARA.

41. Notes by the secretary of defense, November 6, 1961, *FRUS, 1961–1964*, 1: 543–44.

42. McNamara, memo for JFK, November 8, 1961, in *United States–Vietnam Relations*, bk. 11, pp. 343–44.

43. Memo for JFK, November 11, 1961, ibid., 359–66.

44. Notes of a meeting, November 11, 1961, *FRUS, 1961–1963*, 1: 577.

45. Memo for the record, November 6, 1961, *FRUS, 1961–1963*, 1: 532; notes of a meeting, November 11, 1961, ibid., 236.

46. William Bundy, MS, 22–23; *FRUS, 1961–1963*, 24: 358, editorial note; report prepared by the Interagency Task Force on Laos, attachment to memo from Paul Nitze to McNamara, January 23, 1961, ibid., 30; JCS, memo to McNamara, July 12, 1961, ibid., 292–94; Walt Rostow, memo to JFK, August 4,

1961, ibid., 341–42; Rostow, memo to JFK, August 11, 1961, ibid., 374; Rostow, memo to JFK, August 17, 1961, ibid., 373; Rusk, McNamara, and JCS, draft memo to JFK, November 8, 1961, *FRUS, 1961–1963*, 1: 565; William Bundy, memo to McNamara, November 9, 1961, RG 218, Wheeler Papers, box 138, NSC Files, Vietnam, NARA. In the copy of that draft found in Wheeler's files, someone inserted the word "unanimous" before "SEATO agreement," indicating that Kennedy's advisers were urging that Kennedy do an end run around existing SEATO rules. See draft "Recommendations" section, November 8, 1961, RG 218, Wheeler Papers, box 138, NSC Files, Vietnam, NARA.

47. Notes on NSC meeting, November 15, 1961, *FRUS, 1961–1963*, 1: 608–9. This was substantially the same position that Kennedy had taken in a meeting with *New York Times* columnist Arthur Krock on October 11, when he expressed doubt that the United States should intervene in "civil disturbances caused by guerrillas" and said it was "hard to prove that this wasn't largely the situation in Vietnam." Herring, *America's Longest War*, 80.

48. Gelb and Betts, *Irony of Vietnam*, 77.

49. Paul B. Fay Jr., *The Pleasure of His Company* (New York: Harper & Row, 1966), 190. In the conversation just after reading Fletcher Knebel's *Seven Days in May*, about a fictional military takeover of the United States, Kennedy suggested that if a third "Bay of Pigs" occurred, a military attempt to take over the government "could happen." He vowed, however, that it "won't happen on my watch."

50. McGeorge Bundy, memo to JFK, November 15, 1961, *FRUS, 1961–1963*, 1: 606–7.

51. See Pelz, "John F. Kennedy's 1961 Vietnam War Decisions," 378; Kahin, *Intervention*, 137–38; George C. Herring, *America's Longest War: the United States and Vietnam, 1950–1975*, 3d ed. (New York: Knopf, 1996), 82–83; Giglio, *Presidency of John F. Kennedy*, 246; Logevall, *Choosing War*, 29–31, 25, 61–63; Kaiser, *American Tragedy*, 143; Dallek, *Unfinished Life*, 461; Jones, *Death of a Generation*, 190.

52. McGeorge Bundy, "Notes for Talk with Secretary Rusk Nov. 15," memo to JFK, November 15, 1961, *FRUS, 1961–1963*, 1: 613–14.

53. Newman, *JFK and Vietnam*, 141. Kennedy told Michael Forrestal, who replaced Walt Rostow as White House specialist on Southeast Asia, that one in ten of Rostow's ideas was "absolutely brilliant" but that "six or seven are not merely unsound, but dangerously so." He admired Rostow's creativity, he said, but would be "more comfortable to have him creating at some remove from the White House." Townsend Hoopes, *The Limits of Intervention* (New York: David McKay, 1969), 21.

54. Averell Harriman, draft memo, November 11, 1961, *FRUS, 1961–1963*, 1: 580–81.

55. Ibid., 581–82.

56. JFK, memo to Rusk and McNamara, November 14, 1961, *FRUS, 1961–1963*, 1: 603. Kennedy used this memo as a source of talking points at the November 14 NSC meeting, according to a handwritten note on the memo by

McGeorge Bundy. Kennedy has been portrayed as having opposed Harriman's proposal or any other negotiations over Vietnam, based entirely on a quotation attributed to a November 14, 1961, memo from JFK to Rusk and McNamara supposedly arguing that any negotiations on Vietnam while infiltration continued would make his administration appear to be "weaker than in Laos." See Kahin, *Intervention*, 137–38; Herring, *America's Longest War*, 83. The passage attributed to Kennedy was not from the Kennedy memo, however, but from a memo from Rostow to Kennedy urging him to reject negotiations. For the Rostow memo to Kennedy, see *FRUS, 1961–1963*, 1: 602. A copy of the document in which the Rostow page was inserted from the collection of documents used by George McT. Kahin in *Intervention* was provided to the author by Audrey Kahin. The page from Rostow's text clearly was not integrated into Kennedy's memo. The Rostow page begins with a "B," whereas the JFK memo has no "A" section; the paragraph numbers on the page do not follow the numbers in the JFK memo, and the Rostow page ends in the middle of a sentence.

57. Memo of conversation between Averell Harriman and Georgi Pushkin, November 20, 1961, box 534, Harriman Papers, Manuscript Division, Library of Congress.

58. Averell Harriman, telegrams to Department of State, November 21 and 27, 1961, *FRUS, 1961–1963*, 24: 522–24; 526–27. No communication from Harriman to the White House on the subject is in Harriman's own files or in the Kennedy Library files on Vietnam. This does not mean that Harriman and Kennedy never discussed his conversations with Pushkin by phone or in person, but since Kennedy had not changed his mind about the initiative, Harriman had every reason to withhold from JFK the actual contents of his formulation of U.S. policy in those talks.

59. Memos of conversations between Averell Harriman and Georgi Pushkin, December 1, 1961, and January 20, 1962, box 534, Harriman Papers, Manuscript Division, Library of Congress. Harriman noted in comments on a Galbraith proposal in April that such national elections would "result in a Communist takeover." Harriman memo, April 4, 1962, box 463, Harriman Papers.

60. Notes of a meeting, November 9, 1961, *FRUS, 1961–1963*, 1: 573.

61. Harriman ended his November 11 memo to Kennedy by saying: "Major military commitment as well as possible UN initiative should be held in reserve as long as direct negotiations seemed to be making progress." Averell Harriman, draft memo, November 11, 1961, ibid., 581.

62. Stevenson, *End of Nowhere*, 166–69; Winthrop Brown, ambassador to Laos, telegram to Department of State, November 16, 1961, *FRUS, 1961–1963*, 24: 515; JCS, memo for Gen. Maxwell Taylor, January 5, 1962, NSF, box 319, Meetings and Memoranda, "Special Group (CI) Meetings, 6/8/61–11/2/62" file, JFKL; Taylor, memo to McGeorge Bundy, January 5, 1962, ibid.; CINCPAC, message to JCS, January 5, 1962, quoted in Historical Division, JCS, "Chronological Summary of Significant Events Concerning the Laotian Crisis: Fifth Installment: 1 January to 30 April 1962," 15, http://hubcap.clemson.edu/~eemoise/Laos.html (last visited July 29, 2004); memo for the record, January 6, 1962, *FRUS, 1961–1963*, 24: 572.

63. Memo for the record, January 6, 1962, *FRUS, 1961–1963*, 24: 572.

64. Bowles, *Promises to Keep*, 400–403. For the text of his proposal, as circulated in the State Department, see Chester Bowles, "Notes on the China Food Situation," January 15, 1962, S/P files, lot 69D121 (China), box 212, RG 59, NARA. Kennedy did not share his brother Bobby's dislike of Bowles, whose ideas he respected. See Wofford, *Of Kennedys and Kings*, 373; Sorensen, *Kennedy*, 287.

65. United Kingdom, note attached to memo by L.D. Battle to McGeorge Bundy, March 29, 1962, NSF, 196, "Vietnam General 3/29/62–4/28/62," JFKL.

66. Amb. J.K. Galbraith, memo to JFK, April 4, 1962, in *United States–Vietnam Relations*, bk. 12, pp. 461–462.

67. Memo of conversation between Averell Harriman and JFK, April 6, 1962, *FRUS, 1961–1963*, 2: 309.

68. Michael Forrestal, memo to JFK, April 17, 1962, *FRUS, 1961–1963*, 24: 695. On Forrestal's relationship to Harriman, see David Halberstam, *The Best and Brightest* (New York: Random House, 1972), 94.

69. Unsigned note for Harriman, April 17, 1962, box 463, Harriman Papers, Manuscript Division, Library of Congress. The impersonality of the message, the absence of any signature, and the two errors in the text all indicate that it was not from Forrestal.

70. Unsigned note for Harriman, April 17, 1962, ibid.

71. Note for Edward Rice from Harriman's secretary, dictated by Harriman, April 17, 1962, ibid.

72. Edward Rice, draft telegram to Galbraith, April 17, 1962, box 463, Harriman Papers, Manuscript Division, Library of Congress.

73. Harriman's files contain no second draft of the telegram, and no telegram to Galbraith is to be found in the State Department's Central Files. The researchers for the 1962 *FRUS* volume also failed to find any telegram from Harriman to Galbraith on the Desai initiative. See *FRUS, 1961–1963*, 2: 309, editorial footnote 4.

74. Department of State, telegram to U.S. embassies in Phnom Penh, Saigon, Paris, and New Delhi, April 26, 1962, State Department Central Files, 75K.00/4–2662, NARA.

75. Schlesinger, *Robert Kennedy*, 709.

76. Roger Hilsman, draft memo of a conversation, *FRUS, 1961–1963*, 2: 367; Logevall, *Choosing War*, 37 and n. 83, p. 432; Dallek, *Unfinished Life*, 461.

77. Michael Forrestal, memo of JFK's instructions at Laos/Vietnam briefing, May 2, 1962 (document declassified, September 28, 1983, from the Kai Bird Collection).

78. Galbraith, telegram to Department of State for Averell Harriman, May 5, 1962, *FRUS, 1961–1963*, 2: 375–76; id., letter to Harriman, May 10, 1962, ibid., 379.

79. Averell Harriman, undated handwritten note to Michael Forrestal, and undated handwritten note from Forrestal to Harriman, box 463, Harriman Papers, Manuscript Division, Library of Congress. For the text of the telegram, dated May 16, see *FRUS, 1961–1963*, 2: 375–76.

80. After talks with Rusk on May 24–25, the British Foreign Office understood that it had an informal agreement with the State Department on a joint policy of no negotiations on South Vietnam. See Logevall, *Choosing War*, 19, 35.

81. Averell Harriman, "What We Are Doing in Southeast Asia," *New York Times Magazine*, May 27, 1962, 54.

82. On the June 2, 1962, ICC Report, see Jones, *Death of a Generation*, 182–83.

83. Harriman's deputy William H. Sullivan claimed in interviews in the 1970s and 1980s that Harriman had gotten authorization from Kennedy to meet with the North Vietnamese to explore the possibility of a peace agreement on Vietnam, and that Kennedy and Harriman both believed that the Laos agreement "could serve as a model for an agreement guaranteeing Vietnam's neutrality." Gibbons, *U.S. Government and the Vietnam War*, 121–22. For a similar account, obviously based on Sullivan's testimony, see Allen E. Goodman, *The Lost Peace: America's Search for a Negotiated Settlement of the Vietnam War* (Stanford, Calif.: Hoover Institution Press, 1978), 13–14. In his memoirs, however, Sullivan makes no such claim. He merely notes that Kennedy preferred a negotiated settlement to U.S. involvement in an escalating war, an insight that he must have gotten from Harriman—the only official in the State Department who knew. See William H. Sullivan, *Obbligato, 1939–1979: Notes on a Foreign Service Career* (New York: Norton, 1984), 177.

84. Sullivan, *Obbligato*, 177.

85. Memo of conversation, July 22, 1962, *FRUS, 1961–1963*, 24: 869–70.

86. For interpretations suggesting that Harriman's posture in the meeting with Khiem was a good-faith diplomatic effort, see Noam Kochavi, "Limited Accommodation, Perpetuated Conflict: Kennedy, China, and the Laos Crisis, 1961–1963," *Diplomatic History*, 26, no. 1 (Winter 2002): 120; Dallek, *Unfinished Life*, 525; Jones, *Death of a Generation*, 190; Kaiser, *American Tragedy*, 140–41. One interpretation even goes so far as to suggest that Kennedy rejected a proposal by Harriman to negotiate a coalition government in South Vietnam based on the Laotian model. See Bassett and Peltz, "Failed Search," 240. Only Fredrik Logevall is critical of Harriman's "utterly intransigent line" in the meeting, but he attributes that line to Kennedy's policy. See Logevall, *Choosing War*, 38.

87. Sullivan, *Obbligato*, 178

88. Undated note to Sullivan from Harriman's secretary attached to the original typescript of Sullivan's memo, box 530, Harriman Papers, Manuscript Division, Library of Congress. No copy of the Sullivan memo has turned up in the White House national security staff files at the JFK Library. Harriman did send a copy of the Sullivan memo to Walt Rostow, however. The document was attached to a one-sentence, undated note from Harriman to Rostow, which was found in "Records of the Policy Planning Staff (S/P)," lot file 69D121, box 218, RG 59, NARA.

89. Galbraith, telegram to secretary of state for Harriman, September 28, 1962, box 463, Harriman Papers, Manuscript Division, Library of Congress;

telegram from Harriman to Galbraith, October 4, 1962, ibid. Galbraith's report was quite accurate in its appreciation of the importance of North-South trade to Hanoi and its willingness to make concessions in order to obtain it. See 124–26 above.

90. Chester Bowles, memo to JFK, "US Policies in the Far East," April 4, 1962, *FRUS, 1961–1963*, 2: 299–303.

91. Bowles, *Promises to Keep*, 409–10.

92. Chester Bowles, "Notes on the China Food Situation," January 15, 1962, S/P files, lot 69D121 (China), box 212, RG 59, NARA; Bowles, memo to JFK, ibid.; Bowles, letter to JFK, June 27, 1962, with attached paper, "Notes on the China Food Situation," Chester Bowles file, box 438, Harriman Papers, Manuscript Division, Library of Congress.

93. Mose Harvey, "U.S. Policy Re the Sino-Soviet Conflict," March 12, 1962, 18, attachment to memo from Walt Rostow to Undersecretary of State for Political Affairs George McGhee, March 13, 1962, undersecretary for political affairs subject files, 1961–1963, box 6, RG 59, NARA; "Sale of Grain to China and Related Aspects of Communist Policy" (draft), March 16, 1962, S/P files, lot 69D121 (China), box 214, RG 59, NARA; U.S. consulate general, Hong Kong, airgram to Department of State, July 18, 1962, "Implications for U.S. Policy of Internal Developments in Communist China," July 19, 1962, S/P files, lot 69D121 (China), box 214, RG 59, NARA.

94. Harriman, memo to Rusk, April 13, 1962, *FRUS, 1961–1963*, 12: 216–17; Deputy Assistant Secretary of State for Far Eastern Affairs Edward Rice, memo to Harriman, March 28, 1962, ibid., 199; Department of State, draft paper, May 28, 1962, ibid., 231–33; Robert W. Komer, memo to McGeorge Bundy, January 29, 1962, ibid., 181; Roger Hilsman, *To Move a Nation: The Politics of Foreign Policy in the Administration of John F. Kennedy* (New York: Dell, 1967), 317.

95. Chester Bowles, memo to Rusk, July 12 1962, personal office files, box 28, special correspondence, Chester Bowles, JFKL.

96. Harriman, memo to Rusk, July 30, 1962; id., memo to Edward Rice, August 1, 1962, box 438, Harriman Papers, Manuscript Division, Library of Congress.

97. Bowles, memo to JFK, August 16, 1962, personal office files, box 28, Chester Bowles file, JFKL.

98. Draft memo for JFK, November 8, 1961, *FRUS, 1961–1963*, 1: 563.

99. Harriman, letter to Arthur Schlesinger Jr., October 17, 1961, personal office files, box 128A, Vietnam Security 1961 file, JFKL.

100. Harriman, "What We Are Doing in Southeast Asia," 54. In a 1964 oral history, Kennedy speechwriter Theodore Sorensen recalled the commonly held belief within the administration that South Vietnam was different from Laos because it was "accessible" to U.S. military power. See William C. Gibbons, "Lyndon Johnson and the Legacy of Vietnam," in Lloyd C. Gardner and Ted Gittinger, eds., *Vietnam: The Early Decisions* (Austin: University of Texas Press, 1997), 125.

101. CIA, Office of National Estimates, "An Appraisal of Soviet Intentions," December 21, 1961, in Gerald K. Haines and Robert E. Leggett, eds., *CIA's Analysis of the Soviet Union, 1947–1991* (Washington, D.C.: Center for the Study of U.S. Intelligence, 2001), 72, 74–75, 82–83; "Highlights of Discussion at the Secretary's Policy Planning Meeting," January 2, 1962, S/P files, lot files 69D121, RG 59, NARA; "U.S. Policy Re the Sino-Soviet Conflict" (paper submitted by Rostow to Rusk), April 2, 1962, 9–12. S/P files, lot files 69D121, box 208, RG 59, NARA; NIE 11–9-62, "Trends in Soviet Foreign Policy," May 2, 1962, 16, RG 263, NARA.

102. Rusk, testimony before the Senate Foreign Relations Committee, January 15, 1962, in U.S. Congress, Senate, *Executive Sessions of the Senate Foreign Relations Committee together with the Senate Armed Services Committee*, 87th Cong., 2d sess., 1962, Historical Series (Washington, D.C.: Government Printing Office, 1986), 14, pt. 1: 68.

103. Ibid., 161–62. The intelligence to which Rusk and McNamara referred was the capture of top-secret PRC military documents by Tibetan rebels in October 1961. See John Knaus, *Orphans of the Cold War: Americans and the Tibetan Struggle for Survival* (New York: Public Affairs, 1999), 243. McCone sent the CIA assessment of the documents to JFK in late January 1962. Robert W. Komer, memo to McGeorge Bundy, January 29, 1962, *FRUS, 1961–1963*, 22: 181, editorial footnote.

104. CIA, Office of Current Intelligence, "The New Stage of the Sino-Soviet Dispute," February 28, 1962, OCI No. 03161/62, p. 14, RG 263, NARA.

105. Harriman, memo for the files, July 21, 1962, box 530, Harriman Papers, Manuscript Division, Library of Congress. The CIA's Office of Current Intelligence concluded in February that Beijing's defiance of Moscow meant the "indefinite postponement, perhaps for decades, of China's achievement of status as a modern industrial and military power." Office of Current Intelligence, "Prospects for the Sino-Soviet Relationship," OCI No. 0360/62 (n.d.), 17, 22, 26, transmitted by memo from Rostow to Rusk, February 23, 1962, P/S files, lot files 69D121, box 208, RG 59, NARA.

106. John K. Galbraith, *A Life in Our Times* (Boston: Houghton Mifflin, 1981), 478.

107. Roger Hilsman, oral history interview, August 14, 1970, 21, JFKL. See also Hilsman interview quoted in Michael Maclear, *Vietnam: The Ten Thousand Day War* (London: Thames/Methuen, 1981), 87. In his own book, Hilsman makes no reference to Kennedy's willingness to negotiate a settlement. In his interview for Emile DeAntonio's documentary film *Year of the Pig* (1969), however, Hilsman said Kennedy "was fully prepared to lose" the war in South Vietnam. This pattern suggests that the political atmosphere of the early period of the war had constrained what he was willing to write or say about Kennedy's policy.

108. Ellsberg, *Secrets,* 194–95.

109. McGeorge Bundy, telegram to JFK, September 1, 1963, *FRUS, 1961–1963*, 4: 81–83; John F. Kennedy, *Public Papers of the Presidents: John F. Kennedy, 1963* (Washington, D.C.: Government Printing Office, 1964), 653.

110. The argument was originally made in Newman, *JFK and Vietnam*. For works that reject the thesis, see Reeves, *Question of Character*, 409–12; Robert D. Schulzinger, *A Time for War: The United States and Vietnam, 1941–1975* (New York: Oxford University Press, 1997), 123; Larry Berman, "NSAM 263 and NSAM 273: Manipulating History," in Gardner and Gittinger, eds., *Vietnam*, 177–203; Fredrik Logevall, "Vietnam and the Question of What Might Have Been," in Mark J. White, ed., *Kennedy: The New Frontier Revisited* (New York: New York University Press, 1998), 19–61; Logevall, *Choosing War*, 69–74; Edwin Moïse, "JFK and the Myth of Withdrawal," in Marilyn B. Young and Robert Buzzanco, eds., *A Companion to the Vietnam War* (Oxford: Blackwell, 2002), 162–73.

111. See Robert F. Kennedy, third oral history interview by John Bartlow Martin, April 30, 1964, JFKL; Schlesinger, *Robert Kennedy*, 646–54.

112. Michael Charlton and Anthony Moncrief, eds., *Many Reasons Why: The American Involvement in Vietnam* (New York: Hill & Wang, 1978), 82; Collier and Horowitz, *The Kennedys*, 531. On Bundy's recollection that Kennedy was not involved in the issue before October 1963, see William C. Gibbons, "Lyndon Johnson and the Legacy of Viet-Nam," in Gardner and Gittinger, eds., *Vietnam*, 136; Newman, "The Kennedy-Johnson Transition," ibid., 165.

113. Rusk admitted later that he and Kennedy had "a certain arms-length relationship partly because of the Viet Nam war and partly because of the difference in personalities." Dean Rusk, oral history interview with Paige Mulhollan, July 28, 1969, LBJL. www.lbjlib.utexas.edu/Johnson/archives/hom/oralhistory.hom/rusk/rusk.asp (last visited July 29, 2004).

114. See Weisbrot, *Maximum Danger*, 51–75.

115. Memo for the record of a meeting with JFK, January 3, 1962, *FRUS, 1961–1963*, 2: 4. It is not clear whether Kennedy understood that the Air Force Jungle Jim operation, which Kennedy had approved in October only for training, was going ahead with combat operations thinly disguised as training missions. The JCS strategy was to inform Kennedy on December 21, while he was in Bermuda meeting with British Prime Minister Harold Macmillan, that the Jungle Jim aircraft would begin "combat missions with combined U.S.-GVN crew aboard as part of combat crew training requirements." If there was no reaction from the White House, the operations would begin. Gen. Maxwell Taylor, telegram to JFK, December 21, 1961, ibid., 754, and editorial footnote 3. No record of Kennedy's reaction to learning that the training mission was essentially a ruse has been found.

116. Gen. Lyman Lemnitzer, memo to McNamara, "The Strategic Importance of the Southeast Asia Mainland," January 13, 1962, in *Pentagon Papers* (Gravel ed.), 2: 665–66.

117. "Memorandum for Mr. Bundy, Mr. Smith/General Clifton" (no author shown), March 29, 1962, *FRUS, 1961–1963*, 2: 283.

118. George W. Allen, *None So Blind: A Personal Account of the Intelligence Failure in Vietnam* (Chicago: Ivan R. Dee, 2001), 149–50. Allen does not give

the date of the conference in this account, but he confirmed it in interviews with John R. Newman and David Kaiser. See Newman, *JFK and Vietnam,* 254 n. 33, 257; Kaiser, *American Tragedy,* 134 n. 48, 518.

119. *Pentagon Papers* (Gravel ed.), 2: 175–76.

120. In a 1986 interview, McNamara was asked directly about Kennedy's "role and objectives" regarding Vietnam. His answer avoided Kennedy's role in or attitude toward the withdrawal plan. See Robert S. McNamara, oral history interview, pt. 3, July 24, 1976, OSDH, 13.

121. McNamara, telephone interview with the author, January 28, 2004.

122. The authors of the Pentagon history also assumed McNamara was acting "at the President's behest" in initiating the plan for a phased withdrawal, even though they cited no documentary evidence on the point. See *Pentagon Papers* (Gravel ed.), 2: 175.

123. Robert S. McNamara, with Brian VanDeMark, *In Retrospect: The Tragedy and Lessons of Vietnam* (New York: Times Books, 1995), 26–27. McNamara elaborates on this recollection in McNamara, oral history, pt. 3, July 24, 1986, n.p., OSDH. McNamara also brought up the incident and his reaction in a 1968 television broadcast. See Henry L. Trewhitt, *McNamara* (New York: Harper & Row, 1971), 98.

124. Deborah Shapley, *Promise and Power: The Life and Times of Robert McNamara* (Boston: Little, Brown, 1993), 263, 257; George Plimpton, ed., *American Journey: The Times of Robert F. Kennedy* (New York: Harcourt Brace Jovanovich, 1970), 210; Robert S. McNamara, "Introduction," to Robert F. Kennedy, *Thirteen Days: A Memoir of the Cuban Missile Crisis* (New York: Norton, 1969), 13; Schlesinger, *Robert Kennedy,* 451; McNamara, *In Retrospect,* 90–91.

125. Schlesinger, *Robert Kennedy,* 433, 441; McNamara, *In Retrospect,* 94–95.

126. Berman, "NSAM 263 and NSAM 273," in Gardner and Gittinger, eds., *Vietnam,* 273; Logevall, "Vietnam and the Question," 25; Kai Bird, *The Color of Truth: McGeorge Bundy and William Bundy, Brothers in Arms. A Biography* (New York: Simon & Schuster, 1998), 259.

127. McNamara, *In Retrospect,* 48.

128. McNamara, oral history interview, pt. 3, July 24, 1986, 11, OSDH.

129. *Pentagon Papers* (Gravel ed.), 2: 175; 179, fig. 2.

130. Col. R. C. Forbes, deputy secretary, JCS, note to Control Division, March 4, 1963, JCS Central Files, 1963, box 5, RG 218, NARA.

131. Memo for the record of the secretary of defense, Honolulu conference, May 6, 1963, *FRUS 1961–1963,* 3: 268–70; "Record, Eighth Secretary of Defense Conference, 6 May 1963," Assassination Records Review Board JFK Document Exhibits, www.parascope.com/ds/papertrail/arrbJFKdocD.htm (last visited July 22, 2004); JCS, telegram to Adm. Harry Felt, May 9, 1963, OSD Files, FRC 69 A 3121, Vietnam 091.3 MAP Secret, RG 330, NARA; Felt, telegram to JCS, May 11, 1963, OSD Files, FRC 69 A3131, Vietnam 091.3, MAP Secret, RG 330, NARA.

132. Mansfield in Charlton and Moncrief, eds., *Many Reasons Why,* 81.

133. Memo of conversation between JFK and Harriman, April 6, 1963, *FRUS, 1961–1963,* 2: 309.

134. Logevall, *Choosing War,* 38. See also Roger Hilsman, oral history interview, August 14, 1970, 21, JFKL.

135. "JCS-SecDef Discussion, 29 April, 1963," JCS Central Files, 1963, box 5, RG 218, NARA; "Record, Eighth Secretary of Defense Conference," 6, 48, 115.

136. Newman, *JFK and Vietnam,* 363; memo from Taylor to McNamara, JCSM-629–963, August 20, 1963, *FRUS, 1961–1963,* 3: 591–94. It appears from the Taylor memo that three-fourths of the withdrawals would be actual units, rather than half, as had been proposed by CINCPAC.

137. Maxwell Taylor Appointment Book for 1963 Taylor Papers, Archives, National Defense University.

138. *Pentagon Papers* (Gravel ed.), 2: 168, 182; memo from Taylor to McNamara, "Projection of U.S. Military Strength in the Republic of Vietnam," September 11, 1963, Taylor Papers, box 7, RG 218, NARA; Newman, *JFK and Vietnam,* 364.

139. Memo of telephone conversation between JFK and Ball, August 21, 1963, Papers of George W. Ball, "Vietnam I (1/15/62–10/4/63)," box 7, LBJL.

140. McNamara, *In Retrospect,* 57–61; memo for the record of a meeting, August 26, 1963, *FRUS, 1961–1963,* 3: 638–41; memo of a conference with JFK, August 27, 1963, ibid., 659–65; JFK, cable to Lodge, August 29, 1963, *FRUS, 1961–1963,* 4: 35–36.

141. Message from Lodge to Rusk, August 31, 1963, NSF Country File, Vietnam Addendum, Roger Hilsman (Vietnam-Diem), JFKL; Lodge, telegram to Department of State, September 4, 1963, *FRUS, 1961–1963,* 4: 111 n. 3; Lodge, telegram to Department of State, September 13, 1963, ibid., 203; CIA station in Saigon, telegram to CIA, September 2, 1963, ibid., 89; Thomas L. Hughes, director of the Bureau of Intelligence and Research, research memo for Rusk, September 11, 1963, ibid., 84; Logevall, *Choosing War,* 49–50.

142. McGeorge Bundy recalled in a letter to the author, November 13, 1967 (in author's files), "I do remember enough about it to be able to tell you quite flatly that President Kennedy's own policy on this matter was not governed by any view that the real danger was plans by Diem and Nhu to negotiate with North Vietnam. That just was not the problem as the President saw it."

143. Memo of a conference with JFK, September 3, 1963, *FRUS, 1961–1963,* 4: 103; memo from Hilsman to Rusk, September 16, 1963, ibid., 221–30; White House, telegram to Lodge, September 17, 1963, ibid., 252.

144. White House, telegram to Lodge, September 17, 1963, ibid., 252; memo for the record, September 23, 1963, ibid., 280.

145. Interview with NBC, September 9, 1963, in *Pentagon Papers* (Gravel ed.), 2: 827; JFK, memo to McNamara and Taylor, September 21, 1963, ibid., 748–49; memo for the record of a meeting, September 23, 1963, *FRUS, 1961–1963,* 4: 28; Schlesinger, *Robert Kennedy,* 770.

146. Jones, *Death of a Generation*, 370; Logevall, *Choosing War*, 53; Kaiser, *American Tragedy*, 255. Another interpretation is that Kennedy was simply concerned with learning the truth about the battlefield situation. See Newman, *JFK and Vietnam*, 385–86.

147. On Kennedy's maneuvering to impose Taylor on the JCS, see Gen. Maxwell Taylor, first oral history interview by Elspeth Rostow, April 12, 1964, 12, JFKL; McMaster, *Dereliction of Duty*, 22. On Taylor's close friendships with both John and Robert Kennedy and with McNamara, see Taylor's own recollection in Plimpton, ed., *American Journey*, 203; Taylor, oral history interview with Maurice Matloff, Richard Leighton, and R. H. Watson, October 18, 1963, 20–21, OSDH; Schlesinger, *Robert Kennedy*, 448–49; McNamara, *In Retrospect*, 90. Taylor quotation from Taylor, oral history interview, 20.

148. Kennedy, *Public Papers of the Presidents: John F. Kennedy, 1963*, 244, 421, 569, 652.

149. Maxwell Taylor Appointment Book for 1963, Taylor Papers, Archives, National Defense University; Taylor, oral history interview, October 18, 1983, 27, OSDH.

150. Memo of conversation, September 29, 1963, *FRUS, 1961–1963*, 4: 319.

151. Maxwell Taylor, *Swords and Plowshares: A Memoir* (New York: Norton, 1972), 298.

152. Jones, *Death of a Generation*, 353.

153. Taylor and McNamara, memo to JFK, October 2, 1963, in *Pentagon Papers* (Gravel ed.), 2: 752; William Bundy, MS, ch. 9, p. 20.

154. William Sullivan, oral history interview, 6, LBJL; Chester Cooper, oral history interview, June 9, 1966, 49, JFKL; Newman, *JFK and Vietnam*, 403.

155. Maxwell Taylor Appointment Book for 1963, Taylor Papers, Archives, National Defense University.

156. In his memoirs, McNamara mistakenly places the heated debate at the NSC meeting that evening. McNamara, *In Retrospect*, 79–80. The tape recording of the NSC meeting does not show any such debate. Tape recording of NSC meeting, October 2, 1963, POF, Presidential Recordings Collection, tape no. 114/A49 (cassette 2 of 3), JFKL. The meeting McNamara was recalling was certainly the one that followed the short McNamara-Taylor meeting in the morning. That meeting was attended by JFK and was not recorded.

157. "Meeting with Robert S. McNamara," April 29, 1994, 25, OSD Historian's Office. This is the transcript of a meeting between McNamara, Brian VanDeMark, and five members of the staff of the OSD Historian's Office.

158. Tape recording of NSC meeting, October 2, 1963, POF, Presidential Recordings Collection, tape no. 114/A49 (cassette 2 of 3), JFKL.

159. Chester Cooper, oral history, 49; id., *The Lost Crusade: America in Vietnam* (New York: Dodd, Mead, 1970), 215–16; McGeorge Bundy interview with John M. Newman, July 16, 1991, cited in Newman, "Kennedy-Johnson Transition," 165; Bundy, interview with Kai Bird, cited in Bird, *Color of Truth*, 258 and n. 25; 442. Cooper was certainly wrong in recalling that McGeorge Bundy's intervention with McNamara occurred *after* the NSC meeting.

Bundy, who had attended the NSC meeting and heard JFK announce what would be told to the press, would have known that it was too late by then to change the text.

160. "Meeting with Robert S. McNamara," April 29, 1994, 25; McNamara, oral history interview, pt. 3, July 24, 1986, 12.

161. William Bundy (MS, ch. 9, p. 22) recalled that his notes "make it clear that the sentence [on the 1965 withdrawal deadline] was regarded as settled throughout the day after the meeting between McNamara and the President."

162. Tape recording of NSC meeting, October 2, 1963, POF, Presidential Recordings Collection, tape no. 114/A49 (cassette 2 of 3), JFKL. For the length of the meeting, see *FRUS, 1961–1963*, 4: 350, editorial note 1.

163. Tape recording of NSC meeting, October 2, 1963. Newman interprets Kennedy's insistence on this as giving himself the freedom to implement the withdrawal as he saw fit, because he was less optimistic than they were. See Newman, *JFK and Vietnam*, 407. This interpretation ignores the abundant evidence that Kennedy had been behind the adoption of both dates all along.

164. Transcript of off-the-record news conference at the White House, October 2, 1963, in documents assembled for Vietnam Conference, June 1997, by Brian VandeMark, National Security Archive; White House policy statement on Vietnam, October 2, 1963, *Department of State Bulletin*, October 21, 1963, 623.

165. McNamara, telephone interview by the author, January 28, 2004.

166. Gen. Maxwell Taylor, memo to JCS, October 4, 1963, JCS-CM935–63, Taylor Papers, National Defense University. The military command in Vietnam and at CINCPAC headquarters still refused, however, to go along with the withdrawal of U.S. troops down to the 680 military personnel allowed by the Geneva Accords. On December 5, 1963, CINCPAC responded to the Taylor message by submitting a plan that would have left 3,200 troops through FY 1966—i.e., after the end-1965 deadline—and 2,600 even after the end of FY 1967. That plan would have left 1,000 more U.S. troops in South Vietnam at the end of the withdrawal than the plan CINCPAC had submitted seven months earlier. See *Pentagon Papers* (Gravel ed.), 2: 170.

167. The policy discussions and debates among Kennedy, his advisers, and Lodge about the coup plans in October are covered in greatest detail in Jones, *Death of a Generation*, 386–406.

168. Dallek, *Unfinished Life*, 684.

169. Newman, *JFK and Vietnam*, 423–24, 427; Schlesinger, *Robert Kennedy*, 722; William J. Rust, *Kennedy in Vietnam* (New York: Scribner's, 1985), 3–5.

6. JOHNSON, MCNAMARA, AND THE TONKIN GULF EPISODE

1. See Stanley Karnow, *Vietnam: A History* (New York: Viking, 1983), 319–426; Larry Berman, *Planning a Tragedy: The Americanization of the War in Vietnam* (New York: Norton, 1982), esp. 3–7; Lloyd C. Gardner, *Pay Any*

Price: Lyndon Johnson and the Wars for Vietnam (Chicago: Ivan R. Dee, 1995), esp. 98, 124, and 158; Michael H. Hunt, *Lyndon Johnson's War: America's Cold War Crusade in Vietnam, 1945–1968* (New York: Hill & Wang, 1996), esp. 78–85; Fredrik Logevall, *Choosing War: The Lost Chance for Peace and the Escalation of War in Vietnam* (Berkeley: University of California Press, 1999), esp. 389–95; David Kaiser, *American Tragedy: Kennedy, Johnson and the Origins of the Vietnam War* (Cambridge, Mass.: Belknap Press of Harvard University Press, 2000), 412–93. For works documenting some resistance by Johnson to going to war, incidental to other themes, see George McT. Kahin, *Intervention: How the United States Became Involved in Vietnam* (New York: Knopf, 1986); H. R. McMaster, *Dereliction of Duty: Lyndon Johnson, Robert McNamara, the Joint Chiefs of Staff, and the Lies That Led to Vietnam* (New York: Harper-Collins, 1997).

2. See John Stoessinger, *Crusaders and Pragmatists* (New York: Norton, 1979), 183–96; Karnow, *Vietnam*, 321; Doris Kearns Goodwin, *Lyndon Johnson and the American Dream* (New York: Harper & Row, 1976), 176; David Halberstam, *The Best and the Brightest* (New York: Random House, 1972), 414, 434; Logevall, *Choosing War*, 75, 78–79, 298, 390; Bill Moyers, "Flashbacks," *Newsweek* 85 (February 10, 1975): 76.

3. Kearns Goodwin, *Lyndon Johnson and the American Dream*, 309–34; James Reston, *Deadline: A Memoir* (New York: Random House, 1991), 311.

4. Robert S. McNamara with Brian VanDeMark, *In Retrospect: The Tragedy and Lessons of Vietnam* (New York: Vintage Books, 1996), 102; transcript of CNN interview with McNamara in June 1996 for CNN history of the Cold War, episode 11, broadcast December 6, 1998, www.gwu.edu/~nsarchiv/coldwar/interviews/episode-11/mcnamara3.html (last visited July 29, 2004). In Errol Morris's Academy Award–winning film *The Fog of War*, released in 2003, McNamara again portrayed Johnson as having been the primary force for war in Vietnam.

5. John Prados, *Operation Vulture* (New York: ibooks, 2002), 125–27. Prados interprets statements in Johnson's newsletter critical of the Eisenhower administration for failing to prevent Communist victory in Indochina as evidence that he supported military intervention. For an account of how Johnson engaged in a partisan attack on Dulles and the Republicans over Indochina without taking a public position on intervention, see Rowland Evans and Robert Novak, *Lyndon B. Johnson: The Exercise of Power* (New York: New American Library, 1966), 77–78.

6. For Johnson's own account of the April 3 meeting, see William C. Gibbons, *The U.S. Government and the Vietnam War: Executive and Legislative Roles and Relationships*, pt. 1, *1945–1961* (Washington, D.C.: Government Printing Office, 1984), 191. For other sources on Johnson's role in the meeting, see Chalmers M. Roberts, "The Day We Didn't Go to War," in Marcus G. Raskin and Bernard B. Fall, eds., *The Viet-Nam Reader* (New York: Vintage Books, 1965), 59; memo for the file of the secretary of state, April 5, 1954, *FRUS, 1942–1954*, 13: 1224–25; George C. Herring and Richard H. Immerman,

"Eisenhower, Dulles and Dien Bien Phu: 'The Day We Didn't Go to War Revisited,'" in Lawrence Kaplan, Denise Artaud, and Mark Rubin, eds., *Dien Bien Phu and the Crisis of Franco-American Relations, 1954–1955* (Wilmington, Del.: SR Books, 1990), 88–89.

7. LBJ, report, May 1961, *FRUS, 1961–1963*, 1: 156.

8. On McNamara's hunger for power and desire to impose his own policy on the Ford Motor Company, see Deborah Shapley, *Promise and Power: The Life and Times of Robert McNamara* (Boston: Little, Brown, 1993), 58–74; Peter Collier and David Horowitz, *The Ford: An American Epic* (New York: Simon & Schuster, 1987), 289; David Halberstam, *The Reckoning* (New York: William Morrow, 1986), 208, 211–13, 239–40.

9. William Colby, *Honorable Men* (New York: Simon & Schuster, 1978), 220–21; Newman, *JFK and Vietnam*, 435; Edward J. Marolda and Oscar P. Fitzgerald, *The United States Navy and the Vietnam Conflict* (Washington, D.C.: Government Printing Office, 1986), 335. Unfortunately, no documents on military pressures against North Vietnam were included in the record of the Honolulu meeting published in the relevant *FRUS* volume.

10. In February 1963, Kennedy had opposed transferring jet fighter planes to the South Vietnamese Air Force because of "political considerations involving escalation." And five months before his assassination, Kennedy had rejected the idea of air attacks on North Vietnam, arguing that it would do little damage and would risk Chinese intervention. See State Department, telegram to U.S. embassy, Saigon, February 6, 1963, *FRUS, 1961–1963*, 3: 102–3; memo prepared in the CIA for John C. McCone, June 19, 1963, ibid., 24: 1032.

11. Draft of NSAM, unnumbered, November 21, 1963, NSF, National Security Action Memoranda, South Vietnam, NASM 273 file, LBJ.

12. Draft NSAM, unnumbered, November 24, 1963, NSF, Papers of McGeorge Bundy, box 1, Chronological File, November 23–30, 1963, LBJL.

13. NSAM 273, November 26, 1963, *FRUS, 1961–1964*, 4: 637–39.

14. McGeorge Bundy, interview with John M. Newman, August 5, 1991, cited in Newman, *JFK and Vietnam: Deception, Intrigue and the Struggle of Power* (New York: Warner Books, 1991), 445.

15. See Lyndon B. Johnson: *The Vantage Point: Perspective of the Presidency, 1963–1969* (New York: Holt, Rinehart and Winston, 1973), 43–46; Memorandum for the Record of a Meeting, November 24, 1963, *FRUS, 1961–1963*, 4: 635–37; Moyers, "Flashbacks," 76; NSAM 273, November 26, 1963, *FRUS, 1961–1963*, 4: 637.

16. McNamara, *In Retrospect*, 103. William Bundy also asserts that Johnson had "no thought at this stage of a new policy or stronger action." William P. Bundy, oral history interview with Paige Mulhollan, May 26, 1969, 12, LBJL.

17. Gen. Maxwell Taylor to Adm. Harry Felt, December 2, 1963, Taylor Papers, box 12, RG 218, NARA; Kaiser, *American Tragedy*, 291–92; McNamara, telegram to Amb. Henry Cabot Lodge, December 12, 1963, *FRUS, 1961–1963*, 4: 702.

18. *FRUS, 1964–1968*, 1: 27, editorial footnote 2; *The Pentagon Papers: The Defense Department History of United States Decisionmaking on Vietnam. The Senator Gravel Edition* (Boston: Beacon Press, 1972), 3: 50–152; Edwin E. Moïse, *Tonkin Gulf and the Escalation of the Vietnam War* (Chapel Hill: University of North Carolina Press, 1996), 5; Richard H. Shultz Jr., *The Secret War against Hanoi* (New York: HarperCollins, 1999), 36–40.

19. Gen. Victor Krulak, "Report on the Visit of the Secretary of Defense to South Vietnam," December 21, 1963, *FRUS, 1961–1963*, 4: 724.

20. Undersecretary of state for political affairs (Sullivan), memo for the record, "Report of McNamara Visit to Saigon, December 19–20, 1963, December 21, 1963," *FRUS, 1961–1963*, 4: 729. The "Special Group" had been established under NSC 5412 and had also been known as the "5412 Committee" and the "303 Committee" during the Kennedy administration. Its members were the undersecretary of state, the deputy secretary of defense, the president's special assistant for national security affairs, the director of the CIA, and the chairman of the JCS. McGeorge Bundy chaired all the meetings and had considerable latitude in what he reported to Kennedy. See Gibbons, *U.S. Government and the Vietnam War*, 1: 309–10; Shultz, *Secret War against Hanoi*, 289–90; Kai Bird, *The Color of Truth* (New York: Touchstone, 1998), 223–24. The "Special Group" should not be confused with the "Special Group (Counterinsurgency)" established by Kennedy in early 1962.

21. McNamara, memo to LBJ, December 21, 1963, *FRUS, 1961–1963*, 4: 734.

22. *Pentagon Papers* (Gravel ed.), 3: 151, *FRUS, 1964–1968*, 1: 27; Moïse, *Tonkin Gulf*, 5.

23. Gen. Maxwell Taylor to McNamara, January 22, 1964, in *Pentagon Papers* (Gravel ed.), 3: 498. On Taylor's policy of not forwarding JCS papers that the secretary did not agree with to McNamara, see 173 above.

24. Ambassador Henry Cabot Lodge, telegram to LBJ, February 20, 1964, *FRUS, 1961–1964*, 1: 94–95; McMaster, *Dereliction of Duty*, 69; memo for the record of meeting, February 20, 1964, *FRUS, 1961–1964*, 1: 93–94. For further evidence of Johnson's preoccupation with placating Lodge, see the excerpt from a March 9, 1964, memo from Michael Forrestal to William Bundy, *FRUS, 1964–1968*, 1: 132, editorial footnote 3. Bundy notes that it was only in late February—i.e., in response to Lodge's proposal—that Johnson had authorized contingency planning for bombing the North. William P. Bundy, oral history interview with Paige Mulhollan, May 26, 1969, 18, LBJL.

25. Telephone conversation between LBJ and McNamara, February 20, 1964, in Beschloss, ed., *Taking Charge*, 250. This elaboration of the theme that it was a South Vietnamese war to win or lose was Johnson's answer to his own rhetorical question: "How in hell does McNamara think that when he's losing the war that he can pull men out of it?" The quotation in Errol Morris's Academy Award–winning film *The Fog of War* of Johnson's statement earlier in the conversation that he had "always thought it was foolish for you to make any statements about withdrawing" is misleading. A few seconds later, Johnson added, "I asked for your explanation and you gave a good explanation." Ibid., 249.

26. McMaster, *Dereliction of Duty*, 71–72.

27. William Bundy, draft memo for the president, March 1, 1964, in Gareth Porter, ed., *Vietnam: The Definitive Documentation of Human Decisions* (Stanfordville, N.Y.: E. M. Coleman Enterprises, 1979), 2: 240–46. Kaiser, *American Tragedy*, 302–3, cites a draft of the same memo dated March 2. In his own oral history, Bundy claims that, despite "discussion" of bombing the North, "nobody felt this was the time to go ahead," ignoring or forgetting his own draft memo. William P. Bundy, oral history interview, May 26, 1969, 17.

28. JCS, memo to McNamara, March 2, 1964, *FRUS, 1964–1968*, 1: 117.

29. SNIE 50–2-64, "Probable Consequences of Certain Actions with Respect to Vietnam and Laos," May 25, 1964, ibid., 379–80.

30. "Definition of Links between Actions and Political Effects," 3. Johnson Group Papers, March 1964, vol. 2, 2.C, lot file 85D240, box 15, RG 59, NARA. This is one of the suite of papers drafted by the interagency study group chaired by Robert H. Johnson of the State Department's Policy Planning Council. For a description of the study and its conclusions, see DOD, *United States–Vietnam Relations, 1945–1967*, bk. 3 (Washington, D.C.: Government Printing Office, 1971), IV.C.2. (a), pp. 6–8.

31. NIE 11–9-64, "Soviet Foreign Policy," February 19, 1964, *FRUS, 1964–1968*, 14: 24, 30.

32. William Bundy, "Exploiting the Vulnerabilities of the Communist World" (address to strategy seminar, July 18, 1963), 9, subject files of the Office of the Assistant Secretary of State, Bureau of Far Eastern Affairs, lot file 85D240, box 6, RG 59, NARA; memo of conversation between Hilman Bassler, chief of South Asia and East Asia Section, Foreign Office of the Federal Republic of Germany, and Marshall Green, April 2, 1964, ibid., lot file 66D93, box 2, RG 59, NARA. For a similar description of U.S. and Soviet "parallel action lines in containing China," see "Guidelines of United States Policy toward China" (9th draft, March 2, 1964), 10, subject files of the Office of Asian Communist Affairs, 1961–1973, lot file 70 D248, box 1, RG 59, NARA.

33. JCS, memo to McNamara, March 2, 1964, *FRUS, 1964–1968*, 1: 117; Rosemary Foot, *The Practice of Power: U.S. Relations with China since 1949* (Oxford: Clarendon Press, 1955), 154–55; D. M. Mazure, J2, "CHICOM Military Capabilities," memo, March 5, 1964, records of Robert S. McNamara, box 63, "Miscellaneous Reports: VN Trip March 1964," RG 200, NARA; SNIE 50–2-64, "Probable Consequences," 380; John C. McCone, memo for the record, April 2, 1964, *FRUS, 1964–1968*, 30: 33; memo of conversation, April 19, 1964, *FRUS, 1964–1968*, 30: 252.

34. JCS, memo to McNamara, April 29, 1963, *FRUS, 1961–1963*, 7: 689; Assistant CIA Director for National Estimates Sherman Kent, memo to Harriman, July 8, 1963, ibid., 7: 771; summary record, NSC meeting, July 31, 1963, ibid., 22: 373; "Basic National Security Policy" (draft), March 25, 1963, S/P papers, lot file 69D121, box 28, RG 59, NARA; Walt Rostow, memo to Rusk, September 13, 1963, ibid., 3: 509.

35. Robert H. Johnson, "The Implications of a Chinese Communist Nuclear Capability" (undated attachment to memo for LBJ from Rostow), April 30, 1964, *FRUS, 1964–1968*, 30: 57–58. For the expression of a similar view by William Bundy, see "Outline of Oxford Speech," September 19, 1964, William P. Bundy Papers, box 17, lot file 85D240, RG 59, NARA.

36. SNIE 14.3.63, "The Impact of the Sino-Soviet Dispute on North Vietnam and Its Policies," June 26, 1963, *FRUS, 1961–1963*, 3: 417; "Definition of Links between Actions and Political Effects," 3, Johnson Group Papers.

37. McGeorge Bundy, memo for LBJ, March 3, 1964, National Security Files, Files of McGeorge Bundy, box 2, Chronological File, March 1964, LBJL; Kaiser, *American Tragedy*, 305; McNamara, memo for LBJ, March 16, 1964, *FRUS, 1964–1968*, 1: 167.

38. Diary Cards, file box 51, "Robert S. McNamara," LBJL; Logevall, *Choosing War*, 127–28. Logevall interprets McNamara's despondency with Harlech as evidence of his sober realism on the war rather than of his unhappiness at being forced to abandon the bombing of the North.

39. Summary record of NSC meeting, March 17, 1964, *FRUS, 1964–1968*, 1: 172; Logevall, *Choosing War*, 128.

40. Telephone conversation between LBJ and McGeorge Bundy, March 4, 1964, in Beschloss, ed., *Taking Charge*, 267; Bird, *Color of Truth*, 276.

41. McMaster, *Dereliction of Duty*, 86 and n. 4; 362.

42. Richard N. Goodwin, *Remembering America: A Voice from the Sixties* (Boston: Little, Brown, 1988), 271.

43. James Reston, "Vice-President McNamara? The Latest Gossip," *New York Times*, March 27, 1964, 27; notes of LBJ interview with Neil Sheehan, March 24, 1965, quoted in Kearns Goodwin, *Lyndon Johnson and the American Dream*, 177.

44. Paul R. Henggeler, *In His Steps: Lyndon Johnson and the Kennedy Mystique* (Chicago: Ivan R. Dee, 1999), 78; Henry L. Trewhitt, *McNamara* (New York: Harper & Row, 1971), 259. On Johnson's offers of higher office, see McNamara, *In Retrospect*, 123.

45. William Bundy, MS, ch. 13, p. 8.

46. Harold P. Ford, *CIA and the Vietnam Policymakers: Three Episodes, 1962–1968* (Langley, Va.: History Staff, Center for the Study of Intelligence, Central Intelligence Agency, 1998), 59; McGeorge Bundy, memo to LBJ, May 22, 1964, *FRUS, 1961–1964*, 1: 349–50.

47. "Scenario for Strikes on North Vietnam," May 24, 1964, *FRUS, 1961–1964*, 1: 363–68. The memo is attributed by the editors to DOD, but a draft with the same title and dated May 23 found in CIA files is signed by William Bundy, then assistant secretary of state. See Ford, *CIA and the Vietnam Policymakers*, 60 n. 123.

48. Summary record of NSC Executive Committee meeting, May 24, 1964, *FRUS, 1961–1964*, 1: 370–72.

49. Gen. Andrew Goodpaster, memo, "Four Meetings on Extension of Operations against North Vietnam, 24–25 May," Taylor Files, box 12, May 1964, RG 218, NARA.

50. McGeorge Bundy, draft memo to LBJ, May 25, 1964, *FRUS, 1964–1968,* 1: 377; telephone conversation between LBJ and McGeorge Bundy, May 27, 1964, in Beschloss, ed., *Taking Charge,* 371.

51. McNamara, *In Retrospect,* 120–21.

52. Telephone conversation between LBJ and McGeorge Bundy, May 27, 1964, in Beschloss, ed., *Taking Charge,* 370.

53. Jack Valenti, *A Very Human President* (New York: Norton, 1975), 133–34.

54. William Bundy, MS, ch. 13, p. 24; William Bundy, memo for discussion, June 10, 1964, in Porter, ed., *Vietnam,* 2: 282–83; draft congressional resolution on Southeast Asia, June 11, 1964, ibid., 283–84; "Draft Resolution on Southeast Asia," May 25, 1964, DOD, *United States–Vietnam Relations,* bk. 4, IV.C.2 (b), following p. 42.

55. *Pentagon Papers* (Gravel ed.), 3: 180–81; William Bundy, MS, ch. 13, pp. 23–25.

56. The literature on the Tonkin Gulf incidents has continued to grow over the decades. The earliest generation of books challenging the official story of the events includes Anthony Austin, *The President's War: The Story of the Tonkin Gulf Resolution and How the Nation Was Trapped in Vietnam* (Philadelphia: Lippincott, 1971); Joseph C. Goulden, *Truth Is the First Casualty: The Gulf of Tonkin Affair—Illusion and Reality* (Chicago: Rand McNally, 1969); Eugene Windchy, *Tonkin Gulf* (Garden City, N.Y.: Doubleday, 1971). Further documentation was provided by a second generation of studies in the 1980s and early 1990s: "The 'Phantom Battle' That Led to War," *U.S. News and World Report,* July 23, 1984, 56–67; Jim Stockdale and Sybil Stockdale, *In Love and War,* rev. ed. (Annapolis, Md.: Naval Institute Press, 1990), 19–36; Stanley Karnow, *Vietnam: A History* (New York: Viking, 1983), 370–76; George McT. Kahin, *Intervention: How the United States Became Involved in Vietnam* (New York: Knopf, 1986), 218–23. Superseding these sources are now Moïse, *Tonkin Gulf,* and John Prados, "Essay: 40th Anniversary of the Gulf of Tonkin Incident," http://www.edu/~nsarchiv/NSAEBB/ NSAEBB132/essay .htm (last visited August 27, 2004). The National Security Archive website provides the original texts of the intercepts of North Vietnamese messages during the Tonkin Gulf incidents, at http://gwu.edu/~nsarchiv/NSAEBB/ NSAEBB132/tonkin_intercepts.htm. For corroboration from former North Vietnamese Defense Minister Vo Nguyen Giap that the alleged August 4 attack never took place, see Robert S. McNamara, James Blight, and Robert Brigham, with Thomas Bierstecker and Herbert Schandler, *Argument without End: In Search of Answers to the Vietnam Tragedy* (New York: Public Affairs, 1999), 23.

57. McNamara et al., *Argument without End,* 23.

58. David Kaiser notes that none of the telephone conversations between McNamara and Johnson that had been released "suggest that McNamara ever raised these questions with the Commander in Chief" but does not pursue the issue further. See Kaiser, *American Tragedy,* 335.

59. Duty officer in the White House Situation Room, memo to LBJ, August 2, 1964, *FRUS, 1964–1968,* 1: 590; LBJ and McNamara, tape of telephone conversation, August 3, 1964, LBJL.

60. Gen. Maxwell Taylor, telegram to Department of State, August 3, 1964, *FRUS, 1964–1968,* 1: 593; Brian VanDeMark, notes on recordings of telephone conversation between William Bundy and George Ball, August 3, 1964, LBJL, VanDeMark Collection, National Security Archive; Ball later recalled that both Bundy and McNamara had been concerned that right-wing Republicans would put pressure on the administration to escalate to the point that "might involve bringing the Chinese in." George Ball, oral history interview, July 8, 1971, 13, LBJL, www.lbjlib.utexas.edu/johnson/archives.hom/oralhistory.hom/BallG./BallG.asp (last visited July 30, 2004).

61. "Chronology of Events, Tuesday, August 4 and Wednesday, August 5, 1964, Tonkin Gulf Strike" (3d draft, August 25, 1964), 3–12, NSF, Vietnam Country File, box 228, "Gulf of Tonkin (Miscellaneous)," LBJL; conversations between Johnson and McNamara, 9:12 A.M. and 9:43 A.M., August 4, 1964, in Beschloss, ed., *Taking Charge,* 495–97.

62. "Chronology of Events," 21; U.S. Congress, Senate, Committee on Foreign Relations, *The Gulf of Tonkin, the 1964 Incidents, Hearing,* 90th Cong., 2d sess., February 20, 1968 (Washington, D.C.: Government Printing Office, 1968), 11.

63. President's Daily Diary, August 4, 1964, p. 6, LBJL.

64. Transcript of conversation between Sharp and Burchinal, 1:29 P.M., August 4, 1964, NSF, Vietnam Country File, box 228, LBJL.

65. Transcript of telephone conversation between McNamara and Sharp, 4:08 P.M., August 4, 1964, NSF, Vietnam Country File, box 228, LBJL.

66. President's Daily Diary, August 4, 1964, LBJL.

67. "Chronology of Events," 25. This was not merely an alert to be prepared to carry out the air strikes; it was the actual authorization for the strikes. An alert had already been sent to the commander of the Seventh Fleet and the two warships in the Tonkin Gulf from CINCPAC headquarters at 4:14 P.M. "Chronology of Events," 24.

68. President's Daily Diary, August 4, 1964.

69. "Memorandum for McGeorge Bundy," August 4, 1964, no author shown, NSF, Vietnam Country File, "Maddox Incident 8/4/64," box 227, LBJL.

70. Telephone conversation between Johnson and McNamara, 5:09 P.M., August 4, 1964, in Beschloss, ed., *Taking Charge,* 500–501.

71. DOD news release, August 4, 1964, NSF, Vietnam Country File, "Gulf of Tonkin (Miscellaneous)," box 228, LBJL.

72. Author's notes of telephone interview with McNamara, February 24, 2004; McNamara, *In Retrospect,* 134.

73. Summary notes of the 438th meeting of the National Security Council, August 4, 1964, *FRUS, 1964–1968,* 1: 611–12.

74. Author's notes of telephone interview with McNamara, February 24, 2004.

75. McNamara, *In Retrospect*, 134.

76. William F. Levantrosser, "Tonkin Gulf Revisited: Vietnam, Military Mirage and Political Reality in 1964," in Bernard J. Firestone and Robert C. Vogt, eds., *Lyndon Johnson and the Uses of Power* (New York: Greenwood Press, 1988), 308; Karnow, *Vietnam*, 374; Stockdale and Stockdale, *In Love and War*, app. 2, 503–5.

77. Excerpt from CNN interview with McNamara in June 1966 for a documentary on the Cold War broadcast December 6, 1998, http://www.gwu.edu/~nsarchiv/coldwar/interviews/episode-11/mcnamara3.html (last visited July 29, 2004).

78. A handwritten note initialed "BKS" (Bromley K. Smith) and dated in pencil August 7, 1964, said, "Here are additional proof of attack messages." It also said the JCS would be ready with a briefing on "all evidence" on Monday afternoon. NSF, National Security Council History, "Presidential Decisions, "Gulf of Tonkin Attacks of August 64," vol. 1, table 9, LBJL.

79. "Memorandum for McGeorge Bundy," no author shown, August 8, 1964, NSF, Vietnam Country File, box 277, LBJL.

80. "Chronology of Secretary of Defense McNamara's Actions in the PT Boat Crises," August 6, 1964, NSF, "Gulf of Tonkin (Miscellaneous)," box 228, LBJL.

81. "Questions for Mr. McNamara on the Tonkin Gulf Chronology," undated, "Gulf of Tonkin (Miscellaneous)," LBJL.

82. "Transcripts of Telephone Conversations, 4–5 August," "Gulf of Tonkin (Miscellaneous)," LBJL. The transcript of the Sharp-McNamara conversation was not included in that collection of transcripts but is an entirely separate document in the same file.

83. "Chronology of Events," 16, 21, 30, 32, 35. McNamara's handwriting on the document can be verified by comparing it with his handwritten farewell letter to Lyndon Johnson on February 23, 1968, in McNamara, *In Retrospect*, between 206 and 207.

84. The submission of the final draft of the chronology to Johnson by Bundy is mentioned in editorial note, *FRUS, 1961–1964*, 1: 605.

85. "Chronology of Events," 23–24; "Telephone conversation between McNamara and Admiral Sharp," NSF, Vietnam Country File, "Gulf of Tonkin (Miscellaneous)," box 228, LBJL.

86. "Chronology of Events," 27.

87. Ibid., 28.

88. Telephone conversation between Sharp and Burchinal, 5:23 P.M., "Transcripts of Telephone Conversations."

89. "Chronology of Events," 28.

90. Telephone conversation between Sharp and Burchinal, 4:40 P.M., "Transcripts of Telephone Conversations."

91. Edward J. Marolda and G. Wesley Pryce, *A Short History of the United States Navy and the Southeast Asian Conflict, 1950–1975* (Washington, D.C.: Naval Historical Center, Department of the Navy, 1984), 20; George Ball, *The*

Past Has Another Pattern (New York: Norton, 1982), 371; George Ball, oral history interview with Paige Mulhollan, July 8, 1971, 14, LBJL.

92. Moïse, *Tonkin Gulf,* 244; William Bundy, "Next Courses of Action in Southeast Asia," August 13, 1964, *FRUS, 1961–1964,* 1: 673–79.

93. JCS, memo to McNamara, JCSM-746–64, August 27, 1964, *FRUS, 1964–1968,* 1: 713–17; Gibbons, *U.S. Government and the Vietnam War,* 3: 13; *Pentagon Papers* (Gravel ed.), 3: 193, 556–59.

94. Gen. Maxwell Taylor, telegram to State Department, September 6, 1964, *FRUS, 1964–1968,* 1: 733–36; William Bundy, "Courses of Action for South Vietnam" (draft memo), September 8, 1964, in *Pentagon Papers* (Gravel ed.), 3: 560–61.

95. Bundy, "Courses of Action," in *Pentagon Papers* (Gravel ed.), 3: 561–62; McMaster, *Dereliction of Duty,* 150; memo of meeting, September 9, 1964, *FRUS, 1964–1968,* 1: 749–55.

96. Marolda and Pryce, *Short History,* 20.

97. Telephone conversations between LBJ and McNamara, 11:46 A.M. and 6:26 P.M., September 8, 1964, tape WH6409.11, LBJL.

98. Ball, *Past Has Another Pattern,* 379–80; McGeorge Bundy, memo for the record, September 20, 1964, *FRUS, 1961–1964,* 1: 778–81; Ball, *Vietnam-on-the-Potomac,* 17; Marolda and Pryce, *Short History,* 20. The *Pentagon Papers* account claimed that DESOTO patrols were resumed in February 1965. See *United States–Vietnam Relations,* bk. 4, p. 28.

99. Daniel Ellsberg, *Secrets: A Memoir of Vietnam and the Pentagon Papers* (New York: Viking, 2002), 52. Nevertheless, McNamara insists that he was the one questioning the effectiveness of bombing the North, and that Johnson was on the other side of the issue. McNamara, *In Retrospect,* 153.

100. McMaster, *Dereliction of Duty,* 166; Logevall, *Choosing War,* 243–44; "Top Secret: The Prophecy the President Rejected," *Atlantic,* July 1972, 35–49; Ball, *Vietnam-on-the-Potomac,* 169.

7. BUREAUCRATIC PRESSURES AND DECISIONS FOR WAR

1. Dean Rusk, telegram to Amb. Maxwell Taylor, drafted by William Bundy, November 8, 1964 (declassified document in the Kai Bird Collection).

2. John McNaughton, "Action for South Vietnam" (2d draft, November 6, 1964), in *The Pentagon Papers: The Defense Department History of United States Decisionmaking on Vietnam. The Senator Gravel Edition* (Boston: Beacon Press, 1972), 3: 599–600; William Bundy, "III. The Broad Options" (draft), November 17, 1964 (declassified document in the Kai Bird Collection).

3. NIE 10-3-64, "Probable Communist Reactions to Certain Possible US/GVN Courses of Action," October 9, 1964, excerpts quoted in Walt Rostow, memo to Dean Rusk, November 23, 1964, in *Pentagon Papers* (Gravel ed.), 3: 645; "CIA-DIA-INR Panel Draft," November 6, 1964, ibid., 596. The main lines of analysis of that estimate were reiterated in a paper by the intelligence panel on November 24. *Pentagon Papers* (Gravel ed.), 3: 653–56.

4. McNaughton, "Action for South Vietnam," 601; William Bundy, "Analysis of Option C," November 8, 1964, in *Pentagon Papers* (Gravel ed.), 3: 615–16.

5. William Bundy, MS, ch. 18, p. 36.

6. McNamara's handwritten notes on his copy of William Bundy's memo "Issues Raised by Papers on Southeast Asia," November 24, 1964, Papers of Robert S. McNamara, box 63, "SVN Memo to President December 1964" file, RG 200, NARA.

7. "CIA-DIA-INR Panel Draft," 597.

8. William Bundy, MS, ch. 18, p. 33.

9. *Pentagon Papers* (Gravel ed.), 3: 245; William Bundy, "Draft Position Paper on Southeast Asia," November 29, 1964, ibid., 678–79.

10. "Position Paper on Southeast Asia," December 2, 1964, *FRUS, 1964–1968*, 1: 969–74; William Bundy, MS, ch. 19, p. 8.

11. *Pentagon Papers* (Gravel ed.), 3: 251. Both Fredrik Logevall and David Kaiser interpret the result of the December 1 meeting as being the acceptance by Johnson of Option C, at least in principle, and note that the final version of the position paper includes language about "appropriate U.S. deployments to handle any contingency" in connection with the second phase of bombing. They fail to recognize, however, that the paper did not, in fact, commit Johnson to proceeding to the second phase of the bombing. See Logevall, *Choosing War: The Lost Chance for Peace and the Escalation of War in Vietnam* (Berkeley: University of California Press, 1999), 270–71; Kaiser, *American Tragedy: Kennedy, Johnson and the Origins of the Vietnam War* (Cambridge: Mass.: Belknap Press of Harvard University Press, 2000), 376–79.

12. William Bundy, MS, ch. 19, p. 13; notes on meeting, White House, December 1, 1964, *FRUS, 1964–1968*, 1: 966–68; William Bundy, oral history interview with Paige Mulhollan, May 29, 1967, 7, OSDH.

13. LBJ, telegram to Taylor, December 3, 1964, *FRUS, 1964–1968*, 1: 975.

14. Robert J. Dallek, *Flawed Giant: Lyndon Johnson and His Times, 1961–1973* (New York: Oxford University Press, 1998), 444.

15. William Bundy, oral history interview, May 29, 1967, 2–4, OSDH.

16. LBJ, telegram to Taylor, December 30, 1964, *FRUS, 1964–1968*, 1: 1057.

17. Kaiser, *American Tragedy*, 385–86. The complaint to Alsop about Bien Hoa could reasonably have been interpreted as a warning that Johnson should not refuse retaliatory strikes over the Brinks Hotel blast on December 24.

18. Taylor, telegram to LBJ, January 6, 1965, *FRUS, 1964–1968*, 2: 16; LBJ, telegram to Taylor, January 7, 1965, ibid., 41; Taylor, telegram to LBJ, January 11, 1965, ibid., 47.

19. *Pentagon Papers* (Gravel ed.), 3: 684.

20. William Bundy, MS, ch. 20, p. 24; ch. 22, pp. 7, 20–24. Bundy adds, "In hindsight, I do not think this was the case." But he offers no reason for his change of view.

21. Interview with McGeorge Bundy by CRS, January 8, 1979, quoted in William C. Gibbons, *The U.S. Government and the Vietnam War: Executive and*

Legislative Roles and Relationships (Washington, D.C.: Government Printing Office, 1984), 3: 47.

22. "Ambassador Taylor's Situation Report on the RVN, August 10, 1964," in *Pentagon Papers* (Gravel ed.), 3: 531; SNIE 43–64, "Chances for a Stable Government in Vietnam, September 8, 1964," *FRUS, 1964–1968*, 1: 743–45; NIE 53–2–64, "The Situation in South Vietnam," October 1, 1964, ibid., 806–911. McNaughton, "Action for South Vietnam," in *Pentagon Papers* (Gravel ed.), 3: 599; Logevall, *Choosing War*, 479 n. 30.

23. Under the plan, the United States would have provided "quasi-covert support to an anti-coup group," urged such an anti-coup group to proclaim the coup to be "Communist"-inspired, and assured it that "sufficient U.S. combat personnel would be landed immediately to secure and protect key GVN and U.S. installations." "Contingency Planning for South Viet-Nam" (n.d.; probably August–September 1964), 7, Vietnam Working Group Subject Files, 1963–1966, Political Affairs and Relations, 1964, box 5, RG 59, NARA.

24. Taylor, telegram to Department of State, December 31, 1964, *FRUS, 1964–1968*, 1: 1062–63.

25. James C. Thomson, "How Could Vietnam Happen?" *Atlantic,* April 1968, 51. Thomson's account conceals Vice President Humphrey's identity, but it is revealed in George McT. Kahin, *Intervention: How the United States Became Involved in Vietnam* (New York: Knopf, 1986), 272.

26. Telephone conversation between LBJ and McGeorge Bundy, March 2, 1964, in Michael R. Beschloss, ed., *Taking Charge: The Johnson White House Tapes, 1963–1964* (New York: Simon & Schuster, 1997), 263; telephone conversation between LBJ and Senator Richard Russell, May 27, 1964, ibid, 367; LBJ conversation with McNamara, June 16, 1964, ibid., 411; William Bundy, "Draft Position Paper on Southeast Asia," 969–74; William Bundy, MS, ch. 19, p. 8.

27. See the recollection of Wilbur J. Cohen, in Merle Miller, *Lyndon: An Oral Biography* (New York: G. P. Putnam's Sons, 1980), 407–8. On the conflict between Johnson's ambitions for his Great Society legislative agenda and major U.S. combat in Vietnam, see also Jeffrey W. Helsing, *Johnson's War/Johnson Great Society* (Westport, Conn.: Praeger, 2000), 63–65; Bill Moyers, "Epilogue: Second Thoughts," in Bernard J. Firestone and Robert C. Vogt, eds., *Lyndon Johnson and the Uses of Power* (New York: Greenwood Press, 1988), 351; Doris Kearns Goodwin, *Lyndon Johnson and the American Dream* (New York: Harper & Row, 1976), 251–52; Dallek, *Flawed Giant,* 190–99; Jack Valenti in Ted Gittinger, ed., *The Johnson Years: A Vietnam Roundtable* (Austin: Lyndon Baines Johnson Library, 1993), 44, 66; David Halberstam, *The Best and the Brightest* (New York: Random House, 1972), 507.

28. This development is discussed in detail in Kahin, *Intervention,* 267–71.

29. McNamara and McGeorge Bundy, memo to LBJ, January 26, 1965, *FRUS, 1964–1968*, 2: 95–97. McNamara and Bundy explained Rusk's refusal to join them in the memo by citing his belief that "the consequences of both escalation and withdrawal are so bad that we simply must find a way of making our present policy work." It is unlikely, however, that this was the whole story of

Rusk's refusal to join them. Rusk was known to believe that the secretary of state should limit his role to giving advice to the president and should not be in the position of putting pressure on him to adopt a certain policy option. Roger Hilsman, *To Move a Nation: The Politics of Foreign Policy in the Administration of John F. Kennedy* (New York: Dell, 1967), 59; Halberstam, *Best and the Brightest*, 421–22. Rusk may well have seen the McNamara-Bundy memo as going well beyond that line.

30. Paul R. Henggeler, *In His Steps: Lyndon Johnson and the Kennedy Mystique* (Chicago: Ivan R. Dee, 1999), 105–6; Kearns Goodwin, *Lyndon Johnson and the American Dream*, 320.

31. Telephone conversation between LBJ and Senator Richard Russell, May 27, 1965, *FRUS, 1964–1968*, 27: 133. No record of the meeting itself has been found, but the meeting and the Republican senators expected to participate are referred to in McGeorge Bundy's memo to LBJ, May 26, 1964, ibid., 390.

32. Richard Nixon, "Needed in Vietnam: The Will to Win," *Reader's Digest*, August 1964, 37.

33. Moya Ann Ball, *Vietnam-on-the-Potomac* (New York: Praeger, 1992), 154.

34. Gibbons, *U.S. Government and the Vietnam War*, 3: 50–51.

35. Ibid., 53–54

36. John McCone, message to Bundy in Saigon, February 3, 1965, *FRUS, 1964–1965*, 2: 131–32.

37. Ford, *CIA and Vietnam Policymakers*, 73.

38. George W. Allen, *None So Blind: A Personal Account of the Intelligence Failure in Vietnam* (Chicago: Ivan R. Dee, 2001), 184; Harold P. Ford, *CIA and the Vietnam Policymakers: Three Episodes, 1962–1968* (Langley, Va.: History Staff, Center for the Study of Intelligence, Central Intelligence Agency, 1998), 72–73.

39. Allen, *None So Blind*, 184; *New York Times*, February 8, 1965, 1, 15; Gibbons, *U.S. Government and the Vietnam War*, 66. Allen heard the story directly from Reston in Saigon in 1965 but did not identify him in his book. He agreed to reveal Reston's identity to the author in light of the fact both principals are now long deceased. George W. Allen, personal communication to author, March 10, 2004.

40. McGeorge Bundy, telegram to U.S. embassy, Saigon, February 8, 1965, *FRUS, 1964–1968*, 2: 202.

41. McGeorge Bundy, memo to LBJ, February 16, 1965, ibid., 283.

42. Department of State, telegram to U.S. embassy, London, February 16, 1965, ibid., 294–295, and editorial note 3, 294.

43. The story of the Taylor-Westmoreland intervention to oust Khanh was pieced together from declassified messages from Saigon by George McT. Kahin, the only scholar to focus on those developments. See Kahin, *Intervention*, 297–303.

44. Logevall, *Choosing War*, 348, 352, 354–55; memo of conversation between Rusk and Harlech, February 17, 1965, *FRUS, 1964–1968*, 2: 313–15;

William Bundy, draft paper, February 18, 1965, ibid., 316–17; editorial note 1, ibid., 316; memo of telephone conversation between Ball and McNamara, February 18, 1965, ibid., 318–19.

45. Adlai Stevenson, letter to LBJ, February 17, 1965, NSF, Agency File, box 89, LBJL.

46. Memo of a meeting with the president, February 17, 1965, *FRUS, 1964–1968*, 2: 301–2.

47. David Kraslow and Stuart H. Loory, *The Secret Search for Peace in Vietnam* (New York: Vintage Books, 1968), 99; John Bartlow Martin, *Adlai Stevenson and the World: The Life of Adlai Stevenson* (Garden City, N.Y.: Doubleday, 1977), 830; Mario Rossi, "U Thant and Vietnam: The Untold Story," *New York Review of Books*, November 17, 1966, 8. In November 1965, Johnson asked Bill Moyers, then his press secretary, to investigate the U Thant initiative. Ibid., 106.

48. Lyndon B. Johnson, *The Vantage Point: Perspectives of the Presidency, 1963–1969* (New York: Holt, Rinehart & Winston, 1971), 123; memo of discussion at the 549th NSC meeting, February 18, 1965, *FRUS, 1964–1968*, 2: 326–27.

49. Memo of conversation between LBJ and Couve de Murville, February 19, 1965, *FRUS, 1964–1968*, 2: 332–33.

50. *FRUS, 1964–1968*, 2: 352, editorial note 1.

51. Paper prepared by Rusk, February 23, 1965, *FRUS, 1964–1968*, 2: 358; Office of Current Intelligence, memo to McCone, February 23, 1965, ibid., 359–61. See also William Bundy, draft paper, February 23, 1965, ibid., 2: 352–55.

52. "Secretary Rusk's Press Conference of February 25," *Department of State Bulletin*, March 15, 1965, 364.

53. Kahin, *Intervention*, 302–3.

54. *Pentagon Papers* (Gravel ed.), 3: 334–35, 338–44.

55. Thomas C. Hone, "Strategic Bombardment Constrained: Korea and Vietnam," in R. Cargill Hall, ed., *Case Studies in Strategic Bombardment* (Washington, D.C.: Air Force History and Museums Program, 1998), 500–501; Cyrus Vance, oral history interview with Paige Mulhollan, March 9, 1970, LBJL. www.lbjlib.utexas.edu/johnson/archives.hom/oralhistory.hom/Vance-C/Vance.asp (last visited July 25, 2004).

56. See Logevall, *Choosing War*, 299.

57. Helsing, *Johnson's War*, 51–53.

58. "President's Meeting with Congressional Leaders," January 22, 1965, *FRUS, 1964–1968*, 2: 66.

59. Michael Beschloss, ed., *Reaching for Glory: Lyndon Johnson's Secret White House Tapes, 1964–1965* (New York: Simon & Schuster, 2001), 205, 211–13.

60. H. R. McMaster, *Dereliction of Duty: Lyndon Johnson, Robert McNamara, the Joint Chiefs of Staff, and the Lies That Led to Vietnam* (New York: HarperCollins, 1997), 244.

61. LBJ, memo to McGeorge Bundy, March 6, 1965, *FRUS, 1964–1968*, 2: 404.

62. McCone, memo for the record, March 18, 1965, ibid., 458.

63. McGeorge Bundy, memo for discussion, March 14, 1965, ibid., 446–49.

64. McGeorge Bundy, memo to LBJ, April 1, 1965, ibid., 507.

65. SNIE 10–3/1–65, "Communist Reactions to Possible US Courses of Action against North Vietnam," February 18, 1965, *FRUS, 1964–1968*, 2: 323–24; Gibbons, *U.S. Government and the Vietnam War*, 3: 114.

66. McGeorge Bundy, memo to LBJ, April 1, 1965, *FRUS, 1964–1968*, 2: 507.

67. Gibbons, *U.S. Government and the Vietnam War*, 3: 180.

68. Robert S. McNamara with Brian VanDeMark, *In Retrospect: The Tragedy and Lessons of Vietnam* (New York: Vintage Books, 1996), 179; McGeorge Bundy, notes of meeting with LBJ, April 1, 1965, *FRUS, 1964–1968*, 2: 511–12; DOD, telegram to Taylor, April 15, 1965, ibid., 561–62; *Pentagon Papers* (Gravel ed.), 3: 448; William Bundy, MS, ch. 25, p. 6.

69. Kaiser, *American Tragedy*, 427–28; McMaster, *Dereliction of Duty*, 269.

70. McNamara, memo to LBJ, April 21, 1965; Taylor, diary entry, April 20, 1965; Ulysses S. G. Sharp, *Strategy for Defeat: Vietnam in Retrospect* (San Rafael, Calif.: Presidio Press, 1978), 80; *Pentagon Papers* (Gravel ed.) 3: 458.

71. William Bundy, memo to Rusk, March 19, 1965, *FRUS, 1964–1968*, 2: 460–65; John McNaughton, "Proposed Course of Action Re Vietnam" (1st draft, March 24, 1965), in *Pentagon Papers* (Gravel ed.), 3: 694–95; Taylor, paper, April 1, 1965, *FRUS, 1964–1968*, 2: 504.

72. McGeorge Bundy, memo to LBJ, March 6, 1965, *FRUS, 1964–1968*, 2: 404.

73. Ibid.; Logevall, *Choosing War*, 357; Blema Steinberg, *Shame and Humiliation: Presidential Decision Making on Vietnam* (Pittsburgh: University of Pittsburgh Press, 1996), 100; McGeorge Bundy, memo to LBJ, March 6, 1965, *FRUS, 1964–1968*, 2: 405; id., memo for discussion, March 16, 1965, ibid., 446–49.

74. Intelligence memo, April 21, 1965, *FRUS, 1964–1968*, 2: 595–96.

75. McCone, memo for the record, April 22, 1965, *FRUS, 1964–1968*, 2: 598. Reversing his earlier position, McCone strongly dissented from the notion that the threat of bombing would deter deeper North Vietnamese military engagement in the South. John McCone, notes of NSC meeting, April 21, 1965, *FRUS, 1964–1968*, 2: 578–81.

76. McNamara, testimony in *Military Procurement Authorizations, Fiscal Year 1965, Hearings before the Committee on Armed Services and Committee on Appropriations*, U.S. Senate, 88th Cong., 2d sess., February 1964 (Washington, D.C.: Government Printing Office, 1964), 153; John McCone, memo for the record, March 18, 1965, *FRUS, 1964–1968*, 2: 460; McMaster, *Dereliction of Duty*, 71 and n. 52; 359.

77. *FRUS, 1961–1963*, 24: 973, editorial footnote 4.

78. Memo of meeting with LBJ, February 17, 1965, *FRUS, 1964–1968*, 2: 300–301, 307.

79. Kaiser, *American Tragedy*, 432; *New York Times*, April 25, 1965, A3.

80. Gen. William Westmoreland, message to the JCS, June 7, 1965, *FRUS, 1964–1968*, 2: 733–36; JCS, memo for McNamara, JCSM-457–65, June 11, 1965, appendix, George McT. Kahin Collection, National Security Archive.

81. McNamara, *In Retrospect*, 188.

82. Richard Helms, memo for the record, June 8, 1965, *FRUS, 1964–1968*, 2: 739–40; William Bundy, MS, ch. 26, p. 8.

83. Telephone conversation between LBJ and McNamara, June 10, 1965, in Beschloss, ed., *Reaching for Glory*, 349–50, 352.

84. McGeorge Bundy, notes of meeting with LBJ, June 10, 1965, and summary of the meeting by William Bundy based on his notes, *FRUS, 1964–1968*, 2: 745–49; William Bundy, MS, ch. 26, p. 9. McNamara repeated the same proposal in his conversation with Johnson later that same evening. See telephone conversation between LBJ and McNamara, June 10, 1965, in Beschloss, ed., *Reaching for Glory*, 349.

85. Summary notes of NSC meeting, June 11, 1965, *FRUS, 1964–1968*, 2: 757–59.

86. Memo of telephone conversation between LBJ and Ball, June 14, 1965, *FRUS, 1964–1968*, 3: 9.

87. Robert McNamara, oral history interview, pt. 3, July 24, 1976, 20, OSDH. McNamara does not go that far in his memoirs, but he implies as much by indicating that he shared McGeorge Bundy's view that the additional deployments would simply "cover a retreat" in the end. McNamara, *In Retrospect*, 194.

88. Gibbons, *U.S. Government and the Vietnam War*, 3: 319; McGeorge Bundy, memo to McNamara, June 30, 1965, *FRUS, 1964–1968*, 3: 90–91; William Bundy, oral history interview, May 29, 1967, 35, OSDH.

89. Rusk, paper for LBJ, July 1, 1965, *FRUS, 1964–1968*, 3: 105.

90. Earle G. Wheeler, chairman, JCS, memo for McNamara, JCSM-457–65, June 11, 1965, records of Gen. Earle Wheeler, RG 218, box 182, NARA; David L. McDonald, acting chairman, JCS, memo for McNamara, JCSM-482–65, June 18, 1965, ibid.

91. McGeorge Bundy, handwritten notes on June 18, 1965, meeting with LBJ, VanDeMark Collection, National Security Archives. Bundy's notes do not mention the caveat that the decision to withdraw would be subject to later review. However, a draft NSAM prepared at the Pentagon the following day makes that caveat explicit. See Gibbons, *U.S. Government and the Vietnam War*, 3: 317.

92. McMaster, *Dereliction of Duty*, 297; Bundy handwritten notes on June 18, 1965, meeting, VanDeMark Collection, National Security Archive. McMaster quotes Westmoreland as rejecting the idea that his short-term request would be an "upper threshold of our ground commitment; and that thereafter a cut of 3–6 battalions might be enforced." Unfortunately, McMaster's footnote does not identify the document from which the Westmoreland quote was drawn.

93. Memo of telephone conversation between Ball and LBJ, June 14, 1965, *FRUS, 1964–1968*, 3: 9–11. The plan stopped short of calling for allowing the National Liberation Front to participate in national elections, which Ball had

advocated in an April 21 memo to Johnson. See "A Plan for a Political Resolution in South Viet-Nam," attachment to memo for LBJ from Ball, May 8, 1965, Harriman papers, National Security Archive. Johnson had temporarily dropped the plan in May after Taylor had pointed out that the Saigon government was not strong enough to accept it. See Kaiser, *American Tragedy*, 435.

94. See memo of telephone conversation between LBJ and George Ball, June 14, 1965, *FRUS, 1964–1968*, 3: 9; Ball, memo to LBJ, June 18, 1965, ibid., 17, 30–21.

95. See Leslie H. Gelb and Richard K. Betts, *The Irony of Vietnam: The System Worked* (Washington, D.C.: Brookings Institution, 1979), 289; Logevall, *Choosing War*, 249–50; Stanley Karnow, *Vietnam: A History* (New York: Viking, 1983), 404; James C. Thomson, "How Could Vietnam Happen?—An Autopsy," *Atlantic*, April 1968; Dean Rusk, second oral history interview by Paige E. Mulhollan, September 26, 1969, Internet copy, LBJL, www.lbjlib .utexas.edu/johnson/archives.hom/oralhistory.hom/rusk/rusk.asp. For Ball's refutation, see George Ball, oral history interview, 12, LBJL, Internet copy, www.lbjlib.utexas.edu/johnson/archives.hom/oralhistory.hom/Ball-G/ BallG.asp; Ball, *The Past Has Another Pattern*, 384. William Bundy supported Ball's contention that Johnson did not treat him like a "devil's advocate." See William Bundy, oral history interview with Alfred Goldberg and Lawrence Kaplan, March 12, 1990, 23, OSDH.

96. Memo of telephone conversation between George Ball and Bill Moyers, June 21, 1965, *FRUS, 1964–1968*, 3: 33. For an interpretation that Johnson was deceiving Ball by suggesting that he agreed with his memo, see Kaiser, *American Tragedy*, 448, 450–51.

97. Ray S. Cline, deputy director of CIA for intelligence, memo to Jack Valenti, June 21, 1965, with attachment, "Evolution of Communist Positions Concerning Negotiations," NSF, Vietnam Country File, box 19, LBJL.

98. McNamara pointedly observes that Ball's memo was "initially sent only to the President and Dean" and "had not been analyzed and debated by senior officials." McNamara, *In Retrospect*, 192. McNamara repeated that observation in a telephone interview with the author, January 28, 2004. Implicit in this complaint was the concern that Ball enjoyed back-channel access to Johnson on his proposal that was denied Johnson's other advisers.

99. Telephone conversation between LBJ and McNamara, June 21, 1965, in Beschloss, ed., *Reaching for Glory*, 365. Johnson recounted to Moyers that he had told McNamara, "If there is no alternative, the fellow here with the program [Ball] is the way I will probably go." See memo of telephone conversation between Ball and Moyers, June 21, 1965, *FRUS, 1964–1968*, 3: 33. Johnson had not literally said that, but McNamara could have inferred that sentiment from Johnson's comments.

100. McNamara, *In Retrospect*, 191.

101. Gen. Earle C. Wheeler, private diary, 1965, records of Gen. Earle Wheeler, RG 218, box 182, NARA. The time of McNamara's telephone conversation with LBJ is in Beschloss, ed., *Reaching for Glory*, 364.

102. Wheeler, telegram to Westmoreland, June 22, 1965, *FRUS, 1964–1968,* 3: 36.

103. William Bundy, MS, quoted in *FRUS, 1964–1968,* 3: 40–41, editorial note.

104. Westmoreland, telegram to Wheeler, June 24, 1965, ibid., 41–43.

105. Gen. Earle C. Wheeler, private diary, 1965; Kaiser, *American Tragedy,* 452–53; William Bundy, memo to Dean Rusk, June 29, 1965 (declassified document in the Kai Bird Collection).

106. A draft of the memo signed by McNamara that shows both the June 26, 1965, date of the previous version and the July 1, 1965, date is in the VanDeMark Papers, National Security Archive.

107. McNamara to LBJ, July 1, 1965, *FRUS, 1964–1968,* 3: 97–104. McNamara attached without comment the summary of a more optimistic CIA estimate of Hanoi's likely response, based on the twin assumptions that the tide in South Vietnam would be reversed and that Hanoi would be subject to punitive bombing, implying that he did not endorse its conclusions. See *FRUS, 1964–1968,* 3: 86–89.

108. McNamara, *In Retrospect,* 192–93.

109. Robert McNamara, comment in James B. Blight and David A. Welch, *On the Brink: Americans and Soviets Reexamine the Cuban Missile Crisis* (New York: Hill & Wang, 1989), 191; Philip Nash, *The Other Missiles of October* (Chapel Hill: University of North Carolina Press, 1997), 136. On the attack on the Kennedy administration in September 1962, see Robert Weisbrot, *Maximum Danger: Kennedy, the Missiles and the Crisis of American Confidence* (Chicago: Ivan R. Dee, 2001), 76–93.

110. Logevall, *Choosing War,* 368.

111. Telephone conversation between LBJ and McNamara, June 30, 1965, in Beschloss, ed., *Reaching for Glory,* 376–77.

112. Notes of meeting, July 21, 1965, *FRUS, 1964–1968,* 3: 189–205.

113. William Bundy, oral history interview, May 29, 1969, 41–42, OSDH. For a similar assessment by McGeorge Bundy, see Larry Berman, *Planning a Tragedy: The Americanization of the War in Vietnam* (New York: Norton, 1982), 106.

114. Cyrus Vance, telegram to McNamara in Vietnam, July 17, 1965, *FRUS, 1964–1968,* 3: 162–63.

8. DOMINOES, BANDWAGONS, AND THE ROAD TO WAR

1. See Douglas Macdonald, "Falling Dominoes and System Dynamics: A Risk Aversion Perspective," *Security Studies* 3, no. 2 (Winter 1993–94): 225–58.

2. Stephen M. Walt, *The Origins of Alliances* (Ithaca, N.Y.: Cornell University Press, 1987); id., "Alliance Formation in Southwest Asia: Balancing and Bandwagon in Cold War Competition," in Robert Jervis and Jack Snyder, eds., *Dominoes and Bandwagons: Strategic Beliefs and Great Power Competition in*

the Eurasian Rimland (New York: Oxford University Press, 1991), 51–84. For a broader argument that balancing behavior prevails in the international system, see Kenneth Waltz, *Theory of International Politics* (Reading, Mass.: Addison-Wesley, 1979), 125–28.

3. See Robert Jervis, "Domino Beliefs and Strategic Behavior," in Jervis and Snyder, eds., *Dominoes and Bandwagons,* 20–50; Deborah Welch Larson, "Bandwagon Images in American Foreign Policy: Myth or Reality?" ibid., 98–103; Jerome Slater, "The Domino Theory and International Politics: The Case of Vietnam," *Security Studies* 3, no. 2 (Winter 1993–94): 186–224; Macdonald, "Falling Dominoes."

4. Robert Jervis, "Perceiving and Coping with Threat," in Robert Jervis, Richard Ned Lebow, and Janice Gross Stein, *Psychology and Deterrence* (Baltimore: Johns Hopkins University Press, 1985), 25; Jaacov Y. I. Verzberger, *The World in Their Minds: Information Processing, Cognition, and Perception in Foreign Policy Decisionmaking* (Stanford, Calif.: Stanford University Press, 1990), 5. For other references to rationalization and related concepts, see Ralph K. White, *Fearful Warriors: A Psychological Profile of U.S.-Soviet Relations* (New York: Free Press, 1984), 155–57; Dean G. Pruitt, "Definition of the Situation as a Determinant of International Action," in Herbert C. Kelman, ed., *International Behavior: A Social-Psychological Analysis* (New York: Holt, Rinehart & Winston, 1965), 401.

5. NSC 64, "The Position of the United States with Respect to Indochina," February 27, 1950, *FRUS, 1950,* 6: 745.

6. "Military Situation in Indochina," annex no. 2, "Draft Statement of U.S. Policy on Indochina for USG Consideration," October 6, 1950, in *United States–Vietnam Relations, 1945–1967* (Washington, D.C.: Government Printing Office, 1971), bk. 8, pt. 5, B.2, p. 360.

7. "NSC Staff Study on United States Objectives, Policies and Courses of Action in Asia," May 17, 1951, in ibid., 441–42.

8. On the Burmese Communist insurgency, see Hugh Tinker, *The Union of Burma: A Study of the First Years of Independence* (London: Oxford University Press, 1957), 58. On the Huk movement in the Philippines, see Eduardo Lachica, *Huk: Philippine Agrarian Society in Revolt* (Manila: Solidaridad, 1971), 137. On the Malayan emergency, see J. Norman Parmer, "Malaysia," in George McT. Kahin, ed., *Government and Politics of Southeast Asia,* 2d ed. (Ithaca, N.Y.: Cornell University Press, 1964), 293.

9. NIE 5, "Indochina: Current Situation and Probable Developments," December 29, 1950, *FRUS, 1950,* 6: 963.

10. For further discussion of the Truman administration's threat perceptions in Southeast Asia, see Douglas J. Macdonald, "The Truman Administration and Global Responsibilities: The Birth of the Falling Domino Principle," in Jervis and Snyder, eds., *Dominoes and Bandwagons,* 128–32.

11. William C. Gibbons, *The U.S. Government and the Vietnam War: Executive and Legislative Roles and Relationships* (Washington, D.C.: Government Printing Office, 1984), 1: 123–24; U.S. Congress, Senate, *Executive Sessions of*

the Senate Foreign Relations Committee, 83d Cong., 2d sess., 1954, Historical Series (Washington, D.C.: Government Printing Office, 1977), 6: 140, editorial footnote.

12. SE 52, "Probable Consequences in Non-Communist Asia of Certain Possible Developments in Indochina before Mid-1954," November 16, 1953, *FRUS, 1952–1954,* 13, pt. 1: 866–67, 871.

13. See 72 above.

14. *Executive Sessions* (cited n. 11 above), 6: 7.

15. Ibid., 113.

16. Robert Alan Goldberg, *Barry Goldwater* (New Haven, Conn.: Yale University Press, 1997), 104

17. *Executive Sessions* (cited n. 11 above), 6: 170

18. See 75–77 above.

19. Memo of discussion at the 192d NSC meeting, April 6, 1954, *FRUS, 1952–1954,* 13, pt. 1: 1257.

20. Eisenhower, *Public Papers of the Presidents of the United States: Dwight D. Eisenhower,* vol. 2: *1954* (Washington, D.C.: Government Printing Office, 1960), 382.

21. See 81–84 above.

22. *New York Times,* May 12, 1954, 6.

23. *Executive Sessions* (cited n. 11 above), 6: 274.

24. NIE 63.1–4–55, "Consequences of Possible US Courses of Action with Respect to Vietnam," September 13, 1955, in DOD, *United States–Vietnam Relations,* bk. 10, pp. 999–1000.

25. See Tinker, *Union of Burma,* 58; Benedict J. Kerkvliet, *The Huk Rebellion: A Study of Peasant Revolt in the Philippines* (Berkeley: University of California Press, 1977), 233–34; Parmer, "Malaysia," in Kahin, ed., *Governments and Politics of Southeast Asia,* 293; Richard Stubbs, *Hearts and Minds in Guerrilla Warfare: The Malayan Emergency, 1948–1960* (Singapore: Oxford University Press, 1989), 187.

26. Jay Taylor, *China and Southeast Asia: Peking's Relations with Revolutionary Movements* (New York: Praeger, 1976), 195; J. H. Brimmel, *Communism in Southeast Asia* (London: Oxford University Press, 1959), 318. The MCP later blamed "anti-Maoists" in China for the pressure on them to lay down their arms. See Stanley S. Bedlington, *Malaysia and Singapore: The Building of New States* (Ithaca, N.Y.: Cornell University Press, 1978), 82–83; Taylor, *China and Southeast Asia,* 276–80.

27. "Sino-Soviet Bloc Activities in Mainland Southeast Asia," December 18, 1959, annex B to report on Southeast Asia (NSC 5809), January 7, 1959, in *United States–Vietnam Relations,* bk. 10, pp. 1169, 1172–73.

28. NSC 6012, "Statement of Policy on U.S. Policy in Mainland Southeast Asia," July 25, 1960, in *United States–Vietnam Relations,* bk. 10, p. 1282.

29. For intelligence analyses and other official assessments of these trends, see 143–44, 163–64 above.

30. "SNIE 50–61: Outlook in Mainland Southeast Asia," March 28, 1961, *FRUS, 1961–1963*, 23: 59–60.

31. Tinker, *Union of Burma*, 58; Melvin Gurtov, *China and Southeast Asia: The Politics of Survival* (Baltimore: Johns Hopkins University Press, 1971), 209 n. 32; Lachica, *Huk*, 137; Anthony Short, *The Communist Insurrection in Malaya, 1948–1960* (London: Frederick Muller, 1975), 493–95; Stubbs, *Hearts and Minds in Guerrilla Warfare*, 241–42.

32. SNIE 10–62, "Communist Objectives, Capabilities and Intentions in Southeast Asia," February 21, 1962, in Gareth Porter, ed., *Vietnam: The Definitive Documentation of Human Decisions* (Stanfordville, N.Y.: E. M. Coleman Enterprises, 1979), 2: 155.

33. Director, Far East Region (Heinz), memo to Paul H. Nitze, assistant secretary of defense for international security affairs, March 15, 1962, *FRUS, 1961–1963*, 23: 105–6; CIA memo, March 15, 1962, ibid., 107–9.

34. SNIE 10–62, "Communist Objectives," 155. Pol Pot and his group of ultra-leftist Cambodian Communist leaders won control of the CPK leadership in 1960 but had made no preparations for armed activity before the U.S. intervention in Vietnam and had no access to arms. See Ben Kiernan, *How Pol Pot Came to Power* (London: Verso, 1985), 188–221.

35. Ruth T. McVey, "Indonesian Communism and the Transition to Guided Democracy," in A. Doak Barnett, ed., *Communist Strategies in Asia* (New York: Praeger, 1963), 148–95; Rex Mortimer, *Indonesian Communism under Sukarno: Ideology and Politics, 1951–1965* (Ithaca, N.Y.: Cornell University Press, 1974), 50–56, 137, 171–74; Herbert Feith, *The Decline of Constitutional Democracy in Indonesia* (Ithaca, N.Y.: Cornell University Press, 1962), 240–41; Harold Crouch, *The Army and Politics in Indonesia* (Ithaca, N.Y.: Cornell University Press, 1978), 45.

36. "Guidelines of United States Policy in Indonesia," November 11, 1961, 12, Thomson Papers, box 21, Southeast Asia, 1961–1966, Indonesia file, JFKL.

37. SNIE 10–62, "Communist Objectives," 154.

38. Minutes of Special Group (CI) Meeting, January 18, 1962, Special Group (CKI) Meetings, 6/8/61–11/3/62 folder, NSF, box 319, JFKL. The "rebellious elements" quotation is from Deputy Assistant Secretary of State for Southeast Asia Edward Rice. The observation that the insurgency movement in the northeast was based on "nationalism rather than communism" was from the CIA's Richard Bissell. The need to "break up this activity in Thailand" was voiced by U. Alexis Johnson, the new U.S. ambassador to Thailand.

39. "Minutes of Country Team Meeting with General Taylor and Party," October 26, 1961, box 44, Taylor Papers, National Defense University.

40. "Evaluations and Conclusions" (n.d.), *FRUS, 1961–1963*, 4: 481–82; Gen. Maxwell Taylor, paper, November 3, 1963, ibid., 479.

41. Testimony by Taylor before the Senate Foreign Relations Committee, October 8, 1963, U.S. Congress, Senate, *Executive Sessions of the Senate Foreign Relations Committee*, 88th Cong., 2d sess., 1963, Historical Series (Washington, D.C.: Government Printing Office, 1986), 737.

42. McNamara, memo to JFK, November 8, 1961, in DOD, *U.S.–Vietnam Relations*, bk. 11, p. 343

43. Rusk and McNamara, memo to JFK, November 11, 1961, in *The Pentagon Papers: The Defense Department History of United States Decisionmaking on Vietnam. The Senator Gravel Edition* (Boston: Beacon Press, 1972), 2: 110–11.

44. Dean Rusk, oral history interview, July 17, 1986, 21, OSDH; McGeorge Bundy, oral history interview, April 15, 1991, 26, OSDH.

45. *Pentagon Papers* (Gravel ed.), 2: 828.

46. David Kaiser, *American Tragedy: Kennedy, Johnson, and the Origins of the Vietnam War* (Cambridge, Mass.: Belknap Press of Harvard University Press, 2000), 101.

47. Mike Mansfield, memo to LBJ, January 6, 1964, *FRUS, 1964–1968*, 1: 2–3; Kaiser, *American Tragedy*, 295; Robert S. McNamara, with Brian VanDeMark, *In Retrospect: The Tragedy and Lessons of Vietnam* (New York: Vintage Books, 1995), 106.

48. William Bundy, memo to LBJ, January 7, 1964, Vietnam Working Group Files, Political, box 2, RG 59, NARA.

49. McNamara, memo to LBJ, January 7, 1964, *FRUS, 1964–1968*, 1: 12–13.

50. For Taylor's articulation of the test case thesis, see Taylor, memo to McNamara, January 22, 1964, in *Pentagon Papers* (Gravel ed.), 3: 497.

51. Lawrence J. Bassett and Stephen E. Pelz, "The Failed Search for Victory: Vietnam and the Politics of War," in Thomas G. Paterson, ed., *Kennedy's Quest for Victory: American Foreign Policy, 1961–1963* (New York: Oxford University Press, 1989), 235; highlights of discussion at Secretary of State Rusk's policy planning meeting, August 28, 1962, *FRUS, 1961–1963*, 5: 485.

52. SNIE 50–64, "Short Term Prospects in Southeast Asia," February 12, 1964 (document declassified under FOIA, November 4, 1975).

53. William Bundy, draft memo for LBJ, March 1, 1964, in Porter, ed., *Vietnam*, 2: 240–41.

54. McNamara, interview in June 1996 for the 1998 CNN documentary on the Cold War, episode 11, http://www.gwu.edu/~nsarchiv/coldwar/interviews/episode-11/mcnamara3.html (last visited July 29, 2004).

55. McNamara, oral history interview, pt. 3, July 24, 1986, 12, OSDH.

56. "Summary of Discussion at the Honolulu Conference, October 8–9," October 11, 1962, ibid., 973.

57. Michael R. Beschloss, ed., *Taking Charge: The Johnson White House Tapes, 1963–1964* (New York: Simon & Schuster, 1997), 248–49.

58. Summary record of the 521st NSC meeting, January 7, 1964, *FRUS, 1964–1968*, 26: 18.

59. Bundy later justified his linking of the outcome in South Vietnam to a PKI takeover of Indonesia by claiming that it was "implicit" in the statement that he and others considered the Sukarno regime to be "heavily Communist-infiltrated." See William Bundy, MS, ch. 12, p. 13. I have found no such claim in the diplomatic dispatches or intelligence analyses of the period.

60. NIE 54/55–63, "The Malaysian-Indonesian Conflict," October 30, 1963, 7, Thomson Papers, box 22, "Indonesia General, 1961–1963" file, JFKL.

61. Thomas L. Hughes, head of the State Department's Bureau of Intelligence and Research, circulated a memo that again underlined the fact that the PKI "would probably be restrained from attempting a coup by recognition of its limited insurgency potential and its desire to avoid providing the army with a rationale for a complete takeover." Even if the PKI should attempt to seize power, Hughes observed, the army had the capability to counter it. Bureau of Intelligence and Research, "The Succession in Indonesia," RFE-16, March 9, 1964 (declassified document in the Kai Bird Collection). Ten days after that memo was circulated, the Indonesian army commander Gen. Abdul Haris Nasution told U.S. Ambassador Howard Jones that if the PKI organized strikes or riots, "Madian . . . would be mild compared with army crackdown today." U.S. embassy, Jakarta, telegram to State Department, March 19, 1964, *FRUS, 1964–1968*, 26: 81. Nasution was referring to the violent repression of the PKI after it had attempted a coup in Madian in 1948.

62. Department of State, telegram to U.S. embassy, Kuala Lumpur, February 18, 1964, *FRUS, 1964–1968*, 26: 58.

63. NIE 54/55-63, "Malaysian-Indonesian Conflict," 7; Department of State, telegram to U.S. embassy, Jakarta, March 3, 1964, ibid., 66.

64. "Secretary McNamara's speech on Vietnam" (draft, March 17, 1964), "1964 McNamara Vietnam Speech 3/26/64" folder, Thomson Papers, box 24, JFKL.

65. William Sullivan, untitled MS (ca. October 1964 according to a handwritten notation), 9, William Bundy Papers, box 17, RG 59, NARA.

66. William Sullivan, memo to William Bundy, March 17, 1964, Thomson Papers, box 24, "1964 McNamara Vietnam Speech 3/26/64" file, JFKL.

67. For the text of McNamara's March 26, 1964, speech, see *Department of State Bulletin*, April 13, 1964, 562.

68. Telephone conversation with Richard Russell, May 27, 1964, in Beschloss, ed., *Taking Charge*, 364–65.

69. Lyndon B. Johnson, *Public Papers of the Presidents of the United States: Lyndon B. Johnson*, vol. 2: *1963–64*, (Washington, D.C.: Government Printing Office, 1965), 370.

70. Director of the Board of Estimates (Sherman Kent), memo to John McCone, June 9, 1964, *FRUS, 1964–1968*, 1: 484 n. 1.

71. Ibid., 484–87.

72. The analysis assumed a "clear-cut Communist victory" in Laos and South Vietnam rather than a "piecemeal victory, such as one staged through a 'neutralist' phase." The latter outcome, it said, would have "somewhat less sharp and severe" impacts on the region. Ibid., 485, original source n. 2.

73. Kai Bird, *The Color of Truth: McGeorge Bundy and Bill Bundy: Brothers in Arms* (New York: Touchstone, 1998), 285.

74. William Bundy, "Questions and Answers on a Congressional Resolution," 23, in Averell Harriman's folder for June 15, 1964, meeting, box 509, Harriman Papers, Library of Congress.

75. Moya Ann Ball, *Vietnam-on-the-Potomac* (New York: Praeger, 1992), 130.

76. H.R. McMaster, *Dereliction of Duty: Lyndon Johnson, Robert McNamara, the Joint Chiefs of Staff, and the Lies That Led to Vietnam* (New York: HarperCollins, 1997), 117–18.

77. Notes of a White House meeting, September 9, 1964, *FRUS, 1964–1968*, 1: 752–53.

78. William Bundy, "The Choices We Face in Southeast Asia," attachment to memo for Rusk, McNamara, Ball, and McGeorge Bundy (marked "First Draft"), October 15, 1964 (Kai Bird Collection).

79. The CIA's paper on covert action in Indonesia asked, "Is it unthinkable to foment internal tensions such as gave rise to the Chinese riots of last year, and which under certain conditions might force the Army to assume broad powers and restore order?" See CIA, "Prospects for Covert Action," memo for Department of State, September 14, 1964, *FRUS, 1964–1968*, 26: 162–63. See also CIA, "Political Action Paper," prepared for an October 22 meeting with William Bundy, ibid., 181–82 and 181n.

80. William Bundy, "II. U.S. Objectives and Stakes in South Viet-Nam and Southeast Asia" (declassified draft in the Kai Bird Collection), November 8, 1964, 3.

81. William Bundy, "Memorandum of Executive Committee Meeting, November 24, 1964" (declassified document in the Kai Bird Collection), 2.

82. *Pentagon Papers* (Gravel ed.), 3: 658.

83. "U.S. Policy toward Communist China," November 30, 1962, *FRUS, 1961–1963*, 22: 273.

84. NIE 1–61, "Estimate of the World Situation," January 17, 1961, *FRUS, 1961–1963*, 5: 23.

85. Robert W. Komer, "Strategic Framework for Rethinking China Policy" (draft, April 7, 1961), NSF, Country Files, box 22, China file, JFKL.

86. Roland Paul, *American Military Commitments Abroad* (New Brunswick, N.J.: Rutgers University Press, 1973), 105–27.

87. Daniel Fineman, *A Special Relationship: The United States and Military Government in Thailand, 1947–1958* (Honolulu: University of Hawaii Press, 1997), 209–57; Donald Neuchterlein, *Thailand and the Struggle for Southeast Asia* (Ithaca, N.Y.: Cornell University Press, 1965), 123–33; "Progress Report on U.S. Policy in Mainland Southeast Asia (NSC 5612/1)," November 26, 1957, in DOD, *United States–Vietnam Relations*, bk. 10, p. 1109.

88. SNIE 10–62, in Porter, ed., *Vietnam*, 2: 154; McCone, notes, June 11, 1962, *FRUS, 1961–1963*, 23: 947–48; Taylor, paper, September 21, 1962, ibid., 961.

89. McNamara, *In Retrospect*, 125.

90. Bird, *Color of Truth*, 294–95.

91. William Bundy, oral history interview with Paige Mulhollan, May 29, 1967, 35–36, OSDH.

9. CONCLUSION: THE PERILS OF DOMINANCE

1. Leslie Gelb and Richard K. Betts, *The Irony of Vietnam: The System Worked* (Washington, D.C.: Brookings Institution, 1978).

2. Quoted in Graham T. Allison, *Essence of Decision: Explaining the Cuban Missile Crisis* (Boston: Little, Brown, 1971), 148.

3. Roger Hilsman, *To Move a Nation: The Politics of Foreign Policy in the Administration of John F. Kennedy* (Garden City, N.Y.: Doubleday, 1967), 554–55, 561.

4. Gen. Matthew Ridgeway, memo, April 2, 1954, *FRUS, 1952–1954,* 13: 1220–21. For the views of the other service chiefs, see ibid., 1221–23.

5. Thomas J. Dodd, speech to the U.S. Senate, February 3, 1965, in Marcus G. Raskin and Bernard B. Fall, eds., *The Viet-Nam Reader,* rev. ed. (New York: Vintage Books, 1967), 35.

6. See Wohlforth, "The Stability of a Unipolar World," *International Security* 24, no. 1 (Summer 1999): 24–28; Michael Mastanduno, "Preserving the Unipolar Moment: Realist Theories and U.S. Grand Strategy," *International Security* 21, no. 4 (Spring 1997): 44–98.

7. See Christopher Layne, "The Unipolar Illusion: Why New Great Powers Will Rise," *International Security* 17, no. 4 (Spring 1993): 5–51; Kenneth N. Waltz, "The Emerging Structure of International Politics," *International Security* 18, no. 2 (Fall 1993): 44–79; id., "Structural Realism after the Cold War," *International Security* 25, no. 1 (Summer 2000): 27–28.

8. Kenneth N. Waltz, "International Structure, National Force and Balance of World Power," *Journal of International Affairs* 2 (1967): 228.

9. For discussion of this point in the realist literature, see Hans J. Morgenthau, *Politics among Nations,* 3d ed. (New York: Knopf, 1965), 33–35; Michael Mandelbaum, *The Fate of Nations: The Search for National Security in the Nineteenth and Twentieth Centuries* (Cambridge: Cambridge University Press, 1988), 134–42; William C. Wohlforth, "Realism and the End of the Cold War," *International Security* 19 (Winter 1994–95): 107–8; Robert Gilpin, *War and Change in World Politics* (Cambridge: Cambridge University Press, 1981), 146–48.

10. Waltz, "Structural Realism," 13.

Selected Bibliography

PRIMARY SOURCES

Archival, Manuscript, and Oral History Sources

Avery, Dorothy. Collection of translations of captured documents from CDEC, author's files
Ball, George W. Papers, LBJL
Bundy, McGeorge. Letter to the author, November 13, 1967, author's files
Bundy, McGeorge. Papers, LBJL
Bundy, William P. Papers in Kai Bird Collection
Bundy, William P. Papers, NARA
Bundy, William P. Unpublished manuscript, OSDH
Central Intelligence Agency, Office of Current Intelligence, Reports on the Soviet Union, 1949–1991, NARA
Central Intelligence Agency, Office of National Estimates, declassified NIEs, NARA
Dulles, John Foster. Memoranda of Conversations, 1953–1954, NARA
Harriman, W. Averell. Papers, Manuscript Division, Library of Congress
Harriman, W. Averell. Papers, National Security Archives
Hilsman, Roger. Papers, JFKL
Johnson, Lyndon. Presidential Recordings Collection, LBJL
Joint Chiefs of Staff, Central Files, NARA
Kahin, George McT. Papers, National Security Archive
Kennedy, John F. Presidential Recordings Collection, JFKL
McGhee, George. Papers, NARA
McNamara, Robert S. Papers, NARA
National Security Files, Country Files, Vietnam, Laos, and China, JFKL
National Security Files, Vietnam National Security Action Memoranda, LBJL
Oral History Collection, JFKL
Oral History Collection, LBJL
Oral History Collection, OSDH

President's Daily Diary and Diary Cards, LBJL
State Department, Policy Planning (S/P) Files, NARA
State Department Central Files, NARA
Taylor, Maxwell. Papers, National Defense University
Taylor, Maxwell. Papers, NARA
Thomson, James C. Papers, JFKL
VanDeMark, Brian. Papers, National Security Archive
Wheeler, Earle C. Papers, NARA

Interviews by the Author

Bui Tin. Hanoi, June 23, 1984
Forrestal, Michael. New York City, November 27, 1987
Goburdun, Ram. New Delhi, November 15, 1970
Ha Van Lau. Hanoi, June 21, 1984
Hoang Tung. Hanoi, December 24, 1974, and August 2, 1982
Lam Van Phat. Saigon, August 11, 1971
Nguyen Co Thach. Hanoi, August 2, 1982, and June 24, 1984
Nguyen Huu Co. Saigon, November 22, 1971
Nguyen Tien. Hanoi, November 17, 1978
Pham Binh. Hanoi, June 21, 1984
Sheehan, Neil. Washington, D.C., July 12, 1967
Tran Cong Man. Hanoi, June 23, 1984
Tran Van Dinh. Washington, D.C., July 27, 1967, and October 21, 1967

Published Primary Sources

Cameron, Allan W., ed. *Viet-Nam Crisis: A Documentary History*, vol. 1: *1940–1956*. Ithaca, N.Y.: Cornell University Press, 1971.
"Comrade B on the Plot of the Reactionary Chinese Clique against Vietnam." Translated by Christopher E. Goscha. 1979 document from the People's Army Library in Hanoi. Available at the website of the Cold War International History Project, http://cwihp.si.edu (last visited August 29, 2004).
Democratic Republic of Vietnam [DRV]. Institute for Research on Marxism-Leninism and Ho Chi Minh Thought. *Lich su Dang Cong San Viet Nam, tap II (1954–1975)* [History of the Vietnamese Communist Party, vol. 2 (1954–1975)]. Hanoi: Chinh Tri Quoc Gia, 1995.
Democratic Republic of Vietnam. Ministry of Defense. Institute of Vietnamese Military History. *Cuoc Khang chien Chong My, Cuu nuoc 1954–1975: Nhung su kien quan su* [The Anti-U.S. Resistance War for National Salvation, 1954–1975: Military Events]. Hanoi: Nha Xuan Ban Quan Doi, 1980. Translated in Joint Publications Research Service, JPRS 80968, June 3, 1982.
———. *Lich su Khang chien Chong My, Cuu nuoc (1954–1975)* [History of the Anti-U.S. Resistance for National Salvation (1954–1975)]. Vol. 1. Hanoi: Su that, 1990.
———. *Lich su Quan Doi Nhan Dan Viet Nam* [History of the Vietnam People's Army]. 2 vols. Hanoi: Quan Doi Nhan Dan, 1988.

———. *Victory in Vietnam: The Official History of the People's Army of Vietnam*, trans. Merle L. Pribbenow. Lawrence: University of Kansas Press, 2002.

Eisenhower, Dwight D. *Public Papers of the Presidents of the United States: Dwight D. Eisenhower, 1954*. Washington, D.C.: Government Printing Office, 1960.

Haines, Gerald K., and Robert E. Leggett, eds. *CIA's Analysis of the Soviet Union, 1947–1991: A Documentary Collection*. Washington, D.C.: Center for the Study of U.S. Intelligence, 2001.

Ho Chi Minh. *Selected Writings*. Hanoi: Foreign Languages Publishing House, 1977.

Johnson, Lyndon B. *Public Papers of the Presidents: Lyndon B. Johnson, 1964*. Washington, D.C.: Government Printing Office, 1965.

Kennedy, John F. *Public Papers of the Presidents: John F. Kennedy, 1963*. Washington, D.C.: Government Printing Office, 1964.

Koch, Scott A., ed. *Selected Estimates on the Soviet Union, 1950–1959*. Washington, D.C.: History Staff, Center for the Study of Intelligence, Central Intelligence Agency, 1993.

Le Duan. *Letters to the South*. Hanoi: Foreign Languages Publishing House, 1986.

———. *Ta nhat dinh thang, dich nhat dinh thua* [We Shall Certainly Win; the Enemy Will Certainly Lose]. South Vietnam: Tien Phong, 1966.

———. *Thu vao Nam* [Letters to the South]. Hanoi: Su that, 1985.

The Pentagon Papers: The Defense Department History of United States Decisionmaking on Vietnam: The Senator Gravel Edition. 5 vols. Boston: Beacon Press, 1971–72. Cited as *Pentagon Papers* (Gravel ed.).

The Pentagon Papers as Published by the New York Times. New York: Bantam Books, 1971.

Porter, Gareth, ed. *Vietnam: A History in Documents*. New York: New American Library, 1981.

———, ed. *Vietnam: The Definitive Documentation of Human Decisions*. 2 vols. Stanfordville, N.Y.: E. M. Coleman Enterprises, 1979.

Steury, Donald P., ed. *Intentions and Capabilities: Estimates on Soviet Strategic Forces, 1950–1983*. Washington, D.C.: Center for the Study of Intelligence, Central Intelligence Agency, 1996.

Truong Chinh. *Tinh hinh hien tai va nhiem vu truoc mat* [Present Situation and Immediate Tasks]. Report read to the Seventh Enlarged Conference of the Central Committee, 1955. No publication information shown, for international circulation only.

United States–Vietnam Relations, 1945–1967. Study prepared by the Department of Defense. 12 vols. Washington, D.C.: Government Printing Office, 1971.

U.S. Congress. Senate. Committee on Foreign Relations. *Executive Sessions of the Senate Foreign Relations Committee, together with Joint Sessions with the Armed Services Committee, 6. 83d Cong., 2d sess., 1954. Historical Series*. Washington, D.C.: Government Printing Office, 1977.

————. *Executive Sessions of the Senate Foreign Relations Committee, together with Joint Sessions with the Armed Services Committee*, 13, pt. 1. 87th Cong., 1st sess., 1961. Historical Series. Washington, D.C.: Government Printing Office, 1984.

————. *Executive Sessions of the Senate Foreign Relations Committee, together with Joint Sessions with the Armed Services Committee*, 14. 87th Cong., 2d sess., 1962. Historical Series. Washington, D.C.: Government Printing Office, 1986.

————. *Executive Sessions of the Senate Foreign Relations Committee, together with Joint Sessions with the Armed Services Committee*, 15. 88th Cong., 2d sess., 1963. Historical Series. Washington, D.C.: Government Printing Office, 1986.

————. *The Gulf of Tonkin, the 1964 Incidents. Hearing*. 90th Cong., 2d sess., February 20, 1968. Washington, D.C.: Government Printing Office, 1968.

————. *United States Security Agreements and Commitments Abroad,* Part 3: *Kingdom of Thailand: Hearings before the Senate Foreign Relations Committee, November 10–17, 1969.* 91st Cong., 1st sess., 1969. Washington, D.C.: Government Printing Office, 1987.

U.S. Department of Defense. *Soviet Military Power.* Washington, D.C.: Government Printing Office, 1987.

U.S. Department of State. *Foreign Relations of the United States, 1950.* Vol. 6 (East Asia and Pacific). Washington, D.C.: Government Printing Office, 1976. Cited as *FRUS.*

————. *Foreign Relations of the United States, 1952–1954.* Vol. 2 (National Security Affairs); vol. 8 (Eastern Europe; Soviet Union); vol. 12 (East Asia and Pacific, pts. 1 and 2); vol. 13 (Indochina, pts. 1 and 2); vol. 14 (China and Japan); vol. 16 (Geneva Conference). Washington, D.C.: Government Printing Office, 1981–88.

————. *Foreign Relations of the United States, 1955–1957.* Vol. 1 (Vietnam); vols. 2 and 3 (China); vol. 19 (National Security Policy). Washington, D.C.: Government Printing Office, 1985–90.

————. *Foreign Relations of the United States, 1958–1960.* Vol. 1 (Vietnam); vol. 3 (National Security Policy; Arms Control and Disarmament); vol. 8 (Berlin Crisis), and vol. 10 (Eastern Europe Region, Soviet Union, Cyprus); vol. 11 (Lebanon and Jordan); vol. 12 (Near East Region; Iraq, Iran); vol. 19 (National Security Policy). Washington, D.C.: Government Printing Office, 1986–96.

————. *Foreign Relations of the United States, 1961–1963.* Vols. 1–4 (Vietnam); vol. 5 (Soviet Union); vol. 8 (National Security Policy); vol. 22 (Northeast Asia); vol. 24 (Laos Crisis). Washington, D.C.: Government Printing Office, 1988–99.

————. *Foreign Relations of the United States, 1964–1968.* Vols. 1–4 (Vietnam); vol. 14 (Soviet Union). Washington, D.C.: Government Printing Office, 1992–2001.

Vietnamese Communist Party [VCP]. Committee on Party History. *50 nam hoat dong cua Dang Cong San Viet Nam* [Fifty Years of Activities of the Vietnamese Communist Party]. Hanoi: Su that, 1979.

————. Institute of Marxism-Leninism. *Tai lieu huong dan hoc tap nghi quyet Dai Hoi IV cua Dang* [Guidance Document for Studying the Resolution of the Fourth Party Congress]. Hanoi: Nha Xuat Ban Sach Giao Khoa Mac-Le-Nin, 1977.

————. *Mot so kien cua dang ve Chong My, Cuu nuoc* [Some Party Documents on the Anti-U.S. Resistance for National Salvation]. Hanoi: Su that, 1985.

Westad, Odd Arne, Chen Jian, Stein Tønnesson, Nguyen Vu Tung, and James G. Hershberg, eds. *77 Conversations between Chinese and Foreign Leaders on the Wars in Indochina, 1964–1977*. Washington, D.C.: Cold War International History Project, 1998.

SECONDARY SOURCES AND MEMOIRS

Allen, George W. *None So Blind: A Personal Account of the Intelligence Failure in Vietnam*. Chicago: Ivan R. Dee, 2001.

Allison, Graham T. *Essence of Decision: Explaining the Cuban Missile Crisis*. Boston: Little, Brown, 1971.

Allyn, Bruce J., James G. Blight, and David A. Welch, eds. *Back to the Brink: Proceedings of the Moscow Conference on the Cuban Missile Crisis, January 27–28, 1989*. Harvard University Center for Science and International Affairs, Occasional Paper no. 9. Cambridge, Mass.: CSIA; Lanham, Md.: University Press of America, 1992.

Anderson, David L. *Trapped by Success: The Eisenhower Administration and Vietnam, 1953–1961*. New York: Columbia University Press, 1991.

Andrew, Christopher. *For the President's Eyes Only: Secret Intelligence and the American Presidency from Washington to Bush*. New York: HarperCollins, 1995.

Arnold, James R. *The First Domino: Eisenhower, the Military and America's Intervention in Vietnam*. New York: William Morrow, 1991.

Austin, Anthony. *The President's War: The Story of the Tonkin Gulf Resolution and How the Nation Was Trapped in Vietnam*. New York: Lippincott, 1971.

Ball, George. *The Past Has Another Pattern*. New York: Norton, 1982.

————. "Top Secret: The Prophecy the President Rejected." *Atlantic*, July 1972, 35–49.

Ball, Moya Ann. *Vietnam-on-the-Potomac*. New York: Praeger, 1992.

Barrett, David M. "The Mythology Surrounding Lyndon Johnson, His Advisers, and the 1965 Decision to Escalate the Vietnam War." *Political Science Quarterly* 103, no. 4 (Winter 1988–89): 637–63.

————. *Uncertain Warriors: Lyndon Johnson and His Vietnam Advisers*. Lawrence: University of Kansas Press, 1993.

Bassett, Lawrence J., and Stephen E. Pelz. "The Failed Search for Victory: Vietnam and the Politics of War." In *Kennedy's Quest for Victory: American Foreign Policy, 1961–1963*, ed. Thomas G. Paterson. New York: Oxford University Press, 1989.

Berman, Larry. "NSAM 263 and NSAM 273: Manipulating History." In *Vietnam: The Early Years*, ed. Lloyd C. Gardner and Ted Gittinger. Austin: University of Texas Press, 1997.

———. *Planning a Tragedy: The Americanization of the War in Vietnam*. New York: Norton, 1982.

Beschloss, Michael R. *The Crisis Years: Kennedy and Krushchev, 1960–1963*. New York: Edward Burlingame Books, 1991.

———, ed. *Reaching for Glory: The Johnson White House Tapes, 1965*. New York: Simon & Schuster, 2001.

———, ed. *Taking Charge: The Johnson White House Tapes, 1963–1964*. New York: Simon & Schuster, 1997.

Betts, Richard K. *Nuclear Blackmail and Nuclear Balance*. Washington, D.C.: Brookings Institution, 1987.

Billings-Yun, Melanie. *Decision against War: Eisenhower and Dien Bien Phu, 1954*. New York: Columbia University Press, 1988.

Bird, Kai. *The Color of Truth, McGeorge Bundy and Bill Bundy: Brothers in Arms*. New York: Touchstone Books, 1998.

Blight, James G., Bruce J. Allyn, and David A. Welch. *Cuba on the Brink*. New York: Pantheon Books, 1993.

Blight, James G., and David A. Welch, eds. *On the Brink: Americans and Soviets Reexamine the Cuban Missile Crisis*. New York: Hill & Wang, 1989.

Bluth, Christoph. *Soviet Strategic Arms Policy before SALT*. Cambridge: Cambridge University Press, 1992.

Bohlen, Charles E. *Witness to History, 1929–1969*. New York: Norton, 1973.

Boretsky, Michael. "Comparative Progress in Technology, Productivity and Economic Efficiency: USSR vs. USA." In U.S. Congress, Joint Economic Committee, *New Directions in the Soviet Economy*, pt. II-A. 89th Cong., 2d sess., 1966. Washington, D.C.: Government Printing Office, 1966.

Bowles, Chester. *Promises to Keep: My Years in Public Life, 1941–1969*. New York: Harper & Row, 1971.

Bradley, Mark Philip. *Imagining Vietnam and America: The Making of Post-colonial Vietnam, 1919–1950*. Chapel Hill: University of North Carolina Press, 2000.

Brandon, Henry. *Anatomy of Error: The Inside Story of the Asian War on the Potomac*. Boston: Gambit, 1969.

Brigham, Robert. *Guerrilla Diplomacy: The NLF's Foreign Relations and the Vietnam War*. Ithaca, N.Y.: Cornell University Press, 1998.

Brimmel, J. H. *Communism in Southeast Asia*. London: Oxford University Press, 1959.

Brown, MacAlister, and Joseph J. Zasloff. *Apprentice Revolutionaries: The Communist Movement in Laos, 1930–1985*. Stanford, Calif.: Hoover Institution Press, 1986.

Bui Tin. *Following Ho Chi Minh: the Memoirs of a North Vietnamese Colonel.* Translated by Judy Stowe and Do Van. Honolulu: University of Hawaii Press, 1995.

Burke, John P., and Fred I. Greenstein. *How Presidents Test Reality.* New York: Russell Sage Foundation, 1989.

Burlatsky, Fedor. *Khrushchev and the First Russian Spring.* London: Weidenfeld & Nicolson, 1991.

Buzzanco, Robert. *Masters of War: Military Dissent and Politics in the Vietnam Era.* Cambridge: Cambridge University Press, 1996.

Chaffard, Georges. *Les Deux Guerres du Vietnam: De Valluy à Westmoreland.* Paris: La Table Ronde, 1969.

Chang, Gordon. *Friends and Enemies: The United States, China and the Soviet Union, 1948–1972.* Stanford, Calif.: Stanford University Press, 1990.

Charlton, Michael, and Anthony Moncrieff, eds. *Many Reasons Why: The American Involvement in Vietnam.* New York: Hill & Wang, 1978.

Chen, King. "North Vietnam in the Sino-Soviet Dispute, *1962–1964." Asian Survey,* September *1964,* 1023–36.

Cheng Guan Ang. *Vietnamese Communists' Relations with China and the Second Indochina Conflict, 1956–1962.* Jefferson, N.C.: McFarland, 1997.

Chen Jian. "China and the First Indochina War, *1950–54." China Quarterly* 133 (March 1993): 85–110.

———. "China's Involvement in the Vietnam War *1964–69." China Quarterly* 142 (June 1995): 356–87.

———. *Mao's China and the Cold War.* Chapel Hill, N.C.: University of North Carolina Press, 2001.

Chen Xiaolu. "Chen Yi and China's Diplomacy." In *Toward a History of Chinese Communist Foreign Relations,* ed. Michael H. Hunt and Niu Jun. Washington, D.C.: Woodrow Wilson Center for Scholars, 1993.

Christensen, Thomas J. *Useful Adversaries: Grand Strategy, Domestic Mobilization and Sino-American Conflict, 1947–1958.* Princeton, N.J.: Princeton University Press, 1996.

Colby, William. *Honorable Men.* New York: Simon & Schuster, 1978.

Colby, William, with James McCargar. *Lost Victory.* Chicago: Contemporary Books, 1989.

Coleman, David G. "Eisenhower and the Berlin Problem, 1953–1954." *Journal of Cold War Studies* 2, no. 1 (Winter 2000): 3–34.

Collier, Peter, and David Horowitz. *The Kennedys: An American Drama.* New York: Warner Books, 1984.

Collins, John M. *U.S.-Soviet Military Balance, 1960–1980.* New York: McGraw-Hill, 1980

Cooper, Chester. *The Lost Crusade: America in Vietnam.* New York: Dodd, Mead, 1970.

Craig, Campbell. *Destroying the Village: Eisenhower and Thermonuclear War.* New York: Columbia University Press, 1996.

Crouch, Harold. *The Army and Politics in Indonesia.* Ithaca, N.Y.: Cornell University Press, 1978.

Dallek, Robert. *Flawed Giant: Lyndon Johnson and His Times, 1961–1973.* New York: Oxford University Press, 1998.

———. *An Unfinished Life: John F. Kennedy, 1917–1963.* Boston: Little, Brown, 2003.

Devillers, Philippe, and Jean Lacouture. *End of a War: Indochina, 1954.* Translated by Alexander Lieven and Adam Roberts. New York: Praeger, 1969.

DiLeo, David. *George Ball, Vietnam, and the Rethinking of Containment.* Chapel Hill: University of North Carolina Press, 1991.

Dinerstein, Herbert. *War and the Soviet Union: Nuclear Weapons and the Revolution in Soviet Military and Political Thinking.* Rev. ed. New York: Praeger, 1962.

Dingman, Roger. "Atomic Diplomacy during the Korean War." *International Security* 13, no. 3 (Winter 1988–89): 50–91.

Divine, Robert A. *Eisenhower and the Cold War.* Oxford: Oxford University Press, 1981.

Dobrynin, Anatoly F. *In Confidence: Moscow's Ambassador to America's Six Cold War Presidents (1962–1986).* New York: Times Books, 1995.

Dockrill, Saki. *Eisenhower's New Look National Security Policy, 1953–56.* New York: St. Martin's Press, 1996.

Dommen, Arthur J. *Conflict in Laos: The Politics of Neutralization.* Rev. ed. New York: Praeger, 1971.

Duiker, William J. *The Communist Road to Power in Vietnam.* 2d ed. Boulder, Colo.: Westview Press, 1996.

———. *Ho Chi Minh.* New York: Hyperion, 2000.

Dunn, Keith A. "Soviet Strategy, Opportunities and Constraints in Southwestern Asia." *Soviet Union/Union Sovietique* 11, pt. 2 (1984): 182–211.

Eden, Anthony. *Full Circle: Memoirs of Anthony Eden.* Boston: Cassell, 1960.

Eisenhower, Dwight D. *Waging Peace, 1957–1961.* Garden City, N.Y.: Doubleday, 1963.

Ellsberg, Daniel. *Secrets: A Memoir of Vietnam and the Pentagon Papers.* New York: Viking, 2002.

Evans, Rowland, and Robert Novak. *Lyndon B. Johnson: The Exercise of Power.* New York: New American Library, 1966.

Fall, Bernard B. *Anatomy of a Crisis.* Edited by Roger M. Smith. Garden City, N.Y.: Doubleday, 1969.

———. "The Pathet Lao: A 'Liberation' Party." In *The Communist Revolution in Asia,* ed. Robert A. Scalapino. 2d ed. Englewood Cliffs, N.J.: Prentice-Hall, 1969.

Fay, Paul B., Jr. *The Pleasure of His Company.* New York: Harper & Row, 1966.

Feith, Herbert. *The Decline of Constitutional Democracy in Indonesia.* Ithaca, N.Y.: Cornell University Press, 1962.

Fetzer, James. "Clinging to Containment: China Policy." In *Kennedy's Quest for Victory: American Foreign Policy, 1961–1963*, ed. Thomas G. Paterson. New York: Oxford University Press, 1989.

Fineman, Daniel. *A Special Relationship: The United States and Military Government in Thailand, 1947–1958*. Honolulu: University of Hawaii Press, 1997.

FitzSimons, Louise. *The Kennedy Doctrine*. New York: Random House, 1972.

Foot, Rosemary. "New Light on the Sino-Soviet Alliance: Chinese and American Perspectives." *Journal of Northeast Asian Studies* 10 (Fall 1991): 16–29.

————. "Nuclear Coercion and the Ending of the Korean Conflict." *International Security* 13, no. 3 (Winter 1988–89): 92–112.

————. *The Wrong War: American Policy and the Dimensions of the Korean Conflict, 1950–53*. Ithaca, N.Y.: Cornell University Press, 1995.

Ford, Harold P. *CIA and the Vietnam Policymakers: 3 Episodes—1962–1968*. Washington, D.C.: Center for the Study of Intelligence, Central Intelligence Agency, 1998.

Freedman, Lawrence. *The Evolution of Nuclear Strategy*. New York: St. Martin's Press, 1989.

Fursenko, Aleksandr, and Timothy Naftal. *One Hell of a Gamble: Khrushchev, Castro and Kennedy, 1958–1964*. New York: Norton, 1997.

Gaddis, John Lewis. *We Now Know: Rethinking Cold War History*. New York: Oxford University Press, 1997.

Gaddis, John Lewis, Philip H. Gordon, Ernest R. May, and Jonathan Rosenberg, eds. *Cold War Statesmen Confront the Bomb: Nuclear Diplomacy since 1945*. New York: Oxford University Press, 1999.

Gaiduk, Ilya V. *Confronting Vietnam: Soviet Policy toward the Indochina Conflict, 1954–1963*. Stanford, Calif.: Stanford University Press, 2003.

————. "Containing the Warriors: Soviet Policy toward the Indochina Conflict, 1960–65." In *International Perspectives on Vietnam*, ed. Lloyd C. Gardner and Ted Gittinger. College Station: Texas A&M University Press, 2000.

————. *The Soviet Union and the Vietnam War*. Chicago: Ivan R. Dee, 1996.

————. "Turnabout? The Soviet Policy Dilemma in the Vietnam Conflict." In *Vietnam: The Early Decisions*, ed. Lloyd C. Gardner and Ted Gittinger. Austin: University of Texas Press, 1991.

————. "The Vietnam War and Soviet-American Relations, 1964–1973: New Russian Evidence." *Cold War International History Project Bulletin* 5–6 (Winter 1995–96): 22, 250–57.

Galbraith, John K. *A Life in Our Times*. Boston: Houghton Mifflin, 1981.

Gallicchio, Marc S. "The Best Defense Is a Good Offense: The Evolution of American Strategy in East Asia, 1953–1960." In *The Great Powers in East Asia 1953–1960*, ed. Warren I. Cohen and Akira Iriye. New York: Columbia University Press, 1990.

Gardner, Lloyd C. *Pay Any Price: Lyndon Johnson and the Wars for Vietnam*. Chicago: Ivan R. Dee, 1995.

Garthoff, Raymond L. *A Journey through the Cold War*. Washington, D.C.: Brookings Institution, 2001.

——. *Reflections on the Cuban Missile Crisis*. 1987. Rev. ed. Baltimore: Johns Hopkins University Press, 1989.

Garver, John. *Foreign Relations of the People's Republic of China*. Englewood Cliffs, N.J.: Prentice-Hall, 1993.

Gavin, Francis J. "The Myth of Flexible Response: American Strategy in Europe during the 1960s." *International History Review* 23, no. 4 (December 2001). Online at www. utexas.edu/lbj/faculty/ gavin/articles/mofr.pdf.

——. "Power, Politics and U.S. Policy in Iran, 1950–1953." *Journal of Cold War Studies* 1, no. 1 (1999): 56–89.

Gelb, Leslie H., and Richard K. Betts. *The Irony of Vietnam: The System Worked*. Washington, D.C.: Brookings Institution, 1979.

George, Alexander L. *Presidential Decisionmaking in Foreign Policy: The Effective Use of Information and Advice*. Boulder, Colo.: Westview Press, 1980.

Gibbons, William C. "Lyndon Johnson and the Legacy of Vietnam." In *Vietnam: The Early Decisions*, ed. Lloyd C. Gardner and Ted Gittinger. Austin: University of Texas Press, 1997.

——. *The U.S. Government and the Vietnam War: Executive and Legislative Roles and Relationships*. Washington, D.C.: Government Printing Office, 1984–88.

Giglio, James N. *The Presidency of John F. Kennedy*. Lawrence: University of Kansas Press, 1991.

Gilpin, Robert. *War and Change in World Politics*. Princeton, N.J.: Princeton University Press, 1981.

Gittinger, Ted, ed. *The Johnson Years: A Vietnam Roundtable*. Austin: Lyndon Baines Johnson Library, 1993.

Gittings, John. "New Light on Mao: 1. His View of the World," *China Quarterly* 60 (October–December 1974): 750–66.

——. *The World and China 1922–1972*. New York: Harper & Row, 1974.

Glasser, Jeffrey D. *The Secret Vietnam War: The United States Air Force in Thailand, 1961–1975*. Jefferson, N.C.: McFarland, 1995.

Goodwin, Richard N. *Remembering America: A Voice from the Sixties*. Boston: Little, Brown, 1988.

Gormley, Dennis M. "The Direction and Pace of Soviet Force Projection Capabilities." In *The Soviet Union: Security Policies and Constraints*, ed. Jonathon Alford. New York: St. Martin's Press, 1985.

Goulden, Joseph C. *Truth Is the First Casualty: The Gulf of Tonkin Affair—Illusion and Reality*. Chicago: Rand McNally, 1969.

Gribkov, Anatoli, and Gen. William Y. Smith. *Operation Anadyr*. Chicago: Edition q, 1994.

Gurtov, Melvin. *China and Southeast Asia: The Politics of Survival*. Baltimore: Johns Hopkins University Press, 1971.

——. *The First Vietnam Crisis: Chinese Communist Strategy and United States Involvement, 1953–1954*. New York: Columbia University Press, 1967.

Halberstam, David. *The Best and Brightest.* New York: Random House, 1972.

Halperin, Morton H. *Bureaucratic Politics and Foreign Policy.* Washington, D.C.: Brookings Institution, 1974.

Hammer, Ellen. *A Death in November.* New York: Oxford University Press, 1987.

He Di. "The Most Respected Enemy." In *Toward a History of Chinese Communist Foreign Relations,* ed. Michael H. Hunt and Niu Jun. Washington, D.C.: Woodrow Wilson Center for Scholars, 1993.

Helsing, Jeffrey W. *Johnson's War/Johnson Great Society.* Westport, Conn.: Praeger, 2000.

Henggeler, Paul R. *In His Steps: Lyndon Johnson and the Kennedy Mystique.* Chicago: Ivan R. Dee, 1999.

Herken, Greg. *The Winning Weapon: The Atomic Bomb in the Cold War, 1945–1950.* New York: Knopf, 1980.

Herring, George C. *America's Longest War: The United States and Vietnam, 1950–1975.* 3d ed. New York: McGraw-Hill, 1996.

———. "A Good Stout Effort: John Foster Dulles and the Indochina Crisis, 1954–1955." In *John Foster Dulles and the Diplomacy of the Cold War,* ed. Richard Immerman. Princeton, N.J.: Princeton University Press, 1992.

Herring, George C., and Richard H. Immerman. "Eisenhower, Dulles and Dien Bien Phu: 'The Day We Didn't Go to War Revisited.'" In *Dien Bien Phu and the Crisis of Franco-American Relations, 1954–1955,* ed. Lawrence Kaplan, Denise Artaud, and Mark Rubin. Wilmington, Del.: SR Books, 1990.

Hess, Gary R. "Commitment in the Age of Counterinsurgency: Kennedy's Vietnam Options and Decisions, 1961–1963." In *Shadow on the White House: Presidents and the Vietnam War, 1945–1975,* ed. James N. Giglio. Lawrence: University of Kansas Press, 1993.

Hilsman, Roger. "McNamara's War—Against the Truth: A Review Essay." *Political Science Quarterly* 111, no. 1 (1990): 151–63.

———. *To Move a Nation: The Politics of Foreign Policy in the Administration of John F. Kennedy.* Garden City, N.Y.: Doubleday, 1967.

Hone, Thomas C. "Strategic Bombardment Constrained: Korea and Vietnam." In *Case Studies in Strategic Bombardment,* ed. R. Cargill Hall. Washington, D.C.: Air Force History and Museums Program, 1998.

Hoopes, Townsend. *The Limits of Intervention: An Inside Account of How the Johnson Policy of Escalation in Vietnam Was Reversed.* New York: David McKay, 1969.

Horelick, Arnold L., and Myron Rush. *Strategic Power and Soviet Foreign Policy.* Chicago: University of Chicago Press, 1966.

Hsieh, Alice Langley. *Communist China's Strategy in the Nuclear Era.* Englewood Cliffs, N.J.: Prentice-Hall, 1962.

Hughes, Emmett John. *The Ordeal of Power: A Political Memoir of the Eisenhower Years.* New York: Atheneum, 1963.

Hunt, Michael H. *Lyndon Johnson's War: America's Cold War Crusade in Vietnam, 1945–1968.* New York: Hill & Wang, 1996.

Immerman, Richard H. "Between the Unattainable and the Unacceptable: Eisenhower and Dienbienphu." In *Reevaluating Eisenhower: American Foreign Policy in the 1950s,* ed. Richard A. Melanson and David Mayers. Urbana: University of Illinois Press, 1987.

Jacobsen, C. G. *Soviet Strategy–Soviet Foreign Policy: Military Considerations Affecting Soviet Policy-Making.* Glasgow: Robert Maclehose, 1972.

Jervis, Robert. "Domino Beliefs and Strategic Behavior." In *Dominoes and Bandwagons: Strategic Beliefs and Great Power Competition in the Eurasian Rimland,* ed. Robert Jervis and Jack Snyder. New York: Oxford University Press, 1991.

———. "Perceiving and Coping with Threat." In Robert Jervis, Richard Ned Lebow, and Janice Gross Stein, *Psychology and Deterrence.* Baltimore: Johns Hopkins University Press, 1985.

Jia Qingguo. "Searching for Peaceful Coexistence and Territorial Integrity." In *Sino-American Relations, 1945–1955: A Joint Reassessment of a Critical Decade,* ed. Harry Harding and Yuan Ming. Wilmington, Del.: Scholarly Resources, 1989.

Johnson, Lyndon B. *The Vantage Point: Perspectives of the Presidency, 1963–1969.* New York: Holt, Rinehart & Winston, 1971.

Johnson, U. Alexis. *The Right Hand of Power.* Englewood Cliffs, N.J.: Prentice-Hall, 1984.

Jones, Howard. *Death of a Generation: How the Assassinations of Diem and JFK Prolonged the Vietnam War.* Oxford: Oxford University Press, 2003.

Joyaux, François. *La Chine et le règlement du premier conflit d'Indochine: Genève 1954.* Paris: Publications de la Sorbonne, 1979.

Kahin, George McT. *Intervention: How the United States Became Involved in Vietnam.* New York: Knopf, 1986.

Kahin, George McT., and John W. Lewis. *The United States in Vietnam.* New York: Dial Press, 1969.

Kaiser, David. *Vietnam Tragedy: Kennedy, Johnson and the Origins of the Vietnam War.* Cambridge, Mass.: Belknap Press of Harvard University Press, 2000.

Kaplan, Fred. *The Wizards of Armageddon.* New York: Simon & Schuster, 1983.

Karnow, Stanley. *Vietnam: A History.* New York: Viking, 1983.

Kattenburg, Paul. *The Vietnam Trauma in American Foreign Policy.* New Brunswick: N.J.: Transaction Books, 1980.

Kearns Goodwin, Doris. *Lyndon Johnson and the American Dream.* New York: St. Martin's Griffin, 1991.

Kennedy, Paul. *The Rise and Fall of the Great Powers.* New York: Random House, 1987.

Kennedy, Robert F. *Thirteen Days.* New York: Norton, 1999.

Kerkvliet, Benedict J. *The Huk Rebellion: A Study of Peasant Revolt in the Philippines.* Berkeley: University of California Press, 1977.

Khrushchev, Nikita S. *Khrushchev Remembers: The Glasnost Tapes*. Edited and translated by Jerrold L. Schecter and Vyacheslav Luchkov. Boston: Little, Brown, 1990.

———. *Khrushchev Remembers: The Last Testament*. Edited and translated by Strobe Talbott. Boston: Little, Brown, 1974.

Khrushchev, Sergei N. *Nikita Khrushchev and the Creation of a Superpower*. University Park, Pa.: Pennsylvania State University Press, 2000.

Kiernan, Ben. *How Pol Pot Came to Power*. London: Verso, 1985.

Kochavi, Noam. "Limited Accommodation: Perpetual Conflict: Kennedy, China, and the Laos Crisis, 1961–1963." *Diplomatic History* 26, no. 1 (Winter 2002): 95–135.

———. "Washington's View of the Sino-Soviet Split, 1961–1963: From Puzzled Prudence to Bold Experimentation." *Intelligence and National Security* 15, no. 2 (Spring 2000): 50–79.

Kraslow, David, and Stuart H. Loory. *The Secret Search for Peace in Vietnam*. New York: Vintage Books, 1968.

Lacouture, Jean. *Vietnam: Between Two Truces*. Translated by Konrad Kellen and Joel Carmichal. New York: Vintage Books, 1966.

Larson, Deborah Welch. "Bandwagon Images in American Foreign Policy: Myth or Reality?" In *Dominoes and Bandwagons: Strategic Beliefs and Great Power Competition in the Eurasian Rimland*, ed. Robert Jervis and Jack Snyder. New York: Oxford University Press, 1991.

———. *Origins of Containment: A Psychological Explanation*. Princeton, N.J.: Princeton University Press, 1985.

Layne, Christopher. "The Unipolar Illusion: Why New Great Powers Will Rise." *International Security* 17, no. 4 (Spring 1993): 5–51.

Leamer, Lawrence. *The Kennedy Men, 1901–1963*. New York: HarperCollins, 2001.

Lee, Chae-Jin. *Communist China's Policy toward Laos: A Case Study, 1954–1967*. International Studies, East Asian Series, Research Publication No. 6. Lawrence: Center for East Asian Studies, University of Kansas, 1970.

Leffler, Melvyn P. *A Preponderance of Power: National Security, the Truman Administration and the Cold War*. Stanford, Calif.: Stanford University Press, 1992.

Levantrosser, William F. "Tonkin Gulf Revisited: Vietnam, Military Mirage, and Political Reality in 1964." In *Lyndon Johnson and the Uses of Power*, ed. Bernard J. Firestone and Robert C. Vogt. New York: Greenwood Press, 1988.

Lewy, Guenter. *America in Vietnam*. New York: Oxford University Press, 1978.

Linden, Carl A. *Khrushchev and the Soviet Leadership, 1957–1964*. Baltimore: Johns Hopkins University Press, 1966.

———. *Khrushchev and the Soviet Leadership: With an Epilogue on Gorbachev*. Baltimore: Johns Hopkins University Press, 1990. Revised edition of the preceding.

Little, Douglas. "Ike, Lebanon, and the 1958 Middle East Crisis." *Diplomatic History* 20, no. 1 (Winter 1996): 27–54.

Logevall, Fredrik. *Choosing War: The Lost Chance for Peace and the Escalation of the War in Vietnam.* Berkeley: University of California Press, 1999.

———. "Vietnam and the Question of What Might Have Been." In *Kennedy: The New Frontier Revisited,* ed. Mark J. White. New York: New York University Press, 1998.

Macdonald, Douglas J. "Communist Bloc Expansion in the Early Cold War: Challenging Realism, Refuting Revisionism." *International Security* 20, no. 3 (Winter 1995): 152–88.

———. "Falling Dominoes and System Dynamics: A Risk Aversion Perspective." *Security Studies* 3, no. 2 (Winter 1993–94): 225–58.

———. "The Truman Administration and Global Responsibilities: The Birth of the Falling Domino Principle." In *Dominoes and Bandwagons: Strategic Beliefs and Great Power Competition in the Eurasian Rimland,* ed. Robert Jervis and Jack Snyder. New York: Oxford University Press, 1991.

MacFarquhar, Roderick. *The Origins of the Cultural Revolution,* vol. 3: *The Coming of the Cataclysm, 1961–1966.* New York: Oxford University Press and Columbia University Press, 1997.

Maclear, Michael. *Vietnam: The Ten Thousand Day War.* London: Thames Methuen, 1981.

Mandelbaum, Michael. *The Fate of Nations: The Search for National Security in the Nineteenth and Twentieth Centuries.* Cambridge: Cambridge University Press, 1988.

Maneli, Mieczyslaw. *War of the Vanquished.* Translated by Maria de Görgey. New York: Harper & Row, 1971.

Marks, Frederick, III. "The Real Hawk at Dienbienphu: Dulles or Eisenhower?" *Pacific Historical Review* 59 (August 1990): 297–322.

Marolda, Edward J., and Oscar P. Fitzgerald. *The United States Navy and the Vietnam Conflict.* Washington, D.C.: Government Printing Office, 1986.

Martin, John Bartlow. *Adlai Stevenson and the World: The Life of Adlai Stevenson.* Garden City, N.Y.: Doubleday, 1977.

Mastanduno, Michael. "Preserving the Unipolar Moment: Realist Theories and U.S. Grand Strategy." *International Security* 21, no. 4 (Spring 1997): 44–98.

May, Ernest R., ed. *American Cold War Strategy: Interpreting NSC 68.* Boston: Bedford Books/St. Martin's Press, 1992.

May, Ernest R., John Steinbrunner, and Thomas Wolfe. *History of the Strategic Arms Competition, 1945–1972.* Vol. 1. Office of the Secretary of Defense, Historical Office, March 1981.

MccGwire, Michael. "The Rationale for the Development of Soviet Seapower." In *Soviet Strategy,* ed. Gerald Segal and John Baylis. London: Croom Helm, 1981.

McMahon, Robert J. "U.S.-Vietnam Relations: A Historical Survey." In *Pacific Passage: The Study of American East-Asian Relations on the Eve of the Twenty-First Century,* ed. Warren I. Cohen. New York: Columbia University Press, 1996.

McMaster, H. R. *Dereliction of Duty.* New York: HarperCollins, 1997.

McNamara, Robert S., with Brian VanDeMark. *In Retrospect: The Tragedy and Lessons of Vietnam.* New York: Vintage Books, 1996.

McNamara, Robert S., James Blight, and Robert Brigham, with Thomas Biersteker and Herbert Schandler. *Argument without End.* New York: Public Affairs, 1999.

McVey, Ruth T. "Indonesian Communism and the Transition to Guided Democracy." In *Communist Strategies in Asia,* ed. A. Doak Barnett. New York: Praeger, 1963.

Melandri, Pierre. "The Repercussions of the Geneva Conference: South Vietnam under a New Protector." In *Dien Bien Phu and the Crisis of Franco-American Relations, 1954–1955,* ed. Lawrence Kaplan, Denise Artaud, and Mark Rubin. Wilmington, Del.: SR Books, 1990.

Miller, Merle. *Lyndon: An Oral Biography.* New York: G. P. Putnam's Sons, 1980.

Modelski, George, and William R. Thompson. *Seapower in Global Politics, 1494–1993.* Seattle: University of Washington Press, 1987.

Moïse, Edwin E. "JFK and the Myth of Withdrawal." In *A Companion to the Vietnam War,* ed. Robert Buzzanco and Marilyn Young. Oxford: Blackwell, 2002.

———. *Tonkin Gulf and the Escalation of the Vietnam War.* Chapel Hill: University of North Carolina Press, 1996.

Mortimer, Rex. *Indonesian Communism under Sukarno: Ideology and Politics, 1951–1965.* Ithaca, N.Y.: Cornell University Press, 1974.

Mosley, Leonard. *Dulles: A Biography of Eleanor, Allen and John Foster Dulles and Their Family Network.* New York: Dial Press/James Wade, 1978.

Nash, Philip. *The Other Missiles of October.* Chapel Hill: University of North Carolina Press, 1997.

Naughton, Barry. "The Third Front: Defense Industrialization in the Chinese Interior." *China Quarterly* 115 (September 1988): 351–88.

Neuchterlein, Donald. *Thailand and the Struggle for Southeast Asia.* Ithaca, N.Y.: Cornell University Press, 1965.

Newman, John M. *JFK and Vietnam: Deception, Intrigue and the Struggle of Power.* New York: Warner Books, 1992.

———. "The Kennedy-Johnson Transition: The Case for Policy Reversal." In *Vietnam: The Early Decisions,* ed. Lloyd C. Gardner and Ted Gittinger. Austin: University of Texas Press, 1997.

Nighswonger, William. *Rural Pacification in Vietnam.* New York: Praeger, 1968.

Ninkovich, Frank A. *Modernity and Power: A History of the Domino Theory in the Twentieth Century.* Chicago: University of Chicago Press, 1994.

Nitze, Paul. *From Hiroshima to Glasnost: At the Center of Decision.* New York: Grove Weidenfeld, 1987.

Nixon, Richard M. *The Memoirs of Richard M. Nixon.* New York: Grosset & Dunlap, 1978.

Nolan, Janne E. *Guardians of the Arsenal: The Politics of Nuclear Strategy.* New York: Basic Books, 1989.

Nolting, Frederic. *From Trust to Tragedy: The Political Memoir of Frederick Nolting, Kennedy's Ambassador to Diem's Vietnam.* New York: Praeger, 1988.

Ofer, Gur. *Soviet Economic Growth, 1928–1985.* Santa Monica, Calif.: RAND and UCLA Center for the Study of Soviet International Behavior, 1988.

Olsen, Mari. *Solidarity and National Revolution: The Soviet Union and the Vietnamese Communists, 1954–1960.* Oslo: Norwegian Institute for Defence Studies, 1997.

Papp, Daniel. *Vietnam: The View from Moscow, Peking, Washington.* Jefferson, N.C.: McFarland, 1981.

Paul, Roland. *American Military Commitments Abroad.* New Brunswick, N.J.: Rutgers University Press, 1973.

Perret, Geoffrey. *Jack: A Life Like No Other.* New York: Random House, 2001.

Plimpton, George, ed. *American Journey: The Times of Robert F. Kennedy.* New York: Harcourt Brace Jovanovich, 1970.

Polmar, Norman. *Strategic Weapons: An Introduction.* New York: Crane Russak, 1982.

Porter, Gareth. "After Geneva: Subverting Laotian Neutrality." In *Laos: War and Revolution,* ed. Nina S. Adams and Alfred W. McCoy. New York: Harper & Row, 1970.

———. "Imperialism and Social Structure in Twentieth Century Vietnam." PhD dissertation, Cornell University, 1976.

———. "Vietnam and the Socialist Camp: Center or Periphery?" In *Vietnamese Communism in Comparative Perspective,* ed. William S. Turley. Boulder, Colo.: Westview Press, 1980.

Prados, John. *Operation Vulture.* New York: ibooks, 2002.

———. *The Sky Would Fall.* New York: Dial Press, 1983.

Preble, Christopher A. "'Who Ever Believed in the "Missile Gap"?': John F. Kennedy and the Politics of National Security." *Presidential Studies Quarterly* 33, no. 4 (2003): 801–26.

Qiang Zhai. "Beijing and the Vietnam Conflict, 1964–1965: New Chinese Evidence." *Cold War International History Project Bulletin* 6–7 (Winter 1995–96): 233–50.

———. "China and the Geneva Conference of 1954." *China Quarterly* 129 (March 1992): 103–22.

———. *China and the Vietnam Wars, 1950–1975.* Chapel Hill: University of North Carolina Press, 2000.

———. "An Uneasy Relationship: China and the DRV during the Vietnam War." In *International Perspectives on Vietnam,* ed. Lloyd C. Gardner and Ted Gittinger. College Station: Texas A&M University Press, 2000.

Radvanyi, Janos. *Delusion and Reality: Gambits, Hoaxes and Diplomatic One-Upmanship in Vietnam.* South Bend, Ind.: Gateway Editions, 1978.

Randle, Robert. *Geneva 1954: The Settlement of the Indochinese War.* Princeton, N.J.: Princeton University Press, 1969.

Raskin, Marcus G., and Bernard B. Fall, eds. *The Viet-Nam Reader.* Rev. ed. New York: Vintage Books, 1967.

Rasler, Karen A., and William R. Thompson. *The Great Powers and Global Struggle, 1490–1990.* Lexington: University of Kentucky Press, 1994.

Reeves, Thomas C. *A Question of Character: John F. Kennedy in Image and Reality.* New York: Free Press, 1990.

Reston, James. *Deadline: A Memoir.* New York: Random House, 1991.

Richter, James G. *Khrushchev's Double Bind: International Pressures and Domestic Coalition Politics.* Baltimore: Johns Hopkins University Press, 1994.

Roberts, Chalmers M. "The Day We Didn't Go to War." In *The Viet-Nam Reader,* ed. Marcus G. Raskin and Bernard B. Fall. New York: Vintage Books, 1965.

Rogers, Frank E. "Sino-American Relations and the Vietnam War, 1964–66." *China Quarterly* 66 (June 1976): 293–314.

Roman, Peter. *Eisenhower and the Missile Gap.* Ithaca, N.Y.: Cornell University Press, 1995.

Rosenberg, David Alan. "The Origins of Overkill: Nuclear Weapons and American Strategy." *International Security* 7, no. 4 (Spring 1983): 3–71.

———. "'A Smoking Radiating Ruin at the End of Two Hours': Documents on American Plans for Nuclear War with the Soviet Union, 1954–55." *International Security* 6, no. 3 (Winter 1981–82): 3–38.

Ross, Douglas A. *In the Interests of Peace: Canada and Vietnam, 1954–1973.* Toronto: University of Toronto Press, 1984.

Rossi, Mario. "U Thant and Vietnam: The Untold Story." *New York Review of Books,* November 17, 1966, 8–13.

Rust, William J. *Kennedy in Vietnam.* New York: Scribner's, 1985.

Ryan, Mark A. *Chinese Attitudes toward Nuclear Weapons: China and the United States during the Korean War.* Armonk, N.Y.: M. E. Sharpe, 1990.

Schlesinger, Arthur, Jr. *Robert Kennedy and His Times.* Boston: Houghton Mifflin, 1978.

———. *A Thousand Days: John F. Kennedy in the White House.* Boston: Houghton Mifflin, 1965.

Shapley, Deborah. *Promise and Power: The Life and Times of Robert McNamara.* Boston: Little, Brown, 1993.

Sharp, Ulysses S. G. *Strategy for Defeat: Vietnam in Retrospect.* San Rafael, Calif.: Presidio Press, 1978.

Short, Anthony. *The Communist Insurrection in Malaya, 1948–1960.* London: Frederick Muller, 1975.

Shu Guang Zhang. *Deterrence and Strategic Culture: Chinese-American Confrontations, 1949–1958.* Ithaca, N.Y.: Cornell University Press, 1992.

Shultz, Richard H., Jr. *The Secret War against Hanoi.* New York: HarperCollins, 1999.

Shulzinger, Robert D. *A Time for War: The United States and Vietnam, 1941–1975*. New York: Oxford University Press, 1999.

Slater, Jerome. "The Domino Theory and International Politics: The Case of Vietnam." *Security Studies* 3, no. 2 (Winter 1993–94): 186–224.

Sorensen, Theodore. *Kennedy*. New York: Harper & Row, 1965.

Spector, Ronald H. *Advice and Support: The Early Years of the United States Army in Vietnam, 1941–1960*. New York: Free Press, 1985.

Steinberg, Blema. *Shame and Humiliation: Presidential Decision Making on Vietnam*. Pittsburgh: University of Pittsburgh Press, 1996.

Stern, Sheldon M. *Averting the Final Failure: John F. Kennedy and the Secret Cuban Missile Crisis Meetings*. Stanford, Calif.: Stanford University Press, 2003.

Stevenson, Charles A. *The End of Nowhere: American Policy toward Laos since 1954*. Boston: Beacon Press, 1972.

Stockdale, Jim, and Sybil Stockdale. *In Love and War: The Story of a Family's Ordeal and Sacrifice during the Vietnam Years*. 1984. Rev. ed. Annapolis, Md.: Naval Institute Press, 1990.

Stolper, Thomas E. *China, Taiwan and the Offshore Islands*. Armonk, N.Y.: M. E. Sharpe, 1985.

Stubbs, Richard. *Hearts and Minds in Guerrilla Warfare: The Malayan Emergency, 1948–1960*. Singapore: Oxford University Press, 1989.

Sullivan, William H. *Obbligato, 1939–1979: Notes on a Foreign Service Career*. New York: Norton, 1984.

Tang, Truong Nhu, with David Chanoff and Doan Van Toai. *A Vietcong Memoir*. New York: Random House, 1985.

Tannenwald, Nina. *The Nuclear Taboo: The United States and the Nonuse of Nuclear Weapons since 1945*. Cambridge: Cambridge University Press, 2003.

Taylor, Jay. *China and Southeast Asia: Peking's Relations with Revolutionary Movements*. New York: Praeger, 1976.

Taylor, Maxwell. *Swords and Plowshares: A Memoir*. New York: Norton, 1972.

Taylor, Sandra C. "Laos: The Escalation of a Secret War." In *The Vietnam War as History*, ed. Jane Errington and B. J. C. McKercher. New York: Praeger, 1990.

Thayer, Carlyle A. *War by Other Means: National Liberation and Revolution in Viet-nam, 1954–60*. Sydney: Allen & Unwin, 1989.

Thee, Marek. *Notes of a Witness: Laos and the Second Indochinese War*. New York: Random House, 1973.

Thies, Wallace J. *When Governments Collide: Coercion and Diplomacy in the Vietnam Conflict, 1964–1968*. Berkeley: University of California Press, 1980.

Thomson, James C. "How Could Vietnam Happen?—An Autopsy." *Atlantic*, April 1968, 47–53.

Tinker, Hugh. *The Union of Burma: A Study of the First Years of Independence*. London: Oxford University Press, 1957.

Trachtenberg, Marc. *History and Strategy.* Princeton, N.J.: Princeton University Press, 1991.

———. "The Influence of Nuclear Weapons in the Cuban Missile Crisis." *International Security* 10, no. 1 (Summer 1985): 137–63.

———. "A 'Wasting Asset': American Strategy and the Shifting Nuclear Balance." *International Security* 13, no. 3 (Winter 1988–89): 5–49.

Trewhitt, Henry L. *McNamara.* New York: Harper & Row, 1971.

Troyanofsky, Oleg. "The Making of Soviet Foreign Policy." In *Nikita Khrushchev,* ed. William Taubman, Sergei Khrushchev, and Abbott Gleason; trans. David Gehrenbeck, Eileen Kane, and Alla Bashenko. New Haven, Conn.: Yale University Press, 2000.

Tucker, Nancy Bernkopf. "John Foster Dulles and the Taiwan Roots of the 'Two China' Policy." In *John Foster Dulles and the Diplomacy of the Cold War,* ed. Richard Immerman. Princeton, N.J.: Princeton University Press, 1992.

Valenti, Jack. *A Very Human President.* New York: Norton, 1975.

Vickerman, Andrew. *The Fate of the Peasantry: Premature "Transition to Socialism" in the Democratic Republic of Vietnam.* Monograph Series, no. 28. New Haven, Conn.: Yale University Southeast Asian Studies, 1986.

Vigor, John. "The Soviet 'Forward Reach.'" In *Soviet Military Power and Performance,* ed. John Erickson and E. J. Feuchwanger. Hamden, Conn.: Archon Books, 1979.

Walt, Stephen M. "Alliance Formation in Southwest Asia: Balancing and Bandwagon in Cold War Competition." *Dominoes and Bandwagons: Strategic Beliefs and Great Power Competition in the Eurasian Rimland,* ed. Robert Jervis and Jack Snyder. New York: Oxford University Press, 1991.

———. *The Origins of Alliances.* Ithaca, N.Y.: Cornell University Press, 1987.

Walton, Richard J. *Cold War and Counter-Revolution: The Foreign Policy of John F. Kennedy.* Baltimore: Johns Hopkins University Press, 1972.

Waltz, Kenneth N. "The Emerging Structure of International Politics." *International Security* 18, no. 2 (Fall 1993): 44–79.

———. "International Structure, National Force and Balance of World Power." *Journal of International Affairs* 2 (1967): 215–31.

———. "Structural Realism after the Cold War." *International Security* 25, no. 1 (Summer 2000): 5–41.

———. *Theory of International Politics.* Reading, Mass.: Addison-Wesley, 1979.

Ward, M. D. "Differential Paths to Parity: A Study of the Contemporary Arms Race." *American Political Science Review* 78 (1984): 297–317.

Warner, Geoffrey. "The United States and the Fall of Diem, Part I: The Coup That Never Was." *Australian Outlook* 28 (December 1974): 245–58.

Watson, Bruce W. *The Changing Face of the World's Navies: 1945 to the Present.* Washington, D.C.: Brassey's, 1991.

Wehrle, Edmund. "A Good, Bad Deal: John F. Kennedy, W. Averell Harriman, and the Naturalization of Laos, 1961–1962." *Pacific Historical Review* 67 (August 1998): 349–77.

Weinland, Robert G. "The Evolution of Soviet Requirements for Naval Forces: Solving the Problems of the Early 1960s." *Survival* (January–February 1964): 16–25.

Weinstein, Franklin. *Vietnam's Unheld Elections: The Failure to Carry Out the 1956 Reunification Elections and the Effect on Hanoi's Present Outlook.* Ithaca, N.Y.: Cornell University Southeast Asia Program, 1966.

Weisbrot, Robert. *Maximum Danger: Kennedy, the Missiles and the Crisis of American Confidence.* Chicago: Ivan R. Dee, 2001.

Wenger, Andreas. *Living with Peril: Eisenhower, Kennedy and Nuclear Weapons.* Lanham, Md.: Rowman & Littlefield, 1997.

Westad, Odd Arne. "History, Memory, and the Languages of Alliance-Making." In *77 Conversations between Chinese and Foreign Leaders on the Wars in Indochina, 1964–1977,* ed. Odd Arne Westad, Chen Jian, Stein Tønnesson, Nguyen Vu Tung, and James G. Hershberg. Washington, D.C.: Cold War International History Project, 1998.

Whiting, Allen S. *The Chinese Calculus of Deterrence.* Ann Arbor: University of Michigan Press, 1975.

———. "Mao, China and the Cold War." In *The Origins of the Cold War in Asia,* ed. Akira Iriye and Yonosuke Nagai. New York: Columbia University Press, 1977.

———. "New Light on Mao: Quemoy 1958: Mao's Miscalculations." *China Quarterly* 62 (June 1975): 263–70.

Windchy, Eugene. *Tonkin Gulf.* Garden City, N.Y.: Doubleday, 1971.

Winters, Francis X. *The Year of the Hare.* Athens: University of Georgia Press, 1997.

Wofford, Harris. *Of Kennedys and Kings.* New York: Farrar, Straus & Giroux, 1980.

Wohlforth, William Curti. *The Elusive Balance: Power and Perceptions during the Cold War.* Ithaca, N.Y.: Cornell University Press, 1993.

———. "Realism and the End of the Cold War." *International Security* 19, no. 3 (Winter 1994–95): 91–129.

———. "The Stability of a Unipolar World." *International Security* 24, no. 1 (Summer 1999): 5–41.

Wolfe, Thomas W. *Soviet Power and Europe, 1945–1970.* Baltimore: Johns Hopkins University Press, 1970.

Xiaoming Zhang. "Communist Power Divided: China, the Soviet Union, and the Vietnam War." In *International Perspectives on Vietnam,* ed. Lloyd C. Gardner and Ted Gittinger. College Station: Texas A&M University Press, 2000.

———. "The Vietnam War, 1964–1969: A Chinese Perspective." *Journal of Military History* 60 (October 1986): 731–62.

Yahuda, Michael. *China's Role in World Affairs.* New York: St. Martin's Press, 1978.

Yang Kuisong. *Changes in Mao Zedong's Attitude toward the Indochina War, 1949–1973.* Translated by Qiang Zhai. Washington, D.C.: Cold War International History Project, Working Paper no. 34, February 2002.

Young, Marilyn B. *The Vietnam Wars, 1945–1990.* New York: HarperCollins, 1991.

Zagoria, Donald. *The Sino-Soviet Conflict, 1956–1961.* Princeton, N.J.: Princeton University Press, 1962.

Zasloff, J. J. *Origins of the Insurgency in South Vietnam, 1954–1960: The Role of the Southern Vietminh Cadres.* RAND Corporation Memorandum RM-5193/2-ISA/ARPA, May 1968.

Zimmerman, William. *Soviet Perspectives on International Relations, 1956–1967.* Princeton, N.J.: Princeton University Press, 1969.

Zubok, Vladislav M., and Konstantin Pleshakov. *Inside the Kremlin's Cold War: From Stalin to Khrushchev.* Cambridge, Mass.: Harvard University Press, 1996.

Index

Abramov, Alexander, 50, 52–53
Acheson, Dean, 2
aid. *See* economic assistance; PRC
  military assistance; Soviet military
  assistance; U.S. military assistance;
  VPA (Vietnam People's Army)
  assistance to South Vietnamese
  insurgents
Aidit, D. N., 64–65
air forces: PRC, 60, 187; Soviet, 9,
  279n23, 281n52; VPA, 129. *See also*
  bombers; U.S. Air Force
airlift: Soviet capability, 9; Soviet to
  Laos, 49, 62–63, 143; U.S. capability,
  8–9
Alsop, Joseph, 125–26, 206–7,
  345n17
Anderson, Dillon, 99, 100–101
Anh, Le Duc, 135
appeasement policies, of Soviets and
  PRC, xi, 32–69, 113
Army of the Republic of Vietnam
  (ARVN), 115, 118, 124–39, 169,
  205, 221
assassination: Diem, 126, 127, 178;
  Kennedy, 127, 178, 182, 266–67. *See*
  also killings
assistance. *See* economic assistance;
  PRC military assistance; Soviet
  military assistance; U.S. military
  assistance; VPA (Vietnam People's

Army) assistance to South
  Vietnamese insurgents
Associated States: Indochina, 74, 82,
  95. *See also* Cambodia; Laos;
  Vietnam
Australia, 82, 125, 246

balancing behavior, 229–30. *See also*
  bandwagon thesis; power relations
Ball, George, x; Johnson administration,
  193, 200, 202, 213, 221–28, 243, 252,
  254, 342n60, 350–51nn93,95,98,99;
  Kennedy administration, 159, 171,
  176
bandwagon thesis, xii, 229–30,
  236–45, 249–54, 258
Barrington, James, 160
bases. *See* military bases
Basic National Security Policy, U.S.,
  86
Bay of Pigs invasion, Cuba, 116, 145,
  153, 168, 325n49
Berlin: conferences, 73, 98; free city
  status for West Berlin, 63; Kennedy
  speech (1961), 15; South Vietnam
  compared, 152, 219; U.S.
  interventionism, 3, 14, 152
Bien Hoa attack, Viet Cong, 206, 207,
  268, 345n17
Binh Gia battle, 135
Bo, Mai Van, 134, 136–37

Text: 10/13 Aldus
Display: Franklin Gothic
Compositor: TechBooks
Printer: Maple-Vail Manufacturing Group
Indexer: Barbara Roos